Grétry and the growth of opéra-comique

Bust of Grétry by Henri-Joseph Rutxhiel, signed and dated An 13 (1804–5): plaster cast in the Musée Art Wallon, Liège

GRÉTRY

and the growth of opéra-comique

DAVID CHARLTON

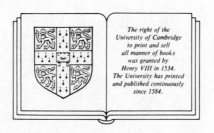

The right of the
University of Cambridge
to print and sell
all manner of books
was granted by
Henry VIII in 1534.
The University has printed
and published continuously
since 1584.

CAMBRIDGE UNIVERSITY PRESS

Cambridge

London   New York   New Rochelle
Melbourne   Sydney

Published by the Press Syndicate of the University of Cambridge
The Pitt Building, Trumpington Street, Cambridge CB2 1RP
32 East 57th Street, New York, NY 10022, USA
10 Stamford Road, Oakleigh, Victoria 3166, Australia

First published 1986

Printed in Great Britain at
the University Press, Cambridge

British Library cataloguing in publication data
Charlton, David
Grétry and the growth of opéra-comique.
1. Grétry, André Ernest Modeste
I. Title
782.1′092′4 ML410.G83

Library of Congress cataloguing in publication data
Charlton, David, 1946–
Grétry and the growth of opéra-comique.
Bibliography: p.
Includes index.
1. Grétry, André Ernest Modeste, 1741–1813.
2. Composers – France – Biography. 3. Grétry,
André Ernest Modeste, 1741–1813. Operas.
4. Opera – France – History and criticism. I. Title.
ML410.G83C35 1986 782.1′092′4 85-9664

ISBN 0 521 25129 X

SE

Contents

Contents

Illustrations

Preface

'Opéra-comique' is a misnomer and Grétry is hardly a household name, yet the composer of *Zémire et Azor* and *Richard Cœur-de-lion*, and the operatic genre that stands behind *Fidelio*, form a vital part of later eighteenth-century culture. The last major monograph on Grétry, by Michel Brenet, appeared a hundred years ago (1884); like its lesser successors, it is in French. The last book in English about opéra-comique was Martin Cooper's remarkable brief study of 1949. I have chosen to turn the spotlight on one period (1760–1790) and to view Grétry's achievement in the genre in which he excelled.

Because Grétry's opéras-comiques are so diverse, each tends to raise questions pertaining to a new operatic or cultural area. Thus readers may survey the field by following the book chronologically, or else use it to locate facts about a given work quickly. Readers seeking information on subjects like local colour, the chorus, the gothic revival or 'functional recollection' of motifs must generally have recourse to the index rather than chapter headings. Performance statistics are recorded in chapters 7 and 26.

Opéra-comique in general, and Grétry's scores in particular, have a deceptively simple look. This tempts writers to generalise, which is dangerous. One, for example, states that opéra-comique in Grétry's day 'was still basically a play with incidental music'. This is untenable. One can only regard Grétry's opéras-comiques as opera with spoken dialogue instead of recitative. Another will discuss 'rescue opera' as having 'several musical traits' separating it from earlier works. Quite apart from the invalidity of the term 'rescue opera', the facts do not support the contention, any more than they prove stylistic exclusivity of authentic sub-genres like *paysannerie* or *chevaleresque*. What this book demonstrates are (a) the operatic individuality of the twenty-three works it reviews in some detail and (b) statistical and historical evidence concerning the growth of opéra-comique.

A number of writers, of course, have shown the way. Earlier this century were Arthur Pougin, Georges Cucuel with his brilliant archival work, Pauline Long Des Clavières with *La jeunesse de Grétry*, and Heinz Wichmann, whose *Grétry und das musikalische Theater in Frankreich* includes Grétry's recitative operas, not analysed in the present book; more recently there have been Clarence Brenner (*The Théâtre Italien*), Georges de Froidcourt, editor of Grétry's *Correspondance générale*, Kent M. Smith, whose thesis on Egidio Duni covers opéra-comique up to Grétry, José Quitin, author of a study of Grétry's Liège period, and Karin Pendle (see notes to Chapters 4, 16 and 26).

I do not underestimate the difficulty of discussing an art so closely linked with a foreign literary culture. This study, at least, provides information about literary sources and quotations rendered into English (by the present writer except when

ix

otherwise stated). Many have stressed Grétry's mastery in *déclamation*, the imitation of human nature through musical imitation of vocal characteristics. Brenet, for one, showed the theoretical and practical ways in which the composer dealt with it, and the significance of Jacques Lacombe's *Le spectacle des beaux-arts* (1758) which Grétry knew (i:441). But although I have discussed Grétry's artistic procedures no detailed account has been given of *déclamation*. It can be over-emphasised. English-speaking readers will appreciate Grétry's range better by reference to form, tonality, orchestration or other devices of the dramatist–musician. In a recent essay, however, I have tackled both *déclamation* and the relation of words to music in the 1760s: see *Essays on Opera and Drama in honour of Winton Dean*, ed. Nigel Fortune, Cambridge University Press (forthcoming).

The primary sources for this book were Grétry's manuscripts, the earliest printings of his music and librettos, the manuscript account and record books of the Comédie-Italienne and many different literary works forming the intellectual background to opéra-comique. Performance statistics up to 1826 were freshly researched. More work remains to be done on bibliographical questions. Operatic criticism ideally relates to theatre performance: less than a handful of Grétry's works have been staged in the last six or seven years. So in Gabrieli Baldini's words, much 'has rather resembled an act of excavation; something more experimental than really critical, something which, as well as revealing treasures, has also brought to light material justifiably buried' (*The Story of Giuseppe Verdi*). It is encouraging, nevertheless, that six Grétry stage works have been recorded either whole or in part; that figure may well increase.

Acknowledgements

I should like to thank the School of Fine Arts and Music of the University of East Anglia for the provision of study leave and research funds. The staff and librarians of the Bibliothèque Nationale and British Library gave valuable personal assistance, and those in Cambridge (Rowe Library), Geneva (Archives d'Etat; Bibliothèque Publique et Universitaire), Liège (Bibliothèque Publique Centrale), Lille (Bibliothèque Municipale), Rouen (Bibliothèque Municipale) and numerous Italian collections, epistolary help. The support of Anthea Baird (London University, Senate House Library), Trevor Fawcett (formerly of the University of East Anglia Library), Catherine Massip (Bibliothèque Nationale) and Nicole Wild (Bibliothèque de l'Opéra) was particularly helpful. My thanks for help with enquiries and provision of materials are due to Stephen Banfield, Michael Cardy, Anthony Caston, Monique De Smet, Valérie Emery, Roger Fiske, Arthur Jacobs, David Kimbell, Yves Lenoir, the Earl of Lindsey and Abingdon, Hugh Macdonald, Caroline Martin, Georges Minet, Alexander Potts, John Renwick, Michael Robinson, Julian Rushton, Stanley Sadie, Kent M. Smith, Dieter Sonntag and Neal Zaslaw. Margaret Rayner kindly allowed me to use unpublished information from her dissertation on Sedaine. For assistance with translation I am indebted to my dear parents, who have been as generously supportive as ever. M. Elizabeth C. Bartlet provided stimulating discussion and the benefit of her specialist advice in certain areas. Michel Noiray has facilitated my research in Paris in numerous friendly ways. My text has benefited from the encouragement and scrutiny of David Van Edwards and John Warrack and for this I am especially grateful. Naturally, no blame attaches to them for my errors. Finally, I record my gratitude to Patricia Scholfield, who shared in the conception and realisation of the book. It is affectionately dedicated to her.

Abbreviations

Note: When a citation is made without any reference except to volume and page, e.g. (ii:60), Grétry's *Mémoires* are the source: see below.

b.   bass

bar.   baritone

CC   *A.-E.-M. Grétry: Collection complète des œuvres*, ed. F. A. Gevaert, E. Fétis, A. Wotquenne and others (Leipzig, 1884–1936). (N.B. The accuracy of these scores and their prefaces cannot be assumed uncritically.)

F:Pn   Paris, Bibliothèque Nationale

F:Po   Paris, Bibliothèque de l'Opéra

Froidcourt   Georges de Froidcourt, *La correspondance générale de Grétry* (Brussels, 1962)

GB:Lbl   London, British Library

Grimm   *Correspondance littéraire, philosophique et critique par Grimm, Diderot, Raynal, Meister, etc.*, ed. Maurice Tourneux (16 vols., Paris, 1877–82)

Loewenberg   Alfred Loewenberg, *The Annals of Opera: 1597–1940* (Cambridge, 1943, revised 3rd edn, 1978)

Mémoires   A. E. M. Grétry, *Mémoires, ou Essais sur la musique* (3 vols., Paris, An v [1796–7], reprinted New York, 1971). (N.B. References to the first edition, of volume one only (Paris, 1789), are made in full.)

Mémoires secrets   [Louis Petit de Bachaumont and others] *Mémoires secrets pour servir à l'histoire de la République des lettres en France, depuis 1762 jusqu'à nos jours* (36 vols., London, John Adamson, 1777–89)

Opéra   The Paris Opéra, properly called Académie Royale de Musique

Réf   A. E. M. Grétry, *Réflexions d'un solitaire*, ed. Lucien Solvay and Ernest Closson (4 vols., Brussels and Paris, 1919–24). (N.B. The four volumes of this, the first edition, do not always correlate with the (incomplete) eight volumes of Grétry's manuscript.)

s.   soprano

t.   tenor

The New Grove   *The New Grove Dictionary of Music and Musicians*, ed. Stanley Sadie (20 vols., London, 1980)

PART ONE

Les arts suivent les mœurs dont ils font la peinture.   Grétry, *Mémoires*, ii:355

L'esprit de parti . . . jusqu'à la fin du monde, se mêlera des Opéra-comiques et des affaires d'Etat.   Masson de Pezay, *La Rosière de Salency*, 'Réflexions'

1. Introduction

This book, designed for the general reader as well as the specialist or student, is about a composer, the company for which he mainly wrote (the Comédie-Italienne) and a type of French opera using spoken dialogue. It was never intended to be a life-and-works study, but I have written some biographical 'profiles' which give the most extensive details about Grétry available in English and are perhaps the first to make systematic use of Grétry's *Réflexions d'un solitaire*, the collected letters of Grétry issued by Georges de Froidcourt, and Monique de Smet's archival work in Rome. Besides, it is difficult not to be interested in an artist of such compulsive talkativeness as Grétry. He aimed to be entertaining as well as thoughtful and he was as frank about his contemporaries and his inner life as possible.

The reasons that Grétry can legitimately be taken as the centre of interest of a whole operatic genre are that he was an ambitious innovator, a fertile producer and a successful composer. The degree to which he was successful merely in terms of performance statistics will be shown in comparative tables in chapters 7 and 26. Grétry's first Parisian opéra-comique was seen publicly in August 1768. After June 1769 the first complete month at the Comédie-Italienne (later the Opéra-Comique) in which *no* Grétry opéra-comique was mounted (excluding of course closed periods) was February 1804; the second was November 1824: two months in fifty-five years. Only then did the gaps become more frequent. Though it is true that the Revolution changed people's taste, as it changed the whole business of theatre production, Grétry's works retained much more of their hold than has often been asserted. With the Consulate and the Empire his opéras-comiques ascended in popularity once more, going into decline under Louis XVIII. At least seven of them were seen during the Victorian era in Paris, some repeatedly. As for the French provinces, where he was even more consistently popular, statistics have yet to be compiled.

Outside France, Grétry's works enjoyed great celebrity. Not all were equally popular, but certain ones were known everywhere and lasted on the stage into the twentieth century. Not for nothing have writers such as Heinz Wichmann and Edward Dent seen opéra-comique as a root source for the Romantics.[1] Its themes, techniques and sounds were staple experiences for much of Europe, including parts of Italy (to Grétry's great satisfaction). England borrowed the ideas but usually found the music uncongenial. Beethoven's father – to take a small example – was singing Grétry rôles as early as 1771 in *Silvain* and *L'amitié à l'épreuve* (see chapter 9). The reader will find a survey of the Parisian performance history of each work at the end of the relevant chapter together with a brief indication of its success on the world scale, drawn from Alfred Loewenberg's *The Annals of Opera*.[2]

Grétry and the growth of opéra-comique

Grétry's opéras-comiques are as inseparable from literary considerations today as they always were. They were influential not least because they were frequently written by dramatists who had new things to say, and said them with style and skill. The opéras-comiques are not 'comic operas': they may be horrific dramas, realistic and political dramas, historically based dramas, sentimental tales, pastorals, comedies of manners, farces. Grétry even wrote a neo-classical opéra-comique. This is interesting enough, but because their plots, unlike the musical tragedies with recitative by Gluck and others at the Opéra, were based on sources much less than familiar today, it has been thought worthwhile to spend time exploring both them and their derivation. Only this can tell us about the values and techniques of a genre too little known. Further, both the operas and their sources are worth exploring in order to discover the connections they have with cultural or political events around them. An imperative need of opéra-comique authors, one shared of course with the early Romantics, was to find new regions of subject-matter and appropriate ways of dealing with it. The process of search was well under way in the 1760s: Grétry appeared at a vital point in its development. All over the world musical theatre at this period was challenging or overtaking spoken theatre in popularity. Opéra-comique answered not just a French, but an international need.

Situated near the hub of the capital where opéra-comique was produced, Grétry met large numbers of people: royalty, nobility, officials, men of letters, all manner of musicians, entrepreneurs, publishers and artists. He was closely in touch with drifts in cultural thought. In Paris, the growth of opéra-comique was keenly followed by educated people and its impact recognised, for as the Comédie-Italienne's royal certificate of 6 March 1780 spelled out, the king

noted that, since 1762, the genre of lyric pieces [i.e. opéra-comique] had made progress which was as astonishing as it was rapid. French music, which previously was the object of the indifference or scorn of foreigners, is now spread through all Europe, since French comic operas (*Opéra bouffons* [*sic*]) are performed in all courts of the North and even in Italy, where the greatest musicians of Rome and Naples applaud the talents of our composers. It is works of this type that have formed taste in France, that have accustomed ears there to a more learned and expressive music, and which finally have prepared for the revolution occurring even at our Academy of Music [the Opéra], where today one sees masterpieces applauded whose merit would have been neither recognised nor appreciated had they been played twenty-five years earlier. Therefore one cannot doubt that this revolution is the fruit of the comic operas composed for the Comédie-Italienne and the continual efforts of the actors who have performed them.[3]

Ample evidence will be found in this book of these 'continual efforts', not least concerning the revision of certain operas, to which attention is given at the close of each relevant chapter.

For readers interested in the technical growth of Grétry's opéras-comiques there is some formal commentary on works, including the management of finales, the evolution of what I have termed 'functional recollection' (i.e. organised musical reminiscence) and the composer's principles of formal structure. To save space, the individual items (e.g. arias) are referred to in the main text by bracketed reference numbers, while the first words in French of these are placed together in the notes as 'Incipits'. In this way an aria on a recording, for example, can be readily identified.

It is essential to remember that Parisian theatre was not in our sense *free*. All theatres had to be licensed and the limits of their repertory defined. The three official theatres, controlled through a hierarchy descending from the Gentlemen of the King's Bedchamber, were (i) the Opéra, properly called the Académie Royale de Musique, (ii) the Comédie-Française, and (iii) the Comédie-Italienne. The first two, whose statutes dated back to the Grand Siècle, jealously guarded their interests and were able to negotiate restrictions on any others (these smaller theatres are described in chapter 26). The Comédie-Italienne itself was, in Grétry's day, the product of the fusion of two companies in 1762: (a) the original Comédie-Italienne and (b) the unofficial Opéra-Comique company. Let us briefly describe their development.[4]

(a) The first permanent Italian players worked in Paris from 1660 to 1697; Louis XIV then disbanded them and in 1716 the Regent brought them back. They acted in the old theatre in the Hôtel de Bourgogne, rue Mauconseil, which was in use up to Easter 1783 and where Grétry's earlier works were mounted. The legal title 'Comédiens Italiens Ordinaires du Roi' was given in 1723. Their repertory widened from harlequin plays to include French plays, notably Marivaux, much ballet and humorous parodies of serious (recitative) operas. Their production in 1746 of Pergolesi's *La serva padrona* was unsuccessful. Though he worked mainly for the Opéra-Comique (see below), Charles-Simon Favart put on several works at the Comédie-Italienne from 1740. The orchestra by 1756–60 possessed six violins, three cellos, two upper woodwind, two bassoons and two horns. From 1760–2 this was augmented by two violins, two violas and a double-bass.

The Italiens were never far from financial crisis, one main reason for which was the superior attendance at the Opéra-Comique. This fundamental factor, according to Georges Cucuel, caused the royal officials controlling the Italiens to bring about the fusion of 1762.[5]

(b) Being a rival to the official theatres and operating only on sufferance, the Opéra-Comique underwent numerous indignities. It had a licence to perform at the Saint-Laurent fair (*c.*9 August to 29 September) and the Saint-Germain fair (3 February to Palm Sunday). From 1713 to 1719 the Opéra permitted the players to sing vaudevilles, that is, the arranging of traditional songs with new words.[6] This kind of verbal-musical wit has persisted in various ways into our own century and is sometimes used in television commercials. A similar experience was provided in *The Beggar's Opera* of 1728. By 1715 the title of the company was fixed as Opéra-Comique, and the genre itself had been born: whole dramatic entertainments were being designed around sung vaudevilles. We still lack much information on the music of early opéra-comique, but by 1723 the young Rameau was writing music for one called *L'Endriague*, and others followed in 1726.[7] In these, original music was heard alongside vaudevilles. By 1743 the important entrepreneur Jean Monnet had become director of the Opéra-Comique and engaged Favart 'as stage manager and répétiteur, and made him responsible for revising the texts in the repertory' (*The New Grove*, vi:438). From that point on, their musical plays became ever more successful. The orchestra was about the same size as that of the Italiens. Following enforced closure between 1745 and 1752 Monnet built a fine theatre at the Saint-Laurent fair with decorations by Boucher.[8]

Then came the events that crystallised the form opéra-comique was to take: the performances of the *bouffons* (the Italian troupe of Bambini) at the Paris Opéra, 1752–4, generating enthusiasm for Pergolesi's music; and Rousseau's *Le devin du village*, first seen at the same theatre in 1753. Rousseau's opera, which had recitatives and so was not an opéra-comique, nevertheless pointed the way: a music based on naturalness and Italianate simplicity, linked with moral dilemmas whose implications might involve social criticism. Though it did not kill off vaudeville comedies, Italian or mock-Italian music was so popular that it became the basis of a new opéra-comique tradition. Favart's *Ninette à la cour* (1755), for example, mostly if not all built on real Italian music fitted with French words, was both elaborate and influential.[9] After many experiments and after Pergolesi's masterpiece had likewise been adapted into *La servante maîtresse*, the composer Egidio Duni was invited to Paris from Parma to write opéras-comiques.

Duni's *Le peintre amoureux de son modèle* (1757) was the first work in an often successful corpus: certain works were still enjoyed up to 1790, as is shown in Tables 6 and 9 of chapter 26. Duni wrote for the Opéra-Comique (except *La fille mal gardée*, 1758), and from the following year a tide of interesting opéras-comiques swept onto the same stage from the pens of Monsigny and Philidor. These seemed to signal the coming of age of the genre and made it more necessary, from the Establishment's point of view, to harness both it and its audiences.

So the two companies joined with effect from 3 February 1762; five Opéra-Comique singers, including MM. Clairval and La Ruette, went over to the Comédie-Italienne. However, the fusion had far-reaching ramifications, since the Comédie-Italienne had to accept the licence already granted to the Opéra-Comique: and when renewed from 1767 it contained cardinal restrictions.[10] First, it was not permitted to mount opera in Italian; some Italian works were played in French adaptation (see chapter 22) because the players interpreted their permission to give parodies (in the literary sense) as licence to adapt in this way. Secondly, it was forbidden to give 'continuous music': no connecting recitative was allowed. Thirdly, 'simple or composed choruses' were forbidden lest the result rival traditional French opera. (We shall see that Grétry's works eroded this restriction during the 1770s; but in 1780, as chapter 26 shows, many prohibitions were tightened up.) Other articles forbade the depiction of murder or suicide by blade or poison.

After some years of consolidation, just after Grétry's advent, Desboulmiers assessed the total strength of the Comédie-Italienne repertory in 1770:

52 Italian *canevas* (i.e. semi-improvised comedies) from one act (8 in all) to five acts (10 in all)
63 French plays mainly in one act (28 in all) or three acts (32 in all)
60 opéras-comiques, most in one act (41), some in two acts (11) and the rest in three acts (7).
The only four-act one was *La fée Urgèle* by Favart and Duni.[11]

A work could be either in verse or prose.

The figures show that there was ample scope for the evolution of larger-scale opéras-comiques. In the event, four-act works remained rare: Grétry's *Zémire et Azor*, *La Rosière de Salency* (first version), *Aucassin et Nicolette* (first version), *Pierre le Grand* (first version) and Dalayrac's *Sargines* (1788). Méhul's *Euphrosine ou le tyran corrigé* (1790) was reduced from five acts to four, then three.

It is noteworthy that the label 'opéra-comique' was rarely used on the title-page of an individual work. In Grétry's case only the sequel to *Le Comte d'Albert* was so called. Why was this? First, a French love of order and logic and secondly, a reflection of the types of musical drama that had evolved since 1700: *comédie*, *comédie-lyrique*, *comédie-parade*, *opéra bouffon*, *drame lyrique*. Unfortunately, the most frequent label, *comédie mêlée d'ariettes* (comedy mixed with *little* arias), is inherently misleading. 'Ariette' originally meant 'musical aria for voice, whose character is light', such as Rameau's Italianate pieces.[12] By extension, 'ariette' was applied to Italianate opéra-comique. But when opéra-comique grew more various, with 'songs which themselves had character and expression', then

from that moment one had to make a distinction between the merely brilliant *ariette* and the expressive, passionate one. But as the usage was established of calling all opéra-comique arias, *ariette*; and although taste had decided that the songs in [Rousseau's] *Le devin du village* were arias, not *ariettes*, since their style was simple and natural, usage prevailed and retained the term *ariette* for all arias sung at the theatre where *ariettes* had shone.

In this book we simply refer to arias.

It is certain that in the minds of many, an opéra-comique of whatever complexion in 1770 was generically still a play with music more than an opera with spoken dialogue. Favart's own works, for one thing, enhanced the literary centre of gravity. There was no accepted rule. But the emergence of Michel-Jean Sedaine as a librettist in the late 1750s meant that the genre was affected fundamentally by a dramatist who was ready to give modern music a modern rôle at the Comédie-Italienne. In 1760 Sedaine wrote, 'Since the toleration of arias, music can be employed [in opéra-comique] in the "familiar" style, extend its dictionary of words, find resources unknown even at the Opéra, which will be turned to its profit.'[13]

When the critical history of opéra-comique comes to be written it will find a certain watershed around 1770. Several extended critiques appeared, such as P. J. B. Nougaret's *De l'art du théâtre* (2 vols., 1769), Laurent Garcin's *Traîté du mélodrame ou Réflexions sur la musique dramatique*, V. de La Jonchère's *Essai sur l'opéra* (1772) and B. Farmian de Rosoi's *Dissertation sur le drame lyrique* of 1775, which is discussed in chapter 17. These are hardly separable from wider debates going on concerning the rôle of French theatre in public life. Put bluntly, these revolve round certain reforms suggested by the Encyclopaedists and developed afterwards: the desire for less artificiality of language, for widening the means of expression, for making theatre relevant to the middle class by showing bourgeois characters and life-styles; the desire to show the conditions of people's work and to make use of realistic and appropriate costumes.

The identification of a ruling élite with a ruling, stultifying set of dramatic conventions was taken up by Louis-Sébastien Mercier in his banned study *Du théâtre, ou nouvel essai sur l'art dramatique* (1773). All the old poetic authorities must be removed before a modern theatre can develop, he says. Mercier claims that

the old system must necessarily change if the Frenchman wants to have a theatre; that our fine, much-vaunted tragedy is but a phantom cloaked in purple and gold, but which has no reality; that it is time that truth were more respected, that the moral purpose made itself better felt, and that the representation of civil life should finally take over the imposing, untruthful apparatus that has up to now decorated the exterior of our plays. They say nothing to the multitude.

Opéra-comique from the 1760s onward is not least interesting for its intimate relation to the reform of theatre in general. Those attached to Voltaire's viewpoint were incensed by the hybrid nature of the genre, a favourite simile being that of a deformed offspring or 'monster', something born of the impotent attempt to mate comedy and tragedy;[14] or a 'dramatic two-headed monster that sometimes sings and sometimes speaks' (Grimm: viii: 314f). Littérateurs such as La Harpe were still writing in 1777 of its 'bizarre alliance, music succeeding word'. In other terms, opéra-comique was 'unnatural' on two counts. It was not a traditional comic or tragic entertainment, and it mixed dialogue and music. Sedaine was particularly vulnerable to criticism since he was influenced by the English theatre and Shakespeare's startling (to the French) juxtapositions, as with the gravedigger's scene in *Hamlet*.

Other critics, like Nougaret, granted only a limited scope to music in opéra-comique. He approved of musical choral endings, especially as designed by Sedaine and Anseaume (who wrote *Le tableau parlant* for Grétry), 'because one supposes then that what is depicted is happening in the mind of the characters', i.e. it is authentically dramatic and not a mere song. He also approved of eliminating the mixture of vaudevilles and original music in a single work (still found, for example, in Philidor's popular *Le maréchal ferrant*, but outlawed by Sedaine). This mixture he found 'shocking'. Nougaret saw little scope for trios, quartets or quintets, exciting though they could be with everybody uttering at once.[15] He even thought overtures might be done away with. In fact, Grétry's ambitious experiments with overtures, which rendered them intrinsic to their parent opera, are important enough to warrant careful examination.

The dichotomy exposed by Mercier was echoed in many critiques of Sedaine's librettos, which approved of his stage sense but disliked his 'style', i.e. literary style. Grimm liked the 'Shakespearian' use in *Le déserteur* (1769) of simple, effective phrases of prose dialogue, but found the varied line-lengths of verse, ideal for musical setting, a 'detestable jargon'. The basic fact that music had to be succeeded by spoken dialogue was itself a critical problem. It was a popular technique, enforced by statute, and now, apparently, masterpieces of a sort were being composed in this way. Simple vaudevilles might not overbalance the finesse of Favart's poetry but what happens when musical expression is allowed to expand radically? Carlo Goldoni and Grétry took a pragmatic approach. The first, coming to the Parisian scene in 1762, initially found the mixture 'monstrous':

However, afterwards I reflected; I was not satisfied with Italian recitative, still less with that of the French; and since in opéra-comique one must do without rules and plausibility, it is better to hear a well-recited dialogue than to suffer the monotony of a tedious recitative.[16]

Grétry's view was that since 'it is impossible to make a recitative interesting when the dialogue is not', parts of a drama are particularly at risk in recitative, especially the scenes of exposition. Spoken dialogue has the ability to lead from one thing to another in many subtle ways, and not least with rapidity: 'The man who knows nature best, knows that effects can only be produced by preparation and leading up to them gently as far as their highest degree. Therefore, let the stage speak. Let us mould at one and the same time actors who declaim and musicians who sing.' (i:131). In fact, there could be – for those in favour – a dramatic continuum between dialogue and music:

Grétry and several authors have shown that music could follow all the activities of the stage and approach, to the point of illusion, the truth of dialogue . . . in the theatre, [music] is an extension of prosody.[17]

However the danger, with less original minds than Grétry's, was sheer musical inconsequentiality. E. T. A. Hoffmann saw this happening in light comedy, lacking for him the 'romantic-fantastic element predominant in Italian *opera buffa*'.

The French have no genuine *opera buffa* but only comedies with an incidental admixture of song, which are then mistakenly called comic operas.
    The music, which therefore appears not as an essential prerequisite but only as an incidental embellishment of the text, is subject to the same tendency. One could call it conversational; for here too the only object is that everything should flow together easily and smoothly, that nowhere should anything obtrude in an unseemly manner and that the whole should be suitably amusing, that is, may be understood and enjoyed without any effort being needed, or indeed any particular attention being paid.[18]

In his 1785 book Michel Chabanon developed a general principle (one for which Grimm attacked him) that musical setting was more appropriate to tragedy than comedy. Opéra-comique demanded a distinct aesthetic; it had no overriding unrealistic convention, i.e. of being sung all through; it was more generally pleasing; it had variety; it took the best advantage of speech and of song; the speech provided a useful rest from music, and renewed one's appetite for music.[19] On the other hand, there was too little consistency in the 'truth of expression' of the dialogue, presumably owing to musical demands cutting in, while the musical level easily suffered from inconsistency in 'mode' (key), character and 'movement'. (The techniques Grétry used to overcome such problems will be seen in chapter 2.) Nevertheless, he concluded, there was no *a priori* reason why opéra-comique should not tackle even tragedy.

It is disappointing that neither Chabanon nor the later critic A. W. Schlegel (see below) come to terms with what F. B. Hoffman meant in saying that 'music could follow all the activities of the stage'. This was, after all, a great period in the operatic evolution of ensemble and finale. Grétry, like Mozart, strove to capture action in music and – as long as it was well-motivated – was consistently inspired by a scene of activity. Since opéra-comique allowed perfect comprehensibility of plot, librettists like Marmontel and Sedaine followed an aesthetic path away from static aria and duet, favouring instead the pace and interest of the dramatic continuum. For example, in duets opéra-comique frequently availed itself of the 'dialogue duo', a logically natural and conversational type whose characteristics were admirably described by Rousseau: they included the use of questions, answers, brief exclamations and comprehensible melody, broken only rarely by dissonances or disordered emotion, and allowing the voices to sing simultaneously only for limited periods.[20] By the time he wrote *Raoul Barbe-bleue* (set by Grétry, 1789), Sedaine had arrived at a point where every solo, duet or ensemble had been subsumed convincingly into a unified flow. Schlegel is perfectly aware of Sedaine, of course, and found in *Richard Cœur-de-lion* unmistakeable 'traces of the romantic'. But his argument that the great value of dramatic freedom in opéra-comique was in danger of being hampered by its employment of musical means is hardly likely to satisfy the modern critic of opera:

Quinault has had no successors. How far the French operas of the present day are below his both in point of invention and execution! . . . With pretensions a great deal lower, the *comic opera* or *operette* approaches much more nearly to perfection. With respect to the composition, it may and indeed ought to assume only a national tone. The transition from song to speech, without any musical accompaniment or heightening, which was censured by Rousseau as an unpleasing mixture of two modes of composition, may be displeasing to the ear; but it has unquestionably produced an advantageous effect on the structure of the pieces. In the recitatives which are generally not half understood, and seldom listened to with any degree of attention, a plot which is even moderately complicated cannot be developed with true clearness. Hence in the Italian *opera buffa* the action is altogether neglected, it is distinguished for uniformity of situation, for want of dramatic progress. But the comic opera of the French, although from the space occupied by the music it is unsusceptible of any solid dramatic development, is still calculated to produce a considerable stage effect, and speaks in a pleasing manner to the imagination. The poets have not here been prevented by the constraint of rules from following out their theatrical views.[21]

The popularity of opéras-comiques by Favart, Sedaine and their successors, he claims, is for German audiences a consequence of their poetical merit, not their music. The study by Gaudefroy-Demombynes shows, however, that this was true only some time after 1800:[22] and what are we also to make of the evidence of Carl Maria von Weber in 1817 in speaking of 'countless' performances of Grétry in Germany, and of his appeal in terms such as these?

Grétry may well be the only French composer to have displayed in his music an unmistakable lyrical, and indeed often a romantic sense. His rhythms are always determined by the dramatic needs of the moment rather than by conventional formulae, and the ingeniousness of his melodies has proved inimitable.[23]

Up to 1783, as mentioned above, the home of opéra-comique was the Hôtel de Bourgogne, whose theatre dated back to the sixteenth century. It was, naturally, remodelled from time to time. By the later eighteenth century its capacity was probably about 1,500,[24] but the stage was quite narrow and the orchestra pit, when Grétry first saw it, held ten violins, two violas, three cellos, two double-basses and the usual six wind players. The timpani were habitually played by one of the violists and were never to have a salaried player before the Revolution. Although the musical scope of the works given steadily increased in the 1770s, the company could only squeeze in eleven violins (1773–7), then twelve (1777–83); the rest of the orchestra remained as at the 1768 levels. Evening performances started at 5.15 or 5.30 and lasted some three hours. The theatre opened every night of the year, with few exceptions other than the annual Lenten closure period. In chapter 26 we shall mention the custom-built theatre into which the Comédie-Italienne moved in 1783: the 'Salle Favart' (Plate v). Whatever the theatre, royalty, nobility and bourgeois sat in the tiers of boxes and the upper galleries. Since so much of the seating was held on subscription it was perfectly respectable for anyone, as long as they were male, to use the *parterre* or pit; but as Charles Burney found out in 1764, one had to have stamina:

I am just come from the Comick Opera, which is here called the *Comédie Italienne*, where I have been extremely well entertained, but am so tired with standing the whole time, which every one in the pit does, that I can hardly put a foot to the ground, or hand to the pen.[25]

Thomas Pennington in the 1780s saw in the pit 'well-dressed people, in bags, ruffles etc., with whom I had dined at the table d'hôte, at half-a-crown a head'.[26]

John Lough has traced the changing composition of the *parterre* but found it difficult to gauge the number of lower-class enthusiasts. What is undeniable is that in the earlier days of the century, even to the 1760s, the pit audience was the arbiter of success or failure of operas and plays in a way that was respected by everybody; the pit embodied a consistency of acquaintanceship and taste. From about 1770 'complaints about the poor taste of the spectators in the *parterre* become more insistent'.[27] The old guard, in other words, was becoming adulterated by bourgeois elements, for in that same period Parisian bankers, merchants and others rose to supremacy. With an estimated 40,000 members, five times as numerous as the nobility, this class was financing major architectural and industrial programmes.[28] Of course, they demanded entertainment. Except for the highest-paid craftsmen, the artisan classes earned far too little to buy admission to the official theatres. When they were allowed in for a *gratis* performance for some royal celebration or other, the working people displayed an innocent gaiety:

A young fishwife who had never been to the theatre before, seeing the prompter open the trap-door and raise his head above the stage, cried, 'Eh! look at that dog there that's made a hole in the stage to get himself a place!'[29]

Returning to the theatre in 1773, Burney reported some rowdyism. By 1786 the

Mercure de France was in absolute despair about the atmosphere of extremism in which works were now heard. The pit at the Comédie-Italienne was the worst of any:

Faithful to the principles of giddiness with which it is imbued, it did not fail to call for the author of the work it had just condemned, in loud shouts; for a quarter of an hour its obstinacy filled the auditorium with yelling virtually identical to that thrown up by the Parisian populace at the noble spectacle of a bull being slaughtered.

(23 December 1786, pp. 181–6)

It is quite wrong to think of organised applause or booing as the product of the nineteenth-century theatre. Grétry himself described a *claqueur*:

What things take place at a first performance! At one of my own, a friend of mine assured me he had found himself next to a man who applauded while shouting, 'I'm being paid to hiss, but it's all the same to me.'

(*Réf*:iii:122)

He also complained about journalists being importuned by authors' enemies on a first night, 'in order to dictate to them tomorrow's sheet' and so bring about ruin (ii:291).

Let us turn our attention to the stage itself and the illusions and sensations it produced. A cardinal principle for Grétry was the need for relative intimacy in the opéra-comique theatre. Everybody remembers Grétry's prophetic formula for an ideal theatre, inspired by ancient Rome, with an invisible orchestra, reflective walls, no boxes and painted brown. Its size, however, was to be sufficient for only a thousand people at most. For his own art, as he said, lives in the acting, by the 'thousand details, by the asides, by a thousand movements of the face in which actors can present the truths of this genre'; and in the music, only by 'a thousand nuances between soft and loud, by a thousand ornaments, tiny notes, trills, broken chords, pizzicatos, arpeggios, can the composer express the truth of moral details constituting a [stage] action which is not exaggerated' (iii:24–33).

In the theatre of his time, the front curtain went up at the beginning of the show and stayed up until the end. There may sometimes have been an upstage curtain to conceal backdrop changes between acts, but changes on the main stage were ordinarily visible: see chapter 15. As for lighting, no more vivid indication of ideals could be given than the following instructions in the libretto of Favart and Duni's opéra-comique *Les moissonneurs* (*The reapers*), first mounted when Grétry was struggling to gain a foothold in Paris in 1768:

Act 1 sc. 1 Dawn begins to appear: the stars are still visible.
[footnote:] N.B. In act 1 the sky brightens gradually, the morning mist clears and the sun rises; in act 2 it is above the horizon and in the beginning of act 3 it appears in its full height and declines towards the end of the day. This progressive movement must be made imperceptibly, but its effect must be noticeable in the three acts.

Oil lamps, however, gave a localised, smoky light; and the main house chandelier remained illuminated for the duration of the performance. In chapter 14 we shall see how one of Grétry's librettists complained bitterly in the 1770s that the scenery and properties made his vision impossible to convey adequately. Yet the tendency towards more costly, specially-designed scenery was inexorable, and with the opening of the new premises in 1783 the way was open for illusions of the sort portrayed in Plates VI and VII. Costume design was liable to be haphazard, as the main singers, those possessing a shareholding, were responsible for their own. When the time came to appoint supervision over the company's chorus costumes, the task went to a principal singer, Mme Dugazon: she would have inspection duties, supervise purchases, and so on.[30] But as was pointed out in 1789 in the context of Grétry's *Raoul Barbe-bleue*:

An actor cannot see everything on his own, do everything and know everything: in the matter of costumes he is obliged to address himself usually to tailors, or to young painters; but tailors are generally ignorant and not all young painters are very knowledgeable. Thereby frequent mistakes are created, anachronisms, and a confusion which can only lead unenlightened spectators and actors astray.[31]

In this book there is not room to explore the sartorial or other particularities of the singers for whom Grétry wrote. However, these would be fruitful fields to study. The Comédie-Italienne built up an exceptional *esprit de corps* in the 1760s and a willingness to develop the genre of opéra-comique through experience and advice. Marmontel pays it more than one tribute.

Mme La Ruette invited us to dinner. There I read my libretto [*Lucile*] and Grétry sang his music. Both being approved in this little council, all due preparations were made for introducing the work upon the stage and, after two or three rehearsals, it was performed.

Our actors showed us, quite sincerely, every consideration: both in acting and singing they understood what was looked for; and they had a presentiment of the effects more infallible than ours.[32]

One cannot say that this almost familial atmosphere lasted into the 1780s but, as has always been normal, a composer would write with individuals in mind. 'When one creates a part for an actor, one must proportion it to his faculties.' (i:331n). Certain players specialised in certain types of rôle, which is why Grétry ran into difficulties in *Silvain* when he wanted Mme La Ruette as Hélène; the actresses ordinarily charged with playing mothers objected (i:199). Needless to say, the tactician and charmer got his own way. Some of Grétry's leading actors, or rather, contemporary engravings of the rôles created by these actors, can be seen in Plates I–III and VI–IX:

Plates I, II, III: Marie-Thérèse La Ruette as Henriette (*Les deux avares*), Corali (*L'amitié à l'épreuve*), Zémire (*Zémire et Azor*).
Plates I, II: Joseph Caillot as Martin (*Les deux avares*), Sander (*Zémire et Azor*).
Plate I: Jean-Louis La Ruette as Gripon (*Les deux avares*).
Plates VIII, IX: Louise-Rosalie Lefèbvre (Mme Dugazon) as Azémia, Isaure (*Raoul Barbe-bleue*).
Plates I, II, III, VI, VII: Jean-Baptiste Clairval as Jérôme (*Les deux avares*), Nelson (*L'amitié à l'épreuve*), Azor (*Zémire et Azor*), Blondel (*Richard Cœur-de-lion*).

Mme La Ruette (1744–1837) was Grétry's leading actress from *Le Huron* to *La Rosière de Salency*, creating ten rôles, obviously specialising in virtuous heroines

13

but also (see chapter 10) allowing herself to be persuaded to change her interpretation from something too proper to something more natural and witty.[33] Caillot (1732–1816), who retired in 1772, created seven rather contrasted Grétry rôles.[34] He had a baritone range, since his voice 'though classified as a bass (*basse-taille*) was rather a tenor (*taille*), or what the Italians call *tenore*, in that the line descends rarely to the bass cords, and that the expressive character of most arias demands more vocal sensibility than power'.[35] His voice was sonorous but was 'the least of the gifts he received from nature': such an actor was he that Garrick, seeing him at work, cried out, 'There's a rare man! That's the most excellent one!'[36] Jean-Louis La Ruette (1731–92) created eight Grétry rôles, often comic servants but also more serious parts.[37]

Who could have forgotten the comic, witty acting of M. La Ruette, and the true, ingenious way he created all his rôles? He adopted early an air of old age and took admirable advantage of it with his trembling, hardly brilliant voice . . . He was by turns buffoon, straight actor, *naïf*, amusing or serious, and knew how to artfully bring to life all the characters allotted to him. He sang with the greatest accuracy . . . he was a born musician . . . Never did he permit himself to change any dialogue and improvise for well or ill to make the multitude laugh.[38]

Mme Dugazon (1755–1821) was perhaps the greatest dramatic soprano of her time at the Italiens, and has been the subject of more than one biography.[39] It is said that Grétry spotted her at the age of fourteen when she was a dancer at the Comédie-Italienne – actresses often joined at this age or younger – and wrote 'On dit à quinze ans' in *Lucile* specially for her.[40] When young, she was supposedly coached by Mme Favart, who herself created for Grétry only one part, Juliette in *L'amitié à l'épreuve*, not long before her death. It was later a commonplace that Dugazon's name on a poster was alone enough to ensure a work's success. After creating Chloé in *Le jugement de Midas*, though she had taken main rôles since 1774, she progressed to parts in which her talent for complete self-identification was seen to full advantage.[41]

No actor served Grétry longer or better than Clairval (1737–95), the tenor who created at least sixteen rôles from *Le Huron* to *Richard Cœur-de-lion*.[42] A 'great actor in a minor theatre, he raised it, almost alone, to the degree of favour we see now, and sustained it with Mme Favart, Caillot and La Ruette . . . The type of pleasure Clairval gives in most of the rôles he plays is not that which provokes shouts of *bravo* every minute; but a smile is on one's lips, reflection in one's eyes, and pleasure in one's heart.'[43] Public payment of their debt to Clairval was paid by Grétry in the *Mémoires* and by Sedaine in the libretto of *Richard Cœur-de-lion*. Space forbids discussion of yet other important actor–singers who created Grétry rôles, such as Marie-Jeanne Trial, Mlles Billioni and Colombe, and MM. Nainville, Philippe (i.e. Philippe Cauvy), Rosière, Trial, Narbonne and Meunier.[44] In giving lists of *dramatis personae* for each opera in this book I have added a voice-type: but as we saw in Caillot's case, concepts of such types were rather different two centuries ago. Grétry's full scores rarely used the alto clef, the one appropriate to the very high tenor (*haute-contre*); his use of the tenor clef is usually consistent, but as some voices ranged widely, like Caillot's and Philippe's, Grétry did sometimes notate a given rôle in both the bass and tenor clefs within a single work. Such vocal types I have called baritone, but there is evidence that our concept of the baritone did not exist for the earlier Grétry. Fétis, talking of the singer and composer Jean-Pierre Solié (who started his career at the Comédie-Italienne just at the closing period of this book), asserted:

The arrival of the famous Italian *bouffons* drawing all Paris to the théâtre de Monsieur, rue Feydeau [i.e. the new permanent, genuinely Italian company which opened in January 1789, though their premises at the Salle Feydeau only opened in 1791] permitted Solié at the same time to study the art of singing at their school . . .
His vocal organ passed imperceptibly from tenor to baritone [*baryton*], a voice type until then unknown at the Opéra-Comique; it resulted therefrom that composers wrote specially for him, and furnished him an employment that has been named after him.[45]

However, Grétry certainly differentiated between bass and tenor, as when he rewrote a *basse-taille* part (that of Narbonne, rôle of Robert) for *taille*: see the end of chapter 30.

Composers themselves nominated which singers they desired in a new work, and in the rather hierarchical manner of the time, a given rôle remained the 'property' of a singer as long as was artistically possible. As earlier opéras-comiques by Grétry and others outlived their original actors, certain rôles were spoiled by less expert and conscientious followers. A particular problem was the lack of rehearsal opportunity made available for younger singers coming into older rôles for the first time. This bears witness to the hydra-headed personality of the company around 1789: it presented many new works every year, also contained a company of non-singing actors (since 1780) and yet was expected to maintain elements of a repertory going back thirty years or more. Modern rehearsal methods did not yet prevail; two violins and a cello were paid to accompany certain rehearsals from May 1774, and in 1790 piano rehearsals were still not used, though they were obviously desirable and were being employed at the Théâtre de Monsieur.[46] Singers were coached as necessary in new parts, as this revealing account shows; Mme Dugazon

knew no music; her singing is neither Italian nor French, but simply itself. She obliges me to teach her the rôles I have written for her, and I admit that I tremble when I indicate my nuances to her, for fear that she will substitute inspirations granted by a greater master than I.

(i:416)

While it is manifestly impossible to be certain, it seems likely that whereas around 1770 singers used a thinner, more declamatory style, this was to become more 'expressive' in the manner here described by Louis-Sébastien Mercier somewhere around 1780:

Modifications are one of the great secrets of music: it is they that give it expression, movement and life. But we have never known among us the inexpressible charm of smoothly-flowing sounds; that is, the art of intensifying and softening the voice, of leading it through all nuances, not from low to high, but from the most constrained [*remisse*] to the most intense, on each of the pitches of which the voice is capable.[47]

If this is reliable testimony, the development of such a style would probably be connected with the spread of ⤐⤏ signs in the 1780s in opéra-comique and elsewhere. Grétry confirms that they could be of varied length and signified 'one note swollen or diminished' (iii:322).

The rehearsal methods applied to new works were equally outdated when the whole company gathered together. The more friendly ways of finishing, testing and improving an opéra-comique could not remain in the enlarged company when there was no 'producer' apart from the librettist, and when individual artistic loyalties could not all be trusted.

> The three final rehearsals of a work are, for authors and actors, a time of torment during which they almost know neither what they are doing nor what should be done. It is then that they cut, slice and mutilate a work which sometimes has need only of a good performance; it is then that librettist and composer commit faults for which they would scold a school class. Exhausted with tiredness, late nights and above all worry, how dare they claim to do what is most difficult in the arts, to cut out part of a whole that has been contemplated at length from all points of view? (ii:308–9)

This seems unanswerable, and accounts for the way works were often improved after first nights. We shall consider in a moment the written evidence for such alterations. What Grétry wanted was a couple of well-prepared rehearsals, in the presence of some people in the auditorium; the difficulty in obtaining this was overwhelmingly due to the actors charged with secondary rôles.

Democratic procedures had long obtained in the selection of texts, though naturally everything had subsequently to be submitted for the censor's approval. All the actors and other shareholders formed an Assembly every Saturday morning, or had the right to; it was then that the coming week's plans were agreed, and important rehearsals fixed. In the early days the Assembly itself heard new texts and voted on them, but eventually a reading committee had to be set up. The allocation of an accepted libretto to a composer was made at the discretion of its author, but of course the musical result had to be approved by the company. This may well have been one of the duties given to Grétry when he became attached to the Comédie-Italienne in 1771 (see chapter 7). Although a composer then had a certain advisory rôle, he did not conduct from the keyboard as was done in Italy and elsewhere: in the absence of recitatives, no keyboard was necessary, and the violinist–director had charge.[48] (At court, Grétry certainly conducted in 1772, possibly from the keyboard: the court manuscript score of *La Rosière de Salency* has a figured bass line. See chapters 7 and 14.) Judging from manuscript indications in printed scores, Grétry's opéras-comiques were performed with flexibility of tempo. A printed *rallentando* would be followed by a (brief) pause where appropriate. Pauses or tempo changes were used to emphasise significant words or changes of emotional direction. Such basic analogies with the drama connect with the critical observations quoted earlier, and accord with Grétry's own aim at the 'truth of moral details'.

Opéras-comiques, then, were 'living' things, even when successful, and liable to change aspects of their appearance in several ways. Easiest to change, when in prose, was spoken dialogue. We mentioned impromptu actor's changes in connection with La Ruette. Unpublished alterations can be seen from manuscript prompter's copies, but these are chiefly lost before 1800. However, dialogue changes to words or phrases are commonly found between the various early editions of a libretto. This leads to the question of librettos themselves.

A typical Grétry opéra-comique was first produced either at the Comédie-Italienne or at court. For a court performance the libretto would be issued only by the official printer, Ballard. When it opened in Paris the work would have its libretto published again by a different *éditeur* and, if it was at all successful, further editions would be issued quite quickly, these varying in size and pagination. The dating and other details of a title-page could be extremely erratic, and work remains to be done on these questions. In earlier days a Grétry libretto would be first printed around the time of the première or even possibly before (see chapter 10 for one copy bearing a first performance date that did not actually transpire). For example, both the very earliest known versions of *La fausse magie* exist as librettos. A catholic study of available librettos, therefore, furnishes valuable details of the evolution of a work. Later on, a libretto might be held back for a time while the opera 'settled down'. The best example here is *Richard Cœur-de-lion*, published as a libretto in 1786 only after two preliminary versions had been mounted. It is also a good example of the danger of accepting dates at face value: the official permission to print the libretto, dated 19 October 1784, still appears at the back.

Yet another source of a libretto exists: the printed score. This will often differ in detail once again from the librettos and, partly because it took longer to publish, may well represent a slightly more authentic version of the words.

Let us turn now to the music. After a first night, the opéra-comique was quite likely to be modified further from the state it had reached in rehearsal: audience reaction was noted and, especially when the daily press began in 1777, that of critics. If the première was at court the criteria were different, in so far as the production and taste of the audience were not necessarily the same as for Paris. *Zémire et Azor's* sumptuous court première generated more enthusiasm than the Paris performances afterwards. The gap in time between court and city performances usually provided the occasion for changes of greater or lesser degree.

Consequently, individual numbers might be cut or shortened or be replaced by others. There was no one method by which any of these changes might be preserved for posterity. (In the case of *Les mariages samnites* the first thoughts of the authors were artificially preserved in score; in that of *Richard Cœur-de-lion* the score preserved only the putative final version.) A clue is sometimes to be found in the unaccompanied aria or duet versions printed for popular consumption at the back of some librettos. If an opéra-comique was felt to be wholly unworkable, as was *Théodore et Paulin* (chapter 27), it could even be transformed as though from a chrysalis into a butterfly. Then, 'parody' technique might be used: new words to old music. More frequently, dissatisfaction with a particular act could give rise to the redesign and amalgamation of material (see *Aucassin et Nicolette* and *Pierre le*

Grand) or even to the subsequent preference for a third or fourth version more closely resembling the first one (*Les deux avares*, *La fausse magie*). Or there might be radical cutting, followed by radical expansion with new characters (*L'amitié à l'épreuve*). Two different full score versions exist for all three of the last-named operas, although this fact is by no means always appreciated.[49] Because Grétry regarded the printed score as authoritative, and perhaps because he used helpers to notate details (see chapter 2), he did not preserve his manuscript scores of opéras-comiques: besides, it was customary not to do so after publication. This deprives us of information concerning versions, leaving the printed score as the focus of our discussions. In a unique case, that of *La Rosière de Salency*, we can compare two different versions, the earlier in manuscript. This, as it happens, is especially fortunate since the evolution of the work presents quite tangled problems.[50]

Information about versions sometimes derives from account-books, when remuneration to authors indicates the number of acts of a given piece at a given time. Authors and composers shared $\frac{1}{9}$ of net profits for a three- or four-act work, $\frac{1}{12}$ for a two-act work and $\frac{1}{18}$ for a one-act piece. We shall, incidentally, see Grétry complaining about these rates in chapter 25.

Full scores never cite a publication date, so dating has to be achieved by newspaper and other evidence. We have adopted the datings issued by François Lesure (see note 49) and in the Grétry work-list for *The New Grove*, except when new research has revealed errors. Often a full score was issued a matter of months after a première; indeed *La fausse magie* came out in a version quite quickly withdrawn from the stage and subsequently twice changed. The score of *Silvain* (première 19 February 1770) says on the title-page, 'The [orchestral] parts will appear on 20 April.' If this is confirmation that the score went on sale on or before 19 April, the press announcement of this fact was indeed tardy, appearing only on 21 May 1770. Much later on there were delays in score publishing, particularly of *Les méprises par ressemblance* and *Le rival confident*. The very notion of 'publication' needs to be treated with care, however. The publisher did not run off a fixed number of copies and dispose of the plates but kept the latter and ran off copies as demanded. In chapter 3 note 1 this is discussed in connection with Grétry's use of opus numbers. When the three scores mentioned earlier were reissued in new versions, the original plates were certainly used where possible but with new pagination. In fact there is only five pages' difference in length between the one-act and two-act scores of *La fausse magie*.

So sometimes a printed score shows a reasonably definitive version of a work as acted in Paris, and sometimes only an outdated one. The 'Versions and performances' sections in this book attempt a summary of each case, drawing also upon the composer's letters, *Mémoires*, *Réflexions d'un solitaire*, newspaper articles, the *Correspondance littéraire* and the *Mémoires secrets* of Bachaumont. This has seemed necessary, since while a certain amount of such information was made use of in the Grétry complete edition (i.e the *Collection complète des œuvres*, 1884–1936: *CC*), by no means enough of it was known about or used to give a consistently truthful picture. The *CC* omitted salient parts of reviews and many bibliographical references. In some egregious cases they remained ignorant of fundamental printed sources: see chapters 23 note 1 and 34 note 17, for example. But even copies of the *CC* can be hard to locate: not even the music department of the Bibliothèque Nationale in Paris stocks them all.

2. Profile 1: from Liège to Paris

André-Ernest-Modeste Grétry (baptised 11 February 1741, died 24 September 1813) was the second of six children.[1] The first-born was Jean-Joseph-Célestin (1739–96) and the first of four daughters was Marie-Catherine-Dorothée (1743–1804). When Grétry first issued his *Mémoires* his mother, brother and one or more sisters were still alive. This is doubtless the reason why the composer left no portrait of them when describing his childhood in Liège. Nevertheless, the *Mémoires* contain a mass of details about the composer's early life, details which modern research has often been able to corroborate.[2]

Grétry's ancestors came originally from the village of the same name near the castle of Bolland, fifteen kilometres from Liège, where they farmed. Jean-Noel, Grétry's grandfather and an amateur musician, moved to Blégny after marrying Dieudonnée Campinado: they lacked her family's consent. Even this circumstance is lent a surreptitious connection with his own works by the composer, who relates how Dieudonnée's illustrious ecclesiastical uncle visited her later to find her 'as happy in her rural household as if she had been born a peasant' (i:2): the reader may compare the figure of Hélène in *Silvain*. Jean-Noel made his living by selling cheap beer and brandy. The eldest surviving son of this marriage was François-Pascal (1714–68), the composer's father. François carved out his own career as a professional musician, which was to place him excellently when guiding his own son's development. Aged fifteen (Grétry says twelve) he won a salaried position as second violin at the church of St Martin-en-mont, Liège. He must also, in due course, have had to give lessons privately; in 1738 he married a pupil, Jeanne Des Fossés (1715–1800). If she (later the composer's mother) had 'little fortune', her family, nevertheless, had more elevated social pretensions. Jeanne's father was 'controller of an office of Prince Jean-Théodore, cardinal of Bavaria' (i:3–4). But Grétry's home background was humble, close-knit and affectionate:

persons of high birth are far from knowing how much stronger this respectable emotion [paternal and filial love] is among the honest bourgeois . . . The custom of living together, of warming oneself at the same fire, drinking from the same vessel, eating from the same dish, would doubtless be repugnant to the artificial nature of the *beau monde*; but however with what delight I remember those dear and good old days! (i:50)

Yet early life had its share of brutality: this future music tutor to the queen of France remembered the convulsions of a nameless wife, the senseless cruelty of her husband's 'cure' (*Réf*:ii:241). Among ordinary people the effects of brandy, the national drink, were only too visible. Recalling this, Grétry added: 'My poor father died of this excess at no advanced age' (*Réf*:iii:68).

Liège had been an independent episcopal principality of the Holy Roman Empire since before the year 1000 and was ruled, often not without opposition, by a prince–bishop. It became part of France in October 1795. Grétry fiercely retained his feeling of Liégeois identity and was welcomed back in triumph in 1776 and 1782. When he was born the capital city of Liège was a compact place of fewer than 57,000 inhabitants: Vienna had some 176,000 at this period; pre-industrial Sheffield only 20,000. During the month that Grétry was born, one of the most fecund of the Liégeois year, only 143 births were recorded in the city.[3]

In June 1748 Grétry's father took employment at the collegiate church of St Denis, Liège, as first violin.[4] The strength of music at this church, which was to be the centre of Grétry's activities for a decade, was as follows: four chorister priests, six chorister lay clerks, six choirboys; four violins, cello, double-bass, bassoon, organ. The instrumental number was augmented by choral students who were given free lessons at the time their voices broke; in Grétry's case it was to be on the violin. There was a choir-school, the normal means by which musical boys were educated at the time: Joseph Haydn in Vienna was placed in one. Grétry became a choirboy on 25 August 1750. Initially he lived at home, since only the four oldest choristers could board at the school. At St Denis the choirmaster's duties specified, *inter alia*:

He must instruct the choirboys in Gregorian chant and in music in lessons of one hour before noon and one hour after Vespers. He must educate them and instruct them in modesty and have them participate in all offices and processions, by day or night.

However, as happened with Haydn, Grétry's musical education within the choir-school was deficient in theory and composition. Additionally, other circumstances militated against his rapid development. It was not just that he loved freedom and the countryside (to which he was to return in retirement at Montmorency), and hated getting up at 5 a.m. and walking to church thrice daily. Fate put him in the charge of young and unexceptional choirmasters. The first, H. F. Devillers, appointed temporarily from June 1750 to the end of 1753, ran a terrifying and violent régime. Grétry did so badly that he had to be withdrawn. However, his father took him to study with François Leclerc, a cathedral musician of gentle disposition. The second choirmaster, C. F. Jalheau (referred to in the *Mémoires* simply as 'J.'), more subtle, had recently taken holy orders in Rome. He seems to have had no propensity towards composition, and in the *Mémoires* he plays rather the opposition part that Cherubini was to play in those of Berlioz.

Then, while Grétry was still away from St Denis, there arrived in Liège an Italian comic opera troupe. It performed between 1753 and Ash Wednesday 1755.[5] This was his supremely formative, and fortunate, musical experience. Grétry's father, who may well have played in the orchestra, took him to all the performances and to many rehearsals; like Berlioz later, Grétry learned by sitting in the pit. His single most important musical model, Pergolesi, was represented, together with operas by Galuppi and others. Fired by 'a passionate taste for music' and at his father's behest, he regained his place in the choir by singing an Italian aria, with Latin words, so well at a Sunday service that the Chapter requested it again the next week. On this occasion came 'all the Italian troupe, women and men: each of them regarded me as his pupil' (i:18). From then on Grétry's obviously attractive voice was heard many times. Doubtless it was bad for his vanity; but it also provided a foundation-stone for his career as an opera composer.

Some time after this Grétry took his first unguided steps in free composition, which he achieved by patchwork and imitation. So his father provided him with two teachers: H. J. Renkin, organist of St Pierre, for keyboard, figured bass and harmony, and later Henri Moreau of St Paul for counterpoint. As Moreau was studying in Rome until Easter 1756 Grétry must have been at least fifteen when he began. But his progress as a composer was held back by their insistence upon prior perfection in contrapuntal and fugal technique (i:33). The normal musical style even in Liège's church music was modern and Italianate, and to judge from the examples by Georges Wenick, who directed music at St Denis up to 1750, blended a high degree of melodic charm with hardly less contrapuntal interest for the chorus.[6] Grétry finally produced a set of six 'symphonies', now lost, whose success in performance brought him the patronage of Simon-Joseph de Harlez, provost of St Denis; this Maecenas organised Grétry's place in Rome at the Liège foundation known as the Collège Darchis.

Thanks to the benefaction of Lambert Darchis in the late seventeenth century ordinary Liège boys could train in Rome for the priesthood, the arts, or sciences. Up to four boys went annually, staying for a maximum of five years.[7] Musicians had attended since 1721 and Henri Moreau himself had been. However, aspiring students first went to qualify at the Jesuit college in Liège. Grétry did not. He had become proficient enough to play second violin at St Denis since January 1759; now he set himself to write a complete Mass 'to induce the Chapter to let me depart', not the usual short Mass ending with the Gloria or Credo. After Moreau's corrections and with de Harlez' support, the Chapter accepted it for the next solemn feast day. With barely decorous glee the *Mémoires* recount how Jalheau was obliged to conduct the piece, his 'bad grace' matched only by the enthusiasm of Grétry's supporters in the orchestra. Neither this nor any other Mass by Grétry survives today.

In many ways Grétry's life began when he walked to Rome. He states that he left at the end of March 1759; however, other evidence points to March 1760, which we shall assume is the correct date.[8] His parents opposed his departure on the grounds of his indifferent health, but it was Grétry's father who was first to die, in 1768, without seeing his son again. For the composer it was a release which had a psychological force parallel to that felt by Goethe:

It was only when I realised that everyone at home was chained, body and soul, to the north . . . that, drawn by an irresistible need, I made up my mind to undertake this long, solitary journey to the hub of the world.   (*Italian Journey*, 1786)[9]

Not only did Grétry avoid the Jesuit college but he succeeded in obtaining 100 Brabantine florins towards study in Rome from the church authorities, granted him on 1 April 1760.

Vivid portraits began to spring up in the *Mémoires*: his guide, his companions, mountains, adventures, conversations, the overwhelming first glimpses of Italy and the papal city itself. The Collège Darchis provided board and lodging but a course of study – medicine, architecture, sculpture, painting – was one's own to organise. Over the next six years Grétry garnered the social and musical expertise that he would need in Paris: his, in other words, was the experience of a Prix de Rome winner over forty years before France made that award available to her young musicians. His new horizons encompassed anatomy classes, friendship with the painter Nicolas de Fassin, and becoming fluent in Italian,[10] to say nothing of meeting a hermit and living with him for three months. Charles Burney, who was in Rome in 1770, noted 'the easy and social manner in which [strangers] live with the natives, as well as each other'.[11] And it was the epoch of major discoveries at Herculaneum and Pompeii, of the publication of Winckelmann's *Geschichte der Kunst des Altertums*; Grétry became as capable as anyone of penning a few pages on the music of the ancient Greeks or Romans (iii:414). If he gives no hint of having met Hubert Robert, who was studying at the French Academy in Rome, he is equally silent concerning the gigantic ensembles of instruments playing on palace balconies that Burney saw, though he can hardly have missed them.

Music in Rome favoured the liturgy rather than the theatres: of the latter there were eight, but opera was given only at Carnival time, from early January to Shrove Tuesday. As far as musical style was concerned this hardly mattered, since 'Church music is not at all grave and serious . . . sometimes one can hardly tell sacred music apart from theatre music.'[12] His idol was the composer Piccinni, whose comic masterpiece *La Cecchina* was first staged in Rome's Teatro delle Dame (Alibert) just before he arrived. Piccinni allowed the young composer and a friend to watch him work for an hour, but we know of no further contact. An operatic apprenticeship was – is – a matter of osmosis; so Grétry's progress in Italy can be no better told than by gathering up the scattered information in the *Mémoires* (i:79–111).

Life	Works
Arrives (?May 1760); following intensive viewing of the city and antique remains he falls ill for 'two months'. Spends 'six or eight' months with a feeble teacher (say August 1760 to February 1761) then 'six weeks' alone studying Durante's fugues. Is accepted for 'two years' as a pupil of Giovanni Casali, *maestro di cappella* of St John Lateran and 'the only master I acknowledge' (to ?April 1763). Then seeks his own way; decides to develop theatre music and art of true declamation; works 'obstinately' and self-critically begins to destroy	Three keyboard fugues Fugues; 'Confitebor' dated 1762;[13] Magnificat in eight parts; psalms; masses[14]

Profile 1: from Liège to Paris

Life	Works
his own efforts. Falls ill for 'six months' (?end 1763) and recuperates spiritually and musically during sojourn with hermit for 'three months' (?April 1764). Writes new music which is performed, leading to a commission for the Teatro delle Dame: a pair of comic intermezzos for Carnival 1765. Probably during 1765 Grétry presents himself in Bologna and successfully sits test for membership of the Accademia Filarmonica.[16] Becomes private composer of concertos to English flute-player 'milord A . . ' (i:110), probably the 4th Earl of Abingdon, resident in Geneva. Leaves Rome (?early 1766); according to the *Mémoires*, 1 January 1767.	Several vocal scenes (lost) and symphonies[15] *La Vendemmiatrice* (*The Grape-picker*), music lost, is well received Proposal received for more intermezzos Flute concertos

Grétry met Lord Abingdon (1740–99) in Rome; the musical Englishman had gone to Switzerland after leaving Oxford in 1761, and mixed in democratic circles. Later he was to know Haydn well in London.[17]

Already Grétry's individuality can be perceived in the words of elder contemporaries. Piccinni gave *La Vendemmiatrice* his approbation because it did not follow 'the common route' (i:109) while Casali – composer of some four operas, not just church music – described him on his departure from Italy as a 'true donkey in music who knows nothing, but is a friendly and well-mannered young man'.[18] Grétry found his own character a constant topic of interest. Slight of build, blond, with regular features and attractive eyes, he thrived in a society of conversation and gallantry: a 'delicate gentlemanlike young man, very well bred and proper', thought Burney.[19] His fascination with women is the recurring motif of his *Réflexions*, where we catch him in an appropriate vignette. The Abbé Galiani (1728–87) 'said to me one day, on seeing my piano surrounded by sirens: "My child, flee the coquettes, they would consume you and your talent." I wanted to hear him speak – I said it was often difficult to resist them.' (*Réf*:ii:146). He was at home amid the passions of theatrical life. The backstage atmosphere and the easy wit are reported to perfection by Bouilly, his collaborator on *Pierre le Grand*. The young author, overcome after the successful première of this work, kisses the perspiring neck of Mme Dugazon, his leading lady. ' "Come, come" says Grétry with his malicious smile, "he's a gourmet; that promises for the future." ' (*Mes récapitulations*, i, 202). The skilful rejoinder or telling of a tale in polite company could be mixed with a benign consciousness of his own status as a member of the Third Estate, or amusement at his learned friends' incomprehension at the skills that musicians take for granted. His, too, were the delicate problems of an invalid. Since adolescence Grétry suffered occasional internal bleeding, usually brought on by stress.[20] This obliged him to take to his bed for several days at a time, and no cure was ever found for it.

Early in 1766 his friend the flautist Charles Weiss induced Grétry to go to

Geneva. The composer's fees for music lessons there were superior to those approved by the authorities, thanks to the influence of certain English gentlemen encountered in Rome (i:129–30). It was in reality a plan of campaign. Grétry had been shown the score of Monsigny's opéra-comique *Rose et Colas* (1764) which, he recalled, 'awakened my desire to work in Paris'. To besiege Paris resources were necessary: besides money, Geneva provided a training-ground whose possibilities were all grasped by Grétry during 1766. He saw opéras-comiques on the stage; he obtained the help and friendship of Voltaire in the quest for a libretto; and he composed a successful setting of Favart's opéra-comique *Isabelle et Gertrude* which drew the crowds for six nights in December.[21] By fortunate coincidence the players whom Grétry saw and for whom he wrote his first French stage work had only been brought to Geneva in summer 1766; they acted *Rose et Colas* and some six other representative opéras-comiques by Monsigny, Philidor, Duni and Gossec.[22] That Grétry found it, as many did, a shock at first to appreciate both singing and speaking in one work, and the sound of sung French, says much about the thoroughness with which he was steeped in Italian music and about the strangely distinctive way in which French singers pronounced and sang at that time. In the provinces Burney thought this was due to the influence of plainsong in church; in Paris he thought the vocal music resembled 'the screaming of tortured infernals': 'the French voice never comes further than from the throat; there is no *voce di petto*, no true *portamento* or direction of the voice, on any of the stages'.

Voltaire received the young composer, presumably in autumn, almost at once, and had it seems already heard speak of him as a musician of *esprit*, with spirit, wit or intelligent interest. Indeed Grétry was invited back more than once, and it must remain for our next chapter to speculate more closely about the meeting of these two minds. Less speculative is that Grétry gained the entrée at Ferney to a section of Voltaire's friendly disciples and correspondents who assisted in the struggle to win Paris: people such as his early patron the Comte de Creutz and the critic La Harpe. Indeed La Harpe reported that at Ferney, 'they also wanted to invite me to write some works for M. Grétry. I replied that I did not at all believe I had that sort of talent'; it is possible that this writer recommended *Isabelle et Gertrude*, for in addition to being derived from a Voltaire poem (*Gertrude, ou de l'éducation d'une fille*) Favart's text received high praise in La Harpe's *Cours de littérature*.[23]

Grétry's music survives only in part and has never been published, though the libretto (which of course had been issued already) has been studied. Nevertheless, the manuscripts as they exist provide precious knowledge, the more so since players' markings suggest they were at one time used.[24] Complete material survives for the overture, (12), and (13); the missing bass part for (14) and (15) can safely be taken from the viola line, as the rest of the opera has them virtually in unison throughout. No voice parts survive for (1) to (11) or the final vaudeville and chorus (16).

The music shows Grétry in command of many moods that appear in later works, ranging from farce through the sentimental to the sturdily energetic. Movements are often developed to over seventy bars in length. In form, the influence of Philidor is detectable in the use of ABA or ABA' with the central section in a contrasting rhythmic metre as well as key: (1), (2), (5), (10), (15). But in other movements types of sonata form appear: (7), (9) and (12). However, Grétry is already experimenting with the placing of the recapitulation: (3), (4), (6). Melodies can suggest Monsigny's rococo grace (12) or Pergolesi's freshness, as do (2) and (8).

In (13), Isabelle's 'Un secret ennui', we see the typically simple string scoring and some untypical faults of word-setting: 'Et le matin' is ungrateful both for the stress on the article 'le' and for the unprepared high entry of the voice, something hard to imagine in the later works (Ex. 2:1). In (13) overall, however, words

Ex. 2.1 *Isabelle et Gertrude* (13) Cf. Ex. 20.6.
('A secret trouble consumes me when I let sleep overcome me. And in the morning on waking [I am still more uneasy]')

determine the form to a large degree. This is entirely characteristic of Grétry's later practice. Crudely speaking, this entailed new music for new lines or images in the text, same or parallel music for identical texts, no musical repetition when no reprise of text. Compared to Piccinni's style, Grétry's obviously sounds the more 'speaking' or declamatory. Piccinni can be virtually Baroque in use of sequence (whether in subjects or in passagework) and instrumental figuration. Grétry rarely used sequence for its own sake and his linear writing is free from instrumental figures. His instruments are subordinated to the nuances of words. The reported difficulties in Rome surely make sense, since Grétry's style signifies a personal response to Italian influence, not total absorption of it.

Variety of key is greater in *Isabelle et Gertrude* than some later works, and the presence of a splendid duet in G minor (15) reveals the composer's affinity with that key. On the other hand, a certain similarity of outline affects leading themes in (4), (5), (7), (10), (12) and (13), though not so acutely as to cause conscious association in the hearer. A later example of this occurrence is Ex. 12.6. Grétry was right to draw attention to the 'encouraging success' the work received, though he does not claim it as more than an apprentice piece. As we shall see, he did not throw away the score.

Sustained by Voltaire's encouragement, Grétry left for Paris some time in 1767; he took lodgings with a painter, Sené.[25] Duni and Philidor showed towards him that spirit of disinterest which often obtained in the world of opéra-comique at this period, by contrast with the intrigues surrounding so much of what happened at the Paris Opéra. When Pleinchesne offered his text of *Le jardinier de Sidon* to Grétry only to confide it three days later to Philidor, that master proposed a joint composition with Grétry, a course he had never yet seen fit to take: the dividing-line between *pasticcios*, using popular tunes and borrowed arias, and opéras-comiques, the work of one musical hand, had been generally clear for a decade now. Sensibly, Grétry refused, though his reasons were wholly selfish (i:148). He then prevailed upon the rather obscure figure of Légier for a libretto, probably the Pierre Légier who had written the unsuccessful *Le rendez-vous* (1763) for Duni.[26] Légier was said by Grétry to have chosen *Les mariages samnites* (*The Samnite marriages*) as a subject, but it is equally likely that the musician, who in any case had ceaselessly to goad this *bon vivant* into what little serious activity he was capable of, was responsible. *Les mariages samnites* (see chapter 17 for the second version) was a Moral Tale by Voltaire's disciple Jean-François Marmontel: the story is set in the fourth century B.C. and concerns the relation of love, the family and heroism in an ideal republic.

It was, to judge from his surviving letters, growing near the end of 1767; any reputation Grétry had brought with him was now in the balance. He played the score to his friends the *littérateurs* François Arnaud and J. B. A. Suard, both advocates of the reform of French opera and future champions of Gluck; they canvassed support in society, enabling Grétry to meet Creutz personally.[27] In Creutz, Grétry found not just a persuasive and diplomatic ally, but also a friendly critic and helpmate to his muse. The first setback then occurred when the Comédie-Italienne turned down the opera's libretto as 'too noble' for their theatre.

Indeed, one has only to glance at the 1776 version to see why. So there began a series of adaptations and new beginnings that was not exhausted until the early 1790s, the unperformed *Roger et Olivier* and *L'inquisition* (p. 147). These facts tell us something of the high aims Grétry entertained for the subject, and something of his practice of re-using music: although the 1767–8 *Les mariages samnites* does not survive as such, we can identify several powerful pieces from it.[28] The work's high style made possible the idea of an arrangement with recitatives for the Opéra, which was done, after which the Prince de Conti caused a private audition of the work to take place in the early months of 1768, reportedly in the presence of 200 influential guests (Grimm:viii:166). This was a disaster. The chorus sabotaged its rehearsal, and in the evening 'nothing produced the least effect; boredom was so universal that I wanted to escape after act one'; his musicians had conspired to ruin him. If the officials present from the Opéra had engineered the conspiracy personally they could not have succeeded better in convincing themselves of Grétry's nefarious influence as a modern Italianate stylist. As Burney was saying four years later, 'The serious opera of Paris is still in the trammels of Lulli and Rameau, though every one who goes thither either yawns or laughs, except when roused, or amused, by the dances and decorations . . . nothing but a kind of national pride, in a few individuals, keeps the dispute alive.'[29] It was after this *débâcle* that Marmontel (see below) was told Grétry was 'on the point of drowning himself'.

Creutz and the literary set effectively determined the course of opéra-comique by persuading Marmontel to write for Grétry (*Réf*:ii:98): the masterly opéra-comique librettist Sedaine was still working with Monsigny, and besides was considered by the Establishment to be a poor writer from the stylistic point of view. Marmontel had style but lacked experience in the genre. Thus it came about that Grétry should compose *Le Huron*, the idea for which Marmontel arrogates to himself in his *Mémoires*: 'I had, just then, on my table one of Voltaire's tales (*L'ingénu*); I thought it might furnish me with the outline of a little opéra-comique.'[30] Again, from this account, Grétry began setting the words before the whole libretto was complete, a process he later rejected. Presumably the libretto went before the Comédie-Italienne Assembly independently of the music; to judge by Grétry's words the finished opéra-comique, created in six weeks, underwent an informal audition after dinner in the presence of the leading male singer Caillot, and then only out of the latter's complaisance towards Marmontel and Creutz. There followed a full hearing with Grétry at the harpsichord which was successfully given before the main actors at Mme La Ruette's (i:159–60) and as events turned out, Mme La Ruette was to create the leading soprano rôle in all Grétry's opéras-comiques up to the end of 1773. Haughty and defensive though Marmontel was, even in private with Grétry, and mercilessly criticised though his style and stage sense were in the endless circle of cultural gossip in Paris, this writer became the backbone of a successful team together with his composer and his interpreting actor–singers, responsible for four of the thirteen most popular opéras-comiques given in Paris during the 1770s (see chapter 7).

Fortunately, we can penetrate some way into the working methods of these artists. Grétry resembles a Romantic musician not least because he became a man of letters, and because all his mature work was created with men of letters. But in the many references to his own art he seeks to reveal and enlighten, not to mystify or idealise. With Marmontel, at least, he would be present at the poet's reading of 'first sketches of pieces' and be encouraged to make suggestions (*Réf*:ii:97). Whereas we shall see in certain 'Versions and performances' sections of this book the way Grétry helped to make changes after a first night, more significant contributions from musician to poet occurred earlier: 'I said not a word in my *Essais* [i.e. *Mémoires*] about the happy ideas that I could communicate to my poets when I went through (*tenoit*) their works at my piano; however, they are numerous. I regarded this revelation as a vulgarity between two artists who, through mutual efforts, sought to perfect the entirety of their common work' (*Réf*:ii:100). For example the composer suggested in *Zémire et Azor* the 'magic picture' trio (19) and the climactic solo (24), originally to have been in spoken form. He decided on the need for the musical close to act 1 of *La fausse magie* (*Réf*:ii:102–3). In a letter to Beaumarchais, Grétry was sufficiently struck by the following simile (made by Le Chapelier) to quote it: 'you are husband and wife when you join together to write a work; you [Grétry] have helped show off the words just as the poet has led you to make fine music by preparing the place where one is to sing' (18 August 1791). The composer tells us he gave much advice to the musician who in a way became his successor, Dalayrac; warm testimony was given by Dalayrac's librettist Marsollier concerning just such creative participation as the above.[31] Once ready to commence composition, however, Grétry was entirely his own man. The following personal description is corroborated by a letter written in 1774 by the composer Désaugiers.[32]

[Dr Tronchin:] You must tell me how you write your music. [Grétry:] Well, just as one writes poetry . . . a picture; . . . I read, I re-read twenty times the words I want to paint in sounds; it takes several days for my head to become heated: in the end I lose my appetite, my eyes get inflamed, the imagination rises, then I write an opera in three weeks or a month.   (i:21–2)

Once in the requisite exalted state, Grétry counselled, one should not reflect overmuch, but let the 'torrent' flow and return later so that 'taste and discernment may put right the deviations of your over-excited imagination' (i:102). For at least certain operas Grétry composed under the secret inspiration of a woman other than his wife (*Réf*:iv:184), which was possibly why 'In youth I often wrote music with my feet in warm water; I felt the need of this palliative to calm my head' (*Réf*:ii:171). At other times he imagined music in bed upon waking, afterwards writing out the details without having played the music on any instrument (*ibid.*:iv:362). It is at least possible that in these circumstances Grétry thought more melodically than harmonically, for his collaborator in 1803 and fellow Liégeois, Jérôme-Joseph de Momigny, considered that

[Being] too little of a harmonist to set down on paper or follow mentally a sequence of selected chords that were knowledgeably interlinked, and draw out from it a melody as original as it was distinguished, it was only after creating his voice-line separately that Grétry sought that bass and those chords which might accompany it.[33]

As reported by Grétry himself, the next stage in the compositional process seems remarkable: a kind of joint elaboration technique.

An intelligent copyist often made a fair copy of my first rough draft, very scanty; after which I dictated to him the immense details of a score. We cannot, like painters, abandon part of our work to our pupils; no composer, however skilful, can fulfil the intentions of another.   (*Réf*:iii:238n.2)

These methods may help to explain the dearth of Grétry autograph manuscripts, and the testimony of Momigny adds substance to the composer's account. Himself a composer, writer and analyst, Momigny published an independent report of daily visits to Grétry specifically to orchestrate *Delphis et Mopsa* (Opéra, 1803), but only that work. During joint sessions, 'I instrumented for him his arias and choruses.'[34]

Like Mozart, Grétry played billiards frequently; he was also addicted to snuff, which he held between two fingers while playing over his music at the keyboard (i:83; *Réf*:ii:171,228). Also like Mozart, Grétry did not compose later operas through from start to finish: 'the first piece of music being written seems to indicate the genre of the entire work. Consequently I often began with the most important scenes of the text, the remainder of which was only, to me, a necessary derivative.' (*Réf*:iv:344). And indeed it is wrong to think of Grétry as even predominantly instinctive, as Momigny insists that he 'had two ways of working to shape his melodies, one from pure inspiration, his emotions high and his spirit exalted; and the other by seeking, *very patiently*, from a certain number of degrees of the scale, a combination of sounds which pleased him'.[35] This process is also described by Grétry himself as taking place *c*1780: Dalayrac, before presenting himself as a composer in public, watched Grétry at work; 'often he was astonished to see me rejecting ideas, inflexions that seemed good to him' (iii:265).

Temperamentally Grétry began and remained a melodist and although in this study we shall see his harmony and orchestration progress with the times, he ended believing 'it is the sensitive melodist and not the harmonist who makes discoveries in music' (*Réf*:i:24). Of course, this demanded a good libretto, both in its relation of words to situations and in its choice of words. The former point Grétry makes many times; the latter he explains by condemning (like all seasoned opera composers) parentheses, inversions and elisions of vowels (*ibid.*:ii:210), complaining too that poets are insufficiently meticulous in providing parallel verses in terms of accent as well as metre and rhyme. Of Grétry's principles of word-setting, or prosody, we shall say more in a moment, as these lie at the very foundation of his belief and practice as an opera composer. On the level of the phrase, rather than the single word,

I begin each piece almost always by a declaimed melody, in order that in having a more intimate relationship with the drama, the beginning might impress itself on the mind of the spectator. Equally, I declaim everything constituting the character of the personage; I leave to melody everything that is only decoration or rounding off of the poetic phrase; melody would harm technical words, it embellishes all the others. If a word needs to be heard well for the understanding of a phrase, let it be a good note that carries it. If you set up a *forte* in one or several bars in your orchestra, let this be on words already heard; for a necessary word, lost in the orchestra, can entirely conceal the meaning of a piece.   (i:77–8)

Arriving in Paris and at work on *Les mariages samnites*, Grétry wrote to his old mentor Padre Martini in very interesting terms:

I have placed myself on a very critical course by wishing to give a royal work in French in Paris . . . Many have tried to write music in the Italian taste, but they have had no success because the prosody of the language was incorrect; I believe I have surmounted this point.

(1 December 1767)

There are two points to distinguish here. First, Grétry is talking about serious, not comic, opera: probably not by chance, he wrote this two days after the first performance of the serious opera by Philidor that is regarded as having made an Italianate breach in the defences of the Opéra: *Ernelinde*. Grétry surely knew it; but he would also have known that the application of correct prosody to Italianate music at the Opéra had had little chance so far of being tried.

The second point is that his 'surmounting' of prosodic problems was somehow a new solution. We know he had discussed word-setting with Voltaire and assume he knew that his friend Arnaud had published on the subject.[36] Voltaire and others could have shown him Marmontel's prosodic defence of sung French dating from 1759.[37] But Grétry's own writings suggest more coherent, practical principles.

The expressive note very frequently wants to be on the verb, quite frequently on the noun, sometimes on the adjective. That is not all: this good note must be situated on the good syllable of the word.   (*Réf*:i:236)

The 'good syllable of the word' means that whose accent is demanded by the normal pronunciation of the French language. Significantly, the inspiration for his style in word-setting was derived not from *littérateurs* but scores:

I analysed Pergolesi's music when I sought to develop my musical faculties; may I not, I wondered (having his music before me), declaim in singing with as much truth and charm?   (*Réf*:i:229)

In the *Mémoires* (ii:191–4) Grétry gives a close analysis of Hélène's aria (3) in *Silvain*. His principles operate on an almost note-by-note level, and are governed in this case by a mixture of three styles (romantic, vague, pious) designed to capture the quality of a mother's love. Both the harmony and the melody relate in detail to the poetry. For example, the triplets appearing at 'A ses peines, ses soucis' ('has its sorrows, its cares') illustrate Hélène's softening of these words 'in order not to frighten her daughter', who is shortly to be married herself. Thus two uninteresting words ('has its') receive meaning. In the central 3/8 section the rise and fall of the line 'But in gentle slavery' is likened by Grétry to 'the chain which wraps round the husband', where we hear a combination of lilting rhythm and minor mode.

Profile 1: from Liège to Paris

In the change from the comic style of *Isabelle et Gertrude* to that of *Les mariages samnites*, Philidor's *Ernelinde* must have been a general inspiration; one can not only isolate certain aria themes in it that might comfortably be by Grétry,[38] but can compare music such as *Le Huron*'s obbligato recitative (see next chapter) and D major march (12) or the G minor aria (1) of *Les mariages samnites* (1776 verson, conjecturally from 1768) to individual items in *Ernelinde*: see Ex. 2.2. However, when one analyses the word-setting in *Ernelinde* and places it beside that in *Le Huron*, one sees that Grétry's is often rather the more supple and effective, partly owing to the principles given above. Example 2.3, where Philidor is musically supple, shows in vivid form Grétry's superior placing of important words. Ringed words show Philidor stressing an article, preposition or adverb, while underlined words show nouns and verbs liable to elude the hearer. Such things may seem obvious now, but the fact is that opéra-comique in France was about to embrace the whole range of emotions that the Classical style in music was capable of suggesting, and that whoever wanted to match this range in France had to embrace French sensitivity to poetry. In their way, Grétry and Marmontel became the Lully and Quinault of opéra-comique, each a stylist who sought to reflect the other's art.

For all his apparent candour, however, the composer kept a tight control over revealing too much about the common practice of self-borrowing. It will be seen in chapters 6 and 9. We have noted the admitted re-use of material from the abortive *Les mariages samnites*; the more concealed sentence in the *Réflexions* (iv:294) states, 'I took some phrases of melody in my French operas from the Italian opera I wrote in Rome.' The identity of these borrowings cannot be

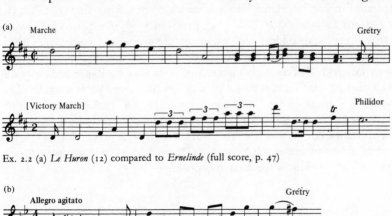

Ex. 2.2 (a) *Le Huron* (12) compared to *Ernelinde* (full score, p. 47)

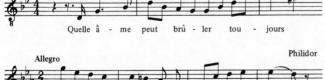

Ex. 2.2 (b) *Les mariages samnites* (1) compared to *Ernelinde* (full score, p. 12)

Grétry and the growth of opéra-comique

Ex. 2.3 *Ernelinde* (full score, p. 21) compared to *Le Huron* (6)
In each case the poetic metre is the same and the singer is concerned with the heroine.

established, as the work in question is lost, but the same process is observable to a surprising extent in the case of *Isabelle et Gertrude* (which Grétry does not mention). Material from this turns up in opéras-comiques over the succeeding twenty years. The overture, eighty-four bars of efficient curtain-raising, was used in a revised version for *Les méprises par ressemblance* in 1786. 'De sa modeste mère', (2), was the thematic starting-point for (2) in *L'ami de la maison* in 1771. 'Un secret ennui', (13), was rewritten for *Le jugement de Midas* (14), given in 1778, using the key, muted strings and main orchestral ideas but of course new words and voice line. Other such examples surely remain to be identified.

Owing to the survival of the early manuscript version of *La Rosière de Salency* we know that a duet rejected from it found its way less than three years later into *Les mariages samnites* – unless, that is, it had come from the 1768 version of the latter to start with. If he portrayed himself as creator of original works whose ethos, by contrast with Italian opera, was that 'they varied their style and melody as many times as they changed texts' (*Réf*:iii:238), Grétry had as few scruples about practicable self-borrowing as the next composer.

3. Le Huron (The Huron)

Comédie in 2 acts, in verse: *CC* 14

Libretto by Jean-François Marmontel. Dedicated to the Comte de Creutz, plenipotentiary minister of the King of Sweden.

First performed at the Comédie-Italienne, 20 August 1768.

Printed full score, Paris, Berault, Houbaut, n.d. [1768] as Œuvre 1.[1]

Dramatis personae: The Huron, an uneducated Canadian (bar.)

> Mlle de St Yves (s.)
> M. de St Yves, her father (b.)
> Mlle de Kerkabon (s.)
> M. de Kerkabon, her brother (b.)
> The Bailli (spoken rôle)[2]
> Gilotin, his son (t.)
> An officer (t.)
> A corporal (b.)

Troupe of soldiers; Bailli's men (non-singing)

ACT 1: A coastal village in Brittany. Mlle de Kerkabon and Mlle de St Yves discuss the attractions of the newcomer, brought up among Huron Indians. St Yves has resolved not to accept the hand of Gilotin (aria 1).[3] Gilotin enters and describes the 'wild man' hunting (aria 2). In an uneasy duet (3) she rejects his advances. The Huron enters and presents St Yves with hares and partridges he has shot. They discuss Huron valour and the Huron's late mistress Abucaba, who has been eaten by a bear (aria 4). Suddenly Mlle de Kerkabon notices a portrait round the newcomer's neck and recognises it. She rushes off, leaving him to declare his affection to St Yves (aria 5). The Huron then disposes of Gilotin's pretensions, boasting defiance (aria 6). Offstage Mlle de Kerkabon and her brother have decided that the portrait is of their sea captain brother, lost some years before. In a humorous recognition quartet (7) they decide, despite the Huron's professed ignorance of his parents, he is after all their nephew. 'Their hearts throbbed, they cried out, they snatched the portraits [they are comparing one of their own], giving and taking them back twenty times a second' (Voltaire). The Huron is thus enlisted as a Frenchman; enjoined to wear French clothes, he refuses until persuaded by Mlle de St Yves. Mlle de Kerkabon is chagrined at finding herself his aunt, for which St Yves lightly chides her (aria 8). Mlle de Kerkabon teases her in return (9). The returning Huron describes the babble of questioning voices of neighbours and worthies in the village (10). He and St Yves confirm their love but then an officer warns of the approach of the English by sea (aria 11). Gilotin demonstrates his cowardice while the Huron takes the sword.[4] A 'Warriors' March' closes the act (12), presumably to cover the exit of the villagers who during (11) have assembled and taken up arms.

ACT 2: (The same.) Mlle de St Yves waits alone anxiously (aria 13). Gilotin cruelly

33

exaggerates her fears for the Huron, which find outward expression in a recitative and aria (14). But he is well and has led the French to victory. The lovers sing ecstatically (duet 15). Afterwards he is urged to describe his defeat of the English (aria 16). This persuades Monsieur de St Yves to give his daughter to the Huron, which provokes the downtrodden Gilotin yet further (aria 17). But meanwhile the Huron embarrasses the St Yves household by his forward method of wooing and has been ejected (aria 18). Mlle de St Yves is to be sent to a convent, which angers the Huron (aria 19). He goes off to rescue her and his inevitable arrest by the Bailli is prevented only by the forgiveness of Monsieur de St Yves (duet and septet 20).

By chance, Grétry's contact with the Voltaire circle in 1767–8 coincided with the publication of two related and politically sensitive works: Marmontel's novel *Bélisaire* and Voltaire's short story *L'ingénu*, the source (as it became) of Grétry's *Le Huron*. John Renwick describes the *Bélisaire* affair as the unexpected but undoubted climax to the Calas and Sirven cases.[5] It was barely four years since the *parlement* of Toulouse – which had condemned Calas to an appalling execution (on faked evidence) – reversed its judgement. Their action was the result of three years' unceasing effort by Voltaire to harness worldwide support against them; the bruises were still felt from this blow to the power of entrenched Catholicism and its political allies in France. In retreat at Ferney, ready at any time to slip onto the refuge of Swiss soil, Voltaire was now redoubling his printed and epistolary campaign for justice and toleration.

Bélisaire (spring 1767) was the most outspoken political statement its author ever made. He seems to have considered it a last testament, believing he was dying. Belisarius, condemned to prison on false evidence and there blinded, has been finally released. He finds the state in decay under the ageing emperor, Justinian, but such is his belief in its future that his wisdom on government is sought. This gives Marmontel the opportunity to lecture on the monarchy ('All confidence is extinguished . . . the prince lives at variance with his subjects'), the leisured classes, uniformity of taxation, and so on. He attacks privilege and 'fanaticism', naturally understood as 'Catholicism'. A storm of protest was released; the future Louis XVI and his brother invented punishments for his presumption;[6] raging debates at the Sorbonne gave rise to the proscription of thirty-nine portions of the novel. As the arguments simmered, Voltaire defended *Bélisaire* in two pamphlets. Then, probably in late spring 1767, he was inspired to write *L'ingénu*. This tale, which quotes briefly from *Bélisaire*, is ostensibly about a seventeenth-century youth, brought up in Canada with the Huron Indians, who lands by chance on the French coast. After falling in love with Mlle de St Yves he goes to Paris to seek his reward for repulsing the British. But he is thrown into prison once his liberal opinions become known, especially on the subject of the Huguenots. In prison he educates himself with the help of a Jansenist who is also a 'prisoner of conscience'. The Huron is rescued only by the exertions and sacrifice of his lover, who herself dies after her seduction by an influential government minister. Obviously *L'ingénu* could be taken as a wry satire on the *status quo* in France, touching on both general issues (the still-used and hated powers of arbitrary arrest or censorship) and particular ones (the dispute of the Breton *parlement*).[7]

L'ingénu was published, under the pseudonym Dulaurens, in July 1767 in Geneva and early September in Paris. It was banned on 17 September. Marmontel, correspondent of Voltaire for over three decades, was moved to hail him again: 'You are an astonishing man!' The sentence from *Bélisaire* that became part of the Huron's prison education is found in chapter 11 of *L'ingénu*: 'Truth shines with its own light, and minds are not enlightened by the flames of the stake.' Marmontel left Paris to recuperate but was back in 1768. He had already taken sufficient interest in opéra-comique to use his own Moral Tale *La bergère des alpes* (*The alpine shepherdess*) for a libretto in 1766, unsuccessfully set by Josef Kohaut. Grétry reports that he intended anyway to use *L'ingénu* for a libretto (i:159): the story had sold well in the short time it had been publicly available. The opéra-comique *Le Huron* cannot be said to be provocative, deference to the censors having caused the removal of most contentious elements. Imagined in the context of its time, however, the opera would obviously bring to mind the jokes and barbs that Voltaire's prose makes so memorable. Marmontel was obliged to omit the religious dimension and the Versailles episode: the Huron's new acquaintance with the Bible and his resulting urges to be circumcised and baptised in a river, for example. A crucial issue of relationship thereby vanished: that since Mlle de St Yves acted as the Huron's godmother the Church automatically forbids her to marry him. In Marmontel the Huron vindicates himself entirely through bravery, which is true to Voltaire but not sufficiently individual. In act 2 the hurried dénouement is effected by St Yves *père*, who first enters in act 2 sc. 6, has no expressed character, and is ready to confine his daughter to a life of prayer at the drop of a hat. On one level we might endorse Grimm (iv:87): 'An insipid and trivial marriage intrigue, relieved by bizarre trimmings.'

Grimm also ridiculed the care with which Marmontel ingeniously incorporated many telling details from Voltaire, but he was a biased witness. The source was unique and had to be preserved in what ways it could. Here the Huron replies to St Yves' enquiry about Indian courtship:

(Voltaire)   En faisant de belles actions, répondit-il, pour plaire aux personnes qui vous ressemblent (By fine deeds, he replied, to please those who resemble you)
(Marmontel) C'est de faire, en aimant, quelque belle action,
            Qui plaise à ce qui vous ressemble.

Though the libretto is in verse, the rhythms and rhyme schemes are free and fluid; Marmontel was nothing if not a fluent stylist. When the Huron protests at European dress it is with well-turned force:

Mlle de Kerkabon: Du pays où l'on est, il faut suivre les goûts.
Huron: Chez des singes, fort bien, mais non pas chez les hommes.
                  (One must follow the tastes of the country one visits.
                  That's all very well for monkeys, but not for men.)

Marmontel cannot quite keep the original order of events, but transposes details from one section to another to assist authenticity. And two of the most vivid numbers, (7) and (10), are directly derived from Voltaire's humour. The quartet enlarges on Voltaire's mocking tone ('Their hearts throbbed') with platitudinous lines ('He's got his father's features') and Grétry responded carefully using pattering vocal quavers rather in the manner of Philidor's opéra-comique ensembles. The aria (10) became a popular favourite. It is an excellently contrived adaptation of the provincial supper scene into solo reportage. In the recreation of certain scenes Marmontel must have felt that the audience could mentally fill in the objects of forbidden satire.

The public success of Le Huron was overwhelmingly due to its score, whose quality 'elevates the composer without contradiction to the first rank' (Grimm:viii:165). It is substantial in size and quality and contains as many numbers or more than some three-act works. It also comprises great stylistic diversity. The very solidity of Grétry's formal constructions is worthy of note. Unattracted now by simple ABA designs, he delights in variety; this results in outlines such as that of (8): ABA'B', or of (13): ABAC, or of (19): AB, recitative, A'. Literal repetition of A sections is normally discarded in favour of recomposed versions – designated in this book as A' – which can thereby resemble the recapitulation of a sonata form. The coherent drive of modulation back to the home key is always felt, revealing Grétry's thoroughness beside Philidor, who could be lazy or stiff in modulating to the return to the home key. (Grimm noted: 'He knows above all how to finish his arias and give them their just length.') Burney summed up the stylistic orientation in noting 'many pretty and ingenious things, wholly in the buon gusto of Italy', while also remarking that 'several of his melodies are wholly French'.[8]

Mlle de St Yves begins in (1) with a melody that may have become a model for the more famous Italian suavity of Zémire et Azor (Ex. 3.1). The French elements, aside from the wistful Gratioso in the overture, are used for comic or countrified matters, and the Huron is sometimes given such material precisely because he is a natural, outdoor being. In (4), for example, he describes Abucaba's virtues with images such as the straightness of cane or rushes (Ex. 3.2). This is square, syllabically orientated, akin to the Romance style as it appears in Philidor's Sancho Pança (1762): Ex. 3.3. Already Grétry proves that he has the dramatist–musician's ear for humour and colour in orchestral writing. It shows in Gilotin's (17), where we really do hear that he is a ninny, as Voltaire calls him: grumbling violin semiquavers, bowed against lame pizzicato quavers and crotchets in C minor.

Most solo work falls to the hero himself, with ten arias. This is too many and one at least, (18), sounds as though it has been ill-adapted from Les mariages samnites: Grimm mentions only the superb (14) in this connection, as we said in chapter 2, note 28. The Huron's music extends from comic description to soul-searching and the comprehensiveness well suits Voltaire's energetic youth, whose good looks and impulsive ways fascinate the Breton locals. The strength of his anger in (19) is enormous, and effectively communicates Voltaire's original text: he would burn down the very convent in which St Yves is detained were it not that he fears for her

Le Huron

Si ja - mais je prends un é - poux

Ex. 3.1 *Le Huron* (1) Cf. Exx. 10.3 and 12.6(a)
('If ever I take a husband')

Les joncs ne sont pas plus droits, Elle en a - voit

la sou - ples - se,

Ex. 3.2 *Le Huron* (4)
('Rushes are not straighter, she had their litheness')

Je ne suis qu'u - ne ber - gèr - e, Je ne vois que mes mou - tons

Ex. 3.3 *Sancho Pança*, Romance
('I am just a shepherdess')

Que ne suis-j'en - core dans nos bois, Loin de ces fu - nes - tes (rivages)

Ex. 3.4 *Le Huron* (19)
('Were I still in our woods, far from these fatal shores')

safety (Ex. 3.4). A probably unprecedented combination of medium and message is allotted the Huron in (5). His declaration to St Yves is scored only for flutes, clarinets, bassoons, horns, violas and string bass, yet is sixty-three bars in length. Grétry's notion was most likely to suggest a rough-hewn upbringing, or an unfamiliar manner of speaking. Clarinets, not to be regular employees for over twenty years at the Théâtre Italien, had formed no part of the orchestra of Duni, Philidor and Monsigny; Grétry was soon to request them again in *Les deux avares*.

Grétry and the growth of opéra-comique

Probably he had heard them in the vigorous score of *Gilles garçon peintre*, music by La Borde, revived at this theatre in February 1767 using specially hired players. But this piece was an old favourite and there is no archival evidence that the same was done for *Le Huron*.[9]

Mlle de St Yves is the first in a long line of Grétry's romantic heroines. Voltaire also idealises this 'fine low Breton girl who had been very well brought up'. We see her in relation to her neighbours in act 1; her eloquent rejection of Gilotin is prepared for by the spacious refinement of (1). To Marmontel's inexperience, perhaps, we owe the lack of a St Yves–Huron duet in the first act, but the lushness of (13) almost makes up for one. Like several arias that were to follow at parallel junctures after act divisions it is musically indulgent, with twenty bars of introduction and a high, virtuoso coda.

At several important points in Grétry operás-comiques the technique of obbligato recitative (récitatif obligé) appears. St Yves' (14) is a noteworthy example, fifty bars long.[10] Such music first came to be used in Italian *opera seria* at the end of Alessandro Scarlatti's career around 1720. To quote Rousseau's *Dictionnaire de musique*:

These alternating passages of recitative and melody clothed in all the brilliance of the orchestra represent all that is most touching, most ravishing, most energising in the whole of modern music. The restless actor, transported by a passion which prevents complete utterance, interrupts himself, pauses, holds back, while the orchestra speaks for him.

Already in 1759 Marmontel named the emotional effect of obbligato recitative and the cantabile aria as 'the only real superiority that [Italian] opera has over ours', and was obviously aware of the fine example that Antoine Dauvergne had composed for the recitative opera *Enée et Lavinie* (1758).[11] Orthodox forms of recitative had appeared occasionally in opéra-comique since the advent of Duni; but Philidor placed an obbligato recitative in act 3 of *Tom Jones* (1765–6). It was entirely in keeping with his importation of Italian material in general. At this point, the heroine Sophia is at her wits' end, alone at Upton, hunted by her father, whereupon Philidor's recitative focuses sympathy for an elopement that 'made her a dangerous model for French girls', the 'character which most perplexed the French'.[12] Then in the recitative opera *Ernelinde*, which Grétry could have seen on its first night at the Paris Opéra, 29 November 1767, Philidor placed a yet more powerful obbligato recitative. At the end of act 2 Ernelinde has to decide between dutiful sacrifice and personal inclination, and her tension and disorder are translated into experimental declamation, harmony and accompaniment. The resulting enacted stream-of-consciousness caught the attention of all Parisian critics.[13]

In (14) St Yves recalls the voice of the Huron, she despairs, she questions social convention, she sees an imagined death scene (just as Ernelinde sees the imagined corpse of Sandomir). The technical apparatus of the music includes horns crooked simultaneously in G and D, tremolando strings, and harmony as startling as that of

Ex. 3.5 *Le Huron* (14)
('What do I say, alas, cruel one, perhaps your lover is on the point of death, I hear him, he calls me')

Philidor (Ex. 3.5). The drooping thirds at 'Je l'entends' ('I hear him'), when she imagines the Huron dying, are a motif first associated with her lover's 'feeble voice' in the twelfth bar of the recitative.

Grétry not infrequently used horns or bassoons to represent or idealise a human voice. In this obbligato recitative he rather experimentally wrote a solo horn B natural on a pause, after a full close in D major. St Yves responds to it with the words 'that fading voice'. When the B was criticised for its apparently unformed tonality the composer defended it as the logical musical analogue of a far-off voice altered by travelling over a distance (i:167–8). But if this is to be classed as 'imitation', we must at least recognise it as 'psychological imitation' whose reality comes through the supposed 'perception' of the stage character. We are obliged to endow the heroine with a memory and an imagination, as well as emotions. Music's part in such techniques of impersonation would be regularly employed in the future by Grétry. Certain features appear again soon in *Silvain* (10), where the heroine is alone at a moment of crisis, suffering apprehension and hearing the imagined 'cry of nature raised in his [Dolmon *père*'s] heart'.

The march closing act 1 of *Le Huron* (Ex. 2.2) was admitted by the composer to have been part of the early *Les mariages samnites* (i:157) and it was a popular success, scored with both clarinets and piccolos. Michel Corrette wrote a set of three variations on it for mixed chamber group as part of his *XXIV Concerto Comique* (a work deemed missing in reference books but which survives in the British

Library). Hearing it in Brussels, Charles Burney found the march was played on stage 'so soft as to be scarcely heard', followed by a crescendo as the band approached the audience, and then back to 'the last audible degree of *Piano*': a 'very fine effect'.[14]

Grétry's dealings in opéra-comique with Voltaire form an intriguing by-way in the history of the genre. The poet and his niece Mme Denis listened to Grétry performing music, including his own for *Isabelle et Gertrude* (i:165). Voltaire, as a practised librettist, offered robust help to his guest concerning word-setting. Yet he habitually despised opéra-comique, as is easily seen from his correspondence, regarding it with personal feeling as a symptom of the decline in the national taste in general and for his plays in particular. He was an admirer of old Lully's music, had written three librettos for Rameau and was already in his seventy-third year.[15] He feared that unconventional works like *Ernelinde* would degrade serious opera and, more prophetically, that opéra-comique would kill the latter off.[16] Nevertheless, the advent of the opéra-comique in Geneva, and possibly too of Grétry, provoked some greater curiosity: the entire company gave two performances at Ferney, in September 1767. First they gave *Le roi et le fermier* by Monsigny and *Annette et Lubin*, a *pasticcio* with Italian music, then *Rose et Colas*, also by Monsigny, and *La chasse d'Henri IV*.[17] 'I had never seen opéra-comique,' he wrote, 'I laughed, I cried; I almost knelt with the little family when Henri IV was recognised.'

What did these experiences produce? Conversations, though we have no record of them, must have ranged round the nature and future direction of the art form itself since, as was soon clear, Voltaire took Grétry's ambitions seriously. As to musical idiom, there seems to be evidence that Voltaire was at one with Grétry: 'I want my Dalila to sing beautiful arias where the French taste should be dissolved in the Italian taste.'[18] In their subjects, Grétry's earlier works show a strong reaction against pure comedy, except for *Les deux avares*, four years later. Instead, he permitted humour incidentally or excluded it totally, as with *Lucile* and *Silvain*. Both *Le Huron* and *Silvain* had contentious overtones, while *Les mariages samnites* portrays duty to the state. If any of the opéras-comiques played at Ferney represented common ground for Grétry and Voltaire it was Sedaine's text for *Le roi et le fermier*. Sedaine would not collaborate with Grétry until 1773 but we find Voltaire writing appreciatively to him in 1769: 'I know no one who understands the stage better than you and makes actors speak more naturally' (letter of 11 April). The king, in *Le roi et le fermier*, is shown as the friend of his rural people and one who will disinterestedly condemn a seducer, be he even the aristocratic lord of the manor. If Voltaire knew Sedaine's English source (Robert Dodsley's *The King and the Miller of Mansfield*; French translation by C. Patu, 1756), he would have recalled its outspoken sallies against title, social privilege and life at court. He and Grétry could not have failed to admire Monsigny's music, whose scope extends to a 'royal hunt and storm' that connects the first two acts. Voltaire later described Monsigny's overture *Le déserteur* as a masterpiece,[19] while Grétry took Monsigny as a model in composing romances (i:149) and more besides.

During 1767, the year of *L'ingénu*, Voltaire produced his first opéra-comique text, *Les deux tonneaux* (*The two barrels*), seemingly destined for his earlier operatic collaborator La Borde in a letter (4 June) that correctly describes the piece as 'in the most singular taste in the world'. It attempts to create a commonly intelligible comedy within a classical Greek setting. The barrels are those of Bacchus' priest containing happiness and sorrow meted out to all of us, descending 'in an eternal rainfall upon a hundred different worlds and on each animal'.[20] Though published (posthumously) with the subtitle 'sketch' it is a complete text and quite capable of being set, extending to three acts.

Voltaire's second opéra-comique text, *Le baron d'Otrante*, was the outcome of his promise to give a text to Grétry, who received it in August or September 1768. Appropriately for a work designed for him and for the public, this libretto has much more action and a more practical moral. In fact it was an adaptation of Voltaire's own poem *L'éducation d'un prince* (1763): the prince (baron in the stage version) has been brought up in luxury by a set of venal privy counsellors. His undefended estates are overrun by the Turks and he is made to work in the stables as a muleteer. With the help of his beloved, Irène, who charms the Turkish leader Abdalla, the baron achieves awareness and organises a successful counter-coup, while also showing mercy to Abdalla. This text – as the Comédie-Italienne decided when it was presented to it anonymously – had promise but required further work: the third (final) act is extremely brief and the character of Abdalla required more than the effective distancing Voltaire provided by giving him only simple Italian to speak.[21] Nevertheless Voltaire believed it could be set as it stood, since he wrote to his niece in October, 'As I told you, I wrote to Mme St Julien that you had taken on Guêtri [*sic*] – I think he might do excellent music for the Beneventin [i.e. the above libretto, whose source poem takes place in Bénévant]. I have all the declamation in my head.'[22] But the libretto's referral put an end to the project: 'For myself, I was most annoyed with this mishap which caused me to abandon setting his piece to music as he on his side abandoned opéra-comique' (i:167). Had Voltaire been able to make all his characters equally vivid for the stage we should have had a typical opéra-comique model for the 1770s: a diverting and pertinent essay on the perils of kingship whose material (uncomfortably for us) parallels the situation of Louis XVI (acceded 1774), his Marie-Antoinette no rescuing Irène.

VERSIONS AND PERFORMANCES

Gaps of months at a time between early sets of performances of *Le Huron* may reflect modifications to its words or music. This will frequently be seen to occur in Grétry's *œuvre*. For example in the duet (3) the voice parts as printed, unaccompanied, in a 1768 libretto[23] show a version of the piece thirteen bars shorter than appears in the full score, and containing a two-bar Adagio. Since it was commoner to remove music than to add it after a first night, the libretto version might represent a revision, the full score version the original; but the reverse is as potentially likely. In this instance Grétry himself reveals that the piece *was* shortened in final rehearsals. But at the fourth performance Monsigny (who was next to Grétry) guessed it had been tampered with, and declared that his complaisance had thereby spoiled it. The passage was subsequently restored (ii:308). In general this sort of information is meagre: most of Grétry's autographs are not extant and we have few authoritative manuscript copies. The essential thing is to guard against imagining that opéras-comiques in Paris possessed anything like the fixity that a printed score tends to suggest. Sometimes even the scores give notice of differences in performance that were the practice at the Théâtre Italien.

Le Huron aroused rather less extreme enthusiasm in the public than it did with Grimm; 17 performances were mounted during August, September and December 1768 but there were only 8 in 1769. From 1770 to 1785 inclusive there followed 111 performances, though the work's popularity dwindled to 2 or 3 a year from 1778. Thereafter there were 3 solitary showings in 1793 and a freak one in December 1806 when the many cuts ruined the dramatic motivation.[24] Grétry had the misfortune to witness – and record – the actors' mistakes and mentions the belief that this revival was pursued as a vehicle for the young tenor Elleviou in his Huron's costume (letter of 2 January 1807). The last showings outside France listed by Loewenberg were at Kassel and Bonn (1783).

4. Lucile

Comédie in 1 act, in verse: *CC* 2
Libretto by Jean-François Marmontel. Dedicated to the Comte d'Oultremont, brother and First Minister of the Prince–Bishop of Liège.
First performed at the Comédie-Italienne, 5 January 1769.
Printed full score, Paris, Aux adresses ordinaires; Lyon, Castaud, n.d. [1769] as Œuvre 11.
Dramatis personae: Lucile, supposed daughter of Timante (s.)
Timante, rich bourgeois (t.)
Dorval *père*, his friend (b.)
Dorval *fils* (t.)
Blaise, a working man (bar.)
Julie, a servant (s.)
A lackey (spoken rôle)
Village girl (s.)
Chorus of village girls and boys
A dressing-room in Timante's country house; Lucile's wedding morning. Her hair is being combed by Julie, and she expresses her hopes for her marriage (1).[1] Dorval, the bridegroom, enters and imagines future happiness with Lucile (2). Timante enters in a dressing-gown, equally expressing the mood of relaxation (3).

Dorval *père* enters and servants produce tea and light wine: round the table they sing the quartet (4). They welcome the arrival of Blaise, widower of Lucile's former nurse. (The original actor, Caillot, appeared bald and in rough clothes.) Blaise's mournful mood is interpreted as due to the recent death of his wife. Alone he sings a solo (5), 'My wife! what have you done?' Lucile returns to sing a brief song (6) after which, in a prolonged spoken dialogue, the crisis is revealed. His wife confessed that she exchanged her own child for Timante's baby whom she suckled, but who died. Lucile is Blaise's true daughter, and hardly in a social class to marry Dorval. Blaise allows Lucile to decide her own fate; he has done his duty. Alone, Lucile sings of her first reaction (7); but when Julie and Dorval come in she can neither restrain her tears nor confess the truth. There is a dramatic trio (8). Dorval questions Blaise about Lucile's evident misery, but she herself enters to admit her identity. Timante is at a loss, knowing the truth, yet determines, 'If fate be unjust, we must correct it.' Lucile rejects Dorval's idea of concealing the facts. Knowing Dorval *père*'s likely objections, Timante places him in the moral position of having to accept Lucile's birth by extracting, in a general conversation with him, the opinions, 'One seeks to know the birth only of insolent parvenus' and 'thinking nobly creates all the worth of nobility'. After the duet (9) Timante enlightens Dorval. Blaise is invited to join the household and be free of work. A bucolic episode continues the action with dance and song by villagers (10) and a chorus with bourgeois and villagers together, its central section a duet for Lucile and Dorval (11).

The vitality of eighteenth-century opéra-comique arose together with the freedom with which its source material was selected: modern, Renaissance or earlier in period, English, German, Italian or French in provenance, poem, play or story in form. The sense of exploration was keen in the 1760s: if Duni portrayed knights and ladies and a transformation scene in *La fée Urgèle* (1765) his *Les moissonneurs*, three years later, was a modern morality tale set amid country reapers. *Tom Jones*, of course, derived from Fielding's novel. Grétry's operas continued this trait: *Silvain* is set in Switzerland, *Les deux avares* in Smyrna, *L'amitié à l'épreuve* in London, *Le Magnifique* in Florence. Continuity in the genre was provided by that of the company, the Comédie-Italienne, and the typology of certain kinds of rôle.

Contrary to what has been said by Loewenberg and Brenner, *Lucile* bears no relation save in the names of its characters to the Moral Tale by Marmontel, *L'école des pères*. This concerns Timante's chastening of his libertine son Volny through the rather cumbersome expedient of faking the loss of his own fortune. Volny develops a 'pure love' for the convent-girl, Angelica. The social setting is as for *Lucile* and the tone is equally artificial: but there is no question of a marriage ceremony, a lowly birth, or someone like Blaise. As in the case of *L'ami de la maison*, Marmontel has created a separate work of fiction. Indeed, he himself in the *Mémoires* describes the libretto as only 'analogous in character' to the Tales.[2]

Little could have prepared the Parisians for the shocking stylistic gap between *Lucile* and the worlds of most preceding opéra-comique. On one level it is an almost repellent enactment of complacent bourgeois 'virtue', at times astoundingly patronising. Good visual parallels exist in canvases by Greuze of wealthier ladies painted for preference 'in their *déshabillé du matin* [morning casual dress], easily identifiable from contemporary fashion prints'.[3] The opening scenes of the opera are replete with small-talk, the quartet (4) sums up the mood of comfortable familial piety (see for comparison Greuze's picture *La mère bien-aimée*),[4] and the crisis which provides the mainspring of the action is resolved with the utmost civility. All the characters are seemingly innately virtuous. Grétry's effective score helped reduce audiences to tears and send them away both 'weeping and enchanted'. 'There reigns from end to end a kind of enthusiasm for goodness and virtue which is communicated to the spectator.'[5] All classes shall be one at the day of judgement but for the moment, wealth ensures that no one has very much to lose. Good old Blaise, we know, will fit perfectly into the household; his discretion is all but purchased at the end.

Given the characters, the libretto reads very naturally. There is neatness of style, grace and felicity in the asides and generally good placing of music. It manages to be elevated without being inflated. And it was a tale everybody could identify with, in fact a sort of reversal of the popular eighteenth-century 'shepherd king' fable (as in *Il rè pastore*), wherein the handsome commoner is discovered to be heir to a throne. The problem of dynastic succession is still the underlying issue, and Marmontel points it up in the revelation scene before and after (9).

Timante: And if I tell you that Lucile had poor people for ancestors, ploughmen.
Dorval *père*: (*abruptly*) Well, ploughmen . . . so much the better. It's a class as honest as it is useful.

In conceiving the musical elaboration possible within his scenario, Marmontel found words for all but three of the suitable crises: the three revelations of Lucile's paternity. No music was envisaged for that of Blaise to Lucile, of Lucile to Timante and Dorval, or of Timante to Dorval *père*. In the second of these cases an excellent *coup de théâtre* was however designed.

Blaise: It is for Lucile to tell you [what the obstacle is].
Dorval: (*with spirit*) It is for you to tell. I wish to know it. Speak, or fear my anger.
                    Enter Lucile with Timante
Lucile: Moderate your language, Dorval, and have respect for my father.

The most curious of these omissions was the final revelation. The duet (9) is anticlimactic simply because it does not musicalise the crux of the conversation Timante and Dorval *père* are having. Words and music describe a closed ABA' form which remains inconsequential.[6]

But at least four of the numbers, (4,5,7,8), form a remarkable addition to the repertory of opéra-comique. In particular, (8) evinces a musical and dramatic logic so skilfully realised that it bears comparison with Mozart. Together with (1) these four give us complete portraits of Lucile and Blaise. The others are more loosely sketched in music, but disappointingly so only in the case of Timante, whose (3) suggests a kind of Gallic Squire Western. In the earlier Grétry operas the solo vocal expositions of character are more conventional, taken as a whole, than many ensembles, where priority given to dramatic progress or opposition resulted in a double possibility: either the words could be relied upon to guide him through what might be called a process of 'logical improvisation', or musical repetition might give rise to something more traditional. Grétry's attitude to musical repetition – and thus coherence – rested on strong tonal foundations. But the repetition of melody or theme existed for him quite independently of tonal repetition. He was not averse to altering the given words in order to achieve a more symmetrical return of a theme or phrase. But he was equally or more likely to respect the integrity of the librettist's word-repetition by paralleling his musical material – in whatever key – to his collaborator's words, and saving a return to the home key for the best moment as he saw fit.

One of the common moulds in which an eighteenth-century librettist cast a solo was simply ABA. The composer took on responsibility for distributing the words within his musical form, choosing perhaps a three-part design like Da Capo or Dal Segno, or else the AA' short sonata, without development section, or the full sonata form. Another popular possibility was the three-part form which combined sonata with Da Capo: the A and A' sections resembled the exposition and recapitulation of a sonata, but the middle section was in a contrasting metre and tempo. Blaise's monologue (5), in F minor, falls however into an asymmetrical form, like the words. It resembles an extended rondo – a recurring refrain with different episodes in between – without a matching close. At the first performance the actor, entering slowly, 'fixed the audience with a stare', telling them, 'Alas! I come in sorrow.'[7] Strings are played muted.

Theme	Key		
A	F minor	Refrain	Ah! my wife! what have you done?
B	A flat	Episode	The poor child! And I come to break her heart!
A	F minor	Refrain	
C	A flat to E flat	Episode	She loves a lover who adores her
A	F minor	Refrain	
D	D flat	Episode	No one will know if I keep silent
	E flat minor	(slower)	(link) What are you saying Blaise? Never . . .
E	F minor	Coda	I know it . . . Sincerity, that's my law.

Ex. 4.1 shows part of the refrain and coda. Blaise progresses from negative despair to decision. After the musical repetitions the final part is strongly marked off by unharmonised unisons and a new dotted rhythm. The link uses vocal declamation, heightening the tension before the decision. The whole monologue is the first polished example of typically Grétryan freedom controlled by selected elements of traditional form. And it naturally gives Blaise the moral authority required by the drama.

The quartet (4) was long celebrated in French-speaking Europe. It epitomised the virtues of hearth and home before and after the Revolution and took on an extended meaning when the French royal family was in danger. The notion of staging an ensemble round a table was not new (Sedaine had conceived it in *Le*

Ex. 4.1 *Lucile* (5)
(a) Refrain ('Ah, my wife, what have you done?')
(b) Coda ('What are you saying, Blaise: that I keep silence? No, never')

Ex. 4.2 *Lucile* (4)
('Where could one better be [than in the bosom of the family?]')

bûcheron (*The Woodcutter*), set by Philidor). But to associate it with another rondo design whose refrain was 'Where could one better be' created a very original musical image of the household ritual (Ex. 4.2). The orchestra is impressively independent, especially in the subsidiary sections. Against the orchestra the moral exhortations fly thick and fast to bride and groom: 'Be liberal', 'Be economical', 'Never deceiving'.

This sums up the idyll to be so effectively threatened by Blaise. Once he has revealed to Lucile the dying confession of his wife, the music of (7) and (8) takes on responsibility for the drama: Lucile alone, then with Julie, then through the entrance of Dorval, his shock at her tears and her confusion prior to a hurried exit. Lucile's (7) uses ABA' form, its mournful G minor relating back to Monsigny's 'Hélas, j'étais' in *Rose et Colas* (1764). Yet it is too brief (thirty-three bars) to bear the dramatic weight at this point, so continues into (8) in C minor without a break. Although the score calls this a 'Terzetto' Dorval's entrance is delayed until the music reaches in effect the development section of a sonata. Afterwards, Grétry employs a systematic process of recomposition in order to match the increasing distress, cleverly integrating the drama's movement with formal musical principles. Achievements such as this show that he was quite capable of sophisticated traditional schemes: often he elected to experiment instead.

A word is needed about the choral finale. In keeping with the small, even *ad hoc* resources available, the music was set out on only two staves, soprano and tenor clefs. As for dancers, there were ample potential resources: twenty-six salaried dancers were listed in April 1769, for example.[8] It was the first of many opportunities for Grétry to display his penchant for memorable rustic dance-tunes.

Marmontel's death on 31 December 1799 readily symbolises the expiry of his reputation in the new century. More recently, writers have redefined his work's importance.[9] His contribution to French music is easily overlooked both because literary critics can be dismissive about opera librettos (he wrote about twenty)[10] and because he did not include in his collected works the many articles he wrote for the *Mercure de France*. His association with opera extended back to four collaborations with Rameau in 1751–3.[11] During that period his allegiance changed to Italianate music, where it remained. Rameau, he says, 'already old, was not disposed to change his style' (*Mémoires*, book iv). As set out in these *Mémoires*, Marmontel's plan was to effect the Italianisation of opéra-comique and recitative opera. In the end he was to write for Piccinni and support him against Gluck (see chapter 16).

Since opéra-comique was in any case firmly set on a course of Italianisation during the 1750s, more significance is to be attached to Marmontel's personal contribution to it. His tale *La bergère des alpes* (1766) was particularly good material since music, played and sung, forms a vital part of its sensibility: 'You sung, I was melted; what my heart feels, my hautboy expresses; I breathe my soul into it.'[12] In making a libretto of it, Marmontel took full advantage of these features. Following the success of *Lucile*, 'seeing that with a musician and actors ready to respond to my intentions, I could create *tableaux* whose colours and nuances would be faithfully rendered, I formed a keen taste for this type of art; for I might say that in raising the character of opéra-comique, I created a new genre'.[13] The shift away from traditional comedy was later identified with the particular contribution of Grétry's music: he being the 'first to have the talent and courage to work on pure, noble comedy [we might say, comedy of manners] without the degradation of mixing the grotesque and buffoonery'.[14] No one who has read Marmontel's words can doubt his intelligent handling of language or his desire to rise above partisanship in uniting French words with Italianate music. Parody arias had since 1753 demonstrated perfectly well that the two were compatible. The problem was to apply the techniques to tragedy, and have the results performed. Grétry drew the telling conclusion that 'Sedaine, who had the most dramatic consciousness, was hardly a musician, sacrificing nothing to the music, that is why his pieces have unity. Marmontel concerned himself greatly with the musical portion, that is why I sometimes shone at his expense.' (*Réf*:iii:97). He had 'that happy poetic mediocrity suiting music, which has nothing more to say when the music has said all' (*Réf*:ii:100). His facility was such that he 'would repeat in good verse what one had just said to him in prose' (ii:134).

Marmontel's first Moral Tales were written as contributions to the *Mercure de France* from 1755–9. The collected edition of January 1761 added a further three, making fifteen, and the second edition of 1761 added three more. When the edition of 1765 appeared, five new Tales were included.[15] Favart's successful adaptation of *Soliman II* for the Comédie-Italienne in 1761 (brief musical score by Gibert) opened the way for a host of other stage adaptations so that, in terms of numbers, the Moral Tales as a source overtook La Fontaine's tales (see Table 1).

Although Marmontel wrote six opéra-comique librettos for Grétry, only two of them come from the *Moral Tales* and *Lucile* is hardly a derivation at all. Closer identity of Moral Tale and libretto obtains in *L'ami de la maison*, but even these are separate entities. Moral Tales provided the source of *L'amitié à l'épreuve* (counted twice in Table 1 since its versions are so different) and for *Les mariages samnites* through other librettists.

Marmontel intended a special relation between the Moral Tales and the theatre, at least for the last eight Tales, since in the preface to the second 1761 edition he alluded to the success of *Soliman II* and declared that in his three new Tales – and henceforth – he favoured 'actions easy to dramatise, to spare authors work'. Statistically speaking his intentions were realised: forty-three dramatisations, both performed and unperformed, resulted from the seven Tales in this category, while an equal number derived from thirteen earlier Tales. For opéra-comique however it was different. Philidor's unsuccessful *Le bon fils* (1774), derived from *La mauvaise mère*, was the only opéra-comique from the Tales to be set by an important eighteenth-century composer besides Grétry.

Marmontel wants to show that men and women have limitless capacity for improvement, that virtue is always rewarded, and that a healthy society depends on the morality of the family. Sometimes he shows moral dilemmas within a family and friends, occasionally he holds up the mirror to fashion through caricature, and sometimes moves quite outside the setting of his own *milieu*: in the latter, 'subjects appear which, without having a moral directly relative to our culture, gave me affecting situations or interesting pictures; these tales are *Lausus et Lydie*, *La bergère des alpes*, *Annette et Lubin* and *Les mariages samnites*; but even in these my object was to make virtue attractive'.[16] Although their subject-matter disqualifies the Tales from wide interest today, the author's serious use of characterisation deserves attention. He did not rely on stock situations. And the actors of the Comédie-

Table 1: *Stage adaptations given publicly in France (most in Paris) of La Fontaine's tales and Marmontel's Moral Tales, 1702–93*[17]

Genre	La Fontaine	Marmontel
Plays 1702–60	13	—
Opéras-comiques 1702–60	23 (15 vaudeville and 8 composed settings)	—
Plays 1761–93	10	21
Opéras-comiques 1761–93	22 (6 vaudeville and 16 composed settings)	19 (1 vaudeville, 1 *pasticcio* and 17 composed settings)
Ballets 1702–60	1	—
Ballets 1761–93	1	1

Italienne found inspiration from some of his rôles, though not from his rehearsal methods.[18]

Caillot's acting in the rôle of Blaise is, I think, one of the most attractive things to be seen on any stage . . . I defy Garrick, the great Garrick, to play this role better.   (Grimm:viii:245)

VERSIONS AND PERFORMANCES

Lucile was the most popular single Grétry opéra-comique for over ten years: see chapter 7, Table 3b. In its first decade it was seen more often than any other Grétry opéra-comique in its equivalent period. It received 29 performances during 1769; *Le Huron* received only 8. In the eleven years 1770–80, *Lucile* attained a total of 166 performances, but its popularity thereafter declined. From 1781–93 inclusive there were only 46 performances, and after that none until a successful revival during the reappearance of several Grétry opéras-comiques under Napoleon. From 1804–14 inclusive it was seen 49 times: the last showing at the Opéra-Comique was on 3 November 1814. The last performances outside France to be listed by Loewenberg were at Liège (1920).

5. Le tableau parlant (The talking picture)

Comédie-parade in 1 act, in verse: *CC* 9
Libretto by Louis Anseaume. Dedicated to the Duc de Choiseul.[1]
First performed at the Comédie-Italienne, 20 September 1769.
Printed full score, Paris, Aux adresses ordinaires; Lyon, Castaud, n.d. [1769] as Œuvre III.

Grétry and the growth of opéra-comique

Dramatis personae: Isabelle, a well-born girl (s.)
Columbine, her maid (s.)
Cassandre, her middle-aged tutor (t.)
Léandre, nephew of Cassandre, in love with Isabelle (t.)
Pierrot, Léandre's valet (t.)

Cassandre's house. The almost-finished portrait of Cassandre stands on an easel, upstage. Isabelle, though young, is not too young to think of marriage (aria 1).[2] Her Léandre has been abroad for two years; her parents have died. Columbine enters singing a melody from Duni's *La veuve indécise* (*The irresolute widow*);[3] she advises Isabelle to accept old Cassandre's offer of marriage (aria 2). But Isabelle cannot stomach even the thought of his pathetic courtship. Cassandre appears and, encouraged by Columbine, quickly badgers Isabelle into agreeing to marriage (aria 4). But he then announces his imminent departure on business. Polite expressions of regret follow (trio 5). Alone Cassandre reveals that he intends to spy on Isabelle (aria 6). He grills Columbine about Isabelle's motives: she scorns his pretensions to be taken seriously as a lover (aria 7). Cassandre leaves angrily. Now Pierrot arrives; he and his master have sought their fortunes as far as Guyana. Pierrot and Columbine declare their love anew. Pierrot's narration of a sea-storm is followed by an optimistic duet (solo and duet 8). There follows their love duet (9), infused with comic touches. Léandre comes in and duly meets his much-relieved Isabelle, whose confessional aria (10) is succeeded by their own love duet (11). They move the portrait of Cassandre downstage, next to a newly-laid table, and leave for a walk in the garden. Cassandre emerges from the cupboard in which he had concealed himself and gives vent to his rage (12). He cuts out the face of his portrait so that he can observe from behind his own canvas. The lovers return and sit down to a meal of Cassandre's food. Isabelle is persuaded to practise approaching her tutor and admitting the truth. She therefore asks the picture's permission to take Léandre's hand and Cassandre, 'forcing his voice', finds himself obliged to give it. They are astounded (quintet 13). Cassandre grudgingly capitulates, and there is a simple close (vaudeville 14).

One of Grétry's great gifts was to be able to write witty music for the stage, something that was to be invaluable when he later came to compose comic finales. Laughter, lightness and speed were in his theatrical blood from his Liège days and he himself recognised an inborn 'natural gaiety' (i:181). Any Parisian author or composer who renounced tragedy had equally venerable comic traditions against which to match himself; indeed one might say classical traditions, since the age of the Italian improvising Harlequins did not close at the Comédie-Italienne until 1780.[4] Here the great Carlin (Carlino Bertinazzi) was Arlequin, Ciavarelli and, from 1769, Camerani were Scapin and the gifted actor and author Antoine Colalto (who died in 1778) played Pantalon. These were not simply comedians in the narrow sense but also commentators on anything and everything, the court jesters of Paris. So although traditional Harlequinades were the epitome of pure, farcial comedy, with characters that possessed no necessary past or future, the Parisian tradition was infused with Gallic verbal wit. *Commedia dell'arte* characters were thus still seen after 1780 in various plays, for example by Patrat and Florian, even at the Comédie-Française.

Some earlier opéras-comiques were basically farcical, for example *Le soldat magicien* by Quétant and Philidor, or to a lesser extent Philidor's perenially popular *Le maréchal ferrant*. These dated from the days of the fair theatres; though they were still performed, other comedies – especially by Sedaine – had demonstrated the effective inclusion of more irony and more interesting exploration of human weaknesses. Opéra-comique was well suited to this because of its variety of musical tone; in fact, as D'Origny pointed out, a light, risqué comedy positively benefited from a reduction in its frothier content when being rearranged as an opéra-comique.[5] Grétry was attracted to comedy which had a wider base than the simply farcical, so that in *Le tableau parlant* the characters do have a past and a future and Cassandre's purpose is to show a perhaps universal weakness of middle age, but also one that he, Grétry, saw as particularly applicable to the society of his time:

> If we glance at contemporary morals . . . what do we notice? Woman more flirtatious the older she becomes. 'What age is madame marquess?' asked one of our kings. 'Sire, forty years old.' 'And you?' he then said to the lady's son. 'I'm the same age as my mother, Sire' he replies. (i:184)

The point about Cassandre is that although he suspects Isabelle's acceptance of him to be merely opportunism, he is also a self-deceiver who wants to be loved for himself as if he were a twenty-year-old:

> Dans ma femme je veux trouver les sentimens
> Qu'inspire une tendresse extrême.
> Je veux enfin, je veux être aimé pour moi même,
> Tout comme si je n'avois que vingt ans.

These fantasies are all resurrected in his presence while he is hiding behind the picture, together with insulting references to his 'thin, dismal face' and rakish slyness.

Nobody in recent times had thought of adapting *commedia dell'arte* figures in a way suitable for more elaborate musical treatment. A contemporary explanation of the genre *comédie-parade* was provided by Grimm (viii:347): 'mixture of buffoonery and nobility; actors taken from common people, making us laugh by imitating tragic declamation and corrupting the pronunciation of words in a burlesque manner. The classic authors in this genre usually put their wit and art into stuffing the dialogue with *doubles-entendres*, almost always with idiotic effect.'[6] By adopting rhyming verse, Anseaume immediately altered the tone and pace to something more gently artful and yet still humorous; once the players found the right level of freedom they discovered the inherent charm of the piece, 'because they knew how to unite decency and grace with the utmost merriment' (i:188).

It is impossible to encapsulate the flavour of this charm as it is contained in the music, but criticism can perhaps suggest the happy balance between simpler emotions such as anger (6) and amazement (13), and more ironic ones such as mocking imitation (3) and sustained deception of feeling as in (5) where all three characters weep crocodile tears. Moreover there is a consciously self-inflated solo (8) which thereby becomes not merely a parody of the actor, Pierrot, himself, but also a parody of the simple 'pictorial' arias that delighted the crowds in, say, *Le maréchal ferrant*: see Ex. 5.1. In addition there is the 'comic song' style as expressed in (7), where an indivisible unity is created between a catchy melody and a witty form of words (Ex. 5.2): this was a tradition in which Monsigny had particularly excelled. Whereas in future Grétry comedies there would be an emphasis on duets and ensembles containing stage action, *Le tableau parlant* (with the obvious exception of 13) exploits contrasts that come rather from words. An unusual feature, too, is the presence of love duets, for it was far commoner to create comedy out of the rejection of a lover than the acceptance of one. The duets (9) and

Ex. 5.1 (a) *Le maréchal ferrant* (1)
('Working away since morning with no ill-humour')

Ex. 5.1 (b) *Le maréchal ferrant* (11)
(Being on the subject of a sick donkey, which is here imitated)

Ex. 5.1 (c) *Le tableau parlant* (8)
('The hapless sailors keep a ghastly silence, interrupted by the roaring and whistling of the elements')

Ex. 5.2. *Le tableau parlant* (7)
('You were what you are no longer, you were not that which you are')

Le tableau parlant

Ex. 5.3. *Le tableau parlant* (12)
('So that's how they take advantage of me')

(11), which contain no hint of parody, are responsible for the balancing element of grace that the text supplies through the verse.

The most animated solo music is Cassandre's, and for him Grétry imagined splendidly overheated; frustrated music of a kind we would associate with Mozart's Osmin. The solo (12) in C major is a sonata form piece with humorous development section: 'I'll get to the bottom of this mystery.' By the subtle interjection of quavers the beginning alone shows a helpless rather than purely animated rage, the blood-pressure sharply rising: Ex 5.3. But Cassandre's first solo (6) contrasts by using a non-repeating form: it is our first important example of a Grétry aria where new thoughts receive new musical motifs and the whole is simply rounded off by a quotation from the introduction. In this case there is not much expressive need to modulate. The shift from the tonic D minor to its relative F major is brief, and descriptions of feminine treachery soon head back to their obsessive main key-area. Thus established thematic form is overruled in the interests of comedy and speed, and the character is depicted by delivery and musical mimicry. For example the normally grandiose interval of an octave slips over, as it were, and lands on a seventh instead (Ex. 5.4). All through, Grétry took the freedom provided by the words to give reign to his command of different forms: apart from the extremes of sonata (6) and non-repeating (12) he used Da Capo in (1) and (4), ABA' as a cross between sonata and Da Capo in (3) and (7), and ABA'B' in (8) and (9).

In the background, naturally, lay the Italian experience, but simple emulation of the Italian *buffo* style occurs only in (13) with its sequential quavers, crescendos and accented off-beats. Elsewhere, as in (2), Grétry's point of departure was the tripping, syllabic style of his acknowledged spiritual and musical mentor, Pergolesi. A different melodic flavour, not regularly to be exploited by Grétry, found considerable expression in *Le tableau parlant*: melody in 6/8 metre. Six main

Ex. 5.4. *Le tableau parlant* (6)
('Wounds, flatters you')

53

sections of music employ it and, placed side by side, display excellent variety of outline and phrase-length.[7] Two are in the minor mode. Such frequency subtly suggests the traditional world of opéra-comique without there being any recourse to popular vaudeville melodies as such. At the end, the composer invented his own vaudeville tune, which is subjected to the traditional verse – refrain – verse structure as suggested by the librettist. But (14) concludes with a 'Dernier Chœur' in 6/8 instead of 2/4 metre. The kind of melodic relation between the two (Ex. 5.5) illustrates the way opéra-comique could change between musical levels, just as the fifty bars' length of the last chorus shows the musical desire to round off a work in a solidly 'composed' way. However, both these things were unashamedly borrowed by Grétry from examples already developed by Philidor and Monsigny.

(a) Allegro

Le Dieu de la ten - dres - se sou - rit à la jeu - nes - se

(b) Allegro

Le Dieu de la ten - dres - se sou - rit à la jeu - nes - se

Ex. 5.5. *Le tableau parlant* (14)
(a) [Vaudeville] (b) Final chorus
('The god of tenderness smiles on youth')

VERSIONS AND PERFORMANCES

Three early sources may be distinguished: the 1769 libretto closely related to early public performances; the full score, seemingly issued in 1769; and the 1770 libretto for the Fontainebleau performance of 7 November (see chapter 7).[8] Six changes, all concerning just the libretto, were made between the first of these and the second. The most revealing cuts, though making for added speed, weakened somewhat the authors' original desire to lend the characters depth: the first mention of the death of Isabelle's parents in sc. 1; the possibility expressed after (2) in sc. 2 of Isabelle's nascent affection towards Cassandre; and her probing after (11) into Léandre's amorous adventure in the West Indies, hints of which the audience has already been given. Improved speeches were inserted before (8) and after (12). Adjustments were made before (11) to allow the principal lovers to sing alone on stage. Three much smaller text changes were made between the full score printing and the 1770 libretto for Fontainebleau.

Le tableau parlant remained at the Comédie-Italienne and its successor, the Opéra-Comique, for close on a hundred years. In its first decade of life, 1769–78, there were 114 performances, and in its second decade, 95. The next two decades saw the halving of this popularity to 50 (1789–98) and 26 (1799–1809). But in 1811 there was a revival, with the unprecedented total of 174 performances in the decade to 1820, 51 in the decade to 1830 and 33 to 1840. There was a lapse of ten years before a further 93 performances from 1851 to 1865. The cumulative total of 636 performances excludes consideration of those given elsewhere; Loewenberg lists productions in four other Paris theatres (1854–1910).[9] The only Grétry operas to be given at the Opéra-Comique after *Le tableau parlant* were *Les deux avares*, revived in 1893, *L'épreuve villageoise*, revived in 1888, and *Richard Cœur-de-lion*, which was still being given in 1893.

6. Silvain

Comédie in 1 act, in verse: CC 27
Libretto by Jean-François Marmontel. Dedicated to Prince Charles de Pologne.
First performed at the Comédie-Italienne, 19 February 1770.
Printed full score, Paris, Aux adresses ordinaires; Lyon, Castaud, n.d. [1770] as Œuvre
IV.
Dramatis personae: Silvain, living as a peasant hunter (bar.)
Hélène, his wife (s.)
Pauline (s.) ⎱ their daughters
Lucette (s.) ⎰
Bazile, villager to be married to Pauline (t.)
Dolmon, Silvain's father (b.)
Dolmon *fils* (spoken rôle)
Dolmon's guards (t. and b.)

In front of Silvain's simple dwelling, a small wood opposite. Silvain's and Hélène's thoughts, prompted by their daughter's wedding next day, turn back to their own marriage in defiance of Dolmon and subsequent estrangement from him. Hélène (aria 1)[1] observes that she and Silvain seem to have grown apart lately. He, quite without resources through having been disinherited, replies that the ownership of the local land has passed from a friendly lord to his own father (whom he has not seen for fifteen years) and will be controlled by the ruthless Dolmon *fils*. Silvain is in awe of his father, and mortified at the thought of perhaps leaving a familiar landscape (aria 2). He leaves to catch game for the wedding meal. Hélène gives her daughters some homely advice (aria 3). There is a sisterly contretemps concerning Pauline's behaviour towards Bazile (arias 4, Lucette, and 5, Pauline). Bazile enters jovially (aria 6). His father has rejected outright any thought of a dowry from Silvain. Bazile and Pauline look forward to happiness together (duet 7). Suddenly Silvain rushes in followed by armed guards. Bazile seizes an axe and defends the cottage with Silvain while the women cower between the parties (ensemble 8). Dolmon *fils* enters, without recognising his brother, to accuse him of poaching. In a bitter confrontation Silvain insults him, and he leaves with the guards. Silvain turns desperately to his wife for support (duet 9). He cannot face his father's approach. Hélène (obbligato recitative and aria 10) is left to summon up the courage to meet Dolmon. In a spoken sequence Dolmon listens to the pleading of a wife and daughters whom he does not know, but whose accents he recognises as educated; the daughters even urge him to live among them (trio 11) and he is moved to tears by their transparent virtue. Finally Silvain and Hélène enter just as Dolmon is embracing the children and are as surprised to see this as Dolmon is to learn that they are his grandchildren. Silvain is recognised and forgiven, amid inevitable tears. Bazile is accepted by Dolmon, who utters the final words: 'Come, Bazile: it is sometimes good to show that simple virtue can replace [the status of] good birth' (ensemble 12).

In this, one of Marmontel's most original librettos, three strands are combined: the well-established popular pastoral setting; the moral lesson, directed at parents; and the question of the common rights of peasants. Many pastoral opéras-comiques from the 1760s echo the courtier's temptation of the country girl with a fine necklace in the 'Pantomime' from *Le devin du village* (1752). Favart, who generally wrote in a more artificial pastoral style than Sedaine, turned to a more realistic exploration of country life in a work that might well have influenced *Silvain*: *Les moissonneurs* (*The reapers*), given in 1768 with music by Duni. Desiring to inculcate a 'love of humanity', as he says in his preface, Favart drew on the Book of Ruth in portraying a family divided among itself, a humane lord of the manor who dresses in unfashionable country attire, and his odious town-dwelling nephew. The country people are eulogised as providers of wealth by their labour. *Silvain*, though, goes further than this or *Le Huron* in dramatising the relevance of a political issue. After all, it comes near to violence in (8) and specifies the antagonist as the landowner – by implication landowners generally – who wishes to cut off a means of livelihood. It is no merely personal or arbitrary act of tyranny. The force of the libretto, and its emphasis on the 'purity' and probity of Silvain's family, can be better appreciated when it is recalled that 'the majority of the rural inhabitants of France were wretchedly impoverished' and that 'in these circumstances, the continued retention by the peasants of their common rights – the right of common pasturage on the open fields, the use of commons, the right of gathering wood for fuel in the forests, the right of gleaning and gathering stubble after the harvest – was indispensable as a means of keeping body and soul together'.[2]

There is no preface in the libretto of *Silvain* and the reader may conclude with Edouard Fétis that Grétry was a simple musician with no care except that of abstract fidelity to his librettists' creations: a sort of disinterested practitioner of accurate declamation.[3] But what is really telling is that *Silvain* was actually regarded as potential subversion:

What is amusing, is that they are deeply convinced at court and in the great world that such subjects are deliberately treated by the *philosophes* to spread their dangerous opinions about the equality of all men and on the prejudice of birth; and that *Silvain*, for example, was composed by reason of a decision taken by the whole body of encyclopaedists to have a sermon preached at the Comédie-Italienne in Lent 1770 by the Rev. Father Caillot and our dear sister in God Laruette, on the chimera of high birth and the abominable doctrine of the liberty of the hunt.   (Grimm:viii:468–9)

To those like the Duc de Noailles it was simply an exhortation to marry one's servant and let the peasants poach. Indeed the beginning of the opera does dilate on the generosity, pity and apparently authentic friendship that the peasants showed to Silvain when he and Hélène first became rural dwellers in total ignorance of the means of cultivating a living. Like Favart, Marmontel is certainly preaching humanity; and, unlike *Lucile*, *Silvain* does not conclude with an unequivocal assumption into the bourgeois fold. Grimm personally considered that there was no suspicion that Marmontel and Grétry had produced an 'outrage against the morality of opéra-comique'. His analysis can be regarded as correct mainly because the librettist puts such emphasis upon filial guilt. The integrity of family unity is as central to *Silvain* as it was to the earlier opera. However, it can only be attained dramatically by heavy use of sentimentality.

Nevertheless, this family unity embraced parental toleration as well, not blind authoritarianism. These elements were derived by Marmontel from his source play, the one-act *Erast* by the Swiss writer and artist Salomon Gessner (1730–88).[4] In his own time and after Gessner was universally celebrated, his work even provoking 'a kind of fever' in the 1760s and 1770s, especially the *Idylls*.[5] His main fame dated from the 1760 translation into French of his *Abel*: it was the first of many. Gessner was an exponent of the prose-poem form more familiar to English readers of Macpherson's Ossianic works. In Gessner's *Idylls* truth is sought through the brevity of a moment transfixed; before a sylvan backdrop, arcadian characters are inspired to sentimental ecstasy and song. However, Gessner did possess a social conscience and his social criticism found its strongest expression in *Evander und Alcimna* and *Erast* (*c*1758, published 1762). *Erast* is about a destitute family of unimpeachable moral probity. Erast's almost starving children pity their even poorer mountain neighbours. Their old servant Simon impulsively waylays a traveller for his gold, justifying himself as follows: 'My blood boils when I see these haughty oppressors, who reckon the poor and the helpless as the beasts of the fields, wantoning in voluptuousness, and consuming in riot and debauchery the riches they have for the most part gained by tyranny and fraud, while the poor languish.'[6] But Erast orders Simon to give the gold back, and the rich traveller turns out to be Erast's father, who originally disinherited him for marrying without consent, but who is now remorsefully seeking his son to repair the wrongdoing. 'There is no egalitarianism here . . . social criticism is included for sentimental effect' is a recent view that overlooks the sincerity and explicitness of Simon's speech.[7]

Erast resembles an eighteenth-century engraving of woodland children with beautifully formed limbs receiving charity from a well-dressed wayfarer. What Marmontel did was transform this 'engraving' into the equivalent of an oil by Greuze, strengthening the psychological tensions and darkening the tints. Simon's theft is replaced by the issue of hunting and the welfare of the poorest sections of society. In common with many other dramatists who explored new material in the French theatre, Marmontel was unable to free himself from characters who are basically well-off, for even Hélène reveals that she was well-born, but the author's happy ambiguity in making Dolmon the double agent of Silvain's misfortune loads the dice effectively against him. It is true that there is a close structural resemblance to *Lucile*: humble birth is made good, a parent is lost and found, a wedding provides the framework. Nevertheless, *Silvain* enlarges the inner and outer scope of its predecessor and the music undoubtedly follows suit in this respect.

In particular, the music focuses on qualities of genuineness in the various relationships within Silvain's family (including Bazile), stressing above all the conjugal love of Silvain and his wife. Not until his *Le Comte d'Albert* did Grétry again have the chance to approach this theme, and by then his style had developed considerably. Through the power of Hélène's solos (1) and (10), the music supports Marmontel's portrayal of her as an authoritative personality, going far beyond Gessner's picture of Erast's wife. Through Silvain's tormented aria (2) we identify with him not as an embittered, shallow person but as someone who has an almost heroic capacity to forgive injustice. Yet he cannot bear to meet his father face to face; his strength is found in Hélène. Their crucial duet (9) certainly benefits from the prior trauma of the confrontation (8), but can stand alone as the musical and dramatic bedrock of the opera. In common with much of the score, (9) is not threatened by the decorative kind of Italianisms that were to come, and breathes with a grace – an intended 'naturalness' – that dignifies certain pieces by the later Gluck. Because Marmontel was ready to provide extended texts in ensembles as well as sometimes in arias, the music was able to take over dramatic responsibility

Ex. 6.1 *Silvain* (9)
('O my supreme possession! O half of myself!')

Ex. 6.2 *Silvain* (9)
(a) ('Your heart will fly to the bosom of a father')
(b) ('Love and faith unite me with you')

and suggest psychological evolution. The form of (9) makes unusual use of musical repetition in order to convey mutual and moral confidence:

Section 1: Larghetto, 111 bars. Essentially non-repeating, with new motifs for new thoughts. The ecstatic phrase, Ex. 6.1, extended to a paragraph of nineteen bars, is the high point.
This is repeated after some new music, during which Hélène weeps.
Section 2: Allegro assai, 65 bars. This re-uses two important themes from the first section, but to different words: Ex. 6.2 shows the first. This technique, like a delayed recapitulation, obviously suggests the resolution of a conflict.

The authors reinforced such musical optimism in Hélène's recitative and aria following. It is her moment of trial as the person whose rejection originally brought about the family catastrophe. Like the heroine of *Le Huron* she becomes the prey to her imagination and fear, the orchestra bringing alive the images of a potentially tragic confrontation. Then in the aria she begins with a prayer-like phrase which involuntarily, perhaps, reveals her guilt not merely in displeasing Dolmon, but possibly for having seduced his son: 'I was young . . . mad love led us astray.'[8] By this time the music has gained confidence, even suggesting a certain self-righteousness, and the piece becomes almost expansive. Dolmon, who of course receives no musical solo, will seem even more of a passive figure in the scenes to follow. To have created a convincing character for Dolmon would have required more than a single-act drama.

The lighter touches in the opera stem from the daughters. The taste for portraying young girls in opéra-comique, and sometimes equally young men, was often mawkish. Yet it is impossible to capture the style of acting proper to this taste, which might have been stylised: the actress who took the part of Pauline (Mme Trial) was twenty-three, and Mlle Beaupré, who played Lucette, nearer thirty.[9] Yet the elder daughter is supposed to be about fifteen and the younger one fourteen or less. The convention simply was that the composer gave such characters as adult-sounding music as he wished. Lucette is strongly drawn, lively, and constantly taking the verbal initiative. Pauline is reticent, even prudish. But that fact accords well with the developing design of the duet she has with Bazile (7): it proceeds from a set of exchanges towards a shared statement, presented as a melodic novelty:

Theme A (F major); theme A (C major); link; theme A (G major); link back to F major; theme B for the final quatrain sung together (Ex. 6.3)

The contrast between this duet and the ensemble that comes hard on its heels is one of the high points of the work. The notion of intruding guards or gamekeepers was itself half-expected, and maybe not original;[10] but given powerful and extended music, the aggression implicit in the act could achieve a thrusting reality out of all proportion to the appearance of mere words in the libretto. Like a tableau, the music is conceived in grouped masses. The guards, of which it is instructed there should be four, or three at very least, occupy the wooded side of the stage; the mother and daughters occupy the centre; and Bazile and Silvain

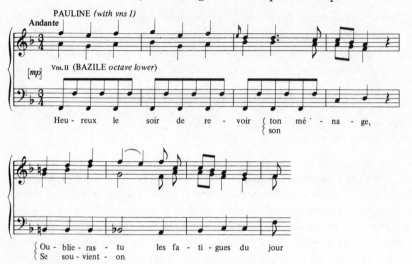

Ex. 6.3 *Silvain* (7)
('Happy in evening to see again one's household, Shall you forget the strains of the day')

defend the cottage. The three positions are dramatised in the music. The male groups threaten each other loudly while the women on one hand have high, fearful music, and on the other, pleading phrases. Ex. 6.4 illustrates some of the contrasts, but cannot convey the very energetic orchestral accompaniment. Acting directions were written into the music where, after a pause, 'the guards make a violent movement, at which the women cry "O Ciel"'. One is reminded of the grouped opposition of men and women in David's *The Oath of the Horatii*, exhibited 1785.

Grétry himself suggests that, if not ahead of its time, his score was at least found difficult at first. Caillot (Silvain) could make nothing of (2) and it took several rehearsals for all the actors to find their way (i:200). Thus it was perhaps the more embarrassing when in 1778 a row broke out in the press between Grétry and La Harpe concerning parody technique in *Silvain* (9). The whole episode is instructive. One meaning of the term 'parody' often used at the period was the fitting of new words to pre-existing music. It was commonly enough done, and was correctly rumoured to have occurred in *Le Huron* (see chapter 2, note 28). But the aesthetic integrity between words and music destined for them was keenly defended in Gluck's time; Gluck's music actually provoked the notion in Paris that he was a 'poet in sound' and that because of this, he had taken musical composition nearer to an ideal of unity of conception. Rousseau, poet as well as composer of *Le devin du village* (1752), was held up as an operatic John the Baptist to Gluck's Messiah. 'The most perfect accord' existed in this opera between music and word because Rousseau 'had conceived words and music at the same time'.[11] Grétry's 'famous duet of *Silvain*', though asserted to be only a parody, proved that 'poet and musician might have one soul without being united in the same person'.

Silvain

Ex. 6.4 *Silvain* (8)
(a) ('Put down your weapons! Alas, do not fire.')
(b) ('The first person who comes forward'; 'You defend him!'; 'O heavens!'; 'What, you resist?')

To the end (*Réf*:ii:107–8) Grétry maintained that *Silvain* (9) was free of parody; but the persistent La Harpe subsequently declared that Marmontel had told him that the duet (7) was parodied. In his *Mémoires* Grétry admits that this was so, and that it came from the privately-performed version of *Les mariages samnites* (i:211). The process, he says, was relatively easy for the poet since the voice-line determined the necessary type of rhythms and rhymes. He does not defend himself against any particular aesthetic charge and actually pays tribute to Marmontel's skill. But he also recalls a much more unorthodox process in the composition of *Lucile* (1) whereby he rejected some of the given words and simply put down the music he wanted to write, leaving Marmontel to make the necessary verbal changes afterwards. (The story is reminiscent of Mozart's composition of *Die Entführung aus dem Serail*.[12]) In fact, the conception of the declamatory voice-line as a thing in itself never left Grétry, as witness his amusingly sincere proposal to harness the skills of fine symphonic composers like Haydn (i:349–55). The composer, acquainted with each place in the opéra-comique requiring music, would set down a score. After a live rehearsal a vocal line would be worked out from the given texture, and lastly the words would be added. However, a wry footnote added between 1789 and 1797 bewails that his advice has been too well taken by the modern school (Cherubini, Méhul etc.) in that their vocal lines, no longer *aimable*, have become 'less obligatory than the viola part'! The duet (9), popular enough to be arranged for chamber performance by Tapray,[13] is Grétry's first surviving dramatic music in 'slow–fast' form. As applied to duets, the form stemmed from two-part arias developed by Galuppi before 1750.[14]

VERSIONS AND PERFORMANCES

Silvain, which seems to have undergone no significant alterations after early performances and publication, was virtually as popular as *Le tableau parlant* up to 1800, becoming less so in the new century. In the decade 1770–9 it received 128 performances, and 91 in the following decade. From 1790 to 1799 there were 41 performances, but only 10 from 1800 to 1809. It was successfully revived in 1813, receiving 80 performances to 1819 and a final 31 performances from 1820 to 1827. The last foreign performances listed by Loewenberg were at St Petersburg (1800).

7. Profile II: the popular composer

The pace of activity was great and the year 1768 a testing time, even for somebody like Grétry who recognised from the start the 'hundred-headed Hydra' opposing his plan 'not to leave [Paris] without defeating all the obstacles to the desire I had to establish my reputation there' (i:144). Parisian tongues were acid. Arriving home after the disastrous hearing of the abortive *Les mariages samnites* Grétry found an anonymous message advising him to pack his bags. Numerous are the occasions on which Grétry speaks of envy and jealousy in Paris, and never more pungently than in describing the jibes even Marmontel suffered, which helped to keep that man's relations with Grétry cool.[1]

Once *Le Huron* was successfully mounted Grétry was talked about as well as musically popular. He was to remain in the public eye for much of his life, and seems to have wanted this. Musical ingratiation was an aim: 'I asked myself, is there no way to satisfy almost everybody?' (i:169). His strategy worked. Cultured patrons and gossip writers made him rather a cult figure; with no regard for his modesty they fastened on him as a composer of the 'new age', of the enlightened style of music, of the age of Haydn.

From its success [*Les deux avares*] on 6 December one will presume that performances of it will be followed, and that the taste for Grétry's talent will increase; his music declaims, so to speak, and is all in expression and images.[2]

The Duc de Choiseul sent him fifty *louis* (*Réf*:iii:82). Philidor, who seems not to have commanded the kind of society patronage that Grétry could call upon, did ultimate harm to his own cause by teaming up with lesser librettists like Poinsinet, after Sedaine went to work with Monsigny. The time was ripe for new talent and Paris at times fell on Grétry as though in love with its own image of the 'man of genius'. 'He is young, pale in appearance, wan, suffering, tormented, with all the symptoms of a man of genius.' (Grimm:viii:165). In October 1769 he became ill, and reported on his cough and weakness. Less than two months later his chest condition gave rise to fears for his life, which were still being expressed the next March. His style of living apparently aggravated his poor health, and could even have been connected with his love-affair with Jeanne-Marie Grandon (1746–1807), 'pretty as a heart and endowed with the most beautiful black eyes in France' (Grimm:viii:468). A daughter was born to the couple and baptised on 1 December 1770, then 'confided in danger of death to a nurse'.[3] This was Andriette-Marie-Jeanne, known as Jenny: she was not to survive her sixteenth year. Grétry's mother, recently widowed, had come to Paris with her own daughter in order to nurse the composer; she decided to stay and continued living in Grétry's household until her death on 14 April 1800, aged almost eighty-five.

Les deux avares and *L'amitié à épreuve* were in rehearsal and first performed at exactly the same time. Grétry gives a quite Berliozian account of his own illness and delirium during the composition of *Les deux avares*: 'my brain was like the central point round which revolved ceaselessly this piece of music which I was powerless to stop' (i.e. the Turkish chorus, (8) or (12) or (15)); 'if Hell be ignorant of this method of torture, it might adopt it in order to punish bad musicians'. And without recounting why, he confesses that the music of *L'amitié à épreuve* was written against formidable odds: 'Never was it more difficult to exalt my imagination to the required point.' He sentimentally alludes to his 'wife' and 'family' by his side in the time of trial, forgetting that his daughter cannot yet have been born and that his marriage did not officially take place until July 1771. In February 1772 he still had the 'pale look of a man of genius' but was 'in better health since getting married' (Grimm:ix:441).

The honour of participating creatively in important royal celebrations was probably itself inducement to nerves and illness. On 16 May 1770 the sixteen-year-old Duc de Berry, dauphin of France, was married to Marie-Antoinette of Austria, then fifteen.

Meanwhile the festivals of Versailles continued. No description can convey any adequate idea of their splendour; they attracted an immense concourse of people from different parts of the kingdom and even from foreign countries. The luxury of dress, the splendour of equipages, the beauty of the court ladies, the magnificence of the *grand concert*, presented altogether a perfect scene of enchantment. The gardens of the palace were illuminated by several millions of variegated crystal lamps.[4]

During May and June Versailles saw performances of Lully's *Persée* and Rameau's *Castor et Pollux*. Then at Choisy on 11 and 12 July the dauphine was introduced to opéras-comiques by Duni, Philidor and Monsigny; she 'condescended to acknowledge personally to the players the pleasure she had received from seeing them'.[5] A new series of theatricals commenced at Fontainebleau on 13 October with Philidor's *Le bûcheron* (*The Woodcutter*), and this time there were no *tragédies-lyriques*; the older style was represented in one-act pastorals by the aged Jean-Claude Trial, and de La Garde. But eight opéras-comiques were represented, and Rousseau's *Le devin du village*. Four were new: Duni's *Thémire* (20 October), Grétry's *Les deux avares* (27 October), Kohaut's *La closière* (10 November) and *L'amitié à l'épreuve* (13 November). Monsigny, warned against impending blindness, had almost ceased composition; Philidor's latest opéra-comique *La nouvelle école des femmes* (January 1770) had failed at the Comédie-Italienne.

Not surprisingly the spotlight fell on the young Grétry, whose duties, at least in 1772, comprised that of conductor. Our eye-witness gives a perhaps unique account of his Italianate vigour which, in an atmosphere of courtly reserve, was interpreted as slight ostentation.

The activity of S.ᵣ Grétry, author of the music [of *L'ami de la maison*], was distinguished by the liveliest and most varied gestures. He conducted, and the whole disorderliness of his person characterised the interest he took in the matter. His pride appeared all the better founded, since the success of these pretty nothings is almost uniquely due to the composer.   (*Mémoires secrets*:v:28)

Lucile and *Silvain* were seen at court in January 1771 with eight other productions of the Comédie-Italienne. The marriage of the Comte de Provence on 14 May was followed later that year by more opera and drama at court. The only new opéras-comiques given, apart from the single-act *Le faucon* by Sedaine and Monsigny, were Grétry's *L'ami de la maison* and *Zémire et Azor*. *Lucile* was to close the year's showings at Versailles.[6]

Thus Grétry was recognised with royal honours; on 24 January 1772 he reported to Padre Martini, 'Your Reverence will not be sorry to learn that . . . the king has just awarded me a pension of 1200 francs and a gratuity of 200 louis.' The pension was granted the day following the triumphant première of *Zémire*. *L'amitié à l'épreuve* was dedicated to the dauphine, who was often to participate in private performances of Grétry's works and gave him the title of her director of music, once she became queen in 1774. At about the same time, 18 September 1771, the Comédie-Italienne itself decided to pay Grétry a salary, not merely in respect of his past services but 'in recognition of his daily offices and [the fact] that he shall work only for this theatre and shall watch over everything concerning this type of music, the voices and the orchestra'.[7] Accordingly he was paid 100 *livres* a month from the end of October. At this time the veteran Duni received only 66 *livres* 13 *sols* per month and the less distinguished Sodi, 25 *livres*. No other composers were paid on this basis; the normal remuneration was a percentage of the net takings of the evening on which one's music was performed. Grétry continued to draw his percentages as well, which rapidly accrued by reason of the popularity of his operas. Thus he was granted official and extraordinary status at the Théâtre Italien and became, on paper, musical supervisor of French opéra-comique in both executive and consultative capacities.

Studies of eighteenth-century instrumental music can rarely quantify the popularity it attained. Yet where there was a centralised point of cultural activity (like Paris) and when accurate records survive (the Comédie-Italienne) it is possible to explore relative popularity in a given area, and to achieve objectivity of a sort. Studies of opéra-comique up to now, where they have mentioned the longevity of a work, have been prone to mislead by quoting a single performance statistic out of context.[8] The picture during the decade 1771 to 1780 is one of domination by Grétry, but he was not the only composer of popular works. Taking, as we have throughout the following survey, composed opéras-comiques at the Théâtre Italien as our basis for comparison, Monsigny was the next most popular and Duni and Philidor the third most popular composers. However, the figures exclude consideration of vaudeville comedies, so cannot be taken as indicators of absolute levels of popularity.

Table 2a: *Total number of opéra-comique performances 1771–1780 inclusive, irrespective of number of acts*

Figures in brackets indicate the number of different operas constituting the relevant total.

Grétry:	1,222 (17)	Philidor:	458 (11)	Gossec:	102 (2)
Monsigny:	661 (10)	Dezède:	160 (8)		
Duni:	461 (10)	Martini, J. P. E.:	139 (3)		

Of course, there were also other composers giving more or less successful opéras-comiques; for example Pierre Vachon with his persistently performed *Les femmes et le secret* (thirty performances) but unsuccessful *Sara* (six). A salient point about

Grétry and the growth of opéra-comique

Grétry's success is, however, that during these years he gave the theatre twelve new works, whereas his nearest rival in this respect produced only eight new ones. The mass of popular works by Monsigny, Duni and Philidor were pieces that had been produced originally before 1771.

Table 2b:
New opéras-comiques given publicly 1771–1780 inclusive

Grétry:	12	Monsigny:	3	Vachon:	1
Dezède:	8	Philidor:	2	Champein:	1
Martini:	3	Rigel:	2	Duni:	—

Turning to individual works apart from those by Grétry we find that, contrary to the impression often given, Monsigny's were more popular than Philidor's. On the other hand the only work by Philidor to drop out of the repertory was *Le jardinier de Sidon*. Monsigny's *Le faucon* failed but his other works all stood the test of time and averaged more performances each than those of Philidor in this period: the most successful new one was *La belle Arsène* (1775), which gained sixty-one performances in six years. The last successful opéra-comique by Philidor was *Les femmes vengées* of the same year, which had forty-six performances in the same time. Included in the figures below are Sacchini's *La colonie*, adapted from his *L'isola d'amore* for the Comédie-Italienne in 1775 (see chapter 22); and Favart's *Annette et Lubin* and *Isabelle et Gertrude, pasticcio* works originating in 1762 and 1765, also using Italian music.

Table 3a: *Most popular operas (excluding vaudeville pieces) other than Grétry's at the Comédie-Italienne 1771–1780 inclusive*

Le déserteur (Monsigny) 154 performances	*Annette et Lubin* 114
Le roi et le fermier (Monsigny) 141	*L'amoureux de 15 ans* (Martini) 107
Rose et Colas (Monsigny) 133	*Le tonnelier* (Gossec) 98
Tom Jones (Philidor) 124	*Isabelle et Gertrude* (Blaise *et al.*) 78
La colonie (Sacchini) 121	*Les trois fermiers* (Dezède) 72
La clochette (Duni) 120	*On ne s'avise jamais de tout* (Monsigny) 66
Les deux chasseurs (Duni) 120	

Philidor's next most popular works were *Le maréchal ferrant* (sixty performances) and *Le sorcier* (also sixty).

When one looks at Grétry's contributions at the period, one must acknowledge their durability as well as their immediate appeal. The only Grétry works to be withdrawn quickly were *L'amitié à l'épreuve*, *Les mariages samnites* and *Matroco*, and the first two of these were to reappear during the following decade (which will be discussed in a similar way in chapter 26).

Table 3b: *Most popular opéras-comiques by Grétry 1771–1780 inclusive showing number of public performances in Paris*

Lucile	143	Les deux avares	116	Le Huron	89
Zémire et Azor	128	L'ami de la maison	110	La Rosière de Salency	86
Silvain	121	Le tableau parlant	105	L'amant jaloux	54
				Le Magnifique	48

It is worth nothing that Grétry had no direct power to recommend the selection of this or that work for the coming week at the Théâtre Italien: such was the duty of the first *semainier* (steward for the week), one of three who changed in rotation. It was the *semainier*'s list which had to be submitted to the assembly of actors for discussion each Saturday.

Of Grétry's younger competitors, Dezède and Martini stand out. Martini's *L'amoureux de 15 ans* (1771) was far more successful than either of his other works, *Le fermier cru sourd*, abandoned after one night, and *Henri IV* (1774), which attained thirty-one performances. The latter was exceptional in dramatic approach and in musical requirements: see p. 130. Dezède's only real success apart from *Les trois fermiers* (1777) was *Julie* (1772) which reached fifty-two performances by the end of 1780: it is discussed in chapters 27 and 32. Its sequel, *L'erreur d'un moment*, lasted twenty-one evenings, and Dezède's other titles received between one and six performances each. In Table 3a, therefore, only two out of the thirteen works listed were newly produced French scores stemming from the decade in question; but in Table 3b five of the works fall into that category. Grétry had hardly a rival.

8. Les deux avares (The two misers)

Opéra bouffon in 2 acts, in prose: CC 20[1]

Libretto by C. G. Fenouillot de Falbaire. Dedicated to the Duc d'Aumont, First Gentleman of the King's Bedchamber (who arranged the wedding entertainments for Fontainebleau).

First performed at Fontainebleau, 27 October 1770. First performed at the Comédie-Italienne, 6 December 1770.

Printed full scores, Paris, Aux adresses ordinaires; Lyon, Castaud, n.d. [1771 and 1773] as Œuvre V (134 and 155 pp.)

Dramatis personae: Gripon, a miser (t.)
            Martin, a miser (bar.)
            Henriette, Gripon's niece (s.)
            Jérôme, Martin's nephew (t.)
            Madelon, Henriette's confidante (s.)
            Ali, first janissary (b.)

Mustapha, Osman, and seven other janissaries (haute-contre, tenor, bass)

ACT 1: A public square in Smyrna. Gripon's house, right, with a door and a window above it. Next to it an upright pyramid, obliquely angled to the spectator and adjoining Gripon's house via the garden wall, above which trees are seen. Opposite, Martin's house seen from the rear, with a barred window downstairs and a plain one above. The sea in the background; another large house upstage with a sizeable inset window on the first floor. Downstage left, a well surmounted by a pulley. Roads enter left and right and by each a modern reflector lamp brightly lighting the scene.[2] Night. Jérôme opens the upstairs window of Martin's house and serenades Henriette, who answers from Gripon's upstairs window interrupting his solo in a low voice (1).[3] Plans for them to descend are thwarted as Martin appears with a lantern, just in time to see Gripon return and go in. Martin gloats about money and profits, overheard by Jérôme (solo 2). He wants to ransack the pyramid but reluctantly concludes that he needs Gripon's help. Gripon hurries back out (to lend money to a young gambler at 2% per hour!) but is unhappy at Martin's proposal; however in the duet (3) they convince themselves it would not be a bad plan to rob the monument. They further agree to prevent Jérôme from proposing to Henriette. Martin fulminates against nieces, nephews and all relations (4). When they have gone, Jérôme – who has been watching – removes a couple of bars from the downstairs window and jumps out, and is joined by Henriette (duet 5). Madelon will assist them in their plans to marry, justifying her action by reference to the wishes of Henriette's late mother. But they need resources. Henriette protests at Jérôme's hatred of guardians (aria 6). Gripon returns, huge profits made; Jérôme leaps back inside. After a sparse supper Gripon leaves, but forgets his keys. Madelon calls the lovers together and goes with the keys to recover Henriette's confiscated jewels from the miser's safe. The lovers keep watch (duet 7). She returns with the box but in their amorous absorption the couple let it fall into the well where they are sitting. As it is almost dry they all go in search of a rope. Martin returns with two hammers, but as he beckons Gripon to follow, the janissaries are heard and appear for parade prior to the evening watch. Ali divides his nine companions into two groups which leave, while singing, from opposite sides of the stage (chorus, march and chorus, 8). ACT 2: The same; later that night. Gripon is seen looking for more tools. Jérôme has arranged a boat back to France and Henriette (aria 9) anticipates the pleasures of Paris. Jérôme is lowered into the well (trio 10) but as he finds the jewels the misers are heard returning and he is perforce abandoned underground. Observed by Henriette, the misers knock their way into the pyramid, which they think contains the Mufti's treasure (duet 11). Offstage janissaries are heard (12) and Gripon is too scared to enter the monument, so Martin does so instead, to his companion's joy (solo, Gripon, 13); but all he discovers are the Mufti's clothes and hat, which he throws out. Gripon is so frustrated that he shuts Martin inside by lowering a grille and throws the clothes down the well. Martin pleads to be let out (duet 14) and the Turkish guard is alerted by the noise. As the janissaries approach,

Gripon realises he has lost his keys, so he climbs a convenient ladder and cowers in the recessed upper window upstage. Drunk and disorderly, the Turkish guard enters (chorus and solo, Ali, 15). Ali goes to draw water but the well bucket, hauled up, reveals Jérôme in the Mufti's apparel; he hits out at them with the supposed wrath of Mahomet, and the guards flee in terror. In leaving they knock over the ladder. The jewels are safe and the lovers ready to escape. In the quintet (16) the trapped uncles are mocked and, at Madelon's instigation, blackmailed into agreeing to the marriage. They are rescued and there follows a short vaudeville (17).

Falbaire was a wealthy author and civil servant who made his name with the play *L'honnête criminel* (1767), on the subject of Jean Fabre: Fabre had been condemned to the galleys in his father's stead to expiate, as a Protestant, the 'crime' of unauthorised religious worship. His eventual release in 1762 was the subject of a high-level power struggle between the parties of reaction and tolerance. The play brought about his royal pardon; it was not permitted to be acted publicly in Paris, though it was taken up all over Europe.[4] Falbaire sent his play to Voltaire, who recommended him to make the acquaintance of Marmontel, which he apparently did; at what stage he met Grétry we do not know, and the composer says nothing about him in the *Mémoires*. Subsequently, Falbaire collaborated with Philidor on a pastoral after Gessner, *Mélide ou le premier navigateur* which, though conceived for the Comédie-Italienne, was stolen for the Opéra by the choreographer Gardel: this was permitted, since the Opéra was the more important theatre.[5]

As his prefatory remarks confirm, Falbaire's inspiration was Italian comic practice, which is why the genre of the work, unusually for Grétry, is 'Opéra bouffon'. Stage activity, farcical coincidences, use of darkness and balconies, all were stock elements of contemporary *opera buffa* (see chapter 22). This is basically why Grimm found it antipathetic (ix:191), and why the author excused it so vigorously:

I do not believe [it] worthy either of the honour of being attacked or the trouble of being defended. If this piece resembles no other, if it is found to contain movement, situations, some pleasing *tableaux*, if it has given rise to charming music and to laughter, I have fulfilled the purpose I set myself in writing it.

Grétry does not appear over-enthusiastic about the opera in the *Mémoires*: 'Low comedy is not the genre to flatter my imagination', he asserts pompously, 'I was happy to ennoble Columbine and Pierrot in *Le tableau parlant* . . . but one cannot, without harming truth, ennoble bad characters', such as misers (i:213). This is Grétry at his least attractive. *Les deux avares* contains music of superb comic energy, eminently worthy of its inspiration. And there are innovations. The serenade (1) incorporates 'Mandolini ad libitum' and the janissaries are associated with clarinets. What had been a large ensemble in *Silvain* has now grown, as it were, into a small chorus (8, 12, 15) singing in three parts, with their own dramatic rôle and music. In sharp contrast to *Le tableau parlant* only six of the seventeen vocal numbers consist of straightforward solos; the burden of music is taken by duets or ensembles. Falbaire went out of his way to put action into the latter. Detailed stage instructions attach to (5), (10) and (11), while the quintet (16) forms an embryonic finale. Grétry's handling of all four is exemplary and forms the best comedy in the genre since Philidor's *Sancho Pança* (1762). Turkish settings had been used before, memorably in Favart's *Soliman II* (1761), since his wife as Roxelane wore a costume made in Constantinople, but also in Lemonnier's *Le cadi dupé* of the same year, set by Monsigny (staged to 1781) and also by Gluck.

Only one Da Capo aria is found: that is Martin's (2), which stands as an exposition. It wonderfully exaggerates the 'low' comic diction of *Le tableau parlant*. Here the gap between certain notes reaches grotesque proportions just as the words paint a grotesque love: 'Sequins and ducats, a whole heaven of money would rather make me believe in the Koran.' But when the misers come together in (3) we move beyond static portrayal: we see mutual distrust, scruples about theft, and finally the overcoming of both in the higher interests of money. At first, tentativeness is suggested by an orchestral motto developed in the background; but Grétry dramatises and verbalises it: Ex. 8.1. The motto is stabilised, the voices come together, but when the misers are emboldened to 'take everything', a new motif replaces the original motto. In 'Nieces, nephews, hateful race' (4) Grétry wrote his most joyous aria of buffoonery to date. Yet the more desperate side of

Ex. 8.1 *Les deux avares* (3)
(a) ('To take this gold, these jewels')
(b) ('By sharing [we shall be together]')

the miser's mentality is not ignored, particularly in the augmented-sixth-chord climax, which outdoes in aggressive originality the 'learned' Philidor. 'Avarice is, however, a passion whose nuances can be captured: the worry, joy, frustration' (i:213).

Such energy is even intensified in (5), in which the lovers escape from their confines. It is brilliantly alive, responding to the physicality of 'I press you to my breast, what happiness'. A seemingly free range of ideas in music mirrors the turmoil of feelings. Once there is a sense of safety ('There they go') the music steps audaciously from A to C major ('Ah, how my soul is satisfied'). After a central section in D, the return to the home key A brings no resumption of theme but a gleeful new refrain (Ex. 8.2). The singers also have virtuoso triplets, reminding us

Ex. 8.2 *Les deux avares* (5)
('Viva Martin, viva Gripon for closing up their houses well')

that Grétry was stretching their techniques. Martin, in (4), has to perform ten adjacent rising semitones. When Henriette sings the rondo (6) she must produce the most beautiful sustained line: she expresses here something deeper than one has the right to expect in comedy, the suggestion of uncorrupted charm conveyed in an elementally serene melody.

With the little chorus and march (8) clarinets made their third appearance in Grétry's operas.[6] The music had already been in existence as a regimental march, this explaining why it sounds totally un-Turkish (i:214). No percussion parts are shown in the score (such absence was normal at the time) but could well have been added elsewhere because cymbals were fashionable and the music long popular.[7]

In act 2 the ensembles are all more noteworthy than the solos (9) and (13); indeed it would absorb much time and an excess of good humour to suggest their every inspiration. The most remarkable of the 'action ensembles' is (10), panic-stricken and in C minor. Jérôme in fact concludes the piece alone, singing helplessly from below ground. A passage of fifty-four bars, prior to this, depicts him scratching about at the bottom of the well; the accompaniment is for pizzicato strings only (*CC* misplaces the *arco* instruction). Somewhat similarly, (11) puts music to various pictorial uses: hammering, levering, the falling of the large stone protecting the entrance to the pyramid. If the inspiration was Philidor's imitative music – riding, wood-chopping, dealing cards etc. – the application here was more dramatically functional.[8] But very little could have prepared the audiences of the

H. Gravelot inv.

De Longueil Sculp.

Remettez-vous, ne craignez pas
Voyez ici, regardez la
LES DEUX AVARES.
Je me vois pris, ah! quel martire!
Act. II. Sc. 7.

Plate 1. *Les Deux Avares* (libretto, Paris, Ballard, 1770). The
appended text is from the 'Fontainebleau' version; nevertheless the
plight of the trapped misers is identical to the stage situation in the
quintet (16). The reflector lamp is specified in the stage instructions.

Les deux avares

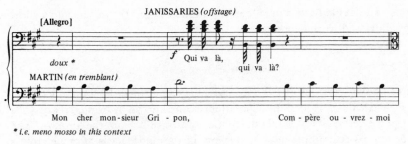

Ex. 8.3 *Les deux avares* (14)
('My dear Monsieur Gripon, kindly let me out, old friend'; 'Who goes there?')

time for the sudden interpolation – from offstage – of the janissaries in (14): see Ex.
8.3. This was Falbaire's idea; at least, it is part of the printed libretto. Ali sings
'Who goes there?', taking the music to the 'developmental' area of B minor,
throwing Martin into a despair that only diminished seventh arpeggios can
portray; thereafter the janissaries break in. Yet this is not the only boldness
associated with the chorus. Their (12) is set in E, but when they arrive on stage in
(15) they sing a developed version of the same music and words in B flat (also the
key of their act 1 music). By analogy with *Le Huron*'s horn note in the obbligato
recitative (14), this must be to suggest the effect of distance. Now their Bacchic
energy is uproarious, if about as likely (as Grimm stiffly pointed out) 'as if the
patrol appointed to guard Paris were to kick up a rumpus during the night or break
some windows . . . singing songs against Jesus Christ' (ix:189): Ex. 8.4.

The quintet and vaudeville (16, 17), played without a break, form a sequence of
287 bars; first there are explosive tuttis, flying orchestral figures, even laughter in
music. This, however, is but the first of four sections in contrasting speeds and
metres, if not contrasting keys. Yet Grétry shrewdly ends it with the whining of
the misers rather than with all singing at the same time. By this means the
'vaudeville' falls into place as a 'lesson', modestly Allegretto in speed. It is not a

Ex. 8.4 *Les deux avares* (15)
('Ah it's good. Ah it's divine')

traditional vaudeville but a single 'verse' shared between the misers and a short 'refrain' addressed to the audience.

VERSIONS AND PERFORMANCES

The three known versions of *Les deux avares* may be termed the 'Fontainebleau', the '1770' and the '1773' versions. The latter two are known by printed scores (134 and 155 pages respectively) while the first is known only from the libretto.[9] The last scene was hissed at Fontainebleau (Grimm:ix:190) and at Paris, after which cuts were made. However, since only ten performances were given there during December 1770 prior to the opera's complete absence in 1771, even these changes were unacceptable. Three showings, of which nothing is known, occurred in January 1772.

Comparing the 134-page score and the 'Fontainebleau' libretto we can ascertain that two arias and three ensembles were excised, as well as four characters who acted in the final scene but never sang.[10] This was evidently too Draconian for, as Grimm thought, 'the mutual influence' between the remaining pieces 'is destroyed'. In 1773 three pieces were inserted, two of which can be related to those cut earlier, even though the words (and presumably most if not all the music) differed. These two were (9) and (16). The third new number was (13).

The exact date at which the '1773' version was finalised is not positively known: Loewenberg suggests 6 June. After four performances in March there was a month's gap, perhaps for adjustments; one or two performances a month ensued, resulting in a total of sixteen for the year 1773.

Even including the periods of adjustment, the performance figures before the Revolution show that the work ran not far short of *Le tableau parlant* in popularity. From 1770 to 1779 inclusive there were 109 performances, with 73 during the following decade. Then in 1790–6 inclusive, 25 performances took place. The opera was revived in 1802, but attained only 28 performances including its last in 1812. However, it was revived in 1893 and had reached a total of 19 showings by the end of that year. The last foreign production noted by Loewenberg was at Kassel (1926).

9. L'amitié à l'épreuve (Friendship put to the test)

Comédie in 2 acts, in verse: *CC* 42 and 43 (for 3-act version see chapter 29).
Libretto by Charles-Simon Favart and C. H. Fusée de Voisenon.[1] Dedicated to the dauphine (Marie-Antoinette of Austria).
First performed at Fontainebleau, 13 November 1770. First performed at the Comédie-Italienne, 24 January 1771.[2]

L'amitié à l'épreuve, 2-act version

Printed full score, Paris, Aux adresses ordinaires; Lyon, Castaud, n.d. [1771–2] as Œuvre VI.

Dramatis personae: Nelson, member of the English parliament (t.)
                Lady Juliette, his sister (s.)
                Corali, young Indian girl entrusted to Nelson (s.)
                Blandfort,[3] captain of a rated ship (b.)
                Hubert, Lady Juliette's chambermaid (spoken rôle)
                An Italian singing-teacher (spoken rôle)
                A notary (spoken rôle)
                Several valets

ACT 1: A study in London, richly furnished in the English style with a writing-desk containing papers and a pair of pistols. Alone, Nelson is beset by a conflict between his growing love for Corali and the honour of his friendship for Blandfort, who is away at sea (aria 1).[4] He decides to confide in his sister. In the duet (2) she claims to know his mind already. In dialogue she reminds him that he is a 'defender of laws' and Nelson (aria 3) convinces himself (though not us) that peace is re-established in his heart. Corali enters; he reacts unsteadily; she describes her great debt to his sympathetic instruction (4). She settles down to read, he to work on the defence of an 'innocent accused and in chains', but neither can concentrate. Corali confesses her affection and Nelson realises he must leave London. A diversion is introduced in the form of Corali's singing-lesson: she is accompanied by Juliette on the harp (aria 5). Nelson explains to Corali that Blandfort, who rescued her as a girl from pillaging English soldiers and so became her guardian, has set his heart on marrying her. She retorts that Blandfort, whom she loves as a father, has always taught that a person should marry by choice (aria 6). This merely compounds Nelson's sense that to love Corali would be to 'overturn the edifice of order, of honour, of society'. He sings an anguished monologue (7). A letter arrives from Blandfort announcing his imminent arrival. A trio (8) for Juliette, Nelson and Corali focuses the discussion on whether Nelson should leave for the country and abandon Corali to unhappiness; he departs before the music has ended.

ACT 2: The same. Corali has decided to return to her homeland. In Indian costume she deplores Nelson's going (aria 9). As Hubert goes to warn Juliette of the situation Corali sings the strophic Romance (10). Ever the guardian of propriety, Juliette comes to investigate; Corali argues implacably against her moral dictates. Suddenly Blandfort arrives, with Nelson behind. A formal quartet ensues (11). Visibly unwell, Nelson again announces his intention to leave for the country, though Blandfort naturally wishes to be near his friend, and sings an aria – unintentionally ironic – apostrophising love and friendship (12). Corali refuses to say why Nelson looks shaken. Blandfort goes to look for a notary for the marriage. Nelson still cannot disappoint his friend and argues desperately against Corali. He asks to be left alone and evidently wishes to end his life, going towards the desk and its pistols. Juliette and Corali rush forward and their pleading lends him the strength to overcome his passion. Corali agrees to constraint. All three pray to friendship (trio 13). Blandfort and the notary enter. Corali collapses as she goes to sign the marriage documents whereupon Blandfort pieces together the truth. He stands down and makes the settlement of his wealth over to Corali and Nelson. There is a gay concluding quartet, 'Let us live together' (14).

Marmontel's *L'amitié à l'épreuve* first appeared in the third collected edition of Moral Tales in 1765. It is a sophisticated and satisfying piece of writing. Although Favart's libretto adhered to the skeleton of events and added little, it gives an impoverished notion of the emotional complexity of the original story. This is best summed up as a psychological drama with a cast of four. Blandfort, serving in India, has rescued the fifteen-year-old Corali during a British attack, presumably during the Seven Years' War. But his soldiers have mortally wounded her father, a Brahmin. Before he dies, the Hindu questions Blandfort's motives and his politics; the latter admits 'It is my duty here to protect the commerce of the English.' In reply to the accusation of non-belief in Vishnu, Blandfort counters that millions have never heard of Vishnu, but yet live. They decide that Corali shall be free to choose between Eastern and Western ethics. (The opera omits most of these details.)

Corali is lodged with Juliette in London during Blandfort's next expedition and becomes attracted to Nelson. Juliette, a rather acerbic widow, imposes constant pressure of restraint on the Indian: thus 'In proportion as the moral ideas increased in the young Indian's mind, she lost her gaiety and natural ingenuousness.' But Marmontel's Corali is utterly self-possessed, sensitive and intelligent, and she conceals her growing feelings towards Nelson in order not to drive a wedge between family and friends. Nelson goes away for an extended time to escape her influence and Corali is kept unaware of the precise rights her guardians feel Blandfort has over her. So the crisis develops slowly, though it is resolved as it is in the opera. Many ironies are exploited by the writer, such as the tolerance of the Brahmin and Blandfort contrasted with the rigidity of Juliette, or the way Corali's final bitterness and remorse do not prevent her understanding Nelson's scruples. Marmontel in fact wanted to jolt his readers out of complacency. Although propriety is observed, it is at such human cost that the scales become weighted towards freedom of action in spite of the profoundest trust between (male) friends. No single code of ethics may be sufficient in real life.

The power of Marmontel's fable has been seen as related to the ramifications of the Calas case which, as we saw on p. 34, provoked the composition of *Bélisaire*.[5] But Corali is Indian and – especially in its second version – the opera cannot be appreciated today if we forget the dimension of colonial expansion and war. India became the theatre of French and English bloodshed in the war of Austrian succession (1744–8). It was the Frenchman Dupleix who 'showed that it was possible for a determined European power with small but efficient military forces to establish political control over large areas of India'.[6] During the Seven Years' War (1756–63) both France and England landed thousands of troops in India; the general defeat of France stimulated only the desire for revenge that was satisfied fifteen years later in the wars of American Independence. By making Corali's family war victims Marmontel shows his disquiet at crude clashes between ancient and modern civilisations and is conscious of cultural exploitation. His story's final tableau depicted a very hard-won victory for honesty and genuine friendship. Blandfort's tolerance in cultural matters, which ultimately deprives him of his expectations of happiness, nevertheless provides the way forward. This remains perhaps the deepest irony in a subtle and prescient response to large problems.

One may posit other fables that seem related to *L'amitié à l'épreuve*, in particular that of Antiochus and Stratonice, popular in eighteenth-century painting, ballet and opera, and furnishing the subject of Méhul's opéra-comique *Stratonice* in 1792.[7] In this, however, amorous competition is between father and son. Since Voltaire was also to use the *topos* of the non-European victim of European customs in *L'ingénu* (see chapter 3) not long after the publication of Marmontel's tale, it would be agreeable to suppose that Marmontel thereby repaid one of his debts to his more brilliant mentor.

The name of Favart (1710–92) is inseparable from the history of eighteenth-century theatre by reason of his plays, his parodies (such as *Bastien et Bastienne*) and opéra-comique librettos. He became a past master in the older style of opéra-comique, for which new words were fashioned around traditional tunes or popular arias, often Italian in origin. But he also wrote librettos for original scores and by 1770 had collaborated four times with Duni (including on *La fille mal gardée*) and with Boismortier, Philidor and others. Friendly authors frequently assisted him, as did his wife, the brilliant actress–singer Marie Justine du Ronceray (1727–72) who created the part of Juliette. In playing the harp in (5) she was to repeat the successful idea exploited in her husband's *Soliman II ou les trois sultanes* (1761), the hardy perennial in which she sang to her own accompaniment.

Less well-known today is the asthmatic, libidinous figure of the Abbé de Voisenon (1708–75), *bon vivant*, Academician, writer of tales, plays and salacious stories, and librettist in his own right to Mondonville, principally of the oratorios *Les Israëlites* and *Les fureurs de Saül* (1758–9). He is the most likely anonym behind the asterisks on the title-page of *L'amitié à l'épreuve*. Outrageous, but usually forgiven, he is thought to have touched in Favart's scenic structures with the epigrammatic style of dialogue for which he was himself so well valued. Further, he had been an intimate friend of Mme Favart for twenty years. We should not be surprised at the possibility of such domestic arrangements in Paris. When Casanova was there in 1750 and was entertained by Carlino Bertinazzi of the Comédie-Italienne, he discovered Bertinazzi lodging with a couple the wife of which had borne him the four children about the house – 'Affairs of this kind are not uncommon in Paris among people of a certain sort' – and the paternity was freely acknowledged.[8] One can only surmise that the choice of our opéra-comique's subject consciously echoed reality: an attractive woman loved by two men who continue as friends. The panegyric to friendship (13) represents a concept that is certainly in the tale, but becomes somewhat more dominant in the operatic form; and of course from the dramatically authentic point of view (13) is at least ambiguous, since the friendship it concerns is the repressed one of Corali and Nelson planned by Juliette, 'friendship' in opposition to 'love'.

JULIETTE.
Vois ta sœur à tes pieds.

CORALI.
Et vois-y ta victime.

Plate II. *L'amitié à l'épreuve* (libretto, Paris, Veuve Duchesne, 1771). This shows the height of Nelson's dilemma before the 'friendship' trio (13), in the first version of the opera. He goes to fetch a pistol from the writing-desk, contemplating suicide.

Marmontel, as we know, envisaged his later Moral Tales being used by others as sources for the theatre. L'amitié à l'épreuve was adapted as a verse play by de Langeac as Corali et Blanford and given at the Comédie-Italienne in March 1783, that is after Favart's one-act adaptation of our opera had been tried on the same stage in 1776. D'Origny, in Annales du Théâtre Italien, was provoked by this play into considering problems faced by adaptors for the stage in adhering to the unity of time.[9]

The subject of the most interesting tale is not always amenable to theatre. In the original form one can extend the plot as far as interest demands it. In the theatre, to conform to the rule of twenty-four hours, one puts the emotions on the rack, as it were, by not allowing them to develop fully. In a tale, verisimilitude may lack truth. In a drama, truth must not lack verisimilitude. A speech that has engaged the interest in one work loses part of its effect in the second; lastly, it is difficult to contrast character equally well, to establish motives for action equally solidly, to give the same perfection to the dénouement.

This applied generally to opéra-comique. In fact one might say that the most successful librettos were those avoiding straightforward adaptation of a tale in favour of either hybrid sources or the use of a pre-existing stage play. Yet D'Origny might have observed that because the conventions of music in opera themselves lack verisimilitude, an opera can turn music to good account in an adaptation. L'amitié à l'épreuve as opéra-comique was a conception worthy of any musical dramatist. But Grétry's librettists failed in one basic respect: the provision of duets. One can readily imagine a text containing little else: the lovers, Juliette and Corali, brother and sister, male friends. In fact Favart conceived no duets, ten solos, two trios and two quartets. In the early librettos (2) is a solo for Juliette; it was converted by the addition of Nelson's protestations. Such a fundamental lack deprived the work of interactions in music that would have conveyed Marmontel's character-development. One must admit too that the libretto reduces the sensibility and moral conflict of Corali. By minimising the ethical dimension and bringing forward into act 1 the element of Blandfort's return the action becomes fixed on the issue of whether Nelson should go or stay. In turn this makes Corali seem more dependent and helpless than she should be, in spite of the vigorously written spoken scenes in which her integrity remains firm. Juliette's character is drawn more successfully in dialogue than in any of her ensembles: she receives no arias.

In spite of this Marmontel was apparently pleased with the attempt, writing to Mme Favart after the première: 'Monsieur Favart . . . has spread over the subject of L'amitié à l'épreuve the graces of his wit and of his style. I am not surprised at the success he has had [although there were but eleven performances the receipts were high]. I share as much a part in it as if I had contributed myself.'[10] Indeed the libretto is far from insensitive. Juliette's exposition shows her unyielding in the face of her brother's 'weakness'. The 'reading' scene aptly particularises the lovers' condition. With the exception of the singing-lesson act 1 moves steadily towards the trio, preceded by Corali's refusal to accept Blandfort in marriage. In act 2,

Grétry and the growth of opéra-comique

Nelson's suicidal desperation is preceded by a genuine discussion of the issues. The subject lent itself ideally to verse, and the mixed Alexandrines and shorter lines give the correct atmosphere of gentility.

If the work conformed overmuch to the French contemporary generic term 'comedy intermingled with arias', this did not prevent Grétry demonstrating both freshness and versatility. No one better than he could accommodate a sudden switch of mood, or an interpolation. This emerges most clearly in Nelson's music, and his character is that which comes closest to an ideal portrayal. The opera plunges into the middle of things with an unconventional monologue (1), where his doubts and swaying moods are pictured in a non-repeating musical form; the music closes in a mood of self-disgust. Then in (3) after Juliette's remonstrating talk he suppresses his love. Grétry confers notable subtlety on the opening, using a type of dramatic irony in the orchestra. The broad deployment of this in French opera is usually credited to Gluck, when in 1779 his violas gave the lie to Orestes' claim, 'Peace returns to my heart' (*Iphigénie en Tauride*, act 2). Nelson similarly claims his soul's peace in the absence of love. But the accompaniment uses a type of texture that, especially in E flat, generally signified to its age the *presence* of amorous feeling: Ex. 9.1.[11] The whole aria is rather too placid to be fully convincing, however, with orthodox word–theme recapitulation in a loose sonata form. Finally in (7) Nelson's torture reaches its height. Grétry's style is again episodic, wayward and even angry towards the coda. Perhaps a suicidal streak is suggested in the B flat minor episode which arrives totally unprepared where we expect a cadence on G minor.

Corali remains, musically, too lightweight a figure, though her breadth is well conveyed. She can be attractively ingenuous (4), culturally adept (5), spirited (6) and heartbroken (9), (10). Nowhere in the music can she express sympathy or guilt for the rift opened up between Nelson and her saviour Blandfort. Her true character resides in (4) and (10). The main theme of the former (Ex. 9.2) surely encapsulates those qualities Nelson finds admirable in her; what is more, Corali confesses in the aria that she has learnt all from Nelson, asking him to 'reveal the truth in her heart'. Her naturalness and instinctive rejection of marriage without

Ex. 9.1 *L'amitié à l'épreuve* (3)
('No, never shall love trouble [my soul's peace]')

L'amitié à l'épreuve, 2-act version

Ex. 9.2 *L'amitié à l'épreuve* (4)
('If I think, it is your doing; I see in you the truth')

Ex. 9.3 *L'amitié à l'épreuve* (10)
Romance ('To what sorrows he abandons me; Nelson, my soul shall follow you')

love is expressed in (6) with an easy yet artificial lyricism that recalls Haydn: see Ex. 32.2. Afterwards, Nelson's anguish in (7) is doubly effective. The only minor-key piece in the opera is Corali's 'Nelson part' (9) in which we admire the pathetic honesty of expression, if not the exploitation of a top B flat. But her Romance (10) in D major transcends grief through noble dignity and beauty. Here the forbearance of Marmontel's Corali is wonderfully captured; the song is distilled into strophic form, which seems to carry the whole weight of the drama: 'To what sorrow he abandons me' (Ex. 9.3). Yet the music was a self-borrowing, originally composed to words by Metastasio, destined for private performance (i:190).

The two trios (8) and (13) indicate what Grétry might have done had the text granted him more opportunity for face-to-face opposition in music. The psychological struggle of the first is contained within a full-scale sonata form, giving prominence to a long, interesting development section: Juliette urges Nelson to leave London; Corali cannot sustain the thought. The tension produced in Nelson results in angry flashes like Ex. 9.4, but the overall urgency of imagery is considerable. As a parallel to this we have the climax of (13) in the next act,

Ex. 9.4 *L'amitié à l'épreuve* (8)
('Betrayed by friendship')

outwardly a prayer sung kneeling but inwardly full of the extremes of emotion that have just been developed at some length in the scene where Nelson's willingness to make a final sacrifice convinces the women only that he has 'conquered himself' and so made Corali's marriage to Blandfort 'legitimate'. Aware of the originality of the conception, Grétry searched (he reports) for a week to discover the right 'colouring' for the piece[12] and finally selected E major tonality, clarinets in B natural (the instrument had not been heard since the overture) and an extraordinary horn solo (Ex. 9.5). Touches of conventional religious imagery like the imitative entries and the plagal cadence at the eighth bar were subsumed into an altogether new language. Rhetoric is balanced by sensuousness. The operatic prayer itself as an idea looks forward to the nineteenth century, but details of Grétry's example were to be reborn in the Republican hymns of the 1790s. Horn solo music, for example, came to express qualities associated with natural religion, after the churches had been secularised.[13] Indeed the horn solo in the trio has more in common with the future than the past, being devoid of conventional motifs.

VERSIONS AND PERFORMANCES

A closing divertissement was designed for the Fontainebleau performances (see chapter 7) and printed in the librettos. Its music, not published in score, is said to have been taken from works by Philidor and Mondonville.[14] There are *entrées* for English sailors and their women, Malabar Coast Indians and negroes. The Calenda and Branbransonnette were performed, the latter showing off the bells on the dancers' limbs. As will be seen, certain of these decorative motifs were expanded in the 1786 reworking.

L'amitié à l'épreuve enjoyed ten performances in January and February 1771 and

L'amitié à l'épreuve, 2-act version

Ex. 9.5 *L'amitié à l'épreuve* (13)
('Fill our hearts, sweet Friendship')

one on 7 March; receipts were good but the run was stopped by the Easter break. If (10) was transposed from C major (1770 libretto, Veuve Simon et fils, p. 67) to D (score) we know of no other musical changes. However, a precious indication of Grétry's active rôle in the improvement of the production is found in a letter to Favart which shows incidentally that Nelson originally went so far as to fetch out the pistol near the end:[15]

Yesterday I was in the third row of *loges* to see and hear the effect of the second act of our piece, and I think we lose entirely by having withdrawn the pistols. The moment that Nelson remained alone, or felt himself to be so, was charming. The moment of the pistol produced emotions which to me were needed for the trio to have effect. At present all appears cold and I think with reason. I conjure you therefore, my friend to replace it. As the return of the two women is disagreeable they could stay upstage and I think that Nelson should not say, 'Yes Corali, I shall take my life' and after that, 'I need to be alone.' This gives away his intentions, which seems pusillanimous.

Forgive me, my friend, I tell you all I think as one who is the most concerned for the success of a work in which he has a share.

This letter is if anything more interesting than that discussed at the end of chapter 28 concerning *Richard Cœur-de-lion*, because it reveals adjustments the evidence for which is otherwise lacking. In fact Grétry's view may well have prevailed with Favart, who in 1776 (see below) did bring the pistol back and did omit the lines quoted by Grétry.

The short run of *L'amitié à l'épreuve* must have been connected with the indisposition of Mme Favart; though she died in 1772 she was overtaken with her final illness in June 1771 and appeared no more on the stage. The opera did however reach audiences elsewhere, and Beethoven's father sang the part of Nelson in 1771.[16]

A one-act revision of the opera made by Favart, not mentioned by Grétry, was seen at Versailles on 29 December 1775 and the Comédie-Italienne on New Year's Day 1776 where it survived for four performances.[17] Favart found himself obliged to cut from the centre of the work, and items (6), (7), (9) and (10) were dropped. Corali's singing-lesson was retained, whereas the presumably duller though more pertinent discursive scenes between her and Nelson and Juliette were not. Such lowering of the moral tension in the story led Favart to make some interesting alterations in the attempt to raise it again, and in the very scene that Grétry had written about. Corali received a new speech of defiance that went beyond the issue of her personal relation to Blandfort and spoke instead of a general defence of freedom; her words suddenly attain a political quality that seems to register the change of identity between the governments of Louis XV and of Louis XVI. The rattle of colonial chains is heard: 'Our soul is free, and is independent. Would you harbour laws to afflict, to oppress innocence, nature, love, and dictate to me my choice?' This public tone was then taken up at the climax of Nelson's despair:

Nelson (*to Corali*): Corali, you can vouch for my probity.
　　　　　　　　　　Every citizen owes himself to society;
　　　　　　　　　　He is accountable to his country . . .
(*showing a pistol*)　No. This would forestall [my remorse] . . .

It will be remembered that Nelson is a parliamentarian. In France the thirteen *parlements*, though legal foundations, also had extensive police powers, even over religion, trade and industry. They had formed an increasingly virulent opposition to the king's policies at home and in fact had to be suspended from 1771 to 1774. Nelson's words above compare with the sentiments both of Rousseau's *Du contrat social* (1762) and of various *parlements*, e.g. that of Rouen in 1771.[18] However briefly, Favart redraws the complicated map of tensions in Marmontel's Moral Tale in more up-to-date terms.

Something more thoroughgoing was needed to re-establish *L'amitié à l'épreuve* on the stage and, when the time came, the political dimension was not neglected. The genesis of the 1786 version was claimed for his own by Grétry: 'I suggested to the librettist adding a comic rôle which would throw some variety on the subject.' (i:219). So extensive were the alterations that the new version is best considered later, on page 251.

10. L'ami de la maison (The family friend)

Comédie in 3 acts, in verse: *CC* 38

Libretto by Jean-François Marmontel. Dedicated to the Duc de Duras, First Gentleman of the King's Bedchamber (who had succeeded the Duc d'Aumont as organiser of court entertainments).

First performed at Fontainebleau, 26 October, 1771. First performed at the Comédie-Italienne, 14 May 1772.

Printed full score, Paris, Houbaut; Lyon, Castaud, n.d. [1773] as Œuvre VIII.

Dramatis personae: Agathe, daughter of Orfise (s.)
Célicour, her cousin, aged 20 (t.)
Cliton, the 'family friend' and Agathe's tutor (t.)
Oronte, Célicour's father (bar.)
Orfise, Oronte's sister (s.)

ACT 1: The drawing-room of a country house near Paris. Célicour has been a page, and is destined for the army. However, he has fallen in love with Agathe. She complains that he follows her interminably, wanting to talk (aria 1).[1] Célicour already suspects Cliton's motives, but Agathe, who enjoys learning from him, finds the idea incredible (duet 2). Célicour declares his love, which Agathe half-parries and half-reciprocates. Oronte enters with the news that Orfise has helped Célicour obtain a captain's commission. Duty must precede love, Oronte asserts (aria 3). Célicour begs permission to marry his cousin before entering service; two days' grace is all that is needed. All three try and anticipate Orfise's reaction (trio 4).

ACT 2: Agathe, overheard by Célicour, says to Oronte she will watch Cliton and snare him in his own trap (aria 5). Orfise enters with Cliton; she has heard the news and reacts quickly and adversely (aria 6), proceeding to banish Célicour for two years. He leaves with his father. Cliton, always flattering to Orfise, warns that Agathe seems to be losing some of her naturalness: perhaps her head is being turned by Célicour (aria 7). Orfise asks him to find out what she thinks, during lesson time. He goes off to fetch Agathe's globe, while she (aria 8) sings of the recognition of love. Cliton proceeds with her lesson on ancient Greece but it becomes a thinly disguised song addressed to the girl (aria 9), after which he impulsively clasps her hand. In a lively exchange she refuses to take his protestation of love seriously (duet 10) and goes; but Cliton imagines his to be the victory (aria 11).

ACT 3: Alone, Agathe reads a love-letter from Cliton (aria 12) and delightedly kisses it, but is surprised by Célicour, whose suspicions are aroused. She teaches him to be more trusting and eventually shows him the letter (duet 13). She will turn it to their advantage. As Célicour kneels to kiss her hand Cliton enters: Agathe quickly pretends to be outraged at her cousin and Cliton duly fulminates against the act (aria 14). Célicour then reveals possession of Cliton's letter and blackmails him (duet 15), to which Cliton can only react impotently (aria 16). Offstage, Agathe tells Orfise of her love. Orfise, not pleased at being the last to know of it, cannot think it a suitable match (aria 17) and tells Cliton she thinks he would be the better husband. But he has taken advantage of his position; all enter, and although Oronte pleads for the young lovers, Orfise calls on Cliton to pronounce judgement. Célicour surreptitiously waves the incriminating letter in front of him, forcing him to nominate Célicour. He is humiliated before a still-unsuspecting Orfise (quintet 18).

L'ami de la maison is a wholesale recomposition originating in Marmontel's Moral Tale, *Le connaisseur*. In terms of its thirteen known stage adaptations, this was the author's most popular story.[2] The present opéra-comique, the only surviving musical version, was his second attempt at reworking, for some time in 1769 he completed a three-act text and read it to Grétry and some leading actors. He recalled, 'Grétry was charmed, Mme Laruette and Clairval applauded, but Caillot was cold and silent', because 'a satire upon false taste is not lively enough for a theatre like ours' (*Mémoires*, book ix). Marmontel burned the script there and then and immediately started work on *Silvain*. Grétry destroyed eight numbers already composed (*Réf*:ii:104). Caillot's remarks as reported above indicate that this early version adhered more closely to the source tale than the opera we know, for 'false taste' as a theme was in fact dropped. The artistic success that Marmontel acknowledged in *L'amitié à l'épreuve* probably convinced him that social comedy ought to be given a better chance to be tried in opéra-comique. At any rate, it is recorded by Grimm that Grétry was at work on *L'ami de la maison* by mid-April 1771, just after the close of the run of the former work.

　　Even with the large changes made to *Le connaisseur* Marmontel was still the sniper's victim, principally for making Cliton a descendant, as it were, of Molière's Tartuffe. But in the original tale the main character, Fintac, is not a devious guest but the uncle to whose house come his niece Agathe and young Célicour, up from the country. Fintac is an intellectual hypocrite, a pretend polymath, shuffling importantly among his manuscripts, books, scraps of natural history, telescope, wax bas-reliefs and so on. He is ultimately kind-hearted.[3] His ruin is the play that he writes and puts on under Célicour's name, which fails utterly. The young people blackmail its real author into agreeing to their marriage. The satire is suavely done, not least in its dialogue, and extremely funny. There are delicious scenes that would have been very hard to capture in opera: a private play-reading; a dinner party with its pseudo-scientific conversation; a fireworks scene. Nevertheless in act 2 of the opéra-comique some of the humorously empty flattery of the original is perceptible in the dialogue between Orfise and Cliton.

L'ami de la maison

In turning the plot round and making Fintac into Cliton, Marmontel brought this character nearer to caricature and buffoonery. His human, not intellectual, weakness is the main target (though Agathe's superior quickness is vital). Agathe becomes the chief figure of interest, a girl whom nobody realises has grown up in front of their eyes, but who is in command of things. Cliton controls his position in the house by flattering Orfise, and a strength of the libretto is that she remains deceived by him. The rôle of Célicour was reduced. The demands placed on the actors by what the *Mercure de France* called 'pure and noble comedy' (see the end of this chapter) bears witness to the way Marmontel and Grétry extended the one-act experiments of *Lucile* and *Silvain* and the more sentimental world of *L'amitié à l'épreuve*. Tears and revelations are replaced by comic irony. Doubtless Grétry achieved less than his *Mémoires* implied, but his desire to impart the necessary tone will be taken seriously:

It was hard, I admit, to give all these mixed characters a tinge of subtlety and wit sufficient not to make them monotonous in the theatre . . . This music that often 'speaks', although of a fairly elevated genre, had not, I think, been handled by any musician.   (i:231)

It must be admitted that Cliton is hardly a profound reflection of weakness. But the authors elsewhere felt their way towards the goal of a musical comedy of manners, which was indeed new. As he had done before, Grétry exploited the suave diction of Italianate melody to express the leisured status of his characters, but with subtle differences. He virtually eliminated roulades and gave even the more taxing passages a syllabic underlay. This represents a blend – some would say a compromise – between national styles, producing an effect analogous to Mozart's in 'Porgi amor' or 'Dove sono'. Other techniques also anticipate *Figaro*: the ability of the music to alternate between the comic style and the high style, giving the illusion of a complex sensibility; preference for duple over triple or compound metres; the use of stylistic parody; and the 'grand' sonata style for Orfise, though with a development section suggesting the frailty beneath. In Grétry's art nothing, even in a straightforward-looking score, can be taken for granted. The orchestra will suggest a mime; a phrase may be an ironic comment by or on a character. The composer clarifies some of this in his analysis of (1): see Ex. 10.1. The first of these extracts comes from the orchestral introduction, and Grétry says, 'The actress who will not give some signs of ironic pity on these four notes, does not understand my music.' The second extract 'indicates irony, I think, and connects with the little ritornello I have just cited', while the third, with the words 'You think that they don't see you', again signifies irony 'made sweet by slurred pairs on each syllable' (i:232–3).

An aspect of Marmontel's construction was the close succession of musical numbers in parts of acts 2 and 3. Very little dialogue occurs between (9), (10) and (11) and little enough between (8) and (9). Similarly there is little separating (15), (16) and (17) and not much between (14) and (15). This kind of continuity had already been explored by Sedaine, and *Les deux avares* also approaches it; Marmontel went on to consolidate the idea in *Zémire et Azor*. However, it was inherently impossible for perhaps the majority of opéras-comiques to contain or even aspire to such a distribution of material. *L'ami de la maison* strikes a reasonable

(a)

AGATHE
Allegretto spiritoso

Sui - vre mes pas   *espress.*

(b)

a - vec   fi - nes - se   bel - le fi - nes - se

(c)

vous cro - yez qu'on ne vous voit   pas

Ex. 10.1 *L'ami de la maison* (1)
(a) ('Following my steps') The four notes are bracketed.
(b) ('With fine finesse')
(c) ('You think they can't see you')

balance between solos and ensembles, including duets, and each act was given a contrasting musical climax.

In view of Grétry's known aims, we shall look briefly at the characters in turn. Table 4 shows the disposition of numbers; since this was perhaps Grétry's 'singer's opera' *par excellence*, it shows the undue concentration on Cliton at the expense of others.

Table 4. *Disposition of numbers in* L'ami de la maison

Arias	Duets	Trio	Quintet
Agathe: (1)(5)(8)(12)	Agathe, Célicour: (2)(13)	Agathe, Célicour,	(18)
Cliton: (7)(9)(11)(14)(16)	Agathe, Cliton: (10)	Oronte: (4)	
Orfise: (6)(17)	Célicour, Cliton: (15)		
Oronte: (3)			

In fact Cliton's style of music overbalances the opera, leaving too many of the contrasting emotional areas to spoken verse.

Grétry described Oronte as 'a straightforward person'; he is an old soldier, whose aria (3) looks at first sight like the model for Mozart's 'Non più andrai' in *Figaro*[4] because it follows his son's confession of love and sounds like an ironic reaction. But the military images come naturally to him and are simply good-natured. Apparently (3) was for a long time regarded as one of the finest military arias in the repertory.[5] Célicour could have been remembered by the quick mind of Beaumarchais, however. Although he is twenty, 'they treat me like a little boy; but I ceased being a page six months ago'. His dogged attention to Agathe is left to the actor to suggest: the authors deleted any solo exposition in favour of the duet (2),

88

and the gentle mockery of (1). This duet shows in music gaiety, teasing, understanding, together with very different reactions to the idea of Cliton as a potential lover. Such principles were well developed in the extended duet (13), rightly singled out by the *Mercure de France* as 'an interesting action' but wrongly interpreted as the seizing and depiction of 'a rapid moment where the emotions of the interlocutors form a contrast and a tableau' (June 1772, p. 173). The 'correction' of Célicour is shown in a sectional sequence of music:

Material A	2/2 Allegro assai	Disagreement, patter
B	3/4 Larghetto	More serious emotions
A		Brief reprise
C	3/4 Larghetto ending with a double cadenza	Professions of good faith; Agathe shows him the letter.

It is this very freedom of form and dramaturgy that characterises the opéra-comique of the 1770s and 1780s: the act 2 'Rose scene' of *Le Magnifique*, the act 2 ensemble with offstage chorus in *La Rosière de Salency*, the act 2 action duet and offstage escape in *Aucassin et Nicolette*, the act 2 prison escape in *Le Comte d'Albert*. These scenes defy the two-dimensional analogy of the 'picture' in order to create the three-dimensional illusion of musical drama.

Orfise was described by Grétry as 'hardly more witty than her brother, but she adds to the delicacy of her sex all the marks of a careful education': her music tells us more. It is as stately as a sailing-ship, rather self-absorbed. The pedal opening of (6) grounds her firmly, as does the spacious theme, so that the timorous C minor centre section is not felt too emphatically (Ex. 10.2). It is a weakness that her (17) is technically similar. Something more dramatically positive – especially opposite her brother in the following scene – could have been devised once it had been resolved to give Orfise more music in 1772; her most characteristic scenes are given to spoken verse.

Cliton, one cannot help thinking, would have been a very interesting person

Ex. 10.2 *L'ami de la maison* (6)
(a) ('They say motherhood is agreeable; saying it, alas, they hardly know')
(b) ('No, a tender heart is never at peace')

had his lonely, pathetic side been permitted some music. Yet his part was little changed in 1772 and must have satisfied the authors. He is a hypocrite and he is punished; but his music only exploits the ridiculous and broadly funny perspectives. From this a good actor would create interest. His hopeless pedantry is shown in operatic parodies which deny the presence of 'genuine' feelings: an extravagant simile aria with overblown storm imitations (7), an old-fashioned minuet (9) and a dullish Baroque dotted-rhythm Andante (14). At the moment he thinks he has captured Agathe, and when our sympathy for him could be kindled, there is an extrovert concert aria (11) rendered ludicrous by the frenetic extravagance of the material. When he is blackmailed (16) he has comic panic, not maliciousness or anger.

Agathe's music, by contrast, has a happy diversity and growth. Her finesse and spontaneity are predominant at first; but by act 2 the aria (5), 'I make pretence of nothing', gives her balance; it is an outstanding, limpid aria in the syllabic-Italian style, with a feeling of strength vis-à-vis the world. This is extended into the self-conviction of love in (8), 120 bars in Andante tempo: Ex. 10.3. Agathe calls on

Ex. 10.3 *L'ami de la maison* (8)
('If sometimes you use cunning, teach me, Love, the art of dissembling')

Love to help her dissemble, it that is Love's way, but this musical feast is essentially a deeply happy lyric monologue.[6] Her last solo (12) is designed around the reading of Cliton's letter, so it is free in form and uses an orchestral motif to stand for the act of reading (Ex. 10.4). Grétry re-used the motif in *Les méprises par ressemblance* (14); in *La Rosière de Salency* he invented a similar one for writing (3).

Once again as if to take forward the gains of the recent past, the ensembles are both static and active. If (2), (4) and (15) are chiefly verbal, then (13) – seen above – and (10) tease essential conflicts of action out of a given situation. (10) cries out to be acted on stage: there are stops and starts, mocking phrases and an ever-active violin line. At first Cliton sings with a near-believable voice, but later, assembling

Ex. 10.4 *L'ami de la maison* (12)

the shreds of his dignity, he falls into self-parody. Agathe teases him and we laugh both at his hopelessness and with her self-possession:

He: Its like a fire that burns me
She: Oh! I'm not that credulous . . .

Comic irony is pursued to the end of the opera. When Cliton is referred to ('There he is, the true model of candour and zeal'), it must be 'en ironie', compounding his humiliation behind Orfise's back. This refrain recalls the spirit of the old vaudeville tunes and indeed Grétry blends vaudeville with sonata principles: refrains in E major; solo and tutti in B major; brief development and transition; refrain and tutti in E major; then final refrain sung by all as a tonic codetta (Ex. 10.5).

Ex. 10.5 *L'ami de la maison* (18)
('There he is, the true model of candour and zeal, the true wise man')

VERSIONS AND PERFORMANCES

'The success which this piece had at Fontainebleau was, to say the least, equivocal. On returning to Paris we relieved the action of several pieces of music.' (i:229). As we shall see, this statement is a vast simplification. Marmontel is much more forthcoming about the personalities involved (*Mémoires*, book ix). He wrote Cliton's part for Caillot who then declined the rôle on personal grounds. Since Mme La Ruette was already cast as Agathe, her husband was called on for Cliton. In this way it was played at Fontainebleau. Subsequently La Ruette 'with his oldish figure, his trembling and broken voice' was replaced by the younger Jullien. Additionally Mme La Ruette's interpretation was altered. Being a little prudish, she did not consider that Agathe's mischievous side behoved an innocent girl, and played the part too stiffly: 'The prankishness was blunted.' This problem was successfully overcome.

Grétry and the growth of opéra-comique

Four distinct evolutions of the opera are identifiable, the first three from librettos, the last from the printed score. The Fontainebleau libretto[7] is essentially the same in content as one now in London whose title-page (though not publication date) shows that the work – with original cast – was scheduled for the Comédie-Italienne on 2 December 1771.[8] However on that evening *Silvain* was acted. For May 1772 a libretto of unique style was issued, with altered scenes contained in a kind of supplement.[9] This shows that music was added as well as subtracted. Further subtraction, perhaps done between June and November, took place before the version known from the score was achieved. This is best shown in tabular form (see below). The substitution in act 1 sc. 1 of the duet (2) for Célicour's 'Oui, désormais' was a manifold gain: the former aria warned Cliton to 'change his tune'. On the other hand 'L'amour le plus insensé' made Agathe's position clearer in 1771: 'If your love is tired of waiting, mine is not so hurried. Yes, Célicour, I do love you.' Act 2 sc. 1 was much improved in 1772, when Orfise enters more emotionally and more musically. The next scene was expanded, notably with Orfise's long speech 'Un homme est un ami'.

Although *L'ami de la maison* was never the most popular of operas, it had a very respectable performance history. A gap occurred between the 13 performances in May and June 1772 until 12 November. But in the ten years 1772 to 1781 it had 119 performances, nearly as many as *Zémire et Azor* in its first decade. Thereafter the rate slowed, so that only 49 performances took place in 1782–91; 13 more took place sporadically in 1792–7. There was a revival in 1804 and the work went on to be seen 62 times in the ten years to 1813, and 43 times in the eleven years to 1824. After odd single performances in 1826 and 1829 it vanished. The last foreign performances listed by Loewenberg were in Geneva (1785).

	Fontainebleau/December 1771	May 1772	Score
act 1			
sc. 1	Agathe: 'Je suis de vous'	'Je suis de vous'	(1) 'Je suis de vous'
		'Vous avez deviné' Duet: 'Quand je louais' Agathe: 'Quoi! vous doutez'	(2) 'Vous avez deviné'
	Célicour: 'Oui, désormais'	'Oui, désormais'	
sc. 2	Oronte: 'Rien ne plaît' Agathe: 'L'amour le plus insensé'	'Rien ne plaît'	(3) 'Rien ne plaît'
	Trio Agathe: 'Je ne fais semblant'	Trio	(4) Trio

act 2			
sc. 1	Spoken	'Je ne fais semblant' 'On dit souvent'	(5) 'Je ne fais semblant' (6) 'On dit souvent'
sc. 2	Orfise: 'La louange est un miroir' Cliton: 'Dans la brûlante saison'	Spoken: ('Il faut que la louange') 'Dans la brûlante saison'	Spoken: ('Il faut que la louange') (7) 'Dans la brûlante saison'
act 3			
sc. 6	Spoken	Orfise: 'Il est bien tems!'	(17) 'Il est bien tems!'

11. The overture (1)

Over the years, Grétry was to explore with tireless interest new methods of relating an overture to its opéra-comique. Indeed this fertility of invention makes his own reported theorising on the subject misleadingly conventional: 'He claimed that the composer should chiefly apply himself to preparing the audience for the emotions he proposed to make them experience; announce to them the siting, period and virtually the characters of the action. "The overture of an opera", he said, "is like the preface of a good book, that disposes the reader to peruse it with interest, and promises him pleasures for the mind and heart." '[1]

The kind of overtures Grétry knew from Italian comic opera were to influence his earlier form and style, however. An overture was historically not an integral part of the whole work, and intermezzos such as *La serva padrona* lacked one altogether. But the standard form was a three-movement sinfonia ending with a gay 3/8 or 6/8 finale. The first movement might use a sonata-form basis but lack defined secondary themes in the dominant or a regular recapitulation. Piccinni's *La Cecchina* is like this, and achieves a casual hold on thematic unity by returning to the motto-like opening near the close (Ex. 11.1): Grétry always adhered to this freedom of approach himself.

Ex. 11.1 *La Cecchina*, overture, opening

Opéra-comique overtures in the 1760s were frequently Italianate; but some were influenced by the symphonic style of Germany and the Mannheim composers, whose music first circulated in Paris in print during the later 1750s and through the agency of musicians employed by La Pouplinière.[2] This tradition was continued in the 1770s by Nicolas Dezède in particular; the opening of his overture to *Julie* (1772), almost certainly witnessed by Mozart during his visit in 1778, looks like *Die Entführung aus dem Serail*. On the other hand, even the younger Philidor did not always publish an opéra-comique overture either in parts or score, for example for *Blaise le savetier* or *Sancho Pança*. Other of his overtures were simply issued in orchestral parts (e.g. *Le bûcheron*), as was Monsigny's for *Le cadi dupé*. Martini's *L'amoureux de 15 ans*, as late as 1773, appears to want an overture.

The usual French designs of the 1760s were either the one-movement sonata or the three-movement Italianate sinfonia. Philidor's *Le sorcier* and Monsigny's *Rose et Colas* follow the first pattern, while Monsigny's *Le cadi dupé* and *On ne s'avise jamais de tout* follow the second. But during this decade opéra-comique sometimes achieved that close relation of prelude to opera demanded by contemporary writers:

A sinfonia should have some connection with the content of its opera, or at least with the first scene of it and not, as frequently occurs, conclude invariably with a gay minuet.
(J. J. Quantz, *Versuch einer Anweisung . . .*, 1752)[3]

The main drift of an overture should be to announce, in a certain manner, the business of the drama and consequently to prepare the audience . . .
(F. Algarotti, *Saggio sopra l'opera in musica*, 1755)[4]

The problem with such a procedure was raised by Rousseau in 1768: how to whet the appetite without detracting from the feast:

Some composers have created strong connections by gathering in advance in the overture all the characters expressed in the play, as if they wished to express the same action twice.[5]

The earliest example found of an explicit connection between overture and opéra-comique is Philidor's *Le bûcheron* (*The Woodcutter*) of 1763, in that the orchestral motif describing the swinging of the hero's axe in his autobiographical aria 'Dès le matin' is woven as well into the beginning and end of the overture. Monsigny, as if following Quantz's prescription, cut out the expected third section of the overture *Le roi et le fermier* (1762), leaving it to end in C minor and in slow tempo. This then led appropriately into the beginning of the opera whose first music is a weighty aria sung by the main character, in E flat.

The high point of the decade was *Le déserteur* (1769), whose overture, probably more than any other, lies behind the Romantic history of the genre. Eschewing convention, it approaches a programmatic tone-poem, since the central portion provides a kind of musical representation of the fulcrum of the opera – the successful petitioning of the king. Additionally the overture begins and ends with the triumphant music that serves in the opera's concluding pages to sum up the whole work. Of Grétry's first eight Comédie-Italienne works, all performed in the forty months beginning August 1768, only *Zémire et Azor*, his biggest work to date, was to use music drawn from its parent opera.

The two early overtures *Le Huron*, in D, and *Silvain*, in C, use the three-movement sinfonia form; but *Lucile*, also in D, stops with the Andante, perhaps to prepare for its sobriety of setting.

The overture *Le tableau parlant* is the first of an adjacent set of three, together with *Les deux avares* and *L'amitié à l'épreuve*, having one movement only. All are in D. *Le tableau parlant* follows a regular sonata outline and, like its predecessors, is in an energetic pre-classical idiom, with kinds of theme, motif and contrast familiar from contemporary symphonies. But with *Les deux avares*, perhaps under the creative pressure of its crazily active plot, Grétry throws tradition to the winds. We hear a loosely organised carnival of tunes strung together in a manner somewhat reminiscent of sonata form. The composer's fertility is nowhere clearer, and it led to new things. One was the style of the third main theme. This already sounds like a nineteenth-century comic opera piece, and the two introductory bars should be noticed, for they are fully characteristic of later instrumental music (Ex. 11.2). The second novelty is the fourth theme as it appears scored for French horn. The first hearing of it extends to eleven bars and the second uses the horn's tone colour to carry forward the melodic development above string ideas which are themselves developing out of earlier figures (Ex. 11.3). This is all redolent of Beethoven or Mahler rather than Boccherini or Mozart and it did not pass unnoticed:

The overture, phrased and in the form of a musical dialogue, had the greatest applause; the experts, however, reproach it as not being an overture, because it completely lacks those large masses of harmony which ought to give it its character, one which assembles together that of the entire work.[6]

Ex. 11.2 *Les deux avares*, overture

Ex. 11.3 *Les deux avares*, overture

Grétry and the growth of opéra-comique

The impulses of facile melody had already pressed strongly forward in *Silvain*'s overture, second and third movements, sometimes highlighted by pizzicato accompaniments: presumably these were not the sections borrowed from the early *Les mariages samnites* (i:156). Grétry's penchant for feminine, falling phrases and *galant* turns stands revealed in *Silvain*'s Andantino before he wrote such things unashamedly into a vocal part (Ex. 11.4).

Ex. 11.4 *Silvain*, overture, second movement

The outer sections of *L'amitié à l'épreuve*'s overture present conventional Italianate material, though it should also be mentioned that it was Grétry's first overture to include clarinets. Yet the central Cantabile section, some sixty bars long, has another 'improvised' form, delighting in solo horn and oboe playing. Indeed the long phrases may constitute a way of preparing the audience for the 'friendship' trio (13), Ex. 9.5, since it appears that the composer did not draw a clear distinction between those overtures making literal use of music from the parent opera and those not so doing. He could deliberately foreshadow music heard later without quoting literally. A good test case is the overture *L'amant jaloux*, where Grétry desired 'to indicate the [act 2] serenade in advance' (i:310), but did so by recomposing it and changing its time-signature. So it is probable that earlier overtures, such as *L'amitié à l'épreuve*, should be regarded as containing emotional and musical ties with what followed them.

L'ami de la maison and *Zémire et Azor*'s overtures returned to three-movement form, yet manifested even more closely such ties. The unusual key of E, for the former, was also used in Cliton's triumph aria (11) and to close the opera in the quintet (18). There is surely little doubt that the overture's second movement, Minuetto lento, was designed to pre-echo Cliton's 'lesson' aria (9), Tempo di minuetto lento. The same character's old-fashioned manners may also be evoked in the quasi-Baroque dotted opening of the first movement, music which contrasts curiously with the up-to-date early Classicism of what follows.

With *Zémire et Azor*'s overture Grétry arrived simultaneously at the discipline of a tighter sonata-form first movement and of a concluding Larghetto and Allegro that could not in fact be separated from the main opera. This is the case because the action of the opera begins during the overture: after twenty-two bars of Larghetto a storm intervenes, the storm that causes Ali and Sander to shelter in the enchanted palace: 'Thunder and winds are heard, especially in the loud parts', reads the instruction. Further, the storm music is mixed up with fragments of Ali's

96

Ex. 11.5 (a) *Zémire et Azor*, overture, final section
'Thunder and winds are heard, especially in the *forte* passages'

Ex. 11.5 (b) *Zémire et Azor* (1)
('The storm is ceasing, already the winds are dying down')

own music, later developed in (1) to the mendacious words, 'Already the winds are dying down', Ex. 11.5. The fragments vanish again and the overture music closes provisionally with an imperfect cadence. Many of these technical ideas were used, on a larger canvas, by Gluck in *Iphigénie en Tauride* (1779). Grétry should be given credit for exploiting them first.

12. Zémire et Azor

Comédie-ballet in 4 acts, in verse: *CC* 13
Libretto by Jean-François Marmontel. Dedicated to the Comtesse du Barry.[1]
First performed at Fontainebleau, 9 November 1771. First performed at the Comédie-
Italienne, 16 December 1771.
Printed full score, Paris, Houbaut, n.d. [1772] as Œuvre VII.
Dramatis personae: Sander, a Persian merchant from Ormuz (bar.)
  Ali, his slave (t.)
  Zémire (s.) ⎫
  Fatmé (s.) ⎬ his daughters
  Lisbé (s.) ⎭
  Azor, a Persian prince, King of Kamir, at first in a frightening form (t.)
  A Fairy (spoken rôle)
  Troupe of genies and fairies

ACT 1: Persia; a fairy palace; night. After the storm-music of the overture Ali and
Sander are seen sheltering from the weather. Ali is scared by the deserted palace, so
pretends that the storm is abating (aria 1), while the accompaniment 'contradicts
his words' (libretto).[2] Sander, however, has lost all his worldly possessions in a
shipwreck and has nothing to lose by staying (aria 2). Suddenly a table laden with
food and wine appears. Ali is too famished to resist. In a solo (3) he jovially
conquers his misgivings. Almost immediately he settles down for a sleep while
Sander, who has seen the dawn coming up, feels like moving on (duet 4).
Remembering his youngest daughter's only wish, Sander decides to take Zémire
back a rose. As he cuts one from the arbour Azor appears in the guise of a
frightening beast, angry at the insult to his hospitality. He demands Sander's life.
Sander recalls that Zémire's request was innocent (aria 5) and Azor agrees that the
life of one of his daughters shall be an acceptable alternative. Although he allows
the merchant to see his daughters once more and to take the rose, he threatens
vengeance for any disobedience (aria 6). Finally, Azor arranges transport – a magic
cloud – and to a descriptive interlude (7) the scene changes.
ACT 2: Azor's simple country house on the gulf of Ormuz.[3] Time goes backwards
slightly, since Fatmé, Lisbé and Zémire are working alone by lamplight, dreaming
of the presents that their father will return with (trio 8). Sander and Ali arrive with
news of the financial disaster. Zémire proposes a simple working life for them all.
On being given the rose she is naturally touched (aria 9) – her sisters had requested
more costly items – but realises something is amiss with her father, who sends the
daughters off and goes to rest himself. Ali sings of the dangers of flying (10). On
Zémire's insistence Ali is about to tell the whole truth, but is summoned offstage
by Sander. Thinking that his children are asleep, he announces that he will sacrifice
himself and, alone, writes a farewell letter (obbligato recitative 11). He leaves. But

in the meantime Ali has confessed the situation to Zémire. She rushes in, determined to give her own life. In the duo with Ali (12) she commands to be led to the palace, gradually breaking her terrified servant's resistance.

ACT 3: An entr'acte (13) is followed by a scene change to a salon in Azor's palace. Azor explains how a cruel fairy has condemned him to his repulsive appearance until such time as he can inspire love. He sings of his tortured existence (14), then hides as Ali and Zémire arrive. Struck by the civilised interior of the palace, Zémire is even more surprised to see her name inscribed over one of the doors. After a duet (15) in which Ali's main object is to escape, Zémire finds herself alone with a group of genies, who pay court to her in a series of dances (16). Then Azor appears and Zémire faints away at the sight. But before long she is struck by his language and sentiments, not least of his aria (17). He makes her the queen of his palace and indeed of his heart, and even promises to re-establish her family's fortunes. She sings a decorative aria for him (18). When Zémire asks to see her family, as she misses them, Azor conjures their images in a magic picture, also transmitting their voices bewailing Zémire's loss (trio 19). The act ends in spoken dialogue as Zémire receives permission to see her family for a final hour before sunset. But Azor gives her a ring which could free her from his power.

ACT 4: The entr'acte (20) uses music of (15). Back at Sander's house Ali is excitedly describing a flying chariot drawn by dragons that he has seen (21); Zémire enters. She tries to reassure her father of her happiness and pity for Azor. The family naturally have little faith in this, thinking her bewitched, and oppose her in an extended ensemble (22). She nevertheless throws away the ring and promptly vanishes.

The scene changes to a part of the palace gardens, overgrown, with a grotto. Azor has given up hope: the sun has set. In an obbligato recitative and aria (23) he gives way to despair and sinks into the grotto. Distantly echoing horn-calls follow the offstage sound of Zémire's voice as she searches for Azor. She approaches gradually and in a cumulative monologue asserts the recognition that she loves him (24). Immediately there is a transformation to another enchanted palace, where Azor is revealed 'in all the splendour of his beauty' on a throne. After some explanation, the Fairy restores Zémire's family to her and presides over the splendours of the couple's wedding (duet and chorus 25).

Zémire et Azor brought back magic into opéra-comique just as the reformers were favouring history and rationalism in serious recitative opera. *Zémire*, however, gave its audience some of the scope and style of serious opera itself. For example, there is the danced sequence (16). Yet it is based on a children's fairy-story, Beauty and the Beast. As a librettist, Marmontel produced his masterpiece; he could identify with the moral dilemmas imposed most obviously upon Zémire (like Lucile, a virtuous daughter who would sacrifice herself for her father) but also upon Azor, the stigmatised outsider who will at last be rewarded for his intrinsic worth. Marmontel's achievement was to give opéra-comique a Moral Tale with the resonance of a myth, though coupled with sufficient humour to balance its

Grétry and the growth of opéra-comique

serious side. Its range of emotions is not small. Grétry, for his part, had recovered from the dangerous indispositions mentioned in chapter 7. 'This work occupied me during the winter of 1770 [–1771]; I had almost constant pleasure during working on it because I felt that its production was at once expressively true and strong; it seemed difficult to me to unite more truth of expression, of melody and of harmony.' (i:222). The scale of the work is connected to the circumstances of its first performance, and the wedding of the prince for whom it was commissioned: perhaps – see p. 64 – it was the first opéra-comique to emulate celebratory court operas like Cavalli's *Ercole amante* and Gluck's *Orfeo ed Euridice*.

The amazing and prolonged international success of *Zémire et Azor* stretched from Moscow (1775) to Philadelphia (1787). In London the King's Theatre put it on in a remarkably faithful version in 1779, though in Italian, whereas most Grétry adaptations were relieved of his music. Both vocal score and full score were printed in London.[4] Other composers used Marmontel's libretto, Linley the elder in London by 1776 for *Selima and Azor*,[5] with Baumgarten at Breslau doing likewise. In the Romantic era Spohr was to compose a successful version of it in 1819. The influence of the work in Germany is suggested by its place in the repertory of touring companies and by the favourable views there of Grétry's art in general. Wieland is a notable example of a critic who appreciated the effectiveness of Grétry's clarity and apparent simplicity.[6] Mozart owned a copy of *Zémire*, and the latter can be compared to *Die Zauberflöte* both in detail (e.g. the magic meal conjured in act 1) and in its general panoply of effects and qualities: the wide formal range of solo and ensemble music; experimental orchestration; the importance of the passage of time and changes of place; the testing and the triumph of virtue. In both, a prince finds his destiny through a girl. As Wichmann observed, however, Grétry's work is the closer to the Romantic model in which a woman, who is idealised, undertakes the rôle of a saviour.[7]

Of the genesis of the work we know next to nothing, and Marmontel's account of it is devoted to the last-minute adjustments he made to Azor's costume, and to the magic picture illusion. Since costumes were the normal responsibility of the actor, Marmontel had to demonstrate to Clairval the unusual art of making himself ugly. The story is interesting in showing that not even the librettist had the right of easy access to what his court designer had prepared: 'But I insisted; and the Duc de Duras, after ordering him [the costumier] to take me to the warehouse, was so good as to accompany me.' An argument ensued, a threat was made by Marmontel to get the king's veto and finally, having specified what he wanted made, 'I forced them to obey me.' The new costume was improvised there and then, with 'a frightening but not deformed mask, not at all resembling a snout'.[8]

Perhaps the basic inspiration for the opera was not actually the fairy-story but Favart's opéra-comique *La fée Urgèle* (*Fairy Urgèle*), set to music by Duni in 1765 and immediately popular. It enjoyed eighty-eight performances in its first six years and was staged until 1782. The conception of a four-act opéra-comique including dances, chorus and set changes stemmed from Favart; both operas end with a magic transformation; both feature an ugly partner who is magically revealed after

Plate III. *Zémire et Azor* (engraved by Pierre-Charles Ingouf after a gouache by François-Robert Ingouf). In act 3 Zémire's father and her sisters appear in a 'magic picture', deploring her loss in the trio (19); they are accompanied by offstage wind instruments. As a matter of record, the accuracy of Azor's costume is verified by Marmontel's own account of its specifications. A gauze fronted the 'magic picture', which also must have had its own light source.

a trial of virtue to be a handsome, royal personage: Favart's in seventh-century France, Marmontel's in Persia. If Favart's was the mould, however, the substance was the children's tale as published by Mme J. M. Le Prince de Beaumont (1711–80). Some of her best stories, which were frequently anthologised and translated, originally appeared in the *Magasin des Enfans* (London, 1756). This was a set of dialogues between a governess and selected pupils 'of the first distinction', Lady Charlotte, Miss Molly etc., and *La Belle et la Bête* is found in Dialogue v. It contains little that Marmontel was obliged to omit, though he made ingenious detailed changes and conflated the sequence of events.[9] Mme de Beaumont made Beauty's sisters malicious and jealous of her (they delay Beauty's last visit home in the hope that the Beast might come and consume her) but Marmontel's sisters are not at all ungenerous. The origin of the celebrated magic picture scene in the opera is Mme Beaumont's magic mirror. Marmontel was even able to take over Beauty's musicality and have Azor provide her with a harpsichord.

A third source was the three-act verse play with music *Amour pour amour* (*Love for love*, 1742) by Nivelle de la Chaussée. (See chapter 19 for its revival in 1777 with music by Grétry.) From Nivelle Marmontel acquired the proper names of his hero and heroine, and the Middle Eastern setting. The play is not about goodness but sentiment, the sway of passions. Azor, a genie, has been enchanted and cannot escape human form until he has inspired true love: the difficulty is that he is forbidden to declare any emotions of love himself. Since Azor is not shown to have any particular virtues the tale has little strength, except perhaps for the fact that Zémire comes to reject the ostentatious gifts of the malevolent rival Assan (the bad fairy disguised). The spell is broken when, in desperation, Zémire declares that 'Azor shall never know it is he alone I love'; the parallel declaration in the opera occurs at the same juncture. After the transformation came a musical divertissement, but without mention of a composer's name.

Marmontel's general synthesis in a four-act frame coheres through the alternation of the domestic and enchanted spheres, at first act by act, but then more frequently. The technique (not present in *La fée Urgèle*) is both shapely and integral to the plot.

Act 1	Act 2	Act 3	Act 4
Palace, ending with journey ordered by Azor.	Ormuz, ending with journey ordered by Zémire.	Palace, ending with unification of places *via* the magic picture then Zémire's journey.	i. Ormuz, ending with Zémire's departure ii. Palace iii. Final transformation.

Partly to compensate for the interest lost in the humanising of the elder sisters, the librettist added the character of Ali; he helps round out act 1, which would otherwise rest solely on two characters. In act 2 Ali is put to most ingenious service as an unwilling pawn in the conflict of sacrifice, and of course as a means of transporting Zémire to the palace. Thereafter Ali's importance lessens.

Grétry's difficulties in *L'ami de la maison* went unresolved chiefly in the disruptive figure, Cliton, who is neither prepossessing nor plausible. But the equivalent figure in *Zémire* is Azor, to whom Mme de Beaumont had already given a virtuous soul. From here it was possible to make Azor sensibility itself. After act 1 he has little to do except express his beautiful feelings. Even physically, the other characters revolve around him: he enchants visually, musically, and to Zémire, emotionally. Deprived of the worldly garb that makes *sensibilité* so hard for modern audiences to accept in exemplary cases like that of Lucile, Azor incarnates the cult:

Ah, what torment to be *sensible*,
To possess a heart made for love. (aria 14)

Anita Brookner sums up the artist of *sensibilité* as one who 'knows how to flatter his audiences by making them feel they share with his characters a fund of irrepressible goodness';[10] in this opera the feeling was heightened by sympathy for the handsome young actor Clairval: 'I have always believed', recorded Grétry, 'that the charming appearance of this actor, anticipated pleasurably by the audience, contributed towards the illusion that he produced in this rôle.'

A discussion of Grétry's music for *Zémire et Azor* might well begin with a recognition of its transcendent qualities, for the opera uses instruments in ways extending far beyond mere 'accompaniment', the eighteenth-century term for the rôle of the opera orchestra. In his imagination music bridges gulfs of time and space. The third act of *Zémire*, in which three months' enchantment of the heroine in the story must be telescoped into mere minutes, gives an illusion of timelessness quite foreign to ordinary opéra-comique. The three dances are the first natural agent of enchantment and lead by virtue of their key (E major) directly to Azor's aria (17): these are the only items in this key. Zémire's reaction – which cannot fail to charm him – is equally enamelled and artificial, a counterpart to her surroundings. When the palace's novelty begins to give way to Zémire's thoughts of home, the flavour of unreality is restored in the magic picture scene. Though (19) precipitates her wish to take action, it is also a tableau outside 'real' time, as it were a hallucination or dream. The unreality is caught in the score by a hypnotic repeated figure (suggested in outline by Diderot) and by the hidden wind sextet accompaniment. The blended tones almost consciously hark back to the offstage trombones of supernatural scenes in Baroque opera (Ex. 12.1). This televisual trick was bound to be enjoyed for itself, but it might be added that it represents a

Ex. 12.1 *Zémire et Azor* (19)
Offstage 'magic picture' music: see Plate III

Grétry and the growth of opéra-comique

Ex. 12.2 *Zémire et Azor* (24)
The wild garden suggested by a double echo

union of special music and the supernatural no less than German Romantic opera
was to do. Grétry's effect was exactly re-used for the ghost of Angela's mother in
The Castle Spectre at Drury Lane in 1797.[11]

The wild garden scene in act 4 equally anticipates Romantic sensibility because
it blends ambiguous musical effect with natural scenery in a manner comparable to
Chateaubriand's descriptions in *Atala*:

The fir trunks, red marbled with green, rising up without branches most of the way, were
like tall pillars, and formed the peristyle of this temple of death; a religious sound, like the
low rumbling of an organ beneath church vaults, reigned here; but at the heart of the
sanctuary, one heard only the hymns of birds.[12]

The music has free form and is experimental in layout: Zémire's voice at first
comes from offstage and her calls are echoed by two hidden French horns and two
offstage flutes: Ex. 12.2. Grimm reports that Grétry had these instruments placed
up in the flies (ix:440), and the archives attest the extra trouble taken over these
things.[13] Only gradually, punctuated by further mysterious calls and echoes, does
the music assume a momentum: Zémire's voice gathers strength against furious
violin arpeggios.

Acts 2, 3 and 4 sc. 1 all conclude with special ensembles (12, 19, 22) that lead
climactically to the subsequent journey and move the story forward to a new stage.
Movement is of the opera's essence, and it might be thought that it was primarily a
work of ensembles. But although all the ensembles and duets except (8) and (25)

Ex. 12.3 *Zémire et Azor* (8)
('Let us watch longer, my sisters')

contain conflict, the following table shows how great a proportion of the music is in fact solo aria. The 'lamplight trio' (8) seems to be unprecedented in style for opéra-comique. Whereas Monsigny's comparable trio in act 3 of *Le roi et le fermier* gave each woman a contrasting type of music, Grétry's does the reverse, providing a rich picture of contentment (Ex. 12.3).

Table 5. *Disposition of numbers in* Zémire et Azor

Arias	Duets	Trios	Quartet
Ali: (1)(3)(10)(21)	Ali, Sander: (4)	Sisters: (8)	Sander, sisters:
Sander: (2)(5)(11)	Ali, Zémire: (12)(15)	Magic Picture (elder	(22)
Azor: (6)(14)(17)(23)	Zémire, Azor	sisters, Sander):	
Zémire: (9)(18)(24)	(includes chorus):	(19)	
	(25)		

Not all the conflicts are serious: (4) is almost buffooning since Ali yawns in music before dozing off and singing in his sleep. (The musical form, a shortened sonata, contradicts the irregularity of the words; but Grétry is suggesting that master and servant have no intention of separating.) Little in Grétry, however, prepares us for the achievement of (12). It is prepared by a strong stage entrance and without further ado the music launches into an intense introduction in G minor. Zémire's uncompromising character is here founded and developed and her strength makes the later part of the opera appear the more credible. She must persuade Ali by any available means to take her to the palace, but for him this is nothing short of putting his head back in the lion's mouth. She harangues him with one argument after another, unremittingly. He is mortally scared, as the Mozartian Ex. 12.4 shows, when his heart really seems to miss a beat. Only by

Ex. 12.4 *Zémire et Azor* (12)
('Lead my steps forward.' 'Who, me? Lead you towards death?')

kneeling to beg him can Zémire get her way; his spirit breaks, and his music too all but falls apart. Formally the music is guided by 'logical improvisation', using subtle developments of initial fragments into longer phrases, and by various parallels. For example, a strong upward motif sung by Zémire, brooking (we feel) no opposition: 'I will see him', is heard later when Ali opposes her: 'I will not go'. Much of the struggle takes place in C minor, the key used for Azor's heartbroken solo (23). The fourteen solo numbers of the opera comprise an enormous range of feeling, graded between the Italianate comic patter of (21) and the pathos of (5) or (23). In form too, the variety is impressive. On one hand there is the elaboration of sonata types, crossed with Da Capo in (6) and (18), and on the other the bare recitative of (11). Some sound more conventional, such as (2), (21) or even Azor's first solo (6), a warrior's aria in D major; others are immediately affecting. Sander's music is all convincing, and much of it after (2) is in the minor mode. 'La pauvre enfant' (5) is in F minor, full of injustice and pity; the orchestra is often important, whether in the tearful bassoon solo or the violent string work in the central section. Later, as Sander writes his farewell letter (11) violins are muted, the bassoons lending a solemnly pathetic tone. With excellent economy Sander leaves the stage straight after this recitative, so confounding all expectations that it will be made fruitful by an aria.

Zémire's three solos are most contrasted, and they proceed from the simple to the complex as if to echo the growth of her character. 'Rose chérie' (9) is no more than a forty-eight-bar song suggesting prettiness and perhaps virtuous simplicity. 'La fauvette' (18) is a breathtaking virtuoso piece, but as well as reflecting Zémire's new-found realm it also contains in its allegorical words a warning to Azor that she can never hope to forget her family, or be happy apart from them. Events show that he understands the warning. In (24), the garden scene discussed above, her music moves completely outside usual formal bounds: through music, she becomes pure will-power and pure desire (Ex. 12.5).

If Azor reveals himself through music as a once-worldly prince in (6), he is completely given to *bel canto* both in (14) and (17); the former, a monologue, is especially memorable. Both are in static ABA form. 'Ah! quel tourment' has the

Ex. 12.5 *Zémire et Azor* (24)
('And in this very moment more than ever, Azor, I love you')

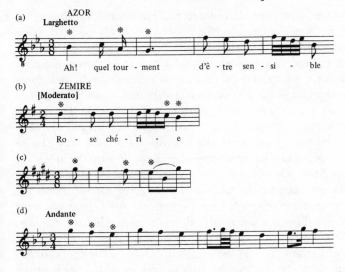

Ex. 12.6 (a–d) *Zémire et Azor* (14) (9) (16a) (19)
Cf. Ex. 12.3

successfully disguised simplicity of a descending scale. Yet the melody itself exists as a paradigm of many of the other themes in the opera (Ex. 12.6), themes all concerning different demonstrations of virtue, active or passive. However, his strength of feeling for Zémire is not musically proven until act 4. At the climax of his despair occurs the second accompanied recitative of the opera: the sun has set and chords for bassoons and violas create a veiled sound. The following aria (improved through new words from one written for *Les mariages samnites*: i:348–9) switches between anguish and anger at the supposed loss of Zémire, with different speeds in the sections: ABA'B'. The orchestral coda is extended to nineteen bars as Azor sinks into the grotto in complete desolation.

In keeping with the atmosphere of a fairy-story, the hero and heroine receive no superfluous love-duet, but only the 'Duo concertant' (25). This is in company with the chorus and sub-principals; their music is treated to the simple device of repetition and refrain, in A major: duet of nine bars; repeat of this by the chorus; continuation of the duet, twenty bars; repeat by the chorus; coda. Although a ballet is specified in all the early librettos no details or specific music survive. However, it is almost unthinkable that performances before 1779 (see p. 208) should not have concluded with dances.

VERSIONS AND PERFORMANCES

The only musical alteration that is proven was Grétry's rewriting of (9). Originally the vocal line was 125 bars long and is seen appended to many early librettos. Grimm (ix:440) reported that Mme La Ruette advised Grétry to shorten it: would that all his soloists had had her discernment.

Grétry and the growth of opéra-comique

Even between the two first ever performances at Fontainebleau 'some light changes' were made, i.e. between 9 and 16 November.[14] Probably the changes are reflected in those seen between the printed court libretto and later editions.[15] Among five dialogue changes in act 1 we may note in sc. 2 the addition of Azor's threat to Sander, 'Tu vas mourir' and the latter's clearer references to his daughters after this. After unimportant changes in acts 2 and 3 we find a quintet originally sited at the start of act 4 sc. 2. Following after (20) and balancing the musical emphasis on Ali, its words contained both a welcome to Zémire and her brief explanation of release by Azor. Later in act 4 six lines originally spoken by Zémire entering for (24) were cut, and (24) itself was lengthened to allow for the following scene-change (*Réf*:ii:103n.l.). Considerable improvements were made in act 4 sc. 5 and 6 by Marmontel, particularly the adding of Azor's request to Sander for Zémire's hand. The persistence of words for a discrete duet for Zémire and Azor followed by a sextet and (Fontainebleau only) chorus in early librettos may also reflect musical reality: we cannot say. That it does is supported only by the persistence likewise of all the words for the long version of (9). The engraved full score indicates on p. 190 a cut of fifty-four bars in (23), evidently made at the Théâtre Italien in the interests of speed of action: 'pour que la Scène marche plus vite'.

The appeal of *Zémire et Azor* was perennial; if other Grétry operas were more popular at certain times, few had its staying power: see chapter 26, Table 10. *Zémire* had 128 performances in its first decade, 75 in the years 1781 to 1790 and 68 from 1791 to 1797. This total of 271 within the first thirty years of life exceeds the totals of 261 and 260 attained by *Silvain* and *Le tableau parlant* in their first three decades, but falls short of *L'amant jaloux* and *L'épreuve villageoise*: they attained 290 and 341 in the equivalent time.

Zémire et Azor was revived after a gap of four years and in the twenty years 1802–21 was seen 195 times. However the following fifteen years, 1822–36, saw only 59 performances. After that there was a sequence of 40 performances in 1846–8 with new orchestration by Adam, and a final one of 27 performances during 1862.

108

PART TWO

13. Le Magnifique (The Magnifico)[1]

Comédie in 3 acts, in prose: *CC* 31
Libretto by Michel-Jean Sedaine. Dedicated to the Duc d'Albe.
First performed at the Comédie-Italienne, 4 March 1773.
Printed full score, Paris, Houbaut; Lyon, Castaud, n.d. [1773] as Œuvre IX.
Dramatis personae: Octave, the Magnifico (t.)
                   Clémentine, daughter of Horace, aged 16 (s.)
                   Alix, her governess (s.)
                   Aldobrandin, middle-aged tutor to Clémentine (t.)
                   Fabio, Aldobrandin's servant (t.)
                   Laurence, married to Alix (b.)
                   Horace, Florentine gentleman (b.)

ACT 1: The overture is an extended mime sequence.[2] A public square in Florence with Horace's large house to one side; on its balcony are Clémentine and Alix watching a procession of former captives bought out of slavery by the Magnifico, together with various soldiers, groups of people, girls with flowers, street musicians. As the procession passes the house, Laurence – also just freed – looks up at the balcony; Alix suddenly becomes animated. She leaves the balcony with Clémentine. The scene changes to the interior of the house; in the duet (1)[3] which follows immediately, Alix is overjoyed at the hope of meeting Laurence again, while Clémentine questions her about him. The generosity of the Magnifico is revealed; he has also financed the horse-race later in the day. Aldobrandin, though a dutiful guardian, has not allowed Clémentine to know about her father's disappearance: Alix explains his presumed death. In the aria (2) Clémentine contrasts her dutiful feelings towards her father and guardian with nascent attraction towards the Magnifico, whom she has seen in church. Alix leaves and Aldobrandin pays court to Clémentine; he has fixed their wedding for the next day but still requires her assent, which she withholds despite his pressure (duet 3). When she has gone Fabio breaks the news that the Magnifico is offering a superb horse to Aldobrandin either for 20,000 ducats or for fifteen minutes' conversation with Clémentine. Fabio describes the animal (aria 4); Aldobrandin considers the deal. In the trio (5) the Magnifico is shown in and strikes his bargain with Aldobrandin. The music links through offstage drumbeats to an entr'acte (6), being a repeat of part of the overture and signifying a further movement of people outside.

ACT 2: Alix leads in Laurence; after years of slavery with Horace he finds himself at home, and abjures future adventures (aria 7). He reveals that the Magnifico knows Horace's identity, but has not gained this knowledge through Horace himself. Horace is preferring to investigate what has occurred in his absence. Clémentine appears in depressed mood. Alix still thinks Aldobrandin the best match for her, at which idea the girl can only weep (duet 8). As Aldobrandin sets the stage for the Magnifico's interview he forbids Clémentine to speak to him. She anticipates the meeting (aria 9). In the long 'rose' scene (10) the Magnifico addresses Clémentine, who remains silent. He realises the reason and breaks out angrily, but then thinks of a plan: since she has been holding a rose, he bids her let it fall if she agrees to accept him. Eventually she does so. Aldobrandin and Fabio, who have been watching out of earshot, think they have won the horse with impunity. Aldobrandin orders preparations for his wedding.

ACT 3: The entr'acte (11) describes Aldobrandin on his horse at the racing. Clémentine is filled with remorse and doubt (aria 12). Horace is shortly to arrive. Alix and Laurence have a comic duet (13). Fabio comes in only to be recognised by Laurence and, for reasons clear later, is chased out by him. Alix wonders whether Laurence is jealous of him (aria 14). Clémentine sings of hope (aria 15) before Horace and the Magnifico enter as friends and, in the girl's presence, the Magnifico declares his love for her. Aldobrandin returns, and is surprised by the visitors; he welcomes Horace and justifies his hopes in requesting Clémentine's hand. He is indignant at the suggestion that he has ignored letters sent by Horace. But Fabio and Laurence come on the scene and the finale (16) begins. Laurence belabours Fabio, who confesses it was he who sold the two into slavery on Aldobrandin's orders. The latter, after an ineffective outburst, is confronted by all, and escapes. A slow last section sets the lovers and the household to rights. To the music of the overture's final march there is a mime in which Clémentine and the Magnifico deliver the remaining captives from their chains.

Relations between Grétry and Marmontel were variable. The latter's treachery was delivered posthumously to the world: 'In general, the folly of composers consists in thinking that they owe nothing to their poet; and Grétry, with all his talents, had this folly in the most sovereign degree' (*Mémoires*). For Voltaire's private ear *L'ami de la maison* and *Zémire et Azor* were 'two little lyric pieces in whose success my dear Grétry is more interested than I'. Shortly after: 'I have said farewell to Grétry and opéra-comique. This year I shall work on the Supplement of the Encyclopédie.'[4] Their sequence of collaboration had been far from unbroken; after *La fausse magie* (see chapter 16) it ceased.

Grétry had generally worked with good texts. But Favart was ageing, and Anseaume's range was limited. Falbaire never worked again with Grétry after *Les deux avares*. Through no action of his own, as we shall see at the end of this chapter, Grétry found himself offered *Le Magnifique*, and seized the opportunity to collaborate with the most distinguished librettist possible.

Sedaine's source was the poem *Le Magnifique*, a tale by La Fontaine. Sedaine often had recourse to this poet in evolving opéras-comiques and in this he was typical of his time: during the eighteenth century when 'one or more of his works [was] being printed in fifty-two of these years', at least ninety-one stage works, including opéras-comiques, were derived from the tales; indeed the number of dramatisations increased after 1760.[5] Sedaine based *Blaise le savetier, Le faucon, On ne*

Le Magnifique

s'avise jamais de tout, *Philémon et Baucis* and *Les femmes vengées* on tales by La Fontaine, and *Le Comte d'Albert* on one of his fables. La Fontaine borrowed the idea of the present poem from Boccaccio's *The Decameron*, Day Three, Novella Five. The Magnifico is a popular war hero in Florence. He is attracted to the wife of Aldobrandin, who has sealed her from the world 'like a fortress'. During the interview that is granted with him, the Magnifico proposes a nocturnal meeting in the garden; the wife keeps silent but the Magnifico makes reply for her. They become secret lovers in Aldobrandin's summer-house. Since adultery was an impossible theme in a modern opéra-comique, it was expected that Clémentine might be made into a young girl; but less so that Sedaine should want an intrinsically sentimental sub-plot in the return of Horace. This does place strains on the libretto, as will be seen. The strength of the work is its unity around the character of Clémentine and its rapid pacing that begins, ends with and is dependent upon the actions of the Magnifico.[6] From the music's point of view the 'rose' scene was both a challenge and a justification of the subject. Sedaine's preface mentions the 'situations on which music might dwell' that had attracted his eye, and continues, 'the musician takes and always merits the greater part of praise. Some reflection is needed to notice the care with which the librettist eliminates ways of appearing at the expense of his associate.'

It was the overture of *Le Magnifique* as much as the 'rose' scene that became such a structural landmark. Grétry recalled reading for the first time Sedaine's basic plan for a procession of captives and the 'chanting of priests' (i:248). But the composer gives only a discreet hint of musical eccentricities worthy of some of Rameau's own overtures. There are four sections:

Fuga: Allegro assai	2/2	G major	314 bars
Andante	2/4	E minor	41 bars
Tempo giusto	2/2	C to (?)E	27 bars
[The same]	4/4	E major	60 bars

Obviously this was conceived as a fairly ambitious spectacle: even the largest opéras-comiques such as Duni's 4-act *La fée Urgèle* or Monsigny's *Le déserteur* were played with no more than about twelve actors, as the contemporary *Registres* show. There was no fixed choral body as such until after the new theatre was built for the Italiens in 1783. Instead, individuals opted to join in any choral music there might be. Though contemporary scores might call such music 'Chœur' the individual staves were as yet only labelled with the names of individual characters, rather than 'sopranos', 'basses' and so on. Nevertheless, it was an era of expansion and there were resources to call in extras; we read that 'Hommes extraordinaires dans les pièces' were paid in March and December 1773, the only months of the year in which *Le Magnifique* was acted. Added to this, the musical requirements of the overture were exceptional: trumpets, horns, side-drum and timpani offstage; in a printed score, at least, the trumpets were unprecedented in opéra-comique. The players were evidently procured through the first hornist, D'Argent, who was paid thirty-six *livres* for 'le Sr Brouin [Braun] Trompette' in respect of three rehearsals and performances during December.[7]

Grétry and the growth of opéra-comique

The 'Fuga' does contain fugal devices, maintaining the verve of orchestral counterpoint throughout; yet in broad terms it follows Classical sonata form. The colourful detail includes an eighteen-bar crescendo for brass and rolled timpani (bar 213), multiple stopping for cellos (bar 170) and an opening side-drum solo. This reappears to connect the 'Fuga' with the Andante, where Grétry wished to co-ordinate the arrival of some priests on stage. He chose the closest secular thing to a hymn he could find, using the popular 'Air d'Henri IV' as a counterpoint to the main theme.[8] But the third section is the most extraordinary of all, the direct forerunner of pieces by Berlioz and Charles Ives (Ex. 13.1).

Ex. 13.1 *Le Magnifique*, overture, third section
The priests' music appears in the bass. The music at bar 13 anticipates the second half of the fourth section.

Le Magnifique

'When a procession passed, I had observed a kind of cacophony, natural when one hears several melodies simultaneously: the priests are to your right, a band of wind instruments is at your left; several trumpets and timpani further off also join the first two groups; all this forms in the distance a characteristic mixture, although disagreeable to the ear. Few people, I think, noticed this mixture in the overture to *Le Magnifique*. The trumpets play a burst; you hear a phrase of the march that is to follow [in the final section]; the priests' chant joins in; they play together; they finish one after the other; general silence supervenes; at last the military band, which is understood to have arrived on the scene, begins forcefully. (i:248-9)

From Ex. 13.1 we can see Grétry's polymetric experiment, primitive both combinatorially and harmonically beside the *Symphonie Fantastique*, last movement (*Dies Irae* section), but nonetheless comparable. In fact the composer forgot to mention the offstage side-drum, clearly demanded in a written instruction. With appropriate staging this episode could be brought to unique effect. The final section, a march, uses horns (presumably back in the pit) but not trumpets. The fragments already heard reappear shortly after the double bar, but are additionally disguised because the whole march is instructed to begin loudly and progressively diminish in volume, in a similar manner to *Les deux avares* (8).

Grétry did not always find it easy to set *Le Magnifique* (i:250), and Sedaine's construction has rather a strange balance, especially in act 3. One understands that the piece occupies a brief passage of imagined time; but the logical sequence of recognition that we know must follow the entrance of Horace comes after excessive delay, compounded by Alix's superfluous (14) and Clémentine's second act 3 aria following it. There also lurks the feeling that large issues are being raised without being accommodated: the return of a beloved father and the enormous crime of Aldobrandin, to say nothing of the latter's real character. Clémentine's personality is very well expounded, but Horace's has no time to flourish and Aldobrandin, who is not caricatured by Sedaine, never receives an individual aria. This is less noticed than the absence of any solo number for the Magnifico prior to the 'rose' scene. As would happen in his later collaborations with Grétry, the rôle of the aria is minimised by Sedaine in favour of complexes and ensembles that bear the action forward. However in *Le Magnifique* the musical balance favours subsidiary rôles, especially that of Alix with three duets and a solo.

This is not, however, to deny the fullness of the music's invention, whether in lamenting solos, buffooning duets or the new style of finale. Clémentine's progress is interesting and beautifully set. She is haunted by the romantic figure of the Magnifico but equally beset by guilt. The twin feelings are composed into the aria (2), where there is mellifluous grace for the Magnifico, who has serenaded her, then quite pained music for the reaction to Aldobrandin. The first music resumes briefly; there is a recitative pondering on her father's possible arrival; and a faster section to end, built partly with ideas from the 'Magnifico' music, in which youthful impetuosity is uppermost. This character-portrait contains a virtuoso close sufficiently difficult to convince us that Clémentine's demands will be satisfied. Indeed in the duet with Aldobrandin (3) she summons considerable resistance against him. Since her personality cannot be shown in the 'rose' scene, the duet and aria (8) and (9) offer alternative means. The duet shows well how, in this opera, more complicated patterns of motivation subsist than had been usual: similar music sung by each character no longer signifies understanding. Alix can only think of the happiness of a husband restored, and projects this on to Clémentine, who herself breaks under the pressure of different feelings. The Magnifico's actions have caused her relation to everyone round her to change, and she cannot confide in anyone. Grétry gives the music a refrain (rondo) structure, since development between the characters is impossible. Then (9), in E major, without double-basses or bassoons, reveals the quiet beauty that so attracts the Magnifico to Clémentine. While in act 3 the aria (15) is an obvious showpiece in static ABA form, the A major monologue (12) returns to the essential strain of guilt: a seven-bar phrase, eloquent melodic leaps (Ex. 13.2); the words centre on the consequences of Clémentine's having made the first independent decision of her life.

Ex. 13.2 *Le Magnifique* (12)
('Ah, how guilty I feel, only with dread do I see the reproach that condemns me')

With a librettist like Sedaine, the search for new forms in music was probably inevitable for Grétry. In *Silvain*, *L'ami de la maison* (5) and *Zémire et Azor* (3) he had written closing sections that freely re-used and developed earlier music. Numbers (1), (2) and (7) of *Le Magnifique* also feature the technique of recomposing a last section using earlier material, in order to suggest progress of emotions. Now, in the act endings (10) and (16), Grétry showed he could write extended scenes with the same freedom and control. The style of (16), dramatically and musically, moves close to the Italian 'chain' finale, which will be mentioned in a moment. Yet perhaps owing to the Florentine setting, the fast-moving, farcical patter style of Italian *opera buffa* has already appeared in the comic sections of (10) and in the trio (5), shown in Ex. 13.3. In both cases this forms a general foil to the portrait of Clémentine, sequestered from the world, and may be classed as a type of local colour (see chapters 21 and 22).

The Italian comic finale built up the stage action in continuous though sectional music to a point of entanglement or resolution at the end of an act. First developed by the librettist and dramatist Goldoni and his composer Galuppi, it is said to have been invented in 1749.[9] Much skill was required to manage the accumulation of events. Although the finale was universally popular by 1760 it did not fit readily into opéra-comique. Above all, the French disliked its dramatic artifice;

Le Magnifique

Ex. 13.3 *Le Magnifique* (5)
('You astonish me, you're joking.' 'No, I'm not joking')

moreover, their tradition of the final vaudeville was not only strong, but susceptible of integration with higher musical forms of development. Nevertheless, Sedaine's penchant for continuity had been seen in his *Le déserteur* (1769); the music is continuous throughout much of act 2 and scenes 10–12 of act 3. Here the keys progress from E flat through G minor and D minor to the main tonality of D major, and the action moves from near-catastrophe to resolution. The treatment is realistic, however, as befitted its serious subject, and because of the rôle of the chorus the listener may think of much of *tragédie-lyrique* as *opera buffa*. Normal opéras-comiques used a single ensemble to conclude, for example *Les deux avares*.

Apart from French adaptations of Italian comic opera, which we shall consider later, there seem to be no Parisian attempts before *Le Magnifique* at the 'chain' construction of Goldoni. In the third act Grétry uses the Italian term 'Finale', not the French 'Final'. Yet we should first consider the long scene (10), which its composer claimed as 'the longest [piece] ever attempted in the theatre' (i:247). Strictly speaking it constitutes an introductory section in A major and three trios in the same key (akin to the refrains of a grand rondo) with contrasting episodes in different keys during which – as Wichmann observed – the action moves forward.[10] The trios are *buffo* exchanges with the Magnifico and Aldobrandin scoring off one another; the episodes detail the Magnifico's one-sided conversation with Clémentine (Ex. 13.4). All this occupies over thirty pages of eighteenth-century score.

Ex. 13.4 *Le Magnifique* (10)
('Fall, charming rose')

With it may be compared the act 3 finale, where the composer used an incomplete circle of keys rather than a refrain. It occupies twenty pages of eighteenth-century score. One of its most un-Italian strokes was the quiet last section, dominated by unity of mind and family and built up over a held bass note (Ex. 13.5).

Ex. 13.5 *Le Magnifique* (16)
('Ah, my friend, I unite you . . .')

Key	Tempo	Action
C major to G minor	4/4 Allegro	Entrance of Laurence and Fabio; Horace recognises the latter, who is prevailed upon to confess something. Aldobrandin quakes. Musical climax.
G major	6/8	Fabio's confession; Aldobrandin incriminated.
D major	4/4	Furious outburst from Aldobrandin.
D minor	2/4 Largo	Brief stunned reaction from the others.
D major to C major	4/4 Allegro	Angry confrontation with Aldobrandin, who escapes; Italianate rapid scales, set syllabically.
C minor	2/2 slow link	Magnifico pronounces sentence: 'Let him go a prey to his avenging remorse'.
C major	2/4 Andante	Binary-form closing ensemble.

At this juncture, as in certain chapters to come, we shall look separately at what will be called 'functional recollection' of music. Grétry is famous for having used, ninefold, Richard's 'own' song throughout all three acts of *Richard Cœur-de-lion* (q.v.); but this notion certainly did not spring fully-armed from the minds of its authors around 1782. It grew from the abiding interest of Grétry in the 'literal' truthfulness of musical drama. In *Les deux avares* we saw this principle at work in the recollection of tonality and music in (15). In *Le Magnifique* (5) Aldobrandin is assigned an octave motif (Ex. 13.6) where he reacts to the Magnifico's proposal for a conversation with Clémentine. Here, Aldobrandin sings the words 'chatting, prattling' in a questioning way. But in the trio sections of (10) he uses the motif again to mock the Magnifico the more effectively, having already duped him. In act 3 (16) the motif is varied when hurled by Aldobrandin to Fabio after the latter has betrayed his master. The interesting, ironic choice of motif here appears to imply that Aldobrandin unconsciously recalls his own betrayal of the Magnifico in act 2. But additionally, of course, the motif serves as a characteristic 'voice-print' over an unexpectedly large period of time.

(a)

Cau - ser, ja - ser

(b)

·Par .- lez, par - lez, par - lez!

(c)

Tu me le pay-e - ras!

Ex. 13.6 *Le Magnifique* (5) (10) (16)
(a) ('Chatting, prattling')
(b) ('Speak, speak!')
(c) ('You'll pay for this!')

It would be almost impossible to catalogue the benefits that Sedaine's imagination brought to eighteenth-century opera. He was born in 1719, became by trade a stone-mason, but made a mark with a volume of poetry.[11] Yet only the persuasion of Jean Monnet brought Sedaine into the theatre, with *Le diable à quatre* (1756), a burlesque with a patchwork for a musical score. Insisting on the compositional unity of any future theatre work, he joined with Philidor in 1759 in *Blaise le savetier* (*Blaise the cobbler*); their *Le jardinier et son seigneur* (*The gardener and his lord*) two years later confirmed Sedaine's comic individuality and taste for social satire. He then determined to write a full-length opéra-comique.[12] *Le roi et le fermier* (1762; see chapter 3) achieved the dramatic maturity he sought, both of characterisation and musical scope. It also showed that he was able to place his art at music's service by guiding the weight of emotional expression towards the arias and ensembles, giving the composer (Monsigny) tasks of conveying action, narration or even simultaneous voicing of contrasting emotion. Sedaine's most famous play was *Le philosophe sans le savoir* (1765), influenced by the ideas of Diderot, portraying a contemporary subject in a realistic middle-class setting. But the difficulties experienced at the Comédie-Française, not least the extensive rewriting required by the censors, guided Sedaine more towards the Comédie-Italienne. At the time when Le Magnifique was completed Monsigny was already in possession of two unset Sedaine librettos. For that reason, he says, the writer offered his new text to Grétry.[13] In fact, had not Monsigny been threatened with blindness as the consequence of continued musical activity, Richard Cœur-de-lion would not have been composed by Grétry. We know, that is, from a partially-reproduced letter that Sedaine pressed his old collaborator hard to accept Richard, and that Monsigny positively urged Sedaine to approach Grétry.[14]

Sedaine continued to look for a type of drama which would explore themes and methods proper to opéra-comique alone. In his earlier career he was influenced by Shakespeare, in particular the juxtaposing of the comic and the serious. Later on (see chapters 24, 33 etc.) he became interested in the mediaeval period as a means not simply of using local colour, although this was sometimes part of the plan, but of forging a theatrical experience based on a limited, intense action (cf. Wagner's designation of Tristan und Isolde as an 'action') between three or even two people. He never went back to simple comedy, and he perennially failed when he attempted works for the Opéra, except for Aline, reine de Golconde, an opera-ballet. The special validity of his late work was felt by La Harpe, who earlier (see p. 8) had had limited time for opéra-comique as a genre. Le Comte d' Albert, he wrote,

is a kind of proverb in pantomine; there is no sort of intrigue; it has tableaux arranged for the stage and for the musician; but the whole thing is effective . . . It is an individual genre that in some ways approaches Shakespeare's dramas. This genre seems to me well enough placed at the Théâtre Italien, which is not a regular theatre, and with music which adopts all tones and likes to vary its tone. One would be mistaken to judge these sorts of piece by the [normal] rules of art.[15]

VERSIONS AND PERFORMANCES

Although Le Magnifique was given at Versailles fifteen days after the Parisian première the Versailles printed libretto appears to be the earliest source.[16] There are only three small differences with the later texts, the main one at the end of act 1. Sedaine originally envisaged (5) merging into a repetition of the overture, rather than the drum-beats; the former would begin softly and then swell to suggest the captives outside. Sedaine's view, expressed in 1778, was that the work 'has never had the success that it could have'; it underwent a bad start, since 'from the fifth performance almost all the rôles have been played by doubling actors, which removes the whole tradition of rehearsals'. Furthermore, M. La Ruette's poor health had caused the final mimed divertissement to be suppressed. This is not apparent from the full score. The early libretto provided three quatrains (not set or at least not surviving) where Clémentine, the captives and the Magnifico sang during the latter's act of generosity. Sedaine rightly regarded this tableau as 'necessary to the dénouement and as a complement to the character of Le Magnifique'.[17]

The opera received sixty performances in the ten years 1773–82. Thereafter it existed as something which would for the next forty years be sufficiently interesting to revive, but never wholly successfully. There were nine performances in 1783–6, then six more in 1790–1. A quite successful run in 1796–8 saw twenty-two performances. The Opéra-Comique did not revive it until 1814, when there were ten performances, followed by an odd two more in 1818. The final set of six performances was in the form of a one-act version, exclusively played during 1823. The last foreign revival noted by Loewenberg was in Moscow (1810).

14. La Rosière de Salency (The Rose-maiden of Salency)

Pastorale in 3 acts, in verse: *CC* 30[1]
Libretto by Alexandre Frédéric Jacques Masson de Pezay. Dedicated to the Comtesse de Stroganoff.[2]
First performed at Fontainebleau, 23 October 1773. First performed at the Comédie-Italienne, 28 February 1774.
Manuscript full score: F:Pn Rés.1336. Printed full score, Paris, Houbaut, n.d. [1774] as Œuvre x.
Dramatis personae: Cécile, the Rose-maiden elect (s.)
           Colin, her betrothed (t.)
           Herpin, her father (b.)
           The Bailli (t.)
           Nina   }
           Lucile   } Cécile's rivals (s.)
           Jean Gaud, miller from the next village (t.)
           The seigneur (b.)
           Chorus of villagers; judges; the seigneur's retinue

ACT 1: A village square with trees, at evening, Herpin's house ceremonially garlanded with flowers and a blue sash. Cécile is peacefully making lace (aria 1).[3] Colin mentions a rumour that the Bailli wants Cécile's hand and has visited Herpin. The lovers sing of their hopes (duet 2). Unnoticed, the Bailli leads in Lucile and Nina to spy. Colin kisses Cécile; she places his hand on her heart; they will meet at dawn to prepare for the seigneur's visit. In a trio (3) the Bailli, Nina and Lucile plot Cécile's downfall, he lustfully, they maliciously, by reporting this 'guilty' farewell. Alone, the girls bicker (duet 4) then greet Cécile in ironic tones. As the moon rises Cécile finds herself alone (aria 5). But the Bailli importunes her directly. She laughs at his offer of marriage. He grows angry (duet and chorus 6), producing a written accusation of her dishonour. Then he raises the village, ordering sergeants to rip the garlands from the house. They demur, so he does it himself, to general consternation.

ACT 2: Entr'acte (7). The same, vestiges of garlands hanging; dawn, gradually brightening. Distant storm. The lovers meet in desperation (duet 8) and appeal to the goddess of love. Colin will seek justice from the seigneur, but as it is too early for the ferry he will have to swim the river (solo 9). He leaves. Herpin emerges, his back to the façade. After his calm solo (10) he eventually notices the disastrous garlands. The storm erupts with the duet and chorus (11), Herpin remonstrating with Cécile as offstage voices witness Colin's efforts; Cécile is prevented from leaving as we hear 'he perishes'. Almost delirious with evil anticipation the Bailli tries to buy his way into Herpin's family, but is resisted. He produces Colin's clothing as evidence of his death (trio 12); Cécile comes out of the house, overhears him and faints. Jean Gaud enters with news (aria 13), so the Bailli, finding himself alone, impersonates Herpin, thus receiving intelligence that Colin has safely crossed the river and been rescued by Gaud from drowning.

ACT 3: Entr'acte (14). Later that day. Pleasant countryside, mountains, river, several peasants repairing storm damage; a knoll to the left overlooking the river. The Bailli supervises peasants preparing for the rose-maiden's ceremony, striking at them distractedly. In the choral ensemble (15) he expatiates on vengeance while overseeing the placing of the throne, then struts around, mocked by the men. All leave. Cécile enters in complete disorder (aria 16) and climbs the knoll, ready to drown herself. Colin, whom she still believes dead, appears on the mountainside. He descends and crosses the river to her, having reported the Bailli's crimes to the seigneur. They have a duet of recovery (17) and another consolidating their happiness (18). To a brief flourish (19) process in villagers, judges, the Bailli and the seigneur with his retinue. The seigneur grasps Herpin's hand, denouncing the Bailli. A rejoicing chorus (20) overwhelms efforts by the Bailli to testify against Cécile. Tactfully the seigneur persuades the elders of her essential virtue. They all echo his sentiments (solo and chorus 21). The Bailli is accused of abusing his authority and only reprieved following pleas by the lovers themselves. The festival begins. Cécile is enthroned; marches and dances follow (22a–d) leading to a sung vaudeville (23a) with closing ensemble (23b).

Grétry's second creative period began with Le Magnifique, continuing with the present work, La fausse magie and Les mariages samnites: a diverse quartet of operas each with considerable musical mastery over its own dramatic world. Le Magnifique evoked Florence using extra actors, but its successors gave the singing chorus an essential rôle and thus unprecedented expressive variety. All four works were in some way problematic; each had a different librettist. They reduce emphasis on straightforward sensibilité and make significant use of functional repetition of music. Special similarities link La Rosière de Salency with Les mariages samnites. These reach into history in order to suggest a more ideal moral climate. Each culminates in a ceremony and each dared to give opéra-comique a (presumed) death and its aftermath. Thus they are important predecessors of the achievements of the 1780s.

In 1766 Billardon de Sauvigny printed an anonymous account of an annual ceremony at Salency (Picardy): 'La fête de la rose',[4] supposedly inaugurated by St Médard, the fifth-century bishop of Noyon. From three 'finalists' the girl with the best reputation for virtue was selected by the local seigneur (lord of the manor) and by general agreement. She was crowned with roses by the priest. Louis XIII, during a visit to Noyon, had also endowed a silver ring and a blue ribbon. In 1770 Sauvigny issued *La rose ou la feste de Salency*, headed by an engraving after Greuze; an augmented edition emerged in 1774. His intention was to evoke ancient, rural simplicity and virtue. Salency's tillers supposedly had no ploughs, only hoes, but 'what good a single wise establishment produces!'[5]

The problem of making an appropriate fictional elaboration of Salency was acknowledged by Sauvigny; he himself wrote a love-story of repressed passion set in sensuously abundant countryside: his rose-maiden tears off her victorious crown and declares her love for the unknown Bazile. The dramatic setting by Favart, *La Rosière de Salenci*, was a three-act *pasticcio* (Fontainebleau, 25 October 1769) with music amalgamated from pieces by Rameau, Philidor, Monsigny and others. The piece was rightly attacked by Grimm (viii:358) for falsity of tone and 'detestable plot': it is an inconsequential affair in rustic dialect.[6] The ideal treatment, thought Grimm, would require much skill to show one's rose-maiden both susceptible and guiltless (x:401).

Grétry could have first encountered Masson de Pezay at Fontainebleau in 1770: two weeks after the première of *Les deux avares* Pezay and Kohaut's one-act opéra-comique *La Closière* was given on 10 November. Pezay had a short but eventful life (1741–77) during which he became an army tactician and secret adviser to the young Louis XVI.[7] He was temperamental, arrogant: to Grimm, 'intense, even extreme' in company. Travelling as Inspector of Coastal Defences he quarrelled with a provincial administrator, who went to the highest level and had him dismissed. Pezay went back to his estate and died the year after his marriage.

In *Les soirées helvétiennes* (1771) Pezay broadcast his love of Swiss mountain countryside, the religious inspiration he drew from it, and his ecstatic response to sunrise over Lake Geneva: 'O most noble of scenes performed here on the most noble of theatres!' The vision of powerful scenery and the almost metaphysical reality of nature in men's lives was to inspire the basic grandeur of *La Rosière de Salency*. The second fresh element was Pezay's vision of the Bailli as an obsessive, manic figure who drives the whole opera forward: 'le terrible Bailli' as he calls him.[8] Pezay evidently saw the legend as the opportunity to do what Greuze would do in *La malédiction paternelle* and *Le fils puni*, exhibited 1777–8: show anguish or tragedy in the village setting, deny oneself the 'easy popularity of the quaint and rustic' and focus, as in a Classical picture, on the 'emotional and moral crisis portrayed' using dark, subdued colours.[9] Thus Pezay reinterpreted Salency completely: in fact his theme of the worm within the bud is quite separable from it. Conversely, this emotional range was balanced by the use of verse dialogue, which distanced the characters from the merely realistic world.

The Bailli as villain was a convention at the Comédie-Italienne, which had 'substituted baillis for the tyrants of the Comédie-Française' (Grimm:x:400).

Perhaps in plays there existed nastier ancestors of Pezay's specimen than the Bailli in Philidor's *Le bûcheron*, for example, who is merely greedy and stupid. Grétry's Bailli in *Les méprises par ressemblance* is unsympathetic and wealthy. In the later eighteenth century a bailli was a 'civil officer who dispensed justice in the name of a seigneur';[10] seigneurial rights, which could be bought, included rents, tolls, dues, mill rights etc., all feudal privileges 'which the peasant proprietors resented all the more because they were now the real owners of the land on which the dues were imposed'.[11] The point about Pezay's Bailli is the realism of his attraction to Cécile which, as he does nothing to check it, makes him an important link in a chain of increasingly effective opéra-comique wrongdoers: Dolmon *fils* (who does not sing), Aldobrandin (who is not arraigned) and – in works to come – Versac in *Les événements imprévus* and Garins in *Aucassin et Nicolette*. The Bailli not only corrupts, lies and bullies, but indulges in pathetic self-pity as in (3) and (15): 'It is easier to take vengeance than pluck love from one's heart.' He is seen with all sections of the community, always in character, and each piece he sings in is disruptive in some way. In (3) the music begins in F major, 4/4, but as the three singers work themselves into a fury of jealousy it turns to an urgent 2/4 in D minor and remains there. In (6) Grétry rose well to the occasion: a twenty-five-page movement in two parts, each in free ABA' form. The opening duet is again in D minor, febrile and rapid. The Bailli accuses Cécile of 'stolen kisses' (Ex. 14.1), second violins suggesting the rising menace of the situation. Then comes Grétry's first fully-fledged choral finale at the Comédie-Italienne, in D major. The 'Chœur' has up to five separate staves. There is great dynamic energy and as Cécile's humiliation is confirmed we progress to F sharp minor (see Ex. 14.2), each chord distended powerfully for four bars: here is the equivalent of Greuze's overtones of tragedy.

Ex. 14.1 *La Rosière de Salency* (6)
('God, what an insult, what outrage'; 'Here noted down on each page . . .')

Ex. 14.2 *La Rosière de Salency* (6)
A unison passage occurs at the goal F sharp as Cécile sings 'Ah, rather tear out my heart'.

In act 2, indeed, the Bailli provokes the most shocking disruption of all: the 'dead' Colin's wet clothes, before (12). The anguish of Herpin and later Cécile is set, Presto, in F minor, with a sad coda as Cécile is carried inside. Again in (15) there are two distinct musical sections, both in D: a sturdy 6/8 Allegretto followed by an urgent 2/4. Whereas the male chorus in the first one is at least working, though not without individual conversations, in the second section it stops incredulously as the Bailli marches about: the strange realism of this scene remained a unique achievement in Grétry.[12]

The chorus throughout does not initiate action, but falls under the sway of the authority of Bailli or seigneur: consequently it intensifies moments of pain as well as eventual triumph. This concept was far more like the rôle of the classical chorus than the anodyne 'acclamation' that the authorities tried to impose in opéra-comique (see chapter 26). And it was at one with Pezay's concept of an overall arch design, somewhat foreshadowing that of *Der Freischütz* almost fifty years later: Cécile's initial security, Colin's kiss, her degradation ending act 1, Colin's 'death' in act 2; the progress back from despair to coronation in act 3. This arch is reflected scenically. The exposition is at evening; in (5) 'the moon is seen rising'; though a new day dawns in act 2, it is a dark one and Pezay even cues thunder into dialogue, as after (10):

Herpin: Cécile, what is this mystery? What is it about?
Cécile (*in consternation*; *thunderclap*): Righteous heaven!

Herpin perceives the storm, in fact, as divine retribution. The repair of storm damage opening act 3, the construction work and the 'high mountains' signify the new order of things. In his choice of keys Grétry shows signs of a parallel organisation, though one is not normally aware of such levels of planning in his opéras-comiques. (1) and (2) create stability in A major (which never returns as a tonic key). Minor keys, as was mentioned, form part of (3) and (6). In act 2 there is more minor mode and more flattening of general tonality: (7), (8), (9) and (12) use D minor, F minor, C minor while (11) – to which we return in a moment – is in B flat. After the important G minor entr'acte (14), related itself to (23a), the keys grow sharper from (16) in E flat, (17) in C, (18) in F to the resumption of D and G majors for the final scenes.

Perhaps (11), the eye of the storm and centre of the drama, shows how Gluck-like opéra-comique might have remained in other circumstances. The foreground father–daughter duet animatedly moves towards C major but with a lurch to the note A an offstage chorus enters unexpectedly. Our imagination is required to 'see' Colin's struggle with the elements. Ex 14.3 gives an idea of the resulting chiaroscuro, together with implied metrical change from 4/4 to 4/2.

Obliged to *watch* Colin's climactic appearance on the mountain in act 3, however, audiences were betrayed by the poverty of scenic resources: Pezay's vision of his victory over injustice and nature was nullified by 'two miserable flats daubed with paint, miraculously raised four feet from the ground', while his small boat sailed on solid boards 'without even the accessory of a poor rotating silver gauze that

Ex. 14.3 *La Rosière de Salency* (11)
('Heaven is angered'; 'Save the poor soul who's swimming')

should have represented the waves'. 'It is really shameful that in the French capital the site of one of the theatres most accredited by public attendance does not permit the resources enjoyed by Nicolet' (the small theatre-owner mentioned in chapter 26).[13]

The quasi-heroic scale of Cécile's and Colin's predicament, so realistically set to music in solos like (9) and (16), with forward-looking irregularity of layout, and duets like (8), demanded a large-scale setting in nature. Yet all was not disorder. Several pieces in the opera emphasise stability through abundance of repetition and/or formal symmetry; the lovers' duets (2), (8) and (18) perhaps even reach the point of self-indulgence. (Curiously, (8) had a non-symmetrical text which Grétry adapted for sonata form.) It is testimony of the work's basic strength that it held the stage notwithstanding such drawbacks.

There is more functional anticipation than recollection in *La Rosière de Salency*. In the entr'acte (14) Grétry used the theme of the vaudeville (23a) as basis for a set of variations. The vaudeville (Ex. 14.4) has five verses during which, the libretto

Ex. 14.4 *La Rosière de Salency* (14) and (23a)
('Sing, dance, be merry, young friends')

says, a round-dance is performed. The minor mode and words lend an equivocal tone to the refrain: 'There is but one evil and one good: to love or to love nothing.' Perhaps this is apt to the rustic sobriety of Salency's moral purpose.

The anticipation during (15) occurs as the heated imagination of the Bailli produces the memory of the music of the rose ceremony, heard in due course as (22a) in G major: the music 'obeys' his memory, the accuracy of which we hear in retrospect. It is surely remarkable that the meaning of the music is first divulged through a character's psychical reality, not literally. The third anticipation occurs in the overture: see chapter 23.

VERSIONS AND PERFORMANCES

'It was only after a thousand alterations that the piece was settled in the repertory' (i:256). 'Never was I more plagued than by the continual changes made by the author . . . every day' (i:437). Their full unravelling is awaited in an edition of the four-act manuscript score.[14] Pezay himself explained that the loss in transit of a corrected text made the Fontainebleau première (from which he was absent) highly unsatisfactory; he disowned the Ballard libretto printed for the occasion.[15] This four-act version contained important differences in structure. Act 1 ended with a supper scene between Herpin and Cécile during which the latter admitted she had had a visit from Colin. Act 2 clarified the point that the Bailli had the right to select the rose-maiden in the seigneur's absence. It continued with a village dance, the spreading of gossip against Cécile and the interruption by the Bailli to denounce Cécile's 'crime'; Colin was detained. Act 3 broadly corresponded to the eventual act 2, but elaborated on relations between the Bailli and Herpin.

Pezay noted in his 'Réflexions' that this inauspicious première was followed by authorial changes that benefited the Parisian public, i.e. four months later. By the time the next printed libretto appeared (Delalain, 1774), actually prefaced by these 'Réflexions', a further court performance had occurred and nine at the Comédie-Italienne. This information[16] allows us to place this statement after 19 March 1774. The basic identity of the opera in February/March 1774 probably accords with its surviving manuscript score, still in four acts but musically similar to the familiar version: however, it contains five vocal numbers and one entr'acte unfamiliar from the latter. These are italicised below:

Old act 1: New (1) to (4) then *solo in E* for Herpin and *duet in D* for Cécile and Herpin. *Entr'acte.*
Old act 2: *Solo in G minor* for Bailli; *duet in F* for Cécile and Bailli, then new (6) and (7).
Old act 3: New (8) to (14).
Old act 4: New (15) to (21) then (23) ending with (22) to which a simple *solo with chorus* was added.

The reduction to three acts must have taken place between the ninth performance on 19 March and the tenth, which was not until 18 June. The libretto for this (i.e. Delalain 1774) suggests that the Cécile–Bailli duet was retained for act 1 and the Bailli's solo retained for act 2. Both are absent, of course, from the printed score and may have vanished by the time of the eleventh public performance, on 10 August. In fact the duet was then used as source for (2) of *Les mariages samnites*. Other detailed textual changes followed. Even without Pezay's claim in 1774 that Grétry had charge of the original libretto over five or six years prior to the 1773 première, the opera's evolution shows how assiduously authors were prepared to refashion promising opéra-comique material.

The work proved far from unpopular, with about the same number of performances as *L'ami de la maison* or *Les deux avares*. The ten years 1774–83 saw 127 performances, and the following decade 46 performances. Between 1796 and 1809 it was seen only 36 times, however, and the final run during 1813–19 saw only 22 performances. In the French provinces it was better liked, being given 'perhaps more often than any other of its author's compositions'.[17] The last foreign performances noted by Loewenberg were in Moscow in 1810.

15. The entr'acte (1)

An entr'acte in eighteenth-century theatre was traditionally a diversion between the acts of any show; the diversion was variously sung, danced or spoken and had no direct connection with the show, but as the theatre curtain remained up the scenery sufficed to preserve continuity:

– all of which put together, must have prepared the reader's imagination for the entrance of Dr Slop upon the stage, – as much, at least (I hope) as a dance, a song, or a concerto between the acts.   (*Tristram Shandy*, vol. ii ch. 8)

At the mid-century Comédie-Française, which had a permanent orchestra, the entr'acte was 'composed of several airs played on the strings which are not listened to'.[1] But at the Opéra

the show follows on consecutively; the entr'acte is a concerted piece which the orchestra continues without interruption, and during which the stage sets change. This continuity of spectacle is favourable to the illusion, and without illusion there is no further charm in the musical theatre.[2]

The attraction of maintaining the illusion was such that entr'actes could also be seen as applicable to the spoken theatre, not merely to sustain a mood but also to develop intellectual continuity, as Beaumarchais hoped in writing scenarios (which were ignored in Paris) for his play *Eugénie* (1767):

I thought that one could try to join an act to the following one by pantomimic action which would sustain the spectators' attention without fatiguing it and would, during the interlude, indicate what happens 'behind the scene'.[3]

At about the same time the orchestra at the Comédie-Française, which 'formerly had no scruples about playing extremely gay tunes in entr'actes of tragedies and noble, serious ones in those of comedies', began to perform music 'connected to the genre and even subject of the play being performed, so far as plausibility permits'.[4]

However, it was opéra-comique that had pioneered these ideas. Towards the end of the first act of *Le roi et le fermier* (1762) there is a duet between the hero and heroine during which 'the stage darkens gradually. It is night by the beginning of the storm.' Sedaine knew his English theatre, and his storm-entr'acte here is not a meaningless intervention but a counterpart to Richard's anger on hearing of Jenny's attempted seduction by the aristocratic Lurewell: as the oak-trees are lashed by the gale Richard measures his own fury against them:

> Aujourd'hui Richard furieux
> Etoit bien plus agité qu'eux.

And the continuity of action is further depicted by the cross-rhythms and motifs of horses and hounds, announcing the approach of the king through the forest ready for his appearance in act 2.

The idea of a storm-entr'acte was followed in *Toinon et Toinette* (1767), music by Gossec; this is printed in the full score but the entr'acte depicting night in Philidor's *Tom Jones* (revised 1766) was engraved only in the instrumental parts. It is 137 bars long and directly relevant to the plot at that point. Of incidental benefit to authors and composers in this connection was a general royal decree on the theatre dated 24 December 1769, aimed at disciplining audiences and the *parterre* in particular, and forbidding them

to commit any disorder when entering or leaving; to shout or make a noise before the show begins, or in the entr'actes, to whistle, boo, wear a hat, or interrupt the actors during performances, in whatever manner and on whatever pretext.[5]

Grétry was obviously interested in developing the functional entr'acte, and although the following sentences sound disingenuous in the light of the work of his predecessors, they may indicate his activities at the Comédie-Italienne as producer and improver of his own works over a period of time:

The ritornello is of great utility in announcing the action that is to follow and giving continuity to that which one fears the spectator will miss. I was the first to suppress the orchestral piece known as an entr'acte, in order to substitute another which should have greater connection with the preceding or succeeding action of the drama.   (iii:320)

The early opéras-comiques, in fact, betray in their scores no entr'actes as such. Then, in the court performance of *L'amitié à l'épreuve*, Grétry tried an experiment. In order to continue the feeling of action, he wrote a 'symphonie concertante' based on the trio ending act 1. It did not succeed and is not preserved (iii:320). A year later he specified minimally-relevant entr'actes in *L'ami de la maison*. The first was indicated by 'One may, for an entr'acte, repeat the first movement of the overture, or its last two movements', and the second by 'For entr'acte repeat the accompaniment of the aria "Ah, dans ces fêtes"' (9). Not until 1773 did he think of anticipating music in an entr'acte. However the path of reform continued with *Zémire et Azor*. The entr'acte after act 1 is indeed functional, expressing 'the flight of the cloud' on which Sander and Ali return to Ormuz. Its musical material is taken both from the earlier storm-music at the beginning of the opera, and – less appropriately – from Ali's 'yawn' motif in (4). Air travel frightens, not bores him. The next two entr'actes involve vaguer forms of continuity. The first is a developed binary-form variation of (8), transposed down a tone to B flat, while the second is a new Da Capo version of the duet (15). This is certainly pertinent to the circumstances ending act 3 since the words of (15), 'Reassure my father', must go through the heroine's mind at that juncture.

Le *Magnifique*, thanks to Sedaine, attained greater cohesion in its two entr'actes. The first re-uses the last section of the overture, connecting with the last part of act 1 through drum-beats underpinning the dialogue. By this means the audience is informed that the captives outside in the public square are again on the move: the overture should itself be an illustrative pantomime. The second entr'acte is a specially-composed piece in ternary form whose central section depicts horse and rider. This, as we know from the dialogue, represents Aldobrandin on his newly-won and coveted charger. Clearly, his absence will enhance the possibility of Clementine's release.

The entr'actes are no less ingenious in *La Rosière de Salency*. The first, a pathetic oboe solo in D minor, ternary form, reflects the devastation of the prevailing mood. The second, Grétry's most elaborate to date, is a theme and four variations: since the theme is drawn literally from an as yet unheard part of the work (23a), it binds the piece together in a new way, as we saw in the last chapter, reflecting the general moral character of the opera. The variations are disposed as follows: oboe solo and violins; bassoon solo and strings; violin solo, strings and bassoon; and viola solo and violins. This viola solo, using triplet figuration, was outstanding for its date (cf. Ex. 23.2, written for the same executant, Monin). The bassoon and violin variations require expert playing, with demisemiquavers. Though this must have been one of the first variation-set entr'actes of all, and an unusual example of orchestral variations outside the symphony, it was certainly not the last. The idea was continued in a healthy line of descendants in French opéra-comique through to the nineteenth century.

Grétry's *La fausse magie*, *Les mariages samnites*, *Le jugement de Midas* and *L'amant jaloux* do not include entr'actes. Other composers, however, continued to experiment during the 1770s. On the accession of Louis XVI in May 1774 considerable national fervour was released and the royal ban on Henri IV theatre-pieces was lifted. The sayings of this enlightened monarch were liberally scattered through two successful opéras-comiques by B. F. de Rosoi: *Henri IV* (November 1774) and *La réduction de Paris* (September 1775). The latter's score, by Francesco Bianchi, is lost, but that of the former, by J. P. E. Martini, was printed. Martini's work centres on the battle of Ivry in 1590, the decisive defeat of the Catholic leader Charles de Lorraine. The 'battle', with its simulated cannon-fire, was elaborately staged as the second entr'acte. The score annotates the music with many instructions suggesting how to render it more effective: Martini even thought that a 'confused' manner of playing might better imitate separated sections of the armies. This sound and fury were heard at the Théâtre Italien with the assistance of twenty military musicians whom, with their corporal, the records show were paid for each performance. Real military signals were specified, e.g. *La charge*, scored for fifes, clarinets, oboes, horns and bassoons.[6] These military musicians, also used in *La réduction de Paris*, are not mentioned as such in Martini's score.

An experiment in the opposite direction, as it were, was made by Nicolas Dezède (whose contribution to opéra-comique is discussed in chapter 32). The first entr'acte in *Les trois fermiers* (1777) anticipated modern convention by requiring the curtain to be lowered; as stipulated in the score,

> The curtain is lowered during the entr'acte although the setting is the same in the second act as in the first, to give the actors who begin act 2 the opportunity to have the fully-laid table carried to the centre of the stage and to sit down at it, which should happen before the curtain is raised.

However, Dezède's music was simply a repeat of the last two parts of the opera's overture.

16. La fausse magie (False magic)

Comédie in verse, in 2 acts: *CC* 25[1]
Libretto by Jean-François Marmontel. Dedicated to the Prince de Poix.
First performed at the Comédie-Italienne, 1 February 1775.
Printed full scores: in 1 act, Paris, Houbaut; Lyon, Castaud, n.d. [1775]; in 2 acts, *ibid.*, n.d. [1778?] as Œuvre XI.
Dramatis personae: Lucette, a recently-orphaned girl (s.)
       Linval, in love with Lucette (t.)
       Mme Saint-Clair, Lucette's aunt (s.)
       Dalin, Lucette's tutor, brother of Saint-Clair (t.)
       Dorimon, Linval's uncle (bar.)
       Gypsy girl (s.)
       Chorus of gypsies
ACT 1: The drawing-room of a country house. A warm spring morning. Mme Saint-Clair finds Lucette pensive. She recalls her own youth and the conflicts forced on modest young women (aria 1).[2] The claims of her old suitor were dismissed by an understanding aunt. Lucette confesses to a similar problem (aria 2) and so appeals to her aunt for help. She loves Linval; he enters and the lovers describe their meeting at a dance (duet 3). Both Dorimon and Dalin have pretensions to Lucette's hand: Mme Saint-Clair ridicules them. Dalin's recent dream and nervous superstition give her an idea for action. Alone, Dalin recounts his dream (4): a young hen is guarded by a gallant old cockerel. A watching kite

abducts the hen; the cockerel promptly changes into a gosling.[3] To him, its message is a warning. Lucette tells him she cannot like or marry Dorimon; in the aria (5) she objects to arranged marriage. Dalin is about to offer himself instead when Lucette (having been instructed by her aunt) pretends she has had exactly the same dream. In the duet (6) they compare dreams and identify with the hen and cockerel, but the kite's identity is kept secret. Dalin informs Dorimon that Lucette is not for him, and Dorimon consoles himself (aria 7). But he is outraged when Dalin claims himself as her partner (duet 8). Dorimon endures the jibes of his nephew before the latter proposes a strategy against Dalin, and Mme Saint-Clair enters to lend her support for Linval as suitor. She (aria 9) has come to terms with age. Dorimon also approves Linval's claim; Saint-Clair lightly warns him to keep faith with Lucette (trio 10). Dalin rushes in with 'formal consent' to Lucette's hand and goes to summon the notary. His reasons become clearer in the quartet (11), when Lucette explains that Dalin has found a document bearing her father's words: 'I transfer to you all my power over my beloved daughter'. Nothing daunted, Saint-Clair finds a solution. Passing gypsy fortune-tellers will be brought in to help.[4] Dalin's credulity will be his snare.

ACT 2: Lucette sings an aria of hope (12). Preparations are in train; Dorimon is instructing the gypsies; Linval in disguise will play a soothsayer. Dalin's interest is kindled, and he invites the gypsies to his wedding celebrations. Linval, who has seemingly had his palm read, shows Dalin his good fortune. A 'Marche des Bohémiens' brings on the gypsies, carrying a large mirror draped with a veil. A girl of their number reads Dalin's palm (15), finding only 'love that flies away'. Linval, disguised, reads Lucette's palm (16). All is fortunate until the orchestra recalls the dream music (6), suggesting its corroboration with the fortune-teller's vision. The gypsies request the signatures of Dalin and Lucette before making their conjurations and forecasts (chorus, 17). Then they ask Dalin to kneel before the mirror. The finale begins (18) and he sees ostensibly a vision in mime, but it turns out to be the actual civil wedding of the lovers, the notary having been disguised as a Turk. Dalin goes off furiously, leaving the others to point the moral: each of us has our own soothsayer.

Justifiable expectations were declared of this comedy, which had been talked of for two years: this only fuelled Grimm's malicious pleasure in its cold première, and some booing (vi: 26). Its most tedious aspect is that it rings the changes on the bachelor tutor theme: one might claim it resembles *L'ami de la maison* writ large.[5] Rather than using pure wit to demolish Dalin's efforts, Marmontel settled for burlesque. Dalin's eccentric credulity, however, sits strangely in the person of Saint-Clair's brother, since through her urbane character the action derives a pleasant individuality. But even she becomes forgotten in act 2 when the chorus takes over in a kind of opéra-comique equivalent to the Turkish ceremony in *Le bourgeois gentilhomme*.

Belief in fortune-telling was a better comic theme than might now appear. For example the chorus, in its pseudo-incantation (17), evokes Mathieu Laensbergh

La fausse magie

His was a household name less than two centuries ago. Prophetic almanacs issued from his name from 1635, at first in Liège, so that 'Almanachs de Liège' were common ways in Europe of foretelling planetary motions or (as in 17) the weather. Added piquancy accrued to Marmontel's satire in April 1774 when Mme du Barry read in her Almanach de Liège that 'a lady among the most favoured will play her final rôle' and became so obsessed by the prophecy that she attempted to buy up every copy to prevent the idea circulating. She naturally failed, and the prophecy came true in May when Louis XV died.

Sedaine in *Le Magnifique* and Pezay in *La Rosière de Salency* gave Grétry extended movements to set to music. Faced with Marmontel's lack of provision for an effective close to act 1, Grétry was obliged to poach dialogue for sung use in (11). 'You'll see, I said to him, what the Italians call a finale, all I require now are some filling-in lines for the ensembles'.[6] One suspects he got his way elsewhere too. There is frequent rapidity of dialogue between numbers, e.g. between (14) and (15) and (16) are only four lines of spoken verse; between (7) and (8) only six; between (4) and (5) only eight, etc. Moreover in act 2 the continuous music of (18) comprises all the important action and the conclusion: in a sense it marries French vaudeville with Italian finale.

La fausse magie surely remained long popular for its unforced melodious quality. Although there are cleverly irregular forms and uses of instruments (see below) the rather faded intrigues of act 1 allow for arias where action ceases and music is paramount. Thus (2) wins our sympathy for Lucette through sheer confident beauty, a vocal slow movement with the limpidness of Paisiello. Its successor (5) is duller, more rococo, failing to capture the spontaneity of 'To love is not to plan – it's the moment that enlightens us'. Dorimon's stoic (7), too, might bore us with static predictability. In act 2 Grétry gave Mme Trial (the Lucette) a coloratura showpiece (12), devoid of dramatic integration. At *c*180 bars' length, this vocal concerto capped a series of soprano virtuoso pieces all of which, nevertheless, had a greater claim to relevance: the singing-lesson in *L'amitié à l'épreuve* (5), the set piece in *Zémire et Azor* (18), or (5) in *La Rosière de Salency*, which changes midway into something more thoughtful. Ex. 16.1 gives some notion of how opéra-comique continued to act as first cousin to Italian opera.

Perhaps more enduring strengths lay elsewhere: Mme Saint-Clair's character, the ensembles in general, and the musical cross-references associated with Dalin's

Ex. 16.1 *La fausse magie* (12)
('Shines and seems to flutter')

Ex. 16.2 *La fausse magie* (10)
('You'd have to reckon with me if you broke faith with her')

dream. The music tells us that Mme Saint-Clair is younger than her years: for example in the coquettish intervals of (1), the self-mocking humour and unusual form (ABCDA') of (9) or the spirited benevolence of (10), which becomes a close-harmony number (Ex. 16.2). Such things, with the cultivated brilliance of the lovers' duet (3), turn the work into a rout of dull age by youth.

Ensemble writing is freshest, however, in the final sequences (11) and (18). The former is no 'chain' finale – the same four singers perform it all – but a sectional quartet: the text alone covers four pages. There are five sections, alternating faster with slower, all in C except the third in F. Ex. 16.3 illustrates how purely *buffo* the music was near the close. In act 2 variety arrives with the chorus, who enter playing 'Turkish' music: 'cymbals, triangles and other singular instruments', though with no more intrinsic local colour. Virtually nothing afterwards is traditional in form. The 'palmistry' solos (15) begin placidly, only to erupt with bad news: the first fizzles out while (16) modulates from G to E flat and never returns. The stage is next set for the choral incantation (17), which is a splendid

Ex. 16.3 *La fausse magie* (11)
('Yes I understand, it's a mystery')

La fausse magie

Ex. 16.4 *La fausse magie* (17)
('And thou who makest New Year's Day')

parody of traditional clichés, from solemn progressions (Ex. 16.4) to a fugal ending on the subject of weather. Grétry's early affinity with choral writing, most fully exploited in recitative operas like *La caravane du Caire*, is not suspected from the *Mémoires*; they belittle Rameau (i:145), but a letter to Padre Martini reads, 'the best things are the choruses of Rameau, which give me infinite pleasure'.[7] All is brought together in (18) through assured handling in timing and subtle musical recollections, with the following scheme:

Key	Tempo	Action
B flat major	4/4 Andante	Peering into the mirror, Dalin sees Linval take Lucette's hand in some kind of ceremony; a musical climax with the general cry 'It's done!'
G minor, D minor, C major	4/4 Allegretto	Chorus joins with soloists in excited explanation.
F major	4/4 Larghetto	Mme Saint-Clair, Dorimon and lovers attempt to reconcile Dalin.
D minor	2/2 Allegro	Dalin's angry exit; brief choral ensemble
B flat major	2/2 [no tempo mark]	Vaudeville: four verses
B flat major	3/8 Presto	General ensemble on the words of the preceding moral.

The persistence of orchestral motifs through the first section, designed to form a continuum of tension, notably looks forward to the even greater orchestral independence shown in *Les mariages samnites*.

The various uses of functional recollection can now be explained, and form an interesting enlargement of concepts in *Les deux avares* and *La Rosière de Salency*. The music in question accompanies not Dalin's comic narration of the dream (4), though this is admittedly in the opera's 'dream' key of E flat major. Instead Grétry used (6): the comparison of dreams where Dalin demonstrates his nervous tendency to jump to conclusions. The oboe has several related 'cockerel' ideas, Ex. 16.5, above characteristic accompaniments (and with presumably humorous acting). In (16) Lucette's palm is read; Dalin observes. The libretto instructs: 'The music recalls the dream.' So the tonality becomes E flat as the 'fortune-teller' affects to see a change in her future, while Grétry recalls thirty-five bars closely

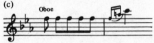

Ex. 16.5 *La fausse magie* (6) and (15)

based on (6) in order (i) to show Dalin's act of memory, (ii) to remind us of the content of the dream, and (iii) to portray Dalin's assumption that the fortune-teller is witnessing the substance of the dream. Through the agency of the orchestra Dalin's imagination is perceptible on both active and passive levels. Lastly Grétry recalls Ex. 16.5(c) jokingly during the vaudeville of (18) just before 'Love shall be our soothsayer'.

In the dream Lucette appears as a hen; an appropriate motif appears also in (6) with its characteristic upper auxiliary note: Ex. 16.6. Later on this is developed as an ironic mocking idea directed against Dalin in (18), and slipped into the vaudeville as a horn solo. These recollections could almost be called ideal forms of 'false magic', or illusory images. The *Mercure de France* review seems to have alluded to this, mentioning the composer's 'special ability to make all the instruments into actors' (*CC*, iii), while Grétry himself alluded to the orchestral

Ex. 16.6 *La fausse magie*
(a): (6) ('Yes I the hen'); (b): (18) ('Love delights in what you've done'); (c): (18), vaudeville

autonomy in the opera, or distinctive balance between melody and accompaniment (i:260).

Projects with Marmontel after *La fausse magie* were begun, only to be given votes of no confidence at the Comédie-Italienne. A published letter by the librettist and critic F. B. Hoffman in 1805 recorded: 'He wrote *Les statues* in four acts. Grétry, in no doubt that the libretto would be refused, wrote two acts of it which he afterwards burned, the libretto having been turned down twice.'[8] Hoffman mentions *Le mari sylphe* and *Le sigisbé* as refused likewise; Grétry repeats this evidence, adding *Le vieux garçon*, which he esteemed the best (*Réf*:ii:104). Brenet dates *Les statues* as 1776–8; in August 1782 Marmontel read a 3-act libretto *La rancune trompée* to the company, with no end result.[9] 'Thus deprived of librettos, I then became friends with D'Hèle and Sedaine' (*Réf*:ii:104).

We have not so far mentioned *Céphale et Procris*, the opéra-ballet Grétry and Marmontel prepared for the wedding celebrations of the Comte d'Artois and Marie-Thérèse of Savoy. It was coolly received at Versailles on 30 September 1773 and at the Paris Opéra on 2 May 1775. The composer wanted to alter the first two acts substantially, which Marmontel refused to sanction. In a mock-criticism placed in the mouth of Gluck, who attended two of the Versailles rehearsals, 'You and your librettist must inject more warmth and interest into the first two acts; he must reduce the excessive number of arias' (i:283). Gluck was in Paris to prepare the 1774 versions of *Orphée et Eurydice* and *Alceste*. Grétry fully acknowledged him as ideal creator of *tragédie-lyrique*, as a 'consummate artist', 'the model', the 'creator of a new genre' (i:283; 354–7). But Marmontel's sympathies gravitated towards Gluck's opposite number Piccinni, following his view of *Céphale et Procris* as a 'fruitless attempt': 'my distrust of my own powers amounted to fear', so he embarked on the idea of adapting the librettos of Quinault and Metastasio, starting with *Roland* and *Atys*.[10] With *Didon* (1783) and *Démophoön* (1788) he made lasting contributions in collaboration with Piccinni and Cherubini.

VERSIONS AND PERFORMANCES

General disagreement exists on this subject, and the present account contradicts *The New Grove*.[11] There are four identifiable versions of *La fausse magie*, of which one is wholly lost and one partly lost. Grétry mentions only the fourth one.

First version   Two acts   1, 4, 6 February 1775
Second version   One act   9 to 20 February 1775, six performances

From the theatre accounts we can differentiate between two- and one-act versions since authors received either 1/12 or 1/18 of takings respectively.[12] Librettos of both were issued; the second version was issued in full score.[13]

Third version   Two acts   18, 21, 23 March 1776

This has vanished; it is discussed below.

Fourth version   Two acts   Presumably 8, 12 January 1778
Possibly 29 July 1779

Grétry and the growth of opéra-comique

The third version involved the most far-reaching changes. In place of a magic mirror ('puerile and contrived': Grimm:xi:221) the deception involved a mandragora. A prophecy was made to Dalin that Lucette's first husband would die the day after his wedding. Linval married Lucette anyway and Dalin was afterwards informed of the trap. Grimm and D'Origny preferred this dénouement, but doubt was cast on its music.

The remaining three versions are not radically different from one another. In 1775 all that was done – that there was time to be done – was to cut. Six items were removed and the dialogue tailored accordingly. The interval was taken out and (12) put at the opening. Five of the six cuts were solos: Linval's two were in act 1, leaving him with only (13). Of the excised arias for Dorimon, Saint-Clair and Dalin in act 2, the second appears the most significant loss. Placed between (13) and (14), its melody (retrieved from an anthology and printed in *CC*) was richly nostalgic. The duet cut, being between Saint-Clair and her brother, was probably a regrettable loss. The opera's course of action was unaffected in general. In 1778 or 1779 this one-act version simply became a two-act one: the final movement of the overture was added; (12) went back to its original position. Minor adjustments were made to the spoken text.

That the one-act score was published at all is less surprising when we recall that Grétry had *La Rosière de Salency* engraved within six months, refusing any undertaking to wait longer.[14] He never relinquished his basic criticism of the later work, however: that the second act involves a too radical change of level from the social comedy of the first (i:261). When an interesting plan to enhance the sense of the fantastic in act 2 was dropped Grétry felt understandably ambivalent.[15] It would have involved a pantomime of spirits after (17) behind a gauze. Further, 'Paris is not bothering with any props, and they are greatly mistaken.'

La fausse magie nevertheless, after its false start, achieved popularity, being seen every year except 1810 and 1819 up to 1823. In its first decade there were eighty-three performances, and in its second, to 1794, there were eighty-six. The ten years to 1804 produced seventy-one performances and the following ten years produced seventy-two. Between 1815 and 1828 inclusive there were fifty-six performances. It was then dropped but had twenty-one further showings in 1863, reorchestrated by E. Prévost. The last foreign production listed in Loewenberg was in Vienna (1809).

17. Les mariages samnites (The Samnite marriages)

Drame lyrique in 3 acts, in prose:[1] *CC* 35
Libretto by Barnabé Farmian de Rosoi. Dedicated to the Prince–Bishop of Liège.[2]
First performed at the Comédie-Italienne, 12 June 1776.
Printed full score, Paris, Houbaut, Lyon, Castaud, n.d. [1776] as Œuvre XIII.
Dramatis personae: Agathis, Samnite youth (t.)
Parmenon, his orphaned friend (t.)
Eumene, Agathis' father (b.)
Céphalide, Samnite girl (s.)
Euphémie, her mother (s.)
Eliane, friend of Céphalide (s.)
Two Samnite girls (s.)
Samnite chief   }
Samnite general } spoken rôles
Chorus of Samnite women, warriors, old men

ACT1: Ancient Italy. A large amphitheatre with high trees in a semicircle and grassy steps downstage. The most valorous Samnites are to receive their chosen wives. Agathis and Parmenon enter hand in hand. This day of battle with Rome and of the marriages only makes the official edict of personal restraint harder to bear, admits Parmenon (aria 1).[3] No youth may yet name his hoped-for wife, except to a parent; though perhaps rivals, the two will never cease friendship (duet 2). To Eumene, Agathis anticipates glory and admits love (aria 3), afterwards naming Céphalide as its object. They pray this love may be protected (duet 4). Eumene impulsively decides to take up arms (aria 5). As the two go upstage Céphalide and Euphémie appear downstage. In the quartet (6) the undeclared lovers are helped by their parents to avoid looking at each other; yet after it Céphalide gives Agathis a telling glance and confides her love to her mother, full of hope (aria 7). Samnite girls, youths, soldiers and old men assemble. The chief addresses them: the enemy is at the gates. Parmenon looks towards Eliane, Agathis and others towards Céphalide (melodrama 8); there follow a warlike duet for Parmenon and Agathis and a march (9) for the departing warriors. Alone, the women sing in chorus, withdrawing slowly (10).
ACT 2: In an obbligato recitative and aria (11) Eliane oscillates between resignation and utter grief at Parmenon's possible death. She debates with Céphalide the 'slavery' of women's function under Samnite law (duet 12). The girls are dressed by their mothers for the marriages (vaudeville and chorus 13). Eliane, taking up her bow, denounces the girls' absence of choice in marriage; she will choose to fight. She defies her peers (choral ensemble 14) and rushes out. Various soldiers appear, beaten back in the fighting. Eumene is carried in

wounded. Agathis tends him briefly and requests Céphalide's help. He rallies retreating Samnites (solo 15) and leaves. Céphalide and Euphémie are dressing his father's wounds when a soldier enters with the rumour of Agathis' own death. The women and Eumene have a trio of grief (16).
ACT 3: Céphalide appeals to the goddess of love (17). Euphémie confirms Agathis' victorious return and dissipates her daughter's worries (aria 18). Eliane has vanished. The march (9) heralds the victory parade. The chief announces three equally heroic combatants. Parmenon (fanfare 19) has saved a friend's life and taken a Roman standard. The unknown second warrior has saved the general's life. The third is Agathis, who first tended his father but then led his side to victory.[4] Eumene appeals on his son's behalf (aria and chorus 20). Agathis renounces the proffered first prize – choice in marriage – in favour of Parmenon; the latter cedes it in turn. They are asked to confer. In the duet (21) they eulogise their respective loves but happily find these are not one and the same. They announce their choices and discover Eliane's absence. A visored warrior enters and reveals herself as Eliane, the saviour of the general's life. She describes her ordeal in battle (aria 22), is pardoned, and united with Parmenon. In the choral ensemble sequence (23) all submit to duty and pleasure under the aegis of love.

This major Grétry work was not the first neo-classical opéra-comique: Philidor's *Le jardinier de Sidon* (1768) based on Fontenelle, is a moral tale about kingship set in Sidon, ancient Phoenicia. That work, however, was domestic in scale. Grétry's opera was as ambitious a canvas as any history painting and its dignified treatment provokes comparison with the Parisian tragedies of Gluck. The Comédie-Italienne, as we saw in chapter 15, staged two opéras-comiques on national themes in 1774 and 1775. Both were by Rosoi and their success helped the passage of *Les mariages samnites* (i:287), a yet more radical offering that outlawed jokes, 'pretty caricatures' and variety for its own sake in favour of 'the noble simplicity of that *true beauty* which attaches to nature alone' (Rosoi's preface to the *Nouvelle édition* (Paris, 1776), vii).

Rosoi was admittedly a self-publicist. He was detained for slander in 1765, imprisoned for libel in 1770 and guillotined as a royalist activist in 1792. But he believed the public should bring its mind and conscience into the theatre; more pertinently he considered opéra-comique was the correct genre in which to treat important subjects. In his manifesto, *Dissertation sur le drame lyrique*,[5] he asserted his right to be free and a *philosophe*; he deplored public squeamishness towards the portrayal of moral dilemma or outrage, evoking the memory of the persecution of the Huguenots. Shakespeare inspired Rosoi, as he did Sedaine. 'By following the idea of Shakespeare while correcting his faults we could create a Theatre of History; a school where the son of a peer and the son of an artisan sitting side by side might learn to judge men . . . to recognise true virtues in all classes and from all ages' (p. 37). Why should these lessons be learnt through opéra-comique? *Zémire et Azor* might gain in visual splendour at the Opéra but 'the details of tenderness, fear, pride or valour; the gradations of hate or jealousy' would be lost

(p. 11). Opéra-comique communicated ideas because it lacked purely musical elaboration and 'always monotonous recitatives' (p. 13). For subject-matter Rosoi propounded especially 'ancient chivalry, another genre more picturesque for us and maybe more necessary as to morality' (p. 9). With the zealot's sweep he declares that the purely comic genre must die out. Meanwhile

a tale from the history of the Samnites presented itself to me . . . of all stories it is possibly the most interesting for its morals. The sanctity of marriage as the recompense of services rendered to the nation . . . The public will judge my efforts, but another painter [i.e. composer] must support me. Several have hesitated; the public voice has said to them: this heroic genre will not be able to survive for long. (p. 14)

As will be seen, Grétry paid a heavy price for his support.

'Heroic genre' here meant neo-classicism in the context of republican morality: a common enough mode in French painting with or without the portrayal of an *exemplum virtutis*.[6] *Les mariages samnites* focuses centrally on that of Agathis, for he puts the defence of the state before the succour of his father.

The Samnites were not actually builders of cities, arches or stadia (see Plate IV). They were successful enemies of Rome who lived in the hills, seemed to have political unity, and fought with cunning and strength in small numbers.[7] Marmontel's Moral Tale *Les mariages samnites* (1761) drew on Montesquieu's *De l'esprit des lois*, also a favourite text of Grétry. But ironically, in the chapter concerned, Montesquieu confused the Samnites with the Sunites, who were central Asians:

The Samnites had a custom which in a tiny republic . . . must have had admirable effects. All the youths were assembled and were judged. He who was declared the best [in valour] took as wife the girl of his choice.[8]

Marmontel and Rosoi needed to evoke an existence of complete dedication and without luxuries. The Tale is sober and measured in tone, relieved only in the description of Samnite girls who lean gracefully on their bows, 'carelessly lifting their light dress above one knee to give more ease and nobility to their bearing' (contemporary translation). The Samnites oppose an ideal social and national unity to the selfishness of eighteenth-century ambition. The former is achieved by the radical intrusion of the state into personal life. Marmontel's Samnites court with the eyes only, revealing their choice to their parents. This strengthens the family bond; at the annual marriage ceremony the females have no choice in the matter and marriage is a state duty. After the victory Agathis wishes to forgo the advantage of choosing a wife first, claiming that desire for Céphalide had overcome paternal love. Parmenon in his *exemplum virtutis* also declines the honours, exactly as in the opera.

Marmontel's Eliane is hardly more than a name. Rosoi's expansion of her character could well have led to the sort of pretty compromise Grétry thought of (i:289). But Rosoi was as true as his word: 'A Samnite whose burning heart and proud soul protest against that law in favour of nature . . . the purpose being to contrast better the peaceable obedience of the rest of Samnite youth' (preface). All

Plate IV. *Les mariages samnites* (J. F. Marmontel, *Contes moraux*, 3 vols., Paris, 1765). Agathis and Parmenon discover that they are not rivals in love. The scene corresponds to (21) in the opera, after the successful battle against the Romans and before the marriage ceremony. Samnite women are in the background and Samnite chiefs in the foreground. The setting and costumes are derived from Marmontel's text, to which the opera's libretto was also faithful.

her music was newly composed (i:288), reaching sometimes Amazonian proportions. In the sixty-one-bar recitative and its aria (11) high a'' flat leaps to low e'
while high g'' leaps to low d'. Her sustained cry convinces us that Samnite law is
exerted at unbearable cost. At the end her exalted aria (22) is accompanied by an
orchestra including trumpets and timpani. And in her act 2 dialogue she inherits
Rosoi's polemical thrust: the law is created and maintained by masculine pride. A
husband is 'a master jealously ruling over a heart'. 'If my hand is not afraid to bear
arms or my heart to brave death, what man has the right to forestall my choice?'
These speeches and such music anticipated the gradual emancipation of women in
1780s opéra-comique; Corali in the 1786 *L'amitié à l'épreuve*, the Countess in *Le
Comte d'Albert*, Sophie in Dalayrac's *Sargines*.

Perhaps the main shortcoming of Rosoi's dramaturgy is that Eliane is
introduced, developed and thrown into battle within the space of act 2. The battle
has been joined since the end of act 1 but we have lost the rhythm of it by (15). To
have grafted Eliane into act 1, involving her more closely with other main
characters, would have allowed the ceremonies of (9) and (10) to form part of act 2,
and the spectator to be more conscious of the ongoing fight. Nevertheless Rosoi
created effective ensembles and conclusions to each act. Outside the speeches
opening act 3 he deployed music with naturalness and variety; there are six short
dialogue links and three fairly brief ones.[9] Those in act 2 are longer. The total of
ten arias might usefully have forgone (5), (18) and the newest showpiece for Mme
Trial (17), its roulades and clichés quite inappropriate to Samnium. Three
ensembles involve chorus; other novelties included Grétry's first *mélodrame* (a fey
flute solo with strings), a fine march (9)[10] and the 'Vaudeville' (13).

Grétry's account of the composition of the 1776 *Les mariages samnites* is simple:
Rosoi found that his libretto was so compatible with that of the 1768 version (see
chapter 2) that 'my music could serve and I had only a few pieces to write for the
rôle of Eliane' (i:288). Rosoi, that is, simply provided new words for the 1768
items not already borrowed for other operas. In the 1776 score twenty numbers are
vocal settings; of these five involve Eliane and a sixth, (2), was left over from *La
Rosière de Salency*. But we may suspect that certain of the remaining fourteen were
also new. For one thing (15) and (20) involve functional recollection (described
below) in a manner inconsistent with 1768. Moreover there is a tremendous formal
variety in the designs.[11] Grétry made 'no apology' for the work in spite of its poor
reception in Paris, and was right to do so.

The *Dissertation* of Rosoi showed his sensitivity to local colour: 'It is not enough
to have written a piece . . . it must produce its effect relative both to the characters
and the spectators. A given local colour suits one location better than another.
Further, the performer's singing must always be at one with his acting' (p. 44).
Grétry responded accordingly to the two chief qualities of Samnium: patriotic
bravery and noble simplicity. These are manifest through martial instrumentation
and idioms, and restraint and grace. The first of these corresponded to the
splendour of the staging in Paris, which entailed 'prodigious expense'.[12] Part of it
involved hiring twenty military musicians for eight rehearsals and the performances,[13] presumably to participate in (9), (19) (whose music does not appear in

score) and (23). These players must explain the uniquely expanded orchestration in (9): flutes, oboes, clarinets, bassoons, horns, trumpets and timpani (Ex. 17.1). Agathis' (3) was Grétry's first opéra-comique aria with trumpets, though not *the* first: the rousing final 'Notre roi' in Rosoi and Martini's *Henri IV* had incorporated the instrument in 1774. Brass formed also a vital part of Agathis' combat music (15) and associated material elsewhere: Ex. 17.5. It was typical of the rich scoring throughout that Grétry twice used soft trumpets: first as subtle character-suggestion for Eliane in (13) and secondly in an opening of complex timbre (21): Ex. 17.2.

Ex. 17.1 *Les mariages samnites* (9)
('The warlike trumpet announces battle')

Ex. 17.2 *Les mariages samnites* (21), showing triplet continuum

Dignified restraint reminiscent of Gluck's neo-classicism is prominent in the women's chorus (10) which Mozart used for his piano variations KV352/374c, a set whose aptness to the operatic mood was stressed by Saint-Foix.[14] Mozart could indeed have seen the opera on 5 or 10 August 1778. But there are other manifestations: the beautiful duets (2), (4) and (12) and Eumene's prayer-like 'Pardonne O ma patrie' in (20), all stressing conjunct intervals, steady tempo and symmetrical phrase-structure: Ex. 17.3.[15]

Ex. 17.3 *Les mariages samnites* (4)
('Tender Love owes her its features')

Yet there is a third basic quality to the music, in 'local colour' of a different order. The moral earnestness of the setting was evoked on a psychological level through the orchestral and expressive intensity of the ensembles.[16] Numbers (6), (13), (14) and (21) portray different clashes between Samnite law and personal inclination, while (16) – which the Parisians could not accept – was a pure tableau of mourning. These elevate the opera to a high position in Grétry's *œuvre*. In (6), (14) and (21) we find impressive conversational interaction, impelled on by repeated motifs (Ex. 17.2), while in (16) the accompaniment might perfectly well be enjoyed without voices, such is its complexity (Ex. 17.4). Also impressive is the design of form to suit circumstance, providing ample food for Mozart's thought (see note 14). Whereas (6) and (14) resemble dialogue duets, proceeding from separate to shared statements, (13) puts the vaudeville finale structure to revolutionary use. As the girls are dressed, each sings a stanza, linked by a refrain; the accompaniment to each is carefully fitted to its particular character. The fifth and last, that of Eliane, has prominent bassoons and soft brass, and her protesting words inhibit the expected final refrain altogether.

Although the opera concludes in triumphal tones the dénouement belongs in (21), an authentic dramatisation of Marmontel: a Larghetto duet of seventy hesitant bars leads to the revelation of Eliane's name, then a sudden recitative of incredulity and a concluding section of hectic C major joy with much noise of

Ex. 17.4 *Les mariages samnites* (16)
('Unhappy father! Alas, what is to be done?')

timpani. The piece offers an ideal example of the fructifying musico-dramatic inventiveness of opéra-comique.

Functional recollection in *Les mariages samnites* continued to explore the way music could signify both a meaningful event and its detached existence in a mind (cf. *La Rosière de Salency*, p. 127). In the new work Grétry devised orchestral material, a complex motif one might say, to accompany Agathis' rallying-cry, i.e. the thirty-eight bar solo (15). Here hammer-blows in brass and timpani reinforce the words almost by enunciating them (Ex. 17.5), while the stage action portrays the central moral action of the opera, Agathis' *exemplum virtutis*. This action would have brought to the contemporary mind historical heroes such as Brutus and the Horaces. The musical motif, however, is first made known in the work's overture (most precisely in its development section), so lending its conceptual authority to that rousing piece as emphatically (if not as clearly) as Liszt's brass 'recitative' standing at the portal of his 'Dante' symphony.[17] Furthermore in (20) Eumene, rousing the people's enthusiasm for Agathis, is musically interrupted by a thirteen-bar codetta for chorus which employs Ex. 17.5 (in E flat) to indicate

Ex. 17.5 *Les mariages samnites* (15)
(He seizes his sword: 'Honour calls you back, soldiers')

146

recollection of Agathis' rôle in their victory. So the audience is provoked into using its musical and conceptual memory to interpret the moment, and what now amounts to a symbolic motif has been heard at the opera's beginning, middle and end.

VERSIONS AND PERFORMANCES

During 1776 the opera was seen on 12 and 29 June, eight times in July and once in December. The first printed libretto agrees in detail with the printed score.[18] On 13 July, after the sixth performance, Grétry sent a speech to Vitzthumb in Brussels replacing the solo portion of (20).[19] This change was one of several printed in a new libretto. Though act 1 was kept, act 2 ended with Agathis' exit after (15).[20] The preface explained that the music of (16) was liked but not the quasi-tragic situation. Rosoi submitted to public taste 'more out of respect . . . than because I believed [changes] to be necessary'. There were only three performances during 1777–8, in Paris. In May and June 1782 a version with verse dialogue was mounted three times at the Comédie-Italienne after some successful performances in this form at Rouen.[21] Various details were changed, Eliane's rôle strengthened and three new musical pieces written. Both (1) and (8) were omitted and (5) placed in the ceremonial end of the act, which was an effective stroke, since Eumene's impulsive decision was directly followed by (9), now a 'Chœur des guerriers'. The entry of youths after (7) was covered by a ritornello and chorus 'C'est à vous'. The act 2 changes were unconvincing. Agathis was not seen. His father sang (20) during the battle; victory was announced; then (16) was used for the expression of satisfaction at this news, amounting to a nonsensical salvage operation for the music's sake. Then (17) and (18) were cut; after an entr'acte the curtain rose to act 3 on the assembled Samnites; a new chorus 'Honneur à nos Guerriers' opened the proceedings (F:Pn ms.13794). Eliane had a self-justifying speech near the end.[22]

Two further attempts were made to rescue the opera. Early in the 1790s a libretto entitled *Roger et Olivier* was concocted which incorporated thirteen musical numbers from the earlier opéra-comique, naturally with some alteration. The work was never performed, though the sources survive.[23] Secondly, a letter written early in 1794 reveals that Grétry's nephew (the fledgling writer A. J. Grétry) 'has written the piece [i.e. *L'Inquisition*] without telling me. He took only one piece from *Les deux couvents* [Grétry's lost *Cécile et Ermancé* of January 1792] that was on his mind and used all the music of *Les mariages samnites* for it, very well parodied'.[24] So perhaps ended a quarter-century of transmutation.

Grétry's view was that Parisians could not accept seeing actor–singers in such unusual rôles while the provinces, where the work was successful, were used to more versatility in their players (i:288–9). The final foreign performance noted by Loewenberg was in Vienna (1806).

18. Profile III: at home and abroad

No intimate or family letters survive from the period 1771–8; the obsequious phrases in the dedications of his operas give us only Grétry's professional manner as courtier. From the dozens of letters that survive from the last twenty years of his life we know that he directed his affairs with insistence, that he was hospitable, charitable, and chiding by turns, a family man always. His connections with the court were not interrupted in 1774 with the fall from grace of du Barry, dedicatee of *Zémire et Azor*. The accession of Marie-Antoinette sealed his friendly relations with Versailles, for not only did she devote much time to singing and playing but she also liked his music and attended many public performances of it at the Théâtre Italien. Rather than occupy a high official court position which, Grétry says, could have been his for the asking, he took the informal position of the queen's private director of music.[1] He taught her music, sometimes watched by the young king, who would always question Grétry about his wife's talents if she happened to go out of the room (*Réf*:iii:269). And the queen requested his attendance when, as often happened, his music was to be performed in some private concert or theatre. Thus Grétry maintained his independence while benefiting from official patronage. The best approbation for him was that of the public.

The refusal to compromise with ineptitude when it was in a position of authority – presumably one direct result of his choirboy experiences – led him to have nothing to do with the machinery of state:

In monarchies, each schemer wants to interfere with everything, since everything is susceptible of intrigue. It is not necessary for the schemer to have the least notion of the arts in order to be placed at their head . . . That is what I have seen in France over thirty years; that is what distanced me from all positions relative to music, which I could not have kept for a month, for it would have been impossible for me to take inept orders from an ignorant minister. (iii:8–9)

The basically personal relation with the monarchy especially affected the Grétry's youngest daughter. While Angélique-Dorothée-Louise ('Lucile'), born in 1772, had a lieutenant-general and the wife of a marshal for her godparents, the queen herself and the king's brother, the Comte d'Artois, fulfilled the same functions at the baptism of Charlotte-Antoinette-Philippine ('Antoinette') in 1774.[2] 'Marie-Antoinette loved her much', Mme Dugazon told Bouilly,

not a month passed without an invitation to Versailles where she always showered her with presents. Each time that Her Majesty comes to our theatre, after having given her three curtseys to the public out of etiquette with admirable grace, she looks for the eyes of her charming god-daughter and sends her a kiss from her box, to the applause of the whole audience.[3]

If favoured in society, the composer did not compromise himself by turning out pretty society music. His artistic probity reacted, albeit rather self-consciously, when necessary to comment directed from within (as in the *Silvain* affair in 1778) or from without: when the occasional piece *Les trois ages de l'opéra* was over-praised by the *Journal de Paris* earlier the same year the composer replied publicly to explain that his motives in writing it were merely 'my tribute of admiration to the genius and talents of these illustrious artists', i.e. Lully, Rameau and Gluck. The 1770s saw wider success but also new setbacks: *Céphale et Procris* (see p. 137), the false starts to *La fausse magie*, the Parisian indifference to *Les mariages samnites*. Since Gluck was occupying so much attention the temptation to succeed with classical subject-matter and recitative opera was natural; it parallels exactly Greuze's desire to break into classical Academy painting with his *Sévère et Caracalla*.[4] Mozart in Paris felt similarly: 'If, on the other hand, I write a grand opera – the remuneration will be better – I shall be doing the work in which I delight – and I shall have better hopes of success, for with a big work you have a better chance of making your name' (letter of 31 July 1778).[5] Like Greuze, Grétry obtained some of his best results when concentrating on extending the scope of his chosen genre. For this one has to recognise his courage, since his operas were written for the market-place: they stood or fell by their takings at the door, competing with the best of Gluck.

Grétry's wider success took place on the stages of Europe. We do not know whether he realised how far his and others' opéras-comiques were staple diet to German and Austrian troupes. On the other hand Burney, who conversed with him in 1770, described witnessing *Zémire et Azor* in Brussels and Mannheim and *L'amitié à l'épreuve* in Lille in 1772, in *The Present State of Music in Germany, the Netherlands and United Provinces*. In 1773 Gustavus III of Sweden (who was in correspondence with Creutz and Marmontel)[6] founded a national opera and promoted the works of Grétry among those of other schools.[7] Even in Italy, wrote the composer Floquet in 1776, Grétry's music was fast taking root, with *Zémire et Azor, Lucile* and *Les deux avares* specifically mentioned: a French travelling troupe had been well received in Florence.[8] It would be interesting to know who solicited Floquet's report for the *Mercure de France*, but its appearance in November 1776 formed the opportunity for the editor to claim Grétry's as 'the universal language of all nations' as witnessed by performances in Germany, Flanders, Sweden, Russia, Holland and so on.

During the same year the composer undertook a trip to Brussels and Liège, his native city. The ground had been prepared by the entrepreneurial efforts of the Grand-Théâtre, Brussels, which since 1774 had made contact with Grétry in order to negotiate agreements with him. These allowed the right to a manuscript copy of a new work, which was to be conveyed to Brussels soon after the première. Thus *La Rosière de Salency* was sent in March 1774, *La fausse magie* in February 1775 and *Les mariages samnites* despatched between 3 and 13 July 1776, together with alterations applicable to the preceding opera.[9] From 1775 Grétry's negotiations were conducted with Ignace Vitzthumb, composer, conductor and director of

Grétry and the growth of opéra-comique

the Brussels theatre. Grétry proved a stout bargainer, obtained twenty-five *louis d'or* for each work, and refused a proposal not to publish operas for a year after their first performance.

He reached Brussels in August 1776, bringing with him his sister Marie-Catherine, who since 1770 had been a nun at the convent of Sainte Aldegonde at Huy. She had spent two or three months with her brother and mother while recovering from an illness. Perhaps she was present with Grétry at the baptism of the second child of their brother Jean-Joseph at Ghent, on 18 August.[10] Grétry had intended to return to Brussels after going on to Liège, but he had a disagreeable shock that caused him to change his plans. In his mind he had built up great hopes for Vitzthumb's productions, not least because Vitzthumb had told him on 25 February 1775 that he would incorporate the pantomime in *La fausse magie* that had been rejected at the Comédie-Italienne. Unfortunately his scores had been 'corrected' by this conductor to such an extent that he wrote a politely outraged letter to him on 21 August, declaring 'You have banished me for ever from the Brussels theatre.' Burney gives a clue to the nature of the adjustments when describing *Zémire et Azor* there in 1772, for although the band was 'powerful, correct and attentive', the first clarinet 'served as a hautboy . . . the whole night'.[11]

In Liège, naturally, Grétry was received in triumph both in public at musical events and in private, at parties. The prince–bishop François-Charles de Velbruck, whom Grétry addressed as 'my sovereign' in the dedication of *Les mariages samnites*, signed a document making the musician his 'conseiller intime'. Returning via Spa, he witnessed both *Silvain* and, on 1 September, *Les deux avares*.[12]

After the rift with Marmontel, Grétry badly needed an interesting librettist. Monvel, who had begun his sequence of librettos for Dezède, never moved far outside the *paysannerie*; Sedaine was still with Monsigny; Laujon, the uneven librettist of *Matroco* (see next chapter) did nothing further for Grétry. In the hope that Rosoi might still serve, Grétry commenced work on his one-act text *Pygmalion* and apparently took it with him on the trip to Liège.[13] But it came to nothing and was eventually set by Bonesi, to be condemned in 1780 by the *Mercure de France* as a 'sad and unintelligible rhapsody'.

From an unexpected direction came Thomas Hales, whose brief but unforgettable collaboration with Grétry occasioned a real friendship. Hales' biography requires authoritative research. It is thought he was born in Gloucester in about 1740. Having joined the navy he travelled as far as the West Indies and settled in Havana in 1763. After making and then losing most of a fortune, Hales arrived in Paris about 1770.[14] Here he was to be known as d'Hèle: a fluent French speaker, thin, fair, blue-eyed (*Réf*:iii:265); an eccentric who was known to have made off with a friend's trousers as well as his money, whose style was laconic, and who never suffered fools gladly. Through Suard, whose salon was always open to English visitors, Hales was introduced to Grétry either during or before 1775.[15] With the idea of recouping his losses, Hales had studied the Parisian theatre at first hand and written two librettos (*Le jugement de Midas* and *L'amant jaloux*); in company with the composer and Clairval the singer at the Théâtre Italien, Hales astonished his companions by the acuity of his dramatic criticism (*Réf*:iii:265). He opened up to Grétry the prospect of an original series of joint ventures. But after giving Grétry his first two texts and creating with him *Les événements imprévus*, he died on 27 December 1780 from a progressive illness, to be long remembered in his adopted country for his distinguished contribution to dramatic literature. Would that he had recorded his opinion of Grétry.

19. Matroco

Drame burlesque in 4 acts, in verse: music mostly not extant.
Libretto by Pierre Laujon.
First performed at Chantilly, 3 November 1777. First performed at Fontainebleau, 21 November 1777. First performed at the Comédie-Italienne, 23 February 1778.
Musical extracts in Grétry's *Mémoires* (i:291–6)

Matroco had five acts when given at Chantilly at the Prince de Condé's and was thereafter reduced to four.[1] The librettist, to whose literary skill Grétry more than once pays tribute, was known for the text of Martini's favourite opéra-comique *L'amoureux de 15 ans* (1771); it is a work of surpassing sentimentality and want of intelligence, graced by very efficient music. In March 1777 Grétry's setting of three divertissements by Laujon was given at Versailles, appended to Nivelle de La Chaussée's *Amour pour amour*. Regrettably, as this play lies behind *Zémire et Azor*, the music has not survived. Laujon was secretary to the Duc de Bourbon and under obligation to that family; *Matroco*, said by Grétry as having been composed to please the court (i:294), amounted more or less to a jolly caper for royal consumption. In this it resembles Monsigny's opéra-comique *L'île sonnante* (1767), written at the behest of his employer, the Duc d'Orléans, as an extravagant satire on the power of music to a libretto by a man who loathed modern opéra-comique.[2]

Against the composer's will *Matroco* was shown in Paris and lasted there for five performances: actually the takings were good (on the final night, 1,797 *livres*) which suggests that the withdrawal was insisted upon from within. Grétry says that he consigned the music to the flames, but he appears to have kept something of it since he discusses the opera in some detail in the *Mémoires* and prints a two-part setting of 'a remarkable vaudeville that was in the overture' and also twenty bars from the concluding march. The libretto is extremely funny and episodes such as the mock sacrifice scenes make one regret that the score is lost.

Matroco is interesting today chiefly as the relic of a radical experiment to unite the old-fashioned use of vaudevilles and pre-composed melodies in opéra-comique with the modern resources of the orchestra and vocal forms like the recitative, the quartet and the finale. The vaudevilles were traditional, national, part of the folk culture of their time; as surely as jingles or singles today, they formed an instant bridge between a tune and a form of words. Thus they had wide utility on the stage: they could be used with their proper words in an appropriate situation or, more often, could have new words applied to the tune to make it more relevant. Many possibilities for irony arose: a comic scene could be overlaid with a second level of wit, or a piquant scene might be debased. A writer in 1771 explained that vaudeville refrains should be 'well enough chosen to make an epigram by themselves and stimulate the audience's wits, malice, even sensual pleasure'.[3] Many people preferred the simple vaudeville style of opéra-comique to the musically sophisticated one with modern arias and ensembles. Even after the reforms of 1780 (see chapter 26) specific room was made for vaudeville pieces on Tuesdays and Fridays when French plays were to be shown; the orchestra on those days was reduced to a handful of players.[4]

From the Comédie-Italienne archives we know that the queen and royal family went to the first Paris performance of *Matroco*; the same source tells us all we know about the work's orchestra, since it records payment for two trumpeters and timpanist.[5]

The cast of *Matroco* (the title-rôle is that of a wicked enchanter) includes giants, dwarves, knights, heralds, a fairy, lovers, shepherds and so on. Act 1 is set at night before a tower in a desert, with rocks around it. Act 2 is in a pleasant garden and act 4 portrays a fortified tower. The point of it all, as the author's preface explains, is to parody the whole apparatus of the chivalric romance, the mediaeval world which Grétry would soon explore seriously in *Aucassin et Nicolette* and *Richard Cœur-de-lion*. Among Laujon's targets were heroes who languish and talk but never act, and 'prudish, precious heroines, always trying to tell their life story'. It was a fairly promising subject, but the technical manner of dealing with the vaudevilles was too awkward to be artistically satisfactory. They had, as Laujon says, 'to blend with the different pieces of music' both as contrast to the composed music and as traditional agents of parody. But it was one thing for a small pit group or just harpsichord to play a rapid series of refrains, and quite another for Grétry to cope with motivic demands such as the following:

ACT 3.
    March . . .
    Recitative, mixed with vaudeville refrains.
    Emphasis [a lover]:[6] Illustrious knights (Three knights salute)
                (Air: *Nous sommes trois foux*)
                You whom, one after the other
                I have delivered while on my way
                (Air: *Dans la rue Chifonière en plein plan*)
                From some wicked enchanter
                (Air: *Dansez mon petit*)
                Whose power destroyed, though greater than ours
                Had even found amusement . . .
                (Air: *Du haut en bas*)

A few lines later even a theme from Grétry's *Le tableau parlant* (7) was worked in. The process was excellently described by Grétry as like fashioning a matching body for an antique sculpted head discovered in some ruins (1:304). Nevertheless it is interesting that after first rejecting them outright, Grétry had recently been incorporating one or two vaudeville elements into his work (see p. 126) and had counterpointed a known tune, 'Vive Henri IV', with an original one for dramatic purposes in the second section of the overture to *Le Magnifique*. In rather parallel fashion the overture to *Matroco* was 'composed of known and graphic tunes, explaining the subject of the opera' (i:290). But for the main work the composer was surely correct to observe that the style of music required was overblown and exaggerated, not epigrammatic and associative. The valid opportunity to juxtapose vaudevilles and new music was about to occur in *Le jugement de Midas*.

The *Mémoires* seem loath to quit the subject of *Matroco* without mentioning its more admired passages, as if to compensate the author for the impossibility of using their music in a subsequent score. Not many pages afterwards he unconvincingly counsels the reader against the expedient of writing down ideas 'which, rejected for the moment, might become precious in the future'. (i:307).

VERSIONS AND PERFORMANCES

Nine small changes were made to the libretto between Fontainebleau and the Paris performances; only those mentioned in note 6 imply changes to the music. Textual alterations occurred in act 1 sc. 2 and 4, act 2 sc. 1 and 7, and act 4 sc. 1–4.[7]

20. Le jugement de Midas (The judgement of Midas)

Comédie in 3 acts, in prose: *CC* 17
Libretto by Thomas Hales, known as d'Hèle. Dedicated to Madame [De Montesson].[1]
First performed privately, Palais-Royal, Paris, 28 March 1778. First performed at the Comédie-Italienne, 27 June 1778.
Printed full score, Paris, Houbaut, n.d. [1779] as Œuvre xiv.[2]
Dramatis personae: Apollon (Apollo) (t.)
    Palemon, a farmer (b.)
    Mopsa, his wife (s.)
    Lise (s.) } their daughters
    Chloé (s.)
    Pan, a woodcutter, affianced to Chloé (b.)
    Marsias, a shepherd, affianced to Lise (t.)
    Midas, the village Bailli (t. or bar.)
    Mercure (spoken rôle)
    Chorus of villagers

OVERTURE (to be mimed with the curtain up): A plain, with mountains behind. Dawn breaks slowly. A storm blows up; thunder and lightning. Apollo is hurled from the sky. A shepherd runs away in fright, leaving his cloak. The storm subsides; sunrise.

ACT 1: Apollo picks himself up, reflecting on his harsh punishment by Jupiter. He sings in order to test his godly powers of art (aria 1).[3] Palemon overhears him, amazed at the unfamiliar style of melody. He offers to employ Apollo and (duet 2) describes his work and family; news of two daughters cheers Apollo, who decides to stay. Palemon explains that the village is musical. Midas has arranged twin marriages between Palemon's daughters, who sing, and Pan and Marsias, who match their skills. Pan arrives, singing from offstage a vaudeville, 'J'en ferai la folie' (3a) while Marsias likewise approaches singing Baroque recitative (3b, 3c). Apollo is horrified and escapes when Pan and Marsias join forces (3d). Palemon's favourite daughter is Chloé, but his wife protects Lise. Palemon bemoans his loss of authority in the home (aria 4). In a compact finale (5) the future sons-in-law continue their musical and general opposition until Mopsa arrives. She is furious that the decision to take in a newcomer was made without her consent. Palemon claims the need for help in labouring but loses the next argument since he does not even know Apollo's name or provenance. Mopsa wants him removed and the act ends in stalemate.

ACT 2: A room in Palemon's house, Lise spinning, Chloé arranging flowers. In a duet (6) they discuss the attractiveness of the stranger. Apollo is heard waking in the hayloft; the girls cannot wait to talk to him, but leave. Apollo (aria 7) is unable to decide which girl he prefers. He confronts Mopsa, but easily gains her confidence, even admiration. Palemon is ordered to keep him on. Preparations continue: in a family scene Apollo stands apart upstage, making eyes at each daughter (quintet 8); he takes the name Alexis. Lise, alone, confesses her feelings towards him (aria 9). Apollo returns from picking fruit; in a duet with him she admits her love (duet 10) and goes off to get Mopsa's help in deflecting Marsias. Chloé, the more carefree daughter, comes in and with her Apollo tries a more direct approach, taking her hand. In their duet (11) she is entranced by his imitations of Pan and Marsias, but refuses his embrace. Nonetheless, she promptly enlists her mother in a plan to get rid of Pan (which is easy, since Mopsa will do anything to cross him and Palemon). In the finale (12) Pan is turned down by Chloé and Mopsa, while Marsias is rejected by Lise and Palemon. Each parent's support for the favoured son-in-law is lost in the *mêlée*.

ACT 3: The same. Midas is brought in by Marsias and Pan; he feels personally affronted, since he matched the four as a musical quartet (trio 13). Palemon's family arrives. The parents each announce a substitute spouse for their favourite daughter, not realising that Apollo has charmed both. Singing will decide. Apollo arrives, says he is a double rival, but is not believed. The first 'trial' song, Apollo's lament for Daphne, is an unpretentious Larghetto (14). Midas condemns it. Marsias begins an equivalent lament in French Baroque style, to be interrupted by Pan's tale of Céphise, sung to two vaudevilles (15), 'O réguingué' and 'Belle diguedon'. They finish together in grotesque opposition and receive Midas's complete approval. Apollo then tries a comic song in the form of an allegory: a singing contest between a cuckoo, an owl and a nightingale, judged by a donkey (16). Midas thereupon banishes Apollo, also in Baroque recitative (17a). He is instantly rewarded with asses' ears, while the orchestra brays. Apollo reveals his true identity; the chorus is astonished (17b). The scene changes to a landscape with Parnassus in the distance. Mercure comes in to announce Jupiter's forgiveness, so that Apollo can resume his place on Parnassus and, moreover, take both daughters with him. Midas must keep his auricles as a general warning against false taste. A chorus and ensemble, with a duet of the daughters, pay homage to Apollo and his music (18).

Le jugement de Midas is probably the only opéra-comique for the pleasures of which we have to thank a professor of music at Trinity College, Dublin. The work's genesis dates back to the 1750s, when an Italian company was giving comic intermezzos with great success in Dublin. These included works like Pergolesi's *Le serva padrona* and they were referred to as 'burlettas'. In fact, 'blended with the exhibitions of the theatre [they] almost triumphed over the best productions in our language'[4] and attracted the attention of Garret Wesley (1735–81); Wesley, a gifted instrumental performer and composer, was created first Earl of Mornington in 1760. He obtained the D. Mus. at Trinity College in 1764 and thereafter became its first professor of music. Seeing the possibilities of the comic intermezzo, he commissioned Kane O'Hara to write an English imitation of one. The result was *Midas*, the first English burletta . . . These early burlettas were in verse throughout and all-sung, and they satirized the mythological and historical conventions of *opera seria*, though the music rarely participated in the joke.   (*The New Grove*, 'Burletta')

At first given privately in 1760, O'Hara's *Midas* was revised and seen publicly in Dublin's Crow Street Theatre on 22 January 1762. The musical arranger is unknown. It reached London's Theatre Royal, Covent Garden on 22 February 1764, in three-act form. Both the libretto and the songs, though not the recitatives, were published in London.[5] Owing to illness the performances were curtailed and the burletta was revived in two acts as an afterpiece. It survived on the boards until at least 1825.[6]

O'Hara's basic idea had the freshness needed to beat the Italians for a limited time. He burlesqued the literary device of imitating the ancients by debasing mythology into farce. Simultaneously, the anonymous arranger in London took music from sources like Handel, Arne, Burney (*Queen Mab*) and Rousseau (*Le devin du village*) together with English, Irish and Scottish national songs. The sources were treated with 'extreme freedom' (Fiske) and sometimes the Italian manner was burlesqued by having a portentous introduction placed in front of a trivial piece of melody. Unfortunately we cannot identify many of the pieces, since the 1764 libretto names few of their original titles and, of course, none of their real origins. The emphasis was on tunefulness, though there were several duets and a quintet (score p. 58, libretto p. 57) of some complexity.

Grétry and the growth of opéra-comique

The three-act *Midas* was more risqué and dramatically confused than its two-act successor but their conceptions were identical. O'Hara borrowed the story of Apollo, Pan and Midas, king of Phrygia. Apollo was ejected from Olympus for his vengeance on the cyclops. On earth he was in musical conflict with Pan, god of forests and shepherds. Midas judged the contest in favour of Pan and was rewarded by Apollo with asses' ears. Like a good *tragédie lyrique*, *Midas* opens with a prelude set on Olympus, where Apollo is arraigned and sent to earth with a thunderbolt after him by Jupiter; he has courted disfavour by gossiping about Jupiter's private life to Juno, who sets the tone of the piece in a complaining song:

> Your favourite jades
> I'll plunge to the shades
> Or into cows metamorphose them.

There is also a chorus, sung to the 'King of Prussia's March'. Scene two reveals a countryside and distant village. A violent storm ensues, Apollo is thrown down, decides to be called Pol and is hired as a farm-hand by Sileno. Sileno's daughters are being courted by a lecherous musical squire Midas and his pander, Damaetas. Pan, the local musician, is a merry old bachelor who plies the bagpipes. The daughters are taken considerably with Apollo ('Sir, you're such an oglio / Of perfection in folio') and Midas contrives a musical contest between Pol and Pan ('Dare you think your clumsy lugs so proper to decide as / The delicate ears of justice Midas?'). Pan is the winner with 'A pox of your pother'. Apollo is revealed, awards the asses' ears to Midas, makes Sileno the new squire but his dreadful wife Mysis 'a Billingsgate Queen'. A chorus sees Apollo back to the heavens.

Certainly there was some satirical intent in the choice of music for the trial songs, though this is not entirely clear today. Pan's song, Air xiv (score p. 64) is quoted below; the moral in stanza four is 'Life is but an Old Song', which in fact is what he sings: see Ex. 20.1. The concealed words originally belonging to this tune are, furthermore, a rejection of Classicism, or rather, of foreign highbrow culture.

> Old Homer – but with him what have we to do?
> What are Grecians or Trojans to me or to you?[7]

Pol's trial song (score p. 64) is, by contrast, decidedly Italianate 'art-music', whose source remains unfortunately unknown. It is introduced by four bars of pizzicato strings (Ex. 20.2). O'Hara and his arranger are obviously making a stylistic point

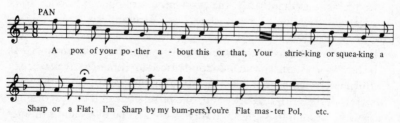

A   pox of your po-ther a - bout this or that, Your   shrie-king or squea-king a

Sharp or a Flat; I'm Sharp by my bum-pers,You're Flat mas-ter Pol,   etc.

Ex. 20.1 *Midas. A Comic Opera* (London, Walsh, n.d.), p. 64 [Air xiv]

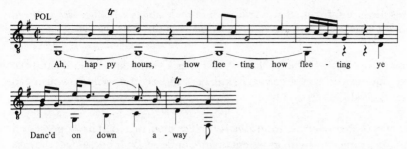

Le jugement de Midas

Ex. 20.2 *Midas. A Comic Opera* (London, Walsh, n.d.), p. 64 [Air xv]

with Apollo's music, even if musical types and their adherents are not the main concern of the piece.

Grétry's new librettist, whom we encountered in chapter 18, challenged in his preface those who imagined he had merely translated the English original. Yet few critics seem to have seen for themselves how extensively the outline of the model was retained, yet how taut and clever was the reworking. Hales's wit is so idiomatic and effective that his *Jugement de Midas* appears to require comparison with nothing else: it is worlds away from O'Hara's rape of English verse. Hales saw that modern opéra-comique, the old vaudeville tradition and the Baroque style of Rameau could fight out their claims in a microcosm of the Parisian battlefield. The satire would be infinitely keener than O'Hara's for having a single composer in charge, by making Apollo the symbol of enlightened taste, and by using opéra-comique itself as the vehicle. To provide a second suitor with Pan, Hales appropriated the mythical satyr Marsyas, a flute-player whose musical challenge to Apollo was also defeated: Marsyas was judged by the Muses and flayed alive by Apollo. Hales retained and developed O'Hara's running domestic battles but ingeniously turned the implacable mutual dislike of Palemon and Mopsa into a series of motivating spurs in the action.

As Voltaire said in the context of translating Pope, a joke explained to the foreign reader ceases to be a joke. Hales's dialogue is nevertheless full of potentially translatable one-line quips which would sound to an English person as natural as any modern play. These are often motivated by the irresistible desire to rise to any bait that might bring higher status. For the disguised Apollo cannot conceal his 'godly' or genteel bearing and it quickly becomes apparent to everyone that it would be a happy accident if they could get him married into the family. The pacing is rapid: we first meet the daughters as nearly married in act 2 yet the same act contrives to end with a complete reversal of their situations. (The exchange of partners, seduction scenes and symmetry perforce bring *Così fan tutte* to mind.) The exposition is pushed into the overture; moreover Mopsa, Pan, Marsyas, Midas and the daughters all make their initial appearance in music, not dialogue. The versification of sung sections was undertaken by Anseaume, but Grétry was adamant that Hales should be owed the tribute for their variety and aptness of design.

The pieces destined for musical setting in each of these librettos [*Le jugement de Midas, L'amant jaloux*] were in prose, but in such a clear style that only the versification was needed. (i:298–9)

This remarkable fact was the result both of Hales's genius and his long study of opéra-comique as a critical observer (*Réf*:iii:261). Indeed, the placing of music can hardly be faulted.

Almost every Grétry overture from *Zémire et Azor*, even that to *Matroco*, possessed some integral connection with its parent opéra-comique. But none, as was the case with *Le jugement de Midas*, was both an acted prelude and the bearer of music destined for functional recollection later. The *Midas* overture is, effectively, a tone-poem.[8] It is both simple and complex, rococo and Romantic, extremely effective in performance. Its single movement is in ABA form with an introduction. The opening bars, interpreting Hales's prescription of 'the silent noise that precedes the dawn', looks innocuous enough on paper; in orchestral sound it becomes a beautiful exploration of half-tints and unresolved seventh chords. This gives way to an Allegretto Pastorale, the sounds and feelings in man of nature coming to life (Ex. 20.3). Later there is the call of a nightingale, identifiable as such from Apollo's (16); it bears the same relation to the whole as Beethoven's quail and cuckoo in the Pastoral Symphony. The storm that occupies the central part of Grétry's overture is surprisingly powerful, and this can best be shown by a harmonic sketch (Ex. 20.4). The jump from chord V in E minor to C minor root position (asterisked) throws together a distant secondary dominant with a tonic long forgotten. It is rudely emphasised by dynamics (*p* to *ff*), orchestration and stage action (Apollo is thrown down).

Ex. 20.3 *Le jugement de Midas*, overture

Ex. 20.4 *Le jugement de Midas*, overture

Le jugement de Midas

The opera's final number (18) re-employs the ABA ensemble–duet–ensemble form heard in *Les mariages samnites* (23). Lise and Chloé are given the oboe melody of Ex. 20.3 to sing in its entirety:

> Is it to be wondered at if our heart
> Was quite defenceless?

This is more than likely a further allegory within the general scheme, an invitation to enjoy again, almost reappraise this typical Grétryan theme. The music is identified with the Apollonian power that has seduced the girls, is 'framed' artificially for that purpose.

This opéra-comique is foremost a comedy of errors, though, not a comedy of ideas. It stands by its characters; but these are not all simple to draw out in music because Hales created much more than caricatures in Apollo and the girls. Apollo, of course, has weaknesses but also remains a dominant intelligence. His opening aria has to impress (Grétry slighted it unnecessarily: i:303). Its sustained, arching phrases do have the required elemental quality for a song about the power of music. The independent orchestra parts create an interesting counterpoint, as though the god were plucking his song from an ever-present continuum. But with Palemon in (2) Apollo discourses in the earthly vernacular, i.e. the syllabic style, also however betraying his quickness by starting phrases before Palemon has finished his sentences. We laugh at Apollo's hesitation at the idea of labouring as we do at his enthusiasm at mention of the daughters. There is further variety in act 2. The solo (7) is luxuriant – he has slept well – yet droll: there is richness in harmony like the dominant major ninth, paused upon, and self-parody as one female image is built up only to be pricked like a bubble in front of the other. A fast close glances at the Italian cabaletta form: 'To court both were too much for a mortal, but for a god . . . it's but a game!'[9] (Ex. 20.5).

Lise is the more serious daughter, fittingly engaged to a devotee of *tragédie-lyrique*. So when Apollo woos her in (10), she is the one to set the pace while he observes the formalities, posing as the courtly lover: 'Ciel! Vous ne me haïssez donc pas?' In gentle musical parody they play with question-and-answer phrases, ending with an ecstatic section just too precious to be taken seriously. And the duet with Chloé (11) is possibly yet more pleasurable, given her more surprising capitulation. As with (10) the form is unpredictable and forward-moving. Apollo

Ex. 20.5 *Le jugement de Midas* (7)
('Lise, Chloé, both are dear to me')

159

Ex. 20.6 *Le jugement de Midas* (14) Cf. Ex. 2.1
('Unhappy victim of your oppressive fate, Daphne, I lose you for ever, I shall never again see your charms. Hear my voice, you whom I adore . . .')

first gets only light mockery for his pains, so he tries a new tack, which works well, by mimicking Pan and Marsias. Only in act 3 does Grétry falter over Apollo. Tension is lost during (14) and (16), both in F, where it should be greatest. Not merely had his aria (7) been in the same key, but the basic ideas of (14) were taken from the 1766 *Isabelle et Gertrude*, Ex. 2.1, and a wholly different context. His music becomes prosaic just where it ought to shine most brightly: see Ex. 20.6.

Lise and Chloé may be village girls but they are creatures of sensibility. It is a pity we hear so little of them in act 3. We languish with them in their masterly duet (6), some 170 bars in length, in E major. The expository duet in *La Rosière de Salency* (2) was a modified rondo in form and so is this: it resembles a sonata-rondo in the weight given to the second episode, its conversation set in D and B minor. As they rise to their feet at the end there is new material and a new metre, but the moment of truth comes earlier with the sense of loss Grétry conveys as the girls compare their young swains to the desirable newcomer in the loft (Ex. 20.7).

Ex. 20.7 *Le jugement de Midas* (6)
('Ah, when I think of him, Marsias': 'Poor Pan')

Although only Palemon has a solo, he, Mopsa, Pan and Marsias have brilliantly drawn characters. Mopsa is one of Grétry's liveliest creations. Palemon may be henpecked but can still engage our sympathy in his own right. It would not be wrong to play him with crude humour in (4) in the fivefold repeated line 'I proved to her I was her husband', since Grétry mentions it himself.[10] We see husband and wife best in the miniature drama of the finale (5), each section only a few pages long.

Key and Tempo	Action
D; 2/2 Andantino con moto	Sons-in-law anticipate their future. Marsias' music becomes a parody of Rameau.
G; 2/4 Allegro	Mopsa launches in, berating Palemon, gabbling incessantly.
D minor; 3/8 Andantino assai	Palemon's response, magnificently suggestive of age, tiredness and resignation. Mopsa mocks his last phrase.
D minor; 2/2 Allegro assai	Palemon explodes, only to be interrogated further; section begins in fugal style.
D minor; 4/4 Allegretto	Palemon tries to reason.
D major; 2/4 Allegro	Hectic argument, powerful use of comic *buffo* style; ends epigrammatically with motto first used in bars 5 and 6.

Ex. 20.8 *Le jugement de Midas* (15)
('Belle diguedon'; 'Your torments do not equal mine')

Pan and Marsias personify musical inflexibility, expressed at its comic apogee when they sing simultaneously in the high tragic and the low comic style (Ex. 20.8). But their language sometimes develops, as when Pan lumbers in during the finale (12) with gauche phrases that embarrass the whole family and employ falsely-accented word-setting in accordance with the vaudeville style.[11] Midas' heir was Beckmesser, as Apollo's was Walther. Wagner made the same stylistic points in *Die Meistersinger* as Grétry here, and both composers used the natural resource of comic delivery to dramatise the issue. Grétry said, adopting the reform position of twenty years' standing,[12] that his satire was directed mostly against the mannered way used by singers at the Opéra. He left instructions that are useful (i:301). First, sing the melody very slowly and unrhythmically; secondly, perform long trills whenever possible; thirdly, lean well on the appoggiaturas; fourthly, make the *martellements* very long; fifthly, adopt an almost smiling face, even in sad arias; draw out all the expression from the lower jaw, which you must stick out in order to give a certain wobbly appearance, and you will sing old French as in the time of Rebel and Francœur.

In conclusion, two particular advances in Grétry's style must be mentioned. The first is the ardent confession of Lise (9) which takes forward the strain of lyricism shown in Lucette's aria (2) in *La fausse magie*. The sense is that rococo taste has been left behind in favour of Classical logic and beauty, but within (as is now normal) an outward-developing variant of a basically simple (ABA') form. The second advance is the integration of mime and mimetic music into an ensemble. *Les mariages samnites* contained a mimed refrain in (12), a melodrama (8) for the silent glances and a quartet (6) in which a pair of lovers communicate silently. In *Le jugement de Midas* (8) we have an ingenious quintet, again with silent glances and communication, but now integrated in order to set the relationships in motion around a group of motivating events. As such, this is the opposite of normal ensembles wherein a static group gives vent to different feelings concerning a single event.

Three kinds of music are heard in the mimed ritornello: the motif of family argument in C major, coloured by the piccolo; the one for Apollo's tender look at Lise in E flat, coloured by slower harmonic rhythm and pizzicato strings; and that for his gay look at Chloé in C minor, with added string activity. The first of these is reserved for the opening and closing parts of the quintet. Before Chloé's vocal entry the orchestra takes up the character of the third motif. As the audience realise by this association what the daughters are actually thinking about, the parents ironically assume that their charges are digesting their recipe for marital bliss. Then Chloé and Lise sing together; the music jumps to F minor and develops the second motif. With justice, as he glances at them longingly, Apollo sings 'I know the object of their secret desire'. Yet the basic pace of the family conference is maintained.

VERSIONS AND PERFORMANCES

As might be expected in the case of an opera tried out in private, there are almost no discrepancies between early published sources. However, the composer recalled that (15) was originally set as two separate items (*Réf*:iii:262). Moreover the *Réflexions* mention two changes made after the première. The first was the withdrawal of a piece so far not identified. The second was the rewriting of the last scene: originally Apollo, Mercure, Lise and Chloé went off, but Midas stayed to beg the others not to make his asses' ears public knowledge. However, they sang a canon mocking him and pursued him off the stage. The final chorus we know was substituted for this to make a more formal close.

Court officials having for some reason refused to mount *Le jugement de Midas*, the work automatically joined the waiting-list of the Comédie-Italienne. Grétry interested Mme de Montesson in it and she allowed it to be performed, with amateur singers, in the private theatre of the Duc d'Orléans. It is possible that Voltaire saw the work, together with a number of uninhibited bishops and members of the Comédie-Italienne (i:299): he certainly addressed a notorious quatrain on *Midas* to Grétry.[13] It is unlikely that the simple parody of *tragédie-lyrique* was a cause for prohibition, especially since Philidor had used the same comic technique for the mock-incantation scene in *Le sorcier* (1764). Some critics have thought that Hales's nationality was the reason, international relations being at low ebb owing to the war of American Independence, which had begun at

Lexington in April 1775. France was to enter a treaty of alliance with the Americans in February 1778 and, as Mozart commented, feelings ran high in that year:

The French [ships] have forced the English to retreat, but it was not a very hot fight . . . Nevertheless there is tremendous jubilation here and nothing else is talked of.

(Letter of 7 August 1778)

The private performances had the desired effect of releasing permission; the public first found the work enticing but its appeal diminished to only a handful of performances each year. From 1778 to 1787 there were 74 performances and only 32 in the decade after that. After 20 performances in 1798–1802 it left the stage until 1807 but from then up to 1813 only 15 further showings took place. There was a revival in 1820, and from then until the last performance in 1824 the work was seen 27 times. This pattern accords with Michael Kelly's explanation: 'In Paris, it in a great degree gained its popularity by the acting of the inimitable Monsieur Trial, who represented the Singing Shepherd; his imitation of the old school of French singing (which he caricatured with irresistible humour) was admirable.'[14] The last foreign revival noted by Loewenberg was in New Orleans (1808).

21. L'amant jaloux[1] (The jealous lover)

Comédie in 3 acts, in prose: CC 21
Libretto by Thomas Hales, known as d'Hèle. Dedicated to J. P. C. Le Noir,
  Conseiller d'Etat and Lieutenant-General of police.[2]
First performed at Versailles, 20 November 1778. First performed at the Comédie-
  Italienne, 23 December 1778.
Printed full score, Paris, Houbaut, n.d. [1779] as Œuvre xv.
Dramatis personae: Lopez, a Spanish merchant (b.)
            Léonore, his daughter (s.)
            Isabelle, friend of Léonore (s.)
            Don Alonze, Spanish gentleman, Isabelle's brother (t.)
            Florival, a French officer (t.)
            Jacinthe, Léonore's maidservant (s.)
ACT 1: Cadiz; a room in Lopez' house with one door leading to a walled garden, another to a closet, and a window concealed by a grille. Lopez is back from a business trip, determined to prevent Léonore's remarriage, since her late husband put money into his own speculations which she might otherwise want to remove. Jacinthe claims to Lopez that her mistress is in mourning and a respectable widow (aria 1).[3] Lopez, not deceived, forbids both Isabelle and her brother access to his house (aria 2). He goes. Suddenly Isabelle appears, having been rescued from

enforced marriage by a stranger who has admired her from afar: Florival. Florival is given leave to return that evening but departs under the impression that Isabelle's name is Léonore. Isabelle describes her rescue (trio 3) and is comforted. Léonore will conceal her from her father and brother, whose family honour has been stained by her escape. Alonze approaches and Isabelle is bundled into the closet, but its door is inadvertently left ajar. His eyes constantly stray towards the closet; Léonore tells him that Lopez has banished him. Noises from within the closet heighten his jealous curiosity; when its door is pulled shut from within he condemns Léonore for infidelity. In the finale (4) his jealousy cannot be quenched even when Lopez (who has never seen him before) enters and demands explanations. Jacinthe has to admit that a certain woman has been sheltered after (so Léonore asserts) having been attacked by Alonze. This suggestion is proved correct to all intents and purposes when Isabelle, veiled, demurely emerges from the closet and is escorted away by Jacinthe. All shame is heaped on Alonze, who is obliged to depart speechlessly.

ACT 2: The same evening. Léonore considers that Alonze's jealousy places him beneath consideration (aria 5). Isabelle is hiding in the garden pavilion, but Lopez suddenly decides to forbid access to the garden and removes the key to it. He rails against the folly of wedlock (aria 6), urging his daughter to let him invest her money instead. Léonore leaves unhappily with Jacinthe. Florival appears bearing a letter of exchange as a pretext for gaining entry. When Lopez goes to cash it Jacinthe just has enough time to tell him to look in the garden. Lopez entertains Florival to a smoke (duet 7), but Florival is wary about discussing his life, believing his new love to be his host's daughter. He escapes and Lopez goes to bed. It is about 9 p.m. An apologetic Alonze turns up; while Jacinthe fetches her mistress Alonze reveals that although he has just inherited money he wishes to be loved for himself. The finale (8) begins with a song for Jacinthe, superseded by a passionate argument between Léonore and Alonze. He protests that he is cured; she melts; they will be happy. A second later Florival's serenade is heard outside. Consumed with new jealousy Alonze rushes to the window. He and Léonore fall to recriminating with cruel irony and the act ends in furious anger.

ACT 3: The walled garden, containing an illuminated pavilion. Isabelle emerges and sings tenderly about Florival (aria 9). He is then seen making an entrance over the garden wall. Isabelle thinks he might be a philanderer but in the duet (10) is persuaded otherwise. Alonze also appears over the wall, and because Isabelle rushes back into the pavilion he is convinced she was Léonore with a lover. In an ensemble (11) each man challenges the other's presence, and then Lopez confronts both intruders, followed by Jacinthe. With one voice they call on Léonore to come out but when she does so, it is from the house. Identities are sorted out, whereafter Alonze appeals to Lopez for Léonore's hand, mentioning his inheritance but forgoing a dowry. In an ensemble (12) Alonze succeeds in his aim. The appearance of Isabelle causes all to prevail on Alonze to sanction her union with Florival and in turn Léonore is urged to forgive the jealous Alonze. They resolve to be less fickle in the future.

Grétry and the growth of opéra-comique

Once again Hales wrought a transformation as poised and stylish as it was radical. In fact La Harpe (the critic) and F. B. Hoffman (the librettist) among others declared L'amant jaloux to be a model of French style and a masterpiece of opéra-comique.[4] The essential basis of plot, setting and humour was The Wonder: a Woman keeps a Secret, in five acts, by Susanna Centlivre, produced at Drury Lane on 27 April 1714. Centlivre's nineteen plays enjoyed prolonged popularity and were selectively reprinted well into the Victorian period. One, indeed, was re-edited in 1969. The Wonder was also published in Polish (1817) as well as French (1784). The vitality of the play is chiefly farcical, complete with brawls, a comic Scots servant, an atmosphere of licence and – almost to the point of tedium – surprise appearances. The scene is set in Lisbon. Violante (Hales's Léonore) defies her father in wishing to marry Felix (Hales's Alonze); Isabella defies hers in avoiding enforced marriage by escaping and being rescued by one Colonel Britton ('a Scotchman'). The 'secret' of the title refers to Isabella's concealment which stimulates some of the farcical deceptions, being doubly difficult to maintain in view of Felix's jealousy; this becomes a Latin weakness erected into a dramatic principle. Beside these bare bones, Hales incorporated various details such as the mercenary motives of the fathers. From act 2 he took over the unwitting interruption of a lovers' scene, making it the climactic serenade in (8). From act 5 he borrowed Felix's challenge to Violante to open a closet, her father's arrival, Violante's incriminating story against Felix, and the silent emergence of the veiled Isabella, as in (4).

Yet the borrowed matter could have been reincarnated only as the inspired result of jettisoning a huge quantity of repetition, scene changes, subsidiary or unnecessary characters, sub-plots and vulgarity. Where the original play is episodic and rather shapeless, the libretto possesses classical economy and design. Whereas the original female characters accept almost any amount of jealous abuse, becoming all but motiveless as a consequence, Hales's and Grétry's are believable people of feeling and even suffering. And whereas Centlivre's Felix is worse than fickle, Hales's Alonze, though always jealous, is still honourable and capable of being humiliated by the situations into which jealousy leads him. Hales brought out and humanised the theme of war between the sexes. As never before in opéra-comique the battle-lines are drawn not between potentially unsuitable lovers or flippant ones, but between responsible partners. The material is on the fringes of 'serious comedy', for example like Shakespeare's Much Ado, focusing on the inner weaknesses that prevent happiness as much as the outer constraints that challenge it. The social context in repressive Spain prevents free dialogue between the sexes. This is why stress is placed on the foreignness of Florival, the agent by whom the women break free of their circumstances. Hales and Grétry responded sympathetically to their heroines both in solos and the trio (3), while the men sing alone only in the ritual smoking scene (7), which is in any case dramatically inconsequential. It is sad that Centlivre leaves us indifferent, other than on the comic level, to the eventual union of Violante and Felix, but remarkable that Hales retains our belief in the underlying forces binding Léonore and Alonze. In the prose we identify with Alonze's virtues and Léonore's self-knowledge; in the music we observe them developing and sparring, to the female's advantage.

Centlivre's Isabella is much more active than the opera's Isabelle, and has time to test her Colonel Britton's motives: this is necessary partly because Britton is a voluptuary. Florival is persistent, but not importunate. The equivalent process of testing is miniaturised into the duet (10). Hales's lines of battle are contrived from the beginning in the Lopez–Jacinthe scenes. Jacinthe has no equivalent in the source play, whose fathers are unmemorable besides, but in the opera these two characters are gifted with intelligent mutual dislike. Each knows the other will be hard to defeat. It is a war of cunning whose final victory is clinched not, as in Centlivre, through a hastily-arranged marriage ceremony but by the cynical fact that Lopez is bought off.

There are fewer musical numbers in *L'amant jaloux* than had previously been normal in a three-act, or even two-act opéra-comique by Grétry. Large portions of dialogue separate the items except in act 3, which uses briefer links. Such a reversal of the pro-musical bias built up with Marmontel and adopted by Pezay cannot be pronounced a complete success. It was bound to set up too many sympathetic resonances in favour of the spoken word.[5] Yet such is the nature of this comedy. Points of tension and action are heightened by music; characters are created in speech. Grétry finds an excellent balance between simple and complex, the inward and the outward gesture. *L'amant jaloux* is also distinguished by its melodic fecundity. Formal non-regularity (which by now we expect) and psychological suggestion aptly produced by this, appear throughout. There is not a single non-developing piece in the opera except (5). Even (6) must be counted as an asymmetrical statement.

Jacinthe's aria (1) dismisses youth and its inconstant *amours* in order to suggest that her mistress is no longer susceptible. But something in the lightness of the general gait conveys to Lopez that all is not above board: perhaps it is the rather frisky bassoon and viola figure at the opening, which vanishes as Jacinthe warms to her task but creeps back, disguised as an octave leap. We are surprised by the heat of Lopez' response in (2). He essentially conveys one order (the banishment), while under rising choleric pressure the themes become distorted (Ex. 21.1). So

Ex. 21.1 *L'amant jaloux* (2)
('Do you understand, my dear?'; 'Do you understand well, my dear?'; 'But if some confidante . . .')

Grétry and the growth of opéra-comique

far, therefore, stalemate: the assertion of paternal will. The next round belongs to the opposite sex. It is what the libretto calls an aria for Isabelle, but with the text for her friends (3) becomes a unique *scena* for three persons, centred on Isabelle's ascent from the fright and darkness of assault to comfort and hope.[6] Although this resembles a structured 'logical improvisation' in five sections its inner fibres are as dramatic as ever in Grétry. Florival's reported words 'Je suis français' in the second section are repeated by Isabelle in a disjunct, almost convulsive way, capturing the possibility of rescue; the same musical motif is developed in the penultimate section, as if to dramatise his swordsmanship exclusively by reference to his personality (Ex. 21.2).

Ex. 21.2 *L'amant jaloux* (3)
(a) ('I am a Frenchman, it is enough to tell you that')
(b) ('He knocks down, he lays low, My tyrant backs off')

In (4) Grétry produced his best finale to date, with a more powerful key-scheme than *La fausse magie* (18). Thanks to Hales' exceptionally vital text (eight pages of printed libretto) the music bristles with comedy. Linear unity in music is pursued first in a recurring rhythm and secondly in an idea epitomising Alonze's compulsive desire to satisfy his jealous suspicions (Ex. 21.3). The more he returns to it, the funnier it becomes, and it even functions on its own in the accompaniment with speech fragments thrown about it. Tonal unity is pursued in a sonata-like procedure. The 'exposition' (D major) covers Alonze's arrival; the 'second subject' (its full resolution prolonged by use of A minor) coincides with Lopez' arrival and demands for explanation; the 'development' (E minor to C sharp minor) goes with Jacinthe's explanation, falsely developed by Léonore, and then Alonze's counter-accusation. There is a musical climax and Isabelle, veiled, comes out. The transition bars are followed by an Andante section in 3/8, E and A

Ex. 21.3 *L'amant jaloux* (4)
('I breathe only vengeance')

L'amant jaloux

* *i.e. Molto moderato in this context*

Ex. 21.4 (a) *L'amant jaloux* (4)
('He no longer knows what to say, he's no longer carried away, he groans, he sighs')

Ex. 21.4 (b) *Le nozze di Figaro* act 2 sc. 7 (Finale, bar 126)

major. Hales' demand for 'Musique à demi voix' (*sotto voce*) is translated into pizzicato strings. As many have noticed (Ex. 21.4) Mozart used exactly the same teasing rhythm as Grétry when his Susanna, not Cherubino, comes out of the Countess's closet. Grétry develops the moment of comic irony to thirty-five bars depicting Alonze's speechless amazement. Da Ponte and Mozart had the advantage that Susanna could be allowed to sing whereas Isabelle's identity must be concealed by means of a quick exit. Finally Alonze slides ignominiously off and the music moves into the joyful release of D major.

One of the great comic *coups* in the opera, and probably all eighteenth-century opera, is the offstage serenade in (8); impeccably placed, it epitomises the basic theme of jealousy. Nowhere had Grétry been able to exploit such pungent irony as in the duet section after the serenade. When Léonore and Alonze first appear in argument he gives them the passionate style of *Les mariages samnites*. It masks their true attachment, which shows through first in soaring G major phrases and, in due time, Alonze's request for forgiveness, delivered kneeling. At this moment of jealousy conquered the strained sound of offstage mandolines, two violins and cello waft in (Ex. 21.5).[7] His faith in her again shattered, Alonze prevents Léonore from discovering who the serenader might be, and Florival disappears into the night. The audience by now is keenly expecting the recriminations to come, but instead each character in turn maliciously recalls the other's earlier love-music while tremors in the orchestra suggest their faithless anger (Ex. 21.6). In the final hectic Allegro Grétry introduces the little 'imbroglio' motif in the orchestra that began and ended the overture.

Ex. 21.5 *L'amant jaloux* (8) Cf. Ex. 23.2
('Here is the time for our meeting')

Ex. 21.6 *L'amant jaloux* (8)
('Never could Léonore's heart [hide her emotions]')

Act 3 does not reach this splendid level of richness; the attention transfers to Isabelle and Florival. Her love is beautifully expressed in (9), 'O sweet night'. Upper strings are muted and the orchestration in general is important in creating an aural image of the Mediterranean warmth. When Florival appears, an artificially sectional form is heard in (10) (ABA'B'C), whereas the obvious thing would have been the love-duet we never hear. Grétry set it as a courtship ritual underpinned by French minuet style, intended to convey the concept of a 'tacit epithalamium' (i:322). Though probably too concise in the context of the general brevity of act 3, the duet can convince on its own terms.

Opera-goers are now familiar with the typically nineteenth-century ensemble in which successive characters enter with the same musical phrases that build up gradually in layers. An example is 'Oh! di qual sei tu vittima' in Bellini's *Norma*. Hales and Grétry anticipated this form in (11), taking the music into quite distant regions and working up considerable tension. Even Jacinthe originally entered with the 'challenge' music, but later in the course of pruning 'there was still something too much [so] I resolved to make [Jacinthe] arrive saying "que voulez-vous?"' (*Réf*:iii:262–3).

Key	Action
F to C	Alonze challenges Florival
C to G	Florival challenges Alonze
E minor	Lopez challenges both men
G to D to D minor	Florival defends the pavilion; the others betray rising anger
A minor	Jacinthe arrives
F	All call on Léonore: when she appears the music deflates rapidly

It is probably inevitable that an anticlimax is felt when we are denied what could easily have been a last section in F in more rapid tempo, as a quintet, playing on the diversity of reactions to Léonore, and her thoughts. Not even the brevity of the spoken linking dialogue afterwards provides compensation: for one thing (12) is in the drastically unrelated key of E major. For the modern listener the plan of (12) is difficult too because it is built simply as a *tableau*, though synthesised with the dénouement of the action and with the vaudeville verse structure. A further vaudeville-like piece in B major points the final moral against jealousy, sandwiched between a 6/8 ensemble proper, in E. Hales clearly was not willing to let music take responsibility beyond this, and Grétry cannot avoid the impression of pattern-making rather than character-making.

Casting back another's music in their teeth has been seen in (8), and functional recollection is again the ironic method used when Jacinthe's principal theme of (1) is brought back in (4). Actually, the moment is so brief and the context so active that only familiarity with the work or Grétry's *Mémoires* makes the recollection evident:

Vous qui rebutez les galans . . . is the motif of the aria *Qu'une fille de quinze ans* . . . it is a subtle way of reproaching the soubrette for her bad faith by adopting her own melody [*accens*]. (i:322)

Jacinthe is adamant in (1) that men are not part of her mistress's life. In (4), faced with the intrusion of a strange man obviously worried about his honour, Lopez cannot resist the tone of sarcasm: 'You who repel the gallants, solemn old matron of twenty', he says to her, using the same music. This recollection falls into the same category as that in *La fausse magie* but now, as happens in part of *Les mariages samnites*, one person's music is quoted by another.

Almost for the first time in Grétry's comedy there is a feeling of creative calculation in *L'amant jaloux*. It takes different forms, some already discussed. Grétry mentions the phenomenon obliquely, seeming to admit to personal increase in craft or skill attained at a cost of decreased spontaneity (i:307). He never lost the gift of spontaneous composition, completing the tragedy *Andromaque* in a month. Although he recognised the desirability of calculation he never ceased to be uneasy with it.

One manifestation was the rather obscure use of imitative figures. Unison bass phrases beginning (3) could be thought of as 'fateful wedding bells' or as *force majeure* (i:319). A very similar association in *Le Comte d'Albert* 'failed in the intention I had given it' (i:403). This concerned the quartet (4) sung by four men and depicting an exciting incident; Grétry used an oscillating tonic–supertonic bass to suggest the bells of a church offstage that the audience was supposed to remember as the destination of Countess d'Albert, herself nowhere in sight.

A happier use of calculation lay in the search for local colour. Grétry writes of the differing qualities of music in *L'amant jaloux* and *Les événements imprévus* using the word 'teinte' (tint, shade). It may be pertinent to remember that his wife and several friends of his were painters.

> *L'amant jaloux* has a sombre, impetuous character: there is nothing comparable in its successor. *L'amant jaloux* is set in Spain, the characters had to take on a Romantic tint inspired by the customs, nocturnal amours and the novels of that nation. (i:333)

Character in nationality determined the French minuet for Florival in (10). More calculated still was the use of the *Folia* bass in (6), though Grétry claimed that 'the reference was appreciated immediately'. Lopez is given a text in which he inveighs against marriage. To set this 'musical dictum' as he called it, the composer had recourse to a kind of pun that depended on local colour: the formula known as *Les folies d'Espagne* (Ex. 21.7). This bass-line, known at the time everywhere for its fifteenth- and sixteenth-century Iberian associations, was associated by Grétry with Corelli, i.e. the violin sonata Op. 5 no. 12 (i:324); but its use as the basis for song had occurred earlier in eighteenth-century Parisian opéra-comique.[8]

Ex. 21.7 *L'amant jaloux* (6)
('Marriage is a desire that once . . .')

As a technical innovation, special mention must be made of the endings of (9) and (11). These provided a bridging passage between the musical level and the spoken level, effectively forming an abbreviated 'melodrama'. In (9) the thematic connection between main aria and bridging passage was obtained by inverting material from the coda of the former, and transposing it. One intention of this bridge was doubtless to prevent audiences laughing too much at Florival's appearance over the wall, and maintain the tone of Isabelle's anxiety. In the case of (11), whose bridging link ends on the dominant chord, the purpose was to dissipate tension rapidly while still respecting the imminent need for explanations.

Bridging passages were to become much used at the end of the century, as were melodramas. Winton Dean has described Méhul's use of them in *Mélidore et Phrosine* as 'psychological transitions' and illustrated their experimental chromatic modulations.[9]

VERSIONS AND PERFORMANCES

Three stages of evolution were preserved for posterity: the Versailles libretto,[10] the early Duchesne librettos[11] and the printed score. Changes were made between

Versailles and Paris, and between 23 December and the second Paris performance on 9 January 1779. Instead of (5) Léonore sang at Versailles a 'demi-character' piece (i:323), well suited to a response made in sorrow rather than anger to Alonze's jealousy. The new (5), composed out of complaisance to Mme Trial, was so criticised that it was shortened for the second Paris performance, according to the *Journal de Paris*. Jacinthe's spoken material now in act 2 sc. 9 was originally in act 2 sc. 13. Alonze had an aria in act 2 sc. 11, situated between (7) and (8), whose text in 1779 librettos may show it was not scrapped immediately. By showing Alonze's jealousy as a volitional trait it was presumably felt to be too unsympathetic a portrait, unworthy of Léonore's faith in him. We have already mentioned the curtailment of (11), also in the 1779 librettos in its full original form. But the most significant improvement was to the finale (8). At Versailles it began much more conventionally, and showed a far weaker Léonore. Léonore wept and asked Alonze to repent; but 'Jamais le cœur de Léonore' was sung first not by him, but by her. In the 1779 librettos Léonore is on the attack, and there is music from the beginning instead of speeches and an obbligato recitative.

L'amant jaloux had an outstandingly successful performance history. The total of 150 performances in the ten years 1779–88 was exceeded by equivalent totals only in the cases of *Lucile* and *L'épreuve villageoise*. In the decade 1789–98 there were 94 performances, and these continued without a break into the new century: in fact the first year in which it was *not* seen was 1821. From 1799 to 1808 there were 52 performances, followed by 42 in the next ten years, and 27 in the ten after that. It was revived in 1850–1, when it was seen 24 times. Loewenberg's last mentioned foreign revival was at Liège (1930).

22. Les événements imprévus (Unforeseen events)

Comédie in 3 acts, in prose: *CC* 10
Libretto by Thomas Hales, known as d'Hèle. Dedicated to the Comte d'Artois.
First performed at Versailles, 11 November, 1779. First performed at the Comédie-
Italienne, 13 November 1779.
Printed full score, Paris, Houbaut, n.d. [1781] as Œuvre xvi.[1]
Dramatis personae: Mondor, a financier (b.)
Emilie, his daughter (s.)
Lisette, her maid (s.)
Philinte, in love with Emilie (t.)
René, Philinte's valet (b.)
The Marquis de Versac (t.)
La Fleur, his servant (t.)
The Comtesse de Belmont (s.)
Marton, her maid (s.)
The Commander, Belmont's uncle (b.)

Grétry and the growth of opéra-comique

ACT 1: A park, Mondor's château seen in the distance. Philinte, young and inexperienced, is too shy to confess his love for Emilie (aria 1)[2] even though his late father was a friend of Mondor. She is now being courted by the dubious Versac; René urges Philinte to be more positive. Versac (duet 2) now describes to Mondor how Emilie has accepted him, admitting however she told him with the eyes only, as is the current fashion. Mondor becomes convinced that only her confirmation is now needed; he goes, and La Fleur and his master discuss a certain countess whom Versac has seduced and then abandoned, using the name Philinte. It is clear that the Marquis only wants Emilie for her fortune. In the finale (3) Emilie is seen with all the characters we have met so far, and is cajoled into declaring her affections. She chooses Philinte, in spite of Versac's persuasiveness. But a letter is brought for Mondor: it is a warning that Philinte is a seducer, addressed from one Countess Belmont, calling herself his wife. Philinte appeals in vain to Emilie amid the general consternation.

ACT 2: A day or two later. A balcony of the château is seen, with an arbour below. After a short introduction (4a) Lisette enters, mortified by the calumny against Philinte, and sings sadly of the foibles of the age (4b). René enters: he and Lisette have always been close to each other, as well as devoted to their master and mistress, whom (duet 5) they hope to restore to happiness. Although Mondor has forbidden Emilie to see Philinte, Lisette thinks she can arrange an interview between them, using the balcony. Versac and La Fleur inform us that Philinte is already packing, as the wedding of Versac and Emilie has been arranged for the next day. Suddenly Belmont and Marton are seen approaching, obliging the Marquis to leave hurriedly. Marton is sent ahead while Belmont (obbligato recitative and aria 6) expresses the righteous fury of an abandoned woman. She tells Emilie she has come to warn against the Philinte by whom she has been ruined during the absence of her guardian uncle. As the women, with Marton and Lisette, express sympathy and pathos, Versac and La Fleur gloatingly comment on these objects of desire (sextet 7). The risk of Versac's exposure is now high and Mondor increases it unwittingly (aria 8) by announcing a plan: he has learnt of the proposed interview from the balcony and wants Versac and Belmont both to witness it, then to denounce Philinte. In a finale (9) Philinte converses with Emilie on the balcony: she still cannot quite reject him. Mondor overhears. Belmont and Marton come on to the balcony whereupon Versac and La Fleur come out of the arbour and take up positions beside Philinte and René. The Countess, ignoring the presence of the real Philinte, whom she has never seen before, denounces her ravisher. After an ensemble the four women go in, with Mondor. There is a closing section for the four men outside before they too leave separately.

ACT 3: Later that day. Scene as for act 1. After the entr'acte (10) La Fleur bemoans the complications caused by Belmont: he is tired of the life of seduction and intrigue (aria 11). The Commander arrives, orders his valet to fetch his pistols, and gives a letter to La Fleur addressed to Philinte which, when he has gone, La Fleur opens to reveal a challenge to a duel. But Versac, upon learning of this, decides that he has had enough of the whole deception and cannot go through with the wedding. He resolves to duel with the Commander himself. The cowardly La Fleur stays behind but René surprises him and threatens him also with a duel (duet 12) on behalf of Philinte. Two shots are heard: the Commander and Versac enter, the latter having fired into the air and unharmed besides. He confesses his sins, offering his hand to the Countess, but not revealing the use of a false name: he is accepted by the Commander, who goes to fetch his niece. Emilie and Lisette are seen, thinking that the real Philinte has duelled and been accepted, and wish only to get away and hide their sorrow. Versac reassures them and in the ensemble (13) all the other characters assemble, overhear this conversation, and realise the change of identity by the use of names: Versac is pleading on behalf of the real Philinte to Emilie. Everybody demands explanations, and Versac provides most of them. Belmont considers (in mitigation) that he did not kill her uncle when he might have taken the chance, and accepts Versac. The closing ensemble (14) simply anticipates future joy.

Les événements imprévus is remarkably unlike any previous Grétry opera. Its music makes grand obeisance to Italian comic opera; its plot adopts characteristics of Italian *dramma giocoso*; its main theme concerns villainy and the diminution of humane values. Its style is melodramatic in the pejorative sense, for Hales puts behind him all the classical elegance and wit of his two preceding librettos. We have been thrust into the final stages of the culture of the *ancien régime* and the world of compulsive seduction where (in fiction) there need not be divine retribution, as in Da Ponte's *Don Giovanni* (1787). Real life was too proximate: the art of the period was compelled to respond with moral equivocation. The very name of the central male figure proclaims his parasitical social position, for 'In France he who wills it is a marquis, and whoever arrives in Paris from the depths of a province with money to spend and a name ending with "ac" or "ille" can proclaim, "a man such as myself, a man of my quality"' (Voltaire).[3] A new vocabulary became lacquered with double meanings. The erotic arts, as in *Les liaisons dangereuses* (1782) could be patterned into fictional yet recognisable forms, in which the figure of the immoralist was placed in the centre of the stage while virtue was left on the sidelines.

So, were Valmont the victim of impetuous passions . . . I should pity him, waiting in silence . . . But Valmont is not a man of that sort: his conduct is the outcome of his principles. He knows exactly how far a man may carry villainy without danger to himself, and, so that he can be cruel and vicious with impunity, he chooses women for his victims. I shall not stop to count the number he has seduced: but how many has he not ruined?[4]

The Marquis de Sade was coming to public notice at the period of our opera, since he was imprisoned at Vincennes from February 1777 and tried at Aix the next year. He was interviewed by Le Noir, the dedicatee of *L'amant jaloux*, in April 1780.[5] Like de Sade, Hales's Versac has had to make himself scarce in certain parts of the country where he would be in danger of questioning. For all their repellent uniqueness, de Sade's fictional characters had predecessors.

Hales, though, seems not to be trying to make Versac into a serious monster. He took the basis of his libretto from what Grimm called an 'old Italian canvas', *Di peggio in peggio*, so far untraced.[6] But he apparently also made his habitual alterations. Although almost unprincipled, Versac has about him a touch of the ridiculous owing to his exaggeration and inconsistency. No Valmont would have risked spending a night in the open simply to avoid a confrontation that would spoil his intrigue, as Versac does. Equally, however, Versac cannot be assumed merely to be a parody. He causes too much suffering and on two occasions his creator suggests that the age and society themselves share some responsibility for him, and produce victims. The deceived Emilie sings of this in (4):

Ah! In this century of ours, how can man be trusted? There is no more loyalty, nor good faith, nor probity. All is ruse and falsity, and the guiltiest are always, alas, the most attractive.

This is understood as a comment literally concerning Philinte but also, by extension, Versac. The second suggestion occurs during act 3 sc. 7 when, in repentant vein, Versac offers as excuses for his behaviour 'My stupid vanity and the example of a frivolous century'.

We shall see later how the plan and characters of *Les événements imprévus* resemble those of Italian comic opera. That Hales had departed too radically from French dramatic propriety was the view of Grimm and others, for 'he has been reproached for not distancing himself sufficiently from the manner and conventions of a genre to which our taste should never grow accustomed' (xii:341). Since the music, too, borrows heavily and untypically from Italy it was recognised at the time as a shaft directed at Piccinni in general and his Italian opera season in particular. After all, *Le jugement de Midas* used opéra-comique to parody other unwanted types of opera. For Piccinni had stolen something of Grétry's thunder in being made the chief opposition party to Gluck, and Brenet considered that Piccinni's adherents 'bestowed on him precisely the praises that Grétry counted on receiving'. The fact is highly significant that, unlike his colleagues, Grétry did not go and visit the Italian master.[7] It was all too ironic a reverse from the Roman days when he had literally sat at Piccinni's feet. The one comment Grétry makes about Italian opera in the chapter on *Les événements imprévus* is adversely critical (i:334): not surprisingly, Piccinni's name is absent.

Once again, as in *L'amant jaloux*, there are fewer musical numbers than in comparable earlier operas: twelve vocal items containing five solos, two finales and a couple of ensembles to conclude act 3. Overall the score contains no more emphasis than its predecessor upon the static or reflective: only (4) and (11) fall into this category. Rather, the composer contrasts the dignified idiom of Philinte, René and Lisette with motoric energy in the Italianate finales (3), (9) and (13). These are inspired, as it were, by the 'modern' and immoral influence of Versac. Philinte, Grétry stressed, is intended to reflect the old-world manners of his late father, a magistrate, and therefore (1) is given 'a nuance of old French melody': Ex.

Ex. 22.1 *Les événements imprévus* (1)
('How cruel it is to love and dare not speak to her for whom one lives')

22.1. The servants are brought to life not in a buffooning way, but in keeping with their riper years. (The dignity of the old servant Antoine in Sedaine's *Le philosophe sans le savoir* had been widely admired.) A variety of musical mood also distinguished *Les événements imprévus* and probably helped it to retain its popularity.[8]

The appoggiatura on chord IV (asterisked) gives Ex. 22.1 its 'traditionalism' and this is taken up in the duet of servants (5) by a stress on chord IVb. Meanwhile Lisette's nostalgia for a better world in (4) is suggested by suspensions and sequences typical of Baroque music (Ex. 22.2). Just as Lisette, the servant, has more solos than Emilie, so the character of René is more rounded out in music than that of Philinte. In the opening scene (1) is and remains the point of definition for

Ex. 22.2 *Les événements imprévus* (4b)
('In this century of ours how can men be trusted?')

Grétry and the growth of opéra-comique

Philinte: he has the help of no counter-plot. It is the servants that more than once prick the bubble of the opera's unbelievability. Unable to jolt Philinte into some rational declaration of love, René goes offstage with the phrase 'He's mad'. In act 3 sc. 8, when the odious Versac suddenly dilates on the general good he plans to bring everybody, La Fleur merely retorts, 'Better late than never'. When these two servants are brought together in the E minor duet (12) Grétry produces an excellently sardonic scene. As before, he adapted rondo form to contrive dramatic development: ABA' (cursory) C (in the major mode) A. René, his venom held in check by his years and breeding, dominates with understated irony. Details are nicely observed ('He shakes La Fleur's hand a little too strongly') and help restore the whole play to reality. The only musical expression of untainted affection in the opera is (5), an endearing scene where René and Lisette, brought together by an external crisis, discover deeper feelings for the first time.

By contrast the musical treatment of villain and victim demanded sharply diverse methods. Like Mozart's Don Giovanni, the Marquis has no full-scale aria, and he is given some genuine depth of harmony only in (13), when he unites Philinte and Emilie. Mostly he performs his machinations in spoken scenes or simply observes the progressive ramifications of his behaviour. Italians would certainly have given him the assertiveness of an aria, whereas Hales and Grétry can convince us perhaps the better of his change of heart in act 3. His lack of personal integrity is expressed brilliantly in (2): the purpose of this duet is to paint the philanderer. Ironically twisting the texture of 'expressive medium' in the orchestra, the composer makes Versac imitate the *supposedly* amorous tone of Emilie in their reported conversation. From what we shall know of Emilie we can be sure that her attempted seducer is manufacturing what she said or at least the way she said it: because the 'expressive medium' is in the minor mode here, whereas the genuine thing was invariably in the major, we intuitively understand his deception (Ex. 22.3). Once this is appreciated, the audience has even less respect for the credulity of Mondor.

The Countess Belmont, a figure typical of contemporary Italian opera, is granted a full-scale entrance scene. She was a character unprecedented in Grétry's

Ex. 22.3 *Les événements imprévus* (2)
('Ah, Marquis, said the girl, spare my blushes')

previous work but a type known to Parisians from Donna Stella in Paisiello's *La Frascatana* and Bélinde in *La colonie*: respectable women who obtain justice with the minimum of intrigue and provide the opportunity for impressive arias of serious emotion. Belmont's obbligato recitative (6) begins rhetorically, the strings in measured tremolando, then reveals an emotional tenderness barely beneath the surface, as she is struck by the beauty of nature surrounding her. Grétry keeps her main aria, in AA' form, to compact proportions, yet allows the singer to sound both energetic and noble, the voice rising to high c'''.

Where villains and victims are juxtaposed in (7), however, the result is yet more noteworthy. This sextet uses Grétry's favoured G minor and an appropriate harmonic anguish but also, as Grimm noticed, the '[adaptation of] Italian melody to the character and genius of our language' (xii:342). Nowhere had Grétry yet exploited vicious irony. The women begin with a kind of funereal lament (Ex. 22.4) but as the music moves to the relative major the Marquis starts to comment on how ravishing the Countess looks. The men's efforts to remain quiet and hidden are interposed to produce a cynical comedy. This part resolves ambiguously with an Italianate 'beating of hearts' section: our first glimpse, outside humorous contexts, of the total subordination of French word-setting to rhythmically even syllables. Shall we laugh or cry? The answer is provided in the climax, designed with considerable pathos, and using the diminished seventh chord: a rare, uncompromising picture of sexual exploitation.

Ex. 22.4 *Les événements imprévus* (7)
('Ah, pity the sad fate of an abandoned lover')

The finales of *Les événements imprévus* are not directly in the tradition of *Le Magnifique* or *Le jugement de Midas*: in the two latter the succession of events is rapid but coherent and the characters generally utter with prominent truth to their own personality. In the former these precepts are relaxed where Grétry appears to adopt a specific 'local colour'. For example, at the opening of (3), Emilie is being asked to make – in public – a crucial decision (Ex. 22.5). Apart from the basic

Ex. 22.5 *Les événements imprévus* (3)
('You must speak, disclose to him the secret of your soul')

inconsequentiality we feel here, and the shock of syllabic repetition, we have too little background knowledge to allow us to believe that Emilie and Philinte would be quite so reticent. The Marquis, however, goes on his knees to beg for her hand: this is the clue to the musical idiom, since Grétry associates his energy with the unreasoning assertion of the music and the use of Ex. 22.5 at several junctures; the musical style becomes a paradigm of the falsity of the occasion. This finale is 377 bars long: its two central sections follow the events on stage with the formal freedom we expect.

Key	Tempo	Action
C to D to (B minor) to A to D	2/2 Allegretto	Emilie cajoled; Philinte's reticence; new urging; Emilie's description of the chosen partner.
G to D	3/4 Larghetto	Marquis kneels, proposes; Emilie chooses Philinte.
	2/4 Andantino	Marquis's humiliation; arrival of the letter.
C to G minor to D minor	2/2 Come prima	General excitement; Mondor reads the letter aloud; Philinte is condemned.
C	2/4 Allegro assai	All oppose Philinte, who appeals fruitlessly to Emilie.

Whereas the third section does not at all neglect the anguish of Mondor, the final one reverts to *opera buffa* style, all six singers holding forth so energetically that Philinte has no chance of halting the proceedings. We accept the spectacle simply because this is an opera, musically overwhelming with pedal-points, artificially hushed voices, thrilling sequences of triplets and so on. It is in the light of this that we shall listen to Ex. 22.2, its simple appeal for traditional values of language and manners; and we recall act 1 sc. 2 where Mondor is shown the changes in social manners among the young with the abandonment of word and reason:

Marquis: Her mouth! Come, come. To be understood does one make use of one's mouth?
Mondor: But that used to be good enough.
Marquis: Yes, Monsieur, it used to be, it was until recently, but we have changed all that; one look, one glance is enough for us.

The dramatic handling of the finale (9), in spite of its being rewritten after criticism, is still more reliant upon the suspension of our disbelief. The misunderstood accusations of Belmont, the confusion of action and motive, are faithfully echoed in buffooning music like that in Ex. 22.5. Yet this same finale contains some of the opera's most tellingly memorable phrases. In a section when they are apparently alone Emilie and Philinte reveal both their hidden trust and their pain: the chromatic underlining of Emilie's questions is a fine revelation of her constancy.

The closing ensembles (13) and (14) are relatively perfunctory, with 94 and 102 bars respectively: the latter will be mentioned in the next chapter.

The score of *Les événements imprévus* reveals curious ultramontane details in addition to those in its finales. There are pointers to performance practice such as 'sans respirer' (do not breathe) over the cadential pause leading to the reprise in (1), and 'lentement le point d'orgue' (slow at the pedal-point) at the final cadence of (11). There are mock-Italian expletives as in the third section of (3) where 'Ciel!' counterfeits the typical 'Si!'. The *Mercure de France* drew the connection with the Italian opera season of 1778–9, which will be discussed in a moment: 'This new composition seems to have been written with the idea of battling or coming to terms with the genre of Italian authors whose comic operas are being performed at the Académie Royale de Musique' (20 November 1779).

Actually, Parisian taste for genuine Italian *buffo* was long established. For more than a generation, the Comédie-Italienne had borrowed from Italy, as had the Opéra-Comique up to 1762. There were translated adaptations ('parodies') of whole works, like *Baiocco et Serpilla* (1753) and *Bertholde à la ville* (1754); there were operas including only some music parodied from Italian, like *Le jaloux corrigé* and *La coquette trompée* (1753).[9] Pergolesi's *La serva padrona*, modified as *La servante maîtresse*, was first seen at the Comédie-Italienne in 1754. Since 1762 it had been acted once every two months on average. Piccinni's celebrated *La Cecchina ossia la buona figliuola* was played from June 1771 in French as *La bonne fille* equally as often. Enormous interest was shown in Sacchini's comedy *La colonie* (originally *L'isola d'amore*): the company gave it from August 1775 with thirty-five performances before the end of that year and regular showings thereafter. Yet other titles were *Le duel comique*, less successful in 1776, *L'inconnue persécutée* and *Pomponin*. In some 'Réflexions' in 1777 the *Journal de Musique* urged the establishment of a true Italian opera in Paris, on the lines of that in London: of performances of the genuine article including *opera seria*, rather than the mixed styles of performance which 'recall sea ports or large fairs where strangers of all nations gather.'[10]

The operas themselves became 'mixed', for great was Parisian sensitivity to the observation of dramatic coherence. *La bonne fille* underwent 'considerable changes to make the intrigue more regular and the situations more realistic'.[11] The published score of *La colonie* has a preface explaining how the translator, N. E. Framery, had felt bound to improve both plot and motivation. He apologises that nothing, even so, could eliminate all the 'vices of structure, entries and exits badly motivated, the *longueurs'* and so on. Even when the Théâtre de Monsieur began mounting Italian opera, its *raison d'être*, in 1789, it was necessary to adapt the librettos of those given in French, to achieve 'that simplicity of plot which we regard as one of the first dramatic proprieties' (Grimm:xv:389).

On the last day of 1776 Piccinni arrived in Paris, began work on *Roland* (successfully mounted at the Opéra in 1778) and was then commissioned by its new director, A. P. J. de Vismes du Valgay, to organise an extended season of Italian comic opera. This policy of throwing open the Opéra's doors indicates precisely that need to diversify in response to taste which the Comédie-Italienne had been fairly well able to meet. De Vismes admitted in 1778 that new works were urgently required since 'The revolution that [Gluck's] new music has produced has recently annihilated the immense repertory possessed by the Académie.'[12] Of Grétry's rôle in de Vismes' plans, and their aftermath, more will be said in chapters 25–6. The Italian company of Caribaldi all but saturated Paris with comic operas from June 1778 to autumn 1779: fourteen works, one each month except February and March 1779, by five masters: Piccinni himself, Anfossi, Paisiello, Sacchini and Traetta. Most of their operas were less than six years old and one, Piccinni's *Le fat méprisé*, a complete novelty. But the Parisians voted with their feet and generally stayed at home. Caribaldi made a derisory profit.

While only a few of the fourteen works can be studied *in extenso*, some conclusions suggest themselves. A superb melodist such as Paisiello made an inevitable impact: *Le due contesse*, fifteen performances, *La Frascatana*, eleven performances. Parisian indifference sprang not from want of curiosity but because too few people understood Italian (according to Grimm:xv:389) and, 'as the newspapers inform us, [because of] the insipidity of inept librettos, whose vacuousness could only shock' Parisian taste.[13] Especially by contrast with opéra-comique, *opera buffa* allowed ridiculous inconsequentialities, neglect of characterisation and reliance on stereotypes. The settings, sometimes unusual or topical (an island; a besieged town) remained in the dramatic background. Affections were not tested so much as asserted, poured out like wine, and enjoyed. Credulity was strained or broken in the chain-finales, apropos which Grétry commented that 'you commonly see very long finales where, against a minimal accompaniment, a young girl of fifteen and an old man of eighty sing the same thing' (i:334). De Vismes' advertisement of his forthcoming season might have turned to ashes in his mouth: 'One will find there . . . those sublime finales which usually express moments of disorder and transport'.[14]

It is worth comparing *Les événements imprévus* with *La Frascatana* (*The Girl from Frascati*). There is a 'serious' pair of lovers, the Cavaliere and his abandoned Donna Stella.[15] Comic rôles include Violante (the Frascatana), her grotesque tutor Fabrizio, and the shepherd Nardone with whom Violante falls in love at the beginning. The Cavaliere is hoping to seduce Violante; Donna Stella arrives in pursuit. Fabrizio abducts the Frascatana in act 2, shutting her in a ruined tower next to his mysteriously windowless house. She is rescued by a complicated plan involving substitution, thereby also evading the Cavaliere's henchmen. In act 3 the Cavaliere goes back to Stella and Fabrizio goes back to good food. Endless dramatic blind alleys are introduced and finales 1 and 2 are based on confusing confrontation. A surprising ingredient is the 'Gothick' tower and its atmosphere of horror. The way that scaring tactics are used in darkness against Fabrizio anticipates features not used in opéra-comique until the 1790s.[16] But a list of comparative elements would include the following:

La Frascatana (F. Livigni, 1774)	*Les événements imprévus* (T. Hales, 1779)
Cavaliere forsakes betrothed for Violante	Marquis forsakes betrothed for Emilie
Forsaken woman arrives and gains general sympathy	The same
Natural affection of Violante and Nardone constant although under threat	Declared affection of Emilie and Philinte undermined but never in doubt
Use of a balcony in finales 1 and 2 to facilitate misunderstandings	Use of a balcony in finale 2 for the same purpose
Violante briefly misled by Fabrizio into believing Nardone is married	Emilie strongly misled by Marquis' actions into believing Philinte is unfaithful
Signs of upright morality in Cavaliere's servant Pagnotta (act 1 sc. 4)	Repentant speeches by Marquis' servant La Fleur
Cavaliere resolves matters by change of heart not *force majeure*	Marquis resolves matters by change of heart as much as by *force majeure*

Hales imagined his characters on a similar social plane, whereas the normal Italian pattern mixed different classes; Monvel and presumably other French librettists had however already used the idea of interaction (see chapter 27). Nevertheless in both the above works the profligate central figure holds most of the dramatic strings, even vulgarly echoing the magnanimity of *opera seria* princes in doing the honourable thing in the end and standing down. In going to hell, one might say, Da Ponte's Don Giovanni clearly seals the fall of that particular aspect of the Old Régime.

VERSIONS AND PERFORMANCES

Les événements imprévus received thirteen performances during November and December 1779. It was then withdrawn until 12 October 1780, after which in a revised version it stayed in the repertory with success. All the changes, which were radical, concerned acts 2 and 3. Apart from text modifications in act 2 sc. 2 and sc. 4 the authors substituted (6) for an earlier aria and substituted (7) for an earlier quartet of women picked out for criticism in the *Mercure de France*. The 1779 act 2 finale had commenced before (8); it contained severe dramatic handicaps. Philinte and Emilie did not have any sympathetic communication; the Marquis was trying to keep Philinte offstage out of the Countess' sight. After the Countess' denunciation of Versac, slight suspicion from Mondor that she was not addressing Philinte (as indeed she was not) was explained away as 'delirium'. On recovering she denounced 'Philinte' by name; the real Philinte declared he did not know her; these cross-purposes were presumably hidden by the general hubbub.

In act 3 scenes 1 and 2 were transposed and (11) added. The original finale was longer but looks potentially to have been more satisfactory only in setting Versac's plea for forgiveness to music. It was less satisfactory in showing a distraught Philinte and then having Mondor enter with the suggestion that he marry the Countess; to explain this red herring the spectator has to recall that confusion of names is still operating, and that Mondor believes the duel was fought between the real Philinte and the Commander. The 1780 version dramatises the confusion of names without asking us to remember too many details. If, as is likely, Grétry used some 1779 music in 1780, he might well have taken the 6/8 solo 'Philinte vous adore' in (13) from the original appeal by the Marquis to both women, 'Soyez à lui, belle Emilie'. The mood and prosody of the latter words perhaps fit better.

In the years 1779–88 the opera was seen no fewer than 123 times, but its popularity lessened in the next decade to a total of 67 performances. It was revived in 1801, achieving 73 performances in the ten years to 1810. The twelve years to the last night in 1823 represented a slow death, but still totalling 48 performances in all. The final foreign revival noted by Loewenberg was in Stockholm (1800).

23. The overture (II)

The years 1773–9 embrace a group of opéras-comiques of extreme diversity. Their overtures, equally diverse, leave us in no doubt that Grétry developed into one of the most interesting composers ever to concern himself with such things. During this time, if we ignore *Matroco*, he wrote eight overtures. Whereas in the first group we considered, there was a roughly even balance (four to three) between three- and one-movement pieces, now all except *Le Magnifique* and *La fausse magie* are single movements. This allowed Grétry to tighten the bond between overture and parent opera. In all other respects it is impossible to generalise: style, form, links with operas themselves were all constantly thought out afresh.

In the matter of tonality Grétry remained conservative. Five of the eight works are in D major, with *Le jugement de Midas* in C major and *Aucassin et Nicolette* in D minor. (In the excerpt of *Matroco*'s overture (i:291) the tonality of D minor is contradicted by the absence of any key-signature.) The overture to *Le Magnifique* does not obey the usual laws of form, style or tonality: it starts in G and ends in E major. This important piece is described in chapter 13. *Le Magnifique* and *Le jugement de Midas* (chapter 20) are the only overtures of this period requiring mime, and whose connections with the parent opera were to that extent palpable. Both are relevant to much later scenes and acts. The distinctive oboe theme of the latter represents the pastoral landscape at dawn, but at the end of the opera it exemplifies modern opéra-comique style, and that of Grétry in particular. And repetition of parts of the *Le Magnifique* overture after act 1 and at the end wrap the whole work in the mantle of the Magnifico's generosity.

The three movements of the *La fausse magie* overture, if traditional, are not mere tokens. The main theme of the opening could almost be by Hérold or Auber, while the final movement is a crazy 'Musette, Presto' that uses quite individual orchestral colours.[1] Restrained as he was in orchestrating vocal movements, at least at this stage, Grétry was showing waxing interest in his overtures and entr'actes in the exploitation of both new textures and harder instrumental passagework.

In *La Rosière de Salency* the connections between overture and opera are both literal and programmatic, in the sense that the overture suggests a crisis that is resolved. Yet it begins as a merry string of themes approximating tonally to a sonata form (cf. *Les deux avares*). The second of the themes will be heard as the 'Simphonie' in act 3 (19) announcing the procession of the rose-maiden. The 'development' section, which presents the sixth and seventh themes, emerges as the pre-echo of shocks to come. Its climax is a sustained four-bar diminished seventh chord. That the following recapitulation also 'resolves' the concealed crisis is felt when Grétry adds a joyous new descant to the first subject, using oboe and horns. Obviously the whole thing owes a debt to *Le déserteur*, briefly mentioned in chapter 11.

With the neo-classical *Les mariages samnites*, first heard three years later, there could be no pot-pourri overture. The form is sonata, the style hard-edged and concise. Trumpets were used for the first time since *Le Magnifique*, but in a rhetorical quality. The exciting string writing surprises us most: the bass-line receives a rare prominence (cf. the opening of *Alceste*) and upper strings respond dramatically in block chords (Ex. 23.1). Subtle permeation of the music with a special motif that is afterwards associated with the heroism of Agathis has been discussed on pp. 146–7. Grétry enshrined the central moral concern of the opera within the fabric of the abstract music preceding it. Again, comparison with *Alceste* is tempting, Gluck having made the oracle's music integral to that

Ex. 23.1 *Les mariages samnites*, overture

overture. But his oracular music is not heard after act 1; Grétry's integration is the more thoroughgoing.

The overture to *L'amant jaloux*, at first sight simply witty and urbane, once again conceals hidden meanings. It begins and ends with an epigrammatic motif stemming from the last section of act 2; here the imbroglio is at its height, and if anything it signifies 'confusion worse confounded'. But there are more certain prognostications. The overture's sonata form breaks off after the second subject and becomes an Andantino in D minor, Ex. 23.2; we hear an oboe theme hauntingly 'felt to be played in the distance' (composer's note), as though a film camera had suddenly switched its lens. This is actually a transformed anticipation of the act 2 offstage serenade. The first part is quite different, and the metre is now 2/4 not 3/8, but the words can still be made to fit, a subtlety to which Grétry himself drew attention (i:311). The second part is a syncopated preview of the equivalent part of the serenade, Ex. 21.5. Grétry seems to have been inspired, as in *Le Huron*, by the notion of acoustic distortion through physical space. Unfortunately he does not explain the significance of the difficult viola countermelody. Between the twin stanzas of the overture's 'ghost' serenade, a juddering diminished seventh chord alerts the unwary to the extra-musical dimension of the episode. No better example of Grétry's economy exists than the fact that when the real serenade is performed, Léonore's attempt between its stanzas to discover the singer is mimed without any music.

Of the overture to *Les événements imprévus* there is less to say, if no less to enjoy. An introductory section in 2/2 is succeeded by a simple ABA' structure. But the

Ex. 23.2 *L'amant jaloux*, overture, central section. Cf. Ex. 21.5
The score directs that the music should sound as though played in the distance.

The overture (II)

remarkable thing is that this ABA' almost literally recurs as the final chorus of the opera. Reflecting the heady atmosphere of the score in general, Grétry requires the solo piccolo to hold forth all through and indeed the central section, of seventy-two bars, is entirely occupied by this instrument, with occasional flute, backed by merest wisps of strings. This compares with the thirty-three-bar episode in the overture to Paisiello's *La Frascatana*, scored just for upper strings (Ex. 23.3). Grétry's coda guys the Italian crescendo, too.

Ex. 23.3 (a) *Les événements imprévus*, overture

Ex. 23.3 (b) *La Frascatana*, overture

Nobody today could hear the overture to *Aucassin et Nicolette* and, as the composer intended, 'step back by a century'. But we would certainly be aware of two 'gothic' themes that appear, the first unharmonised except for a pedal D, the second bereft of harmony (Ex. 23.4). These can be distinguished from the kind of music Grétry would have composed for Graeco-Roman antiquity, since he believed that the Greéks did exploit 'the delights of harmony'.[2] Incidentally, such 'gothic' music seems to have been remembered by J. F. Le Sueur when he came to write his 'Songs of Selma' evoking the fourth century A.D. in the opera *Ossian ou les bardes* (1804).[3] However, the musical impact of this overture is really dominated by a primitive kind of violence. Sedaine wanted the overture to represent the sound of battle between the counts Bongars and Beaucaire, so that the action of the

Ex. 23.4 (a,b) *Aucassin et Nicolette*, overture

Grétry and the growth of opéra-comique

story, as in *Le Magnifique*, might begin from the first page of score. Grétry
therefore devised pounding paragraphs that are something like the eighteenth-
century equivalent of Stravinsky (Ex. 23.5). The next astonishing invention,
nowhere implied by Sedaine's libretto as we know it, introduced the singing voice
of Beaucaire into the overture itself. (In retrospect, the connection with the
L'amant jaloux overture is logical.) He calls the name of his son Aucassin twice,
from offstage. The curtain is down so that the surprise is all the greater. The first
call is in bar 24 after a *fortissimo* climax on the dominant, and the second comes after
the first twenty-four bars have been repeated. The sonata form works its way
through, and roughly at the juncture where we expect Beaucaire to be heard again
in the recapitulation, the curtain rises: but all we see is Aucassin alone, listlessly
dreaming of Nicolette. The music flows without interruption into sc. 1 – this was
new in Grétry – modulating its tone for Aucassin's beautiful apostrophe to his
absent lover. When this has been sung, Beaucaire enters.

The *Aucassin* overture, in its fury, its suggestion of prancing horses, looks
forward across the decades to Wagner and *Die Walküre*. Of Grétry's immediate
successors only Méhul dared to develop this music's modernity when, in the
overture *Uthal* (1806), he brought in the voice of Malvina at the height of his
storm-music, itself Wagnerian in sound if not orchestral strength.

Ex. 23.5 *Aucassin et Nicolette*, overture, opening

24. Aucassin et Nicolette ou les mœurs du bon vieux temps (Aucassin and Nicolette or the customs of the good old days)

Comédie in 3 acts, in verse: *CC* 32
Libretto by Michel-Jean Sedaine. Dedicated to the Duchesse de Grammont.[1]
First performed at Versailles, 30 December 1779. First performed at the Comédie-Italienne, 3 January 1780.
Printed full score, Paris, Houbaut; Lyon, Castaud, n.d. [1782] as Œuvre xx.
Dramatis personae: Count Garins de Beaucaire (b.)
                      Aucassin, his son (t.)
                      Vicomte de Beaucaire (t.)
                      Nicolette, his ward (s.)
                      Count Bongars de Valence (b.)
                      A shepherd (b.)
                      Marcou (t.) and Bredau (b.), guards
                      Officers, soldiers, members of Garins' retinue.

ACT 1: The guards' hall in the castle of Garins at Beaucaire, during the thirteenth century. The overture describes the latest battle between the rivals Bongars and Garins. The latter's voice is heard calling his son's name, but when the curtain rises Aucassin is seen languishing alone. The music continues into his solo and thence as Garins enters to the duet (1),[2] in which father summons son to fight. Aucassin dreams only of Nicolette. Since Bongars is gaining the upper hand, Aucassin agrees to defend the castle provided that his father allows him to see Nicolette once more and for the last time, for they have been prevented from associating. Garins agrees, Aucassin arms for combat (aria 2) and leaves. But the father immediately rescinds his decision (aria 3), for he cannot accept Nicolette's unknown parentage. He summons the Vicomte, who describes Nicolette's attractiveness (aria 4). When she arrives, Garins asks her to reject Aucassin voluntarily, but she explains this would be a useless deception and asks to be placed in 'some holy retreat' (aria 5). Aucassin's victory is heard (offstage chorus 6) and Nicolette is despatched to a secret chamber in the tower. Garins sings of his own victory (aria 7). Bongars and his men are brought in captive, but when Garins goes back on his word Aucassin releases Bongars and makes him swear to continue the war against his father. Bongars is sent off armed and in the ensemble (8) Garins has Aucassin seized and imprisoned.

ACT 2: After the entr'acte (9) we see an inner courtyard fortified with towers, portcullises and drawbridges. Marcou and Bredau patrol in different directions. After the introduction (10a) Aucassin's voice bewails the loss of Nicolette from a tower. In the ensemble (10b) the guards chat about his supposed offence, hear his voice again, then see Nicolette escaping from her prison down an improvised rope. They retreat to watch. She enters, exhausted, hears Aucassin's voice and tells him of her escape and her love for him; she tries to reach his window. Bredau takes pity on her by 'improvising' a warning song (11). She flees. After a fruitless search Garins and the Vicomte conclude she will find only death in the surrounding forests, and release Aucassin. The Vicomte sympathises with him, but Aucassin (aria 12) reaffirms his commitment to love. A shepherd brings a cryptic message signifying Nicolette is waiting in the forest. The drawbridge being unexpectedly lowered for the arrival of Bongars in peace, Aucassin escapes. In the finale (13) it transpires that Nicolette is Bongars' daughter: he had assumed that she was deliberately abducted. It becomes imperative to find the couple.

ACT 3: Entr'acte (14). A forest; Nicolette, alone, is still for the most part confident (aria 15). She hides as the shepherd enters, carrying Aucassin's shield and lance; he wonders what to do with the gold he has been rewarded with (aria 16). Aucassin enters and is reunited with Nicolette. She urges him to obey Garins since her love is unworthy but he pleads otherwise, even suggesting their double death (duet 17). But already they have been surrounded. The final ensemble (18) shows Aucassin ready to commit suicide rather than yield, but after rapid explanations the lovers are restored and the chorus celebrates their devotion.

To attempt an opera on this subject was perhaps the most ambitious artistic decision Grétry took. It signalled a return to subject-matter requiring to be taken seriously when even this preparatory step was liable to meet censure. The following critique was published only months after *Aucassin et Nicolette*'s première:

This work [Sacchini's *Olympiade*] is of the heroic type; consequently it is of that number which the Comédiens Italiens ought to banish from their theatre. We have often repeated it, but without effect. The habit of playing opéra-comique of the low or pastoral type can but seriously harm the nobility of the necessary means for the presentation of works of an elevated type. The rustic simplicity of Blaise or Mathurin cannot prepare their actor for the dignity suitable to a knight or king. (*Mercure de France*, 20 May 1780, pp.134–5)

For his part, Sedaine had recently become interested in mediaeval subjects and produced *Raimond V, Comte de Toulouse* in 1778. Though a satire directed at the unjust treatment he felt he was receiving from the Gentlemen of the Bedchamber, this play contained a fair number of archaic references, and we have it on Grimm's authority that he and Sedaine went looking for mediaeval pictures in the royal library in February 1779.[3] Here too Sedaine probably looked at the manuscript of the original Aucassin fable, dating from the thirteenth century and possibly containing Moorish and Byzantine influences.[4] For he had been asked to dramatise it by its editor, the remarkable historian Jean-Baptiste de La Curne de Sainte-Palaye.[5] The latter's anonymous translation of 1756 as *Les amours du bon vieux tems*, issued again in 1760, recommended to the public the 'authentic picture of our ancient customs' and 'naiveté of emotions'. Sainte-Palaye carefully described how the manuscript is divided into sections alternately designed for recitation and song.

He supposed that the twenty-one lyric interludes were performed by a group of minstrels, and Sedaine eventually took over parts of them for setting in the opera. While the poetic sections were more freely modernised, the editor 'scrupulously rendered' the dialogue and, unlike some of his successors, did not omit parts of the story which might have been found odd or uncongenial.[6]

Aucassin et Nicolette is a strange and powerful fable, whose apparent simplicity of means focuses on each detail, and whose details in turn contribute to the impression of a parable as much as an entertainment. Its relentless pursuit of passion, involving the rejection of parental ties and authority, places it closer to the story of Tristan and Yseult than most eighteenth-century opera plots. Perhaps its touches of the supernatural bring it closer to myth, as indeed do the elemental things narrated. The first part of the fable is the same as the opera, except for the vital difference that Nicolette is known to have been bought as an infant by the Vicomte from passing Saracens. She is imprisoned by the Vicomte, not Garins. After her presumed death in the forest Garins gives a feast to distract Aucassin, but the latter goes to the forest himself, receives Nicolette's cryptic message, and fails to find her. After he has given charity to a giant-like drover he discovers Nicolette during the night. She cures him of a broken arm; they escape on horseback. Crossing the sea they reach Torelore, where Aucassin rouses the king, who claims to be in labour, from his bed; his wife has been leading the army. On the battlefield, where apples and eggs are the weapons, Aucassin learns not to kill. Three years later Torelore is sacked by Saracens and the lovers separated. Nicolette reaches Carthage, which she recognises as her country, and is eventually united with Aucassin in Beaucaire, of which he is now master after his parents' death.

The fable might be taken as an allegory of every son's relation with his family, of the acquisition of wisdom. Aucassin's love is at first almost impersonal in its selfish intensity; but he returns to lead his community and Nicolette's identity is guaranteed. Such themes gave the adaptor the cruel task of encompassing a world that was morally alien and also a perfect construct in its own right. Sedaine's original four-act version was closer to the fable than the final one, but it still 'legitimised' Nicolette's birth. (Legitimacy was a sensitive issue; even Tom Jones had to be legitimised in Philidor's opéra-comique.[7]) This basic weakness apart, everything that could show fidelity to the source seems to have been considered. Qualities of tone and language were made especially close to Sainte-Palaye. Bredau's warning song (11) is almost exactly transferred from the sentinel's equivalent lyric. In act 3 sc. 5 Aucassin has a couplet originally spoken when the lovers escape on horseback: 'Que m'importe où nous irons, Puisqu'ensemble nous allons? ('What matter where we go, Since we shall go together?'). Types of imagery were borrowed:

Nicolette fleur de lis	Simple, naïve et joliette
Douce amie au clair vis	Nicolette est la fleur des champs
Plus êtes douce que raisin	Les lys vous paraîtront moins blancs
Et que soupe en vin.	Si vous regardies Nicolette.
(Sainte-Palaye, p. 27)	(Sedaine, (4))

191

The use of a negative construction by the librettist here nicely echoes a ubiquitous trait of the original, as seen when Aucassin goes at first dreamily into battle.

Think not that he dreams of taking oxen, cows, goats, or that he delivers any blow to the knights, or that he receives the same: by no means, so far did he take no account of them, but so dreamed of Nicolette his sweet friend (*sa douce amie*) that he forgot to hold his reins.

'Sa douce amie' was not only adopted by Sedaine in his last scene, but taken up by Grétry, who gave it a 'gothic' musical setting, as he called it (i:336), both in (18) and – without the sanction of the printed libretto – in (1) as well.[8] It is illustrated in Ex. 24.1, complete with parallel fifths.

Ex. 24.1 *Aucassin et Nicolette* (1)
('Gentle hope of my life, Nicolette my gentle friend')

To some extent Sedaine could adopt his own archaisms like 'guerdon' in (8) which he footnotes as 'recompense'. A greater problem for the audience was the decision to use verse, and Grimm's opinion appears trustworthy: 'The excess of verses, slovenly as these are, often makes the style of dialogue slack and diffuse and above all has lost him the pure and touching naiveté of the original model' (xii:364). In *Richard Cœur-de-lion* Sedaine kept to prose. And there was another, if local, distortion, in that the shepherd seems conceived as a semi-comic rôle. In the original the shepherds' grudging attitude towards Aucassin is more to the point.

The dramatic sweep of act 1 is good, though it attracted Wichmann's unanswerable judgement that it was 'a dramatic implausibility'.[9] However, the revisions of acts 2 and 3 and the conflation of their essential actions led to yet more unlikely juxtaposition: the release of the hero, the arrival of Bongars, and that of the shepherd. Grimm remembered in 1782 that the old third act had been 'unworthily played', but it seems true nevertheless that this opera was an artistic casualty of public taste: that is, to be tolerated only in a less plausible version because the action went quicker,

and today [rapidity] is the greatest merit that one may possess in the eyes of a public bored by so many masterpieces of vaudeville, of pantomime, of the trestle-stage jugglers. Impatience, so to speak, is the first emotion that one takes to the theatre. (xiii:65)

The music of the opera was composed in an upsurge of new ideas; we are in the presence of a musician who is quite sure of his way. As in earlier four-act canvases there is the sense of seriousness and variety, tempered by a little comedy in (16): as Grétry put it, no one will thank the artist for mere truth, if he does not also please (i:336). *Aucassin et Nicolette* is not to be considered a trial run for *Richard Cœur-de-lion*; it is a complete, fine musical object, mainly vitiated by problems concerning drama. For example, little chance was given the composer to write ensembles except in the final numbers of each act where, however, the hero and heroine are either absent or in positions of dramatic negativity. The whole disposition was as follows:

Solos	Duets	Trios	Ensembles
Aucassin (2), (12)	Aucassin, Garins (1)	None	(8) with male chorus
Garins (3), (7)	Bredau, Marcou (10)		(13) with four-part chorus
Vicomte (4)	Aucassin, Nicolette (17)		(18) with four-part chorus
Nicolette (5), (15)			Offstage brief acclamation (6)
Bredau (11)			
Shepherd (16)			

It shows the same attention to ancillary characters that became more pronounced still in *Richard Cœur-de-lion*; paradoxically, however, the later work conceals such characters better in ensemble work. The main characters develop more, musically speaking, in *Aucassin et Nicolette* than those in *Richard Cœur-de-lion*, the focus coming with the third act duet.

The strength of act 1 is worth describing. The violent visions of the overture give way to a paragraph of the purest Grétryan truth: oblivious of everything around him Aucassin has a meditative arioso of thirteen bars. Never, until the end, will he again be permitted to think or sing about Nicolette in these idyllic terms (Ex. 24.2). The yearning of the note B sharp at the end is echoed subsequently in

Ex. 24.2 *Aucassin et Nicolette* (1)
('Nicolette, my Nicolette, no, I shall never forget you')

the score where thoughts are associated with Nicolette. Garins then appears but this does little to promote a dialogue in (1). Aucassin is by turns reflective and angry, and the reflective music is the 'old-fashioned melody for gothic words', Ex. 24.1,[10] achieved as elsewhere in the score by sequential 6–3 chords and non-directional harmony. The 6–4 chord is not resolved classically but passes to chord vi, in turn imparting a modal tint. At the opposite pole, his anger betrays instrumental and harmonic colours of the Romantic era, introverted instead of rhetorical (Ex. 24.3).

Ex. 24.3 *Aucassin et Nicolette* (1)
('I should only want victory')

Numbers (2) and (3), separated by only four lines, have to be considered together. Brass and drums in C major depict Aucassin's authority or resolve, which we must project onto the offstage combat. There is no repetition of music, and he leaves after stentorian calls. But (3) plunges into a black prelude, connected with (2) in harmony, showing the dangerous, brooding father. A high E flat in the voice clashes thrillingly against the strings' F sharp, shown in Ex. 24.4. It is an uncommon example of arioso, fuller than an obbligato recitative, and looks to the nineteenth century in consequence of its declamatory style and heightened orchestral content. Grétry keeps the conventional following Allegro to twenty-three bars, decisively fixing his dishonourable 'No, you will never see her more'.

Before we see Nicolette we picture her through the strange simplicity of (4) which, though there is no evidence that he knew it, brings to mind Berlioz' *chanson gothique* 'Le roi de Thulé'. Grétry imports grace-notes, stresses the flat seventh and dominant minor chord, and hints at 'early' canonic counterpoint. But Nicolette's own (5) has the expressive palette of modern music; in fact it ends in F minor, although properly in the major, after a passionate eruption of chromatic phrases.

Ex. 24.4 *Aucassin et Nicolette* (3)
('Insensate son, did you think I would approve of your affection?')

That she is a far more interesting character than Garins is suggested by the vast octave and a half's sweep of her opening line; in fact it is regrettable that Garins afterwards has such a prolonged aria of triumph in (7), particularly as the dramatist has given us too little background knowledge to understand the scale of his feeling. Act 1 comes rapidly to its head in dialogue with the releasing of Bongars, leaving Grétry to exploit our sympathy for Aucassin in (8) by building up the opposition of the officers (to Garins) from a tiny three-line hint in Sedaine. It is strongly developed in contrapuntal conflict so that Garins is compelled to assert authority by shouting 'Obey!' The orchestra sums up the accumulated injustice in the depressing and uncommon key of E flat minor, as the hero is led manacled away.

If there is evidence of the authors' having succumbed to the gothic-picturesque, it would surely be the way Nicolette is treated in act 2. Although this is 'her' part of the story, she is denied any music to sing. The original fable shows her courage in escaping from the tower, in entering the castle of Beaucaire, finding Aucassin and then escaping by hacking footholds out of the dry moat. Sedaine could have given her an entrance aria and still kept his cherished sentinels' duet, which is really an animated counterpart to the stage scenery. The duet (10b) is of course intriguing and clever: one again thinks of Berlioz, since the sentinels in *Les Troyens* patrol and sing and stop occasionally in identical fashion.[11] If the arioso in (3) was evidence of the composer's continuing desire to break the formal moulds of opéra-comique, then (10b) is even better proof of it: an audacious mixture of three levels of action in which four actors participate, only two of whom are visible.

Key	Tempo	Action
D major	4/4 [Andante con moto]	The guards patrol, pausing to chat (Ex. 24.5); Aucassin's singing voice joins with plaintive phrases.
D minor	2/4 Somewhat faster	Excited motifs accompany the reactions of the sentinels observing Nicolette's descent. A climax as she is understood to have reached safety coincides with Tristanesque calls from Aucassin.
D major		Bredau is moved to pity; with 'strength and emotion' he asserts 'they are made for one another', which focuses the episode prior to a coda for orchestra.

Ex. 24.5 *Aucassin et Nicolette* (10b)

Bredau's warning (11), using fewer musical archaisms than (4), still adopts not only Sainte-Palaye's words but also his poetic organisation in the vocal line, i.e. AA', BB', CC', DD', EE'. It is memorable, to the point, and a good close to the better half of the act. In comparison, Aucassin's monologue (12) is problematic; he 'cannot live' and the voice-line is to be sung quietly, but the music seems simply too heroic and confident. And whereas the finale (13) begins excellently with the device of some officers discussing the revelations concerning Nicolette, the musical scene between Garins and Bongars is curious. What is under discussion is the cause of years of misunderstanding and enmity. But the fathers cannot manage more than a bad-tempered series of repetitions and cadences, while the chorus urges that Nicolette is in danger.

Act 3, too, stands by its splendid music for the lovers, not that for their elders. Nicolette in (15) receives a perfectly etched solo of simple, concentrated beauty. While Ex. 24.6 can show how this blends with the 'archaic' tint of 6–3 chords, it cannot give the extent to which orchestral detail was lavished on the accompaniment, especially in the horn part. The words, but not the music, of the opening are repeated; and symmetry is also avoided in the duet (17). It employs C minor, not in an orthodox way but to convey a delicate acquaintance with death. Nicolette's opening 'Content your father, let me die' omits a routine bass-line. Instead, bassoons and cellos alone play a pathetic countermelody, like a stunted avowal. And Grétry ends this unique piece sombrely in the home key, uninterested in sentimental exploitation. The musical resolution, C major, comes in the finale (18), where trumpets serve to extinguish our misgivings and force home the only sentence that matters: 'Nicolette est sa fille!'

We mentioned earlier the more original first part of (18), where functional recollection occurs. The lovers hardly utter at all, and the chorus is withheld for twenty bars. Aucassin's 'gothic' phrase and Nicolette's reply to it (Ex. 24.1) recur from (1), though now in C, and it is important that the whole entity is brought back: melody, harmony, principal orchestration details. By this means Grétry

Ex. 24.6 *Aucassin et Nicolette* (15)
('Alone and in this wild place, Heavens! what shall become of me?')

underlines the proper theme of the fable, for the subtitle to its 1756 edition was 'One loves no longer as in time past'.

More mundane is the functional recollection of the patrolling music from (10) in the course of (13), heard as the same two guards 'begin walking' back to their posts just before the entrance of Bongars.

A looser association of motifs connects (13) with (18). The unifying motif that opens and closes (13) is transformed in (18) and finally verbalised at the words 'Long live the loves of Aucassin and Nicolette!'

On pp. 143 and 172 we used the term 'local colour', and at this point it is probably as well to provide a musical use of that phrase. It was written in 1788 about the mediaeval subject of Dalayrac's opéra-comique, *Sargines*, discussed in chapter 32.

Since M. Monvel's drama offers a great variety of tones and characters, M. Dalayrac likewise varied his expression in the different pieces to be set to music, and he has always seized, with as much thought as skill, what we shall call the local colour of each of them.[12]

The 'gothic revival' is often thought of as more English and German than French: Walpole and his circle at Strawberry Hill up to 1785, and the enthusiastic essays of Goethe and Herder from 1773.[13] England and Germany identified the appeal of 'gothic' architecture in terms of national artefacts and history, opposed as such to the strong classicising of the French tradition. Yet in France the painstaking scholarship and antiquarian interest of the mid-century on was devoted to the Gallic language, customs and indeed music of the Middle Ages. This was all, eventually, grist to the mill as far as opera was concerned, in a way that research into architecture could only partly be. We shall see in chapter 28 how French research fed into *Richard Cœur-de-lion* in a surprisingly thoroughgoing way.

An interesting paradox, in Lennart Breitholtz' view, was that opera in France, specifically Lully's *Amadis*, *Roland* and *Armide* (1684–6), 'ordinarily the genre least concerned with the real world, was the first to attempt something redolent of historical "local colour" '.[14] This was particularly due to the sets. In the spoken theatre French history already ceased to be treated in an exclusively classical manner after Voltaire's *Tancrède* in 1760. In the same year actors of the Comédie-Française attempted fifteenth-century Genoese costumes,[15] and the Opéra had a set painted after Piranesi's *Carceri* for Rameau's *Dardanus*. A year later, when *Armide* was staged there, a critic deplored that Renaud and his knights were not in the dress of the crusades, but in costumes mixed between Greek, Roman and oriental.[16] As a result of such revivalist thought, the first representative opera became *Adèle de Ponthieu* (1772), music by La Borde and Berton, whose preface explained its desire to 'see on stage the pomp and respectable employment of the chivalric without any admixture of the supernatural'. Certain of its details were authenticated through the research of Sainte-Palaye, while the story itself was a simple one of love, honour and paternal authority. Later revivals became associated with contemporary nationalism, and this strand of development naturally connected with Rosoi's ideal of a 'theatre of history'. Promisingly, its music caused some problems of comprehension: 'a chaotic tangle, where all the modes are confounded'.[17]

At the Comédie-Italienne a simple taste for gothic detail went hand in hand with ambitious dramatic scale in *La fée Urgèle* (1765) by Duni and Favart. 'The production, besides, was decorated very well and dressed in the costume of the time in which the action is supposed to happen' (the seventh century), said the *Mercure de France*. The reviewer particularly mentioned the court of love in act 3 'presided over by Queen Berthe and attended by troubadours', though the latter are not specified in the libretto. This did contain mention of La Hire's upper armour and his knightly master's helmet, with linguistic archaisms like *bachelette* (adolescent girl), *grabat* (pallet) and *courtine* (curtain). Queen Berthe herself appears in act 1 attended by falconers. Musical archaism made a much more tentative appearance in act 3, in the Romance sung by the Old Woman. Ex. 24.7 shows its restricted accompaniment and the avoidance of G sharp, the leading-note; but for more comprehensive examples we must wait until chapter 28.

La fée Urgèle, a fairy-story, hinges on the supernatural. *Aucassin et Nicolette* avoids it. By 1779 the popular theatre had moved into the gothic revival, merely emphasising Sedaine's austerity of handling and avoidance of nationalism. In spite of the publication of Sainte-Palaye's material in 1774 as *Histoire littéraire des troubadours* and Legrand D'Aussy's *Fabliaux ou contes du XIIe et du XIIIe siècle* in 1779, Sedaine's and Grétry's local colour, even the parts the authors considered 'most affecting' (i:337) was met with resistance or laughter. But Sedaine refused to bow to this reaction. Like Rosoi, he insisted on publishing his unaltered text rather than that as heard on stage 'because [the former] seemed necessary to me. The directors of provincial theatres will have recourse to the published score to know

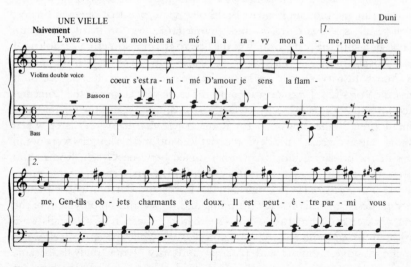

Ex. 24.7 *La fée Urgèle*, act 3, Romance
('Have you seen him, my beloved, he has ravished my soul')

Aucassin et Nicolette

what was withdrawn at subsequent performances.'[18] Like Pezay, Sedaine kicked against the circumstances wherein ill-prepared audiences forced changes in an hour to material conceived and executed over weeks and months. 'Thus I think that an author should adopt only with much circumspection the changes that the public's reaction seems to prescribe at the first performance.' His avowed aim was fidelity to the morals and characters of the original fable, though not without considering Paris' 'disdainful delicacy'. After the work's revision, however, even the Parisians liked the work's special quality. Perhaps this was in Rosoi's mind when he wrote a preface somewhat later in 1782 for Les mariages samnites:

Since this theatre [Comédie-Italienne] has extended the sphere of its efforts, people have been less surprised to see Heroic Works presented there. I shall not repeat here what I showed, to the point of obviousness, in my Dissertation sur le drame lyrique; time has proved the justice of my assertions. No genre is a stranger to this theatre, and there remain a thousand subjects which would succeed less well on the stage of the Comédie-Française or on that of the Opéra.[19]

VERSIONS AND PERFORMANCES

An equivocal reception and certain deficiencies of acting (especially in the part of Garins) caused the four-act Aucassin et Nicolette to be withdrawn after public performances on 3, 5 and 15 January 1780. Grimm reported that act 3 was least liked (xii:364). Even so, there was time to make dialogue changes between Versailles and Paris versions, and to add a concluding ballet.[20] The original act 2 ended in verse, Garins dishonourably claiming to Aucassin that Nicolette had run away with a young soldier. Act 3 was originally set during the feast in Garins' great hall, seen from the entrance. Aucassin had two arias, one becoming (12), met the shepherd, and slipped away. Bongars arrived and an old nurse, Eudelinde, gave evidence of how Nicolette came to be the ward of the Vicomte's wife. Aucassin's farewell message was found, and the search begun. The music contained a festive opening, two arias for the Vicomte, a march for Bongars, and a quartet for Garins, Bongars, Eudelinde and the Vicomte. The original act 4, with minor improvements, simply became the new act 3. In 1779–80 Garins' character was more relentlessly antagonistic towards Aucassin. The original text of (7) matched this attitude, as did Garins' insinuation that Nicolette practised magic (act 2 sc. 5). This antagonism and the feast, but not Eudelinde, were in keeping with the source.

In 1782 the necessary features of the old third act were incorporated with act 2, creating the juxtapositions discussed earlier. Even so, further cuts were necessary after the première on 16 January. Comparing printed librettos with the score, we find that as well as minor adjustments to dialogue, two arias were taken out of the second act. First was the Vicomte's 'Qui d'amour', giving advice to Aucassin, as in the source, to release his frustration in activity. Second was his aria 'Mais voyez donc' which led to the entrance of the officers: both were from the old third act. The loss of the first was sad amid so much spoken dialogue, but the transference of lines from 'Mais voyez donc' into the new second finale was a distinct gain.[21]

199

From 1782–1791 the work had 88 performances, with a further 11 in 1792–3. It was revived in 1802 with 48 performances to the end of 1810, and then 30 performances from 1812 to 1816. The final foreign production noted by Loewenberg was in Berne (1801).

25. Profile IV: Grétry at the Opéra

Illness continued to make its occasional inexorable demands. Grétry caught a chill in the winter of 1777 while journeying to perform at Fontainebleau.[1] But four years later illness brought him close to death, so that he wrote on New Year's day 1781 to the Italiens to ask them, in that final eventuality, to transfer his annuity to his wife. News of the illness was publicised in a poem addressed from Liège by Reynier, printed in the *Mercure de France* on 20 January: Caron refuses to let Grétry cross the Styx and orders him back to enchant the world with more music.[2] This ordeal perhaps reflects other fluctuations in fortune to which Grétry was now liable as a figure of some power, and a friend of princes. While it is true, for example, that as a musician who lived essentially by composing he did not live poorly, it was an event to be remembered when his brother-in-law Jacques Lacombe made business losses around the spring of 1778, was lent 30,000 *livres* by Grétry, and never repaid him.[3]

But pleasanter things were keeping Grétry busy. On 1 April of that year the young A. P. J. de Vismes du Valgay took over as director of the Paris Opéra. He must have favoured Grétry as an agent of change, for he opened his refurbished auditorium on 27 April with Grétry's *Les trois ages de l'opéra*: the 'ages' were depicted with music by Lully, Rameau and Gluck. This ran for an honourable eleven nights. Perhaps he even thought that Grétry should inaugurate a 'fourth age' with Piccinni, since he had already sanctioned the former's setting of *Andromaque*, after Racine. Although this was in advanced rehearsal by May, its performance was blocked by a dispute with the Comédie-Française (which held the acting monopoly of the play) until 6 June 1780. It then failed. This opera, completed in thirty days (i:355) probably counts as one of Grétry's most acute artistic frustrations because it was considered by him to represent a viable alternative to Gluck's style.

The text of *Andromaque* demands a profound sensibility which the too energetic Gluck could not command. It was in the hope of being superior to him in this respect, and wholly persuaded that I was inferior to him in strength, that I undertook this work.   (iii:87)

Grétry also completed a now-lost tragedy *Electre* in 1780 or the next year, which had been accepted by the Opéra but which was passed over in favour of Lemoyne's setting of 1782.[4] Piccinni's progress in *Roland*, to Marmontel's words (1778), and after, was viewed with chagrin by Grétry. This was compounded when *Andromaque* had to be withdrawn on 21 November 1780 and the third act

Profile IV: Grétry at the Opéra

refashioned. Grétry's illness may have had its psychological elements, not least in the realisation that he was not even in the field as official opposition to Gluck, whose masterpiece *Iphigénie en Tauride* appeared in 1779. For even in 1794, at the close of his final volume of *Mémoires* and in what he could reasonably have expected to be a parting message to posterity, he paired himself with Gluck: Gluck had learned from the German symphonists, he says, as he himself learned from the Italians in Rome. 'Gluck expressed in dramatic terms the harmonic effects with which he was imbued; I expressed the melodic tones of Italy that were suitable to the spirit of the French language. If we have both acquired some reputation, it is for having known how to profit from our models.' (iii:438)

Grétry's crisis also came after several years of continuous creative work, of which the following timetable is a conjecture, beginning after the watershed of *La fausse magie*.

1775–6	*Les mariages samnites*
1776–7	*Le jugement de Midas, Matroco, L'amant jaloux*
1777–8	*Andromaque, Les trois ages de l'opéra*
1778–9	*Les événements imprévus, Aucassin et Nicolette*
1780–1	*Electre, Emilie* (1–act miniature within Gardel's ballet *La fête de Mirza*: 22 February 1781)

After this, an eighteen-month absence of new works performed indicates the preparations for an event which, though de Vismes had by then left the scene, surely did constitute a 'fourth age' of opera. This event was the 1782–5 series of works by Grétry that abandoned tragedy for dance, spectacle, genre subjects, the oriental and comedy: *Colinette à la cour* (1 January 1782); *L'embarras des richesses* (26 November 1782); *La caravane du Caire* (30 October 1783); and *Panurge dans l'isle des lanternes* (25 January 1785). If de Vismes did not commission all of these he certainly laid the groundwork for them:

> To fulfil the first object [i.e. to satisfy the public], I believe I can do no better than to welcome all genres, and show no partiality in selecting them.
>
> (From an address to the Opéra staff, 10 December 1777)[5]

Grétry said:

> When I took lyric comedy on to the stage of the Opéra I was regarded as a reprehensible innovator.[6] However, I saw the public tired of endless tragedies. I heard the many enthusiasts of ballet grumble to see it reduced to a subsidiary, often useless rôle in tragedy. I saw the administration, in seeking variety, unsuccessfully take up fragments or old pastorals; I declared on all sides that two opposing genres had complementary attractions; that the Comédie-Française gave alternately tragedy and comedy . . . At last, these three works [and later *Panurge*], above all *La caravane*, given in a short space of time, determined public opinion on the need to establish lyric comedy at this theatre.   (i:360–1)

Musically, Grétry stayed true to himself in 'lyric comedy' by exploiting the forms and styles used in opéra-comique, but paying particular attention to the choral and balletic forces of the Opéra. Since the Comédie-Italienne was denied the right to play new Italian comic music in the 1780s (see chapter 26) Grétry's new pieces for the Opéra acted as a substitute for *opera buffa*. People were at first shocked, but soon learned to smile at this theatre. Almost obsessively, Grétry avoided complications of harmony in *Colinette à la cour*, instead emphasising colour and instrumentation, but in *La caravane du Caire* he drew on fuller resources and was rewarded by public approval amounting to a total of 506 performances (taking over one million *livres*) which were being given into the age of Berlioz. However, owing to the generally feeble handling of recitative and the poverty of the librettos, the one thing Grétry did not do was create a dramatic form to be taken seriously. The way forward in theatre on this scale required constructional powers of a different order. Later in the decade Grétry was involved in setting Sedaine's version of Molière's *Amphitryon*. It failed in 1786 at court and in 1788 at the Opéra.

In June 1782 the Opéra awarded Grétry an annuity of 1,000 *livres*; in March 1784 alone, he received 1,400 *livres* for *La caravane du Caire*;[7] after *Panurge* his annuity was raised to 2,000 *livres* and again to 3,000 *livres* in 1787. But this was only part of the new tide in his fortunes. Since 1771 he had benefited from an annuity for performances given in court, standing at 1,200 *livres*, the same as his concurrent annuity from the Comédie-Italienne.[8] In 1778 the royal annuity was fixed at 2,400 *livres* and in 1786 it was augmented to 6,000 *livres*.[9] That from the Comédie-Italienne also went up, to 1,800 *livres* in 1785, and two years later Grétry became an 'inspector' of this theatre, realising with it the status of a shareholder in the company with entitlement to its profits.[10] Added to this was the share of nightly takings at the box-office, divided with the librettist; even so, there was cause for complaint:

All my works are played throughout the year. No other musician has had as many works put in the repertory and played as frequently as mine are. My dues are therefore paid *pro rata* according to the number of performances. However the most that they have brought me did not equal half the income of a singer, that is ten thousand francs.[11]

Thus the mid-1780s must have seemed an ideal plateau from which to survey the world, as well as dictate to it; and by that time – in his early forties – Grétry seems to have been at work on the *Mémoires*. There was at first only one volume, published in 1789. The remaining two, written in 1790–4, were issued in 1797 together with a new edition of the first volume. Indeed, they may have been started before 1780 since, having described the adolescent onset of his blood-spitting and his remedial practices, the writer says, 'that is the system I have adopted, and I probably owe to it an existence upon which one must have counted little, twenty years ago' (i:24). So strong was Grétry's pleasure in writing that he was thereafter constantly engaged on one literary enterprise or another. After 1795 he began *De la vérité* (*On truth*), three volumes issued in 1801; and from then to his death he worked, often daily, on *Réflexions d'un solitaire*, sustaining himself with a mixture of memory, philosophy and details complementing his earlier works. His sense of pride at being the first modern French musician to leave a literary monument was considerable, notwithstanding the fact that this was a period of intense literary activity that saw, for example, Goldoni's memoirs issued in 1787. (Pride is perhaps the human weakness to which he most often returns in all his writings.) The

Profile iv: Grétry at the Opéra

Mémoires are not an exercise in imaginative self-projection. Like his music, they are clear, varied, amusing, limited. Only in parts of the *Réflexions* do we meet episodes of dream and fantasy, and this manuscript was not published until 1919–22.[12]

As a man of undoubted stature in Paris, Grétry's word and influence were sought in musical and personal affairs. Although he had the artistic support of his orchestra leader in furthering the aims of one Simon Cornu, a provincial violinist, Grétry did not scruple to accept Cornu's gift of twenty-five bottles of champagne.[13] In 1784 he intervened on behalf of Prince Ferdinand de Rohan-Guémenée, to whom he had been attached for some years, in the matter of the succession to the prince–bishopric of Liège.[14] An official post was found for him when a small stamp duty was planned for printed music in 1784–5: that of Royal Censor for music. Froidcourt comments, 'this post, created specifically for him, was a true sinecure' (p. 125). Grétry was thereafter able to certificate his approval, on what possible grounds one can only benevolently surmise, of Pleyel quartets, Haydn symphonies, Mozart chamber music and operas like Salieri's *Tarare*. Specimen certificates survive from between November 1786 and April 1789.[15]

Even Grétry's likeness was sought. Padre Martini requested a portrait in 1778, and was promised one painted by J. S. Barthelemy (unknown today). On 23 September 1780 the composer's bust, sculpted in white marble by Everard after Pajou, was installed with much ceremony in the Liège city theatre. Fabre d'Eglantine read his poem 'Le triomphe de Grétry'. Pajou's plaster model was in turn exhibited in the Paris salon of 1781, exciting admiration for its veracity, even to 'that burning fever' which, averred the *Mémoires secrets*, overtook him when he composed. A Paris street was named after him in 1780,[16] and in the same year Grétry sent a miniature portrait to his old friend Henri Hamal in Liège (illustrated in Froidcourt, p. 112). The more familiar oil by Elizabeth Vigée-Lebrun, now in the Musée de Versailles, was executed in 1785. Hamal's picture makes him into a powdered French courtier, while Vigée-Lebrun shows him as an enlightened human being, very simply attired and unbewigged, basking reposefully in the contemplation of his own genius. This oil was in turn made into engravings by L. J. Cathelin and by Riedel.

A brief but rapturous final return to Liège took place on 21–3 December 1782. The city burgomasters placed him in their midst at the theatre and the elderly prince–bishop de Velbruck was everywhere present to pay homage to his musician friend and 'conseiller intime'. Several of Grétry's operas were given, and poems and addresses were read. The architect Victor Louis accompanied the composer, and their return to Paris was made via another triumphant reception at Lille.[17] Liège's independence and identity as Grétry's fatherland were significant intertwined strands in his life and in dedicating the score of *L'embarras des richesses* to the magistrates of Liège in 1783, he wrote:

Tell [Liège] that the love I bear my fellow citizens was always the warmest emotion of my heart; that from the banks of the Seine where the bounties of a great king and the favour of an enlightened people have retained me, my arms reach always towards her; the object of

203

my work and of my wishes is to interest and please her, to prove to her how dear she is to me.

In return Liège gave Grétry its freedom, in the form of membership of the 'thirty-two trades'. In 1807 he wrote of his 'unique wish' to return to his birthplace but was unable through infirmity to go back there either then or in 1811 when the Place Grétry was inaugurated.

Obviously related to the still-unpublished *Mémoires* was an intention of Grétry's to issue a complete edition of his music. This would also have given him some financial protection over his earlier published scores. We know nothing more of this plan than the document discovered by Barry S. Brook: the royal *privilège* taken out on 19 June 1787 to 'faire graver ses œuvres complètes en musique'.[18]

Probably Grétry's greatest joys and sorrows were caused by his family. His second daughter, 'Lucile', composed a one-act opéra-comique which demands notice, first because it was quite a success and secondly because it forms a pendant to *Richard Cœur-de-lion*. *Le mariage d'Antonio* was produced in July 1786, the month of her fourteenth birthday. It attracted forty-six performances by spring 1791. The story portrays the return to his village of Antonio, Blondel's young guide. Gifts of gold from Blondel enable him to take Colette in marriage. That the librettist, Beaunoir, could graft a work on to the peripheral world glimpsed in (1) and (2) of *Richard Cœur-de-lion* was indeed testimony to Sedaine's imaginative command of detail. With typical flair for publicity Grétry seized the occasion to write a long letter to the *Journal de Paris* not just to say he had corrected and orchestrated his daughter's work, but to dilate on teaching in general. Her subsequent work *Toinette et Louis* (March 1787) had only one performance. One review referred to 'smutty jokes in some scenes' and Grétry shrouds the episode in obscurity (ii:407), connected with her unhappy marriage. But this belongs to our final chapter.

In an interesting section of her monograph, Michel Brenet discusses the fact that apart from Lucile, Grétry had only three pupils: Mlle Changran, later Mme de Bawr; young François-Joseph Darcis (1759–86) who was killed in a duel in Russia; and Caroline Wuiet (1766–1835) whose opéra-comique *L'heureuse erreur* (intended as a sequel to *L'épreuve villageoise*) was given a trial hearing at the Comédie-Italienne in 1786.[19] Letters to her show Grétry's warmth even after twenty years of separation.

The first shadows fell across his personal life with the death of his eldest daughter Andriette ('Jenny') in 1786 or 1787, aged sixteen. It was presumably brought about by tuberculosis. But Grétry, a successful parent wanting successful offspring, blamed himself for having forced her development in opposition to her inclinations (ii:399–403). Harsher lessons were to come.

PART THREE

26. Opéra-comique in the 1780s

Great strides had been made in opéra-comique since the advent of Grétry yet, as we saw in chapter 7, earlier masterpieces continued to be popular, so that the repertory gained a healthy coherence, even a classical one. The dramatic unities were preserved; between actors, writers and audience there was a continuing core, as it were, of moral presumption. If new popular theatres (see below) had established themselves shortly after Grétry's arrival, yet there remained a stratified stability between the levels of public entertainment. At the top stood the Opéra and the Comédie-Française; next came the Comédie-Italienne; below were the acrobats, child actors and marionettes at the fairs and the Boulevard du Temple. However, well before 1780 and in the next decade interlinked influences began to multiply between levels of the hierarchy. The Comédie-Italienne itself expanded, moved to a new theatre, and incurred large debts; the Opéra mounted spectacular and comic works, conspicuously those by Grétry; and public taste everywhere fastened on the melodramatic, the historical, the gothic and the exotic.

The growth of the Boulevard du Temple as a place of public enjoyment occurred after 1760. Partly this was owing to a need for such a site all the year round: the St-Germain fair, although centrally situated, only ran from 3 February until Palm Sunday, while the St-Laurent fair usually ran from 9 August until 29 September. The Temple area was spacious and possessed few houses.[1] The first theatre moved there in 1759 and in 1778 the boulevard was paved for the first time, so attracting a new class of client.[2] In the 1780s La Harpe wrote that 'There are at the moment seven theatres in Paris, and all are crowded . . . The little theatres have placed themselves on a level with the great ones. They poster new plays and count performances . . . it only remains for them to receive critical notice in the newspapers.'[3] Later, under the Consulate, the critic Geoffroy noted that Nicolet's and Audinot's companies 'were in the last years of the French monarchy theatres of respectable company and correct form'.[4] In the following summary, T denotes a theatre's situation on the Boulevard du Temple.

T J. B. Nicolet's company, founded by his father, active from 1759, presenting farcical plays etc. from 1764. Re-named *Les grands danseurs et sauteurs du Roi* in 1772 as a sign of royal patronage; as well as acrobats and mixed shows the playwright Beaunoir produced almost two hundred pantomimes and plays there (see p. 353 n. 10).

T N. M. Audinot's *Théâtre de l'Ambigu-Comique*, founded in 1769 as *Théâtre des comédiens de bois* (i.e. marionettes); gave pantomimes, vaudevilles etc. using child actors. By 1772 one of their shows (*Puss-in-boots*) had been seen by royal command at Choisy. Became the Parisians' favourite cheap theatre; chief writer was J. F. Arnould (Mussot).

T *Théâtre des Associés*, founded in 1774 by N. Vienne and L. G. Sallé, one of Nicolet's ex-actors; gave marionette plays, farces, comedies etc., also specialising in parodies of Comédie-Française successes.

Grétry and the growth of opéra-comique

T   *Variétés-Amusantes*: a small hall opened in 1777 by Lécluse de Thilloy, featuring young musicians and actors. Sold in 1784 and in 1785 moved by new owners Gaillard and Dorfeuil to the Palais-Royal, where a more sophisticated type of comedy now prevailed, by authors such as Dumaniant; now called *Variétés du Palais-Royal*.
Théâtre Beaujolais, opened in 1784 as 'Petits Comédiens de S.A.S. Monseigneur le Comte de Beaujolais' by Delomel and Gardeur at the northern corner of the Palais-Royal; it had been a private theatre. Specialised in comedy and opéra-comique using child actors who mimed to adult voices from the wings; composers who worked for it included Rigel, Chapelle and Piccinni *fils*.[5]

T   *Théâtre des Délassements-Comiques*, founded 1785; gave successful plays by its founder, A. L. P. Plancher-Valcour, and Ducray-Duminil but was subsequently restricted to pantomime, three actors at most on stage, and a gauze separating audience from players.

The various restrictions we have noted above, together with several others such as the permanent appearance of a tight-rope at Nicolet's enterprise, were all imposed by the institutions at the top of the cultural hierarchy, the Opéra and the Comédie-Française. They could also impose financial dues, and exercised the right not merely to vet their competitors' material, but to take ideas from it when they pleased. Looked at from the point of view of the Opéra, the Comédie-Française and the Comédie-Italienne, such controls were indispensable in maintaining great traditions and keeping together the box-office takings they needed; but from the point of view of the majority lacking the means to pay for tickets, it was an outworn system of privilege that prevented people from gaining access to fine theatrical works. Such was the attractiveness of the smaller theatres that in 1784 the Opéra obtained a royal decree giving it the right to license and exploit all of them. A running battle also raged between the Comédie-Française and its lesser rivals.

The Comédie-Italienne was caught between enforced submission to the Opéra and the competition from the popular theatres. On 19 July 1779 the *Journal de Paris* reported that the Italiens had not only augmented their *corps de ballet* but also hired a stage designer (*décorateur*) and a *Maître de ballets*, Auguste Hus. Soon new ballets were being added to repertory works, including *La fausse magie*, *Zémire et Azor* and *La Rosière de Salency*. An official report completed in 1779 drew attention to the financial burden to the company caused by the Italian actors, declining receipts and a lack of good new plays. As a result, the Italian repertory was dropped at the end of the 1779–80 season, leaving just its name to the theatre.[6] But in their stead French actors were reinstated. They had not been part of the company for ten years and indeed it would have been advantageous to it and the history of opéra-comique if something fresh had been done, and greater stress placed on the musical repertory. But the hegemony of the Opéra was asserted in a new thirty-year agreement with it dated 1 January 1780. Three of the provisions in particular must be mentioned: the giving of spoken plays twice a week; the ban on freshly-imported Italian music; and the constraints applied to the use of the chorus.

The presence of an acting troupe created at least two disadvantages: that of finding a good repertory overnight (since of course traditional successes were mostly the property of the Comédie-Française), and the burden of ten extra salaries to pay. While expediency dictated the mounting of L. S Mercier's plays (successes snatched from the boulevard theatres: *Jenneval*, *L'indigent*, *La brouette du vinaigrier*), by 1788 the company was apologising publicly for the 'unremarkable' merit of its recent authors.[7] Jealous of its audiences, the Opéra insisted on denying the Comédie-Italienne the sure success that new adaptations on the lines of Sacchini's *La colonie* would have, and made it promise 'in future not to make any use of Italian or other parodied music, accommodated to French words'.[8] In vain the smaller company argued on the grounds of 'the progress of good music in France and taste in general', grounds still being gloomily rehearsed ten years later by Framery, who added that singing style itself would have improved.[9] The ridiculous thing was that, as a critic in the *Mercure de France* lucidly said in 1787, the Opéra thereafter made no attempt to use its monopoly on Italian comedy; that as a result the capital was denuded of the best foreign operas; that people (the year before) had crowded to Versailles and Fontainebleau to catch Paisiello's *Le roi Théodore à Venise*; and that Italian *opera buffa* was anyway not suited to the Opéra, since its theatre was too large, its actors were unused to the necessary style, and such comedies were too long and lacked any ballets.[10] It is hardly surprising that the Théâtre de Monsieur (later Théâtre Feydeau) was founded in 1789 specifically to fill the gap. Ironically, Framery argued, even this new theatre was to exist in breach of that part of the 1780 agreement giving the Comédie-Italienne sole right to perform comic opera within a four-league radius.[11]

The Opéra tried to nip any growth of opéra-comique choral music in the bud. Article III began by forbidding the evolution of any chorus music that would give a new work the 'form' of (traditional) French or Italian opera; it continued by forbidding the means of realising this:

The Comédiens Italiens may not perform, or have performed, any ornamental chorus, but only ensemble pieces in several parts and performed by those taking part in the dialogue and other actors in the troupe united naturally and necessarily on stage by some incident in the action and not hired for choruses in the strict sense.

It graciously allowed current repertory works like *La Rosière de Salency* to continue to be seen, however, and concluded by attempting to define the limitations of style of future opéra-comique choruses:

they may even introduce extra persons in future plays in the same style [i.e. as *La Rosière*, *Le déserteur* etc.] in which the extra persons shall be necessarily introduced by the subject as in the above pieces and shall have as their purpose more the rendition of a tumultuous acclamation than a chorus in the strict sense.[12]

Nothing could restrain the public's liking for choral music, illicit though the pleasure might have been after the move to a larger theatre in 1783, when more extended choral scenes in, say, act 1 of Martini's *Le droit du seigneur* or Grétry's *Richard Cœur-de-lion* obviously went beyond a 'tumultuous acclamation'. In its old building the company had maintained no regular, separate choral body and choruses were performed by regular actors with two or three voices to a part. By 1786 it seems that a specifically choral subgroup of ten names was in existence with whom, as before, some of the regular actors would have performed.[13] The early history of the chorus was fraught with problems: the first (volunteer) chorus master could not maintain standards, odd copyists or dancers could receive permission to join the chorus ranks, and already in 1784 certain ladies of the chorus were disciplined for dereliction of duty and indecent comportment on stage! In 1788 the whole chorus was re-auditioned and a replacement trainer appointed; in that year Le Vacher de Charnois recorded:

The singing troupe is very numerous; the personnel crowd there uselessly one on another, and several of them would be absolutely without purpose if the mania for choruses had not been introduced at this theatre, where they are almost always out of place because they are always badly performed. There results from this considerable expense, on which pretext the acting troupe is denied that of which it has need.[14]

By 1790 there were fourteen regular chorus members, this number rising to thirty-five in 1795–6.

The Comédie-Italienne had always been awkwardly situated in the midst of narrow streets in the old Hôtel de Bourgogne, which required periodic repair and was too small for the stage effects in some newer operas. It had three tiers of boxes, a *parterre* and a gallery, and in 1781 was reckoned to hold a capacity audience of 1,528.[15] Plans crystallised for the construction of a new building, the Duc de Choiseul providing a site in his grounds off the rue de Richelieu. (The present Opéra-Comique stands near the same spot.) It was built for 300,000 *livres* and the first performance in it took place on 28 April 1783, in the Queen's presence. The work was Sedaine's and Grétry's *Thalie au nouveau théâtre*, a one-act occasional piece containing some vaudevilles. Sedaine's writing was found so lifeless that it was virtually booed, was never shown again, and is lost. The new theatre was found to have design faults in the front of house: these mistakes by J. F. Heurtier had to be rectified by C. de Wailly in 1784 at a cost of 80,000 *livres*.[16] After this alteration its capacity exceeded 2,000. The company paid off its building debts over ten years but it also had financial burdens additional to those mentioned earlier. These included the poor tax of 55,000 to 60,000 *livres* a year, and authors' royalties. Consequently the company only just covered its outgoings in 1783–4 and in the appalling winter of 1788–9 a loan of 50,000 *livres* was required to pay salaries. Other loans of 120,000 and 180,000 *livres* are recorded by Pougin for decorations, costumes and the pension fund over the same period.

More space in the pit allowed the expansion of the orchestra in 1783. The total size of the band since 1777 had been twenty-five, comprising twelve violins, two violas, three cellos, a double-bass, two upper woodwinds (oboe/flute), two bassoons and two horns. In May 1783 the total swelled to thirty-three, dropping to thirty-two in June. There were now thirteen regular violins, including the leader, two violas, five cellos, two double-basses, three upper woodwind and the usual two bassoons and two horns; two other violins and one cello were employed as relief players. However in May 1786 the number of pit violins was increased to sixteen, a figure maintained until 1790.[17] Several players doubled on different instruments; this is how the timpani part was managed. But when clarinettists and trumpeters

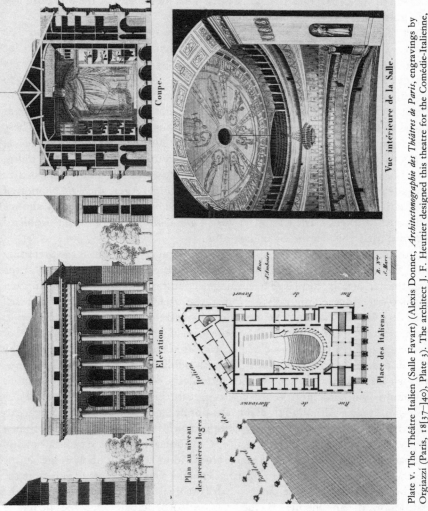

Plate v. The Théâtre Italien (Salle Favart) (Alexis Donnet, *Architectonographie des Théâtres de Paris*, engravings by Orgiazzi (Paris, 18[37–]40), Plate 3). The architect J. F. Heurtier designed this theatre for the Comédie-Italienne, opened in 1783. The main entrance faced south. After adjustments made in 1784 the capacity was around 2,000. The original interior was a marbled green, set off by much gilt decoration. Original plans at the Bibliothèque de l'Opéra reveal that (as was normal) resonating space was allowed under the orchestra pit. The *Mémoires secrets* of May 1783 judged the theatre 'quite favourable to the voice'.

were called for, the company often brought in players from outside. The total of five cellos was fairly high in relation to the violins by comparison with other European orchestras of similar constitution.[18] Unfortunately we do not know how far Grétry's own preferences were expressed in these facts, or simply Parisian taste. At any rate, in the *Reminiscences* of the widely-travelled singer Michael Kelly in 1787, 'my favourite theatre of all was the Théâtre Italien . . . the orchestra was very good, and the actors and singers equally so.'

Yet the orchestras of some smaller theatres were not of negligible size. The Théâtre Beaujolais, for example, employed eight violins, two violas, three cellos and a double-bass with double upper woodwind, bassoons and horns; by 1787 they even had a trumpeter and a timpanist.[19] When theatre yearbooks started to record their personnel (1790–1) the Ambigu-Comique orchestra had a total of seventeen players.[20] Music, after all, whatever its quality or provenance, was crucial to these theatres, especially in the ubiquitous genre of pantomime. These scores are regrettably no longer extant, but they must have had coherence, particularly when, by 1779, certain productions were staking considerable claims to be taken seriously. As they inevitably turned towards historical subjects they took advantage of the fashionable taste for the Middle Ages, and some notion of their activities will help illustrate the background against which Grétry and his colleagues worked, especially on *Richard Cœur-de-lion*, and the wider problems caused during this decade by competition.

Aucassin et Nicolette did not appear until December 1779 but in the preceding April Dubreuil's and Cambini's opéra-comique *Rose d'amour et Carloman*, at the same theatre, already displayed 'charming decorations. All the costume of ancient chivalry was observed there.'[21] (Carloman was Charlemagne's younger brother.) Then on 1 May the 'Petits Comédiens du Bois de Boulogne' gave *Le puits d'amour*; the music was by Philidor, probably in the form of simple songs, and the source of the play was the pseudo-gothic tale *Histoire amoureuse de Pierre le Long* (1765) by Billardon de Sauvigny. Philidor's songs as published in this show no sign of archaism. In August the same year the Ambigu-Comique staged a long-famous pantomime with an eighth-century setting featuring Charlemagne himself, *Les quatre fils Aymons*. Although this fable was purely legendary, Arnould's preface to the printed scenario ostentatiously cites his source book, stressing the production's accuracy. The bulk of the action – in four acts – consists of battles and combats set against the castle of Mantauban and its working drawbridge. In the fourth act the castle is set on fire and Charlemagne's nephew Roland falls from the drawbridge. However the action extols chivalric valour rather than the destruction of an enemy, as the Aymon sons actually get the better of Charlemagne. Also in 1779 Arnould gave *Jérusalem délivrée*, based on Tasso and naturally set in the same period.[22] And in October 1779 Nicolet's troupe gave *La prise de Grenade*, with further combats and military manoeuvres. It marked the beginning of this company's use of developed plots instead of traditional stories. Dialogue was used by them from February 1781 and by 1786–7 even verse dialogue had appeared![23]

Another well-known pantomime, *Dorothée*, was first seen at the Ambigu-Comique in 1782. It was a simple modernisation of motifs seen in such works as Sedaine's *Le roi et le fermier* but set in the 'troubadour' style. Dorothée's knightly husband is away and she is imprisoned by the local mayor when she rejects his advances; condemned to the stake, she is rescued by a valiant knight who fights for her. The piece is noteworthy not just for its cruelty and sentimentality (Dorothée has a child) but its elaborate prologue with five pages of scenario, ending with the reception of a young warrior into the company of knights: it is this young man who rescues the heroine. The paraphernalia of spectacle included a company of supporting actors and a gothic tower as Dorothée's prison.[24] With this may be compared the ruined tower in *La Frascatana* (1778: see p. 183) and those in act 2 of *Aucassin et Nicolette*. The same ideas were used in August 1781 at the Ambigu-Comique in *Pierre de Provence*, in which the knight's lover Maguelonne appeared at a grille-covered window of a tower, bewailing her fate.

References to historical accuracy, seen again in the preface to *Pierre de Provence*, were in no way isolated cases, but a general tendency perhaps occasioned by the abandonment of antique subjects, an anchorage in a world where 'confusion of genres' overturned accepted divisions. Now people were seeing not simply the usual 'downward' movement of themes and ideas from high theatre and culture, but also an 'upward' one. For example, in comedy, when *La musicomanie* was given at the Ambigu-Comique in 1779 it was 'servilely copied' for the Comédie-Italienne in a libretto by Grenier (1781), thereby furnishing the vehicle for the composer Champein's masterpiece, *La mélomanie*, revived as late as 1825.[25] Or for example in tragedy one could take Benda's melodrama *Ariadne auf Naxos*. This was played at the Comédie-Italienne in French, amid some publicity, on 20 July 1781. Although not very successful, in spite of extra musicians being hired for offstage effects, the subject was purloined by the Opéra and presented on 23 September 1782. The text was by Moline and the score by Edelmann.[26] Although recitative was used instead of the spoken word, its dramatic and musical techniques were obviously indebted to popular theatre, not least in orchestral colour and imagery.

The drift of taste towards the sensational and spectacular appears to have influenced a return in the later 1780s to a certain extravagance of costume at the Comédie-Italienne, to peasants with expensive coiffures or bonnets; moreover there was a readiness on the part of some to improvise in the dialogue of older opéras-comiques in order to attract easy laughter. The position was starkly summed up by Le Vacher de Charnois in 1788: 'Our modern productions are skeletons whose hideous constitution is concealed by musicians and scene-designers.'[27] The conditions for Revolutionary opéra-comique were created long before 1789; themes of rescue, imprisonment and combat were simply adapted to Revolutionary needs from what was there already, just as in music the use of rich, detailed or assertive orchestration in the 1790s forms an unbroken continuity with the 1780s.

We saw in chapter 7 how dominant Grétry's position was at the Théâtre Italien from 1771 to 1780. The picture for the succeeding decade is quite different as a

Grétry and the growth of opéra-comique

whole, but in effect Grétry's dominance was assailed, not destroyed. The overall figures for performance show that, just as in the earlier period, Grétry's opéras-comiques received about twice as many showings as those of the next composer, who was now Dalayrac, replacing Monsigny. The popularity of older works from the 1760s declined gracefully but most of them remained in the repertory even if given less often. However, a third group of works by new composers appeared, together with those of the persistent Dezède. As before, the first table does not include vaudeville comedies.

Table 6. *Total number of opéras-comiques publicly performed 1781–1790 inclusive, irrespective of number of acts*

Figures in brackets indicate the number of different operas constituting the relevant total.

Grétry	1,418 (24)	Champein:	212 (8)	Gossec:	78 (2)
Dalayrac:	703 (16)	Philidor:	208 (11)	Berton:	66 (5)
Monsigny:	374 (8)	Duni:	180 (8)	Rigel (Henri-Joseph):	40 (3)
Dezède:	323 (8)	Martini:	138 (3)		

Dalayrac's long and prolific career opened at the Comédie-Italienne in 1782 with *L'éclipse totale*. Most of his operas had the capacity to remain in the repertory and they included, apart from those in Table 8, *L'amant statue* (1785) and *Azémia* (1786). His energetic rate of production continued unabated into the next decade, when, inevitably, it was to overtake Grétry's, and when Dalayrac's works were to receive about twice as many performances as those of Grétry at the Comédie-Italienne.[28]

Monsigny and Gossec had ceased the composition of opéras-comiques in the 1780s, and Duni had died in 1775; Martini produced one publicly-performed work (see Table 8), others receiving only court performances. Philidor's final effort, *L'amour au village* (1785), disappeared after six nights. The initiative had passed to a new generation. Grétry, whose energies in this decade were not confined to opéra-comique, produced numerically only two-thirds of the number of new pieces in this genre that he had brought out in the previous ten years, and only half the number that Dalayrac brought out.

Table 7. *New opéras-comiques given publicly 1781–1790 inclusive*

Dalayrac:	16	Dezède:	5	Philidor:	1
Grétry:	8	Berton:	5	Martini:	1
Champein:	8	Rigel:	2		

As indicated in the next table, the ten most popular opéras-comiques by composers other than Grétry now contained six works originating from the decade in question. (This compares with a total of two new French opéras-comiques out of the thirteen works listed in Table 3a of chapter 7.) The best of the new more than matched the best of the first generation. Moreover the substantial total of ninety for *Les deux petits savoyards* was attained in only two years.

Table 8. *Most popular operas (excluding vaudeville pieces) other than Grétry's at the Comédie-Italienne 1781–1790 inclusive, irrespective of the number of acts*

Blaise et Babet (Dezède, 1783)	129	performances
La mélomanie (Champein, 1781)	108	
Le déserteur (Monsigny, 1769)	91	
Les deux petits savoyards (Dalayrac, 1789)	90	
Le droit du seigneur (Martini, 1783)	88	
Les trois fermiers (Dezède, 1777)	87	
Nina (Dalayrac, 1786)	86	
Félix (Monsigny, 1777)	86	
Les deux tuteurs (Dalayrac, 1784)	79	
La belle Arsène (Monsigny, 1775)	77	

The rise to popularity after a slow start of Monsigny and Sedaine's *Félix ou l'enfant trouvé* has often been remarked upon. Dezède's *Alexis et Justine*, listed below, was its composer's only other successful opéra-comique at the Comédie-Italienne; but *Blaise et Babet*, the sequel to *Les trois fermiers*, was enormously successful throughout the civilised world. Apart from *La mélomanie*, Champein's works at this theatre were all unsuccessful except *Les dettes* (1787) and, like Rigel, he wrote for the Théâtre Beaujolais: two works in 1783 and one each in 1786 and 1787.

Dalayrac's ability to attract interesting librettos in widely differing dramatic styles, and to set them well, makes him the only composer whom one can readily compare to Grétry or those who came before; some of his work will be discussed in chapter 32. It is only when the list of the next most popular works is examined that the composers Duni, Philidor, Gossec and Sacchini appear.

Table 9. *Next most popular operas (excluding vaudeville pieces) other than Grétry's at the Comédie-Italienne 1781–1790 inclusive, irrespective of the number of acts*

L'amant statue (Dalayrac, 1785)	74	performances
Alexis et Justine (Dezède, 1785)	72	
Les deux chasseurs (Duni, 1763)	72	
Le tonnelier (Gossec, 1765)	69	
La colonie (Sacchini, 1775)	68	
Rose et Colas (Monsigny, 1764)	66	
Les femmes vengées (Philidor, 1775)	64	
La dot (Dalayrac, 1785)	64	

The rarely-discussed *Les femmes vengées*, a lively comedy with text by Sedaine, is as unexpected here as the fact that it gained almost twice the number of performances of Philidor's next most popular work, *Le soldat magicien*. Less surprising is the decline in attractiveness of the *pasticcio* works *Isabelle et Gertrude* and *Annette et Lubin* (thirteen and fifty-nine performances respectively): compare Table 3a, chapter 7. The beginnings of Henri-Montan Berton's career must be mentioned, though his name has appeared only in Table 6, since he was later to achieve prominence as a composer and teacher. His *Les promesses de mariage* (1787) reached a respectable total of twenty-one performances. After a gap of time which saw the rapid rise of anticlericalism he wrote the popular *Les rigueurs du cloître* in 1790, in which the corrupt régime of an abbess is terminated by the intervention of the National Guard in the chorus, 'O liberté, déesse de la France'.[29]

Turning in conclusion to the picture presented by Grétry's output we find that, numerically speaking, individual works from his pen had no greater appeal than the most popular ones listed in Table 8; the huge total of Grétry performances in Table 6 was a function of the quantity and durability of his opéras-comiques overall. Furthermore, Table 10 reveals that only two works (actually the first two) were first performed during the decade in question: the rate at which Grétry issued really popular opéras-comiques – popular in Paris, that is – slowed to zero after *Richard Cœur-de-lion* even though no fewer than six of them were first staged between *Richard* and the end of 1790. Of these six the most popular was *Le Comte d'Albert*, with forty-eight performances.

Table 10. *Most popular opéras-comiques by Grétry 1781–1790 inclusive showing number of public performances in Paris*

L'épreuve villageoise	129	Silvain	83
Richard Cœur-de-lion	125	Le tableau parlant	83
L'amant jaloux	118	Aucassin et Nicolette	78
Les événements imprévus	112	La Rosière de Salency	76
La fausse magie	104	Zémire et Azor	75

Grétry's next most successful opéra-comique of the decade, *Les deux avares*, was less popular than any in Table 9: sixty-one performances. In non-revolutionary times *Richard Cœur-de-lion* would undoubtedly have had many more performances than the above number: its performance history will show that this work always fell out of favour at points of revolutionary crisis in Paris, even later in the nineteenth century.

27. L'épreuve villageoise (Trial in a village)

Opéra bouffon in 2 acts, in verse: *CC* 6
Libretto by P. J. B. Choudard, called Desforges. Dedicated to Mme de La Ferté.[1]
First performed at Versailles, 5 March 1784 and at the Comédie-Italienne, 18 March
  1784 as THEODORE ET PAULIN. First performed in revised form at the
  Comédie-Italienne, 24 June 1784.
Printed full score, Paris, Houbaut; Lyon, Castaud, n.d. [1784] as Œuvre xxiii.
Dramatis personae: Mme Hubert, wealthy farmer's widow (s.)
                     Denise, her daughter, aged 16 (s.)
                     André, fiancé of Denise (t.)
                     La France, a valet (bar.)
                     Chorus of peasants

ACT 1: A village close to Paris. The local château is in the background. Mme
Hubert's farmhouse is downstage left, with grassy banks and trees shading right.
Several cottages indicate the hamlet. It is about 7 a.m. in summer. La France is
causing concern since, having paid court to Mme Hubert for five years, he now
betrays signs of preferring Denise. Denise is angered by André's jealous attitude to
her. Mother and daughter will teach both men a lesson. In the couplets (1)[2] Denise
remembers meeting André three years ago: now she despairs of him. Mme Hubert
considers La France's advantages, chiefly pecuniary, while Denise deplores his
vanity. He arrives and obliquely confesses to Mme Hubert his change of heart
(duet 2), while she insists on marriage. In dialogue he confesses the truth. Mme
Hubert unexpectedly gives him permission to ask Denise's hand; he leaves
ecstatically. André approaches with a rose for Denise, but hides in the trees to
survey the house. She observes him (duet 3), uncovers him angrily, rejects him for
La France and packs him off. In the aria (4) she considers what fools lovers make of
themselves, but is no more confident of husbands. A large bouquet arrives,
obviously from La France, but as she pulls out its message she reveals she cannot
read. André has been lurking and now snatches the message, tearing it up as the
finale (5) begins. Denise is calmed only by La France, unperturbed by her illiteracy
and André's ridicule of it. He kneels before her; Mme Hubert comes in and, despite
André's appeals, decrees La France as the new betrothed. The chorus joins in to
summon all to the village festival.

ACT 2: Later the same day. After an entr'acte (6) Denise appears, exhausted by the
dancing and celebration (couplets 7). André has been eyeing the other girls. Mme
Hubert tells La France that her permission is official: all the village may be told.
Seemingly alone, he muses that all the women he has known find defeat before
Denise's attractive naturalness (aria 8). But she has heard his farewell to them.
André now decides to feign a cooling of relations, as well as a new attachment for
himself. He is very direct with La France and Denise prevents a quarrel. In a trio

(9) La France requests her hand. She prevaricates out of consideration for André's feelings: but André is strangely solicitous towards them. When La France has gone André pricks Denise's curiosity so much that he provokes outright jealousy. She realises she has been repaid in her own coin; they are reconciled (duet 10). Mme Hubert has a plan for La France's downfall. Sounds of revelry (11a) show him roistering with the villagers. In the final sequence (11b) the chorus comment on Denise's new partner. La France sings of the delights of the city to which he will introduce Denise – fashion, theatre, painting, the court – but all are rejected by the villagers in humorous responses. Finally La France's claims are publicly rejected when Denise quotes from (8), effectively blackening his character vis-à-vis Mme Hubert. There follow his exit, a vaudeville and an ensemble and chorus.

L'épreuve villageoise was a successful, escapist comedy but its parent opera *Théodore et Paulin* was one of a group of 'moral education' pieces set not in Marmontel's drawing-room surroundings but in a village with its great house. *Théodore et Paulin* itself is known only from a libretto, described in the last section of this chapter. But because of the social and political interest of its genre, some space will also be devoted to other works.

Both *L'épreuve villageoise* and *Théodore et Paulin*, though different entities, were new excursions for Grétry into *paysannerie*, the eighteenth-century term for make-believe village life. In those *paysanneries* where love interest was central the basic format was often that of Rousseau's *Le devin du village*, the celebrated recitative opera first seen in 1752 and staged in Paris for nearly eighty years. One partner rejects the other, flirts with a new and often socially superior one, discovers the incompatibilities, and is reunited with the first lover. The *status quo* is ruffled, but not damagingly so. We shall see in due course how far the later drama placed the established conventions as it were under threat.

Desforges (1746–1806) came from a bourgeois background. He had been an actor since 1769, performing and travelling with different troupes, and writing plays. His later success came with the plays *La femme jalouse* (1785) and *Le sourd* (1790). Grétry must have met him and his wife (who played Mme Hubert) through their employment at the Comédie-Italienne. *Théodore et Paulin* is Desforges' first known libretto; his three later ones were set by H. M. Berton and L. Jadin.[3] He embraced the Revolution and issued a pornographic 'autobiography'.

There are good reasons why *L'épreuve villageoise* was being revived a century after its opening night. It is a simple comedy but a very well paced one. Desforges' skill in humorous dialogue makes the two pivotal deception scenes for Denise and André extremely amusing: these occur after (3) and (9). All the characters save La France speak in rustic accents and slang, but this only isolates La France's character and pretensions, and makes his downfall more memorable. Yet the libretto engages our sympathy for him before the egg finally lands on his face. Whether or not he has been a philanderer he is quite in love with Denise, for his fatal solo (8) is all too obviously a weak moment of grandiloquence. Grétry shows that this valet apes his masters: the music, alone of any in the score, uses the static bass-line and conventional figurations, the 'high style' of some wooden prince in an *opera seria*.

But Denise is no simple creature of pleasure either: she even has a bitter strain of worldly wisdom, for both her solos (1) and (4) are in D minor. Such an exploitation would have been inconceivable in Grétry some years before. In (1) she decides to make a serious stand against André's intolerance, while in (4) the tone and perhaps even cadential mannerisms of (1) are developed. The form of (4) is a freely-developing AB(in D major)A' whose thoughtful stance is underlined immediately by a pause on the diminished seventh (Ex. 27.1). Mme Hubert and André are less romantic characters whom we encounter musically only in duets or ensembles. Yet André of course is no puppet, and his decisiveness perhaps even suggests that he has his own reasons for suspicion. The good sense of librettist and composer allowed André to act in four numbers opposite Denise: (3), (5), (9) and (10). All these are thoroughly alive with comedy. The duet 'en sourdine' (3) expresses their separation, since they sing only to themselves and the audience. Short motifs suggest the outrage and indignation of both, but acting must carry the piece through as much as music. By act 2 and (10) they are rapturously at one again. Vivid string writing on one hand and the latest Italian style on the other give the impression of a civilised finality to their relationship (Ex. 27.2). After this we can only await La France's downfall with relish.

The wit of word and plot in *L'épreuve villageoise* is, in the end, dominated by the excellence of its two finales. These rank with the very best Grétry of their type: (5) occupies over 400 bars and in spirit and style resembles the finales of *Le jugement de Midas*, writ large and broadened into farce.

Key	Tempo	Action
C	6/8 Allegro	André tears up the *billet-doux* and Denise loses her temper.
B flat to C to G	2/4 Allegro	La France's arrival; André ridicules the pair.
C	3/4 Larghetto	La France declares his love but is constantly interrupted by André, who is instructed to emit an 'interior cry'.
C to E flat	2/4 Allegro	Arrival of Mme Hubert; André appeals to her.
E flat	3/4 Andante	La France is decreed as the betrothed.
C	2/4 Allegro	Chorus enters to imbroglio music and festivities.

Ex. 27.1 *L'épreuve villageoise* (4)
('I'm beginning to see that in life half the people laughs at the other half')

Ex. 27.2 *L'épreuve villageoise* (10)
('You doubted my fidelity and I wanted to prove it to you')

The second finale (11b) also uses the chorus; this opera marks its first appearance in Grétry comedy at the Italiens since *La fausse magie*. It does not simply lend decoration but takes part as actively as, say, the officers in *Aucassin et Nicolette*. On one hand the villagers burlesque La France: when he proposes Denise's visits to the theatres (*spectacles*) they enquire as to what 'espectacles' actually are. On the other hand Grétry gives them a noble phrase, almost religious in its awe, as they reject the idea of 'brilliance of court pomp' and recall the natural glory of the sunrise they know so well (Ex. 27.3). (Possible influences on this chorus are mentioned in chapter 32.) The form of (11b) is a perfect amalgam of music and action, in five sections. Like a rondo, the first, third and fifth use the same basic

Ex. 27.3 *L'épreuve villageoise* (11b), second section
('I have seen the sunrise: that must be very similar')

material which is associated with merrymaking, the village fiddler and dancing. The second section, the only one not in A major, is constructed broadly on the lines of question and answer. But its courtly minuet tempo adds an ironic musical layer of humour over the proceedings by lending an equivocal tone to much the villagers say to La France; by extension everything he says becomes portentous. Some of the elusiveness of such processes was summed up by John Lahr: 'Farce is not so much a literary exercise as a comic mass manoeuvre, requiring the logic of a mathematician and the kinetic imagination of the clown. Farce is the intellectual slapstick which has traditionally thrilled audiences and confounded critics . . . The stereotypes confirm and comfort the bourgeois world who applaud them.'[4]

The last main point of musical discussion is Grétry's new 'village' music. The often-remarked freshness of his rustic tone became tinged with the accent of Desforges' characters. Repeated-note phrases, a restricted melodic range and rather stiff rhythms gave rise to a music that seems to walk on short country legs (Ex. 27.4). With a start of recognition the English-speaking music-lover

Ex. 27.4 *L'épreuve villageoise* (11b), fourth section
('Far from terrifying me, [marriage] only delights me: my Denise is back')

identifies the end of this vaudeville (the fourth section of 11b) as the prototype of ditties in Arthur Sullivan's Savoy operas. *L'épreuve villageoise* was revived in Paris in 1853 and Sullivan could have heard it there in 1867, perhaps on 7 or 21 July (when he was in Paris for the Exhibition) or 29 September (when he was en route for Vienna with George Grove).[5] And of course he could have bought the work in various editions. The epitome of this style is (7), Denise's famous verses that Michael Kelly heard in Strasbourg.[6] Grétry boastfully declared that although this was his first attempt at writing 'pretty couplets' the resulting music was 'sung unrestrainedly in the streets and danced everywhere, even on the stage of the Opéra', though he does not say in which ballet. It is not hard to see why: the piece

Ex. 27.5 *L'épreuve villageoise* (7)
(a) ('Good God, how M. La France was decent at the party!')
(b) ('You're more lovable to my mind')

swings along, running from verse to verse without a break and exhaling an almost impudent gaiety, attaining a high point at the held note of the last cadence as though the girl could hardly bear to have the festivities come to an end (Ex. 27.5). It already enshrines the spirit of the American musical.

Denise's functional recollection of (8) within (11b) is extremely funny as well as cruel. For all his tiresome superiority La France suffers double humiliation: not simply are his own words flung back in his face, but he has no idea that they were overheard to begin with. The recollection creates such conclusive irony that La France is speechless. The *coup* has been dealt; he has lost everything and can do nothing, except go; and the authors' evident delight in making the audience fill in the musico-dramatic source of the quotation is clearly akin to the systematic and serious use of functional recollection which was so important in Grétry's next-performed opéra-comique.

The fondness of the *ancien régime* for make-believe rusticity has often been described. 'The queen played the peasant in the meadows by the Trianon, and the theatre incessantly portrayed the villager and the proletarian in the falsest colours.'[7] Yet Brenet and others ignore the darker side of *La Rosière de Salency* as they do the degree to which social comment could be manifested within *paysannerie*. Many pieces were bound only to decadence, and of them Grétry's *Colinette à la cour* is an egregious example (see chapter 25). Exactly as in *L'épreuve villageoise*, the jealous peasant lover hides and acts impulsively. His coquettish mistress, Colinette, is consoled by Alphonse, Duke of Milan, and taken off to his birthday celebrations. During various entertainments at court his friend, the Countess Amélie, is provoked by Colinette's presence into jealousy; but in a masked episode she plays her trump·card by agreeing to marry Alphonse. The noble couple claim in the end that peasant love 'has passed into their hearts'. Such sententious rubbish was doubtless inevitable in what was really a kind of updated rococo opera-ballet but without a classical theme.[8]

In opéra-comique the librettist J. M. Boutet, known as Monvel (1749–1812) was important not only as a leading practitioner of *paysanneries* with a moral conscience, but also as probably the most able author who never worked with Grétry.[9] He wrote instead for Dezède (1772 to 1785) and then Dalayrac (1766 to 1793). With Dezède he gave *Julie* (1772), its sequel *L'erreur d'un moment* (1773), *Le stratagème découvert* (1773), *Les trois fermiers* (1777), *Le porteur de chaises* (1781), *Blaise et Babet* (1783) and *Alexis et Justine* (1785). The important works were indeed popular. *Julie* had 54 performances in its first decade, *Les trois fermiers* 137 over the equivalent period and *Blaise et Babet* 145 performances in the same way. These three and *Alexis et Justine* were all still staged in the 1790s. Most of Monvel's operas for Dezède use rustic dialect, while emphasising the moral uprightness or superiority of the peasants. This was something that Grétry had only approached in *Silvain*, and there it was complicated by family ties and the issue of poaching. *Julie* and its sequel are forthright, and *Julie* was one of the models for *Théodore et Paulin*. It demanded a different set in each of its three acts: inside the château, a forest clearing, with moonrise, and the grounds of the château. Julie, daughter of Marsanges, the *seigneur*, is being forced to marry a decrepit, stammering count. She escapes just before the wedding into the forests at dusk, where she is treated sympathetically by the woodcutter Michaut, his daughter Catau and her new husband Lucas. Julie's lover Sainte-Alme also appears. Michaut organises a plan for rescue. In act 3, next day, he contrives a meeting between Marsanges and

Catau. Catau pretends that her father is forcing her to marry the local bailli instead of sensibly giving her to Lucas, and appeals to the *seigneur*. A masterfully acted-out scene involving Michaut results in the *seigneur* taking Catau's side in the dispute. So Michaut reveals the deception, morally obliging Marsanges to reject the Count in favour of Sainte-Alme.

Not only did Monvel make the Count a figure of the grossest ridicule, but in the elderly, dominating figure of the woodcutter he anticipated clearly the better-known character of Mikéli, the water-carrier in Cherubini's opéra-comique *Les deux journées* (1801). Michaut and Mikéli both personify generosity and humanity, and engineer events on stage to the greater good of people outside their circle, and in both operas this involves a race against time. In fact the demonstration of 'humanity' by Monvel's peasant family as a whole is exemplary, and the word is used of them by Sainte-Alme in act 3 sc. 1. Moreover the continuing moral influence of Michaut into the next generation is illustrated after his demise in *L'erreur d'un moment*. After Julie's marriage to Sainte-Alme and the birth of their child, the 'momentary error' is Saint-Alme's sudden flirtatious passion for Catau. Catau has of course informed Lucas of it and he makes Sainte-Alme see sense and return to Julie with renewed love.

While in opera or play the moral failings of a privileged class were found to be legitimate entertainment when so gently reproved, the case of *Rose* is valuable, since it shows at what definite point established critics felt uncomfortable with this sort of *paysannerie*. *Rose ou la suite de Fanfan et Colas* was a three-act prose comedy by 'Mme de Beaunoir' which passed the censorship and appeared at the Comédie-Italienne in September 1785.[10] Its subject-matter is quite close to *Théodore et Paulin*; the two leading parts, adolescent males, were played by women, and with great effect. Colas and Rose, both peasants, are in love and Colas leaves the area to earn money for her dowry. In his absence the young Marquis Fanfan, Colas's *frère de lait*, falls in love with Rose. When Colas returns only to have his earnings depleted by a debt-collector, Fanfan proposes his own marriage to Rose. Colas becomes furious, threatens the Marquis and seeks further vengeance.

Colas: Eh! que m'importent donc votre naissance, votre rang? Laissons-nous seulement
tranquilles: retournais, croyais-moi, dans vot'châtiau . . .   (act 2 sc. 7)

He outrages his mother and Rose; eventually the Marquis's tutor counsels Fanfan to quench his affections and support instead those of Colas. The *Mercure de France* saw in this action a real and political threat; it was only seventeen months since the stormy public première of *Le mariage de Figaro*. The objectionable aspect was that the peasant gains by force of will what he feels is his, and seeks to injure the Marquis.

However respectable may be the rights of humanity perceived collectively, one must agree that in morals as in politics the distinction between the estates of men is as necessary as it is useful to the good of society; and that it is dangerous to seek to establish a system fatal to that distinction, without which a kingdom would lose its equilibrium and fall into a kind of anarchy. In proposing to set man against man, the author has not noticed that he neglected to observe the conventions; a very serious fault which ought in the general interest to be rigorously banished from the theatre. (8 October 1785 pp. 87–91)

VERSIONS AND PERFORMANCES

Théodore et Paulin, in three acts, was submitted initially as a text to the Comédie-Italienne on 13 July 1783.[11] By that time Grétry had probably been working on *Richard Cœur-de-lion* for several months (see chapter 28 note 10) and could thus afford the time to work with Desforges. After the first public performance *Théodore et Paulin* was withdrawn by Grétry, against the advice of the author and the actors (Grimm:xiii:507), and the musician proposed the basis of a transformation (i:362). In the printed libretto of *L'épreuve villageoise* Desforges claimed that he had felt a 'metamorphosis' to be needed and that 'Grétry gave me ideas which fixed and enlivened my own' (*Lettre à Monsieur de Corancé*). From its manuscript libretto we gain partial entry into the authors' workshop, and can agree with Grimm's blunt verdict that *Théodore et Paulin* was misconceived and too improbable.

The young Marquis de Verval is pining in secret for Théodore Dupré, daughter of the estate's farmer, who was brought up in the Verval château. Verval's mother, the Marquise, rules as a benevolent dictator over happy tenant workers, among whom are Denise (a farm girl), André (her lover) and La France (Verval's valet, also in love with Denise). Paulin is the son of a landowning farmer, now dead, from a nearby town, who is trying to repay family debts by working on his own inherited land: but he is in some danger from attack by unspecified local characters. Paulin's mother is dying and he quickly engages Théodore's sympathy. On La France's advice Verval writes a *billet-doux* to Théodore but La France, who has been dancing with Denise at last night's festivities, uses it to woo her, and although André tears it up, Verval ends act 1 by announcing that Denise may marry La France. In act 2 Paulin is given shelter by Mme Dupré. The Marquise discovers the cause of her son's lovelorn depression and peremptorily decides to help. Denise, hearing La France's farewell to past loves, decides to reject him. As Théodore enters, Mme Dupré reveals to her, Paulin and the assembled peasants Verval's love for Théodore and the Marquise's permission for it. The act ends with a desperate duet for the hapless girl and her undeclared lover Paulin. Only in act 3 does the Marquise decide to check Théodore's view of matters. At this point Denise narrates to her the example of her own unhappiness with the socially desirable La France, whereupon Théodore admits that she is in a parallel situation. Watched by the concealed Marquise, Théodore faces Verval and describes the truth; he magnanimously unites her with Paulin. La France is publicly rejected by Denise as she quotes his 'Adieu Marton'.

The act 3 verses sung by Denise, 'No happiness in marriage without equality' were seen by parts of the audience as plagiarised from *Julie* (*Mercure de France*, 17 April 1784), and indeed the whole thing is a diffuse reworking of Monvel, but with the added comedy of Denise and La France. Out of ten solos, five duets, a trio and four ensembles in *Théodore et Paulin* we can guess with some confidence that four items were re-used somehow, to give (3), (5), (7) and (8). The functional recollection of 'Adieu Marton' was not specified within a finale (only the first act possessed one) but within dialogue.[12] As for the music of Verval and his circle of characters, Grimm suggests that it was equal to the frigidity of the plot. Poet and composer had not only to prune much but compose much new material: it was far from possible just to lift out the good. Almost none of the Denise–André banter was in the earlier libretto and almost none of La France's individuality. Mme Hubert had to be invented; and André's jealous disposition had to be dramatised, not simply reported. To all intents and purposes the authors made a new opera with *L'épreuve villageoise*, cleverly interleaving the wholly unaltered, the partially altered and the wholly new.

The opera was an immediate success and went on to become the third most often performed work by Grétry at the Comédie-Italienne, later Opéra-Comique, after *Richard Cœur-de-lion* and *Le tableau parlant*. By the end of 1888 it had reached a total of 545 performances. The first years in which it was not performed were 1829–30. In the ten years 1784–93 there were 157 performances, then 137 in the next ten years and 47 to 1813. From 1814 to 1831 there were 49 performances. It was revived in 1853 with new orchestration by Auber, gaining 102 performances to 1861, 50 in 1866–8 and 3 in 1888. Loewenberg lists productions at three other Paris theatres (1863–1918); the last foreign one was at Graz (1895).

In the *Mémoires* Grétry gave two recommendations for cuts in (5) and (11b). Following his own practice, these were to assist in conditions of private performance and to speed the action wherever the opera was given (i:363–6).

28. Richard Cœur-de-lion (Richard the Lionheart)

Comédie in 3 acts, in prose: *CC* 1
Libretto by Michel-Jean Sedaine. Dedicated to Mme Des Entelles.[1]
First performed at the Comédie-Italienne, 21 October 1784.
Printed full score, Paris, Houbaut; Lyon, Castaud, n.d. [1786] as Œuvre XXIV
Dramatis personae: Richard I of England, Duke of Aquitaine, Count of Poitou (t.)
        Blondel [de Nesle], troubadour (t.)
        Sir Williams, an expatriate Welshman (b.)
        Laurette, his daughter (s.)
        Florestan, governor of Linz castle (b.)
        Marguerite, Countess of Flanders and Artois (s.)
        Béatrix, her lady-in-waiting (silent rôle)
        Antonio, a local boy (s.)
        Colette, his girl friend (s.)

Richard Cœur-de-lion

Mathurin, an old man (b.)
Mathurin's wife (s.)
Guillot, a peasant (t.)
Urbain (b.) and Charle (t.), Marguerite's men
A peasant (b.)
Local villagers; Marguerite's retinue; officers and soldiers of the castle.

ACT 1: The exterior of the fortified castle of Linz, with towers and battlements, surrounded by barren mountains and dark forests. On one side, a gentleman's house owned by Williams; on the other, a bench. During the brief overture, which proceeds directly into the opera, peasants are seen returning home from work. In the chorus (1)[2] they anticipate tomorrow's golden wedding of Mathurin and his wife; the couple themselves sing; Colette wonders where Antonio is; a second group of workers enters and leaves. Blondel, feigning blindness and disguised so as to avoid detection in his search for Richard, enters with his guide Antonio. Antonio describes the surroundings, chatters about local events and sings about Colette (couplets 2). He goes to find a lodging for Blondel. Alone, Blondel realises that the castle is important enough to hold his master: he sings of Richard's plight and his own fidelity (aria 3). Williams comes out berating Guillot for conveying a letter to Laurette. In the ensemble (4) Guillot says it is from the 'governor', while Blondel hopes this means the castle governor. Laurette joins the ensemble, claiming innocence in the matter. She is ordered back inside; Williams cannot decipher the letter but when Antonio reads it, it reveals Florestan's identity, his devotion to Laurette and the existence of a valuable prisoner in the castle. Williams tells Blondel that he has served King Richard at the crusades; he is now a widower. Laurette questions Blondel privately about the letter and in the aria (5) confesses her love for Florestan, whom she has certainly met. Blondel honours her love with a song, which she learns by repeating each note (6). Sounds of horses and waggons are heard: a 'great lady' is to stay at Williams' house. Marguerite enters with a retinue of knights and ladies. Blondel instantly recognises her since she is the object of Richard's love. He plays on his violin the last phrases of the song 'Une fièvre brûlante', a composition by Richard himself addressed to Marguerite. She recognises it and questions Blondel, who pretends to have learnt it from a squire returning from Palestine. She asks him to repeat it, in return for which she will find him lodging for the night. Blondel plays the whole Romance (7), embellishing it with variations. Marguerite goes in, her luggage is unloaded, and a table is set by the door. A servant gives Blondel wine, for which he plays and sings a crusader's song (8), the servants joining in the chorus. A lengthy orchestral coda suggests the activities of nightfall and removal of lamps.

ACT 2: A mysterious entr'acte (9) forms a march during which soldiers change guard. The front stage reveals a terrace within the castle surrounded by iron grilles, angled so that from it the back of the stage, representing a parapet above the moat, cannot be seen. Dawn is breaking and the stage brightens gradually. Florestan is leading Richard on to the terrace for his daily exercise. Alone Richard sings of his old glory, of Marguerite, and his desperate situation (aria 10). Blondel

227

appears near the parapet. He sends Antonio off and profits from the silence of morning to play the beginning of 'Une fièvre' on his violin. Richard, although he cannot see its source, is instantly alert. Blondel begins to sing the Romance again (11) and Richard, recognising the troubadour's voice, completes the first verse. With growing delight Blondel begins a second verse: 'In a dark tower a powerful king was languishing', and as Richard's hopes rise, the men sing the refrain together. Blondel, dancing about and playing variations on his violin, deliberately catches the attention of soldiers who arrest him even as the king is led back inside. In an ensemble (12) Blondel manages to persuade the men to let him speak to the governor. Still feigning blindness, he pretends to bring Florestan a message from Laurette: she will meet him that evening during the festivities for Marguerite. Finally another ensemble (13) sees Blondel escorted from the castle assisted by the timely return of Antonio.

ACT 3: Later that day. In the great hall of Williams' house. In the trio (14) Blondel is being prevented from speaking to the Countess by Urbain and Charle, but he bribes them and they leave. As Marguerite emerges, thanking Williams for her stay, she announces that she has decided to retreat to a nunnery, being consumed by 'a long sadness'. Béatrix enters with the news that the blind man, no longer blind, seeks an audience. Blondel reveals his identity to her and that he has located Richard in the castle. Marguerite, her knights, Williams and Blondel sing an ensemble (15) determining to deliver the king. The men agree a strategy: Blondel says a dance for the villagers must be organised so that Florestan can be captured at it. If he will not agree to Richard's release, force will be used. Available armed strength is assessed; Blondel has noticed a weak place in the castle defences. Preparations for the dance begin (the music is virtually continuous from here to the end) and in a trio (16) Laurette is forewarned by Blondel to expect Florestan; Williams is more equivocal. The music becomes a divertissement (17 a-d): a peasant song, a jig, a contradance and a waltz. Florestan appears during (17b) and converses with Laurette. In (17d) a drum roll is heard. Florestan attempts to leave but is restrained by armed officers. He refuses to release Richard, though urged to do so by the chorus.

The scene changes to show the castle already under siege.[3] Battle music is heard throughout (18); Blondel leads part of the attack in knight's costume, as Richard struggles against three armed guards. The wall is breached; Blondel kills one of the guards and rescues the king; the chorus sing 'Vive Richard'. To a march (19)[4] Marguerite and her followers appear and she is led before Richard, almost fainting in her womens' arms. In the closing sequence (20) Richard and Marguerite are reunited and all celebrate the glories of the day, but not without a final reminder of the Romance melody that was so necessary a part of the action.

Richard I (1157–99), fiery and impetuous, reigned from 1189 until his death in battle. He spent little time in England. Two of his poetic compositions are extant, one with music ('Ja nus hons pris') about his imprisonment. He left for the Holy Land in 1190, joined the crusaders at Acre and helped to capture Joppa. But the taking of Jerusalem, object of the third crusade, eluded the allies. Richard quarrelled with his friend Philip Augustus of France and with Leopold of Austria, who had him captured on his return through Austria and imprisoned at Dürrenstein on the Danube in 1192 or 1193. A gigantic ransom was raised in England (150,000 marks) whereupon he was released in February 1194. Little is known about the man Blondel de Nesle (*fl.* 1180–1200) but his songs are among the most widespread of those in the trouvère (i.e. northern French) repertory.

The legend of Richard's discovery by Blondel was told, *inter alia*, by Claude Fauchet in 1581;[5] but a more immediate source of Grétry's opera was *La Tour ténébreuse* (*The dark tower*), anonymously published in 1705 by Marie-Jeanne Lhéritier de Villandon (1664–1734).[6] She was daughter of the poet Nicolas Lhéritier and author of various prose and verse publications. In the preface to *La Tour ténébreuse* she names some of her sources, including a privately-owned manuscript of 1308, the 'Chronique et Fabliaux de la Composition de Richard Roy d'Angleterre'. Emphasising Richard's skill as 'true protector of letters' she quotes his poem mentioned above; but points out that Fauchet, while mentioning the rôle of Blondel in the rescue, does not quote his song. To rectify this she includes several poems set to music by her contemporary Cheron de Rochefources, one of which is purportedly the 'rescue' song. It is quoted below, Ex. 28.8. *La Tour ténébreuse* was intended as the first of two or more books using the framework of Richard's imprisonment. Most of the volume consists of two stories of her own invention, *Ricdin-Ricdon* and *La robe de sincérité*. Blondel, after sixteen months in disguised wandering, has located Richard; he has himself hired as a servant and musician on the castle staff, makes contact with the king and hears Richard confess his love for the princess of Flanders, now wife of the Comte de Hainaut.[7] Mlle Lhéritier's stories are told by Richard to Blondel, not *vice-versa*. The latter plans a rescue involving counterfeit keys, but the book concludes before it is attempted. (Ending the legend was a continuing problem. The rescue of the king in the opera was dramatised to Sedaine's satisfaction only after two trial endings had been rejected. See last section.)

Amid continuing and, by now, more expert antiquarian interest in the subject, Mlle Lhéritier's book was used for a retelling of the tale in the *Bibliothèque universelle des romans* in 1776.[8] The author–arranger is not known, but was convincingly argued by Cucuel to have been the Marquis de Paulmy (1722–87), the founder of the *Bibliothèque*.[9] So far from being a slavish précis of the 1705 publication, the new version in its own right became the single most important kernel from which Grétry's opera grew. Paulmy, if it was he, gave the tale dramatic life, drastically shortening *Ricdin-Ricdon* and omitting *La robe de sincérité*. Moreover he threw the character of Blondel into sharp relief historically and musically, at the expense of Lhéritier's interest in Richard as an artist. Blondel is enabled to rescue Richard by contriving to get the castle governor drunk, taking his keys, and escaping with both his monarch and the governor's daughter, who has assisted him. All reach England safely.

Blondel, in this 1776 version, was made to accompany himself on the violin; a footnote provided historical justification in 'the proof in miniatures decorating the oldest chanson manuscripts of the King of Navarre, where this prince is shown with this instrument' (see below concerning Thibaut de Navarre). But equally pregnant was Paulmy's invention of a dramatic sequence for the vital locating of Richard by Blondel. So complete was it that Sedaine could adopt almost its every detail: the choice of a 'lai' supposedly written by the king in Palestine; the instrumental prelude; the first verse; the refrain sung by Richard; the extempore singing of another verse by Blondel with words apposite to the king's imprisonment; the king's interruption of it with the improvised words 'Si Marguerite étoit ici, Je m'écrirois, plus de souci' ('If Marguerite were here I should exclaim, my care is ended'); and even Blondel's dancing about, resulting in a reprimand by the castle guard. (In imagining the above lines Paulmy unwittingly gave Sedaine a clue as to how to develop the libretto using Marguerite's presence; in the 1776 version she is already dead by the time Richard reaches Flanders.)

Sedaine's own libretto makes it clear that he believed that the words of this lai, 'Une fièvre brûlante', were simply a modernisation of lines stemming from the twelfth century.

it is my duty to thank the author of the two verses of the romance I used in this piece, and which are drawn from the interesting *fabliau* [i.e. early French narrative poem] that gave me the idea of it; I allowed myself to change only one expression [the seventh word was originally 'dévoroit' not 'terrasoit']. I could not have invented a complaint more favourable to the texture of my drama . . . and the melody it has inspired in the composer seems to be of the same century.

There was no hint in the 1776 story that Blondel should feign blindness, but Paulmy gave him a drinking-song that plays its part in the rescue plan: it would have been possible to dramatise this episode too. Sedaine however used it as his inspiration for (8), slightly altering the refrain for more vivid projection.

Sedaine's libretto of *Richard Cœur-de-lion* was not ready for submission to the Comédie-Italienne until 8 April 1782.[10] Meanwhile the story of Richard and Blondel was published, briefly, twice more in 1777–8.[11] And an entirely different opéra-comique project appeared that actually went further than Grétry was to do in its incorporation of 'authentic' musical substance from the Middle Ages. *Aucassin et Nicolette*, of course, had blazed the way with its modest use of quasi-gothic music, i.e. pastiche even to Grétry. But now Lhéritier's and Paulmy's *Ricdin-Ricdon* was taken as a source by A. D. M. de Vismes and the composer Henri-Joseph Rigel. Their *Rosanie* was produced by the Comédie-Italienne in July 1780. Although the full score has been lost, one of the solo-voice extracts that survives proves what a publicity letter claimed: 'the music and the words are by King Richard himself; and M. Rigel has added only the accompaniments to them'.[12] Rigel's source, which as far as he was concerned was 'authentic', can be found in J. B. de La Borde's *Essai sur la musique* as a 'Chanson composed by Richard Cœur de Lyon and taken from a tale by that prince made in 1195' (Ex. 28.1). This music was originally in four parts and is perhaps by La Borde himself. It was adapted by Rigel into 'Song of the enchanter and the goblins, words and music by

Richard Cœur-de-lion

Ex. 28.1 'Chanson composée par Richard Cœur de Lyon . . . en 1195'
(*Essai sur la Musique*, ii, supplément, p. 6)

Ex. 28.2 'Air de l'Enchanteur et des Lutins, Paroles et chant du Roi Richard' (F:Pn Y.515)

King Richard' (Ex. 28.2).[13] These examples show how Rigel smooths the rough edges of the original: its 3–2–4 opening bar structure becomes 2–2–2 in equivalent (6/8) values, and the 'primitive' repeated note calls of 'Ricdin Ricdon' are cut out.

Sedaine's treatment of drama in *Richard Cœur-de-lion* marks an evolutionary stage. If he adhered to the three unities, his freedom and independence came this time with the elaboration of his *donnés*. Grétry's librettists of serious works like *Les mariages samnites* had always felt obliged to adhere to and condense the literary source; and Hales was exceptional in selecting plays rather than prose fiction as his. The tendency was to defer to a literary model, to adapt or *précis* part of it. Comedy and *paysannerie* librettists were less inhibited: the 'lowlier' subject-matter seemed to permit more licence. Stated in simple terms, *Richard Cœur-de-lion* treats a semi-serious theme in a 'new and popular manner'. With its less than canonical literary ancestry it could be worked so as to focus on a musical and dramatic kernel: the Romance 'Une fièvre brûlante', the 'rescue' song. As Grétry wrote, 'Never was a subject more proper for musical treatment' (i:367). But in the wider sense the story of Richard was a catalytic subject: in Sedaine's hands it encompassed gothic taste, local colour, historical fact, a moral imperative, the spectacle of armed combat, and released royalist sentiments without being directly patriotic.[14] Its fundamental principles of design were, however, more revolutionary than all this might suggest. That is, whereas most opéra-comique librettos employed a good deal of action but confined it to a small and unified circle of characters, *Richard Cœur-de-lion* uses a restricted field of action yet includes a great many characters not at all closely connected to the primary events. Sedaine gives us a panorama as much as a play, an ambitious canvas comprising figures of all estates; as in a painting there is a principal action (the story of Blondel and Richard) supported by a substructure of organised secondary incidents. This is not to accuse it of diffuseness: on the contrary, almost every detail contributes to the whole.

The number of singing parts is remarkable: old Mathurin, his wife and Colette in (1); Guillot in (4); Charle and Urbain in (14); a peasant in (17a): all sing on one occasion only. Antonio sings in (2) and (3) only. Leading characters have short solo rôles, as for example Richard himself and Marguerite, who is given no aria, and Williams, who sings alone only in (4) and (16), both trios. Florestan has no aria and little enough else. Blondel alone is allowed a normal distribution of music. Yet one does not feel this to be odd when witnessing the opera: somehow the strength of its construction holds the threads together. One vital agent of musical unity remains to be mentioned: the chorus. It plays a full part in all three acts, whether as peasants, domestic servants, knights and retainers or Florestan's soldiery. Thus it becomes woven into the panorama, with its style of music changing accordingly from piece to piece. In this sense it becomes an agent of local colour, in a manner only tentatively used before. Describing the action in the chorus (1) the *Mercure de France* wrote, 'It is like so many magic lantern pictures one after another' (30 October 1784, p. 229).

An underlying affinity of design connects *Zémire et Azor* with *Richard Cœur-de-lion*. We noticed in chapter 12 the former's alternation between the enchanted and the domestic spheres; Sedaine's pattern also uses alternating sites of action, with analogous significance of liberty *versus* detention:

Act 1: Williams' house, exterior
Act 2: Castle from within
Act 3: (a) Williams' house, interior; (b) castle besieged.

Grétry undoubtedly played a large part in the early evolution of operatic local colour. Reviewing the biblical opera *La mort d'Adam* (1809) the critic Etienne Sauvo considered the composer, Le Sueur, had

entered into the circumstances of man in his primitive state; he has wanted to give his music a particular character, a local colour, to research (those are his expressions) a kind of antique melopoiea . . . Local colour is a word easy to use and very easy to misuse. Grétry's works have this merit to a supreme degree, e.g. *Aucassin* and *Richard*: one hears this term when, for example, bards or troubadours are concerned. (*Moniteur universel*, 1 April 1809)

Criteria of local colour seem to include, therefore, expressions of distance and difference, or simplicity opposed to sophistication. Twenty-five years earlier the critics used similar terms.

Grétry seems in this new composition to have forgotten his accustomed manner in order to transport us, by turns of melody at once simple and *romantique* which he places in the mouths of his different characters, to the distant times in which the action of the libretto occurs. The Romance sung by Blondel and King Richard reminds us of those so sweet and touching melodies that one still finds in our southern provinces like monuments which testify that they were the cradle of our minstrels and troubadours.   (Grimm:xiv:61)

Passages like these show Grétry's importance as a father of musical Romanticism, and also why the composer Weber considered that 'Grétry may well be the only French composer to have displayed in his music an unmistakable lyrical, and indeed often even a romantic, sense.'[15]

The visual setting, created to vie with comparable efforts in the other Parisian theatres, was a vital ingredient of the opera's atmosphere. From Claude Bornet's engravings, dated 1786, an impression is gained of the strengths and weaknesses of its sets and costumes (see Plates VI, VII). The illustration for act 1 depicts Blondel and a small group of chorus in (8). Apart from Williams' house, left, the entire stage is dominated, almost crushed by the sombre walls of Linz castle. Its weight and perspective come to symbolise the depth of anguish Blondel feels, the motivation behind the task of discovering and freeing Richard. The illustration for act 3, on the other hand, shows the horizontal line of the walls being breached. The artist has mirrored the stage directions printed in the score: the king is being handed a sword by Blondel which the latter has snatched from a soldier he has slain; at the same time Richard is struggling with three guards. Marguerite is falling into the arms of her women. Some of the anachronisms of dress have been discussed by René Lanson: Blondel's lace wristband in act 1, with the men's overcoats *à brandebourgs*; the woman's shaped dress and plume of feathers; and the vaguely Louis XVI clothes of the peasants.[16]

Lighting effects of dusk and dawn and moonrise had been in use long before act 2 of *Richard*, though the introduction of smokeless lamps in 1782 must have given welcome assistance to the illusion. But the libretto provides a stage direction that suggests that gesture as well as lighting was now essential to the whole effect. The king has just sung (10) and must strike a pose: his 'elbow resting on a stone ledge, he seems plunged into the deepest sorrow: his head is partly concealed by his hand'. This image, and of course the aria, largely replace orthodox characterisation, for which Sedaine's arrangement of events provided no room. Instead there is a romantically suggestive picture, or *tableau vivant*. Even Blondel is given some of this sort of characterisation. While (3) establishes his fidelity and strength, he has to relate to other people in the literal exercise of his profession as troubadour, since he is incognito. Grétry writes him an aggressively modal two-part song in (8), for example, where the roughness and the clashing Fs and Es show that he really has been out to the Middle East (Ex. 28.3). But this is followed by the orchestral postlude providing opportunity for mime as he 'pretends to take Béatrix for his boy; Antonio leads him off', as well as allowing the producer to recreate other touches of life in the twelfth century.

Local colour in the purely verbal sense, as in *La fée Urgèle* and *Aucassin et*

Plate VI. *Richard Cœur-de-lion* (engraved after his own drawing by Claude Bornet, 1786). In the first act Blondel is seen playing his violin in the crusader's song (8) while a servant pours him wine in return. As is better revealed by costume illustrations, Blondel's troubadour robe consisted of a simple cassock-like garment, coloured rose pink. The historical authenticity of the stage designs is obviously superior to that of the costumes.

Plate VII. *Richard Cœur-de-lion* (engraved after his own drawing by Claude Bornet, 1786). This portrays the assault in act 3 on Linz Castle, while the orchestral piece (18) is played. Richard himself on the parapet is being given a sword by Blondel, who has thrown his disguise to the ground. Marguerite swoons in the arms of her women.

Ex. 28.3 *Richard Cœur-de-lion* (8)
('To amuse himself in the morning, fine! That doesn't bother us')

Nicolette, has a modest presence: (8) includes 'jouvencelles' (damsels) and Marguerite arrives in act 1 on a 'palfrey', while Williams cannot read or at least decipher Austrian writing. However, Blondel's violin is a far more ingenious archaism. Obviously it was appropriate to an itinerant musician. Yet it also conformed to the 1780's belief that this was a standard troubadour instrument, and thereby Grétry's violin solos head a line of distinguished Romantic viola obbligatos: Berlioz's 'Chanson gothique', *Le roi de Thulé* in *Huit scènes de Faust* (1829) as well as *La damnation de Faust*; Raoul's Romance, 'Ah, quel spectacle enchanteur' in Meyerbeer's *Les Huguenots* act 1 (1836); and 'Gretchen', the second movement of Liszt's *A Faust Symphony* (1857). In their research, Frenchmen had happened upon pictorial and sculptural representations of violin-like instruments from the period before 1500, and also references to the *vielle* in troubadour texts. In his seminal study of 1742, de la Ravalière printed engravings of four violin and rebec-shaped instruments from fourteenth-century sources, and concluded that 'the violin, as we know it, was loved at all [past] times'.[17] Since the illustrations he used were all of bowed fiddles he felt justified in interpreting *vielle* in old texts not in its current eighteenth-century meaning of 'hurdy-gurdy' but simply as 'violin'. He was followed in this belief by D'Aussy and La Borde.[18] The latter also printed many engravings of early bowed string instruments and considered the three-string rebec as 'the oldest violin known in France', noting its presence in Romance and troubadour literature. These pictures perhaps stimulated Sedaine and Grétry into realising their aims: we know that Grétry owned his copy of La Borde's book before *Richard Cœur-de-lion* was performed (see note 9).'

Blondel's violin, an embodiment of local colour, obviously had to have appropriate music played on it: and with unerring judgement the librettist created a perfect frame for Grétry when he had the violin play the first statement of the Romance 'Une fièvre brûlante'. Marguerite immediately recognises this 'melody which in happiest times her lover made for her' (Blondel) and the violin itself becomes a vital, if inanimate, character (Ex. 28.4).

Ex. 28.4 *Richard Cœur-de-lion* (11)
The Romance shown in its complete act 2 form; for translation see p. 248

After composing it, Grétry noted in the margin of La Borde's *Essai sur la musique*:

I have just set to music this piece by Sedaine, I have not yet seen its effect in the theatre. If I could have discovered the Romance by Blondel and King Richard, I should have had it sung in Paris, but in default of theirs I have written one in the ancient manner [*genre ancien*].[19]

Later Grétry qualified this: 'what I sought [was] the old style [*vieux style*] capable of pleasing modern listeners' (i:369). His private statement shows what we might have surmised, that Grétry was as aware as anyone of his time of the choices open to those wishing to evoke early secular song. We can now draw some conclusions about his stylistic models in reaching the pastiche of 'Une fièvre brûlante'.

Back in 1742 de la Ravalière had provided some astute comments on trouvère song, based in part on nine musical texts which he appended in their original neumic form, by Thibaut of Navarre. He notes that the poets also composed the music, which was less difficult than that of his own day; that it was beautiful, true plainchant, without indications of rhythm; the speeds and decorations depended on the individual singer; that the melodies had less overall range than modern ones; and that the singer usually accompanied himself, particularly on the violin or harp.[20] From Thibaut's examples it could be seen that the vocal range was usually about an octave, that stepwise movement was more prevalent than leaps, and that most songs began with a repeat of the opening phrase.

It seems likely that the earliest effective reinterpretation of such elements occurred in Jean-Jacques Rousseau's opera *Le devin du village* of 1752. In this work the climax of the reconciliation between the youth and girl is the lovely chorus 'Colin revient à sa bergère'. After two dances, Colin sings a 'Romance' beginning with the words 'In my obscure hut, always new cares; wind, sun or cold, always suffering and work' (Ex. 28.5). Rousseau gives the music, in the context, a

Ex. 28.5 *Le devin du village*, sc.8, Romance

uniquely primitive flavour. There is 'no trill' in the orchestra at the sixth bar; simple accompaniment with two flutes; a repeated use of irregular phrases of six bars; a passing modulation to the dominant only; use of reversed (short–long) triple rhythms; restriction to four notes only up to the double bar; strophic construction (two verses); range of one octave; limitation of the leap of a sixth to the second half of the song. In defining the term 'Romance' Rousseau said the following in his *Dictionnaire de musique*, published in 1768 but 'very largely drafted by 1756':[21]

Since the [words of the] *romance* should be written in a simple, touching and archaic [*antique*] style, the melody should match the character of the words.

Grétry cannot have ignored this as a model. But he probably also had in mind the post-Rousseauists who drew directly for inspiration on the troubadour repertory.

The author who attempted to have this early music appreciated by his own age was F. A. Paradis de Moncrif (1687–1770), a friend of the Argenson family (see note 9) and fashionable writer, secretary to the Duc d'Orléans. In his *Choix de chansons* (1755, new edition 1757) he combined genuine with pastiche poems, providing the music for many of them himself. His popular 'Las! si j'avois

pouvoir' paraphrased Thibaut.[22] Moncrif's melodies provide close precedents for
Grétry's Romance. The following two show affinities with it in triple metre with
cadential short–long rhythms and preference for stepwise motion. The first,
moreover, as well as anticipating the melodic design of 'Une fièvre brûlante', uses
a return to the opening melody at the close: this was also used by Grétry (Ex. 28.6).
'Pourquoi rompre' (Ex. 28.7) has the same kind of pleasing wistfulness as Grétry's
theme, together with the quaintness of meandering, irregular phrase-lengths.

Ex. 28.6 *Choix de chansons*, 'Las si j'avois'
Last bars showing 3/4 notation emphasising similarity to Ex. 28.4.

Ex. 28.7 *Choix de chansons*, 'Pourquoi rompre', a strophic Romance

Moncrif did not favour triple metre: out of the thirty melodies he prints, half are
in 3/4, one in 6/4 and the rest in duple or quadruple metre. But he always restricted
the (implied) harmonic scope of the material. Some ('Pourquoi rompre', 'Viens
m'aider', 'Sensibles coeurs' etc.) contain no modulation. Others, like Ex. 28.6,
modulate briefly to the dominant. If anything, Grétry's Romance is more
conventional than some of Moncrif's music since it adheres to four-bar phrases
and is less 'authentic' in that it does not use a repeated opening phrase (compare
Exx. 28.1 and 28.2). Grétry obtains his irregularity by making his melody match the
ABBA pattern of the rhyme scheme (Ex. 28.4). If we can believe the composer, the
effect of 'Une fièvre brûlante' was such that 'a hundred times I was asked whether I
had found this air in the *fabliau* that provided the subject' (i:368). Only later did
theorists codify what came to be known as 'modal rhythm'. It is just as wrong to
grant Grétry the gift of prophecy as to call his Romance style arbitrary.[23] It
encompasses an octave, favours stepwise motion and restricts modulation. Its

Grétry and the growth of opéra-comique

short–long rhythm perhaps goes back to Rousseau. Comparison with the 'rescue' song composed for Mlle Lhéritier's *La Tour ténébreuse* will show how far historical taste in music had progressed over eighty years (Ex. 28.8). Grétry's *Mémoires* also call attention to the chorus (12) from the point of view of local colour: 'The chorus . . . is in the tone [*ton*] of old counterpoint; the soldiers of that time returning from the Holy Land, the ideas one creates of that religious era, suggested to me this type of music.' (i:375). Here he adopted a bald style with suspensions and Aeolian modal movement.

Ex. 28.8 *La Tour ténébreuse*: 'recognition' song for Blondel and Richard

If traditional opéra-comique was built round the depiction of character and a moral lesson that clearly defined right and wrong, *Richard Cœur-de-lion* to an extent de-emphasised both factors. Sedaine's *Le roi et le fermier* in 1762 showed the king amid the people as a potential middle-class hero. *Richard Cœur-de-lion* showed the monarch worth saving, but the rescue is justified by very little taking of rational positions and the king makes no fine speeches. The opera is politically quite vague. All we know is that Florestan is the faithful servant of an allegedly unworthy master, never named. Richard is simply a victim: as Duke of Aquitaine and lover of a French countess he must inevitably be rescued from unjust Austrian action. The chivalrous devotion and intelligence of Blondel are the stronger factors, and they help make the dramatic coincidences acceptable. Yet there are also deeper levels of justification to consider. Richard loves and is loved by both man and woman. His quasi-mythical status is reinforced early on by Blondel's crucial comparison: 'Impelled by love, Orpheus opened up Hades; perhaps the gates of these towers will open to the tones of friendship.'[24] That is, Blondel will triumph over the apparently impossible by performing an act, using music, that is almost superhuman. (We forget for the moment that physical force will be used; but that was actually the last solution Sedaine wanted.) Furthermore, Richard is an artist, a composer, one whose art ('Une fièvre brûlante') in a real sense is his salvation. When one recalls the painting by Delacroix, the play by Goethe and the poem by Byron depicting the poet Torquato Tasso unjustly imprisoned and a martyr to his volatile personality, one can see that Sedaine, anticipating these, is also celebrating his historical protagonist as a creator, as much as for what he stands for as Christian monarch.

Sedaine was a master craftsman: if he understood the extended rôle of the chorus and the transcendent power of the Romance, he also pieced together the plot with expert rapidity. It appears to have inevitability because it keeps at least one step ahead of expectation and is highly economical. Although little enough is spoken, one feels a weight of suggestion behind everything. This principle, alien to French dramatic logic but derived from Sedaine's admired Shakespeare, extends to the musical numbers. So, for example, when act 3 opens with a trio involving two people whom one has not noticed before and certainly never heard, one fits the occasion into a mental picture of Marguerite's retinue. Act 2 is admirable for the way that Blondel's invented explanation to Florestan (that he has been sent by Laurette) economically unites both parts of the plot, i.e. Blondel's private mission and his public strategy. Moreover this episode is entirely plausible. The choral ensembles on either side of this spoken conversation promote, however, almost none of the advances in the plot, in spite of their length. This fact is symptomatic of a change of musico-dramatic emphasis as compared to Grétry's earlier opéras-comiques. One can perhaps describe it using the simile of a painting. Equally as Sedaine provided highlights, middle ground and background, so Grétry's music is designed to make its maximum impact at the high points where the king and Blondel have monologues and where the Romance is heard. The 'middle ground' music consists of solos for minor characters and of the small ensembles; and the 'background' music creates continuity and local colour while little of importance to individuals is going on visually. Such pieces are the opening and closing numbers of act 1, the entr'acte, the Blondel–soldiers ensembles in act 2 and the divertissement in act 3. All the foregoing combinations of solo, ensemble, chorus, Romance theme, and orchestra music are brought together in the sequence from (16) to the end forming a natural climax. Grétry consciously planned the 'foreground' effect of the Romance at least. He insists that it is 'understood' even by the stage characters as being sung, while in other places singing is only explicable by the dramatic conventions of opera itself (i:368).

Technically this was Grétry's ideal libretto since it allowed him to apply 'natural' non-symmetrical forms without prejudice to the overall character of the play, while encouraging lyrical highlights in the foreground monologues (3) and (10). How tempting it must have been to give an aria in act 3 to Marguerite, and how extraordinary that this was denied! Consequently the ideal image of her that is created through Richard's courtly love, expressed formally in the Romance, is maintained inviolate. Perhaps this was the only eighteenth-century opera without a straightforward aria in its last act.

Act 1 begins visually with what the score might call 'overture', but the only musical aspect of the latter not shared with (1) is the nine-bar flourish that opens the work in G minor. This flourish is no formality: it surely evokes the 'dark tower' itself, fiercely and with grim strength provided by the trumpets. This music never recurs but seals the prime object of the play's action in our minds. One can regard (1) and the G major 'overture' music introducing it as a single, sung overture. The voice, after all, had entered the Grétry overture in *Aucassin et Nicolette*. Its simple frame is made by Grétry's old device of an orchestral refrain at beginning and end. The music never leaves G major: contrasting, short sections – delightfully tuneful – are sung by different groups or soloists. One might compare the loose construction with an overture like *La Rosière de Salency*, as well as the rustic tone and triple metre.

It is typical of the opera's economy that (2) maintains the mood of (1) by the use of G major and 6/8 tempo. The convention of beginning an opera with strophic couplets (cf. *Euryanthe*) had been favoured by Dezède but only once before by Grétry, in *Les événements imprévus*. Musically, therefore, nothing prior to it can detract from the superb impact of (3). Not even its twenty-two bars of introduction anticipate the singer's opening phrases (Ex. 28.9). Contrary to classical principles Grétry gives the singer his highest note, a', in the opening section. And while the text implies a rondo, the music ignores this in favour of a two-part form (slower, faster) and avoids any but the briefest modulation. Ex. 28.9 obviously expresses kingship in music. When the same words are sung to the new music later, they convey the reality that Richard is no longer in glorious state. At this point the hammered iterations, Beethovenian in style, describe the qualities that this king (and monarchs in general, says Blondel) requires for his protection.

It is in (4) that we hear the balance swing away from the primary needs of the drama. Perhaps we are surprised at the simultaneous setting of different words;

Ex. 28.9 *Richard Cœur-de-lion* (3)
('O Richard! O my king! the universe abandons you')

perhaps at the prevailing *bonhomie*. Laurette's first words, a protestation of innocence, are set to the same music earlier heard as her father is telling Guillot to warn off Florestan. Moreover the voices enter in quasi-fugal imitation. It compounds the problem of Laurette, namely that the girl has to be deceived until the end about the political importance of her relationship with Florestan. (Her love for him has a potentially tragic conclusion and is resolved briefly and unconvincingly during (18).) Grétry's excuse is that he has used 'a form of counterpoint appropriate to Sir Williams' (i:372). In contrast to this creative calculation he resolved the piece with traditional truth. Blondel appeals for peace between father and daughter, using a phrase that signified, and was understood as, the accents of an old man (Ex. 28.10). The music was applauded, which is impressive evidence of the different way we hear music today (i:372).

Ex. 28.10 *Richard Cœur-de-lion* (4)
('Peace, my good friends!')

Laurette's character is not devious, as her music in (4) might imply: her solo (5), marked *Andante spiritoso*, has the simple honesty of Mozart's music for Barbarina and shares with it the delicate tonality of F minor.[25] The bassoon contributes a final impression of pathos, which seems apt. After this the slightness of (6) would seem irritating, were it not for the enhancement of Blondel's character as a person and a troubadour.

Blondel's art is, in fact, central to (6), (7) and (8). In the theatre (7) becomes an almost magical juncture, though on paper it looks insignificant. Two effects can be discerned here which justify the word 'transcendent' in connection with the Romance. The first is the instantaneous connecting of time and space, but with a power in inverse proportion to the one single strand of music making that connection. The music 'speaks' more clearly than words because it generates a multitude of unspoken emotions and meanings relative to each character in the minds of the audience. Secondly, when the Romance is taken up by the pit orchestra, the ostensibly simple provision of harmony and orchestration seems to lend the Romance not just a clothing, but the quality of a tangible object. The orchestra apparently 'comments' on the Romance, making us feel that this musical object will 'surmount' any obstacles in its way. (The castle, of course, still stands before the audience's eyes.) The variations then played by Blondel on the violin may have been intended to evoke the playing of 'divisions' in the seventeenth century, but in this context we are equally likely to feel the proximity of the Romantic future. The mixture of 'meaning', feeling and 'infinite' suggestion is, after all, close to the view of music we find in the fiction of Wackenroder and E. T. A. Hoffmann.

The strophic crusader's song (8) has already been quoted. Again, Blondel's playing forms part of the entertainment. The variety of orchestration conspicuous all through the opera is noticed in the important parts for bassoon and lower strings during the orchestral variations closing the act. Moreover, the entr'acte (9) makes unexpected history in the same area. Trumpets and horns are muted, while the timpani have 'two pieces of cloth tied to the sticks'. This instruction, omitted from CC_1, remains the only such evidence for covered sticks in France before 1807.[26] The key of E flat, muting, soft fanfares and nebulous atmosphere of (9) are both a counterpart to the image of the castle before dawn (the music means little without the stage set in view) and a musical preparation for (10).

Rarely can a single operatic aria have had to serve as such a complete portrait, for the king sings little else, and no further solo. For that reason it is interesting that his music here is not in contrasted sections: one might have anticipated an ABA'B' form like Azor's aria (17), or an obbligato recitative to begin with. Richard's music is martial, though the muted fanfares 'recall with sorrow the glory of the hero' (i:375). Yet it is not depressed in tone, in spite of his words as he looks at a portrait of Marguerite: 'Sweet image of my friend, come and console my heart, come, take away my sorrow for one moment.' Only the sonata form's fourteen-bar development dwells on the prospect of failure and death. Richard retains the stature of an ideal figure. As was the case in (3), Grétry withholds some thematic ideas from the orchestral introduction until a late (second subject) stage in the recapitulation. The singer, in order to be fully effective, has to command a range of over two octaves.

There follows the central emotional scene of the opera (11). The Romance, at first simply on the violin, but progressing to its first vocal rendering in the opera, and finally to duet form, secures the hope of release for Richard. The overwhelming effect of this scene on stage is of a celebration of freedom. Music itself seems to defy physical reality. Blondel's act 1 evocation of Orpheus becomes beautifully clear. Clairval's acting 'was electrifying: his joy, his surprise at having found his king, the trembling of his voice, and the expression altogether, made an impression on me that can never be effaced', wrote Michael Kelly.[27] For the third time Blondel's violin executes 'divisions', now with leaps and double-stops, but there is no break for dialogue before the soldiers are upon him as a result, in (12). Its special colouring has been mentioned above. Blondel, pretending to be afraid, sings in whining minims, but the music follows the increase in his confidence. The strengths noted in the *Aucassin et Nicolette* ensemble (8), again military in context, are here reinforced by boldness of scale and musical conception. The soldiers are animated, aggressive, quick to react, and have to sing at times in three parts. Even though the material of (12) is used again in (13) the outcome is different since it is redistributed and since Antonio is given fresh music with which to plead with the soldiers. Act 2, therefore, has little spoken dialogue and little outward action; it is chiefly filled and made intelligible with music.

Act 3 commences with three 'middle ground' ensembles, sufficient rather than memorable. (14) is as good-humoured as its form is orthodox: its sonata basis matches the propriety of Blondel's dealings with honest servants. But (15) bursts out of harmonic convention. It begins in B flat (a chivalric key for the Romantics) when Blondel informs the knights of Richard's proximity. They react instinctively, but their joy turns to breathless enthusiasm when Blondel throws off his blind man's disguise. The music turns rapidly to D major, 6/8 metre, and stays in that key. Had Grétry prepared the modulation more substantially the larger-scale importance of the moment would have been apparent, since D major is kept as the main key until the end of the opera. Notwithstanding this. Blondel receives music fit for a hero. As the evening's preparations begin, the trio (16), again in D, takes its cue from the lightness of Laurette's heart. It virtually becomes an Italianate comic piece, so that Laurette as the object of deception is ignored. Instead Blondel, doubtless hoping for a successful outcome, leads her further into belief in Florestan's constancy.

The sweep of music continues into (17), half in D minor and half in D major. Like the supper-entertainment music in *Don Giovanni* these pieces provide both a background (for mime rather than conversation) and a means of increasing tension. And as Don Giovanni's last struggle takes place against the forces of orchestra and chorus, here those same forces take responsibility for the drama, as soon as the governor is arrested. It is the chorus which challenges him to release Richard and the orchestra that depicts the assault on the castle. The combat music is hardly very original, but Grétry keeps the harmony moving and is not prolix (fifty-seven bars). Drama becomes melodrama, perhaps. But without relying on the Italianate finale form, the authors created again the through-composed 'French' finale pioneered in *Le déserteur*. Harmonically speaking, Monsigny far exceeded Grétry in the ingenuity of his finale, making the climactic chord of D major coincide with the triumphant melody signifying Alexis' salvation. Grétry substituted the lesser interest of temporary excursions outside D; thus the march from *Les mariages samnites* (9) was easily added (see note 4) after the combat, being in the same key and adding another link to the chain. There follows in (20) a sober conversational section for the three main characters, rather akin to parts of *Die Zauberflöte* in being neither recitative nor set piece. Using Italian techniques of building excitement with chorus and soloists together, Grétry then expands his musical material in a formal close, never modulating. Particularly effective is the upper a'' held by the voice of Marguerite, an idea whose force was often used in Paris after Gluck, and which also appeared in the last section of (15): Ex. 28.11. The penultimate link in the chain is the trio setting of 'Une fièvre brûlante', which cannot fail to be a powerful stroke. Perhaps even this idea stemmed from *Le déserteur*.

Although the ground had been well prepared since 1770 for the functional recollections of 'Une fièvre brûlante' nothing could have allowed us to anticipate the leap forward taken in *Richard Cœur-de-lion*. We have seen how Grétry used literal or 'natural' repetition of a chorus (*Les deux avares*) or of descriptive music (*Zémire et Azor*); how he showed the spontaneous recollection in memory of a

Ex. 28.11 *Richard Cœur-de-lion* (20)
Celebratory ensemble and chorus

march (*La Rosière de Salency*) or referred, by repeating the orchestral description of a dream, to the operation of memory on several occasions unspecified (*La fausse magie*); how musical recollection might indicate the centrality of an action and a concept (*Les mariages samnites*), and facilitated comic irony and sarcasm (*L'amant jaloux, L'épreuve villageoise*). Quite close to *Richard Cœur-de-lion*, of course, was the recollection of the 'gothic' music in *Aucassin et Nicolette* at the end of that opera: not only did the music embody archaism, but it also summed up the theme of the work, the indestructible love of hero and heroine. The Romance in *Richard Cœur-de-lion* took such techniques forward by itself signifying memory and emotion, by supposedly having been composed by King Richard, and also by being played instrumentally in the sight of the audience, not in the pit. Grétry said that the 'public realised that this tune was the pivot on which the whole piece turned' (i:374). In the *Mémoires* the composer detailed its nine appearances:

Act 1: Solo violin, then embellished version (7)..2
Act 2: The introduction, two verses and variations (11) 4
Act 3: A non-notated offstage hearing in sc. 3 by Blondel, as Béatrix says 'Do you hear his voice?'; then (15) and the end of (18)..3

Each appearance is differently scored or arranged. The first six are in C; (15) is in B flat and (18) in D. We have examined the unique effects produced in acts 1 and 2 by the Romance, and which do not necessitate any actual alteration of the melody, though it may be embellished in variations, or be harmonised. At first only the melody is made known, in (7): the words are added in act 2, initially in a solo rendering punctuated by histrionic pauses as Richard exclaims in astonishment, then in more continuous form (Ex. 28.4) culminating in a duet version and an instrumental variation. In act 3 the melody undergoes radical disguise in (15) and conveys a hidden meaning under the words to which it is sung. Blondel is reporting his discovery of the king and having heard his voice. At this juncture the Romance appears woven into the vocal line as smoothly as a motif in Wagner (Ex. 28.12). The dramatic intention was the presumably private communication of the fact that recognition was achieved specifically through Marguerite's song (i:374):

BLONDEL
Allegro

p Sa voix a pé - né - tré mon â - me, Je la con - nais,
[Sung over pedal B flat]

oui, oui, Ma - da - me.

Ex. 28.12 *Richard Cœur-de-lion* (15)
('His voice penetrated my soul, I recognised it, yes, Madame')

MARGUERITE
Lent

[+ strings]
BLONDEL
RICHARD

Orch. bass *très doux*
C'est l'a - mi - tié fi - dè - le qui fi - nit mon mal - heur

Ex. 28.13 *Richard Cœur-de-lion* (20) trio section
Marguerite's words: 'It is faithful friendship that ends my misfortune'

Blondel, that is, is telling something to Marguerite while concealing it from her knights. Or it may be that the composer was giving Blondel's words a purely 'subconscious' significance: his explanation does not define his intention. Finally the Romance is recalled in tranquillity (18) and is held out before us like the abstract character in the drama that it has become (Ex. 28.13).

Although 'Une fièvre brûlante' gave musical history much, we have seen that it also partook of a tradition going back to Rousseau: Ex. 28.5. This tradition had particular relevance for opéra-comique. It was first widened when Moncrif's archaising Romances were followed by numerous later collections. Commentators have noted that while Rousseau's definition of a Romance unequivocally included the quality of a narrative, like a ballad, Moncrif observed as early as 1757 that writers were applying the title Romance to any strophic love-song, even in the ode style.[28] This was the kind of Romance that appeared in earlier opéra-comique. For example, all four of Monsigny's from 1760 to 1762 contain a Romance, either in G or G minor and in 2/2 metre. The music always forms a set piece although the context may be humorous as well as amorous. The lover may be absent or present. Such could be their attractiveness that a Romance 'sometimes prevented the failure of an opéra-comique'.[29] Philidor and Gossec continued the practice, as in *Sancho Pança* of 1762 (Ex. 3.3) or *Le tonnelier* of 1765, no. 4 in B minor. These were not, however, mere interpolations. They almost all tell us something about the character singing and they often form part of the dramatic action. One example occurs in Philidor's *Le bûcheron,* the 'Vaudeville en Romance', which is actually in Da Capo form and in which Suzette tells an older suitor that she prefers Colin. Or one may instance *La fée Urgèle* (Ex. 24.7), whose Romance is part of the divertissement: as knight Robert, condemned to marry the Old Woman, tries to escape between the dancers in the court of love, the Old Woman sings 'Have you seen him, my well-beloved?' In the next generation, Dezède specialised in Romances, sometimes to the virtual detriment of aria in balanced character-exposition. Grétry rejected this on principle, and came near the tradition only in *L'amitié à l'épreuve* (10).

'Une fièvre brûlante' renewed the tradition at a stroke, not simply in the numerous ways already described, but because it stood in an allegorical relation to the whole opera. That is, its words presented a microcosm of the dilemma of the entire piece.

Stanza 1. A burning fever assailed me one day and drove from my body my languishing soul. My lady approaches my bed and death flees from me.

Stanza 2. In a dark tower a powerful king languishes. His servant bewails his sad misfortune. If Marguerite were here I should exclaim, my cares are ended.

In short, it becomes a tale within a tale. Older Romances epitomised an operatic situation rather in the way that the old vaudevilles did in early opéra-comique: their first line and melody universalised the basic circumstance of that scene. The Romances of the 1760s in a sense replaced the vaudevilles that were in any case being pushed out of opéra-comique scores. Grétry's Romance took the concept and applied it to the opera as a whole. This, accidentally, proved influential. One song, perhaps recurring, would epitomise the essential theme of a work. So in Dalayrac's *Léhéman* (1801) the strophic song 'Un voyageur' appears in different forms throughout, functioning as an allegorical symbol of hope, and reviewed in understanding terms by C. M. von Weber.[30] The process can be compared to Wagner's in *Der fliegende Holländer*, where the ballad of Senta is a tale within a tale, and was seen by its composer as vital to the unity of the whole work.

VERSIONS AND PERFORMANCES

Richard Cœur-de-lion did not attain definitive form until fourteen months after the première. It was then published in score, parts, and as a libretto.[31] The three versions differed mostly in their handling of the dénouement, the king's release. The first version ran for eleven months, 21 October 1784 to 24 September 1785, during which it was seen thirty-four times.[32] Although its third act was universally criticised, this version's popularity remained high. The *Mercure de France* of 30 October considered it ended 'drily' and gave the account from which we can judge for ourselves. During the dance in act 3 Williams addressed Florestan and requested Richard's liberty in exchange for Laurette's hand. Blondel and Marguerite then informed the governor of his prisoner's identity. After half-hearted resistance Florestan, demanding only secrecy from those present, went to comply with their wishes. Although the others thought they had been tricked, Florestan returned as promised, with his guards, and handed the king over. There was a final divertissement.

Grétry reported that the public censured Florestan for dereliction of duty, but this version clearly compromised plausibility, not to mention political possibility. On 23 October Grétry wrote to Sedaine a very full letter which has since been widely reproduced.[33] Taking it for granted that a new ending was required, not least because 'all Paris is making dénouements for *Richard*', he proposed more or less what we now recognise as the final version. However, his concern with character-motivation was meticulous and he suggested details that found no place in Sedaine's ever-economical text. Blondel was to propose, in formulating the rescue, the strategy that Florestan be persuaded his master is a traitor. During the (now-lost) chorus 'Rendez-moi ce héros' from the first version Florestan was to protest that he will not release the king. After Blondel has left to organise the siege Laurette was to have a 'short aria of lively reproach to her lover'. Then

two or three cannon shots or a drum-roll will be heard, though gunpowder was perhaps not yet invented. The back-curtain will rise as in your *Déserteur* and Blondel will be seen, sword in hand, leading Richard out, with the garrison arrested by the knights escorting the countess. This tableau must be designed by an artist: Robert will do it for us. The countess will want to run into Richard's arms, will consider it ill to rush forward; Richard throws himself at her feet. Williams and Laurette hold back Blondel – and the last chorus as at present.

You see, my friend, that only a quarter of an hour's work is needed for us to make these changes which, I think, will be of the greatest effect.

But this was precisely the ending that Sedaine did not want, since he went to the trouble of composing another whole act to avoid doing what he was bidden. He knew what was drawing crowds at the Ambigu-Comique.

The second version was given on 22 December 1785, once only, not more as Grétry implies. Its text, though unknown to the editors of *CC*, was first published in 1822–5, but without including the changes to act 3 that must also have been made.[34] Sedaine ended the third act with the challenge to the governor, the moment of scene change in the final version. The new fourth act was of full length, with no internal scene changes. It is set in a prison in the basement of Williams' house. Blondel has been detained there in his rôle as blind wanderer on suspicion of acting as go-between for Laurette and Florestan. The latter enters under guard: he has been given two hours to agree to release Richard. Blondel, feigning blindness still, ingratiates himself with the governor. In the hope of escaping he encourages Florestan to write a message to his garrison lieutenant instructing him to release the person designated by Blondel. Its ambiguity of meaning is unsuspected. Laurette descends to say that obduracy will result in Florestan being taken to 'the land of his sovereign' and eternally away from her. They part. Williams appears and, whether or not genuinely, does not recognise who Blondel is. He sets him free out of pity. To Williams' appeals for the king's freedom are joined the threats of Marguerite, who wants to take back Florestan for trial in her own lands. But news of Blondel's approach is brought by Antonio. Florestan thinks he is about to be delivered by his troops, but of course they escort Richard himself in. Florestan's chivalrous loyalty to his masters is recognised by Richard, who attaches him to his own service.

This unsuccessful version shifts the attention away from the Richard–Marguerite–Blondel core, and in concentrating on Florestan's dilemma loses the momentum built up in act 2. Should we admire Blondel's cunning, Florestan's sacrifice of happiness or Richard's personality and inspiration? At the end there is no recognition scene for Blondel, but one seems required to resolve his double rôle. In the *Annales du Théâtre Italien* D'Origny noted that in the third and fourth acts 'the superb pieces of music that M. Grétry had added . . . were admired' although the drama itself was adjudged 'cold, insipid'. The musical shape of act 4 looks to have been unconvincing, there being no chorus and the end being spoken, but Lepeintre's text may well have differed from that actually seen on stage. Grétry was provided with words for three new arias for Blondel, one for Florestan, a 'farewell' duet for the latter and Laurette and a trio for the two prisoners and Williams, covering Blondel's release.

Sedaine thereupon wrote an open letter to the *Journal de Paris*, also printed by D'Origny, admitting the unsatisfactory nature of the four-act version. Given that this would take time to revise and that the Comédie-Italienne wished to continue performing the opera, the librettist consented 'following an idea that has always prevailed in the mind of my musician, that the king should be rescued by force at the end of the third act'. In the printed libretto Sedaine returned to the problem of the assault by force:

I had the greatest repugnance for using this means, it seemed to me too well-known, too common; I had not sufficiently reflected; the situation of Blondel and Richard makes it, in some way, new by the necessity of ending thus.

If this sounds like casuistry, it should remind us of those other 'difficult' operatic endings: Monteverdi's *La favola d'Orfeo* and Gluck's *Orfeo ed Euridice*. Sedaine, no less than Monteverdi and Striggio, had problems with his last scene precisely because he was *not* writing a rescue opera, but his own Orpheus opera.

It took only a week to alter the four-act version to the final one, given on 29 December 1785, but even so it seems to have been well performed, the siege carrying 'the stamp of talent of M. Vestris who drew up the plan of it'.[35] There were special circumstances governing the performance history of *Richard Cœur-de-lion* in France (though it was to become Grétry's most frequently played opéra-comique) but the work's career on the world stage took wing immediately since it was translated into all European languages and held the stage virtually to 1900. Vienna saw productions in 1788, 1802 and 1810, but Beethoven's variations WoO 72 on 'Une fièvre brûlante' may have stemmed from hearing the theme in a ballet version produced in 1795, music arranged by Weigl.[36]

Counting all three versions, the opera had 126 performances before its interpretation as a royalist piece put a stop to all showings. In fact there was only one performance in 1791 (September), and it was to be the last. An effort to salvage it as a Revolutionary piece survives in the Bibliothèque Nationale, dated 1791,[37] but none is known to originate from Sedaine. Its revival was in 1806, after Napoleon had crowned himself Emperor; in the ten years to 1815 it attained 208 performances, with 146 in the next decade. Towards the 1830 revolutionary crisis it was again out of favour, with 4 performances in 1826–7 and then another hiatus. In 1841–7 inclusive, rescored by Adam, it reached the enormous total of 236 performances, but again acted as a political barometer with the approach of 1848. Under Napoleon III it was not the Opéra-Comique which did it most justice (35 performances in 1856), but the Théâtre Lyrique, with a run of 302 performances from 1856 to 1868, again in Adam's version.[38] In the revival after the Franco-Prussian war it reached 321 performances at the Opéra-Comique in 1873–93 and was still showing when Soubies compiled his statistics. For the Comédie-Italienne and Opéra-Comique alone this makes a total of 1076 performances.

29. L'amitié à l'épreuve (Friendship put to the test)[1]

Comédie in 3 acts, in verse: *CC* 42–3
(for two-act version see chapter 9)
Libretto by Charles-Simon Favart. Dedicated to the dauphine (the score took this over from the 1770 version. By 1786 Marie-Antoinette had been queen for twelve years.)
First performed at Fontainebleau, 24 October 1786. First performed at the Comédie-Italienne, 30 October 1786.
Printed full score, Paris, Aux adresses ordinaires; Lyon, Castaud, n.d. [1787] as Œuvre VI.
Dramatis personae: Lord Nelson, member of the English parliament (t.)
    Lady Juliette, Nelson's sister (s.)
    Corali, young Indian girl entrusted to Nelson (s.)
    Blanfort, superior officer of the English navy (b.)
    Amilcar, negro in the service of Blanfort (t.)
    Timur, Indian gentleman, brother of Corali (t.)
    Betzi, Corali's servant (s.)
    A notary (t.)
    A singing-teacher (spoken rôle)
Note: square brackets below indicate correspondence with 1770 numbers.
ACT 1: Lord Nelson's house in London. A large study with a library and bureau with books on top, fitted with drawers containing papers. Four or five armchairs. Juliette is chiding Nelson: 'I was an expert, my brother, you're in love' (duet 1) [2].[2] They discuss Corali's debt to Blanfort, who rescued her and raised her.[3] Juliette counsels Nelson to curtail his conversations with Corali. Nelson feels that he can conquer his love (aria 2) [3]. Corali enters, to Nelson's obvious emotion. She asks him to 'reveal the truth in her heart' (aria 3) [4], then openly avows her love. They sit down to read and work but are unable to concentrate (melodrama 4). Betzi announces the singing-teacher. Corali leaves to prepare for the lesson and

Nelson, weeping, tells Juliette that Corali's ingenuous love for him is too tempting. He must leave London. Corali sings her aria for the teacher (5) [5]. Hardly has Corali been made aware of Nelson's decision than Amilcar is announced (solo and ensemble 6). As Corali's former family servant he dances with joy at rediscovering her and describes the voyage that he, Blanfort and Timur have just made from the East Indies to Europe for the wedding of Corali and Blanfort. While Blanfort's letter is read Amilcar sings and dances a short Calenda (7), then leaves with Betzi. Corali flatly refuses the idea of marriage to Blanfort. Nelson begs Corali to keep silence and, satisfying Juliette's expectations, leaves before the end of their trio (8) [8].

ACT 2: A richly decorated drawing-room, a table, armchairs; a side door leads to Corali's room. Timur and Amilcar enter but find nobody about. Timur asks after Corali and Amilcar describes her (9), afterwards going to look for her while Timur sings a eulogy to Blanfort (10). Amilcar returns troubled by the sound of Corali's weeping (duet with Timur, 11). Corali emerges, intending to depart, and is reunited with her brother. She admits to him her love for Nelson, which provokes an urgent duet (12). He decides she should return with him to India and undertakes to obtain her liberty from Blanfort. Alone Corali bids farewell to Nelson (Romance 13) [13] and takes leave of Juliette; but Blanfort's arrival with Nelson is announced. Juliette makes ready with Betzi and Amilcar, while Corali is simply overjoyed (quartet 14). Amilcar is left to pay court to Betzi, first in the verses (15); she demands equality rather than subordination. They sing a duet and dance (16).

ACT 3: as for act 2. Corali has an extravagant aria of hope (17). Juliette enters with Nelson and Blanfort (quartet 18) [11]. Blanfort notices Nelson's pallor, but its true cause is not divulged. Blanfort is content to be home (aria 19) [12]; he goes to seek a notary. The remaining three, with effort, decide to keep silence and pray to friendship (trio 20) [13]. As Corali goes to sign the marriage documents she faints. Timur enters and explains. Blanfort quickly realises the truth and forbids any kind of confessions. In the ensemble sequence (21) Corali recognises her many debts to Blanfort who, in turn, gives her in marriage to Nelson. All determine to be one family. Amilcar requests Betzi's hand and is accepted; all sing 'May friendship bring us together'.

The remaking of this opera was noticed in the simple report of the *Mercure de France*:

M. Favart had too faithfully followed the progress of the tale, which is interesting and moral but a little sad; the changes with which he has newly brought out his comedy throw upon it a tint [*teinte*] of gaiety which, far from spoiling the interest, contrasts happily with it and adds to its effect. M. Grétry has also reworked the music he had written for this opera, he has interspersed new pieces that have had great success, mainly those sung by Mlle Renaud *l'aînée*. (18 November 1786, p. 141)

A new leading singer, some new, amusing characters and a deal of diverting music for them: it was enough to keep the work on the boards, especially with a score genuinely striking and unpredictable in colour and design. But there was a more

serious facet to it: the problem of slavery, the wars against the British, the identity of India and the friendship between peoples as well as between Nelson and Blanfort.
Let us summarise first how the authors changed the 1770 scenario.

1770	1786
Act 1	Act 1
Exposition of dilemma; anguish of lovers; letter heralding Blanfort's return	Exposition of dilemma; Corali's love asserted; arrival of Amilcar with news of Blanfort's return and letter
Music rejected: (1), (6), (7)	Music added: (4), (6), (7)
	Act 2
	Corali confides in Timur; decides against a relationship with either Nelson or Blanfort; courtship of Amilcar and Betzi. All new music except (13)
Act 2	Act 3
Corali's attempt to leave; return of Nelson and Blanfort; trio; dénouement (spoken)	Corali's hope; return of Nelson and Blanfort; trio; dénouement (sung); Betzi's acceptance of Amilcar
Music rejected: (9), (14)	Music added: (17), (21)

Note: all older music was retained in its original order.

We saw earlier the predominance of solos over duets in 1770: there were nine solos out of fourteen numbers (64%). In 1786 three duets were added, a quartet and two larger ensembles, so the ten solos amounted to 48% of the whole. Nevertheless, no attempt was made to give Corali a duet with Juliette or Nelson or Blanfort; Nelson's three arias were cut to one. But the new characters received six solos or duets, and participated in all three new larger ensembles. The singing cast was doubled to eight, a small part being given to the notary in (21). These outward dispositions indicate broadly the new flavour of the piece: the interplay of ideas and emotions has become exotic and anecdotal ('Love put to the test' might have been an apt re-titling) with some conspicuous musical local colour to support it. The new male parts were relatively well insinuated, particularly that of Timur in its unamended (Fontainebleau) form. Some subtle changes strengthened the figure of Blanfort. The new characters inspired Grétry's musical fantasy and may well have been more precisely suggested by him than the single 'comic rôle' he admits to (i:219). Amilcar and Betzi are Grétry's Papageno and Papagena. Amilcar's jocularity almost comes to dominate the closing stages of act 1, and his wooing of Betzi becomes a more than fortuitous mirror of the cross-cultural match between Corali and Nelson: 'Lorsque l'on s'aimer bien, Couleur ni faire rien', he sings in (15).

The opening of act 1 presents a far different picture to that of 1770, striking a jaunty musical pose in the duet (1). Furthermore, in the absence of both Nelson's impassioned arias – old (1) and (7) – his musical exposition falls to (2), which sounds bland after the dialogue that precedes it and discloses the dilemma. In the court première, clearly, a limit was felt to the degree to which Nelson could react to

Corali's attractive expository aria (3) so the last-minute provision of the melodrama (4) was made.[4] It is a welcome occurrence, virtually in lieu of a duet for them. Music intensifies the temperature, just as Favart made the dialogue more forthright. The new Corali is far less likely to take 'no' for an answer.

1770	1786
Corali: . . . for I love you With so much pleasure!	Corali (*carried away by passion, she addresses Nelson as 'tu'*): Yes, Nelson, for I love you so frankly, with so much pleasure . . .
Nelson (*troubled*): You love me? Corali: Yes, Nelson [. . .] Does my friendship annoy you?	Nelson: Corali . . . you love me! . . . Corali: A hundred times more than myself, And to my dying breath.

The 1770 version allegorised the difficulties of their position in the words of (5), 'Braving Cupid's power, one becomes vulnerable', and the 1787 libretto cut the following dialogue (after Fontainebleau) where the lovers had previously discussed Blanfort's position and its possible inconsistencies, given his liberal precepts as taught to Corali. It makes Corali simpler and more headstrong against Juliette, with whom she will come into blunt opposition before the trio (8): 'By truth I was always guided. That is the only counsel I follow.' Such a simplification of the original into a clash of wills is fortified by the appearance of Amilcar, something which promotes merely circumstantial reasons why Corali should accept Blanfort: the near-loss of his life at sea, the presence of Timur specially for the wedding.

Amilcar bursts on the scene in (6), his joyful greeting doubled by a piccolo. Like many of the new numbers, this is in no orthodox form; it could be described as a sectional solo with some ensemble framing. In fact, Favart had not even intended the entrance to be sung, or the text after Amilcar's 'Ah quel plaisir' solo: Grétry commandeered the words to form a through-composed sequence dominated by the character of Amilcar. He recognises Corali and dances with her as he had done when she was a child. No sooner is he constrained to give his news of the voyage than he embarks on a graphic account, comically interrupted by the 'serious' characters at the same time when the excitement grows too strong. Indeed, the principal plot is nearly burlesqued when Amilcar gets to the point where Blanfort was swept overboard. All come in prematurely with 'He is dead', countered by an exaggerated setting of Amilcar's 'Not yet, not yet!'

Although Amilcar's diction is a kind of pidgin French his musical style in (6) is not outlandish. But once alone with Corali in (7) he relapses into the language of the Calenda. This short piece is as engaging as it is important. Encouraged no doubt by the success of his 'Chinese' opera *Panurge dans l'isle des lanternes* (1785), Grétry now set about further exoticism. *Panurge* had two 'oriental' themes in the overture, the second of which (Ex. 29.1) is strongly hexatonic and exploited novel timbres and a drone.[5] The Calenda also has a drone, asymmetrical phrasing and

L'amitié à l'épreuve, 3-act version

Ex. 29.1 *Panurge dans l'isle des lanternes*, overture

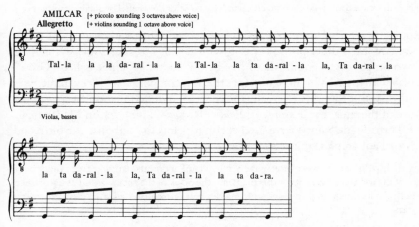

Ex. 29.2 *L'amitié à l'épreuve* (7), end of Calenda replacing an expected eight-bar phrase.

exotic timbre (piccolo three octaves above the voice). Grétry aims for even greater realism in writing a 'composed' accelerando, his phrases getting shorter and shorter, finally whirling to a sudden stop (Ex. 29.2). If Grétry had read Père Labat's description of this favourite dance of slaves, he may well have intended his bass-line to represent drums.

The dancers are drawn up in two lines . . . Those who are waiting their turns, and the spectators, make a circle round the dancers and the drums. The more adept chants a song which he composes on the spur of the moment.[6]

And it is Amilcar's solo (9) that is so memorable at the beginning of act 2; the main key of B major, previously used simply for subsidiary sections, e.g. the vaudeville-like episode at the end of *L'amant jaloux* (12), now itself stands as a metaphor for

Grétry and the growth of opéra-comique

Ex. 29.3 *L'amitié à l'épreuve* (9)
('Touching expression, dark eyelids and two little ivory coconuts that Love herself seemingly embellished')

the exotic (Ex. 29.3). Unprecedented harmonic side-slips and changes of mode illustrate Amilcar's description, starting with Corali's 'tender soul' and ending with 'two little ivory coconuts that Love herself seemingly embellished'. Grétry could play with harmony as inventively as the next composer: see for example Exx. 33.3 and 36.3. But this music is really the equivalent of fictional landscapes in the literature of the time, for example in *Paul et Virginie* (1788), set on Madagascar. Indeed, Bernadin de Saint-Pierre used coconut-palms to symbolise the birth and growth of Paul and Virginia.

Already their palm-leaves were interwoven, clusters of coconuts hanging from them over the pool of the fountain. Except for this planting, the nook of the rock was left as nature had adorned it. On its moist, brown sides wide maidenhair ferns glistened with their green and black stars . . .

By comparison, Timur's music in (10) is completely Westernised; it was the only newly-written sonata-form piece. The interest, energy and even nobility of its close are used to confer distinction on the character of Blanfort, but cannot deflect the fact that he will not be seen until act 3. Then there is a grotesque swing into buffoonery in (11), followed by yet another emotional gulf leading to the duet of brother and sister, in G minor. This interesting piece (12) uses high G horns instead of B flat ones. The Larghetto opening exposes the wounds of Corali's love, after which the Allegro forms an image of desperate commiseration: Grétry exploits some acute dissonances, with triple-stopped violins. Its companion duet was cut after Fontainebleau; but perhaps the ideal solution would have been to site one single duet somewhat later, when Timur could have pictured India and comfort to Corali. For he accepts subsequently that marrying Blanfort would be an 'outrage', while she, influenced by thoughts of a beloved India, imagines herself scattering flowers on her father's tomb. This is the cue for the magnificent

Romance (13), shown in Ex. 9.3, and a finer cue than in 1770. The rich imagery has its visual parallel in paintings like Wright of Derby's 'Indian widow' (1785), sitting nobly alone in her sorrow.[7]

It is against this strength that we see certain changes of emphasis in the next scene (sc. 7, formerly act 2 sc. 4, and not present in the 1776 version). Here, Juliette confronts Corali. Perhaps the crux in 1770 was Corali's couplet, 'Ah! what customs! what corrupted country! Nature is the only stranger here.'[8] These and her sharp preceding lines are now transformed into an almost shrill speech stressing 'laws' instead of customs: 'But I declare that I wish to go far from these climes, where the barbarous injustice of your laws would dispose of a heart not freely given' etc., to which Juliette cannot find the words to reply. Building on his intentions first glimpsed in 1776, Favart makes Corali something of a representative. Her 'victory' is assured in the next music (the quartet, 14) when she sings dancing chains of notes while the others on stage are thinking about the guest bedrooms.

The emotional impact of this is followed comically, as a moral pendant. To Betzi, Amilcar is 'black, but not such a devil'; they sing alternate verses in (15), whose popular playfulness gives the impression that in creating the music of Papageno and his homilies, Mozart was merely summing up an already fashioned idiom (Ex. 29.4). Betzi demands equal rights, not polygamy, no matter how ardently men may treat women as a divine gift. She shows flashes of temper in the 'dialogue aria' (16), actually a duet in slow–fast form culminating in a dance. Grétry had hardly created a more compact developing scene, or more chances for actors to build characters, or a more cosy image of partnership using twinned musical phrases.

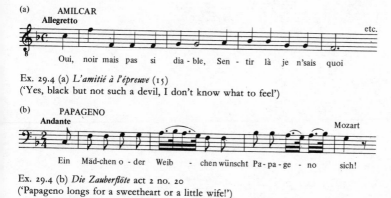

(a) AMILCAR
Allegretto

Oui, noir mais pas si dia - ble, Sen - tir là je n'sais quoi

Ex. 29.4 (a) *L'amitié à l'épreuve* (15)
('Yes, black but not such a devil, I don't know what to feel')

(b) PAPAGENO
Andante   Mozart

Ein Mäd-chen o - der Weib - chen wünscht Pa - pa - ge - no sich!

Ex. 29.4 (b) *Die Zauberflöte* act 2 no. 20
('Papageno longs for a sweetheart or a little wife!')

As we show at the end of this chapter, Corali's virtuosic (17) was not retained in Paris, and the composer doubtless wished he had never been seduced by the singer's capacities, to the detriment of dramatic integrity.[9] The retention of later items in act 3 from 1770 conceals significant changes to words and indeed music. After (18), which gives Blanfort little personal to say, sc. 2 (formerly act 2 sc. 5) was altered more than once in its dialogue; but Blanfort's aria (19) was also improved by cutting repeats and adding a coda. Scene 3 was recast to omit all reference to pistols, so reducing the risk of melodrama that had been taken in 1776. The attention shifts towards Corali. Her earlier spirited reasoning was modified in favour of assertion and a hectoring tone updated from the 1776 revival: 'No: but my soul is independent. And who gave you rights to afflict and oppress innocence, nature, love, and dictate my choice?' Yet she will break into continued weeping as the celebrated trio approaches, so that ultimately the new version lessens the lofty resolve of 1770, not to mention the sheer toughness of Marmontel's Corali. The trio (20) stands out more sentimentally.

The original plan of Favart after it was to remove Corali from the stage while the men decided how best to settle matters. Happily, the fairly substantial proportions of the final music (21) succeed in dignifying the characters of both her and Blanfort. The sense of fulfilment here is comparable to the ending of *Le Magnifique*, but since Grétry is dealing with such a diverse group of individuals, the theme of 'one family' quite replaces the original one of 'sacrifice rewarded'. For the musical expression of this in the Presto, with piccolos, Grétry composed an idea that Wichmann was to call 'the original image of the "seid umschlungen"' (in the finale of Beethoven's Ninth Symphony (Ex. 29.5)). It may be accidental that

Ex. 29.5 (a) *L'amitié à l'épreuve* (21) last section
('May friendship bring us together, let us spend our days together')

Ex. 29.5 (b) Ninth Symphony, op. 125, 4th movement, Maestoso
('Be embraced, ye millions! This kiss to the whole world!')

Beethoven's music is similar, but it is worth remembering that Schiller's ode 'To Joy' dates from 1785 and that ideas for a setting of it were credited to Beethoven as early as 1793.[10] What is undeniable is that both works celebrate universal brotherhood. When 'Les indiens' visited the Comédie-Italienne in August and September 1788, they saw *L'amitié à l'épreuve* twice, the performance on 15 September being 'by order'.[11]

Since Grétry's finale does, thanks to Favart, offer such an unusual development of amity linking Europe with the East Indies, it may be of use to elucidate related textual points not so far brought forward. The character of Timur provides the first two, making it clear that audiences were meant to recall France's recent wars. In act 2 sc. 4 he tells Corali that he was imprisoned by the English for two years and went on to serve under Haider Ali. Then after (12) he had an eighteen-line speech evoking the natural beauties of India, concluding with: 'The time of sacrifices and trouble is past: a king, monarch of the French, assures us the fruits of tranquillity. Everywhere he has planted the olive of peace.'[12] Corali listens with growing enthusiasm, rises and says, 'I shall follow you.'

Since the 1770 *L'amitié à l'épreuve* Anglo-French antagonism had hardly ceased, particularly in the East Indies, and in 1778 France joined the war of American Independence. Haider Ali was the most successful Indian ruler to combat the British and the French allied with him in 1778–82, the years of his greatest military triumph. His biography appeared in French in 1783 only a year after his death in battle. Favart's reference alludes to the Treaty of Versailles (1783) under which 'the French recovered their trading stations in India [although] moral victory lay with the British.'[13] Timur, like his sister, partly becomes a representative in the narrower sense.

Yet this is also true of Amilcar, by implication, the selfless black servant who has not only rescued Blanfort from the boiling sea but refuses to accept the reward that Nelson publicly offers him in act 1. He signifies a condition of man as much as a character; in fact the *Mercure de France* perceived him as a 'negro slave newly arrived from America' (18 November 1786, pp. 141–2) even though nothing in the libretto supports this. For an explanation one has only to recall the great critique of colonialism by Raynal, almost synchronous with Grétry's dramatisation of that other colonial being, the Huron.[14]

It is only the fatal destiny of the Negroes which doth not concern us. They are tyrannised, mutilated, burnt, and put to death, and yet we listen to these accounts coolly and without emotion . . . fourteen or fifteen hundred thousand blacks, who are now dispersed over the European colonies of the New World, are the unfortunate remains of eight or nine millions of slaves that have been conveyed there.

In France generally the experience of America was seen as 'a working example of the sovereignty of the people'.[15] And in 1788 was founded the Société des Amis des Noirs, a year after the free black state of Sierra Leone.

Amilcar's 'exotic' music and Timur's utopian picture of India in act 2[16] anticipate *Paul et Virginie* opéras-comiques by Kreutzer (1791) and Le Sueur

(1794). However, most pre-Revolution stage works that exploited exotic settings approached neither the dignity of Lemierre's play about the Indian widow Lanassa (*La veuve du Malabar*, 1770, popularly revived ten years later) nor the notion of 'one family'. Perhaps the prevailing tone was most durably set in the ballet *Mirsa* (Opéra, November 1779), holding the stage until 1808 with 158 performances. Sporting a Caribbean setting and ending with a Franco-American military parade,[17] it included acts of violence, the association of the sea with death, and excessive histrionics: all three factors would be associated with future opéra-comique.[18]

As a fully-fledged exotic opéra-comique, nothing could compete with Dalayrac's *Azémia* (Fontainebleau 1786): shipwrecked English travellers, villainous Spaniards, threatening natives, even realistic use of gunfire. The visual demands of the libretto were considerable, with different levels, natural vegetation, rocks and sea (see Plate VIII). A further element, more famously employed in *Paul et Virginie*, was natural love. The love of Aucassin and Nicolette in Grétry's opera certainly falls into an adjacent category but contains the counterbalancing theme of filial disobedience. In *Azémia* Prosper discovers Azémia's sex in act 1 (she has been brought up as a boy) and they have a love-scene at night in act 2.[19] Their affection is approved by Lord Akinson who is so liberated from 'the prejudices of Europe' as to 'let nature speak' and marry them. Some remarks on the music of this work will be found on page 284.

Some remarks on the music of this work will be found on page 284.

VERSIONS AND PERFORMANCES

The following is a summary of the musical alterations Grétry made to those items taken over from the 1770 version into the 1786 one.

Old (3): new (2): elimination of fourteen-bar *fioritura* on 'flamme' near the end and substitution of eleven bars of composed music
Old (4): new (3): small cadenza added to final section
Old/new (5): end of opening ritornello improved; many new technical difficulties composed into passagework; four bars cut before cadenza; new cadenza supplied, using an obbligato oboe, taking the voice to e''' natural.
Old/new (8): eleven bars cut from repeated material in recapitulation
Old (12): new (19): transposed from G to E flat; rescored without horns but with flute instead of oboes; binary-form repeats omitted; eleven-bar coda added, with substantial interest in vocal part
Old (13), new (20): clarinets omitted in favour of flutes, who receive appropriate upper octave transposition.[20]

Comparisons between the Fontainebleau libretto and later librettos and the score betray several significant areas of alteration, though none involved restitution of the pistols.[21] Most, however, now seem of doubtful value. The opera began at Fontainebleau as it had previously done, with Nelson's anguished 'Mon âme est dans un trouble extrême'. Timur's status was higher both because he was a nabob (a provincial governor, as the libretto explained in act 2 sc. 4) and because he had the responsibility of explaining the truth to Blanfort after his sister collapsed near the end. Further, after Corali was taken off to recover, Timur offered Blanfort two thirds of his (Timur's) estate in India in compensation for his disappointment and the girl's return there. Timur's rôle as rescuer had been cemented by a second duet with Corali, after (12), where he had persuaded her that in leaving England she would, like Nelson, successfully triumph over love. When this duet was removed Timur's eighteen-line 'colonial' speech was inserted.

For her part, Corali originally had a new cavatina (thus entitled) in the act 1 'reading' scene; it looks undramatic in context; the melodrama (4) appeared instead. Its removal may have swayed Grétry in favour of the virtuoso aria (17), heard after Fontainebleau on 30 October, excised, and put back in a more suitable position in late November.[22] Yet it seemed 'more and more out of place' subsequently, since Corali has at the time no reason to assume future happiness simply because Nelson is returning (i:221). Between the printing of the score and the 1789 edition of the *Mémoires* (17) was dropped. It only makes the continued lack of a duet with Nelson the more keenly felt, particularly since after (5) – again after Fontainebleau – the dialogue scene between the lovers was cut out. But then, even Blanfort's characteristic speech prior to fetching the notary vanished, and that had survived every printed version to date.

L'amitié à l'épreuve had twenty-nine performances in 1786–9, then three in 1792, and lastly eleven in 1816–17.

30. Les méprises par ressemblance (Errors through resemblance)

Comédie in 3 acts, in prose: *CC* 5
Libretto by Joseph Patrat
First performed at Fontainebleau, 7 November 1786. First performed at the Comédie-Italienne, 16 November 1786.
Printed full score, Paris, chez l'auteur, n.d. [1791] as Œuvre xxvii.[1]
Dramatis personae: (with Patrat's costume instructions)[2]

> M. Robert, rich innkeeper, father of Louis Sansquartier and Louison. Dressed as a comfortable bourgeois. (b.)
> The Bailli, wealthy friend and relative of Robert, and father of Thérèse and Louis Latulipe. Dressed first in a short coat and then in judicial robes. (t.)
> Thérèse, younger daughter of the Bailli, neatly dressed as a petite-bourgeoise. (s.)
> Louison, friend and relative of Thérèse, daughter of Robert, dressed rather like Thérèse. (s.)

strong
physical
resemblance

{
Sansquartier, son of Robert, lover of Thérèse. Grenadier's uniform. (t.)

Latulipe, illegitimate son of the Bailli, but not known as such. Grenadier's uniform of the same colour but with different buttons. (b.)
}

Sansregret, travelling-companion of the above. Dragoon's uniform. (b.)

Jacquinot, half-witted godson of the Bailli, promised in marriage to Louison. First dressed in Sunday clothes, crumpled and torn, afterwards more neatly. (t.)

Margot, ageing servant at the inn, dressed as a peasant living near Paris. (s.)

A brigadier, armed (spoken rôle)

Four constables; company of peasants

ACT 1: The main square of a large market town near Paris. Above a new house on one side, a notice 'ROBERT, Wine-seller, caterer, does weddings and banquets'. Bailli's house opposite, upstage. Downstage, a small café with winning lottery numbers in the window: 63, 11, 84, 28, 40. Before the action begins Jacquinot has been in a brawl with two grenadiers (actually Latulipe and Sansregret) at a family party some way away. Sansquartier, who has been away on service for some ten years, is expected home imminently.

Thérèse and Louison sit sewing. Although Thérèse looks forward to marriage with Sansquartier, Louison dreads the prospect of Jacquinot (duet 1).[3] She blames the Bailli's abandonment of his long-lost son, only to be told the story of his illegitimacy, how he was fostered with one Mathurin, and his supposed death in the West Indies (Thésèse's Romance 2). Louison still wants to stay single (solo 3). Robert and the girls anticipate the return of Sansquartier (trio 4). Latulipe and Sansregret enter, recalling the fracas of last night's dance and the loss of their money. They are extremely hungry. Latulipe likes women but Sansregret prefers drinking (duet 5). Finding that Latulipe has drawn winning numbers in the lottery, they discover on looking for his lottery tickets that he has mistakenly picked up an unknown soldier's kit-bag on leaving last night's lodgings. Then Latulipe encounters Louison and soon sings ardently to her (aria 6). Thérèse draws her companion away and Sansregret resolves to defend this latest assault on his companion's heart (aria 7). Margot has been staring at Latulipe and, thinking he is Sansquartier, asks his identity: at his friend's insistence and to protect them both from possible incrimination concerning the brawl, he admits to the name Sansquartier. Margot is delighted (aria 8). Sansregret decides they must press on with the deception, at least until they have eaten. Latulipe goes to look for Louison, leaving Sansregret to answer Robert's questions about his newly-returned 'son'. In order to conceal certain inconsistencies he makes out that his friend suffers from sporadic amnesia, curable by a good intake of alcohol (trio 9: Sansregret, Margot, Robert). When Latulipe appears, his lack of recognition of his 'father' is thus explained away. Moreover, apparent confirmation of his identity is found when papers extracted from the unknown soldier's kit-bag turn out to be those of the real Sansquartier. In the Finale (10) Latulipe, although discovering Louison is his 'sister', staunchly refuses to take any amorous interest in Thérèse. All go in to supper.

ACT 2: The same; 7 p.m. After the entr'acte (11) a dishevilled Jacquinot describes being attacked at the party (aria 12). The constables have been summoned. Now the real Sansquartier arrives, encountering first Jacquinot, who takes him for his attacker and runs away, and then Thérèse, who is very struck by his likeness to her 'fiancé'. Sansquartier gradually realises that an imposter has taken his place, and is even rejected by his own father (duet 13). Jacquinot and the Bailli bring in the brigadier and constables. In the finale (14) Sansquartier is arrested as Latulipe; his filial protestations almost convince Robert that he is genuine, until the contents of his kit-bag, mistakenly left with him at the lodging-house, apparently reveal his identity as Latulipe. He is led away to detention in an old building in Robert's grounds.

ACT 3: A large room furnished in antique style. A side entrance, with two large cabinets opposite. Upstage, a grated window with half-drawn curtain. Nightfall. Sansquartier is imprisoned and overwhelmed by grief (recitative and aria 15). Thérèse has taken pity on him and come to release him, without accepting him as her true fiancé. She hides as Latulipe arrives for a rendezvous with Louison. Challenged, Latulipe throws down his sword; as Sansquartier picks it up the brigadier enters, assumes his prisoner to be Latulipe, and sends Sansquartier away. Thérèse is almost discovered. The Bailli, now robed, comes to interrogate the prisoner, who gladly confesses to the name Latulipe and acknowledges a certificate signed by his foster-father Mathurin discovered by the Bailli in the kit-bag impounded in act 2. The Bailli tearfully recognises him as his own son (trio 16 with Thérèse, still hidden). He is embarrassed enough by the discovery to ask Latulipe to stay where he is for a while. It is now dark. In the finale (17) Thérèse is discovered, almost faints in Latulipe's arms, and so has to face an angry Louison when the latter enters. They hide as, by turns, Sansquartier, Sansregret, Jacquinot and Margot creep in for different reasons. Sansquartier pairs off inadvertently with Jacquinot, and Latulipe with Margot. When Robert and the Bailli enter together they have already solved the mistaken identities. Sansregret confesses to instigating the hoax. Jacquinot is paid off and the correct couples group for their weddings, to the music of an old-fashioned vaudeville and last chorus.

The patient reader vexed with such complication may take comfort from knowing that audiences always found Patrat's last act less than crystal clear. Certain changes were made to it after the première (see last section). But eighteenth-century theatre-goers also knew a tradition of 'resemblance' comedies that we have lost.

The urge to invent new types, new mixtures of genre was strong, and in *Les méprises par ressemblance* themes of filial rejection and imprisonment were mixed with farce. The daring balance was not equitably managed, with the result that a potentially very good work became fatally flawed. The farcical crux went back to the *Menaechmi* by Plautus (3rd century B.C.) who invented or at least handed down the comedy of twin brothers, separated since infancy. The action takes place when the travelling brother returns to the city where his twin has married. Shakespeare's early *The Comedy of Errors* remains the most complex descendant of the *Menaechmi*. Seventeenth-century French adaptors at first kept closely to the original (Jean Rotrou, *Les Ménechmes*, 1632) but gradually grafted on more individuality. Grétry's librettist proclaimed a Spanish source on his title-page, but this has not been found and may have been a decoy. Patrat's was a free reworking, most closely akin to *Le rival par ressemblance* (1762) by Charles Palissot de Montenoy. Both differ from their predecessors first because the resemblance is not between brothers, and second because the doubles each travel to the place of the action. Palissot's comedy, set in Paris, has only one girl at the centre of the confusion, betrothed to the unattractive Cléon. As Cléon is not brought in until act 4, his double, Clerval, has all the best cards to play.

Patrat nevertheless included features evolved by others. In Jean Regnard's *Les Ménechmes*, acted in 1705, luggage mistakenly directed from one twin to the other furnishes a vital mainspring of the action. Regnard also caused documents to be produced, uselessly, as evidence of identity: these parallel the identity papers and Mathurin's certificate in Patrat's third act. Regnard's valet, like Sansregret, promotes the deception and (act 3 sc. 11) explains away inconsistencies uttered by one double by claiming that he is suffering from amnesia.[4] From Eustache Lenoble's *Les deux harlequins*, played at the Comédie-Italienne to 1757, might have come the idea of a farcical encounter in half-darkness. The Comédie-Italienne owned two other comedies before Patrat's on the same theme. Antoine Colalto's *Les trois jumeaux vénitiens* (*The three Venetian twins*), first acted in 1773 and derived from Goldoni, used a single actor playing all three triplets. From this play Patrat could have drawn the idea of a woman becoming engaged to one brother at the outset, only to be deceived by the emergence of his double. There is a more significant parallel in that the most sympathetic triplet, Zanetto de Venise, is detained at the end of the third act, like Sansquartier, as a direct consequence of his appearance and apparent duplicity. The other comedy, Florian's one-act *Les jumeaux de Bergame* (*The Bergamask twins*), 1782, is an elegant treatment in which the harlequin brothers become embroiled with a pair of lovers.

Joseph Patrat (1732–1801) was originally a law student who turned actor and author and ended his career as secretary of the Odéon theatre, Paris. He published many comedies, perhaps the best-known of which was *Le fou raisonnable* (*The rational madman*), 1781. *Les méprises par ressemblance* was his third opéra-comique libretto.[5] Although he never collaborated again with Grétry *père* he provided the libretto of *Toinette et Louis* for Lucile Grétry in 1787 and went on to write eight further librettos for minor composers.

The mechanics of a farce should be completely polished, and one cannot deny that Patrat left in too many creaky joints as the piece proceeded. For example, Thérèse twice imparts the same piece of information to Sansquartier, in acts 2 and 3.[6] Louison's jealousy in (17) at seeing Thérèse fainting in Latulipe's arms is logical only if she already thinks of him as a lover, not brother. Comic business might have dealt with this point, but it is symptomatic of the generally too underdeveloped love story between Louison and Latulipe. After all, theirs is the happiest, most unexpected fate of all. Moreover, while act 1 forms a superb crescendo of musical and dramatic interest the best comic scenes in act 3 are in prose. Patrat's dialogue, particularly in the first act, is seductively quick and humorous. The speed of action and brevity of musical numbers compel comparison with *L'amant jaloux*. In the brief second act the farcical mode alters so quickly that we regret the lack of an extra comic scene based on Sansquartier's resemblance, the development of the plot, as it were. Sansquartier becomes instead a figure with whom we are obliged merely to sympathise; however, we are told very little about his character, though Grétry makes up for this later in the heroic music of (15).

In the sense of new types of character or situation, Grétry was given relatively little, and precisely because he sensed no overriding novelty (one suspects) he used already-tried ideas.[7] The virginal daughters, the imbecile, the Bailli, the lover falsely arraigned, all had appeared before in his *œuvre*. It would be wrong to misrepresent the experience and novelty in his score. The collection of characters was not unpromising, and is quite extensive. However, they engage only perfunctorily in duets or ensembles, save for (9), (13) and (16). So the bulk of what Grétry has to say in music that is new comes in the finales, which are all quite substantial.

Latulipe's declaration (6) stops short after thirty-nine bars.[8] Sansregret has an excellent rôle in act 1 but thereafter fades into the background. Jacquinot, a clear descendant of Gilotin in *Le Huron*, receives in (12) a perfectly judged suggestion of idiotic simplicity, often using only three different bass notes. The Bailli gets no aria, but as he is always sarcastic to his godson in dialogue his 'paternity' trio (16) can be acted with great effect and insincerity, until exploded by Latulipe's wonderful line, 'Everyone wants to be my father today!' Sansquartier is not ideally served in (13), where urgent patterns and pulsing bass paint the anguish of the son, but seem predictable and insufficient for the cross-currents of emotion in a complex stage situation. More unexpected is the obbligato recitative in (15), thirty-eight bars long. The following aria is filled with 'heroic' figurations and old-fashioned static bass-lines, so that one wonders whether these were remnants of a discarded piece from *Théodore et Paulin*.

The term 'finale' suggests Italy but (1), (4), (5) and (9) have already adopted that artificiality of drama implied by characters singing together seemingly for the sake of singing. Yet the finales of *Les méprises par ressemblance* do not adhere to Italian 'chain' convention and forge an alternative kind of Gallicised buffooning music. If the 'Finale' (10), thus named in the libretto, begins and ends in one key (D major) it also imposes a second harmonic architecture. As the tension rises with Latulipe's attraction to Louison instead of Thérèse, not to mention the attendant embarrassment, the harmony progresses up to the dominant of C sharp minor. Then the tension dissipates in a comically artificial series of steps, culminating in Ex. 30.1 in D major. This exhilarating music forms the melodic apotheosis of the whole Finale and (remembering (1), (4), (5) and (9)) of the brilliant first act itself.

Ex. 30.1 *Les méprises par ressemblance* (10)
('Let's go in, let's eat, let's drink, let's sing, let's dance')

The unusual unifying idea of the second finale (14) is the maintenance of a 2/4 time-signature throughout its total of some 475 bars. The only tempo indication is Allegretto, though one assumes fluctuations. By contrast the keys vary widely and include B flat major and B minor within an overall sequence starting in F and concluding in D major. This of course matches the wide range of action, vividly portrayed. The Gallic influence might be summed up as a lifelike pace of action and motivic meaning at the expense of key-symmetry or cantabile aria sections, even for poor Sansquartier. Included in 'motivic meaning' would be the recurring orchestral figure Ex. 30.2 underscoring his persecution by the assembly. The orchestral symbol personal to Grétry for reading (a reiterated violin pedal-note) appears when the Bailli examines the contents of the grenadier's kit-bag.[9] More dramatically telling was the provision of words extra to the published libretto for a group of sympathetic womenfolk, their music counterpointed against myriad cries of 'Quick! to prison!' (Ex. 30.3).

Alternating between 2/4 and 6/8 time, the third finale is built on a sequence of nine related keys; but, like *L' épreuve villageoise*, goes back at the end to a vaudeville and final chorus. The vaudeville has two structural connections with the finale. The opening section of the latter quotes from and is built on the opening of the vaudeville tune proper; and the downward octave leap in the refrain of the

Ex. 30.2 *Les méprises par ressemblance* (14)

266

Les méprises par ressemblance

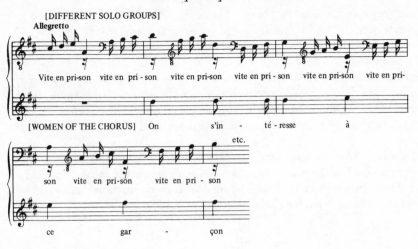

Ex. 30.3 *Les méprises par ressemblance* (14)

vaudeville finds its way into various other phrases in prior sections of (17). Curiously, the vaudeville commences in G and closes in C major: was Grétry attempting here too a structural bridge between these four verses and the final chorus, in C?

Some noteworthy examples of Grétry's orchestral modernity occur in (17), such as the difficult horn solo (reaching top c''') in the imbroglio of sc. 14 – unlike anything earlier in his opéras-comiques – and icy D minor chords held on flutes, violas and bassoons in sc. 11 as Sansquartier creeps on stage. But the list could be continued, especially with uses of pizzicato. It seems certain that Grétry was responding to public taste for colour by making his new music a definite totality of orchestral and vocal sound, and by writing more rhythmically and independently for upper strings.

VERSIONS AND PERFORMANCES

Grimm (xiv:487) noted the successful Fontainebleau première whose version (revealed by comparing court libretto and press review[10]) was retained for the Comédie-Italienne. But the audience had difficulty unravelling act 3, so a modified (17) was readied by Patrat for the fifth performance on 30 November.[11] The letter announcing it also mentioned Grétry's part in the alterations. In this revision (17) was changed up as far as Sansregret's confession. After Louison and Thérèse hid, the Bailli, brigadier and officers entered with Sansquartier, who challenged Latulipe. Latulipe challenged back. Sansregret dragged Jacquinot in, followed by the locals. There was almost a fight as Sansregret defended his travelling-companion. The Bailli's interrogation revealed the mysteries of identity; the girls came out of hiding.

Although the *Mercure* mentioned them, it did not consider the changes to be sufficient (review, see note 10). Nevertheless the 'Paris' libretto was issued to incorporate them.[12] But in publishing the score Grétry reverted to the original version, at least of words. As note 1 records, there was unusual delay before the score appeared.

A major set of changes not seen from the score is revealed in Grétry's letter of 27 September 1788: '*Les méprises par ressemblance* is not being given since there are no baritones to replace Narbonne. I have just arranged his part for a tenor.'[13] This must have been a doubly unwelcome task as three male rôles were already for tenor.

In the years 1786 to 1793 inclusive, the opera had sixty-two performances. It did well when revived in the years 1817–22, with sixty-six performances, and had a further thirty showings in 1858–9. The final foreign production mentioned by Loewenberg was an arrangement at Stockholm (1877).

31. Le Comte d'Albert (Count d'Albert)

Drame in 2 acts, in prose and verse; followed by its SEQUEL, *Opéra-Comique* [*sic*] in 1 act, in prose and verse: CC 26
Libretto by Michel-Jean Sedaine. Dedicated to Elizabeth-Louise Vigée-Lebrun.[1]
First performed at Fontainebleau, 13 November 1786. First performed at the Comédie-Italienne, 8 February 1787.
Printed full score, Paris, Houbaut; Lyon, Castaud, n.d. [1787] as Œuvre xxv.
Dramatis personae (in acts 1 and 2): Count d'Albert (t.)
Countess d'Albert (s.)
Chloé (or Eglé) }
Rosine } their daughters (s.)
Maidservant (s.)
Tréville, friend of d'Albert, a general (t.)
Duval, an officer (t.)
Antoine, a street-porter (t.)

Police informers and agents	Servants of d'Albert	A prison lieutenant
Guards	Neighbours of d'Albert	Jailer
		Prison guards

(in the Sequel):All the above main characters except Duval, plus
Froment, a farmer (b.)
Mme Froment, his wife (s.)
Mlle Froment }
Delphine } their daughters (s.)
The Bailli (t.)
Benjamin, his son, engaged to Mlle Froment (t.)
The village schoolmaster (b.)
La Fleur (spoken rôle)
Three wandering Italian singers (s., s., b.)

ACT 1: A square in Paris with several roads leading into it. Downstage, a shop, half-open, provided with a window-ledge.[2] The frontage of d'Albert's town-house is seen. Two police informers enter. One, acting on the evidence of a letter which proves d'Albert guilty of killing a duelling opponent, has followed him from Brussels. They await his arrival (chorus 1),[3] then hide as d'Albert's children and the maid emerge from the house; the girls, having seen their mother's recent agitation, are pacified (trio 2). The Countess tells her valet to admit only a certain person, and takes the children away. Antoine enters with a heavy basket which he rests on the shop's ledge. He grumbles about his work, its hazards and his single existence. His 'song' (3) describes his philosophy. A well-dressed officer, Duval, passes by just as Antoine takes up his load, but its strap breaks, causing it to overbalance and splash mud on the officer. Duval goes to kill him with his sword but in the quartet (4) d'Albert enters and prevents the murder; the officer is restrained by the appearance of Tréville, his superior, and leaves contritely. Antoine, much embarrassed, is helped on his way. D'Albert explains he has come to collect his family secretly and take them to Brussels; he is under sentence of death for defying the courts. Suddenly (ensemble and chorus 5) the agents arrest d'Albert and bear him away, Tréville's resistance notwithstanding. The Countess re-enters at the noise, learns what has happened, and faints: servants support her. Chloé and Rosine enter but the truth is concealed from them. The anguished Countess departs with Tréville and her daughters, leaving a chorus of neighbours to comment.

ACT 2: Inside a prison chamber.[4] D'Albert meditates alone on his fate (6). The jailer and a turnkey bring food: the turnkey, who is none other than Antoine, sees d'Albert but remains silent. Tréville, whose efforts to obtain clemency have failed, can only commiserate (aria 7). The Countess tells Tréville to deliver the children to a certain uncle, since she has resolved to die should d'Albert be executed. D'Albert cannot accept this decision. The children are brought in, pleading not to be separated from their parents (duet 8) but are sent away. D'Albert and his wife resume their argument (duet 9) but the Countess is resolute. Antoine appears with a plan to save d'Albert, in recognition of d'Albert's actions earlier. He dresses d'Albert in his own wig, hat, gaiters and coat and instructs him how to get past the main gate. Outside, Tréville is waiting with a carriage. D'Albert goes. In the duet (10) the Countess prays while Antoine listens for signs of d'Albert's success. When no alarm is raised, Antoine sets up a tableau to ensure his own survival: as he cries for help, lying face down, she will stand over him with a knife. In the ensemble (11) this is done, and the lieutenant and guards rush in. The Countess defiantly takes credit for the rescue.

THE SEQUEL: After a pastoral overture the scene is set on d'Albert's estate near Brussels: a village square, the gates of Froment's farm to one side. Wandering minstrels sing an Italian trio (12) and are admitted for food and drink.[5] The Bailli tackles Froment about tomorrow's wedding between Benjamin and Mlle Froment, but Froment is bad-tempered on account of the lack of news from their respected seigneur, d'Albert (aria 13). Froment decides to make his own investigations. Benjamin and his fiancée are teased by the independently-minded Delphine, who announces she will find the partner she wants – and propose to him (trio 14). Villagers and neighbours crowd in: halfway through mealtime Froment has decided to go to Paris in search of d'Albert (sextet 15).[6] But then La Fleur announces d'Albert has been saved, and all spontaneously break into dance and song (16). When they have gone inside to hear the story Benjamin expresses his devotion to Mlle Froment (17). Delphine has been moved to tears by the story of Antoine's action. Froment orders a special celebration. D'Albert and his wife arrive, after separate journeys; their reunion is watched by the villagers (duet and chorus 18). There is a speech and a general dance (19). Chloé, Rosine, the maid and Antoine now arrive; d'Albert embraces Antoine, who is acclaimed. Delphine offers herself in marriage to an incredulous Antoine, who accepts her. All hurry to offer a dowry (ensemble 20). There follow a double chorus of peasants (21), a general ensemble expressing unanimity between villagers and their lords of the manor (22) and a contradance (23).

Le Comte d'Albert, like the 'theatre of fact' which was to depict important events under the Revolution, showed Paris to the Parisians. Some assumed that the prison scene was in the Bastille (see note 4) and Antoine's living counterparts were at street corners

to move in or move out our furniture and carry the heavy goods of commerce. You summon them with a sign and they and their hooks are at your side; leaning on boundary-stones, they wait for work. You would think that these men would be one size out of the ordinary, stout, strong-legged, ruddy of complexion; no, they are pale, squat, lean rather than fat; they drink far more than they eat. At any hour you can find them ready to put their back to the heaviest weights. Slightly bent over, sustained by a walking-stick, they carry burdens that would kill a horse; they carry them with suppleness and dexterity, between the hindrances of carriages and in bottleneck roads.

Their job was not the preserve of men:

What is painful to see are those unfortunate women who, a heavy load on their back, red-faced, their eyes almost bleeding, anticipate the dawn in streets of mire, or on a pavement whose icy covering shrieks under the first steps that press on it . . . How are women reduced among us to a labour so disproportionate to the strength given them by nature?[7]

It is interesting that in 1786 porters and carriers had commanded widespread sympathy for their strike and march to Versailles to seek the king's support against a rival monopoly.[8] (This protest was one of several workers' actions that are a background to the Revolution.) The outlines of Sedaine's story were commonly supposed to be factual, though Sedaine is silent on this: one Count d'Albert, condemned in France to execution for duelling in 1721, escaped from prison by sawing through the bars of his window.[9] Duelling was a specially-punished crime of lèse-majesté in France up to the Revolution.

Today duels are uncommon . . . Not sixty years ago the mania for fighting reached such a point that the wisest, most circumspect man could not avoid a bloody quarrel . . . The words of certain *philosophes*, pleading the cause of reason and humanity, obtained from these furious men what the latter had refused to a monarch and his solemn laws.[10]

Sedaine had been an ally of these *philosophes*. Duelling formed the central dilemma of his *Le philosophe sans le savoir* (1765), being one of several themes he himself listed: the equality of men's estate; respect due to commerce; the extravagance of duels, which caused French blood to run that should never be spilled except to defend France; and the need for freedom of religious expression.[11] That d'Albert escapes the worst consequences of his actions, and that these are never discussed, are surely dramatic weaknesses of the opera.

In *Le Comte d'Albert* the first of the above themes led Sedaine to give Antoine moral stature all through, not simply as a result of 'one good turn deserves another'. That is the reason for (3), where Antoine elevates the thinker above the chatterer, the honest girl above the coquette, and any honourable man living over 'A nobleman without merit, be he descended from an Armagnac'. The fact that Antoine would suffer grievously if detected in his complicity in act 2 places him beyond the mere rescuing figure of the rat in La Fontaine's fable *The lion and the rat*: this was Sedaine's dramatic kernel, a kind of truth-giving proverb woven inside the libretto.[12] (A lion lets go a rat in his power, so the rat later gnaws through a snare, freeing the beast.)

Sedaine described the genesis of the libretto, however, as some earlier dramatic sketches for young people of the 'highest rank': Grétry read the manuscript and was attracted to the possibilities of the prison scene. The idea of a sequel betokens a hasty elaboration, one usually described as a bucolic appendage conceived with Grétry's tunes in mind. But the theme of Delphine's independence and sense of worth, her ability in a sense to 'rescue' Antoine, is obviously a mirror of the Countess's intending self-sacrifice in act 2. As an experiment in forgoing the unity of place it was not unique; in September 1785 the Comédie-Italienne rejected a play partly because its scene changed location within the course of an act.[13] Sedaine did not expect to escape censure for breaking the unities of time and place in the third act, which was termed 'Sequel' precisely because it occurs 'fifteen days and sixty leagues' outside the main action.

Grétry says he composed the score rapidly, within a month, so that for example (5) 'could have been treated on my part with greater use of harmony and modulation if time had allowed me to wait and seek' (i:402–4). But there is plenty of interest, despite occasional brevity of numbers. A sign of the age is the dearth of solos, but choruses and ensembles gave Grétry everything that music could cope with: entrances, exits, argument, struggle, offstage activity. The expanding choral body allowed the authors to dramatise different sections of society, although (1) is musically too light-hearted for the occasion and in (5) the police agents (of whom the spoken dialogue optimistically refers to seventeen) perform mostly from the wings. The important chorus and ensemble is (18). Grétry employed a very slow harmonic rhythm to express the ecstatic meeting of his main couple, allowing the chorus to partake in their music from a distance. The result, extended to seventy-five bars (Ex. 31.1) is not unlike parts of the first act finale of *Fidelio*. Thus it

Ex. 31.1 *Le Comte d'Albert* (18)
('Near to you, near to our children')

becomes a focus for the entire opera. Later in (22) all classes are shown united within a steady minuet tempo.

Regrettably, Grétry and Sedaine did not give Antoine a musically distinguished part. In (11) where his heroism might have found voice, it is the Countess who dominates and Antoine who maintains his supposed rôle to the end. Even (3) lacks the polish of a memorably defiant statement. And in (4), only forty-two bars long, Antoine can do little except stammer his relief. D'Albert's daughters provide the story's sentimentality, though Grétry is alive to the details provided by their words, especially in (2).

As in Beethoven's *Fidelio*, where admittedly Leonore is far more courageous than Sedaine's Countess, the consistent thread in Grétry's opera is that of conjugal love. It is quite clear from all evidence that Mme Dugazon created a remarkable portrait of wifely devotion, and had the measure of the character admiringly referred to by Tréville: 'quelle femme étonnante'; she has pleaded d'Albert's case before the king and swayed his courtiers.[14] A little of this depth is heard in (5) where she sings mostly in D minor and where her incomplete harmony on exit suggests the reality of a dread that has come to pass. Act 2, however, is the crux. D'Albert's prison solo (6) avoids a repetition of what is heard at parallel junctures beginning the second act of *Richard* and the third of *Les méprises par ressemblance*. Its tonality of C minor and its sombre mood have been prepared for in the opera's

Ex. 31.2 *Le Comte d'Albert* (6)
('But on children! my children! and on their mother . . .')

overture. The latter recalls Gluck's French style (see chapter 35) and (6) also does, in part. Using a non-repeating structure (though the words are set out in ternary form) the emotions of the condemned man are explored progressively, ending with no hint of catharsis. Ex. 31.2 illustrates the arioso style, the continuity of harmony, and the Gluckian fall as d'Albert recalls his wife's memory. Clearly his fate is not separable from hers. The orchestra helps create an image of the cell as a place of dread rather than a stimulant to nostalgia or anger, as in the earlier Grétry operas mentioned. The introduction develops three ideas, all articulated through their orchestration. In the most interesting of them, sophisticated horn writing and descending bass make a metaphor of the unnatural (Ex. 31.3) which was not lost on Pierre Gaveaux when he composed his 'dungeon' prelude in *Léonore ou l'amour conjugal* in 1798.

The finest music in the opera is probably that for the extended husband–wife

Ex. 31.3 *Le Comte d'Albert* (6)

duet (9), and the height of the conflict – the Countess's duty to her children as opposed to her belief in her own destiny – reaches the foreground in the third and final section. This naturally adopts a progressive form (AA'B). The soprano rises eventually to top B flat with no hint of meretricious appeal, and the force of her determination to abandon the children reaches Medea-like strength; it is seconded by orchestral writing that owes apology to no one. Music such as this was worthy of Gluck's example, just as the Countess's devotion recalls that of Alceste (Ex. 31.4). Then, cemented by the rapidly effective transitions that opéra-comique can make in dialogue, the drama takes its unexpected turn. In the composer's view at least, Sedaine's straightforward dialogue had a Shakespearian quality, partly since

Ex. 31.4 *Le Comte d'Albert* (9)
('You shall live for your/our children'; 'No!')

it was given depth by the piquancy of circumstances on the stage. Antoine, now a 'tutelary deity' (i:400), seems to echo the words of the Saviour at the Last Supper: 'Take my coat, take these dishes', and consequently to partake of Christ's nature.[15] Continuing the tone, the duet (10) makes much of religious emotion. Sedaine had intended the Countess to fall to her knees immediately but Grétry gives her a passionate appeal, alternating the more vividly with the laconic phrases of Antoine; the music still has those ideally religious qualities Grétry said he would like to see in actual church music: 'Few notes, melody simple and analogous to the subject, susceptible of a good bass and harmony' instead of 'tedious psalmody' (i:414). The Countess kneels only after Antoine is sure d'Albert is safe, whereupon Grétry gives her not a sung prayer but a silent one, leaving the orchestra's devout, low suspensions to portray her thoughts. It was a masterly stroke, and indeed to compare Sedaine's bare lines of text with the duet as realised is to see the great range of emotion the composer was able to inject, and the ingenious psychological design that made one follow logically from the last. It clearly inspired him: 'Is there anything more sacred in the world than true conjugal love?' (i:413).

Exhausted, the Countess falls lifeless in a chair. But the deception has to be continued and so the act concludes with her victorious proclamation, set to the music of an upward trumpet-figure, the whole orchestra in unison: 'Tout mon sexe sera pour moi' ('All women shall be for me').

It is easy to call the Sequel 'a collection of sentimental idiocies', as the *Mémoires secrets* did, but the unity of action is not actually broken: the tension caused by the delay in news from Paris is apparent straight away. Comic style does not negate theatrical purpose for Sedaine. We have already mentioned (18), but it must be stressed how fresh and enjoyable are Grétry's lighter pieces and dances, almost all in simple symmetrical forms. Does one despise Rameau for furnishing analogous contrasts? One piece in particular achieved inspired simplicity at the moment it was most needed to avoid anticlimax: this was (17), ready equipped with what was to become a cliché bass-line in the nineteenth century (Ex. 31.5). But it was a new style in Grétry.

Also new in his opéras-comiques and probably anybody's was the idea of a double chorus (21), that is a set of interrelated verses sung and danced alternately by one group downstage (stanzas, 1, 3, 5 in 2/2 metre, G major) and by another one upstage (stanzas 2, 4, 6 in 6/8 metre, E minor). Again, to us, hindsight suggests the nineteenth century and Berlioz' soldiers' and students' choruses in *La damnation de Faust*. However, Grétry was here using an idea from his recitative operas *Colinette à la Cour* (1782) and *La caravane du Caire* (1783), where metrically opposed double choruses had in fact been musically superimposed in exactly the way Berlioz was to adopt.

In a sense *Le Comte d'Albert*, its appeal to humanitarian ideals and to a 'higher' kind of moral authority, was already Revolutionary. The law, after all, is being defied. The work itself (see below) held the stage into Napoleon's era and even beyond it.

Ex. 31.5 *Le Comte d'Albert*, Sequel, (17)
('I am happy in all, Mademoiselle, You are more beautiful than the new-blown rose . . ')

Perhaps more obviously, it formed the model for Bouilly's and Cherubini's opéra-comique *Les deux journées*, the celebrated masterpiece about the water-carrier who saves the life of a titled parliamentarian (1800). But seen in the context of Sedaine's theatrical productions, *Le Comte d'Albert* represents a good solution to the task of writing something not predominantly comic or sentimental, but wide-ranging and involving a mixture of classes and types: not propaganda but dealing with relationships in the light of contemporary life. Far more polemical had been his libretto *Félix ou l'enfant trouvé* (set by Monsigny, 1777), 'a bitter satire on the privileged classes which are here represented by Morin's three sons. They are depicted as thoroughly corrupt and selfish, always ready to use the privileges attached to their professions [the army, the law, the church] for their own ends, and united only in their common hatred of Félix', the foundling who wins his happiness and finds his real father.[16] But *Aucassin et Nicolette* and *Félix* make idealistic compromises over the birth of their characters, for 'it was inevitable . . . that playwrights should show a certain timidity when it actually came to depicting on stage even honest bourgeois, let alone the lower orders'.[17] In this sense, *Le Comte d'Albert* discovers a formula without compromise: Antoine will marry a peasant and d'Albert, the reproved dueller, will return not to the vain city, but to an ideal rural pattern of life where all classes are respected.

Many pre-Revolutionary operas place a certain emphasis on freedom of choice, not least for women. Few, though, seem to stress that natural love and relationship which binds *Le Comte d'Albert*; in the context of Wordsworth Raymond Williams has seen such a stress as 'necessary not only within the immediate suffering but against the aggressive individualism and the primarily economic relationships which the new society embodied'.[18] Paris was a prime example of advanced economics in action; there is plenty of evidence suggesting that the self-determination displayed by Countess d'Albert was an ideal, not a reality. Even up to 1791 women in general 'were still without rights, without property, without power';[19] and Beaumarchais' Marcelline was declaiming, from 1784, 'Even in the highest classes women receive only your most derisory consideration: lured on by seeming respect but in real servitude; treated as children when it comes to possessions but as adults when we transgress!'[20]

The political soil out of which such plays and operas grew was no longer stable. In the month that *Le Comte d'Albert* opened in Paris, the Assembly of Notables met: 146 men headed by seven princes of the blood, summoned to solve the nation's tottering economy and taxation. The following ditty went the rounds: 'King befuddled, Controller-general, convulsive fever, Nobility, aphasic, Clergy, fever redoubled, The people in agony'.

In a performance of Paisiello's opera *Le roi Théodore à Venise* in Louis XVI's presence late in 1786, the wandering king Theodore had just been informed by his squire that they had no more money and did not know where to find more. A voice came up from the audience: 'The only thing is to assemble the Notables!' Louis decided to laugh and restrained the guards from moving in.[21] Public disorder erupted at the Comédie-Italienne in 1786, as we saw in chapter 1, and did so again on 26 December 1787, partially as a result of the failure of a new Grétry opéra-comique, *Le prisonnier anglais*. The *Mercure de France* noted with distress the shouts, whistles and insults that lasted until 11 p.m. and Grimm for one heard political reasons advanced: 'It is the nation preparing for the States-General' (xv:192).

Le prisonnier anglais, libretto by Desfontaines (G. F. Fouques-Deshaye), was simply unbelievable: through the helpful efforts of his jailer a wrongly-accused young man escapes threat of execution, leaving the jailer perhaps to lose his own life in return. At the eleventh hour the true murderer gives himself up. Act 1 was set in a prison cell. The authors then prepared a second version which received six performances from February to April 1788. It incorporated a completely new part for Mme Dugazon. Grétry prevented further performances since he had in mind an improved plan for act 3 with Desfontaines (letter of 27 September 1788). A third version, as *Clarice et Belton*, had eleven performances in 1793 and it is this music whose manuscript survives in Liège and in *CC* 48–9.[22] But as the spoken dialogue has not survived from any version it is impossible to discuss the opera with propriety.

VERSIONS AND PERFORMANCES

Le Comte d'Albert was acted each year to 1793 in a total of seventy-nine performances. From December 1794 it was stripped of references to aristocracy and the feudal system and the Sequel was set outside Frankfurt.[23] The title became *Albert et Antoine* and the last act was not advertised as a 'Sequel'. It had fifty-seven performances, being given each year to 1804, then an odd one in 1806, sixteen in 1812–13, followed finally by eighteen in 1823–4. The last foreign production listed in Loewenberg was in St Petersburg (1822).

32. Confident rivals

As we saw in chapter 26, Grétry's newer opéras-comiques proved to be less attractive to Parisians than his earlier ones. By contrast, certain works by Martini, Dezède and Dalayrac were recognised as being of more lasting interest. *Le rival confident* (Comédie-Italienne, 26 June 1788: *CC* 45), a new two-act comedy by Grétry, was granted only ten performances in 1788, seven of them when a revised version was mounted in October. There followed a mere four in 1789 and three in 1790. (This record makes it, by a hair's breadth, Grétry's least successful opéra-comique before *Cécile et Ermancé* in 1792 and *Joseph Barra* in 1794.) A valuable letter of 27 September 1788 bares Grétry's feelings about his latest work, as well as *Amphitryon* and *Les méprises par ressemblance*, not given since the preceding January: 'You had the courage to talk about rope in the house of the hanged man.' Significantly, Grétry says the revision of *Le rival confident* was not called for by the librettist, N. J. Forgeot, but was the result first of an actress's injury and second of his own initiative: 'I turned the occasion to advantage by asking the author for a dénouement much more amenable to music; I rewrote a finale which will be worth much more.'[1]

Forgeot (1758–98) had provided the libretto for Champein's successful opéra-comique *Les dettes* (1787) and, apart from continuing to write verse comedies, went on to write the unsuccessful *La caverne* for Méhul and two librettos for Lemoyne. His failure to give Grétry a worthy comedy resulted in the ruin of some splendid material. Whereas his characters remain one-dimensional, Grétry's musical details are interesting; whereas his plot design inspires a pallid response in us, Grétry's ensembles are vivid and polished; whereas his wit turns all on the single figure of the opportunist lawyer, Grétry is almost prodigal with witty melodies. Indeed, the score quarries the artless style of *Les méprises par ressemblance* to strike a new vein of gaiety (Ex. 32.1). It is an extraordinary fact that the score abjures traditional aria style in favour of simple song forms and styles. Of the ten numbers, including two finales, four are designated 'Couplets' (i.e. verse songs), the solo for Dolmont (3) is in the style of a popular song, and the closing section of each finale is a resolution into song.[2] Their bass-lines may be very simple, but there was nothing repetitive about the melodies above them, which prophecy the styles of the Victorian era.

Also for the first time, Grétry wrote a guitar accompaniment, added to the orchestra, in the verse song (6). The ordinary convention had been for the plucked strings to imitate it, as in Dalayrac's *Renaud d'Ast* the previous year and in numerous earlier opéras-comiques.[3] Furthermore, nobody seems to have noticed a self-borrowing in *Le rival confident*: the first section of the finale (5). Grétry recomposed the attractive main theme of the aria (6) sung by Corali in the 1770

Confident rivals

Ex. 32.1 (a) *Le rival confident* (3)
('Far from my son, from my daughter, I was for long [a stranger]')

Ex. 32.1 (b) *Le rival confident* (4)
('Who could displease Rosalie? Is it my profession, I pray you?')

L'amitié à l'épreuve, but later rejected (Ex. 32.2). It became the through-composed background idea to a dialogue duet between brother (the Chevalier) and sister (Rosalie), and was even submitted to thematic development to dramatise a question-and-answer later in the scene.

The confusing plethora of opéras-comiques written, performed and frequently published in pre-Revolutionary Paris can be distilled with the help of the tables in chapters 7 and 26. For ease of comprehension we can place Grétry's rivals in two divisions: the first, represented by Dezède and Martini, reaches to the earlier 1780s, and the second, represented by Dalayrac, occupies the period 1783–9. Obviously much more will be written in the future about this subject than the reader will find here. But some consideration is needed at this point, when we must consider questions of relative quality. What did it signify when in January 1787 Grimm wrote of *Les méprises par ressemblance* that 'the public often seemed to notice in this opus the sort of carelessness with which [Grétry] works on everything he does today; it is regretted that this charming musician, disdaining too much a care for his glory in order only to concern himself with his fortune, thinks now only of multiplying his output instead of taking care over it' (xiv:527)? Or when the same source opined that the music of *Le Comte d'Albert* represented 'perhaps Grétry's weakest work' (xv:9–10)? The best of Dezède and Martini was not slow to receive approbation. The thirty-two performances in 1777 of Dezède's *Les trois fermiers* far outstripped the totals for any other single work that year; the same goes for the forty performances of his *Blaise et Babet* in 1783. The thirty-three that Martini's *Le droit du seigneur* received in 1784 exactly equalled the total of *L'épreuve villageoise*; the

(a)

Ex 32.2 (a) *L'amitié à l'épreuve* (1770) (6)
('When one marries without love, one knows nothing of one's misfortune')

(b)

Ex. 32.2 (b) *Le rival confident* (5)
('My Rosalie, O you whom I love'; 'Whom I love'; 'In his mouth the charming word')

thirty-four that Dalayrac's *Nina* received in 1786 outdid the number attained by *Richard Cœur-de-lion*.

Both Dezède and Martini wrote characteristic music; their style in this period is antithetical to Grétry's in that its melody tends to be instrumental, to respect four-bar phrases and to use repeated notes, as did the Classical Viennese composers. Grétry's style, on the other hand, originated against a background of pre-Classical style, less symmetrical. Dezède and Martini were sophisticated harmonists; Grétry subordinated harmony to melodic declamation. Dezède and Martini orchestrated expertly and freely; Grétry's orchestration achieved its purpose through poetically functional detail rather than colour for its own sake. Although it is totally wrong to claim, as many have, that Grétry was ignorant of orchestration, he himself realised, in later years, that the earlier handling could have been somewhat different.

I shall not conceal the fact that often, hearing fuller compositions, richer in wind instruments than mine, I have regretted not using them in my first works. I often neglected the viola part, which is so necessary . . . Besides, it would be easy for me to increase the

Confident rivals

contribution of viola and bassoon; however, I don't know why, I have never been tempted to do so. (ii:63–4)[4]

As early as 1772 Dezède's *Julie* introduced strongly Germanic elements into the overture and some arias (see chapter 27). Obbligato wind instruments play quite often, and all through Louison's act 1 aria. Even the act 2 trio, in a peasant-like 6/8, sounds more like Haydn than Grétry. Dezède's inexperience showed in some overlong, indulgent solos, and elsewhere his French side inclined to established rustic or vaudeville style. The act 2 opening 'Villageoise' that Mozart used for a set of variations, KV315d (264) (Ex. 32.3), can stand as example of the composer's priorities: artificial rather than dramatic in its context and (though sung by a peasant) classless in its musical imagery.

Ex. 32.3 *Julie* (8) used in Mozart, KV264/315d
('Lison slept in a grove, one arm this way, the other that')

But *Les trois fermiers* (1777) is Dezède's musically richest work. The librettist's handling, unfortunately, is almost as poor as that of its sequel, *Blaise et Babet*; the interest is in the 'everyday life of country folk' and it foreshadows more than one characteristic of twentieth-century soap opera.[5] But allied to this are highly sophisticated pieces of writing and attractive melody. A first-act duet of sisters, Andante in sonata form, is as poised and rich as Mozart. There are tonal surprises: Louis' Romance following has a refrain pausing on a root IV[9] chord, and both this piece and the penultimate act 1 solo for Alix commence in keys other than the true tonic (Ex. 32.4). The great tune 'Sans un petit brin d'amour', an act 2 'Vaudeville', beats Grétry at his own game. The Théâtre Italien orchestra had probably never made such a roistering tumult of sound as Dezède designed for it in Jacques' act 1 solo 'Le bon seigneur'; on the other hand, sometimes using *ppp*, he well understood how to give a four-bar theme added 'significance' by having it initially delivered in hushed tones. There is a quickness and intelligence in Dezède's music that we appreciate in pure terms, but which audiences of the time saw as a perfect complement to the finesse of the productions. This is especially so in the case of *Blaise et Babet*, whose paper-thin plot means nothing to the reader, but which was then found to excite 'a rapture of inexpressible admiration'; its music was 'delicious, always cheerful and fresh, its expression strong and local [i.e folk-like in places], the motifs piquant and the melody agreeable'.[6]

A far finer work was Martini's *Le droit du seigneur*, though set once more in the

281

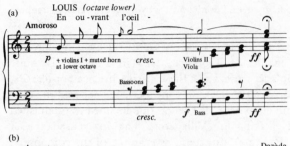

Ex. 32.4 *Les trois fermiers*, Romance en rondeau (4)
(a) refrain (b) opening

surroundings of the village, even with some of the same names (Mathurin, Babet) and displaying the same ideal trust between the tenant farmers and their lord of the manor, a marquis. Desfontaines' libretto engages us with credible psychology and sets out the text with remarkable aptitude for Martini's expression. Here, for once, are a Bailli who takes a dignified rôle and peasants who do not stand and regale us with Romances. The treatment of the theme is quite opposite to that used by Voltaire in his eponymous play (1762) where the girl, it transpires, has blue blood. Now, in 1783, the seigneur's forgotten feudal right to interview the new bride is being resurrected solely for the pleasure of his son, the Count, who is infatuated with Babet and plans to abduct her during the interview and install her as his kept mistress in some distant estate. Eventually his plan is thwarted jointly by his father and the villagers themselves.

The excellence of Martini's musical invention (the subject of a lengthy review by Grimm, January 1784) is inseparable from his constructional ambitions. In the whole of act 1 there are only two very short and one normal-length spoken scenes at all. The overture, which is actually a long tone-poem describing the awakening of nature, runs into the opening choral tableau. A good example of the work's extended tonal control is shown in Ex. 32.5, part of the last sequence (perhaps

Ex. 32.5 *Le droit du seigneur* act 1, final ensemble; page references to full score (Paris, Brunet, n.d. [1784])

'complex' would be a better term) in act 1. The prevailing tonality is E flat, which is interrupted (see the chromatic elision at 'mais son fils') when the Count's name is mentioned, provoking Babet's tale of his earlier attempted seduction: this appears in G major, to be followed by a dramatised modulatory lead-back. In act 2 an exceedingly interesting ensemble portrays the Bailli, girl's parents and villagers in dialogue with the Marquis, and gradually changing his attitude from defensiveness and disbelief to sympathy for them and willingness to investigate his son's actions. Martini's music is stylistically dominated by four-bar phrases and richness of texture, but with a sensitive response to words. It is a guide to what Mozart might have written for the Italiens and suggests (as Grimm said) 'the study of our great masters'.

If Desfontaines gave the peasants moral victory (capped at the end in a hysterical 'Tocsin', with the orchestra battering at thirty-six unison D's) Martini conveyed their moral authority in the sophistication of his music[7] and through the unprecedented responsiveness and flexibility of the chorus writing throughout. This was, simply, ahead of its time by comparison even with the choral episodes in *Richard Cœur-de-lion*. Some notion of the Martini chorus may be seen from Ex. 32.6, the moment in act 1 at which the villagers first hear of the restoration of the *droit du seigneur*. Instead of a simple or histrionic reaction, Martini gives them a phrase that can only be called an outburst of compassionate feeling.

Ex. 32.6 *Le droit du seigneur*, full score p. 48
('Ah! Julien, what a custom')

This process continued what Dezède had begun. Nobody could reasonably make an indictable offence from something as intangible as musical style. But because musical style at this time was broadening so quickly the very use of a new and fashionable idiom conferred upon 'simple' characters could not go unremarked. Already the sophistication of Dezède's music in *L'erreur d'un moment* (1773), the sequel to *Julie*, was mentioned in the *Mémoires secrets*: 'By a peculiarity hardly appropriate to the characters, the arias are more elegant than the ordinary dialogue' (vii:14). The *Mercure de France*, on 29 January 1785, commented on Dezède's 'rather elevated tone' in *Alexis et Justine*, while Monvel's dialogue 'appeared to us much too elevated for the rank of the characters. Virtue and nobility are doubtless common to all estates of men, but their outward expression is not the same.' For Grétry there was rarely any question of such 'inappropriateness' as this.

Grétry and the growth of opéra-comique

Dalayrac's career at the Comédie-Italienne, to which Grétry was party from the start (iii:265), built up through modest successes, willigness to attempt a range of subject-matter, with stress on comedy, and a reliable rate of production. The *Correspondance littéraire* often criticised him for unoriginality. The first rehearsal of his first opéra-comique at the Théâtre Italien was on 24 December 1781;[8] by September 1785 he was selected by the Assembly of that theatre as the composer most likely to guarantee success, after *L'amant statue*, in being assigned Carmontel's *L'abbé de plâtre* to set.[9]

1782	*L'éclipse totale*	1-act comedy (given only until 1786)
1783	*Le corsaire*	3-act comedy (revised 1785; given until 1786)
1783	*Les deux tuteurs*	2-act comedy (revised 1784)[10]
1785	*La dot*	3-act comedy
1785	*L'amant statue*	1-act comedy
1786	*Nina ou la folle par amour*	1-act sentimental drama
1786	*Azémia ou le nouveau Robinson*	3-act adventure drama (revised 1787)
1787	*Renaud d'Ast*	2-act comedy
1788	*Les sérénades*	2-act comedy (a failure)
1788	*Sargines*	4-act national drama
1788	*Fanchette*	3-act comedy
1789	*Les deux petits savoyards*	1-act comedy

Dalayrac's skill in ensemble writing was recognised even in reviews of *L'éclipse totale* and this was quickly turned to account in writing sectional finales. A fuller range of technical skills emerged in *Les deux tuteurs*: if he was also Grétry's heir in giving a varied tone to his solos, he manipulated sonata forms, wrote an entr'acte of 205 bars as an orchestral showpiece, and revealed that he was heir to Dezède in creating artless, even exquisite Romances. Perhaps *Azémia* could not fail to have a certain success (see chapter 29 and Plate VIII), but in fact it is carefully composed. The overture was a scene-setting mime in the tradition of *Le Magnifique*. Of Edouin's first aria 'Ton amour', *Les tablettes de Polymnie* rhetorically asked in 1810, 'Who does not know this beautiful air by heart?' The selfconscious *naïveté* of this decade of Classicism well suited the not-quite-innocent boy and girl in act 1. Colourful, varied music was found for Akinson's prayer in act 2, the Spanish sailors and Alvar, and of course the island's natives in act 3 who sing *Yak-mala* all through in varying tones of aggression. It does not aim to be more than a superficially attractive work, but perhaps no other opéra-comique of its age attained such picaresque energy.

From ultramontane japes the Comédie-Italienne chorus switched in *Nina* to an opening scene that may be claimed as opéra-comique's equivalent to a *tombeau*, or mourning scene in tragedy. Driven to amnesiac distraction by her father's removal of Germeuil, her lover, Nina sleeps surrounded by the good villagers who tend her. Their lullaby, 'Sleep, my child' forms another compassionate type of choral piece, far from anything Grétry wrote, and slightly similar to the 'Shepherds' farewell' in Berlioz's *L'enfance du Christ*. Nina's Romance, which Berlioz tells us he heard in church as a child, is an example of how Dalayrac used good tunes to

Plate VIII. *Azémia* (J. C. Le Vacher de Charnois (ed.), *Costumes et annales des grands théâtres de Paris*, ii, Issue III, p. 21). Dalayrac's opéra-comique, with Mme Dugazon in the title rôle, had a stage set showing a desert island with rocks on different levels and vegetation concealing the entrance to a cave. Azémia is here seen in act 2 during the moonlit love-scene between her and Prosper who, however, modestly remained higher up in his own part of the habitation. Azémia's costume was grey-brown, edged in rose pink, with green foliage.

Ex. 32.7 *Nina*, Romance
('When the beloved returns to his friend who languishes, Then spring will be born again, the grass decked with flowers')

encapsulate, rather than dramatise, an operatic situation (Ex. 32.7). It does not invite us to find any insight into Nina's mental condition, but only to weep in self-righteous sympathy. Dalayrac was prone to let a good melody find its own course, and give it to two characters to sing whether or not the second person's words suited the duplication dramatically. For the first few years of his career he adopted and to some extent remodelled the various stylistic options already opened by others: one we have not mentioned is the Italianate *buffo* style which occurs in *Le corsaire* and lies behind *Renaud d'Ast*.

However, in *Sargines* Dalayrac reached out at a different area. Power, patriotism, heroism, terror all at once came to his pen with unexpected command. Given first on 14 May 1788, *Sargines* codified in opéra-comique the formal accents of patriotic song and chorus, shortly to be adapted for the Revolution. The opera superseded *Henri IV* and *Richard Cœur-de-lion* as a national work because it addressed itself allegorically to the monarchy of 1788 in an urgent voice. It tells two stories: that of the defeat of the English by Philip II Augustus of France at the battle of Bouvines (1214); and that of the conversion of the twenty-year-old Sargines from ineffective youth to defender and saviour of Philip in battle by receiving the blows intended for the monarch.[11] While Sargines' father despises him, the valiant horsewoman Sophie inspires him and rouses him from lethargy. Acts 1 and 2 are conventionally set in countryside and act 3 shows a mediaeval hall, but act 4 takes on the attributes of *tragédie-lyrique*: it shows the outskirts of a village (Bouvines) being burned and destroyed in the course of battle. Soldiers pass back and forth, villagers run to escape the flames and carnage, mothers clutch their infants to their breasts, men drag wives or dying grandmothers from their cottages.

This appalling scene reflects the pressure building up between the monarchy and its opponents in 1788, the *parlements* in particular. 'In 1787 their popularity was such that they seemed to be in a position to dictate their will to the king.'[12] The king exiled them to Troyes after a stalemate in the fight over taxation, but public pressure had them restored in September 1787; then the Paris *parlement* 'harassed the Ministry [of finance] with protests . . . To add to the financial distress of the Crown, the collection of taxes was beginning to break down. Even the loyalty of the Army, under its noble officers, was in doubt.' On 8 May the *parlements* were again suspended and 'only the presence of troops prevented an angry crowd from burning down the Law Courts.'[13] Thus *Sargines* depicts Philip Augustus being acclaimed and summoning those around him to 'defend your king, your families, your property, and the honour of France'. At the same time the opera courted approval in the re-enactment of a scene of humility. 'The pomp of the spectacle at the end of act 3, the historical event of Philip Augustus laying down his crown and offering to fight under the orders of he whom the nation believes most worthy to wear it . . . made one forgive the *longueurs* and slowness of the first two acts.' (Grimm:xv:262–4).

Marmontel's Belisarius had lectured on kingship, indirectly to Louis XV. Now Louis XVI could see a simulacrum of his predecessor urging national unity under the Crown from the stage of a royal theatre. *Sargines* could be regarded as the political reply to Beaumarchais' and Salieri's recitative opera *Tarare* (Opéra, 1787). *Tarare* ends with the popular crowning of its eponymous hero and the overthrow of the tyrannical monarch Atar. The moral, pressed home as in any opéra-comique, exalts democratic reason: the adoption of the fittest person as king and the denial that one's birth alone bestows good or suitable character.

Act 4 of *Sargines* requires offstage drum, timpani and horns and trumpets 'Pavillon en l'air'. The music is as sombre as the key of D minor can imply (Ex. 32.8); it is presaged in the overture by twenty-four bars of unrelieved diminished sevenths for the *tutti*: eight bars each on C sharp, F sharp and G sharp. Earlier in the work we find an important prototype: the patriotic call sung by Sophie in act 1 (Ex. 32.9).

As Grétry put it the following year in speaking of *Raoul Barbe-bleue*, 'The situations are terrifying and one must provide powerful things today now that we begin to be satiated by everything.'[14] Sheer power filled the last pages of *Sargines* in an orgiastic, C major choral acclamation of the king. But this, *Aucassin et Nicolette* and *Richard Cœur-de-lion* were far from the only works to call for one or more extra brass players. The Comédie-Italienne archives reveal a host of identical demands beginning in November 1787:

1787	Deshayes	*Berthe et Pépin*
1787	Bruni	*Célestine*
1788	Lescot	*Les solitaires de Normandie*
1788	Trial	*Julien et Colette*
1788	Propiac	*Les trois déesses rivales*
1789	Cambini	*Rose d'amour et Carloman*
1789	Dalayrac	*Raoul de Crequi*
1790	Grétry	*Pierre le Grand*

The expenses for extra instruments in these and certain plays rose to 2,630 *livres* in the twelvemonth prior to Easter 1790 and since this amounted to more than the monthly salary bill for the entire orchestra the management thereafter employed a permanent trumpeter (at 800 *livres* p.a.) and moved one of their existing players permanently from violin to trumpet. Clarinets, infrequently used up to that time, were also taken into the orchestra.[15]

Ex. 32.8 *Sargines* act 4, opening
(Annotated facsimile of original score)

One final, and crucial, element of rivalry must serve to conclude this chapte
the foundation of the Théâtre de Monsieur and its operatic performance
beginning on 26 January 1789. 'Monsieur' was Comte Louis de Provence, th
king's brother, 'who wanted to enjoy the same right as Louis XIV's brother, tha
of having under his name a company of players with the same rank and privilege
in the dramatic hierarchy as the royal theatres' (Grimm:xv:385). The troup

Ex. 32.9 *Sargines* act 1, ensemble (4)
('We shall give combat to the enemies of the fatherland, every Frenchman risks his life for the king he follows')

survived just over a decade, not without periods of closure in 1796 and especially 1799, before expiring on 12 April 1801.[16] By then the Comédie-Italienne (renamed Opéra Comique National in 1793) was itself in some difficulties, and the two were merged to form the new Opéra-Comique, which opened on 16 September 1801.

The Théâtre de Monsieur, renamed Théâtre Feydeau after its splendid new building inaugurated on 6 January 1791, did not initially present opéra-comique: that was ostensibly the privilege of the Comédie-Italienne, whose artistic monopolies had anyway been broken by the newcomer. Instead there were plays in French, Italian operas under the direction of the violinist–director G. B. Viotti and the composer Cherubini, and Italian opera translated into French with appropriate alterations (see chapter 22). The orchestra was excellent and some offerings were very successful. It was not long before an indigenous composer had a platform, and thus the first 'official' opéra-comique outside Grétry's troupe became *Le nouveau Don Quichotte* on 25 May 1789, music by Champein, with a respectable forty-six performances.[17] A mere handful of comparable works followed before the landmark that signalled a new era: Cherubini's opéra-comique *Lodoiska* on 18 July 1791.

33. Raoul Barbe-bleue (Raoul Bluebeard)

Comédie in 3 acts, in prose: CC 18
Libretto by Michel-Jean Sedaine. Dedicated to Godefroid de Villetaneuse.[1]
First performed at the Comédie-Italienne, 2 March 1789.
Printed full score, Paris, l'Auteur, n.d. [1790] as Œuvre XXVIII
Dramatis personae: Isaure, in love with Vergy (s.)
                     Vergy, a knight (t.)
                     Raoul de Carmantans, a wealthy feudal tyrant (b.)
                     Marquis de Carabas (b.) ⎫
                     Vicomte de Carabi (t.)   ⎬ Isaure's brothers
                     Ofman, Raoul's old retainer and majordomo (t.)

Jacques, peasant youth (s.)
Jeanne, peasant girl (s.)
Laurette, Isaure's confidante (spoken rôle)
A shepherdess (s.)
Chorus of subjects of Raoul; soldiers

ACT 1: The finest hall of a dilapidated mediaeval castle, partly shored up, belonging to Isaure's family; very thick walls, narrow windows; various helmets, breastplates, bucklers, lances, clubs hanging up. Vergy has delivered Jeanne and Jacques from a knight who abducted them. As he has done this for love of Isaure the peasants tell her the story; she is moved by it (trio 1).[2] Isaure and Vergy would like to marry but the depressed state of both family fortunes makes this prospect difficult. In the duet and quartet (2) they express their devotion, after which the Marquis and Vicomte announce they have arranged Isaure's marriage to Raoul. They threaten Vergy's person should Isaure not agree to the plan, and intimate that Raoul is not to be trifled with. In the solo, march and aria (3) Isaure reaffirms her fidelity to Vergy; Raoul and his retinue enter bearing magnificent gifts; he asks her to be his wife. Isaure, alone, gradually becomes entranced by the gifts, particularly a fine mirror and crown (solo, recitative and aria 4). Yet she will not forgo Vergy without his assent. In the duet (5) they reconcile themselves to the inevitable. He leaves and Isaure's hand is given to Raoul; all leave ceremoniously (chorus and march 6).

ACT 2: A magnificent room in Raoul's castle, containing statues and pictures. On one side the ornate door of a chamber. Entr'acte (7). Some time has passed since Raoul's marriage to Isaure. Now he plans to test her curiosity, as he has tested that of his three former wives, commoners from his estate. In a duet (8) Ofman tries to dissuade Raoul from this, since the earlier wives have all been murdered for failing the test. Isaure enters in magnificent apparel. Announcing his departure on business, Raoul gives her the freedom of his possessions but forbids her to enter the chamber; he gives her its bejewelled key. She is not curious by nature and (trio 9) is indignant at being asked to swear to obey Raoul. Unexpectedly a noble lady is announced wishing to see Isaure. It is Vergy, disguised as her late sister, Anne. Raoul leaves them together. Isaure is deeply divided between still-vivid feelings towards Vergy and duty to Raoul, who has never treated her badly. Vergy realises from the pictures and statues that there is danger in succumbing to curiosity. But Isaure is forced to compare Raoul's prohibition with the complete trust she knows from Vergy. She rejects Vergy, who withdraws. In the extended scene and duet (10) Isaure considers the meaning of the chamber. Eventually she unlocks it and enters. She screams and runs out; Vergy reappears, goes in himself and discovers the bloody corpses of the murdered wives. When the couple close the door the key breaks in the lock. Ofman refuses to help Isaure but agrees to throw a written message to Vergy's page waiting outside the castle, addressed to her brothers. Ofman tells them to remain calm during the entertainments that follow, thoughtfully ordered by Raoul as a diversion: dance (11), shepherdess's solo (12), pantomime (13) and dance (14).

ACT 3: The same. During the entr'acte (15) a trumpet signal announces Raoul's return. Isaure feels guilt towards Vergy, who blames her brothers (duet 16). Vergy is escorted out as Raoul enters; Isaure is asked to fetch the key and while she is gone Raoul (aria 17), noting the chamber door has been opened, sings of his blighted destiny. Isaure returns to meet an immediate sentence of death. Vergy in vain tries to take the blame. Raoul enters the chamber with four sword-bearing soldiers and Isaure is given a few minutes to pray. Vergy watches from a turret window, Isaure questions him, and Raoul's voice is heard from within (trio 18). Horsemen are seen approaching. Raoul emerges, furious; Vergy throws off his disguise. During a mimed scene (19) Isaure is dragged into the chamber; Vergy is held by the soldiers; the brothers force an entry together with the fathers of the murdered wives, and release Vergy; one drags Raoul in to the chamber and kills him. A chorus and ensemble of triumph against the tyrant follow without a break.

Sedaine's treatment of the Bluebeard legend deserves attention both for its intrinsic merits and because of its originality as a subject for opera..The *Mercure de France* was revolted and disturbed.

The work has interest; but such interest always leads to incidents or situations that are dreadful. We fear that this is not truthful. Such subjects ought never to be shown on stage, above all the lyric stage. We would desire it so. *Raoul* has been entitled a 'comedy' and wrongly. Yes, people are wrong; but tragedy is forbidden at the Théâtre Italien: the author has need of a [different] title.

Yet the writer recognised prophetically that 'the more that this composition is heard, the more it will be appreciated'.[3]

As presented in popular literary form *Barbe-bleue* was published by Charles Perrault in 1698, together with *Sleeping Beauty*, *Cinderella* and other tales.[4] Here it is a morality tale warning children against curiosity; Vergy does not appear and the nameless daughter who marries the monster is simply seduced by riches. When Bluebeard goes away to test her she immediately descends a staircase and opens the chamber. Condemned to execution, she has with her only her sister Anne, watching for the brothers who are by chance due to visit the castle. Her urgent indications alert them to the need for rescue. So well known were Perrault's stories that when they were included in the bi-monthly journal *Bibliothèque universelle des romans* in 1775 they received cursory treatment in favour of new moral and critical reflections.[5] These recalled that there had already been theatrical treatments, not identified, and averred that the subject was 'actually very theatrical'.[6]

Sedaine chose to preserve the essentials of the source, making very economical additions. Not simply did Vergy 'become' Anne, but Isaure remarks in act 1 that he reminds her of the sister in appearance. This economy leads to logistical problems. It is inconceivable that Raoul will not have heard of the dead Anne by the time of act 2 and (for the same reason) that Vergy would risk the name 'Anne' as a blind introduction. However, in his exploration of psychological detail, Sedaine added much. He envisaged the libretto as a drama between three characters, not a melodramatic thriller. That is why, though the mediaeval setting

Plate IX. *Raoul Barbe-bleue* (J. C. Le Vacher de Charnois (ed.), *Costumes et annales des grands théâtres de Paris*, iv, Issue IX, opposite p. 75). This engraving was made partly as a visual record of the original performances and partly to correct what were seen as falsely heterogeneous costumes in the production at the Théâtre Italien. So the artist here substituted authentic mediaeval costumes worn by the counts of Flanders and their wives, taken from 'figures engraved in an old work'. The authenticity of architectural details was also 'strictly observed'.

is crucial, the details are left to the designer to fill in: Raoul's retinue enter dressed like 'playing-card knaves' but this is surely a joke at the expense of the over-authentic historicism of the 1780s. (The point was not taken by Le Vacher de Charnois, who spent some energy devising correct iconographic motifs: see Plate IX.[7]) 'Curiosity punished' is indeed the legend that Vergy reads within the chamber, but that is no longer the only point. First, there are the references to nobility and feudalism. Act 1 makes clear that Vergy defends injustice suffered by all estates of people: the peasants, a pilgrim, a merchant. The Marquis remarks in act 1 sc. 5 that Vergy is 'gentle with his vassals, proud with us'. Raoul's tyrannical regime of fear, occasionally alluded to, is exposed in the final chorus: 'His death avenges us all.' For her part, Isaure in act 1 admires Vergy's charity; but in act 2, under Raoul's influence, she brands her serving-women (and with what irony!) as 'inquisitive and indiscreet' merely because they are plebeian. As for nobility itself, Sedaine pictures ridiculous values that obey expediency: Isaure's title, like Raoul's, regresses into 'the mists of time' while Vergy's is only half a millennium old.

Brief but memorable play is made with the myth of Cupid and Psyche in act 2 sc. 5; this second new strand can be compared to the allusion to Orpheus in *Richard Cœur-de-lion* or the La Fontaine fable in *Le Comte d'Albert*. Psyche was twice punished for curiosity: once after Cupid made love to her in the darkness, in order to conceal his identity, and again when she opened a box entrusted to her by Venus. It contained a deadly sleep. Psyche's trials, moreover, were the result of her beauty: Isaure (see below) is beautiful. Vergy, who understands the parallel, also notices an image of Pandora.[8] Such richness of allusion helps reinforce the figure of Isaure as a victim, perhaps (like Psyche in *The Golden Ass*) even a rather simple-minded one. The third strand Sedaine introduces is an attempted motivation or explanation for Bluebeard's character in (17). Here, as will be seen, Bluebeard is made a 'noble villain' kind of character, anticipating figures such as Lysiart in *Euryanthe*.

Sedaine's dramatic treatment of Isaure could have been quite simple, even given the existence of Vergy. But in act 1 the lovers know from the start that they are doomed, that in separation they will destroy a vital part of themselves. In Vergy's words, 'Like a plaintive, wandering shade, my soul shall follow my loves; near to you shall I always be' (5). Yet Isaure cannot remain insensible to Raoul's largesse in act 1; the way Sedaine reconciles the conflict is to make her proud of her beauty (the first words of the libretto contain the phrase 'belle Isaure') so that the mirror and the crown provoke the aria in (4) 'Is there beauty I cannot surpass?' By act 2 Isaure appears in the rôle of the respected wife: this subtle invention is strong enough in itself to be the motivating force behind her curiosity. But the appearance of Vergy is traumatic and in sc. 5 Isaure is thrown into a confusion of past (love for Vergy), present (duty towards Raoul) and future. The rejection of Vergy is followed by the rejection of his advice not to enter the chamber. In this way the moment of curiosity is transformed into an act symbolising her divided loyalties and the truth of her love for Vergy. Or in modern terms, in repressing the latter she forces open the inferno of her spiritual destruction. After this terrible climax the drama unfolds regularly until the near-tragedy of act 3. Dramatically speaking, Raoul's death is expected; but it is worth making the point that the Théâtre Italien, in this violent ending, echoed the mass murder (offstage) in Salieri's *Les Danaïdes* (Opéra, 1784) and that of the tyrant Atar in the same composer's *Tarare* (Opéra, 1787).

Sedaine's balance between mediaeval setting and human motivation exactly fitted Grétry's preferences, which the composer described in terms of painting: 'I sought to reinforce the musical colour, i.e. the harmony and orchestral working; but I proceeded like [Joseph] Vernet, I did not alter my system' (ii:47).[9] Indeed for all its novelties Grétry's score cannot be described as an imitation of a Martini or a Dalayrac: apart from offstage calls, trumpets are heard only in the overture and (19). What it reveals is an immensely considered composition; what it lacks, possibly as a consequence, is the melodic distinction of the earlier works. There was nowhere, after (1), for Grétry to exploit simplicity or innocence, or much humour.

Sedaine created a theatrical frame in which all music sat with propriety in its place. When Raoul has an aria in act 1, it functions as a formal contract. In act 3, his (17) covers the space of time during which Isaure pretends to look for the key. Moreover, its coda portrays her reluctant return on stage as a functional transition into dialogue. Progressively since *Aucassin et Nicolette* Sedaine had minimised arias and withdrawn the Italianate finale, substituting his own musico-dramatic continuity all through. When we admire the fluid concurrence of music and drama in, for example, act 2 of *Der Freischütz*, we are admiring one fruit of a seed cultivated by Sedaine. As Weber himself wrote, reviewing *Raoul* in 1817, 'Indeed Grétry has inaugurated a new musical era in France, and his melodic forms and the treatment of the musical numbers in his works have provided a kind of accepted model for all other composers who have wished to catch the public ear.'[10]

In act 1 almost everything the lovers sing is slow in tempo. Their devotion recalls the languid Aucassin and Nicolette, but instead of 'gothic' music we hear in (2) modern Italianate phrases that are as beautiful as Raoul's in (3) are dull. However, the duet (5), an extended rondo in form, breathes resignation, not hysteria, and suggests the eternal nature of their love even as the words of the refrain apparently signal the end of it: 'I release you from the vows you made me.' Its key of C major will be swept aside by the G major march (6) and chorus, as Isaure too is borne away visibly. G major is also the key of Raoul's formal aria (3): this is not yet the frightening figure described by Perrault.

The complexities of Isaure's music start in (3) before the march: stressed seventh chords suggest she is vulnerable, if not suggestible. Then in the scene (4) we see a realistic progression from thoughts of Vergy to delight in jewels and beauty; the keys move violently sharpwards:

Form	Key	Tempo	Action
Aria (broken off)	B flat to F	Larghetto	She will live for Vergy alone.

Obbligato recitative	F to A minor to A major		She realises the richness of the fabrics; discovers the mirror.
Short arioso	A major	Larghetto	She wishes Vergy could offer her such things.
Aria (non-repeating)	E major	Allegro	Imagines the glory that wealth and beauty will bring her and her brothers.

Only the downward tendency of phrases suggests, in (3) and (4), the underlying sacrifice.

In act 2, which is musically richer, Grétry makes a striking portrait of Ofman, who in the libretto has no marked individuality. The duet (8) is an extraordinary mixture: Raoul threatening and powerful, Ofman toadying and duplicitous, the dark mingling of the voices at one with the effect of E major. Ex. 33.1 also

Ex. 33.1 *Raoul Barbe-bleue* (8)
('Does it deserve death to say she is kind?'; 'Guilty one, I would kill you')

exemplifies the occasional discordant progression. Unease also stalks through the 'oath' trio (9) in the form of a grumbling bass-line. It was however in the through-composed (10) that Grétry excelled himself: aria, mime, recitative and duet, anchored in D major-minor but ranging to F sharp minor, B flat and F minor. All through the first Andante Isaure's disturbance is suggested by nagging violin triplets (see Ex. 33.2) which also highlight the dislocations imposed in the music: tonal exploration of areas necessitating double sharps or (q.v.) skipping from the dominant ('Would I do ill, would I do well?') to mediant (the question cannot be answered: the chamber can only be opened). All the music for the mime, starting in B flat, the discovery and the duet (D minor) is powerful. Grétry even uses a reverse progression from V to augmented flat VI (German) to reach a secondary tonic where Vergy describes the three corpses: see Ex. 33.3.

The opera's first reviewer in *Mercure de France* found that the dances and song ending act 2 hung fire; yet for those with ears to hear, this music is hauntingly

Ex. 33.2 *Raoul Barbe-bleue* (10)
('Would I do evil? Would I do good? All right, doubtless it's a dream')

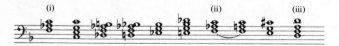

Ex. 33.3 *Raoul Barbe-bleue* (10), transition to recapitulation
(i) Vergy describes the corpses (ii) he recounts the warning inside: 'Curiosity punished' (iii) Recapitulation

apposite, being chiefly in the minor mode. The sad denizens seem to perform under duress, as it were. The 'Danse finale' (14) in D minor doubles a clarinet with first violins, thus providing the perfect illustration of Grétry's memorable sentence, 'If one danced in a prison I should wish it were to the sound of the clarinet' (i:238), here giving rise to a sadly etiolated pastorale.

What is impressive about the first part of act 3 are two self-revelations. The slow–fast duet (16) is no time-serving piece, but an act of humility in which Isaure, unnecessarily, begs forgiveness and offers her death as a sacrifice, and where the immense dignity of her closing B minor phrases possesses the cathartic quality of Gluck.[11] The other revelation occurs in the second, B minor, episode of Raoul's (17), otherwise graced with a hackneyed phrase of a refrain. It expresses Raoul's belief in the predictions mentioned in act 2 sc. 1, namely that his wife's curiosity shall cause his death, so that he is in some way cursed and, like the Flying Dutchman, condemned to seek (Ex. 33.4).

Ex. 33.4 *Raoul Barbe-bleue* (17)
('Does she exist' etc.)

> I wanted to make you happy,
> Offer my wealth and my heart.
> My destiny is truly frightful,
> All my misfortune was predicted.
> Fear the too-curious wife,
> Fly from beauty's charm.
> Is there no woman
> Who does not carry
> Curiosity?
> > Does she exist?
> > Where then is she?
> > Come, cruel one,
> > I call to you,
> Happiness will follow in your path;
> But I shall not discover it.

In the obsessive repetitions of Ex. 33.4 we glimpse some of this torment, later held in check by the D major of the main aria. However it was the trio (18), once more in B minor, that caught the imagination of Grétry's contemporaries. Technically there was nothing in it he had not done before, but the confluence of different people separated by distance, the suggestion of horses in the orchestra, the musician's ingenious raising of one's pulse-beat, undoubtedly stretched the tableau to breaking-point.

Whereas the combat music in *Richard Cœur-de-lion* was simply a self-borrowing, that in *Raoul Barbe-bleue* is a carefully-cast binary form piece that exploits the thrill of trumpets and piccolo, in the minor mode; timpani are held back for the chorus. Here perhaps in (19) Grétry allowed himself a sidelong glance at the Dalayrac of

Sargines. The choral finale, 135 bars long, captures the tones of popular liberation in a similar way to *Sargines*, especially in the 'fanfare' material used as a coda. It could hardly do otherwise with lines such as 'Tyran, tyran, tyran exécrable!' But the subtleties of motivation and rôle of the rescuers become submerged. Even in Perrault the tale ends with a sense of continuity, not the murder scene.

Sedaine's libretto was not independently published until 1791, by which time all legal restrictions limiting Parisian theatres had been abolished. Early alterations can be conjectured by reference to 'some features that prompted murmurs' reported in the *Journal de Paris*. By 2 January 1791 Grétry acted on information that provincial theatre directors had mounted the opera not simply without authorisation but were using his manuscript score 'which has been given them by unfaithful hands'. He publicly requested them to use the published score and alluded to the forthcoming laws affording authors and composers some copyright protection.[12]

The trappings of privilege caused difficulties in 1792 when in Lyon certain volunteers from Montpellier formally objected to Isaure's crown.[13] Sedaine made an altered version of the libretto for Paris to exclude feudal references; for example, 'château' became 'maison' or 'logis'.[14] This was put on in a series of performances beginning October 1794, and presumably shares its other features too with the manuscript prompt copy in the Archives Nationales. The latter contains several effective stage directions for Isaure, many small verbal changes, and two larger improvements. The first is in act 2 sc. 10 when Ofman's agreement to help in the escape is tied to a general desperate hatred for Raoul himself. Then at the very end Sedaine, acknowledging that Isaure's brothers must logically form part of the rescue, gave new stage directions incorporating them.[15]

Raoul Barbe-bleue enjoyed 103 performances in its first decade at the Théâtre Italien (later Opéra-Comique) but there were only 19 peformances in 1799–1801. It was revived in 1806 but became only a sporadic attraction, being seen a total of 30 times to its last night in July 1818. However, the opera was popular in German-speaking Europe. Loewenberg's last foreign production listed was in Vienna (1840).

34. Pierre le Grand (Peter the Great)

Comédie in 3 acts, in prose: *CC* 40
Libretto by Jean-Nicolas Bouilly.
First performed at the Comédie-Italienne, 13 January 1790.
Printed full score, Paris, l'Auteur; Lyon, Garnier, n.d. [1791] as Œuvre xxix.
Dramatis personae: Pierre le Grand, Emperor of the Russias, working incognito as
    Pierre (t.)[1]
    Le Fort, minister and friend of Pierre, incognito as André (b.)[2]
    Catherine, young widow, retired to the village (s.)[3]
    Georges-Morin, master carpenter, with whom live Catherine, Pierre
    and Le Fort (b.)
    Geneviève, wife of Georges-Morin (s.)
    Caroline, their daughter (s.)
    Alexis, young orphan, son of a rich farmer (t.)[4]
    Mathurin, great-uncle and tutor of Alexis (t. or bar.)
    Mensikoff, governor of Moscow (spoken rôle)
    Notary (spoken rôle)
Carpenters working for Georges-Morin, Peasants, Officers of Pierre, Guards and
soldiers.
ACT 1: A Russian village by the sea; village square with Georges' house
downstage left, a large door at the end of which stands as entrance to his shipyard.
Trees opposite forming an arbour. Sea in the background, the shore covered with
piles of building timber; a vessel under construction. Pierre and Le Fort work with
the carpenters on the vessel (chorus 1).[5] The workers leave; Pierre thanks Le Fort
for his friendship and education (duet 2). Le Fort suggests leaving the village,
where they have stayed a year. But Pierre is in love with Catherine and wishes to
marry her before she discovers his identity. She arrives and describes her pleasure
in doing good works among the unfortunate (aria 3). She agrees to marry Pierre,
but not until Georges agrees to let Alexis marry Caroline. Caroline (chanson 4)
tells her mother about Georges' strange unfriendliness to Alexis. Alexis' sad oboe
tune is heard (5): he is welcomed but forced to hide when the intemperate Georges
enters in high spirits (aria 6). Discovering Alexis, he is constrained with difficulty.
Rustic music (7a) announces the villagers, who come to praise Catherine (chorus
7b) and instigate an annual festival in her honour. Mathurin crowns her with
flowers. In the finale (8) Catherine breaks into tears as the celebrations continue.
ACT 2: Interior of Georges' house. After the entr'acte (9) Georges explains to
Pierre that he wants him as his son-in-law. Alexis is a farmer, and he needs a
carpenter to succeed him. Pierre admits he has won Catherine's affections, but also
that his happiness depends on Alexis' wedding with Caroline. To this Georges
agrees delightedly. There will be a double wedding. Alone, Pierre eulogises his
fiancée (aria 10). Catherine comes to question Pierre about his family, only to be

told he is a foundling. She is naturally undeterred, and they look forward to marrying (duet 11). Old Mathurin is helped in by villagers who sit in a circle to await Georges; Le Fort sings a Romance (12) about the travels of Peter the Great. Georges enters with the notary; he will make over his yard and ships to the supposedly penniless Pierre (dialogue ensemble 13). But Mensikoff arrives and, while keeping Pierre's identity secret, asks the company to withdraw. He reports political trouble in Moscow and requests Pierre to address the troops he has brought along. Pierre departs with Le Fort and Mensikoff, leaving Catherine and the others to imagine that he has deserted them (finale 14).

ACT 3: A solitary place near the village, a hill upstage. Following the entr'acte (15) Catherine is comforted further by Georges, Geneviève and Caroline (quartet 16). Alexis rushes over the hill, saying he has seen Pierre with 200 soldiers. Mensikoff arrives to announce they have been in the emperor's presence, and that Pierre wishes to take Catherine to the throne. She and the overwhelmed villagers react in the ensemble and march (17) in which Pierre appears in robes of state. He bids his village friends farewell; Catherine is very unwilling to leave them. There is a chorus of acclamation (18). Peter signs the marriage documents and Catherine is persuaded to adopt a new life. Verses and refrains (19) celebrate the monarch who puts the care of his people above all, and the last lines become a prayer for Louis XVI of France.

Grétry's overtly political operas began with the Revolution, not in the years 1792–4 whither they are usually relegated. Thus *Pierre le Grand* and *Guillaume Tell* constitute a pair and a logical point at which to close our survey. Externally, the growth of opéra-comique under the conditions of the 1790s would require its own detailed history; moreover the words and music of Grétry's opéras-comiques of 1792–4 have wholly or partially disappeared. Both *Pierre le Grand* and *Guillaume Tell* were written in the critical but idealistic stages of the Revolution when the monarchy might in other circumstances have survived, and before the king and his family attempted to flee the country. We shall see below more exactly how each fits into the political picture.

J. N. Bouilly (1763–1842), whose first libretto this was, became a well-known writer and dramatist whose musical collaborators included Dalayrac, Méhul, Gaveaux, Boïeldieu, Isouard and Auber.[6] He grew up near Tours and studied law there and at Orléans. In 1787 he left for Paris and was presented at the bar of the *parlement*. Being a frequenter of the theatre, he wished to write a work for Mme Dugazon (who indeed acted Catherine), as well as one that would express his desire for a constitutional monarchy. The reading committee of the Comédie-Italienne recommended *Pierre le Grand* on 7 June 1789.[7] After its acceptance, Dugazon agreed to introduce Bouilly to Grétry; Bouilly became a friend and eventually the fiancé of Antoinette Grétry. The composer offered to set the libretto in three months, taking it with him to Lyon, his now-preferred place of work and his wife's birthplace.

Bouilly mentions Voltaire's *Le siècle de Louis XIV* as his source, but this must be a slip for *Histoire de Russie sous Pierre le Grand* (dated 1759 but issued 1760). Voltaire gives a full account of the expedition to Europe and Peter's humble style of living, together with many other details about his eagerness to study the sciences. Voltaire also painted a more attractive picture of Catherine than he had done in 1731 in the *Histoire de Charles XII* when 'she had none of the virtues of her sex', though was allowed the courage to 'rectify her education and her weaknesses'. In the later book, she was 'superior to her sex and her misfortune' as well as the perfect partner for Peter.[8]

In the important preface to his original libretto (not in *CC* 40) Bouilly explained:

Struck with astonishment and admiration at the sight of France's regeneration, I sought in history some feature which should have a connection with it, and that I might put on the stage. I saw that in Russia Peter the Great scorned the splendour and delights of the throne in order to give himself completely to the happiness of his people; as LOUIS XVI does today for the happiness of the French.

From a multitude of uncivilised barbarians lacking principles and talent, Pierre-Aléxiowitz formed a society both educated and policed; in calling the French to participate in the rights of royalty, LOUIS creates a people of kings of whom he becomes the tutelary deity.

It must be said immediately that Bouilly created a very worthy libretto, not a legal tract; but he was certainly obliged to idealise his characters. Catherine was actually discovered some five years after Peter's shipyard days and Peter, notwithstanding his enormous achievements, could be brutal and despotic. Indeed he was already married when he met Catherine, but had relegated his wife Eudoxia to a convent and was later to have their son killed. In the opera the villagers speak in country dialect, but Catherine does not. Bouilly's originality lay in the well-judged blend of history and *paysannerie*, and in the choice of grouped events that, in the definitive version of the opera, move together quite satisfactorily: the crowning of Catherine, the arrival of Mensikoff, the marriage. It forms a singular blend of high and low styles both in the music and the dialogue, obviously deriving from Sedaine and *Richard Cœur-de-lion*. Added to this is the 'tragic' close of act 2 and the mutual devotion of Pierre and Catherine, which though so obviously 'humane' (shades of *Le Comte d'Albert*) is sealed by Pierre's transformation into a prince charming, redolent of *Zémire et Azor*. The librettist was judicious, yet his dialogue too was skilful, and tinted by what Lucien Solvay called 'touching naiveté and emphatic phraseology, already imprinted with that slightly affected sentimentality later to earn Bouilly the sobriquet of "poète lacrymal"' (*CC*: p. v). Like Sedaine, Bouilly was meticulous about character motivation, which is surely why he initially refused to countenance a three-act version (see last section). What proved Bouilly's musical sensibility, however, was his provision of extended dialogue ensembles in which a highly flexible conversational style was invited, suiting Grétry perfectly. In fact Bouilly called (13) and (17) 'Dialogue en chant', not 'ensemble' or 'chorus'. The opera's solos and duets are dramatically to the point and their overall distribution balanced: one solo each for Pierre, Le Fort,

Catherine, Caroline and Georges. However, what the audience was intended to leave the theatre singing to themselves were the patriotic verses (12), whose music Grétry brings back with enormous effect in (17) as the march, and of course the final verses (19). We should therefore begin our discussion with these two pieces.

The artificial siting of (12) came straight from the 'brin d'amour' in Dezède's *Les trois fermiers*, though the idea that the music is supposed to have been taught the villagers by Le Fort is related to the Romance in *Richard Cœur-de-lion*. There is no revolutionary fervour among the people; words and melody are direct enough (Ex. 34.1):

> Great kings, superb potentates,
> Leave your courts, your diadems,
> As he did, leave your estates,
> Travel, work yourselves
> And you shall see that greatness
> Does not always make for happiness.

Ex. 34.1 *Pierre le Grand* (12)
('Long ago a famous emperor handed over the keys to his empire'; 'Treasure, rank, greatness do not always make for happiness')

When the music comes back as the march, first softly and *staccato*, it suddenly embodies the whole personality of Pierre by taking on life as an actual military tune. In (17) the watching chorus and soloists have separate commentating phrases while the march continues: if this reminds us of *Les Troyens*, so does the way the march comes to symbolise journeys over and above the confines of the opera itself. In the France of 1790 it might be identified with the journey of the court back from Versailles to Paris in the preceding October.

The verses (19) are an updated final vaudeville, with each strophe orchestrated differently, as in *Les mariages samnites* (13). The refrain forms a rousing appeal (Ex. 34.2).[9] The 1790 libretto printed it after all four stanzas, but a first performance review shows that the ending substituted in the score was also sung on the first night: 'It is a sort of prayer for our Majesty, who acquires each instant new titles to our love. The final lines are sung to the air *Charmante Gabrielle*, so that the tune and words might simultaneously recall the image of good King Henri IV.'[10] In Ex.

Pierre le Grand

Bé - ni soît à ja - mais no - tre Prin - ce dont la ten - dres - se S'oc-

cu - pe sans ces - se du bon - heur de ses su - jets.

Ex. 34.2 *Pierre le Grand* (19)
('Blessed be today our Prince, whose concern is always for his subjects' happiness')

Cru - el - le dé - par - ti - e, Mal - heu - reux jour! Que

ne suis - je sans vi - e ou sans a - mour.

Ex. 34.3 (a) 'Charmante Gabrielle', refrain

Ciel en - tends la pri - è - re qu'i - ci je fais,

Con - ser - ve ce bon Pè - re à ses su - jets.

Ex. 34.3 (b) *Pierre le Grand* (19)
('Heaven, hear my prayer, preserve this good father from his subjects')

34.3 we can compare the way Grétry moulded the traditional melody into a musical *envoi*, a melody which was popularly, if wrongly, thought to have been composed by Henri IV himself in memory of his wife.[11]

But if *Pierre le Grand* had only consisted of a reasonable plot with occasional good melodies, it would never have survived with numerous performances even into the nineteenth century. Grétry responded to almost every musical opportunity, particularly in those numbers involving the chorus, which by the Revolution had become fully institutionalised with a trainer and some fourteen regular members. Their numbers were about to rise dramatically, but their singing still drew Framery's fire: 'These choruses, in large part composed of bad musicians placed there by favour and intrigue, are always poorly performed'.[12] Nonetheless, Grétry's choral writing was his best and most varied yet in opéra-comique. In (1), for example, he imagined a six-part male double chorus full of characteristic detail – the sounds of hammering, the 'Russian' cadencing into the relative minor (A minor), the brassy 'forced' notes on French horns, and the 'Sailor's Cry' which periodically emerges on lower strings and bassoons, specially labelled by the

Ex. 34.4 *Pierre le Grand* (8)
('I feel my tears flow remembering her good deeds')

composer, and always confined to the orchestra. Innovation continued in (8), whose central section is in B minor. Here the chorus 'speak to one another with emotion'. They have music with which to act (Ex. 34.4) as they respond, still in dialect, to Catherine's emotional thanks. Contrapuntal detail was rare indeed for Grétry, and he developed it further against climactic phrases for the soloists.

After the unison choral refrains of (12) the choir returns to four-part writing in (13), here knitted into the texture of the various responses to Georges' extraordinary generosity.[13] At last Grétry and Bouilly attained the give-and-take that Martini demonstrated in *Le droit du seigneur*:

6 bars for Pierre
6 bars for Georges
4 for the chorus
4 for Catherine, and so on.

The choral *pièce de résistance* comes in (14), however, which is a unique movement for several reasons. Catherine believes she is abandoned, virtually at the altar; after a paroxysm of grief she faints, alone on stage, and is discovered by the others. There follows a through-composed movement of 161 bars in 12/8 metre, a rare instance in Grétry's opéra-comique of this signature. The music begins in E flat, before the villagers realise what has occurred, but as the depth of the apparent tragedy is borne in on them the music turns to C minor, where it remains. At first the chorus does not believe what Catherine tells them. Once convinced, they react with power (Ex. 34.5). Such is the grief expressed in Catherine's piercing phrases and by the general development of the tableau, that one is obliged to consider the music as a personal outpouring connected with the dying Lucile Grétry.

In (18) and (19) the chorus returns to more straightforward, though wholly

Pierre le Grand

Ex. 34.5 *Pierre le Grand* (14)
('What, the day before her marriage? What betrayal')

modern styles, and these two bring to nine the total number of items including choir: over half the sixteen vocal items in the opera.

As expected, there are ample and attractive peasant solos for Georges and Caroline, the humorous and naïve (6) and (4). Unfortunately the solos for Pierre and Catherine (10) and (3) suffer from the stiffness of set pieces, probably because Bouilly did not find sufficiently convincing motivation for either. Catherine's words express her goodness and charity, but no such person could believably indulge in a monologue about their virtue, and the music reflects the composer's unease. For his part, Pierre's beginning in (10) is as unmemorable as his opening words are platitudinous. But suddenly his central section takes chromatic flight: 'My wife, my friend, by your virtues and genius you shall guide me.' More satisfactory overall are the duets (2) and (11). The first of these rejects Bouilly's label of 'dialogue duet' in favour of a subtle refrain form centred on a basic image of trust: music, form and dramatisation are at one. Another musical image of devotion dominates the opening of (11). Here as everywhere else, decorative figures are avoided, but in the Allegro Grétry gives his principals top C's in octaves as the climax to a movement full of urgency and warmth. It was a finely calculated, essential moment: Ex. 34.6.

We mentioned 'Russian' modulations in (1), but the local colour pointed out in the contemporary press was linked to a Russian dance seemingly popular at the Opéra.

M. Grétry, in order to give his melody the turn of phrase appropriate to the place of the action, has cleverly placed in the overture and in an aria the principal motif of the *Pas Russe* seen danced so gracefully at the Opéra by Mlle Guimard.[14]

This can be conjectured as the horn motif Ex. 35.4, one which also begins Caroline's song (4). In fact the melodic portion of Ex. 35.4 is also echoed in the

Ex. 34.6 *Pierre le Grand* (11)
(a) ('To burn with eternal love . . .')
(b) ('The happy bond')

orchestral introduction to (7), with the first entrance of Russian villagers. Possibly yet other 'Russian' motifs remain to be found.

The purely theatrical success of *Pierre le Grand* long outlasted its political moment. Even before the opera had been seen, though, the passage of revolutionary events threatened to overtake its message. We can, unusually, cite documentary evidence of the reaction to this of the Comédie-Italienne, whose committee recorded on 18 November 1789:

It has been unanimously agreed that the work Pierre le Grand by MM. Grétry and Bouilly being regarded and written as a *pièce de circonstance* shall pass [into production] immediately after *Caroline*, which is currently in rehearsal.[15]

The last-named work, music by T. Lefèvre, was given on 2 December; Grétry's opera duly became the next première. We saw earlier part of Bouilly's preface, praising the king's supposed call to his people to participate. This is to be understood in the context of the meeting of the States-General. The crisis during 1788, as we saw in chapter 32, was between monarchy and the *parlements*. But once the States-General was decided upon in September 1788 the polarisation shifted ineluctably to the Third Estate (its elected representatives from all over France) *versus* the nobility and clergy. Immense public concern built up in the winter 1788–9, people realising that it made all the difference whether the States-General would operate as in 1614, their own representatives permanently outvoted by two to one, or whether a different type of constitution could be brought about. On 27 December 1788, when the royal council met, the Minister of State, Necker, proposed doubling the elected size of the Third Estate. He argued

that the royal authority had everything to fear from the two higher orders and everything to gain by allying itself with the people. This was, indeed, the way in which the declaration in favour of doubling the representation of the Third Estate was interpreted in the country: the king, it was believed, had thrown in his lot with the people. He became overnight a popular idol.[16]

Pierre le Grand belongs to this juncture, before the fatal stubbornness and weakness of the monarchy destroyed all hope of co-operation. And because the Swiss, Necker, was still held to be he who would mediate successfully between the parties, Bouilly translated him into Le Fort.

I saw besides the famous LEFORT, a Genevan, leading the emperor of the Russias in everything great and memorable which this Prince did; as in France M. NECKER directs and assists the beneficial designs of the monarch. The analogy was striking. And no one mistook it; and I had the sweet satisfaction of seeing love, respect and fidelity break out in all hearts, precious emotions with which I am imbued for my Fatherland and my King.[17]

By 20 June 1789 the Third Estate took its oath of disobedience to the king and slowly proceeded to recast the constitution on its own authority. During the summer months, as the 'Constituent Assembly', it passed a Declaration of Rights – individual freedom, liberty, equality before the law – which the king refused to sign. The Bastille had fallen, unemployment and food prices were rising, and Necker's rôle shrank; it was hungry Parisians themselves who processed to Versailles on 5 October and obliged the royal family to return next day with them to Paris, and the king to accede to the Declaration. Bouilly had referred to the king creating 'a people of kings'. It is a moot point whether this was written before or after a subsequent act of the Constituent Assembly, by which they changed Louis' title from that of ruler by divine right alone to 'Louis by the grace of God and the constitutional law of the State, King of the French'. But at this point, things become more stable. Bread prices were high but steady, the monarchy quietly tried to worm its way out of a democratic rôle, the Constituent Assembly proceeded to vote out the abuses of the feudal past. The harvest was good, and the year 1790 was for the most part peaceful. Necker left France, to 'no effect either on the public mind or public funds' in September 1790.[18]

When *Pierre le Grand* was eventually seen, it was interpreted as 'left of centre'. The more progressive *Moniteur universel* voted strongly in favour. 'It was difficult to select a subject more worthy of great interest . . . above all at a time when the rights of men appear to be assured and citizens have hopes of becoming freer and happier through the bringing together of all conditions of men.'[19] But Grimm had nothing to say about the subject-matter (xv:585), and the *Mercure de France* wanted the leading figure to be more commanding; it could not condemn the subject outright:

Although the moral of the subject is not of wide application (for after all few kings need to make themselves into artists and artisans) the framework is nonetheless interesting. We believe only that the author could have extracted greater advantage from it . . . He should have provided his hero with positions better asserting the dignity of his rank and greatness of his character.

It also thought that the final verses should have been more obviously flattering to Louis.[20]

From the outset, *Pierre le Grand* was criticised for being diffuse. It was in four acts, a version that had nineteen performances between 13 January and August. A letter of 12 February confirms that Grétry and Bouilly had 'cut out more and more of the drawn-out parts' but also that Bouilly considered it 'impossible' to recast it in three acts.[21] The printed four-act libretto, probably reflecting the work prior to cuts, shows how smoothly Bouilly eventually altered it. Broadly speaking, he removed as much as possible of the original act 2 and placed its indispensable scenes into his new first act (new sc. 5 and 6). The largest sacrifice was made in Georges' motivation, for when he originally learned of Pierre's betrothal to Catherine he more aptly refused his daughter's marriage to Alexis. The original act 2 finale therefore consisted of the villagers persuading him to relent. Apart from this finale, the four-act version contained three musical numbers later rejected: an aria for Le Fort in act 2 sc. 1, a duet for Alexis and Caroline in act 3 sc. 1, and an aria for Catherine in act 4 sc. 1.[22] Various pieces of dialogue had to be cut or reshaped as well.

The impulse to do the work came not from Grétry (in Lyon working on *Guillaume Tell*) but from the general assembly of the Comédie-Italienne, which resolved on 11 August 1790 to write to Bouilly in Tours. Their letter would ask him politely but firmly to put right the work's 'considerable faults', reduce it to three acts and so give it a better chance of survival.[23] By cutting the original second act finale Bouilly could have acceded to their request without needing Grétry's help; the new version was first seen on 2 November.

Obviously the opera could not be shown in later stages of the Revolution; it had fifty-two performances in 1790–3. But it was revived in 1801 and steadily reached another thirty-eight performances to 1810, plus seven in 1814–17. The final foreign production noted by Loewenberg was in Amsterdam (1811).

35. The entr'acte (II) and overture (III)

After the middle-period operas without notated entr'actes Grétry resumed his interest in 1779 and thereafter employed them regularly. Exceptions apart, he used one of three simple formulae. The first, going back to *Zémire et Azor*, was to arrange a vocal solo heard already, in order to call the attention to a particular character about to become important. The second, which was new, involved closely anticipating the music of an aria about to be sung at the start of a new act. The third formula was to compose a piece that would loosely suggest the action meant to be continuing between the acts. This type, too, derived from the early 1770s.

The entr'acte (ii) and overture (iii)

The first formula (*Aucassin et Nicolette*, both entr'actes, *Les méprises par ressemblance*, first entr'acte) was the least dramatic. It could easily be taken for a merely pleasant reminiscence, since no significant recomposition or arrangement was done. But the second type (both entr'actes in *Les événements imprévus*, the first in *Raoul Barbe-bleue*, *Le rival confident*, and the second in *Pierre le Grand*) could represent a challenge to an audience, simply because the music – deprived of its correlative, the voice line – might sound strange or even eccentric. Forced to concentrate on the general mood, the audience was prepared by a miniature overture, as it were, in the same key and tempo as the piece about to be sung. The orchestration would naturally conform in great measure to the effect of the anticipation. If there were a scene change the audience would perceive it in conjunction with the music, and each would heighten the effect of the other. Possibly the actors habitually came on stage, blurring the distinction between entr'acte and ritornello.

The third type, of course, admitted many possibilities. In *L'épreuve villageoise* a simple binary dance-like music is heard three times, each faster than the last, clearly signifying the offstage celebrations about which Denise will sing in (7). In *Richard Cœur-de-lion* the single entr'acte, using muted violins, brass and covered timpani sticks,[1] is the accompaniment to the mimed movement of troops going about their duties at daybreak. One could never think of performing it as a separate piece of music: it is at once too comfortable and too odd. Its key of E flat was surely intended to prepare for Richard's solo aria, this link forming a third, psychological strand of suggestion, together with the misty tone-colours and the distant trumpet-calls. In *Raoul Barbe-bleue* Grétry returned to the conception of *L'épreuve villageoise*, seeming to continue the dances within the castle that ended act 2. But he added an electrifying call on offstage trumpet, which signifies the first intelligence of the return of Raoul. The same call will return during the lovers' duet (16) at the join between slow and fast sections, seeming to provoke them into either action or bravery.

A unique notion was conceived for the first entr'acte in *Pierre le Grand*. This apparently self-sufficient solo for oboe with strings in D major is however a free continuation of the gloomy D minor oboe tune (5) played by Alexis: Ex. 35.1. It

(a) Andantino

Oboe solo [+ strings]   etc.

(b) Allegro

Oboe [+ strings]   etc.
Doux et gayment

Ex. 35.1 *Pierre le Grand*
(a): (5) (b): (9)

obviously suggests the rise in his hopes, following his defence by Pierre after Georges' belligerence. In a sense it is a surrogate aria for a character who never actually sings one.

Not until *Guillaume Tell* did entr'actes in mime definitely return, and the hand of the ageing Sedaine had lost none of its dramatic cunning. The first entr'acte, repeated three times, is a 6/8 tempo giusto and during it the audience sees the all-important scene of Swiss citizenry being forced to salute Guesler's cap stuck on its pike. The heaviness of timpani and brass seems to represent the underlying pressures. However, the second entr'acte is totally unambiguous: a seventy-five-bar storm scene traced from beginning to end. Sedaine wanted a full-scale mime:

Had the piece been given at the Opéra or a large theatre, the back of the stage being able to show an expanse of lake, one would have seen the embarkation [of Tell] in the entr'acte, filled by a great piece of music; would have seen the storm rise, the boat in trouble, lost under the waves, vanish; reappear after a loud clap of thunder; Tell directing it and leaping on to the rock [to escape].

These momentous events are described by Tell's son in act 3 sc. 3. The orchestration, including piccolo and trumpets, is both detailed and very suggestive. One figuration clearly pictures water lapping, near the beginning. As Beethoven was often to do, so Grétry superimposes tonic and dominant chords during the tense approach to the first tutti (Ex. 35.2), not timidly, but with conviction.

Ex. 35.2 *Guillaume Tell* (13)
Score: 'Distant thunder'

Finally, the exceptions should be mentioned. Since the second entr'acte in *Le Comte d'Albert* actually precedes what is technically a new work, a sequel rather than simply a third act, it received the status of a second overture. There is a brief 'Larghetto pastorale' which is followed by a rapid *moto perpetuo* of fifty-four bars' duration. In the 3-act *L'amitié à l'épreuve*, on the other hand, the orchestra is simply to play the overture's Cantabile section between the first two acts.

Although his aesthetic idea of the overture did not alter between 1784 and 1791, Grétry's formal and musical approaches continued to grow. The overtures were now single movements, the final three all adding a short slow introduction. This was to remain the standard format in Paris and elsewhere.[2] New keys were used: C minor, G minor, F major. Moreover, the composer was even more willing than hitherto to make extensive musical cross-reference between these three overtures and their parent operas.

The innovative tendencies of the overtures described in chapter 23 surely culminated in *Richard Cœur-de-lion*, where Grétry and Sedaine fused mime, song, prelude and first scene into one. In other words, the G minor orchestral prelude and (1) formed a single, sung overture (which is how the contemporary printed orchestra parts labelled it). By contrast, the least pretentious overture of the 1780s was *Le rival confident*, part of a D major group with *L'épreuve villageoise*, *Les méprises par ressemblance* and *Raoul Barbe-bleue*. In *Le rival confident* Grétry used a very straightforward refrain form (like an extended rondo), whereas all remaining overtures of the period engaged at some level with sonata concepts. Nevertheless the urge to novelty prompted him to include a tambourine all through, an improvised part played either behind the curtain or in the pit.

Placed beside this, the overture to *Les méprises par ressemblance* seems equally unmemorable: simple contrasts of material and texture in buffooning style, a miniature sonata in AA' form. In fact, the work is a retouched version of the overture *Isabelle et Gertrude* written for Geneva in 1766. The sources have been described in chapter 2. Grétry sometimes added extra bars in order to define an idea or a cadence more clearly, and sometimes deleted repetitious ones. The main theme was made more interesting by the addition of a dotted rhythm. Only in the transition to the coda did Grétry contribute a quite new idea, replacing a feminine paragraph with the fanfares now at bar 63 (possibly inspired by the dragoons). Surprisingly little, then, was changed and the new overture is only five bars longer than the original one. Nowhere does Grétry mention this self-borrowing, let alone the aesthetic inconsistency it implies.

The last of the 'light' overtures, *L'épreuve villageoise*, gives us the confidence of the 1780s. Not only is it vigorous and strong, but is carefully orchestrated. Perhaps its hint of monothematicism, sonata-form regularity and cadential prolongation display the hearing of mature Classical symphonies, for Grétry writes warmly about Haydn in the *Mémoires*. The overture's most original motif (Ex. 35.3), which looks as though it was stolen by Beethoven for *his* peasants' merrymaking, recurs upside down, though recognisably, in (3), where it is associated with the words 'la belle fête'.

Symphonic principles now entered the Grétryan overture to darker purpose,

Ex. 35.3 *L'épreuve villageoise*, overture, development

beginning with that in C minor to *Le Comte d'Albert*. The entire piece remains at the slowish pace of Andante risoluto, prefiguring neither the Count's rescue nor the light to come in the Sequel. It resembles ABCA' in its form; confusion is often created within the sonata by Grétry in returning to the tonic (as here after B) instead of taking the second subject area straight into a development section. This also occurs with *Les méprises par ressemblance* and *Raoul Barbe-bleue*. *Pierre le Grand* in this aspect is more conventional. The symphonic duality felt in *Le Comte d'Albert* lies between flute themes that seem likely to represent the children (cf. a motif in their (2)) and stern, rigorous figures. Yet the persistently steady pace stamps the overture with overwhelming gloom, found unattractive by some at the time (i:403).

Raoul Barbe-bleue sounds loose by contrast, its Allegro maestoso in 2/2 imposing a simpler rigour through diminished seventh chords and brass played 'Forcé'. Yet once one knows the identity of its motifs, the piece can be heard as an exciting 'discussion' of issues from the opera: Grétry had – in short – arrived at the formula we know from Beethoven's *Leonora* overtures. The *Raoul Barbe-bleue* overture contains (a) a second subject reproducing Ofman's cringing dotted-note music from (8); (b) seventeen bars in the development section taken (except for instrumental details) from the mime in (19) depicting the violent rescue of Isaure; (c) a tutti theme in its recapitulation that occurs twice in the final chorus, to the words 'Mais ce tyran abominable'; and (d) a coda theme taken from the 'Fanfare', a trumpet-like idea ending the opera. There is no musical reference (as in *La Rosière de Salency* or *L'amant jaloux*) to a central dramatic event in the opera. The overture attempts instead a synthetic drama given form, if not symphonic coherence, by the exterior design of the sonata.

In *Pierre le Grand*, his first overture in F, Grétry took a copybook approach to the sonata, almost slavishly adhering to four-bar phrases and using stressed rhythmic cells worthy of Cherubini. In the first subject and development areas he imposed no individuality upon the style pioneered at the Théâtre Italien by Dalayrac's *Sargines* and taken up by the younger generation. But we have suspected from the introduction that thematic use of grace notes might signify local colour, and suspicion is confirmed at the second subject. This is once more our musically anarchic composer flinging expectation to the winds (Ex. 35.4). Octave horns, as we said in the last chapter, probably evoke the *Pas Russe*. Further, in the recapitulation, Grétry completely recomposes this 'theme' except for its final five bars.

The still-uncommon trumpet in F was included, and clarinets doubling oboes. The doubling presumably reflects the fact that although the opera was staged in January 1790 clarinets were not salaried players until Easter that year, by which time it was too late to publish a special part for them. In *Guillaume Tell*, however, the solo clarinet received utmost prominence, and from the first bar. Sedaine demanded the sight of a Swiss valley at sunrise with mountains, Tell's son in the distance playing on his pipe the *ranz des vaches*, with various herds of animals grazing. The *ranz des vaches* duly opens the overture, as it was to open Schiller's

Ex. 35.4 *Pierre le Grand*, overture

William Tell and feature in that of Rossini. It signified a national musical melody, a set of calls so evocative of the Swiss fatherland that it was supposed to prompt uncontrollable nostalgia when heard abroad by the born Swiss.[3] Apparently taking Rousseau's *Dictionnaire de musique*, plate N, as his source, Grétry diluted the melody's flavour by neglecting the sharpened fourth degree (see Ex. 35.5). That he was not averse to this inflexion is proved by the *Panurge* overture, where it was meant to be an orientalism. The *ranz* is pursued for no fewer than thirty-nine bars, and is counterpointed against the astonishing addition of a 'corne', maybe a cow-horn, floating on the air from time to time with a 'plaintive sound' on the notes c'' and (later) d'' and e''. Was it 'faked' on a conventional instrument? The evidence is lacking.[4] Furthermore, Grétry thought of an accompaniment using the cello

Ex. 35.5 (a) *Ranz des vaches* after Rousseau, *Dictionnaire de musique*

Ex. 35.5 (b) *Guillaume Tell*, overture, opening

harmonic note g'' against the low viola open note c. At one stroke, he destroyed the conventions of the Classical orchestral and beat the noisy innovators (whom he so distrusted) at their own game.

The pastoral prelude then turns into a violent G minor Allegro, occasionally punctuated by 6/8 music for passing troupes of oxen and further 'corne' notes. The motif of a descending scale now made its appearance, one which will in the course of the opera proper come to symbolise the crushing strength of Austria. Most strikingly, Grétry used the motif when quoting, in the overture, from the music for the attempted rape or abduction that ends act 1 (see Ex. 35.6). Doubtless it was bold to mix the mimetic with the abstract. Sedaine, for one, made his dissatisfaction known.[5] However, this flexible thematic integration between overture and parent opera constituted an important departure. It developed that of *Les mariages samnites* on a wider scale, since the use of the downward motif was introduced into the orchestral part on a larger number of occasions than had been Agathis' motif. From Grétry's point of view it was imperative to prepare the audience for it, and so for the true subject of the opera.

Ex. 35.6 *Guillaume Tell*
(a) Overture, main subject group. Cf. Ex. 36.5 for later uses of the 'tyranny' motif
(b) Overture and (7). Bracketed accidentals refer only to (7).

Finally, it is well worth quoting Bouilly's account of the overture, since he was an intimate of the Grétry household when the piece was being composed, and one of the first people to whom Grétry played it.

At one time you believe you hear shepherds leading their flocks to pasture, repeating the old Swiss refrains; at another you can imagine seeing these citizen–farmers meeting together, exchanging their agricultural tools for the pikes with which they founded their liberty; finally, amid the cries of the combatants and the rousing choruses of their women who incite them against tyranny, you distinguish that *ranz des vaches*, that *Lé Zarmailli dei colombettè*, ancient and solemn signal of the independence, the union and the prosperity of the Thirteen Cantons.[6]

36. Guillaume Tell (William Tell)

Drame in 3 acts, in prose and verse: *CC* 24
Libretto by Michel-Jean Sedaine.
First performed at the Comédie-Italienne, 9 April 1791.
Printed full score, Paris, l'auteur, n.d. [1794] as Œuvre XXXI.
Dramatis personae: Guillaume Tell (t.)
     Madame Tell (s.)
     Marie, their daughter (s.)
     Guillaume, their son (s.)
     Melktal *père* (b.)
     Melktal *fils* (t.)
     Guesler, commandant of the Austrian emperor (b.)
     Officer (b.)
     Old man (spoken rôle)
     Surlemann (spoken rôle)
     A traveller (t. or bar.)
     His wife and daughter (s., s.)
     Officers and soldiers of the emperor; Swiss citizens

ACT 1: A Swiss valley at sunrise; mountains. Tell's son seen in the distance on a rock playing the *ranz des vaches* on his pipe; shepherds, flocks. Guillaume wakes Marie; she is to be married today to Melktal *fils*, who arrives in turn (trio 1).[1] His father, the canton's chief, has been detained by Guesler. Tell's wife sets the table and, with Tell and Guillaume, sings of family happiness (verses 2). A traveller and his family report new outrages being committed by Austrian troops. The commandant has had a person's eyes put out. The traveller comforts his child (song with refrains 3), then they leave. Villagers arrive singing a folksong, joined by Guillaume (4). The meal begins. The company invokes the blessings of family life (ensemble and chorus 5). Other villagers enter (chorus 6) and Tell gives the word to proceed to church: Melktal's father can meet them there. Surlemann appears in fright. In representing the people Melktal has irritated Guesler and refused to salute his hat. It is his eyes that have been put out. Tell seizes his bow and commands young Melktal to follow. The people break up disconsolately (ensemble, mime 7) after which a soldier pursues a girl into the room, obviously intending an assault. Tell's wife seizes a knife and drives him off.

ACT 2: A square in a town; market stalls, distant mountains, and a lake. Upstage, a pike with Guesler's cap on top. Armed troops force the citizens to doff their own hats to it (entr'acte 8). Melktal *fils* reports to Marie that Tell has also refused to salute the cap, and been condemned to death: Marie refuses to be comforted (duet 9). Guesler enters with soldiers (aria 10) then orders Tell to be fetched. In an extended movement (11) Tell's wife and children appeal fruitlessly to Guesler, as do the people. When Tell is led in, chained, Guesler orders him to demonstrate his skill by shooting an apple from Guillaume's head at fifty paces. Amid popular acclaim, he eventually fires successfully. Guesler discovers the second arrow with which Tell had intended to kill him in the event of failure. He is immediately borne away, while Austrian soldiers swoop on the people and disperse them. The Swiss men (chorus 12) express their anger with restraint, but women mock their supineness; the men break out in open revolt and trample Guesler's cap underfoot. ACT 3: Countryside, Guesler's castle in the background built on a rocky escarpment. Fortress entrance left, its ramparts extending to the right. Other rocks higher and lower. In the entr'acte (13) a storm is depicted descending on the lake (Lucerne), and the boat bearing Tell to prison.[2] The danger of shipwreck prompts Guesler to use Tell's help as steersman; Tell drives the boat close to some rocks and thereby escapes. On stage, the emperor's soldiers are in activity: a Swiss revolt has started. Tell's wife watches them pass (aria 14); Guillaume, descending the rocks, informs her of Tell's escape, which he has seen. Entering with young Melktal, Tell summons the cantons with a horn call. In a trio (15) with his wife and Melktal, he urges her into action through his implacable spirit of vengeance. Seeing the blinded Melktal escorted in, she retires, overcome with emotion. Armed inhabitants begin to arrive and Tell is placed in charge of the uprising. They wait for compatriots' signals: lighted torches on neighbouring peaks. Women arrive bearing wine and bread; they are prepared to die alongside the men. The song of Roland is sung (16). As the surrounding mountain signals are lit, all leave and climb the mountainside, leaving only old Melktal and the children. During the combat (17) there are several engagements; the castle is set on fire; young Melktal fights Guesler and is only rescued by a fatal arrow from Tell's bow; Madame Tell successfully defends herself with an axe; gradually the troops are put to rout and disarmed. A final chorus (18) appeals to future ages to follow the example of 'all for liberty'.[3]

Sedaine's printed libretto contains both a prefatory note and a poem dedicated to the spirit of Antoine-Marin Lemierre (1723–93), poet and playwright, author of the verse tragedy *Guillaume Tell* (1766). This, Sedaine's source, we shall turn to in a moment. Lemierre was a friend of Sedaine, but the latter's poem of dedication is couched in terms of the revolutionary struggle to which Lemierre's own *Tell* had acted as one of the curtain-raisers:

But your art, more fatal to despotic power, did better by portraying the greatness of the Swiss. In a striking image, in your lofty poem, you showed France a whole people rising up to the strains of proud Liberty.[4]

Lemierre's origins, like Sedaine's, were humble. Like Sedaine, he entered the literary world by publishing poetry. Soon he produced a distinguished series of tragedies, some of them subsequently translated into the principal languages of Europe: *Hypermnestre* (1758), *Térée* (1761), *Idoménée* (1764), *Guillaume Tell* and *Artaxerce* (1766), *La veuve du Malabar* (1770). He was elected to the Académie Française in 1781, and he gave the reception speech for Sedaine before the same body in 1786. Lemierre experienced considerable public resistance to some of his work. Such was the case with both *La veuve du Malabar* and *Guillaume Tell*. The latter was coolly received in 1766, not surprisingly when one considers its main theme was armed insurrection led by a hero of lowly birth. To have introduced such a hero, Lough maintained, was an innovation impossible to be followed up, in spite of all the idealistic pressure to broaden the narrow social base of French serious dramatic characters.[5] It was on its revival in 1786, together with many minor changes of composition, that it was well received. On this occasion a mimed portrayal of Tell's trial shot was included.[6]

Lemierre's writing is powerful and filled with revolutionary fervour. The ringing rhetoric, incidentally, is wholly from the 1766 version. The play adheres to the unity of place (in the mountains near Altdorf and Lake Lucerne) which creates problems in a theme of this kind, but allows for extended speeches describing, for example, the rigours of Austrian tyranny. All sub-plots are relegated to the sidelines, leaving the struggle to play itself out between Tell and Gesler, who is shot dead by his adversary in act 5. Melchtal's narration of his father's tragic blinding sets the play off to a strong start and plunges us into an atmosphere of rebellion and indignation. In fact, Melchtal *père* is never seen, as he has died following the shock of torture. Gesler, who is seen in all acts except the first, is unremittingly evil. By act 3 Tell has been arrested for refusing to kneel to the cap: he unflinchingly faces up to his persecutor. The shooting of the apple and its aftermath complete act 4; between it and act 5 the storm on the lake and escape of Tell are supposed to occur. In a fine *coup de théâtre* it is Gesler who appears first to the terrified Cléofé (Tell's wife) before being murdered in act 5; the play ends with calls to liberty and to arms.

Lemierre reserves a forthright place for Cléofé. She demands in act 1 full participation in the righting of general wrongs, not the rôle of a housewife. In act 3 she pleads with Gesler before the trial shot and (in the rewritten version) snatches back her son from the arms of his soldiers, though to no avail. Lastly, in act 5, Cléofé berates Tell's compatriot Furst for his supposedly cowardly reaction to events so far; and although in fact the preparations for mass action have been carried out, her intention to raise support herself sets the seal on her character.

Although Sedaine took what he needed from Lemierre, including the recognition of Tell's wife as a major character (an emphasis only partially taken on by Schiller in his play of 1804), it cannot be said that his libretto comes close to Lemierre either in dramatic character or in success of realisation. With typical verve, Sedaine imagined a number of musical tableaux that are, for various reasons, powerful: the act 1 arrival of guests, the trial scene, the storm entr'acte, the waiting for the mountain-top signals in (16). Yet for once, his technique of supplying a number of different soloists with arias seems not to solidify with these tableaux into an adequate whole. As in Gluck's French operas, perhaps, the broader scenes with chorus ought to have been interwoven with a consistent picture of the family at the heart of the action. Rather too much of the first act is devoted to scene-setting, and when the shock of the report of Melktal's blinding occurs, it is too late and too sudden a contrast. It is not Grétry's fault that most of the musical local colour finds itself in act 1, or if neither Madame Tell nor Melktal is given much chance to affect the course of subsequent action, or forward the insurrection, or provide some greater point of contrast. Tell's part itself is musically restricted in scope.

To read Sedaine's prefatory material one would imagine that he was a fanatical republican and anti-monarchist. But certain expressions are ambiguous:

Arrogant sovereigns! in the bosom of indolence, enjoy the happy days that the fates allow you, and shepherds of a flock too great for you, fear the anger of a people aroused; let Tyranny expire at the feet of Reason.

According to Margaret Rayner, *Guillaume Tell* was a work of expediency. Sedaine, a constitutional monarchist, was listed in 1790 as suspected of being 'attached to the Old Régime'.[7] The *Almanach général des spectacles* for 1791, discussing *Tell* as a work in preparation, sarcastically attacked Sedaine for wanting to incite unrest and for bending his principles for financial gain.[8] Lemierre himself is supposed to have died in poverty and distress at the course the Revolution was taking; Sedaine died in 1797.

The only evidence for Sedaine's motives is the apparent haste with which the libretto was composed, and that is neither conclusive nor proof of a political position; though if his listing as a suspect was well founded, one must allow that *Guillaume Tell* was an ideal choice for any attempt at self-redemption. Open political involvement of the theatres became acute in winter 1790–1. The case of Voltaire's *Brutus*, for example, shows that royalists and their opponents took up positions before the start and applauded those lines relevant to their own cause.[9] This was the order of the day, and since Sedaine's text 'breathes hatred of oppression and love of liberty, all that had a connection with these two sentiments was applauded' (*Journal de Paris*, 11 April 1791). Grétry, for whatever personal reasons, took on the task of setting this profoundly musical scenario: and nobody who has seen the score will deny, as Brenet put it, the composer's 'self-identification with the libretto', his 'uncommon energy' in the piece.[10] For all Bouilly's tendency to invent when it suited him, his account of Grétry's motives is perfectly plausible: honest, bourgeois self-interest. In 1790 appeasement of the libertarians was still contemplatable.

[*Tell*] flattered the opinion of the day by the detail and tableaux it offered in favour of liberty. Grétry, born a Liégeois, was not insensible to the idea of equality of rights . . . he wished to co-operate with the new political system whose purpose was to render all men equal before the law, and accord distinction only to personal celebrity.[11]

Having an abundance of the latter, says Bouilly, Grétry was the more predisposed in favour of such a system.

That Sedaine gave a restricted individual rôle to his Tell may have been to avoid the part's identification with any of the leaders of the early Revolution. Grétry therefore sought musical unity outside the area of personal characteristics, placing heavy emphasis on Swiss local colour which he pictured, or at least felt, in symbiosis with national identity. So he portrayed the people with 'some rustic phrases indicating the ingenuousness of the Swiss; these seem to say, "It is to preserve our virtues that we rise up"' (ii:50). The composer tells of dining with some Swiss officers garrisoned in Lyon, requesting them to sing for him both ancient national songs and mountain songs that possessed 'most character' (ii:20).[12] He absorbed them, without copying them, and so was able to reproduce something of the *ton montagnard* (mountain tone) to which – he claimed – Swiss and others felt themselves drawn in his opera.

Given the shortcomings of the libretto, it seems that Grétry worked the harder to compensate for them; but there was scant opportunity to introduce musical irony in the first six numbers of the score. The drama here depends upon irony; that Melktal's father is due at any moment, and that what should be the happiest day of these families' lives will be turned into the saddest. If the lullaby (3) was intended by Sedaine as ironic counterpoint to the eternal night that has befallen Melktal *père*, it remains a conceptual, not an operatic stroke. The first three musical numbers are indeed frail, but contain colouristic details that are new such as the 'yodel' in Ex. 36.1 from (1). As the villagers assemble, (4) takes on a more original colour: this pseudo-folksong is entirely constructed over a hypnotic F sharp pedal. With its swaying rhythm and unusual harmony it attains a haunting quality which at last begins to imply layers of irony or, at least, melancholy: (Ex. 36.2).[13] Further, the composer completely renewed himself in (5), which outwardly resembled (4) in *Lucile*: the wedding-morning ensemble sung at table. Now there is a chorus, in five parts, but also a new style of refrain for the secular benediction, 'May your loves be blessed': a sequence of chords so original that Cherubini apparently remoulded it for the wedding procession in his opéra-comique *Médée*, act 2 sc. 6 (1797): see Ex. 36.3.

The various and memorable contributions of Grétry's chorus – and we now have to imagine an ensemble of at least sixteen singers – render this body one of the principal 'characters' in *Guillaume Tell*: they are heard in eight of the fifteen vocal numbers. Tell himself has no separate aria. In act 1, as throughout, he is literally of

Ex. 36.1 *Guillaume Tell* (1)

CHORUS OF VILLAGERS

Noi - set - te, noi - set - te, Je ne veux point te cueil - lir sous la cou - dret - te.

Ex. 36.2 *Guillaume Tell* (4)
('Hazel-nut, I do not wish to cull thee under the hazel-tree')

[Moderato]

Violins

SOLOISTS & CHORUS

Bass: *tenues*
[+ strings + bassoon]Que bén- is soient, que bén - is soient vos a - mours (Orchestra)

Ex. 36.3 *Guillaume Tell* (5)
('May your loves be blest')

the people: with his family in (2) and (5), then in a public rôle in (7). His authority after the news of the outrage is established in commanding phrases; later he assures his wife of his prudence in a passage almost growling 'with concentrated rage' (score), supported only by bassoons and string bass. In the sequence (11), Tell twice has a powerful if short G minor monologue denouncing Guesler; a closer adherence to Lemierre could have produced a more solid piece. Then in the trio (15) the fury of Tell is again heard, where the strings seem to seethe with him in their off-beat chords. Madame Tell's misgivings are unavailing, and Tell makes her resolute. Yet even here Grétry was perhaps more interested in reproducing the aural effect of the distant horns from replying cantons than in developing the portrait of Tell as such.

Madame Tell agrees to share the dangers of combat, and in (17) is shown to prove as good as her word. At this we are hardly surprised, having witnessed her at the end of act 1 threatening a soldier, and heard her pleading with Guesler in (11). Her character is annealed in the fires of uncertainty during the wonderful aria (14), in F minor. Not knowing Tell's fate, she is torn between action and waiting. The siting and circumstances relate to Mlle de St Yves' (13) in *Le Huron*; but the medium is now non-repeating aria, not preceded by obbligato recitative. No thumbnail account could convey the wealth of intervallic difficulty in the voice line, or the continuity of its high passion. Perhaps its climax is the main transition back to F minor (Ex. 36.4) as she seems to see Tell, bloody and calling for help. Surely this was the most violently moving phrase in all Grétry's opéras-comiques.

Ex. 36.4 *Guillaume Tell* (14)
('I see him, bleeding: Ah! cruel ones, stop, I die, I give way to my sorrow')

The other main aria in the work is Guesler's (10): but owing to Grétry's ingenious motivic scheme we cannot fully judge its effect in isolation. Faced with the dramatic concept of two opposing nationalities, Switzerland and Austria, Grétry apparently decided to characterise the latter solely in terms of their aggressiveness. We find that the music – including (10) – expressing this quality is freely identified with a set of short falling motives, suggestive of a hammer-blow or a descending fist. As we saw in Ex. 35.6, the overture makes use of more than one of them. A number of these 'motives of tyranny' are grouped for comparison in Ex. 36.5: (a) from (10); (b) from the beginning of (11); (c) from (12), where the Austrians charge at the Swiss to disperse them; and (d) from the combat (17) where, metaphorically, the Austrian strength is equally matched by the rising power of the insurgents. Other examples could also have been quoted. Just as the mime ending (7) approaches, for example, we hear prefatory hints of the scalewise notes even as the last of the villagers goes offstage, just before the soldier chases his victim in.

Thus Guesler's tyrannical ranting in (10), in C minor, takes its place at the centre of a web of influential motives, which allegorise his commanding rôle in the drama. The aria itself is a stubborn ABA (Dal Segno) form and even its central section preaches his gospel of hatred. Every other vocal item is either non-repeating, strophic, or possesses some type of unorthodoxy. (1) for example, although in ABA' form, begins as a duet and finishes as a trio.

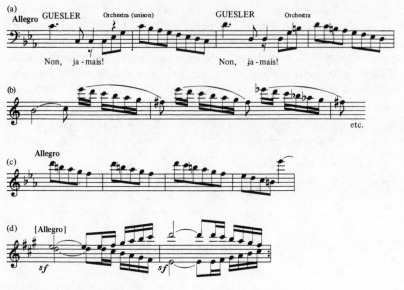

Ex. 36.5 *Guillaume Tell* (10), (11), (12), (17)
Themes using Austrian 'tyranny' motifs. Cf. Ex. 35.6.

The solution adopted for the setting of the fable's central action was that of *Le Magnifique* (10) or *Raoul Barbe-bleue* (10): a substantial musical complex translated in this case into twenty-five pages of score. Tonal unity was not pursued to the end of (11) however (a triumphal chorus of citizens in D major) as it was in the above-mentioned pieces. Presumably it was because the key of C minor forms an even larger natural continuity in act 2, from (10) through the opening part of (11), to the important chorus (12) and even to the entr'acte (13). Although there is a much larger cast of characters in *Guillaume Tell* (11), Grétry delights in the very diversity of music he offers, unifying the whole by organising simple repetition of material from within. For example, drawing on his experience with mimetic music, Grétry made the music for the trial shot rise above abstract accompaniment by recalling a pathetic little motif previously associated with the boy Guillaume. Even for an opéra-comique with a singularly small quantity of spoken dialogue, (11) must be recognised as an ambitious fusion of all possible components: recitative, aria, ensemble, chorus, mime.

Let us return to the music for chorus, noting incidentally the subtle calculation in not giving the Austrian forces any music for ensemble or chorus. *Pierre le Grand* had seen the appearance of serious choral tableaux in Grétry's opéra-comique; they heralded (7) and (12) in *Guillaume Tell*. A range of turbulent textures appears in (7), headed by the new impulse to contrapuntal or fugal writing, now that the individual voice-lines have sufficient aural strength to justify it. Answering (antiphonal) groups of phrases are exploited for the same reason. The key, C minor, was also used in *Pierre le Grand* (14) for mourning. In (12) it is used throughout all four sections, and indeed this chorus – splitting sometimes into six voice parts – dramatises spontaneous insurrection in an operatic way that could have no direct equivalent in the plays of Lemierre or Schiller. The men are cowed by Austrian force (conveyed by the orchestra, Ex. 36.5 (b)) and sing a second section slowly, 'with muted fury': their words echo Lemierre's Tell's couplet near the end of act 2:

O comble de l'outrage et de la tyrannie!
O jour de la bassesse et de l'ignominie!

To this the women respond in a three-part fugato that rises to a powerful climax: 'What! do you fear death?', and as a storm gathers, men and women unite in the last section. Here the music can have a Handelian grandeur, especially when sopranos enter together on their top g'', Ex. 36.6. Seemingly with this in mind, Grétry designed his act 3 closing triumphal chorus in A major, adding a piccolo to the instrumentation. So when the appeal goes out in it to 'imitate our courage, do everything for liberty', the sopranos attain top b'', supported by high F sharps in the brass parts.

Ex. 36.6 *Guillaume Tell* (12)
('Do you hear the thunder? War must begin without delay, All run, all run . . .')

In complete contrast is the song of Roland (16), employing a male chorus in two parts with solos for old Melktal and Tell; again this is a peculiarly operatic moment, though echoed at the opening of Schiller's last act. This piece, with (4), anticipates Grand Opera in its nostalgic combination of the mood before battle, the appeal to the greatness of the past, and the visual splendour of illuminated mountain-tops. Also Romantic is the fact that its music and words fade away on the dominant chord in mid-sentence. Roland's actual song had not survived (i.e. concerning the battle of Roncevalles as celebrated in the *chansons de geste* of the Middle Ages) so, as in the case of Richard the Lionheart, attempts were made to reconstruct it.[14] Even though Roland was killed at Roncevalles, his name signified one of the greatest of Charlemagne's knights, and his evocation by Sedaine was simply an appeal to French patriotism: 'Let us die for our country'. So far from being a mediaeval or Swiss pastiche, this melody was a gift by Grétry to his contemporaries and, indeed, their descendants: Ex. 36.7.

Ex. 36.7 *Guillaume Tell* (16)
The song of Roland

VERSIONS AND PERFORMANCES

Guillaume Tell was much more than the 'almost negative success' claimed by Pougin.[15] It ran for ten years and was seen eighty-two times, chiefly in 1791–4. In 1828–9 a much modified version, with extraneous music, was mounted in order to compete with Rossini's *Guillaume Tell* at the Opéra (3 August 1829). There were thirty-two performances. The last foreign revival noted by Loewenberg was in New York (1831).

CONCLUSIONS

Lucile Grétry, who had suffered an unhappy marriage, died in March 1790, and was followed in death by Bouilly's fiancée, Antoinette, the following December. The first attained seventeen years, the second only sixteen; both may be presumed victims of tuberculosis. Bouilly's moving account pictures the composer's family keeping from Grétry the truth of Antoinette's decline, while he completes what he feels will be an important production in *Guillaume Tell*. In October 1790 Sedaine had already urged the Comédie-Italienne to mount it as soon as possible,[16] but Grétry's personal tragedy obliged the rehearsals of the work to be suspended.

The following few years saw a lessening of Grétry's popularity, while for his part he loathed the 'howling of dogs', his phrase for what he termed 'revolutionary music' (letter of 14 February 1796). The years of eclipse are summarised in Table 11.

Table 11. *Grétry's popularity in 1793–1801*

	Number of different Grétry opéras-comiques given at the Comédie-Italienne/Opéra-Comique	Total Grétry performances at this theatre
1793	20	141
1795	12	131
1797	14	84
1799	11	50
1801	9	50

In 1793 the Comédie-Italienne became the Théâtre de l'Opéra Comique National, or Opéra-Comique for short. In 1801 it shut on 20 July with debts of 1.5 million francs and was merged with the Feydeau company (see chapter 32). When the new Opéra-Comique company arose from these ashes on 16 September 1801 a renaissance of interest in Grétry's opéras-comiques gradually began.

Several now partly- or wholly-lost opéras-comiques were staged after *Guillaume Tell*: *Cécile et Ermancé* (1792), *Basile* (1792), *Joseph Barra* (1794) and *Callias* (1794). The last was the most successful, but still attained only 14 performances. Grétry, though, was indefatigable. He urged Beaumarchais to turn *La mère coupable* (1792) into an opéra-comique, and Ducis to collaborate similarly with him on the tragedy *Abufar ou la famille arabe* (1795).[17] This evidence belies the public statement that after Antoinette's death, Grétry's taste for music diminished with the virtual extinguishing of his imagination (iii:xvii). In 1797 the single-act opéra-comique *Le barbier de village* was mounted at the Théâtre Feydeau with text by A. J. Grétry, his nephew. Its music was drawn from the 'principal pieces' of *La rosière républicaine*, an occasional piece with recitatives from 1794.[18] Then *Lisbeth* (1797) kept the boards for eleven years and was revived in 1813–14 with a total of 104 performances. And *Elisca*, his last opéra-comique, received 21 performances in 1799, with a further 12 on its revision in 1812–13.[19]

The long years of middle to very old age, occupied with family and friends, were still those of continuing celebrity. Many more letters survive from the period 1793–1813 than from all the years before, so it remains a separate task to trace Grétry's life through their help, through the *Réflexions*, the memoirs of his nephew and other documents.[20]

Grétry's career embraced the transformation from aria-based comedy to finale-based comedy, from solo-based drama to chorus-based drama, and from formally traditional music to completely nonconformist designs. Chabanon (see chapter 1) thought that the movements of an opéra-comique were bound to be diffuse as compared to the flow of a sonata or of recitative opera. Grétry proved him wrong by evolving a personal style and by harnessing that style consistently to the needs of the libretto. Further organisation, enhancing larger-scale coherence, was developed through functional recollection; in *Guillaume Tell* this became a more organic technique, perhaps derived from the initiatives of J. B. Lemoyne at the

Opéra in *Electre* (1782) and *Nephté* (1789).[21] We have seen that Grétry's orchestra, often the bearer of such motivic or other recollections, was by no means as weak or aesthetically superfluous as used to be claimed. If Grétry openly regretted earlier doubling in his viola and bassoon parts (see chapter 32) he always founded the ensemble (as did Gluck) on the active pre-eminence of the violins and basses; and he sought after new effects, brought in new instruments, became more complex in his textures and finally took up the challenge of portraying the horrifying and the heroic.

We have seen that Grétry's harmony is uncomplicated on one level but also unpredictable. On another level it follows the drama into the anguished, the antique or the natural world. There is a constant thread of minor-mode (often G minor) invention, right from *Isabelle et Gertrude*. But as was also observed in chapter 1, Grétry defined his own art as one of nuance rather than the large-scale or the tragic. In short, it is an art that we must appreciate in the theatre and under conditions where singers, in particular, must learn to give back verbal values to their melodic lines, learn to control the purely sensuous aspects of musical expression. It is an art that stands at a distant remove from the architectural symmetry of classical sonata form, such as used by Mozart. Grétry, like C. P. E. Bach in his instrumental works, exploited expressive nuance to wholly personal aesthetic ends. High points of expression could be tied in many different ways to the stable ground-plan of musical tonality.

Grétry's melody was not of course mechanical, even when deferring to word or situation. Its intrinsic quality was such that it was later freely claimed that his music had attained the status of 'proverbs' (Jouy's term) or a 'monument' (Momigny's) in French-speaking cultural life.

His tunes, having become *proverbs*, if I dare express myself thus, have been repeated by three consecutive generations.[22]

Or as Ronald Crichton more recently observed of 'Une fièvre brûlante': 'it seems always to have been there'. The task lies ahead for the bibliographer to catalogue the multifarious arrangements through which these tunes were enjoyed outside the confines of the theatre.

Any opera composer wrestles with the problem of balancing music and drama. As a composer who happened to work in France, Grétry laboured under particular difficulty in consequence of the high standards of dramatic verisimilitude that were normal there. This resulted sometimes in a 'double punishment', for alterations to new works, when not carried out under the best conditions, could oblige him to cut against his own better judgement. The public of the time liked speed of action in opéra-comique (if not necessarily in other theatrical genres) and not even Grétry stood above the power of the box-office. But this was his own choice as a basically freelance artist within a basically capitalist economy.

With good reason did Mozart, it seems, study Grétry scores in 1778 and presumably visit the Théâtre Italien. Mozart's acquaintance with works like *Zémire et Azor* and *L'amant jaloux* (q.v.) helps us to understand how the fluid structures in *Die Zauberflöte* may relate to Grétry's attainment of musico-dramatic freedom, either within or without sonata form. The latter's occasional use of mime and its integration into musical numbers, is likewise not to be forgotten. His actors' movements were constantly suggested by orchestral figures (see p. 87) on a moral as well as a histrionic level.

Local colour in its twin aspects of research and application, a musical inheritance of vital significance to the nineteenth century, was one that stemmed with perhaps unique power from Grétry in the eighteenth. And his tireless exploration of new overture forms and methods of integration with an opera must have pre-empted almost everything that the new century was to conceive.

Coherence; use of motives; orchestration; moulding the vocal line around syllable, word and character: these are only the technicalisms of an art which would not be worth reviving if it did not also betray the humanity of Grétry the dramatist–musician. He had the wit to caricature human weakness, but always used his ability to harness our understanding of it. Consider Silvain's and Hélène's youthful indiscretions, later validated by conjugal devotion; Lucile's paternity revealed and the way her mother's deed is effectively expiated by Blaise's honesty; Alonze's jealousy that rises in spite of himself in *L'amant jaloux*; Agathis torn between love of progenitor and fatherland in *Les mariages samnites*.

Leading female parts assume the rôle of rescuer as frequently as male ones: Hélène (*Silvain*), Agathe (*L'ami de la maison*), Zémire, Countess d'Albert, and others. The nature of a victim's suffering is always felt, whether it be the obsessional Aucassin, the betrayed women in *Les événements imprévus* (7), or even the bedraggled Jacquinot in *Les méprises par ressemblance*. All this was possible since the composer had that *sine qua non*, the inborn gift of suggesting musically memorable characters in extremely different moulds, ranging from the simpleton to the tyrant, the coquette to the miser, the heroic wife to the magnanimous Indian woman. Grétry was not free of sentimentality, but this is always limited and never puerile. He was well nicknamed 'the Molière of music'.

As the Revolution approached and broke, opéra-comique developed too quickly for him to grasp all its implications. But, paradoxically, it was he who had urged the genre forward, fuelled its ambition, and hated tackling the same dramatic problem twice. When he did so, for example where he employed Italianate finale structure, he certainly gained in sophistication. Possibly he would have achieved more had he attempted less. But that is an imponderable, for originality was essential to his achievement.

Notes

1 Introduction

1 Heinz Wichmann, *Grétry und das musikalische Theater in Frankreich* (Halle, 1929); Edward J. Dent, ed. Winton Dean, *The Rise of Romantic Opera* (Cambridge, 1976).

2 All the performance statistics up to 1826 were compiled by the present author using F:Po, *Registres de l'Opéra-Comique*. The figures for the Opéra-Comique from 1826 to 1893 were taken from Albert Soubies, *Soixante-neuf ans à l'Opéra-Comique en deux pages* (Paris, 1894).

3 *Les spectacles de Paris . . . 1782* (Paris, n.d.), pp. 110–14. An adapted version is printed in Antoine D'Origny, *Annales du Théâtre Italien depuis son origine jusqu'à ce jour* (3 vols., Paris, 1788, reprinted Geneva, 1970), ii, pp. 154–7. The 'revolution' referred to means the advent and acceptance of Gluck, whose French version of *Alceste* was seen in 1774. This certificate and its various articles reformulated the Comédie-Italienne's structure; legal confirmation was in the Letters Patent of 31 March 1781, registered in the *parlement* of Paris on 1 May following.

4 The standard institutional history of the Comédie-Italienne in English is by Clarence D. Brenner in his introduction to *The Théâtre Italien, its Repertory 1716–1793*, University of California Publications in Modern Philology, lxiii (Berkeley, 1961).

5 Georges Cucuel, 'Notes sur la Comédie Italienne de 1717 à 1789', *Quarterly Magazine of the International Musical Society (Internationale Musikgesellschaft)*, xv, part 1 (1913), pp. 159–63.

6 Georges Cucuel, 'Sources et documents pour servir à l'histoire de l'opéra-comique en France', *L'année musicale*, iii (1913), pp. 253–5, 271.

7 Graham Sadler, 'Rameau, Piron and the Parisian Fair Theatres', *Soundings*, iv (1974), pp. 13–29.

8 J. G. Prod'homme and E. de Crauzat, *Les Menus Plaisirs du Roi, l'Ecole Royale et le Conservatoire de Musique* (Paris, 1929), p. 45.

9 Thirteen tunes are as yet unattributed. This and the whole period in question are clearly explored in Kent M. Smith, 'Egidio Duni and the Development of the *Opéra-Comique* from 1753 to 1770', unpublished dissertation, Cornell University, 1980, pp. 55ff, 75.

10 Cucuel, 'Sources et documents', pp. 264–6.

11 [Jean Auguste Jullien, called Desboulmiers], 'Répertoire' in *Histoire anecdotique et raisonnée du Théâtre Italien* (7 vols., Paris, 1770), vii, p. 467. I have omitted ballet.

12 Jean-François Marmontel, 'Ariette' in *Elémens de littérature: Œuvres complettes [sic] de Marmontel* (10 vols., Paris, 1787), v, p. 260. An example of Rameau's work in this style would be the *ariette* 'Brillez, brillez' near the conclusion of *Castor et Pollux*.

13 From *Poème sur le vaudeville* (1760), quoted in L. Parkinson Arnoldson, *Sedaine et les musiciens de son temps* (Paris, 1934), p. 218

14 e.g. *Journal encyclopédique*, 15 June 1769, pp. 428–39.

15 [P. J. B. Nougaret,] *De l'art du théâtre* (2 vols., Paris, 1769), ii, pp. 305–7, 331.

16 *Mémoires de M. Goldoni*, ed. Paul de Roux (Paris, 1965), p. 293.

17 François Benoît Hoffman, 'Théâtre de l'Opéra Comique' in *Œuvres* (10 vols., Paris, 1829), ix, p. 511. It is interesting that, following Rousseau's lead, one person wrote both words and music of an opéra-comique: N. E. Framery in *La sorcière par hazard* (1768, 1783). But the application of music was found less satisfactory than the management of plot (Grimm:xiii:360–1).

18 Review of Boïeldieu's *Le nouveau seigneur de village* (1813) in *Allgemeine Musikalische Zeitung*, xvi (5 October 1814), columns 669–73. Translation kindly provided by Martyn Clarke.

19 Michel Paul Guy de Chabanon, *De la musique considérée en elle-même et dans ses rapports avec la parole, les langues, la poésie et le théâtre* (Paris, 1785, reprinted Geneva, 1969), pp. 337–40.

20 Jean-Jacques Rousseau, 'Duo' in *Dictionnaire de musique* (Paris, 1768, reprinted Hildesheim, 1969).

21 August Wilhelm Schlegel, *A Course of Lectures on Dramatic Art and Literature*, trans. John Black (2 vols., London, 1815), ii, pp. 75–6. From the German original of 1809–11.

22 J. Gaudefroy-Demombynes, *Les jugements allemands sur la musique française au XVIIIᵉ siècle* (Paris, 1941); for example, Carl Spazier's 1800 translation of part of Grétry's *Mémoires* 'greatly contributed in fixing the eyes of the German public on the personality of Grétry as a writer and philosopher still more than as a composer and aesthetician' (p. 237).

23 *Carl Maria von Weber: Writings on Music*, ed. John Warrack (Cambridge, 1981), p. 224.

24 Brenner, *The Théâtre Italien*, p. 16.

25 *The Early Diary of Frances Burney 1768–1778*, ed. A. R. Ellis (2 vols., London, 1889), i, p. xlv.

26 *Continental Excursions* (London, 1809), cited in John Lough, *Paris Theatre Audiences in the Seventeenth and Eighteenth Centuries* (Oxford, 1957), p. 199.

27 Lough, *Paris Theatre Audiences*, p. 202.

28 George Rudé, *The Crowd in the French Revolution* (Oxford, 1959), pp. 12, 14.

29 D'Origny, *Annales du Théâtre Italien*, ii, p. 130.

30 F:Po, Registre de l'Opéra-Comique vol. 117 f. 111, 16 February 1785.

31 J. C. Le Vacher de Charnois (ed.) *Costumes et annales des grands théâtres de Paris*, iv, Issue IX [1789], p. 76.

32 Jean-François Marmontel, *Mémoires*, ed. John Renwick (2 vols., Clermont-Ferrand, 1972), i, p. 261.

33 Rôles created: Mlle de St-Yves, Lucile, Columbine, Hélène, Henriette, Corali, Agathe, Zémire, Clémentine, Cécile. She retired in 1777.

34 The Huron, Blaise, Silvain, Martin, Blandfort, Oronte, Sander.

35 Le Vacher de Charnois (ed.), *Costumes et annales*, i, Issue XLIV [1787], p. 3.

36 Le Vacher de Charnois (ed.), *Costumes et annales*, i, Issue VI (2 June 1786), p. 5.

37 Gilotin, Timante, Cassandre, Gripon, Cliton, Ali, Aldobrandin, the Bailli (in *La Rosière de Salency*).

38 Le Vacher de Charnois (ed.), *Costumes et annales*, i, Issue XXIV (15 October 1786) pp. 5–6.

39 Arthur Pougin, *Figures d'Opéra-Comique* (Paris, 1875), pp. 1–75; J. J. Olivier, *Madame Dugazon de la Comédie-Italienne* (Paris, 1917); H. and A. Le Roux, *La Dugazon* (Paris, 1926).

40 Pougin, *Figures*, pp. 11–12. It forms the third stanza of (10) and, deservedly, became a popular song.

41 Grétry rôles created: Chloé, Jacinthe, Lisette, Nicolette, Laurette, Comtesse d'Albert, Isaure, Catherine.

42 The Officer, Dorval *fils*, Pierrot, Basile, Jérômè, Nelson, Célicour, Azor, Octave (the Magnifico), Colin, Linval, Apollon, Don Alonze, Marquis de Versac, Aucassin, Blondel.

43 Le Vacher de Charnois (ed.), *Costumes et annales*, i, Issue XI (8 July 1786), pp. 10–12.

44 Biographical notes on certain of these are in Emile Baux, *Notes et documents inédits sur l'Opéra-Comique et quelques-uns des artistes pendant la Révolution* (Paris, 1909).

45 Baux, *Notes et documents*, p. 36.

46 F:Po, Registre de l'Opéra-Comique vol. 56, May, June 1774 etc., 'Frais courants', for *Répétitions particulières*, meaning either 'special' or 'private' rehearsals. Perhaps as many as eight instruments were used by 1790, to judge from the implication 'on répugnerait à faire recommencer de même sept à huit instruments': [N. E. Framery,] *De l'organisation des spectacles de Paris, ou essai sur leur forme actuelle* (Paris, 1790), p. 132.

47 Louis-Sébastien Mercier, 'Gluck' in *Tableau de Paris* (12 vols., Amsterdam, 1782–8), vi., p. 245.

48 David Charlton, 'Orchestra and Chorus at the Comédie-Italienne (Opéra-Comique), 1755–1799' in Malcolm H. Brown and Roland John Wiley (eds.), *Slavonic and Western Music: Essays for Gerald Abraham* (Ann Arbor, Oxford, 1985), pp. 87–108.

49 As with *La fausse magie* in François Lesure (ed.), *Catalogue de la musique imprimée avant 1800 conservée dans les bibliothèques publiques de Paris* (Paris, 1981).

50 The manuscript score will be edited in the series *French Opera in the Seventeenth and Eighteenth Centuries*, ed. Barry S. Brook (75 vols., New York, 1984–) by M. Elizabeth C. Bartlet, who first drew recent attention to its existence.

2 Profile I: from Liège to Paris

1 Grétry himself gives 11 February as his birthday (i:3) and this was accepted by Pauline Long Des Clavières in *La jeunesse de Grétry et ses débuts à Paris* (Besançon, 1920), pp. 5–7. She also gives a family tree dating back to the sixteenth century. But Georges de Froidcourt has argued strongly for a birth date of 8 February in 'Le lieu et la date de naissance de Grétry', *Le Vieux-Liège*, lxxix (1952), p. 166.

2 José Quitin, *Les maîtres de chant et la maîtrise de la collégiale Saint-Denis à Liège, au temps de Grétry: esquisse socio-musicologique* Académie royale de Belgique, Classe des beaux-arts: Mémoires, 2nd series, xiii, fasc. 3 (Brussels, 1964).

3 Etienne Hélin, *La démographie de Liège aux XVIIᵉ et XVIIIᵉ siècles*, Académie royale de Belgique, Classe des lettres: Mémoires, lvi, fasc. 4 (Brussels, 1963), pp. 41 n1, 54, 250.

4 Quitin, *Les maîtres de chant*, pp. 27–9. The exemplary research by Quitin has furnished almost all the specific details and datings that follow.

5 Archival evidence in Long Des Clavières, *La jeunesse de Grétry*, p. 18 n3. It was run by Crosa and Resta, whose name Grétry cited accurately.

6 See Wenick's 'Kyrie' and 'Laudamus te' from the Mass in B flat and the Mass in D (both 1742) in the appendix to Quitin's *Les maîtres de chant*. Georges Wenick was a clearly engaging character who so enjoyed Rome that he simply refused to come back to St Denis and is supposed to have died in Italy. He had been choir-master since 1740.

7 For a biography of de Harlez, see Froidcourt, p. 24. On the foundation of the Collège Darchis, endowed in 1696, erected 1699, see Long Des Clavières, *La jeunesse de Grétry*, pp. 33–5 and, more particularly, Monique De Smet, *Le Collège Liégeois de Rome: sa fréquentation au XVIIIᵉ siècle* (n.p., 1960). Originally the students were chiefly theologians. The college did not survive the Revolution.

8 Grétry's name was first inscribed in the parish register of San Lorenzo in Lucina, Rome, during the few weeks prior to Easter 1761 (22 March), with those of the other students at the Collège Darchis. It was entered there for the last time prior to Easter 1765. The names were gathered at the same time annually in an official census. The actual attendance documents of the Collège have been lost: see De Smet, *Le Collège Liégeois*, pp. 33–6. The day-by-day account given by Grétry of his journey's beginning also fits the year 1760, when Easter was on 6 April: after three-and-a-half days a young abbé with the group gave up the attempt and was instructed first to rest and then go home on horseback. Grétry's mother remembered seeing him reappear in church on Easter day (i:58). I do not accept José Quitin's view that Grétry stayed in Liège until 1761; for one thing Easter fell very early and the walk to Rome would have had to begin during winter; Quitin points out elsewhere in *Les maîtres de chant* that students bound for Rome often left in May or June.

9 Translation by W. H. Auden and Elizabeth Mayer (Harmondsworth, 1970), p. 128.

10 'J'ai vu disséquer des chiens vivans à l'hôpital du St-Esprit, de Rome': *Réf*:iv:283. See also *Réf*:ii:122. Nicolas-Henri de Fassin (1728–1811) is referred to in *Réf*:iv:311.

11 *An Eighteenth-Century Musical Tour in France and Italy*, ed. Percy A. Scholes (London, 1959), p. 303. Burney gives an account of music in the Sistine Chapel (p. 230) and claimed the Romans as 'the most fastidious judges of music in Italy' (p. 303).

12 From an eye-witness quoted in Michel Brenet, *Grétry, sa vie et ses œuvres* (Paris, 1884), p. 12. Burney, who also found this practice 'indecent', reported that in 1770 Carnival began on 7 January; however, the starting date could vary. In Venice, Carnival usually began on 26 December.

13 Copy (one of three that survive, but non-autograph) in F:Pn: 'par André Grétry, élève de Casali'. It may be the 'Confitebor' sent to his parents (i:110) which won him a position in Liège of *maître de chapelle* that he never, of course, took up. Long Des Clavières analyses it in *La jeunesse de Grétry*, pp. 44–7.

14 Only six religious compositions survive apart from the 'Confitebor': 'Dixit Dominus', 4 voices, orchestra (incomplete); 'O Salutaris', 5 voices, organ; 'Laetatus sum', soprano, orchestra; 'Laudate', tenor, orchestra; 'Laudate', soprano, orchestra; 'Mirabilis', 4 voices, orchestra. The last four appear to be nineteenth-century arrangements. See José Quitin, 'Les compositions de musique religieuse d'André-Modeste Grétry', *Revue Belge de Musicologie*, xvii (1964), pp. 57–69.

15 Possibly the works published in Paris and reviewed in 1773: 'SEI QUARTETTI Per Due Violini, Alto E Basso Del Signor Grétry Composti a Roma OPERA IIIa' and issued by 'le Sʳ Borrelly, rue et vis-à-vis la Ferme de l'Abbaïe St Victor'. One should add here that the so-called 'opus 1' flute quartets and 'opus 2' set of six keyboard sonatas first listed by F. J. Fétis, *Biographie universelle des musiciens*, 'Grétry . . .', have never been found, although supposedly published. See Albert Vander Linden, 'Broutilles au sujet de Grétry', *Revue Belge de Musicologie*, xii (1958), pp. 74–7. Similarly, the parts for a Grétry 'Symphonie' published in Liège in *L'année musicale ou Choix des nouvelles musique en tous genres*, no. 7, 1 April 1774, are merely transposed arrangements of three movements taken from the second and the fourth (authentic) string quartets, Op. IIIa.

16 Grétry simply places this event 'several years after' he completed his instruction with Casali, but boastingly at 'an age when it is rare even to dare to aspire to it' (i:91–2). Letters to Padre Martini of the Accademia from Grétry survive from the Geneva period (29 March 1766) and the Paris period (eight letters, 1766–79).

17 Abingdon commissioned flute music from many composers, but at the end of his life began publishing his own music in various genres: see *The New Grove*. His life is described in the *Dictionary of National Biography*, 'Bertie, Willoughby'. The commission for concertos was terminated in 1768 (i:158). Abingdon was already back in London at the end of June 1767: see his letter to Wilkes (GB:Lbl, Add.ms.30869, f. 133) also mentioning that '[I] did not pass through Paris on my way back to England'.

18 From a letter Casali wrote to a friend in Geneva, cited by F. J. Fétis, 'Casali, Jean-Baptiste', *Biographie universelle des musiciens* (8 vols., Brussels, 1837–44), iii, p. 62.

19 L. V. Flamand-Grétry, *L'ermitage de Jean-Jacques Rousseau et de Grétry* (Paris, 1820), pp. 140–1, cited in Froidcourt, pp. 301–2. Charles Burney, *Music, Men and Manners in France and Italy*, ed. H. E. Poole (London, 1969), p. 22.

20 He himself mentions suffering bronchial bleeding or haemoptysis (i:21–4), for which tuberculosis would have been the most likely cause at that time. His longevity would be explained by the fact that tuberculosis can be active, cause lung damage, become quiescent and still leave an individual with recurrent haemoptysis. (The early death of Grétry's daughters also suggests tuberculosis of one or another type.) However, recurrent haemoptysis can also be caused by rarer conditions, foremost among which is hereditary telangiectasia (a condition of the blood vessels). I am obliged to Dr John Collins (London) for this diagnosis.

21 *Isabelle et Gertrude* (Comédie-Italienne, 1765) was a *pasticcio* work, not one with originally composed music, and contained two arias taken from the music of Gluck, furnished of course with new words. See Smith, 'Egidio Duni', pp. 285–6. According to *The New Grove*, 'Blaise, Adolfe Benoît', this musical director of the Comédie-Italienne wrote most of the music.

22 The company was active by the beginning of July. They acted Monsigny's *On ne s'avise jamais de tout* (1761), Philidor's *Le maréchal ferrant* (1761), *Le bûcheron* (1763) and *Tom Jones* (1765), Duni's *La fée Urgèle* (1765) and Gossec's *Le tonnelier* (1765): Long Des Clavières, *La jeunesse de Grétry*, pp. 84–5.

23 La Harpe's recollection of events at Ferney is in the *Cours de littérature*, xii, p. 130, cited in

Long Des Clavières, *La jeunesse de Grétry*, p. 112; his critique of Favart's libretto is in vol. xii, p. 370 of the *Cours*, cited in Long Des Clavières, *La jeunesse de Grétry*, pp. 91–2.

24 F:Pn Vm5.98^bis: disbound, unfoliated manuscript of vocal and orchestral parts in a single hand, probably a copyist. They were first rediscovered by P. Long Des Clavières and reported in *La jeunesse de Grétry*, p. 92. Her music examples, although single-stave, are useful but quite often inaccurately reproduced, as are one or two portions of text. The manuscripts are not attributed to any composer but internal evidence (see end of chapter 2) proves Grétry's authorship.

25 Long Des Clavières, *La jeunesse de Grétry*, p. 115, places Grétry's departure from Geneva too late, i.e. November 1767, since by 1 December (letter to Padre Martini) he had established a footing among 'academicians' – probably Arnaud and Suard (see below) – prepared to recommend him. Sené, mentioned in *Réf*:ii:99, must have been the Genevan Louis Sené, born 1747 (E. Bénézit: *Dictionnaire critique et documentaire des peintres*, Paris, 1976).

26 Grimm (viii:166), not Grétry, divulges Légier's name. One Pierre Légier published an *Amusements poétiques* in 1769. Grétry took possession of the text bit by bit and set it to music in that order, contrary to later habit (i:149–50). In *Réflexions* (iv:342–3) he described his 'little musky poet, who promised me an opera, received from me a hundred begging visits while he did his perfumed toilet, which gave me frightful headaches'.

27 Creutz gave a dinner-party (i:150). Gustave-Philippe, Comte de Creutz (1731–85) was born in Finland and became Swedish ambassador in Paris. Both Marmontel and Grétry provided reminiscences of his extraordinary mental gifts and persuasive charm. He loved Grétry's music and received the dedication of *Le Huron*. See Grétry's account of him in *Mémoires*: i:191–6.

28 Grimm (vii:166) had word that some of the finest pieces entered *Le Huron*, especially (14). Grétry admitted self-borrowing from it in *Le Huron* (12), *Silvain* (part of the overture and (7)) and *Zémire et Azor* (23), as well as the 1776 reworking (i:288).

29 Charles Burney, *The Present State of Music in Germany, The Netherlands, and United Provinces* (2 vols., London, 1775, reprinted New York, 1969), i, pp. 54–5.

30 Jean-François Marmontel, *Mémoires*, ed. John Renwick (2 vols., Clermont-Ferrand, 1972), i, pp. 260–1. In a chapter about Marmontel written in the *Réflexions* (ii, ch. 29) in sorrow and anger following the demeaning stance towards him Marmontel showed in the posthumous *Mémoires* (1804), Grétry rebutted his librettist's implication that he, Grétry, sought to approach Marmontel using Creutz as go-between.

31 'I owe much, and I like to say it on every occasion, to the zeal, friendship, taste and advice of Dalayrac . . . the works [opéras-comiques] were done through discussion, and he helped to make them better by his severity, by the attention he paid in observing everything, weighing everything, foreseeing everything': B. J. Marsollier, 'Ma carrière dramatique' in *Œuvres choisies de Marsollier* (3 vols., Paris, 1825), i, pp. 6–7.

32 Marc-Antoine Désaugiers to his cousin, dated 16 October 1774, in *Musiciens peints par eux-mêmes*, ed. Marc Pincherle (Paris, 1939), pp. 10–13.

33 Jérôme-Joseph de Momigny, 'Opéra' in *Encyclopédie méthodique. Musique, publiée par MM. [N. E.] Framery, [P. L.] Ginguené et [J. J.] de Momigny* (2 vols., Paris and Liège, 1791, 1818), ii, p. 231.

34 Momigny, 'Opéra', p. 231: 'je lui instrumentois ses airs et ses chœurs'. This evidence seems not to have been discussed, though Fétis published the assertion, totally without evidence, that 'The orchestration of [Grétry's] last twenty operas was written by Panseron', which of course appears to imply that the composer did 'abandon' part of his work: F. J. Fétis, 'Grétry, André-Ernest-Modeste', *Biographie universelle des musiciens*, 2nd ed. (8 vols., Paris, 1860–5), iv, p. 105. The manuscript of *Elisca*, Grétry's last opéra-comique, contains some non-autograph pages, but more are wholly by the composer (letter from the late Professor Albert Vander Linden to the writer).

35 Momigny, 'Opéra', p. 231.

36 François Arnaud, *Lettre sur la musique à M. le comte de Caylus* (Paris, 1754). Arnaud does not however enter into significant musical detail here. Arnaud, abbé of Grandchamp (1721–84),

had published in the Querelle des Bouffons and was to take Gluck's part in the disputes with Piccinni.

37 'The prosody of our language is perhaps not sufficiently specific [i.e. compared to Italian]; but it is more than docile to the movements one wants to give it. Our absolutely silent syllables are banished from lyric poetry and the feminine "e", sustained by a consonant, is perceptible enough when sung, as in poetic diction, given a short note.' Unsigned article, 'Examen des réflexions de M. Dalembert sur la liberté de la musique', *Mercure de France*, July 1759, second part, p. 101.

38 *Ernelinde, tragédie lyrique* (Paris, n.d.), p. 44 ('S'il faut que tu me sois ravie'); p. 116 ('Cher objet'); p. 200 ('Tu vois une fille').

3 Le Huron

1 The purposeful placing of opus or *œuvre* numbers on the title pages of his published full scores was not conceived by Grétry from the outset, but it was not long in establishment. Œuvre VII (*Zémire et Azor*), score issued 1772, seems the first production to include the opus number on initial engraving. Even a presentation copy (F:Pn Rés.F.421) apparently given to its dedicatee, and lacking the usual word 'Prix' ('Price'), is headed 'Œuvre VIIᵉ'. Certain exemplars of all earlier opéra-comique scores lack any *Œuvre* designation; others have one. This mixed situation is possible since, once engraved, the plates were not destroyed. When copies of Œuvre I to Œuvre VI were drawn off to supply demand, presumably during or after 1772, the *Œuvre* designation would be engraved at the top of the title page. A copy of *L'ami de la maison* (F:Pn L.5425(1)), publicly performed 1772 and supposedly printed 1773, also lacks an *Œuvre* designation.

2 The Bailli, usually a figure of fun in opéra-comique, was a petty official almost like a cross between a local magistrate and a policeman. See p. 124.

3 Incipits (1) 'Si jamais' (2) 'Comme il y va!' (3) 'Ne vous rebutez pas' (4) 'Les joncs ne sont' (5) 'Vous me charmez' (6) 'Qu'on mette à prix' (7) 'Il a les traits' (8) 'Ma bonne amie' (9) 'L'amour naissant' (10) 'Dans quel canton est l'Huronie' (11) 'Vaillants Français' (13) 'Toi que j'aime' (14) 'Ah, quel tourment' and 'Ah! mon cœur' (15) 'Ah! que tu m'attendris' (16) 'Sur nos étendards' (17) 'Me prend-on pour un sot' (18) 'Qu'ai-je donc fait?' (19) 'Que ne suis-je encore' (20) 'Plus de larmes'.

4 This aspect of Gilotin's character was noted at the time and used in a political pamphlet, having been taken as an allusion to the Duc d'Aiguillon as acting governor of Brittany: see J. H. Brumfitt and M. I. Gerard Davis (eds.), '*L'Ingénu*' and '*Histoire de Jenni*' (Oxford, 1960), pp. xxv–xxvi.

5 John Renwick, *Marmontel, Voltaire and the 'Bélisaire' Affair*, Studies on Voltaire and the Eighteenth Century, cxxi (Banbury 1974), Introduction and p. 72.

6 Bernard Faÿ, *Louis XVI or the End of the World* (London, 1968), p. 56.

7 The background, including the complications of the Breton issue from 1764 to 1767, is well explained in Brumfitt and Gerard Davis (eds.), '*L'Ingénu*' and '*Histoire de Jenni*', pp. vii–xviii.

8 Charles Burney, *The Present State of Music in France and Italy* (London, 1773, reprinted New York, 1976), p. 50.

9 F:Po, Registres de l'Opéra-Comique. In a printed copy of the score stemming from the Musique du Roi (F:Pn H.902) and containing numerous performance marks, this aria is shown as cut. Grétry demands clarinets in D but a note in the score (p. 42) says that oboes might be substituted. *Gilles garçon peintre* dated from 1758; its printed score has been dated c1765 in François Lesure (ed.), *Catalogue de la musique imprimée avant 1800 conservée dans les bibliothèques publiques de Paris* (Paris, 1981), and shows that clarinets in B flat and D were used, playing in the overture and two closing pieces, pp. 113 and 122. In the latter the clarinets are heard together with oboes and horns. Other information on *Gilles* is in Georges Cucuel, 'Notes sur la Comédie Italienne de 1717 à 1789', *Quarterly Magazine of the International Musical Society (Internationale Musikgesellschaft)*, xv (1913), pp. 164–5.

10 Grimm (viii:166) estimated this to be borrowed from *Les mariages samnites*. The 1768

librettos designate (16) also as a *Récitatif obligé* but it was not set as one. This confirms that Marmontel had a definite stylistic approach; part of (19) was also labelled in the same way and Grétry set it as such save for the first four designated lines. On Marmontel's musical sensitivity, see *Réf*:iii:97.

11 [Anon.], 'Examen des réflexions de M. Dalembert sur la liberté de la musique', *Mercure de France,* July 1759, second part, pp. 73–103, attributed to Marmontel in J. G. Rushton, 'Music and Drama at the Académie Royale de Musique (Paris) 1774–1789', unpublished dissertation, Oxford University, 1969, p. 20.

12 W. L. Cross, *The History of Henry Fielding* (3 vols., New Haven, 1918), iii, p. 181.

13 Analyses in Rushton, 'Music and Drama', pp. 27–33 and Daniel Heartz, 'Diderot et le théâtre lyrique: "le nouveau stile" proposé par *Le neveu de Rameau*', *Revue de Musicologie,* lxiv (1978), pp. 229–52. Rushton observes that the absence of all supernatural elements and the final sudden reversal of fortune likens the work to opéra-comique of a later type. *Ernelinde* even contains orchestral combat music in D (full score, p. 275) as does, for example, *Richard Cœur-de-lion* by Grétry.

14 Charles Burney, *The Present State of Music in Germany, The Netherlands, and United Provinces* (2 vols., London, 1775, reprinted New York, 1969), i, p. 27.

15 Voltaire wrote *Samson, La princesse de Navarre* and *Le temple de la gloire* for Rameau. In a slight exaggeration Decroix wrote in the 1780s, 'It is quite remarkable that M. de Voltaire was the first to give an opera to Grétry as he had been the first, around 1730, to give a tragedy [*Samson*] to Rameau, before these two great musicians were yet practised in the genres in which they excelled.' Introduction to Kehl edition of *Le baron d'Otrante* reproduced in Louis Moland (ed.), *Œuvres complètes de Voltaire,* (52 vols., Paris, 1877–85), vi, p. 574. At the time of meeting with Grétry, Voltaire was collaborating with J. B. de La Borde on the *tragédie-lyrique Pandore.* La Borde was actually at Ferney in September 1766, though Grétry does not mention him.

16 Letter of 7 December 1767 to Chabanon (*Ernelinde* derived from Norwegian history and a libretto by Matteo Noris, 1684) and 9 September 1768 to the same.

17 P. Long Des Clavières, *La jeunesse de Grétry* (Besançon, 1920), p. 85. The identity of the Henri IV work is in doubt but could have been Charles Collé's *La partie de chasse d'Henri IV* (1764), permitted public performance only in 1774.

18 Long Des Clavières, *La jeunesse de Grétry*, p. 113. No source given.

19 Letter of 13 May 1774 to J. B. N. de Lisle, in which he hopes Gluck will be 'as good'.

20 From Voltaire's epistle to the King of Prussia, 1751: *Œuvres complètes de Voltaire*, x, p. 360.

21 As Grétry points out (i:166) bilingual comedy was nothing new at the Comédie-Italienne, though it was not part of modern opéra-comique.

22 Letter of 15 October 1768 to Mme Denis; a more cryptic letter of 7 November also refers to 'Guetry'.

23 Paris, Merlin, 1768 (56-page edition), music supplement, pp. 70–1; cf. score, pp. 34–6.

24 *Journal de l'empire,* cited in Long Des Clavières, *La jeunesse de Grétry,* p. 144.

4 Lucile

1 Incipits: (1) 'Qu'il est doux' (2) 'Quel réveil' (3) 'Autour de moi' (4) 'Où peut-on être mieux' (5) 'Ah! ma femme!' (6) 'Tout ce qui peut toucher' (7) 'Au bien suprême' (8) 'Ah! ma belle maîtresse' (9) 'N'est-il pas vrai' (10) 'Chantons deux époux' (11) 'De la fête'

2 J. F. Marmontel, *Mémoires* ed. John Renwick (2 vols., Clermont-Ferrand, 1972), i, p. 261.

3 Anita Brookner, *Greuze, the Rise and Fall of an Eighteenth-Century Phenomenon* (London, 1972), p. 118 and Plate 53, Greuze's portrait of Mme de Porcin.

4 Brookner, *Greuze,* p. 110 and Plate 43; although exhibited in 1769, this painting had attracted enthusiastic comment from Diderot when he saw a sketch of it in 1765: 'It says to every man who has a heart and soul, "Keep your family in comfort; give your wife children . . ."'.

5 *Mercure de France,* February 1769, p. 192.

6 This duet was shown as cut in a printed score stemming from the Opéra-Comique (F:Pn H.904) and containing a number of performance indications.

7 *Mémoires*: i:175. Caillot wore a special wig to achieve the effect of baldness, which excited the great admiration of Grimm (viii:245–6).

8 F:Po, Registre de l'Opéra-Comique vol. 51.

9 Jean Ehrard (ed.), *De l'encyclopédie à la Contre-révolution: Jean-François Marmontel (1723–1799)* (Clermont-Ferrand, 1970) where the writer's dramatic and operatic criticism is discussed by Jacques Wagner (p. 88) and where Annie Becq deals, *inter alia*, with Marmontel's aesthetic ideas on music (pp. 167–87). A critical bibliography exists: John Renwick, *La destinée posthume de Jean-François Marmontel (1723–1799)* (Clermont-Ferrand, 1972). See too Michael Cardy, *The Literary Doctrines of Jean-François Marmontel*, Studies on Voltaire and the Eighteenth Century, ccx (Oxford, 1982).

10 'The great majority of his contributions to the stage therefore had musical settings and required no great skill in dramatic construction, nor a large amount of originality.' From Clarence D. Brenner, 'Dramatizations of French Short Stories in the Eighteenth Century', University of California Publications in Modern Philology, xxxiii (Berkeley and Los Angeles, 1947), pp. 1–34.

11 *La guirlande, acte de ballet* (1751); *Acante et Céphise, pastorale-héroïque* (1751); *Lysis et Délie, pastorale* (unperf.); *Les Sybarites, acte de ballet* (1753).

12 Marmontel, 'The Shepherdess of the Alps', in *Moral Tales* (3 vols., London, 1766), ii, p. 73.

13 Marmontel, *Mémoires*, i, p. 261. By *genre* he means, I think, predominantly bourgeois comedies or Moral Tales, not 'philosophical' opera, as Karin Pendle argued in '*Les philosophes* and *opéra comique*: The Case of Grétry's *Lucile*', *The Music Review*, xxxviii (1977), pp. 177–91. Dr Pendle gives a useful account of a 68-page pamphlet anonymously criticising *Lucile* for inexpert vulgarisation of the *philosophes*' tenets: *Lettre à M. de Voltaire sur les opéras philosophi-comiques* (Amsterdam and Paris, 1769). Doubtless this was part of the anti-Marmontel cabal mentioned in chapter 7 below.

14 Written of *L'ami de la maison* by Antoine D'Origny, *Annales du Théâtre Italien depuis son origine jusqu'à ce jour* (3 vols., Paris, 1788, reprinted Geneva, 1970), ii, p. 79.

15 S. Lenel, *Un homme de lettres au XVIII*e *siècle. Marmontel* (Paris, 1902, reprinted Geneva, 1970), p. 565. Seventeen new tales were published between 1790 and 1806 (*Œuvres posthumes*).

16 *Contes Moraux* (3 vols., Paris, 1768), i, p. 13.

17 Source: Brenner, 'Dramatizations'; but I have ignored this author's statistical conclusions, which are too general, and excluded versions of *Bélisaire*, in order to present the facts in a new form. Brenner actually omits consideration of three Moral Tales, without comment: *Alcibiade*, *Les deux infortunées* and *La femme comme il y en a peu*. Table 1 omits adaptations of La Fontaine's *Fables*, opéras-comiques derived from which include Philidor's *Le jardinier et son seigneur*, Duni's *Les deux chasseurs*, Dalayrac's *Eclipse totale* and Grétry's *Le Comte d'Albert*. I have counted Grétry's *L'ami de la maison*, mistakenly omitted by Brenner.

18 'It must be acknowledged that Marmontel's imperious tone made him more enemies at our rehearsals. He was ambiguous: good-natured when he spoke to the actors in private, supercilious when he made observations to them in front of witnesses.' (*Réf*:ii:102). At the first performance of *L'ami de la maison* at court, 'He seemed ready to devour any actor who stumbled in his role': *Mémoires secrets*, vi, p. 28 (29 October 1771).

5 Le tableau parlant

1 For the gushing, arrogant letter which unsuccessfully proposed Grétry's idea to dedicate this work to the Comte de Rohan-Chabot, see Froidcourt, p. 46. Anseaume (1721–84) had for years been a member of the Comédie-Italienne as répétiteur and secretary, and had written many librettos including *Les deux chasseurs et la laitière*, set by Duni, and *L'ivrogne corrigé*, set by Gluck. The subject-matter of *Le tableau parlant* was thought by D'Origny to be related to the story of the painter Ranc who tricked his critical friends by placing his

model's features behind a hole in the canvas: *Annales du Théâtre Italien depuis son origine jusqu'à ce jour* (3 vols., Paris, 1788, reprinted Geneva 1970), ii, p 62.

2 Incipits: (1) 'Je suis jeune' (2) 'Il est certains barbons' (3) 'Tiens, ma Reine' (4) 'Cet aveu charmant' (5) 'Il faut partir' (6) 'Pour tromper un pauvre vieillard' (7) 'Vous étiez ce que vous n'êtes plus' (8) 'Notre vaisseau' (9) 'Je brûlerai' (10) 'La nuit, dans les bras du sommeil' (11) 'Votre amant souffrait' (12) 'C'est donc ainsi' (13) 'O Ciel!' (14) 'Le Dieu de la tendresse'.

3 'Il nous faut au village', the single line of music in A minor quoted in the score. The known tune and ready-made words function like a vaudeville, throwing ironic light on the present situation. See *Matroco*, p. 152.

4 They were discontinued both because audiences were always poorer on the nights they acted and because it had proved impossible to find adequate replacement comedians in Italy. See the terms of the royal letters patent concerning the change of policy in D'Origny, *Annales du Théâtre Italien*, ii, pp. 154–8.

5 See D'Origny's discussion of the changes made to Desfontaine's comedy *L'amant statue* (1781) when adapted for Dalayrac's opéra-comique (1785): *Annales du Théâtre Italien*, iii, pp. 214–15.

6 The level of certain *parades* can only be guessed from enticing titles such as *Le marchand de merde*, F:Pn Ms.fr.9341.

7 i.e. (3) central section, (6) central section, (8) last section, (9) second section, (10) and (14), last chorus.

8 Libretto, Paris, Veuve Duchesne, 1769 (editions of 43pp. and 64pp., both with extra music pages); and [Paris,] P. Robert-Christophe Ballard, 1770. Score publication date, *The New Grove*.

9 Research for the period up to 1826 derived from the F:Po Registres de l'Opéra-Comique. Research for 1826–93 taken from Albert Soubies, *Soixante-neuf ans à l'Opéra-Comique en deux pages* (Paris, 1894). This has been used throughout the present book. However, Soubies' totals, drawn from press advertisements, are not wholly accurate. A check made for the year 1825 against F:Po, Registre de l'Opéra-Comique vol. 114, shows that Soubies missed two out of a total thirteen Grétry performances that year at the Opéra-Comique.

6 *Silvain*

1 Incipits: (1) 'Nos cœurs cessent de s'entendre' (2) 'Je puis braver' (3) 'Ne crois pas qu'un bon ménage' (4) 'Je ne sais pas si ma sœur aime' (5) 'Hé comment ne pas le chérir?' (6) 'Tout le village' (7) 'Avec ton cœur' (8) 'Arrête! mets bas les armes' (9) 'Dans le sein d'un père' (10) 'Il va venir'; 'Vaine apparence' (11) 'Venez, vivre avec nous' (12) 'Rien de si tendre'.

2 A. Goodwin, *The French Revolution*, 4th edn., (London, 1966), pp. 20–1.

3 *Silvain*, CC 27, preface, p. v.

4 *Silvain*, CC 27, p. xx wrongly gives Marmontel's *Le connaisseur* as the source.

5 Editor's assessment in Salomon Gessner, *Idyllen*, ed. E. T. Voss (Stuttgart, 1973), p. 321. Gessner is important to the history of opera not because he helped to write any, but because his writing inspired them. *Inkle und Yariko*, *Der Tod Abels* and *Der erste Schiffer* each gave rise to two or more stage works in Germany, France or England. Gessner is impersonated in Grétry's own opéra-comique *Lisbeth* (1797).

6 *The Works of Solomon* [sic] *Gessner* (3 vols., Liverpool and London, 1802), iii, p. 184.

7 John Hibberd, *Salomon Gessner* (Cambridge University Press, 1976), p. 69.

8 Marmontel is clear that Silvain's banishment has lasted fifteen years, so his eldest daughter ought to be about fourteen. However the future age at which Dolmon *père* agrees to give the younger Lucette her dowry is fifteen (sc. 13). Pauline must be at least fifteen, which may imply that she is supposed to have been conceived out of wedlock, a fact which doubtless would have exacerbated Silvain's harsh treatment by Dolmon.

9 Mlle Beaupré had been acting since 1758. See Henry Lyonnet, *Dictionnaire des comédiens français* (2 vols., Paris [1904]), i, p. 114. Jean-François La Harpe commented that Mme La

Ruette 'became on stage the age that it pleased her to be; when she wanted she looked like a girl of fifteen, although she was forty'. *Correspondance littéraire* (6 vols., Paris, 1801–7), ii, p. 72.

10 Three possible sources for *Silvain* are given in D'Origny, *Annales du Théâtre Italien depuis son origine jusqu'à ce jour* (3 vols., Paris, 1788, reprinted Geneva, 1970), ii, p. 66: *Inès de Castro*, tragedy by Antoine Houdard de la Motte (1730); *L'enfant prodigue* by Voltaire (1736) and *La vie de Marianne*, novel by P. C. de Chamblain de Marivaux, first published 1731–42, from where Marmontel's gamekeepers are said to have been drawn.

11 *Mercure de France*, 5 October 1778, p. 20, cited in *CC* 27, p. xx. Grétry's reply was published in the *Journal de Paris* on 13 October (Froidcourt, p. 103). It is interesting that Voltaire inveighed against adapting words to music written in advance. The opera composer J. N. P. Royer had, before his recent death, 'engagé ce Sireuil . . . à faire des mauvais vers, car assurément on n'en peut pas faire de bons sur des canevas de musiciens'. Letter to N. C. Thieriot dated 23 January 1755 in *Voltaire's Correspondence*, ed. Theodore Besterman (Geneva, 1953–65), xxvi, p. 42.

12 'I have explained to Stephanie the words I require for this aria – indeed I had finished composing most of the music for it before Stephanie knew anything whatever about it.' Mozart to his father, 26 September 1781, from *Mozart's Letters*, trans. Emily Anderson, ed. Eric Blom (Harmondsworth, 1956), p. 181.

13 J. F. Tapray, *Duo de Silvain dans le sein d'un père. Trio de Zémire et Azor veillons mes sœurs. Ariette de la dernière pièce en sonate* (Paris, De Roullede; Lyon, Castaud). Not in British Union Catalogue or in the public collections found in Paris; see Travis and Emery Sarum Catalogue no. 9, item 543.

14 E. O. D. Downes, 'The Operas of Johann Christian Bach as a reflection of the dominant trends in Opera Seria', unpublished dissertation, Harvard University, 1958, p. 417.

7 Profile II: the popular composer

1 One need hardly mention in this connection Bazile's speech on calumny in act 2 of *Le barbier de Séville*. But where else in operatic history but eighteenth-century Paris could the composer's art in setting a supposedly poor (Marmontel) libretto be conceived of as 'pickling turds' (*Réf*:ii:101–9)?

2 Antoine D'Origny, *Annales du Théâtre Italien depuis son origine jusqu'à ce jour* (3 vols., Paris, 1788, reprinted Geneva, 1970), ii, p. 70.

3 Baptismal certificate, cited in Froidcourt, p. 52.

4 Abraham Fleury, *The French Stage and the French People*, ed. T. Hook (London, 1841), cited in A. M. Nagler (ed.), *A Source Book in Theatrical History* (New York, 1959), p. 299.

5 *Etat actuel de la Musique du Roi* (Paris, 1771), p. 30.

6 *Recueil des fêtes et spectacles donnés devant Sa Majesté à Versailles, à Choisy et à Fontainebleau, pendant l'année 1771* ([Paris,] 1771), pp. 5–28.

7 Archives Nationales o¹.847, cited in Froidcourt, p. 61.

8 Such quotation is understandable, but occasionally one finds blatant exaggeration or worse as in Fétis's comment on Gossec's opéra-comique, *Les pêcheurs* (1766), which 'had such success that it was almost the only opera to occupy the stage for the rest of the year'. *Biographie universelle des musiciens*, 1st edn, (8 vols., Brussels, 1837–44), iv, p. 373. Actually it was a virtual failure.

8 *Les deux avares*

1 Score says OPERA BOUFON, as does author's preface to libretto, but title page of some librettos bears 'Comédie'.

2 Amid much interest in the subject a prize was proposed in 1765 to reward the inventor of an improved method of lighting. Bourgeois de Châteaublanc won it with an oil lamp using a

metal reflector. These were placed centrally over roads in Paris and in 1777 lights were laid from Paris to Versailles. The cylindrical wick developed by the Swiss inventor Argand was not known in France until the 1780s. *La grande encyclopédie . . . par une société de savants* (31 vols., Paris, n.d.), xv, p. 336.

3 Incipits: (1) 'Du rossignol' (2) 'Sans cesse auprès de mon trésor' (3) 'Prendre ainsi cet or' (4) 'Nièces, neveux, race haïssable' (5) 'Les voilà partis' (6) 'Plus de dépit' (7) 'La douce espérance' (8) 'La garde passe' (9) 'Fuyons ce triste rivage' (10) 'Tiens la corde' (11) 'Frappons, frappons' (12) 'Ah! qu'il est bon' (13) 'Saute, Gripon' (14) 'Mon cher Monsieur Gripon' (15) 'Ah! qu'il est bon' (16) 'Viens, Jérôme!' (17) 'De tous nos projets'.

4 One of the numerous ironies produced by the contradictions of the age was that Marie-Antoinette, as queen, elected to see it staged at Versailles. Like other liberals Falbaire wanted to use the theatre as a 'school of morality' dealing 'more directly with the present interests of society' (Preface to *L'honnête criminel*).

5 Manuscript librettos for opéras-comiques by Falbaire entitled *L'amour captif, Le peintre et sa fille* and *Thérèse* are in F:Pn, Nouv. Acq. Fr. 2848, 2968, 3001.

6 However no archival evidence has been found to show special hiring of clarinets, not a regular instrument at the time at the Théâtre Italien. The score has them in unison with oboes. This march, and the janissary chorus (15), were the only items by Grétry taken into *The Two Misers, A Comic Opera in Two Acts* (London, [1775]), seen at Covent Garden.

7 Burney noted the great improvement between 1770 and 1772 in French military music, and participation of the cymbals, which he also described, in *The Present State of Music in Germany, The Netherlands, and United Provinces* (2 vols., London, 1775, reprinted New York, 1969), i, pp. 5–6.

8 i.e. in *Le maréchal ferrant, Le bûcheron* and *Le soldat magicien*.

9 [Paris,] Pierre-Robert-Christophe Ballard, 1770. The *CC* is unusually helpful concerning the versions of *Les deux avares*. The printed scores are dated 1771 and 1773 respectively in *The New Grove*.

10 The Cadi of Smyrna, the French consul, the consul's secretary and the young gambler. The last two are silent rôles. The consul extracted 10,000 ducats from each miser for their release and penance. Texts can be found in *CC*. The words of the final vaudeville were entirely changed, also implying musical alteration.

9 *L'amitié à l'épreuve*, 2-act version

1 Actual wording: 'Les Paroles sont de MM^{+++}, & FAVART.' Voisenon (see below) was Favart's friend and, to an extent that is disputed, literary assistant; his collaboration here is (following tradition) assumed, not proven.

2 Not 17 January as stated on the title-pages of the full scores in two acts and three acts and as reproduced in certain later publications.

3 His name was variously spelled as 'Blanford' (1765 edition of Marmontel's *Contes Moraux*), 'Blandfort' (1770 librettos, 2-act score and 1-act libretto, as in note 16 below), 'Blanfort' (1786 libretto and 3-act score) and 'Blandford' (libretto, Paris, Veuve, Simon & Fils, 1770, *dramatis personae* only).

4 Incipits: (1) 'Mon âme est dans un trouble extrême' (2) 'Je m'y connois' (3) 'Non, jamais, l'amour ne troublera' (4) 'Si je pense, c'est votre ouvrage' (5) 'Du Dieu d'amour' (6) 'Sans l'Amour' (7) 'Non, j'aurois horreur' (8) 'Je pars, rien ne m'arrête' (9) 'Nelson part' (10) 'A quels maux il me livre!' (11) 'Quel bonheur extrême' (12) 'Qu'il est doux' (13) 'Remplis nos cœurs, douce amitié' (14) 'Vivons, tous ensemble'.

5 John Renwick has explored this in *Marmontel, Voltaire and the 'Bélisaire' affair*, Studies on Voltaire and the Eighteenth Century, cxxi (Banbury, 1974), p. 44: 'we tend to believe . . . that Marmontel was insinuating in the *Contes Moraux* that an amelioration in the conduct of people would inevitably bring in its wake an amelioration in the state and running of the country'.

6 Joseph Dupleix was active until 1754; it was the French example that Clive was soon to follow in Bengal, leading eventually to European domination. Accused of mismanagement, Clive killed himself in 1774. Glyndwr Williams, *The Expansion of Europe in the Eighteenth Century* (London, 1966), p. 116.

7 The list of adaptations is too numerous to mention here; most proximate musical examples were Cahusac and Rameau's opéra-ballet *Les fêtes de Polymnie*, act 2 (1745) and B. F. de Rosoi and Langlé's ballet *Stratonice* (1786), given at Versailles. For a discussion including music, see Wolfgang Stechow, ' "The Love of Antiochus with Faire Stratonica" in Art', *The Art Bulletin*, xxvii (1945), pp. 221–37.

8 Giacomo Casanova, *History of My Life*, trans. Willard R. Trask (6 vols., London, 1968), iii, pp. 146–7. Bertinazzi is there said to have had a homoerotic relationship with his mistress's husband but there is no suggestion of one between Favart and Voisenon. Grétry described Voisenon 'much in society, where he always wore a smiling expression accompanied by signs of death ... employing in his remarks [to the ladies] all the roses of love and the most amiable gallantry' (*Réf*:ii:86). Marmontel addressed some malicious verses to Mme Favart apropos her version of his tale *Annette et Lubin*, which Voisenon was supposed to have helped write: 'New song regarding a woman (wife) author whose play (room) is that of an abbé'. *Biographie universelle ancienne et moderne* (Paris, L. G. Michaud, 1827), xlix, p. 407. Generally contemptuous of Voisenon, the *Mémoires secrets* (vi:90) said in January 1772 that '[il] vit chez elle depuis plus de vingt ans'.

9 Presumably the playwright was the writer L'Espinasse de Langeac; the work was not published. See Antoine D'Origny, *Annales du Théâtre Italien depuis son origine jusqu'à ce jour* (3 vols., Paris, 1788, reprinted Geneva, 1970), iii, pp. 58–9.

10 *CC*, p. v., citing an edition of Marmontel without its date, not so far traced.

11 That is, 'expressive medium' texture, analysed in D. Charlton, 'Orchestra and Image in the Late Eighteenth Century', *Proceedings of the Royal Musical Association*, cii (1975–6), pp. 1–12. Grétry was to exploit the same texture ironically in *Les événements imprévus* (2), and Columbine mocks Cassandre's wooing in the same way in *Le tableau parlant* (3).

12 Grétry's term is 'le coloris', then 'les couleurs' (i:218–19); he was not proud of having to search for a week, the reason for which he gives as the illness described in chapter 7. It is noteworthy that (13) was the most traditional-sounding piece in the opera to the elderly court musical officials Rebel and Francœur (i:219).

13 The evidence is iconographical as well as musical; see D. Charlton, 'Orchestration and Orchestral Practice in Paris, 1789–1810', unpublished dissertation, University of Cambridge, 1973, pp. 470–4.

14 Philidor, *Ernelinde* and Mondonville, *Daphnis et Alcimadure*, according to *CC*, p. vi.

15 Froidcourt, p. 134, where this undated letter is mistakenly placed in 1786. That it was written in 1771 is proved by the allusion to 'second act': the 1786 version has its dénouement in the third.

16 French-language libretto dated 1771, without place of publication, but completely different in appearance to all French librettos of the time: F:Pn Yth.677. Nelson, 'Mons. Jean van Beethoven', Juliette, 'Mlle Anne Marie Ries', Corali, 'Anne Marie Salomon'. This performance is not mentioned in *Thayer's Life of Beethoven*, rev. and ed. Elliot Forbes (New Jersey, 1970).

17 *L'Amitié à l'épreuve, comédie en un acte et en vers* (Paris, Veuve Duchesne, 1776), *Avertissement*: 'M. Favart l'ayant réduite en un Acte ...'

18 Alfred Cobban, *A History of Modern France* (3 vols., Harmondsworth, 1963), i, pp. 67, 130.

10 *L'ami de la maison*

1 Incipits: 'Je suis de vous très mécontente' (2) 'Vous avez deviné cela' (3) 'Rien ne plaît tant' (4) 'Voyez je suis bon père' (5) 'Je ne fais semblant de rien' (6) 'On dit souvent' (7) 'Dans la brûlante saison' (8) 'Si quelquefois' (9) 'Ah, dans ces fêtes' (10) 'Plus de mystère' (11) 'Ah, je

triomphe' (12) 'Bon, bon, mieux encore' (13) 'Tout ce qu'il vous plaira' (14) 'Tremblez, jeune insensé' (15) 'J'ai fait une grande folie' (16) 'Ah, quelle adresse' (17) 'Il est bien temps' (18) 'Le voilà, le vrai modèle'.

2 Clarence D. Brenner, 'Dramatizations of French Short Stories in the Eighteenth Century with special reference to the "Contes" of La Fontaine, Marmontel and Voltaire', *University of California Publications in Modern Philology*, xxxiii (1947), pp. 1–34. However this article omits the opéra-comique with which we are concerned and also the anonymous play *L'auteur par amour* (Comédie-Italienne, January 1783) mentioned in Antoine D'Origny, *Annales du Théâtre Italien depuis son origine jusqu'à ce jour* (3 vols., Paris, 1788, reprinted Geneva, 1970), iii, p. 132.

3 Marmontel's preface to *Le connaisseur* (Paris, Merlin, 1768) suggests that he toned down the character and would have liked to make him more jealous and tyrannical. This, he says, would have been over-realistic.

4 If not the speech 'Adieu, mon petit Chérubin', *Le mariage de Figaro*, act 1 sc. 10.

5 [J. D.] Martine, *De la musique dramatique en France* (Paris, 1813), p. 168.

6 The key, A major, had been used before by Grétry for love duets rather than solos, as in *Les deux avares* (5) and *Le tableau parlant* (11).

7 [Paris,] P. Robert-Christophe Ballard, 1771.

8 GB:Lbl 11735.b.2 (vol. 7); Paris, Vente, 1777, this dating bearing no relation to the nature of the opera in 1777.

9 F:Pn 8°. Yth.635; Paris, Vente, 1772.

11 The overture (1)

1 J. N. Bouilly, *Mes récapitulations* (3 vols., Paris, n.d.), i, pp. 417–18.

2 i.e. A. J. J. Le Riche de La Pouplinière, who may have attracted Johann Stamitz to Paris in 1754, and whose private orchestra Stamitz conducted in 1754–5. An assessment of La Pouplinière's symphonic influence will be found in Georges Cucuel's *La Pouplinière et la musique de chambre au XVIIIe siècle* (Paris, 1913, reprinted New York, 1971), pp. 376–80. The overtures of La Pouplinière's later employee, Gossec, are rich in orchestration and symphonic style, e.g. *Les pêcheurs* (1766) and *Toinon et Toinette* (1767), the latter being in C minor.

3 Translated by Oliver Strunk in *Source Readings in Music History* (New York, 1950), p. 588. Quantz wants also to improve the intrinsic musical quality of opera overtures. But even before this publication, Johann Mattheson's *Der vollkommene Capellmeister* (Hamburg, 1739), p. 234, had described the 'chief property' of the overture as 'a brief idea and prelude, a brief representation' of what follows.

4 Strunk, *Source Readings*, p. 665.

5 Jean-Jacques Rousseau, *Dictionnaire de musique* (Paris, 1768, reprinted Hildesheim, 1969), p. 358.

6 *Mémoires secrets*, v, pp. 233–4 (7 December 1770).

12 *Zémire et Azor*

1 The dedication copy, F:Pn Rés.F.42, bears the dedication (printed) and no indication of a price. Other copies include a price indication. Later copies omit the dedicatee's name by re-engraving part of the title page and omitting the dedication page. Mme du Barry (Marie-Jeanne Bécu), 1743–93, succeeded Mme de Pompadour as official mistress to Louis XV. On his death in 1774 she became *persona non grata* at court.

2 Incipits: (1) 'L'orage va cesser' (2) 'Le malheur me rend intrépide' (3) 'Les esprits, dont on nous fait peur' (4) 'Le tems est beau' (5) 'La pauvre enfant' (6) 'Ne va pas me tromper' (7) *Symphonie qui exprime le vol du nuage* (8) 'Veillons, mes sœurs' (9) 'Rose chérie' (10) 'Plus de voyage' (11) 'Je vais faire encore un voyage' (12) 'Je veux le voir' (14) 'Ah! quel tourment'

(15) 'Rassure mon père' (16) a 3/8 dance, a 2/4 'Pantomime' and a 3/8 'Passe-pied' (17) 'Du moment qu'on aime' (18) 'La fauvette avec ses petits' (19) 'Ah! laissez-moi la pleurer' (21) 'J'en suis encore tremblant' (22) 'Ah! je tremble' (23) 'Le soleil s'est caché'; 'Toi, Zémire, que j'adore' (24) 'Azor! en vain ma voix t'appelle' (25) 'Amour! quand ta rigueur'.

3 The 'simplicity' is there only to indicate Sander's unostentatious character. In the source by Mme Le Prince de Beaumont (see below) the family is already poor.

4 It was, apart from Grétry's *Richard Cœur-de-lion*, virtually the only French opera seen and heard in authentic form in eighteenth-century London: Roger Fiske, *English Theatre Music in the Eighteenth Century* (London, 1973), pp. 327, 466, 525. Yet the spoken text of Richard was altered to favour Marguerite's rôle at the expense of Blondel's: *Journal de Paris*, 5 November 1786, p. 1274.

5 Fiske, *English Theatre Music*, p. 419.

6 J. Gaudefroy-Demombynes, *Les jugements allemands sur la musique française au XVIIIᵉ siècle* (Paris, 1941), pp. 221, 234, 238–9 etc.

7 Wichmann, *Grétry und das musikalische Theater in Frankreich* (Halle, 1929), p. 65.

8 The tailor had already made 'a pantaloon just like the skin of a monkey with a long bare tail, a naked back, enormous claws for each of the four paws, two long horns in the headpiece and the most deformed mask, with boar's teeth'. Marmontel wanted something not beastly: 'mottled pantaloons, shoes and gloves of the same, a dolmon of purple satin, a wavy black mane, picturesquely dishevelled'. J. F. Marmontel, *Mémoires*, ed. John Renwick (2 vols., Clermont-Ferrand, 1972), i, pp. 268–9. This account shows that the sumptuous engraving 'Tableau Magique de Zémire et Azor' by Voyez le jeune after J. L. Touzé makes Azor exaggeratedly inhuman compared with the one by Ingouf; Voyez's command of perspective is also less convincing than Ingouf's.

9 Mme de Beaumont's Beauty has three brothers, but they take no part in the story. The author resided in London for over fifteen years, publishing works of history, geography and fiction. Contrary to some statements, Beauty and the Beast was not one of Perrault's tales.

10 Anita Brookner, *Greuze, the Rise and Fall of an Eighteenth-Century Phenomenon* (London, 1972), p. 30.

11 Fiske, *English Theatre Music*, pp. 572–3

12 François-René de Chateaubriand, *Atala*, translated Rayner Heppenstall (London, 1963), p. 36.

13 F:Po, Registre de l'Opéra-Comique vol. 53, accounts for December 1771: payments to Flieger and Gaspard [Proksch], clarinets, and to Mozer, cor de chasse for no fewer than five rehearsals plus performances. These or equivalent performance payments were made whenever *Zémire et Azor* was given publicly. An extra flute was also hired for such performances, beginning in March 1774.

14 *Recueil des fêtes et spectacles donnés devant Sa Majesté, à Versailles, à Choisy & à Fontainebleau, pendant l'Année 1771* ([Paris,] 1771), p. 28.

15 Court libretto, [Paris,] P. Robert-Christophe Ballard, 1771; various others such as Paris, Vente, 1771.

13 *Le Magnifique*

1 In French the title has connotations of open-handedness and liberality, not just power.

2 The full score, p. 179, says 'Si on désire employer l'Ouverture de manière qu'elle donne plus de mouvement à la Pièce . . .', giving long instructions which I have summarised. The mime or 'Balet très intéressant' for the close of the opera is also here referred to.

3 Incipits: (1) 'C'est lui, c'est lui!' (2) 'Pourquoi donc ce Magnifique' (3) 'Ma chère enfant' (4) 'Ah! c'est un superbe cheval!' (5) 'Vous m'étonnez' (7) 'Ah! si jamais' (8) 'Je ne sais pourquoi je pleure' (9) 'Quelle contrainte' (10) 'Clémentine, mettez-vous là' (12) 'Ah! que je suis coupable!' (13) 'Te voilà donc' (14) 'O Ciel! quel air de courroux!' (15) 'Jour heureux!' (16) 'Ne me bats pas!'

4 Letters of 14 November 1771 and 27 December 1771.

5 See chapter 4, notes 10 and 16.

6 Sedaine's *Avertissement* to the libretto refers to the play based on the same tale, by Houdard de la Motte (1731), which he read only after writing the libretto. La Motte's Aldobrandin, so far from being a schemer, is 'duped by all around him'; 'The exposition, the kernel, the dénouement, even the characters are different.' Grimm is very rude about it (x:209), accusing la Motte of 'all the implausibility and licence of the fairs'.

7 F:Po, Registre de l'Opéra-Comique vol. 55, May 1773 *Mandement* 4; December, *Mandement* 16. No record indicates the second trumpeter, but this is normal up to 1790; the part would have been doubled from within the orchestra, presumably by a string player.

8 *CC*, pp. xx, xxi notes the tune's popularity in 1773–4 and connection with the Henri IV stage works by Collé and Rosoi. The earliest printed source apparently calls it 'Air de la Cassandre' in C. de Bordeaux, *Noëls* (Paris, 1581). There is a good recording of the whole overture conducted by Richard Bonynge.

9 Daniel Heartz, 'The Creation of the Buffo Finale in Italian Opera', *Proceedings of the Royal Musical Association*, civ (1977–8), pp. 67–78.

10 Heinz Wichmann, *Grétry und das musikalische Theater in Frankreich* (Halle, 1929), p. 110.

11 Margaret Ann Rayner, 'The Social and Literary Aspects of Sedaine's Dramatic Work', unpublished dissertation, University of London, 1960, p. 13ff.

12 He wanted it to occupy the same length of time as a 5-act work at the Comédie-Française: 'Quelques réflexions inédites de Sedaine sur l'opéra comique', in *Théâtre choisi de G. de Pixérécourt* (4 vols., Paris, Nancy, 1841–3), iv, p. 507.

13 'Quelques réflexions inédites de Sedaine', p. 513. Grétry simply reports that the libretto was offered him by Mme. [Louise] de La Live d'Epinay (i:247).

14 Incomplete transcription by P. Hédouin in *Mosaique* (Valenciennes, 1856), reproduced in Arthur Pougin, *Monsigny et son temps* (Paris, 1908), p. 194. Ends, 'c'est au contraire moi-même qui vous dis: je ne puis faire votre pièce, prenez Grétry'. Monsigny's music for *Philémon et Baucis*, a recitative opera, is not extant; Sedaine's words are in the Archives Nationales, O³.281. Rayner, 'Sedaine's Dramatic Work', p. 143. Both words and music of Sedaine's and Monsigny's unpublished *Robin et Marion* survive in F:Po Rés.2140 (1–2), libretto dated '18 germinal an iii de la République' (Rayner, 'Sedaine's Dramatic Work', pp. 104, 282).

15 Jean-François La Harpe, *Correspondance littéraire* (6 vols., Paris, 1801–7), v, pp. 138–9.

16 [Paris,] Pierre-Robert-Christophe Ballard, 1773; see pp. viii, 71. Later libretto, Paris, Claude Hérissant, 1773, which agrees with the score.

17 'Quelques réflexions inédites de Sedaine', p. 513.

14 *La Rosière de Salency*

1 'Pastorale' was only one designated genre, though it was that carried by the score. The first libretto (Pierre-Robert-Christophe Ballard, 1773), presumably on account of the work's novel features, had 'Opéra lyri-comique en quatre actes'. The Delalain librettos dated 1774 and 1775 describe it as 'Pastorale en trois actes'. That of 1788 has 'Comédie en trois actes'. The score and certain librettos have 'Salenci'.

2 Catherine Petrowna Troubetzkoi, 1744–1815, wife of Count Alexandre de Stroganoff; they spent some years in Paris: see Froidcourt, p. 72.

3 Incipits: (1) 'Quel beau jour' (2) 'La plus douce espérance' (3) 'Vous l'avez, je crois, entendu' (4) 'Ecoute-moi, Lucile' (5) 'Quand le rossignol' (6) 'Oui, si je ne peux te plaire' (8) 'Colin, quel est mon crime?' (9) 'Eh! que me fait l'orage' (10) 'Du poids de la vieillesse' (11) 'O malheureuse' (12) 'Cruel, détourne ces objets' (13) 'Ma barque légère' (15) 'A l'instant' (16) 'J'ai tout perdu' (17) 'Reconnais ton amant' (18) 'Après l'orage' (20) 'Bonheur suprême' (21) 'Que lui reprocher' (23a) 'Chantez, dansez' (23b) 'Chantons, célébrons'.

4 *L'année littéraire . . . par M. Fréron* (Amsterdam, Paris, 1766), iv, pp. 217–24. Edmé-Louis

Billardon de Sauvigny (1736–1812) was a prolific writer, later government censor and eventually civil servant under the Consulate.

5 *La rose ou la feste de Salency* (Paris, 1770), p. xv.

6 To the anonym M.D.L.D.E.M.D.A.D.P.E.L.R. we owe another stage version, entitled *La couronne de roses ou la fête de Salency, comédie en deux actes* (Paris, 1770).

7 *Œuvres agréables et morales, ou variétés littéraires du marquis de Pezai* (2 vols., Liège, 1791), i, introduction. Also Bernard Faÿ, *Louis XVI or the End of a World* (London, 1968), pp. 90, 171. The former says Pezay, whose mother was Swiss, introduced Necker to Louis: see chapter 34.

8 'Réflexions sur la Rosière mêlées de quelques observations générales sur les Spectacles', in *La Rosière de Salenci* (Paris, Delalain, 1774), p. xx.

9 Anita Brookner, *Greuze, the Rise and Fall of an Eighteenth-Century Phenomenon* (London, 1972), pp. 121–3.

10 Pierre Larousse, *Grand dictionnaire universel du XIX siècle* (15 vols., Paris, 1864–76), ii, p. 60.

11 Alfred Cobban, *A History of Modern France* (3 vols., Harmondsworth, 1963), i, pp. 155–6.

12 And perhaps ultimately allowed the authors to omit the Bailli's original act 2 aria 'Ah! le Ciel est bien en colère', expounding the hate people feel for him and the love destroying him from within.

13 'Réflexions sur la Rosière', pp. xxi–xxiii.

14 *French Opera in the Seventeenth and Eighteenth Centuries*, ed. Barry S. Brook (75 vols., New York, 1984–), vol. lxi.

15 See note 1: 'Réflexions sur la Rosière', p. xv.

16 'Réflexions sur la Rosière', pp. xviii–xix.

17 [J. D.] Martine, *De la musique dramatique*, p. 172.

15 The entr'acte (I)

1 Article 'Entr'acte' in Denis Diderot and Jean Le Rond D'Alembert (eds.), *Encyclopédie ou Dictionnaire raisonné des sciences des arts et des métiers* (17 vols., Paris, 1751–65), v, p. 726. They were still not listened to at the close of the century, drowned by talking (iii:24, footnote).

2 *Ibid.*

3 A. M. Nagler (ed.), *A Source Book in Theatrical History* (New York, 1959), pp. 328–30.

4 [P. J. B. Nougaret,] *De l'art du théâtre où il est parlé des differens genres de spectacles, et de la musique adaptée au théâtre* (2 vols., Paris, 1769), ii, p. 99.

5 *Etat actuel de la Musique du Roi et des trois spectacles de Paris* (Paris, 1771), non-paginated final section.

6 The signals appear as *Airs sur les Batteries des Tambours françois* in J. B. de La Borde, *Essai sur la musique ancienne et moderne* (4 vols., Paris, 1780), i, illustrations to p. 286.

16 *La fausse magie*

1 The editors of *CC* 25 reproduced the 1775 one-act version, not the final published version: see last section of this chapter. They failed to locate a copy of the two-act score, which had awkward consequences for the overture: see chapter 23.

2 Incipits: (1) 'C'est un état' (2) 'Je ne le dis qu'à vous' (3) 'Il vous souvient' (4) 'Si je croyois' (5) 'Je ne dis pas' (6) 'Quoi ce vieux coq' (7) 'Quand l'âge vient' (8) 'Quoi, c'est vous' (9) 'En conscience' (10) 'Vous auriez à faire' (11) 'Qu'ai-je entendu' (12) 'Comme un éclair' (13) 'Voyez-vous ces lignes' (15) 'Ah le beau jour' (16) 'Autour d'elle' (17) 'O grand Albert' (18) 'Ne troublez pas le mistère'.

3 The French for this ('oison') also means a credulous person, a mug or dope. ⸺

4 In some versions of the libretto Dorimon is enjoined to invite various friends who favour amateur dramatics.

5 The plot has no connection with *La fausse magie* by Paradis de Moncrif, a comedy of 1719: F:Pn ms.fr.9310, f.294.
6 *Réflexions*, ii, p. 103. This also reveals Grétry converted (10) from a solo to a trio, seen in Ex. 16.2, also discussed in *Mémoires*, i, p. 263 in terms of the separate character of the vocal lines.
7 Letter dated 1 December 1767: Froidcourt, p. 31.
8 Michel Brenet, *Grétry, sa vie et ses œuvres* (Paris, 1884), pp. 118–19, citing *Le journal de l'Empire*, 12 pluviôse an XIII (1 February 1805). Jean-François La Harpe wrote, probably in summer 1775: 'The Italiens have just turned down two librettos that he [Grétry] presented to them, one called *Midas*, the other *Les statues*, a magic opera by Marmontel on which Grétry wanted to work and which the players did not want to undertake, on the pretext that it was not suitable for their theatre. However since the piece, taken from the *Thousand and One Nights*, presents agreeable [stage] situations and is scenically most beautiful (I have heard it being read) they think that Grétry wants to have it performed at Fontainebleau, where it will be successful.' *Correspondance littéraire* (6 vols., Paris, 1801–7), ii, p. 114.
9 F:Po, Registre de l'Opéra-Comique vol. 115, 22 August 1782: it was agreed to be read in full assembly but evidently to no avail.
10 See Marmontel's *Mémoires*, book 9; his last attempt at comic opera was *Le dormeur éveillé*, unsuccessfully given in 1783 at the Comédie-Italienne in Piccinni's setting. Marmontel (*Mémoires*, book 11) concludes, 'I ought to have been more timid; and my vanity was punished by theatrical failures.' For his operas after Grétry see Julian Rushton, 'Music and drama at the Académie Royale de Musique (Paris) 1774–1789', unpublished dissertation, Oxford University, 1969.
11 *The New Grove*, article 'Grétry', work-list, p. 709. The explanation by Karin Pendle seems quite erroneous in 'The Opéras Comiques of Grétry and Marmontel', *Musical Quarterly*, lxii (1976), p. 421.
12 See F:Po, Registre de l'Opéra-Comique vol. 56. The first three performances had *La fausse magie* as main work, while the other six coupled it with other opéras-comiques.
13 Two-act libretto, Paris, Veuve Duchesne, 1775; one-act libretto as 'nouvelle édition', Paris, Veuve Duchesne, 1775.
14 He declined an agreement with the Belgian Ignace Vitzthumb (1720–1816) to wait a year in cases where Vitzthumb had bought manuscript copies for Brussels performance; letter dated 29 January 1775 in Froidcourt, p. 75.
15 Letter to Vitzthumb dated 21 February 1775 in Froidcourt, p. 77.

17 Les mariages samnites

1 The 1782 version became a *Comédie-héroïque* in verse. See note 21. Rosoi's *Henri IV* (1774) and *La réduction de Paris* (1775) were both styled *drame lyrique*. The subject is discussed in a work too recent to have been used: James B. Kopp, 'The "Drame Lyrique": a Study in the Esthetics of Opéra-Comique, 1762–1791', unpublished dissertation, University of Pennsylvania, 1982.
2 François-Charles, Comte de Velbruck. See Froidcourt, p. 95.
3 Incipits: (1) 'Quelle âme peut brûler' (2) 'C'est dans ces lieux' (3) 'Quand mon cœur' (4) 'D'une nimphe' (5) 'Au cri de la nature' (6) 'Je la vois' (7) 'Mon amant' (9) 'Trompette guerrière' (10) 'Dieu d'amour' (11) 'Ou vais-je?' (12) 'Eliane, que m'as-tu dit?' (13) 'Que d'attraits' (14) 'O toi que j'aime' (15) 'L'honneur, soldats' (16) 'Malheureux père!' (17) 'Dieu d'Amour' (18) 'L'amour folâtre' (20) 'Dans les airs' (21) 'Ami, quel moment' (22) 'Les traits qui volent' (23) 'Que de plaisir'.
4 Rosoi augments Agathis' culpability by suggesting the Romans profited by his tending his father, while in Marmontel Agathis does not assist Eumene until he has seen the Romans give way and believes the battle won.
5 Barnabé Farmian de Rosoi, *Dissertation sur le drame lyrique* (The Hague and Paris, 1775 [1776]).
6 i.e. 'virtuous example' or 'virtuous action'. See 'The *Exemplum Virtutis*' in Robert

Rosenblum, *Transformations in Late Eighteenth Century Art* (New Jersey, 1970), pp. 50–106. 'It was around 1760 . . . especially in France [that] the zealous re-examination of Greco-Roman antiquity was gradually combined with the new demand for stoical sobriety of form and emotion.' (p. 50).

7 *The Cambridge Ancient History*, ed. J. B. Bury, S. A. Cook *et al.* (12 vols., Cambridge, 1924–39), vii, chapter 18.

8 Charles Louis de Secondat, Baron de Montesquieu, *Œuvres complètes. De l'esprit des lois*, ed. Roger Caillois (Gallimard, n.p., 1951), book vii, chapter xvi, p. 348.

9 Short links between (2)–(3), (3)–(4), (4)–(5), (6)–(7), (9)–(10), (11)–(12), (17)–(18). Fairly brief links between (1)–(2), (5)–(6), (22)–(23).

10 This was later incorporated into *Richard Cœur-de-lion* as (19).

11 Arias (in order): ABA', truncated sonata, AABA', AB(new metre)A', ABA'B', free form, ABA', ABA', AB(new metre)C, free form. (1), (6) and (16) are in the minor mode.

12 *Mémoires secrets*, 2 June 1776, cited in *CC*, p. xxvii.

13 They and their corporal together with the two trumpeters and timpanist also needed cost 567 *livres* in June and 924 *livres* in July 1776. F:Po, Registres de l'Opéra-Comique, vol. 59.

14 Especially in the 'absence of all virtuoso artifice' and 'persistent serenity'. T. de Wyzewa and G. de Saint-Foix, *Wolfgang Amédée Mozart* (5 vols., Paris, 1912–46), iii, p. 277. Mozart is supposed to have shown Joseph Frank French operas he was currently studying in 1778, especially in respect of 'dramatic effectiveness': Grétry, Gluck, Piccinni, Salieri. See O. E. Deutsch (ed.), *Mozart: a Documentary Biography* (Stanford, 1974), p. 561.

15 Grétry captured the religious feeling required in (4) by Marmontel's source ('un devoir religieux et sacré de ne confier leur intention qu'aux auteurs de leurs jours') but he risked irrelevance by retaining the bird imitations on flute in (2), originally appropriate to *La Rosière de Salency*.

16 By the same token the old-fashioned viola and bassoon obbligato parts in (11) do not sound untoward.

17 *Eine Symphonie zu Dantes Divina Commedia*, i ('Inferno'), bars 12–17, horns and trumpets: 'Lasciate ogni speranza, voi ch'entrate!'

18 Paris, Veuve Duchesne, 1776: no preface.

19 Froidcourt, p. 86. A manuscript score and printed libretto had already been sent. (20) was found to slow the action too much in Paris.

20 Paris, Veuve Duchesne, 1776, 'Nouvelle édition'. See note 21. Dialogue changes were also made.

21 Paris, Belin, 1782, preceded by a new preface. This says, 'I cannot forbear regretting that the end of the second act is not given in the theatre as I had written it, and has never been performed thus . . . But it was feared that the effect of this scene might appear too close to tragedy, and I gave in.'

22 Antoine D'Origny, *Annales du Théâtre Italien depuis son origine jusqu'à ce jour* (3 vols., Paris, 1788, reprinted Geneva, 1970), iii, p. 8, claims also a new third act duet and new solos for Céphalide (Mme Trial) and Eliane (Mlle Colombe) but there are no words for them in the 1782 libretto.

23 F:Pn ms.13805 and mss.13793–4; also perhaps University of Western Ontario. The author has been identified as Jean Marcel Souriguère de Saint-Marc in a notable recent exegesis: M. Elizabeth C. Bartlet, 'Politics and the Fate of *Roger et Olivier*, a Newly Recovered Opera by Grétry', *Journal of the American Musicological Society*, xxxvii (1984), pp. 98–138.

24 Froidcourt, p. 164, dating the letter 1793. See Bartlet, 'Politics and the Fate of *Roger et Olivier*', pp. 107–8, giving full title, *L'inquisition de Madrid*.

18 Profile III: at home and abroad

1 *De la vérité*, i, 163, cited in Michel Brenet, *Grétry, sa vie et ses œuvres* (Paris, 1884), p. 206.

2 The exact dates of her birth and baptism are not known. The evidence is in Brenet, *Grétry*, pp. 93–4.

3 J. N. Bouilly, *Mes récapitulations* (3 vols., Paris, n.d.), i, pp. 153–4; Brenet, *Grétry*, p. 207.
4 Greuze, who enrolled at the Académie in 1755, aged thirty, painted his reception canvas of the emperor Severus reproaching his son for having attempted to kill him; when presented in 1769 it failed to gain him the place of history painter and he was obliged to remain labelled as a genre painter. See Anita Brookner, *Greuze, the Rise and Fall of an Eighteenth-Century Phenomenon* (London, 1972), pp. 67–70 and 109–110.
5 *The Letters of Mozart and his Family*, trans. and ed. Emily Anderson (3 vols., London, 1938), ii, p. 871.
6 P. Long Des Clavières, *La jeunesse de Grétry et ses débuts à Paris* (Besançon, 1920), pp. 128, 133.
7 Brenet, *Grétry*, p. 107.
8 Froidcourt, pp. 91–2; Brenet, *Grétry*, pp. 108–9.
9 Froidcourt, pp. 71, 77–8, 85–6.
10 Froidcourt, pp. 87, 175.
11 Charles Burney, *The Present State of Music in Germany, The Netherlands, and United Provinces* (2 vols., London, 1775, reprinted New York 1969), i, pp. 26.
12 Details of eighteenth-century performances of Grétry at Spa and elsewhere in Paul Culot, *Le jugement de Midas, opéra-comique d' André-Ernest-Modeste Grétry* (Brussels, 1978), pp. 12–13, 83.
13 Letter from G. Moreau to Vitzthumb: Froidcourt, p. 89.
14 The necrology in Grimm (April 1781) says he was not yet forty at his death and came to Paris 'ten or so' years before; this is corroborated in Antoine D'Origny's *Annales du Théâtre Italien depuis son origine jusqu' à ce jour* (3 vols., Paris, 1778, reprinted Geneva, 1970), ii, p. 216. The date 1763 is from the biographical notice in Pierre Marie Michel Lepeintre Desroches, *Suite du répertoire du Théâtre Français* (81 vols., Paris, 1822–3), lvi, p. 85. The only study of Hales is by Sylvain E. M. Van de Weyer, 'Lettres sur les Anglais qui ont écrit en français. Thomas Hales', *Philobiblon Society. Bibliographical and Historical Miscellanies*, i (London 1854). Grétry devoted a chapter to Hales, in addition to the information expressed in his *Mémoires*, in *Réf*:iii:261 (vol. 5, ch. 10).
15 Van de Weyer, 'Lettres', p. 11; since *Le jugement de Midas* was ready by 1776 (q.v.), the authors must have been together by 1775 at the latest.

19 Matroco

1 Michel Brenet, *Grétry, sa vie et ses œuvres* (Paris, 1884), p. 125.
2 i.e. Charles Collé, who was a virulent supporter of the old vaudeville opéra-comique: Grimm, 15 January 1768.
3 'De la Comédie Italienne' in *Etat actuel de la Musique du Roi et des trois spectacles de Paris* (Paris, 1771), pp. 111–14. Grétry's own mature analysis of the musical value of vaudevilles is in *Mémoires* (ii:74–5).
4 Clarence D. Brenner, *The Théâtre Italien, its Repertory 1716–1793*. University of California Publications in Modern Philology, lxiii (Berkeley, 1961), pp. 13–14; six violins are mentioned as the obligatory number for vaudeville opéras-comiques in F:Po, Registre de l'Opéra-Comique vol. 115, entry for 13 January 1782.
5 F:Po, Registre de l'Opéra-Comique vol. 60, payments for March 1778.
6 In the 1778 libretto (Paris, Veuve Duchesne) some of these lines are re-assigned to Fleurdiris, his son.
7 Original libretto, [Paris] P. Robert-Christophe Ballard, 1777; second libretto as in the preceding note.

20 Le jugement de Midas

1 Mme de Montesson (Charlotte-Jeanne Béraud de La Haye de Rion), 1737–1806. She was secretly married to Louis-Philippe, the Duc d'Orléans, having first been the wife of the Marquis de Montesson.
2 Facsimile of part of this full score and one of the 1778 librettos in Paul Culot, *Le jugement de*

Midas, opéra-comique d'André-Ernest-Modeste Grétry (Brussels, 1978), together with historical notes, pictures and documents.

3 Incipits: (1) 'Doux charme de la vie' (2) 'D'abord je donne' (3d) 'Banissons la mélancolie: Rions, chantons' (4) 'Dans mon jeune âge' (5) 'Quand je songe au bonheur' (6) 'Non, non, ma mère' (7) 'Par une grace touchante' (8) 'Je te donne, ma chère' (9) 'Toi qui fait naître' (10) 'Dans mes regards' (11) 'Ce cœur peut-il être inflexible?' (12) 'Pour une femme' (13) 'Non, cela n'est pas possible' (14) 'Du destin qui t'opprime' (15) 'Amans qui vous plaignez' (16) 'Certain coucou' (17a) 'Nous, Midas, Bailli de ces lieux' (17b) 'Est-ce un prestige?' (18) 'Au Dieu des Arts'.

4 [Kane O'Hara,] *Midas; an English Burletta* (London, 1764), 'To the Reader'.

5 Libretto, London, G. Kearsly, 1764; music, London, Walsh, n.d. as *Midas. A Comic Opera*.

6 Roger Fiske, *English Theatre Music in the Eighteenth Century* (London, 1973), pp. 318–24. Libretto, two-act edition, London, W. Griffin, 1766.

7 Pan's song was supposedly Derry Down, these being the words of the refrain in the song called 'Liberty Hall'. Fiske, *English Theatre Music*, p. 677 and personal communication.

8 The best recorded performance is conducted by Raymond Leppard on Philips SAL 3674. A miniature score edition is published by Heugel.

9 The slow 'cavatina' and fast 'cabaletta' pairing is often thought of in formal terms as a nineteenth-century one. In French serious opera the (aria) form goes back at least to Philidor's *Ernelinde* (Sandomir's 'O toi, cher âme', act 1). See p. 62.

10 'I had not thought of [this repetition] while composing, but it was perhaps the only way to explain the writer's idea in its totality, without saying anything to offend decency': *Réf*:ii:62, footnote.

11 In fact Grétry's string accompaniment and piccolo on p. 31 of the full score may be an accurate guide to the way vaudevilles were given at the time; we know that a reduced orchestra was employed; see chapter 19 note 4.

12 That is, of D'Alembert and Marmontel, among others, who objected not to French classical recitative as such but to abuses in its performance, without which there might be 'the noble simplicity of a more natural and rapid delivery', as in earlier times. 'Examen des réflexions de M. Dalembert sur la liberté de la musique', *Mercure de France*, July 1759, second part, p. 88.

13 'La cour a dénigré tes chants / Dont Paris a dit des merveilles; / Grétry, les oreilles des grands / Sont souvent de grandes oreilles.'

14 Michael Kelly, *Reminiscences*, ed. Roger Fiske (London, 1975), p. 282.

21 *L'amant jaloux*

1 The score is entitled *L'amant jaloux*. The printed librettos are entitled *Les fausses apparences ou l'amant jaloux (False appearances, or the jealous lover)*.

2 Le Noir (1732–1807), though discharged by Turgot in 1775 for incompetence during the grain riots, had been reinstated the next year.

3 Incipits: (1) 'Qu'une fille de quinze ans' (2) 'Plus de sœur, plus de frère' (3) 'Victime infortunée' (4) 'Plus d'égards' (5) 'Je romps la chaîne' (6) 'Le mariage est une envie' (7) 'La gloire vous appelle' (8) 'D'abord, amants soumis et doux' (9) 'O douce nuit' (10) 'Je sens bien' (11) 'Seigneur, sans trop être indiscret' (12) 'Prenez pitié'.

4 J. F. La Harpe, who discusses almost all Grétry's opéras-comiques and many others, thought that it was probably the overall best; he appreciated the excellence of the finales, which incidentally demonstrated that he was not confining his judgement to the literary side. See *Lycée, ou Cours de littérature ancienne et moderne* (16 vols., Paris, An VII – An XIII), xii, pp. 537–8.

5 We have a reported opinion of Hales concerning musical participation in the drama: 'He often complained of the stupidity of certain of our composers who, to assert their claims for their art, spoil and corrupt everything, destroy the disposition of a play and put in ill-timed arias, duets and trios that harm the effect of situations and the development of the subject.'

Cited in *Chef-d'œuvres dramatiques de DHele* [*sic*], (2 vols., Paris, 1791), i, p. 4.

6 Grétry expressed his own satisfaction with (3) while denigrating the simpler descriptive arias in *Le Huron* (16) and *Le tableau parlant* (8): *Mémoires*: 36–7.

7 There are two mandolines according to the score but the Registres de l'Opéra-Comique show payment only ever for one player: F:Po.

8 Richard Hudson, 'Folia' in *The New Grove*, vi, pp. 691–2.

9 Winton Dean, 'Opera under the French Revolution', *Proceedings of the Royal Musical Association*, xciv (1967–8), p. 93.

10 [Paris,] P. R. C. Ballard, n.d.

11 Paris, Veuve Duchesne, 1779. But libretto dates are unreliable taken in isolation. The copy with this imprint, 64 pp., in London, Victoria and Albert Museum, theatre collection, still contains the words of the old (5) (see below).

22 Les événements imprévus

1 Score and parts were announced in the *Journal de Paris*, 9 February 1781.

2 Incipits: (1) 'Qu'il est cruel d'aimer' (2) 'L'autre jour sous l'ombrage' (3) 'Il faut parler' (4b) 'Ah! dans le siècle où nous sommes' (5) 'J'aime Philinte tendrement' (6) 'Voici donc le séjour funeste' (7) 'Ah! d'une amante abandonée' (8) 'Je vais vous dire' (9) 'Approchons nous' (11) 'Oui, c'en est fait' (12) 'Serviteur à Monsieur Lafleur' (13) 'Que vois-je!' (14) 'Ah! quel bonheur'.

3 Voltaire, *Lettres philosophiques*, no. 10. He is supported by other contemporary evidence quoted in Gustave Lanson's edition of this work (2 vols., Paris, 1924), i, p. 129: 'Le désordre et le ridicule outré est dans la multitude de ces faquins de comtes et de marquis dont toutes les provinces sont remplies . . . [aussi] Paris et la cour.'

4 P. A. F. Choderlos de Laclos, *Les liaisons dangereuses*, trans. P. W. K. Stone (Harmondsworth, 1961), letter 9, p. 38.

5 *The Marquis de Sade: the complete 'Justine', 'Philosophy in the Bedroom' and other writings* trans. and ed. Richard Seaver and Austryn Wainhouse (New York, 1966), pp. 92–5. Le Noir also signed the permission to print the 1780 libretto of *Les événements imprévus*.

6 A 'canvas', or basis of improvised comedy by Italian comedians, entitled *Les événements imprévus* was given at the Comédie-Italienne on 13 March 1748, according to both Desboulmiers' *Histoire anecdotique et raisonnée du Théâtre Italien* (7 vols., Paris, 1770), vii, 323 and Antoine D'Origny, *Annales du Théâtre Italien depuis son origine jusqu'à ce jour* (3 vols., Paris, 1788, reprinted Geneva, 1970), i, pp. 223–4. Both say it was neither funny nor successful, and it seems not to have survived.

7 Michel Brenet, *Grétry, sa vie et ses œuvres* (Paris, 1884), p. 143, citing a letter from Galiani to Marmontel, 30 November 1778: *Correspondance Inédite de l'Abbé Ferdinand Galiani* (2 vols., Paris, 1818), ii, pp. 291–2.

8 The *Mémoires secrets*, xiv, noted that Grétry's 'vein has become more abundant and more varied' (17 November 1779, p. 269) and Grimm (xx: 342) also noted the maturing style, the loss of sheer brilliance, but gain in subtlety.

9 See Kent M. Smith, 'Egidio Duni and the development of the *opéra-comique* from 1753 to 1770, (unpublished dissertation, Cornell University, 1980), pp. 47–53. Other information kindly supplied by Michel Noiray.

10 *Journal de Musique*, (1777, issue 5), pp. 9–10; reprinted in 3 vols. (Geneva, 1972), iii, pp. 2453–4.

11 D'Origny, *Annales du Théâtre Italien*, ii, p. 72.

12 Arthur Pougin, *Un directeur d'opéra au dix-huitième siècle* (Paris, 1914), p. 24. De Vismes (1745–1819) ran the Opéra from 1778 to 1780 and again briefly in 1800. He was the brother of the dramatist A. D. M. de Vismes who wrote the text of Grétry's *Les trois ages de l'Opéra* (1778): Froidcourt, p. 247.

13 Pougin, *Un directeur d'opéra*, p. 35. Goldoni's help in improving one of these librettos was solicited too late: *Mémoires de M. Goldoni*, ed. P. de Roux (Paris, 1965), pp. 361–2.

14 Pougin, *Un directeur d'opéra*, p. 29.
15 *La Frascatana* (London, G. Bigg, 1778), parallel Italian–English libretto.
16 Such as Dalayrac's *Léon ou le château de Monténéro*. But towers as prisons were soon seen in profusion on the Parisian stage: see chapter 26.

23 The overture (II)

1 The first movement is a sonata, the second ABA and the last a rondo. It is particularly ironic that the editors of *CC* 25, ignorant of the full score of the opera's two-act version, therefore lacked access to Grétry's authentic scoring of this rondo: they provided their own orchestration.
2 Against La Borde's assertion that the Greeks never suspected the delights of harmony, Grétry wrote, 'That must be false'. Ernest Closson, 'Les notes marginales de Grétry dans l' "Essay sur la Musique" de Laborde', *Revue Belge de Musicologie*, ii (1948), p. 119.
3 These are further discussed in D. Charlton, 'Ossian, Le Sueur and Opera', *Studies in Music*, xi (1977), pp. 37–48.

24 *Aucassin et Nicolette*

1 Béatrice de Choiseul-Stainville, sister of the Duc de Choiseul.
2 Incipits: (1) 'Nicolette, ma Nicolette' (2) 'Allez! qu'on apporte mes armes' (3) 'Fils insensé' (4) 'Simple et naïve, joliette' (5) 'Au fond d'une sainte retraite' (6) 'Victoire!' (7) 'Il est vainqueur' (8) 'Perfide, c'est contre ton père' (10b) 'Comment, après ce combat' (11) 'Pucelle avec un cœur franc' (12) 'Non, je ne puis vivre' (13) 'Ah! quel bonheur' (15) 'Cher objet de ma pensée' (16) 'Que de pièces d'or' (17) 'Contente ton père' (18) 'Le voici'.
3 Rayner, 'Sedaine's dramatic work', pp. 166–70.
4 Now F:Pn, fonds fr. 2168.
5 Sedaine says this in the libretto, Paris, Veuve Ballard & fils, 1780, p. iii. Sainte-Palaye (1697–1781) became a member of the Académie des Inscriptions et Belles-Lettres in 1724. With astounding energy he copied hundreds of manuscripts in France and Italy, studying the evolution of both French language and chivalry. Five papers read before the Académie from 1746 sparked off an inextinguishable enthusiasm for the age of chivalry. These papers became *Mémoires sur l'ancienne chevalerie considérée comme un établissement politique et militaire* (Paris, 3 vols., 1759–81). Sainte-Palaye's material on troubadours was written up by C. F. X. Millot and issued in 1774 as *Histoire littéraire des troubadours*.
6 By coincidence, the tale of Aucassin and Nicolette was again published in 1779 in P. Legrand D'Aussy, *Fabliaux ou contes du XIIe et du XIIIe siècle*, vol. ii. But this enthusiast and colleague of Sainte-Palaye suppressed or amalgamated the lyric portions and omitted the Drover and Torelore episodes.
7 *Tom Jones* by Poinsinet, revised by Sedaine (1765, 1766), after Henry Fielding's novel. Sensitivity existed partly because of the high incidence of children being born out of wedlock; 31% of baptisms in Paris between 1770 and 1789 were of foundlings, most being illegitimate: Louis Henry, 'The Population of France in the Eighteenth Century', in D. V. Glass and D. E. C. Eversley (eds.), *Population in History* (London, 1965), p. 451.
8 Where it corresponds to Sainte-Palaye's text (1756 edition, p. 15) at the equivalent point in the story: 'Avant que vous m'ayez donné Nicolette ma douce amie'.
9 Heinz Wichmann, *Grétry und das musikalische Theater in Frankreich* (Halle, 1929), p. 72.
10 Cf. the nineteen-bar theme from the overture *Panurge*, cited in the *Mémoires* (i:378), which Grétry says reflects 'the country where one is never hurried' and described as 'one of the longest I have composed': Ex. 29.1 quotes the opening.
11 They also chat about their superiors, like Grétry's men. See *Les Troyens* act 5, no. 40, 'Par Bacchus'.
12 J. C. Le Vacher de Charnois (ed.), *Costumes et annales des grands théâtres de Paris*, iii, Issue XIII [1788], p. 100.

13 J. W. von Goethe, *Von deutscher Baukunst* (Frankfurt, 1773); J. G. Herder, *Von deutscher Art und Kunst* (Hamburg, 1773).

14 Lennart Breitholtz, 'Le théâtre historique en France jusqu'à la Révolution', *Uppsala Universitets Årsskrift*, xii (1952), pp. 62–3.

15 In Colardeau's *La Caliste*. Favart's description of the costumes is reproduced in Nagler (ed.), *A Source Book in Theatrical History*, p. 324.

16 Breitholtz, 'Le théâtre historique', pp. 165–6.

17 *Mémoires secrets*, vi, pp. 277–80 (2 December 1772).

18 Libretto, Paris, Veuve Ballard & fils, 1780, preface.

19 B. Farmian de Rosoi, *Les mariages samnites* (Paris, Belin, 1782), pp. x–xi.

20 Cf. librettos [Paris,] P. R. C. Ballard, n.d. [1779] and that in note 18. Dialogue differences in act 1 sc. 6, 9; act 2 sc. 2, 5; the dénouement was modified and in the ballet a throne of branches was raised to Aucassin and Nicolette who were duly honoured, the shepherd sang a *pastourelle* and there was a dance.

21 Librettos: Paris, Brunet, 1782 and Paris, Delalain, 1782, giving identical texts.

25 Profile IV: Grétry at the Opéra

1 Letter of 14 December 1777 in Froidcourt, p. 97.

2 Michel Brenet, *Grétry, sa vie et ses œuvres* (Paris, 1884), p. 140 n1.

3 Froidcourt, p. 84; Brenet, *Grétry*, pp. 133, 251.

4 *Mémoires*, i:356 and iii [472]; Brenet, *Grétry*, p. 153.

5 Arthur Pougin, *Un directeur d'opéra au dix-huitième siècle* (Paris, 1914), p. 12. One should also note the successful ballet *Le premier navigateur*, which we mentioned in chapter 8, choreographed by Gardel the elder; with music taken from various Grétry scores, it was seen from 26 July 1785 until the end of the century.

6 Note by Grétry: '*Le Seigneur bienfaisant* [by E. Floquet, 1780] had appeared previously, before the works discussed; but I wonder whether the vocal part was treated there by the composer in an epoch-making way?'

7 Brenet, *Grétry*, p. 168.

8 Letter of 24 January 1772 in Froidcourt, p. 60. He also earned 1,200 *livres* for the score for *Amour pour amour* in 1777 (see chapter 19): Ernest Boysse (ed.), *L'administration des menus: Journal de Papillon de La Ferté* (Paris, 1887), p. 405.

9 Archives Nationales o¹.677, cited in Froidcourt, p. 135.

10 Archives Nationales o¹.848, cited in Brenet, *Grétry*, p. 205.

11 Private note entered during or after 1780 in his copy of J. B. de La Borde's *Essai sur la musique*, reported in Ernest Closson, 'Les notes marginales de Grétry dans l'"Essay sur la Musique" de Laborde', *Revue Belge de Musicologie* ii (1948), p. 121.

12 Few surviving letters mention the 1789 *Mémoires*; in September 1788 Grétry made one of his habitual complaints about the publisher, Prault: 'I can only snatch from him one sheet a week . . . this slowness is killing me.' See Froidcourt, pp. 144, 146, 148. By 4 April 1789 Grétry instructed Prault to hold off publication since public attention was diverted: the States-General were to meet on 5 May. Later letters show Grétry had help in proof-reading, indexing and compiling the table of his works in the second and third volumes: see Froidcourt, pp. 166–8, 172, 175, 178–80.

13 Cornu originally wrote to Grétry at the end of 1782 and was told to compete for his place: see Froidcourt, p. 117. Grétry's other surviving letter to him, dated 25 January 1786, shows that this procedure was not necessarily going to be invoked. In fact, Cornu joined the orchestra after Easter 1786, as second violin; at this time the total number of violins was increased from sixteen to eighteen. F:Po, Registre de l'Opéra-Comique vol. 70.

14 Prince–Bishop de Velbruck, the composer's friend, died in 1784. Prince Ferdinand was not elected, since 'large sums of money backed the candidate preferred by Brussels and Vienna': Froidcourt, p. 123.

15 Froidcourt, pp. 135–48. Grétry described himself as 'Royal Censor' on the title page of

Richard Cœur-de-lion, publication announced in March 1786. However the *Mémoires secrets* (xxvii:45) referred to his nomination as Royal Censor on 29 November 1784. The Order in Council imposing stamp-duty is dated 15 September 1786 but doubt has been expressed as to whether the tax was ever collected; most recently in F. Lesure and A. Devriès, *Dictionnaire des éditeurs de musique française* (2 vols., Geneva, 1979), i, p. 10. On 30 November the *Mémoires secrets* (xxxiii:223) reported that objections had been registered from dealers and that it had been agreed in principle to limit the tax to new music. This decision itself was to be suspended until 1 January 1787.

16 In the second *arrondissement*, on the site of outbuildings of the Hôtel Choiseul-Stainville, near where the new Théâtre Italien would soon be built. Paul Culot, *Le jugement de Midas, Opéra-comique d'André-Ernest-Modeste Grétry* (Brussels, 1978), p. 17 n10. See chapter 24 n1.

17 Brenet, *Grétry*, p. 162.

18 Barry S. Brook, *La symphonie française dans la seconde moitié du dix-huitième siècle* (3 vols., Paris, 1962), i, p. 329. For the protection afforded by a *privilège*, see *ibid.*, i, p. 38.

19 This was given with instruments, and on stage: F:Po, Registres de l'Opéra-Comique, vol. 118, f. 69, 9 February 1786. At the Revolution Wuiet left for England and Holland, returning under the Directory: Froidcourt, p. 298. Needing money, and in some trouble with the police owing to wearing men's clothes, she petitioned Josephine Bonaparte. See Nina Epton, *Josephine, The Empress and her Children* (London, 1975), p. 73. For information on other pupils see Brenet, *Grétry*, pp. 191–4 and *Mémoires*: iii: 382–4.

26 Opéra-comique in the 1780s

1 Maurice Albert, *Les théâtres de la foire* (Paris, 1900), pp. 225–8; Emile Campardon, *Les spectacles de la foire* (2 vols., Paris, 1877), i, Introduction.

2 Nicolas Brazier, *Chroniques des petits théâtres de Paris*, ed. G. D'Heylli (Paris, 1883), p. 302; E. C. Van Bellen, *Les origines du mélodrame* (Utrecht, n.d. [1927]), pp. 78ff.

3 Quoted in F. Gaiffe, *Le drame en France au XVIIIᵉ siècle* (Paris, 1910), p. 229.

4 *Journal des débats*, 18 June 1803, quoted in James F. Mason, *The Melodrama in France from the Revolution to the Beginning of Romantic Drama* (Baltimore, 1912), p. 4.

5 On this theatre see Louis Péricaud, *Théâtre des petits comédiens de S.A.S. Monseigneur le Comte de Beaujolais* (Paris, 1909).

6 Clarence D. Brenner, *The Théâtre Italien, its Repertory 1716–1793*, University of California Publications in Modern Philology, lxiii (Berkeley, 1961), p. 13.

7 Speech given by the actor Granger at the start of the 1788–9 season, discussed in J. C. Le Vacher de Charnois (ed.), *Costumes et annales des grands théâtres de Paris*, iii, Issue IV, [1788], p. 31.

8 Georges Cucuel, 'Sources et documents pour servir à l'histoire de l'opéra-comique en France', *L'année musicale*, iii (1913), pp. 265–6. The company could and did continue to give Italian pieces already in the repertoire.

9 [N. E. Framery], *De l'organisation des spectacles de Paris* (Paris, 1790), pp. 118–19. The Opéra also breached the agreement by staging at least one ballet (*Le coq du village*) on a subject that belonged to the Comédie-Italienne.

10 *Mercure de France*, 3 March 1787, pp. 39–44. *Le roi Théodore* actually came to the Paris Opéra in September the same year for a run of thirteen performances, which perhaps proves the *Mercure*'s general point. The Opéra was of course mounting serious Italian opera to French librettos at the time. The main composers were Piccinni (with *Didon*, 1783 and others), Salieri (with *Les Danaïdes*, 1784) and Sacchini (the best of whose French works was *Oedipe à Colone*, 1787).

11 N. E. Framery, *De l'organisation des spectacles*, pp. 118–19.

12 Document dated 16 October 1779, Archives Nationales E.2557, quoted in Emile Campardon, *Les Comédiens du Roi de la troupe italienne pendant les deux derniers siècles* (2 vols., Paris, 1880), ii, pp. 352–3.

13 David Charlton, 'Orchestra and Chorus at the Comédie-Italienne (Opéra-Comique), 1755–

1799' in Malcolm H. Brown and Roland John Wiley (eds.), *Slavonic and Western Music: Essays for Gerald Abraham* (Ann Arbor, Oxford, 1985), pp. 87–108.

14 Le Vacher de Charnois (ed.), *Costumes et annales*, xii, Issue xlviii [March 1788], pp. 189–90.

15 Brenner, *The Théâtre Italien*, pp. 16–17.

16 Arthur Pougin, *L'Opéra-Comique pendant la Révolution de 1788 à 1801* (Paris, 1891), p. 12, mentions a loan for this of 100,000 *livres*; Brenner, *The Théâtre Italien*, p. 21, cites a contract for 80,000.

17 F:Po, Registres de l'Opéra-Comique vols. 60, 68–9; see David Charlton, 'Orchestra and Chorus'.

18 Neal Zaslaw, 'Toward the Revival of the Classical Orchestra', *Proceedings of the Royal Musical Association*, ciii (1976–7), pp. 158–87, especially Tables I and II.

19 Louis Péricaud, *Théâtre des petits comédiens*, p. 27.

20 *Almanach général de tous les Spectacles* (Paris, 1791); *Les Spectacles de Paris* (Paris, 1791). For comparison, the Théâtre Français Comique et Lyrique, formerly the Jeunes-Artistes, had seventeen strings and seven wind players.

21 *Mémoires secrètes*, 28 April 1779; see Brenner, *The Théâtre Italien*, p. 24. It appears to have had a weak plot: *Les spectacles de Paris . . . 1780* (Paris, n.d.), p. 233.

22 Mason, *The Melodrama in France*, p. 9.

23 Van Bellen, *Les origines du mélodrame*, p. 75.

24 The tower is not mentioned in the printed scenario but in M. H. Winter, *Le théâtre du merveilleux* (Paris, 1962), p. 32.

25 Gaiffe, *Le drame en France*, p. 233.

26 *Ariane dans l'isle de Naxos, drame-lyrique* (Paris, P. de Lormel, 1782), unpaginated preface. The second paragraph begins, 'En adaptant à la Scène-Lyrique ce Sujet, (imité d'un Mélodrame Allemand,)'.

27 Le Vacher de Charnois (ed.), *Costumes et annales*, i, Issue xxiv, 15 October 1786, p. 6 mentions the decadence in costume design, while iii, Issue vi [1788], p. 41 contains the quotation. Improvising in dialogue was, however, not something new, for in October 1769 the actors in *Le tableau parlant* 'ont ajouté de verve plusieurs traits forts plaisants qui ne sont pas dans la pièce, et qui ont grandement diverti le parterre' (Grimm:viii:349).

28 2,063 to 1,066; Dalayrac was also producing a few works at the Théâtre Feydeau, whereas Grétry gave there only *Le barbier de village* (6 May 1797).

29 Further analysis is in Karin Pendle, '*A bas les couvents!* Anticlerical Sentiment in French Opera of the 1790s', *Music Review*, xlii (1981), pp. 22–45.

27 *L'épreuve villageoise*

1 Wife of the powerful Intendant-contrôleur (administrator) of the Menus Plaisirs de la Chambre du Roi. The printed libretto is dedicated by Desforges to D. P. J. Papillon de La Ferté himself (1727–94). The Menus Plaisirs housed stores, workshops etc. but also a small theatre used for rehearsals.

2 Incipits: (1) 'J'n'avions pas encor quatorze ans' (2) 'Bonjour, monsieur' (3) 'J'ons fait un bouquet' (4) 'J'commence à voir' (5) 'André, to me l'païras' (7) 'Bon dieu, bon dieu' (8) 'Adieu Marton, adieu Lisette' (9) 'Je vous revois' (10) 'Viens, mon André' (11b) 'Allons tous rendre hommage'.

3 Berton's *Les promesses de mariage* (1787), his first opéra-comique to survive, was designed by Desforges as a sequel to Grétry's opera. Desforges disowned changes made in rehearsal without his consent: *Journal de Paris*, 12 July 1787, p. 857.

4 John Lahr, 'Life's a farce', *New Society*, lxvii (22 March 1984), pp. 443–4.

5 But it was not given in 1862 when Sullivan and companions 'visited all the operas': Herbert Sullivan and Newman Flower, *Sir Arthur Sullivan. His Life, Letters and Diaries*, 2nd edn. (London, 1950), p. 42.

6 Michael Kelly, *Reminiscences*, ed. Roger Fiske (London, 1975), p. 145.

7 Michel Brenet, *Grétry, sa vie et ses œuvres* (Paris, 1884), p. 181.

8 Libretto by Lourdet de Santerre, after Favart's *Ninette à la cour*, and thence Ciampi's opera *Bertoldo in corte*. Note the Italianate confluence of jealousy, with low and high-born lovers, as in *La Frascatana* etc.

9 *Blaise et Babet* was apparently offered to Grétry after Monvel quarrelled with Dezède, but Grétry counselled artistic *rapprochement*: Brenet, *Grétry*, p. 182.

10 Mme de Beaunoir, or simply Beaunoir, was the pseudonym of Alexandre L. B. Robineau, attached to the king's library (Grimm, December 1782) and a prolific author during the 1780s. He was to write the libretto for 'Lucile' Grétry's *Le mariage d'Antonio*.

11 F:Po, Registre de l'Opéra-Comique vol. 115. Unpaginated manuscript libretto in F:Pn, Th.B.2115, 'Théodore et Paulin. Comédie Lyrique, en vers, Et en trois Actes. Par Mr. Desforges. La Musique de Monsieur GRETRY'. It has the appearance of a fair copy and the plot conforms entirely to the accounts of the work in the *Mercure de France*, 17 April 1784 and Antoine D'Origny's *Annales du Théâtre Italien depuis son origine jusqu'à ce jour* (3 vols., Paris, 1788, reprinted Geneva, 1970), iii, pp. 138–9.

2 Act 3 sc. 9: 'Elle chante les premiers mots de l'air qu'elle a entendu au 2ᵉ acte, "Adieu Marton etc."'

28 Richard Cœur-de-lion

1 Sedaine dedicated his libretto to Prince Henry of Prussia.

2 Incipits: (1) 'Chantons, chantons' (2) 'La danse n'est pas' (3) 'O Richard! ô mon Roi' (4) 'Quoi! de la part du Gouverneur' (5) 'Je crains de lui' (6) 'Un bandeau couvre les yeux' (8) 'Que le Sultan Saladin' (10) 'Si l'univers entier m'oublie' (11) 'Une fièvre brûlante' (12) 'Sais-tu, connais-tu' (13) 'Ah! Monseigneur' (14) 'Il faut que je lui parle' (15) 'Oui, Chevaliers' (16) 'Le Gouverneur, pendant la danse' (17a) 'Et zig, et zig' (20) 'O ma chère Comtesse'.

3 The score gives more extensive details of the stage action than does the printed libretto, amounting to over 250 words. In Plate VII the artist has brought together certain actions that should take place consecutively.

4 Actually the march from *Les mariages samnites* (9). A footnote explains candidly that it was drafted in on the day of the première of the opera's final version, to fit the stage action recently decided upon.

5 Claude Fauchet, *Recueil de l'Origine de la langue et poesie françoise, ryme et romans* (Paris, 1581).

6 Marie-Jeanne Lhéritier de Villandon, *La Tour ténébreuse, et les jours lumineux, contes anglois, Accompagnez d'historiettes et tirez d'une ancienne Chronique composée par RICHARD, surnommé CŒUR DE LION, Roy d'Angleterre* (Paris, 1705).

7 Modern belief is that Richard was probably homosexual. He married during the Cyprus campaign on the way to Palestine but did not stay with his wife. Lhéritier's account of Richard's courtly devotion from afar is reflected in the song which Blondel uses to identify the king, Ex. 28.8.

8 The second volume for July 1776, pp. 163–194. An historically-based account of Richard I together with texts of his poems had been published recently in *Histoire littéraire des troubadours* (3 vols., Paris, 1774), i, pp. 54–68 (see chapter 24 note 5). The tale of Blondel's discovery of the king was however included as 'ce que Fauchet raconte d'après une ancienne chronique'.

9 Georges Cucuel, 'Le Moyen Age dans les opéras-comiques du XVIIIᵉ siècle', *Revue du Dix-Huitième siècle*, ii (1914), p. 69. Without investigating the relation of the whole 1776 version to the Grétry opera, Cucuel noticed that the second stanza of Sedaine's 'Que le Sultan Saladin' (8) appeared, credited to Paulmy, in La Borde's *Essai sur la musique ancienne et moderne*. A. R. Voyer d'Argenson, Marquis de Paulmy, was a career diplomat until 1770 and owner of some 100,000 volumes and manuscripts now preserved in the Bibliothèque de l'Arsenal, Paris.

10 F:Po, Registre de l'Opéra-Comique vol. 115, 8 April 1782: 'Fait lecture d'une pièce nouvelle

de Mr Sedaine en trois actes en prose et Ariettes, intitulée Richard Cœur de Lion. La d^{te} Pièce acceptée pour être lue à l'assemblée.'

11 *Journal de musique, par une société d'amateurs* (1777), second part, pp. 19–20, reprinted in *Journal de Paris*, 9 January 1778, p. 34. The anonymous author gave the tale another new ending: Blondel hurries to England to initiate negotiations for the king's release.

12 *Journal de Paris*, reported in Barry S. Brook, *La symphonie française dans la deuxième moitié du dix-huitième siècle* (3 vols., Paris, 1960), i, p. 359.

13 *Airs Détachés DE ROSANIE Comédie Lyrique en trois Actes* (Paris, chez l'Auteur, n.d.), pp. 22–4. For Rigel's source in Ex. 28.1 see J. B. de La Borde, *Essai sur la musique ancienne et moderne* (4 vols., Paris, 1780), ii, supplement, p. 6.

14 Richard in a sense replaced Henri IV as a royalist hero. Breitholtz points out that Louis-Sébastien Mercier's forbidden plays such as *La Destruction de la Ligue ou la Réduction de Paris* (1782), published abroad but secretly circulated in France, 'by mixing the personality of Henri IV with frankly revolutionary propaganda, made it difficult, until the end of the Ancien Régime, to write plays with this popular idol as hero. From that moment, in practice, this theme was abandoned!. Lennart Breitholtz, 'Le théâtre historique en France jusqu'à la Révolution', *Uppsala Universitets Årsskrift*, xii (1952), p. 338.

15 *Carl Maria von Weber: Writings on Music* ed. John Warrack (Cambridge, 1981), p. 224, from review of Grétry's Raoul Barbe-bleue, 13 May 1817.

16 René Lanson, *Le goût du moyen âge en France au XVIIIe siècle* (Paris, Brussels, 1926), p. 31.

17 Pierre Alexandre Lévesque de la Ravalière, *Les poësies du Roy de Navarre* (2 vols., Paris, 1742), i, p. 254.

18 La Borde, *Essai sur la musique*, i, pp. 305, 356.

19 Grétry's note was made in volume one, p. 113, just before the story of Richard told in the context of the history of secular song, not the second volume containing the examples of secular song. Transcription in Ernest Closson, 'Les notes marginales de Grétry dans l' "Essay sur la Musique" de Laborde', *Revue Belge de Musicologie*, ii (1948), p. 121.

20 De la Ravalière, *Les poësies du Roy de Navarre*, i, pp. 241ff. The music reproduced corresponds to nos. I, LIV, LIII, XXXIV, LII, XL, XXXVIII and XI in Pierre Aubry and A. Jeanroy (eds.), *Le chansonnier de l'Arsenal (MS 5198)*, (Paris, 1909–10). Further discussion of the topic is in Théodore Gérold, 'Le réveil en France, au XVIIIe siècle, de l'intérêt pour la musique profane du moyen âge', Publications de la Société Française de Musicologie (series 2), iii–iv: *Mélanges de musicologie offerts à M.Lionel de La Laurencie* (Paris, 1933), pp. 223–34.

21 Philip Robinson, 'Jean-Jacques Rousseau, Aunt Suzanne, and Solo Song', *The Modern Language Review*, lxxiii (1978), p. 294 n11.

22 Gérold, 'Le réveil en France', pp. 232–3. It is a paraphrase of the second verse of the chanson 'De nouviau m'estuet chanter'. Gérold notes that this version by Moncrif was reprinted by others in 1765 and 1782 and that Herder translated it in his *Stimmen der Völker*, whence it passed to Brahms's notice and inspired his setting, Op. 14 no. 4.

23 Cucuel, 'Le Moyen Age', pp. 65–6, considered that 'The first two rhythmic modes [trochaic and iambic], revealed by the publication of texts, were quickly exploited by the authors of romances' and that Moncrif's and Paulmy's songs in duple metre were different in nature, nearer to the French rondeau and vaudeville. For Gerald Abraham, 'Grétry had not the faintest notion what a twelfth-century *trouvère* song was like': *The Tradition of Western music* (Berkeley, Los Angeles, 1974), p. 121.

24 Act 1 sc. 2. Grétry claimed that Sedaine's original word was not 'tones' but 'violin': this of course strengthens the connection with Orpheus (who sang to his lyre). Grétry with difficulty persuaded Sedaine that 'violin' would be unintentionally funny: *Réf*:iii:256.

25 Mozart, *Le nozze di Figaro*, no. 23, 'L'ho perduta'.

26 That is, the instruction 'baguetes garnies' in Dalayrac's overture *Lina*. See David Charlton, 'Orchestration and Orchestral Practice in Paris, 1789–1810', unpublished dissertation, University of Cambridge, 1973, p. 339. The term 'voilée' (i.e. 'veiled' or 'muffled') used later in speaking of this passage (i:375), was adopted by French composers around 1790.

27 Michael Kelly, *Reminiscences*, ed. Roger Fiske (London, 1975), p. 147. In performance, the Romantic sensibility seems close to this episode, particularly in the unreal juxtaposition of a meaningful music with the limitations of the mundane. In his tale *Don Juan*, E. T. A. Hoffmann uses Mozart's music as the mystic bridge between two people one of whom is a singer, the other having a profound sympathy for Mozart's music.

28 See *The New Oxford History of Music*, vii: *The Age of Enlightenment 1745-1790*, ed. Egon Wellesz and Frederick Sternfeld (London, 1973), pp. 342-4; Gérold, 'Le réveil en France'; Robinson, 'Jean-Jacques Rousseau', p. 295; and an article appearing after I had written this section which fills in many details, and stresses the rôle of the Romance as a song for its own sake: Daniel Heartz, 'The Beginnings of the Operatic Romance: Rousseau, Sedaine, and Monsigny', *Eighteenth-Century Studies*, xv (1981-2), pp. 149-78.

29 [P. J. B. Nougaret,] *De l'art du théâtre où il est parlé des différens genres de spectacles, et de la musique adaptée au théâtre* (2 vols., Paris, 1769), ii, p. 299.

30 David Charlton, 'Motif and Recollection in four operas of Dalayrac', *Soundings*, vii (1978), pp. 38-61.

31 Score announced in *Gazette de France*, 10 March 1786. Libretto, Paris, Brunet, 1786.

32 Primary statistical evidence, F:Po, Registres de l'Opéra-Comique, Easter 1784 to Easter 1785, has been lost. Normally replacement figures are drawn from newspaper evidence collated in Clarence D. Brenner, *The Théâtre Italien, its Repertory 1716-1793*, University of California Publications in Modern Philology, lxiii (Berkeley, Los Angeles, 1963). But the Registre commencing after Easter 1785, vol. 69, says that the April 7 performance was the twenty-fourth; Brenner gives the twenty-fifth. I follow the Registre.

33 Froidcourt, pp. 124-5; Michel Brenet, *Grétry, sa vie et ses œuvres* (Paris, 1884), pp. 188-9; Julien Tiersot, *Lettres de musiciens écrites en français du XVᵉ au XXᵉ siècle* (2 vols., Turin, 1924), i, pp. 103-4.

34 Pierre Marie Michel Lepeintre Desroches, *Suite du répertoire du Théâtre Français avec un choix des pièces de plusieurs autres théâtres* (81 vols., Paris, 1822-3), lviii, p. 63. In the reprint (Geneva, 1970) it is in xx, p. 451.

35 Antoine D'Origny, *Annales du Théâtre Italien depuis son origine jusqu'à ce jour* (3 vols., Paris, 1788, reprinted Geneva, 1970), iii, p. 230.

36 *Thayer's Life of Beethoven*, rev. and ed. Elliot Forbes (Princeton, 1970), p. 199.

37 F:Pn, ms.fr.9259, ff. 92-110, 'La fête patriotique ou La fédération d'un grand empire. Comédie en deux actes en prose et en vers mise sur la musique de richard cœur de lion. Roüen, 1791', anonymous. It is set in Persia.

38 T. J. Walsh, *Second Empire Opera* (London, 1981), pp. 72, 308.

29 *L'amitié à l'épreuve*, 3-act version

1 Main title in the printed librettos: *Les vrais amis* (*The true friends*).

2 Incipits: (1) 'Je m'y connois' (2) 'Non, jamais' (3) 'Si je pense' (5) 'Du Dieu d'amour' (6) 'Bonjour à toi' (7) 'Grande, grande réjouissance' (8) 'Je pars, rien ne m'arrête' (9) 'De fraîcheur, de grâce' (10) 'O Blanfort!' (11) 'Qu'entends-je?' (12) 'Par un charme puissant' (13) 'A quels maux il me livre' (14) 'C'est cet appartement' (15) 'Oui, noir, mais non si diable' (16) 'Je veux qu'on ne me gêne en rien' (17) 'Je vais jouir' (18) 'Quel bonheur extrême' (19) 'Qu'il est doux' (20) 'Remplis nos cœurs, douce amitié' (21) 'Par vos soins'.

3 But not the precise nature of her ethical education as described by Marmontel in the original Moral Tale; see chapter 9.

4 The actual wording in the libretto is, 'Les quatre vers suivans sont précédés & entre-coupés par des traits de Symphonie . . . qui expriment leur émotion, ce qui forme une espèce de Mélodrame.'

5 *Panurge* was set 'dans l'Isle des Lanternes, qu'on suppose voisine de la Chine'. The inspiration for its music could have been La Borde's *Essai sur la musique ancienne et moderne* (4 vols., Paris, 1780), ii, chapter 12 (secondary pagination), pp. 174-7. There are two pages of

Chinese melodic transcriptions using pentatony and hexatony. For other excursions into Grétry's local colour, see chapters 21, 24, 28.

6 *Nouveau voyage aux isles de l' Amérique* (Paris, 1722), cited in R. Nettel, 'Historical Introduction to "La Calinda"', *Music & Letters*, xxvii (1946), pp. 59–62. La Borde's *Essai* included no African dances, only details of instruments. The article 'Calinda' in the *Encyclopédie ou dictionnaire raisonné*, ed. Diderot and D'Alembert, says the dance was accompanied by 'a type of guitar and some toneless drums, which the negroes strike with the flat of the hand'.

7 Other pictures Favart and Grétry could have seen in the 1783 Paris Salon include J. J. Lagrenée *l'aîné*'s 'Two widows of a Hindu officer', likewise celebrating dignity and virtue.

8 'Ah! quelles mœurs! quel pays corrompu! / La nature en ces lieux est la seule étrangère'.

9 The singer was Mlle Renaud, and the piece allowed the 'musical luxury' of happiness anticipated (i:221). Later, Grétry was distinctly petulant about her, without admitting he had pandered to her wishes: 'each musician prides himself on reaching a note above his colleague; Italian sopranos and Mlle Renaud, topping everything else, already strike up in half the third octave; however, it will be well to finish that and return to nature' (i:397). The new cadenza for (5) reached to e'''.

10 Heinz Wichmann, *Grétry und das musikalische Theater in Frankreich* (Halle, 1929), p. 107; *Thayer's Life of Beethoven*, rev. and ed. Elliot Forbes (New Jersey, 1969), p. 121. As we noted earlier, Beethoven's father sang the rôle of Nelson in 1771.

11 Clarence D. Brenner, *The Théâtre Italien, its repertory, 1716–1793*, University of California Publications in Modern Philology, lxiii (Berkeley, Los Angeles, 1961), p. 460.

12 This speech appeared, together with a caveat saying it had been cut for reasons of length, in the 1787 librettos: see note 21 below. It parallels the final speech of Lemierre's play *La veuve du Malabar* (published 1780), in which King Louis of France is credited with the humanitarian extinction of barbarous customs in India. 'Vous, peuples, respirez sous de meilleurs auspices' etc.

13 Glyndwr Williams, *The Expansion of Europe in the Eighteenth Century* (London, 1966), pp. 132–3. The biography was by Maistre de la Tour: *Histoire d' Ayder-Ali-Khan*. The resistance was continued by Haider Ali's son, Tipu Sultan, also a skilled tactician, who died in battle in the fourth Mysore war against the English, 1799. A manuscript libretto for a three-act opera on the subject of Haider Ali exists in preliminary form in F:Pn, Ms.n.acq.2929, f. 119, unsigned and undated. The English appear to play no direct part in it.

14 G. T. F. Raynal, *Histoire philosophique et politique des établissmens et du commerce des Européens dans les deux Indes* (6 vols., Paris, 1770). The translated quotation is from J. O. Justamond's 2nd edition (6 vols., London, 1798), iv, pp. 97, 102.

15 Williams, *The Expansion of Europe*, p. 234.

16 Begins: 'Dans nos heureux climats l'astre du jour se lève. / C'est là qu'on voit de toutes parts / Les fleurs, les fruits, l'ombrage, la verdure.'

17 MIRSA, BALLET EN ACTION (Paris, 1779). Music by Gossec, Dezède *et al.* Not to be confused with Gardel's *La fête de Mirza* (1781): see chapter 25.

18 At least one dancer in the part of the evil Corsair uttered a cry at the moment of death: see *Mercure de France*, September 1780, p. 233. This was found 'absolutely out of place' in a 'simple amusement'.

19 This *topos* could have stemmed from Shadwell's reworking of Shakespeare's *The Tempest*: Hippolito, 'one that never saw Woman', has been raised on the island separately from Miranda and her sister. Grimm assumed this borrowing (xiv:483). But the theme of sexual ambiguity was somewhat fashionable. The adolescent Chevalier de Faublas dresses as a girl in J. B. Louvet de Couvray's eponymous novel (1785–7). In the opéra-comique *La fille garçon* (1787) by Desmaillot and St Georges, a boy is brought up as a girl companion of the farmer's daughter Nicette (Grimm:xv:132–3).

20 Even the printed orchestra parts bear this surprising change out. No archival evidence exists for specially-hired clarinettists in this work.

21 [Paris,] P. Robert-Christophe Ballard, 1786; Paris, Veuve Duchesne, 1787; Paris, Prault, 1787.

22 Presumably at the beginning of act 3, though this cannot be proved. After the third performance Grétry wrote to the *Journal de Paris*, which carried his text on 7 November 1786 (omitted by Froidcourt); he explains that (17) – or at least 'un Air de bravoure' – was withdrawn owing to unsuitability for its 'situation dramatique'. Following appeals from 'several persons' to reconsider it, and by agreement with Favart, the composer would restore it to 'une situation convenable', allowing the perfection of Mlle Renaud's performance to be enjoyed.

30 *Les méprises par ressemblance*

1 This was Grétry's first opéra-comique without dedication, a practice that faded at the Revolution. On 12 February 1790 Grétry wrote that 'The *ressemblances* has just been engraved', adding less clearly, 'and will appear when the assembly [of the Comédie-Italienne] has pronounced on the fate of our productions': Froidcourt, p. 150. By this time, according to a printed catalogue in the scores of the opera in GB:Lbl, both *Le Comte d'Albert* and *Le rival confident* had been printed. It is possible that Grétry and Patrat disagreed over which version of (17) was preferable: see the end of this chapter. Patrat's dissatisfaction caused him to mount a version of the libretto as a spoken comedy, *Les deux grenadiers*, at the Théâtre de la Cité in 1792, afterwards Théâtre Montansier. This was printed in Pierre Marie Michel Lepeintre Desroche's *Suite du répertoire du Théâtre français* (81 vols., Paris, 1822–3), lxxii, p. 187 (reprint, Geneva, 1970, xxiii, p. 154).

2 Costume instructions were exceptional in opéra-comique, though typical of burgeoning factual detail of all kinds in theatre texts. Patrat had already put costume instructions in his play *L'heureuse erreur* (1783), as Beaumarchais had also done in *Le barbier de Séville* (1775).

3 Incipits: (1) 'Vive, vive la liberté' (2) 'Mon père avoit' (3) 'Oui, je veux rester fille' (4) 'Ah! quel plaisir' (5) 'Un peu d'amour' (6) 'Pardonnez au désordre extrême' (7) 'Non, non, j'en suis incapable' (8) 'Mon Dieu! mon Dieu!' (9) 'D'abord dans un morne silence' (10) 'Le voilà' (12) 'Dam! fallait me voir danser' (13) 'Jamais le cœur' (14) 'O juste ciel' (15) 'Méconnu par mon père' (16) 'Embrasse-moi, mon cher enfant' (17) 'Qui va là?'.

4 Regnard's valet puts the cause down to seeing military action; Latulipe has supposedly lost his memory as the result of some shipwreck.

5 The first, *Les deux morts*, 1781, simply used vaudevilles; the composer of the second, *La kermesse*, 1783, was G. J. Vogler.

6 Act 2 sc. 6: *Sansquartier*: Comment le savez-vous? *Thérèse*: Je l'ai vu . . . Il est arrivé. Act 3 sc. 2 *Sansquartier*: l'évidence? . . . *Thérèse*: Apprenez, pour vous confondre, que le fils de Monsieur Robert est arrivé.

7 This would be supported by comments in the *Mémoires* (ii:85), where in response to an unsuitable new libretto Grétry would say to an author, 'I wrote the music of your play a long time ago; I would be in danger of plagiarising my own work if I took charge of yours.'

8 The only other Andantes not in recitative are the Andante staccato (7) and that beginning (17), when Thérèse is discovered.

9 Cf. *La Rosière de Salency* (3); *L'ami de la maison* (12); Ex. 10.4.

10 Libretto, [Paris,] P. Robert-Christophe Ballard, 1786; *Mercure de France*, 9 December 1786, pp. 83–90.

11 He announced it in a letter dated 28 November to the *Journal de Paris* of 30 November 1786.

12 Paris, Brunet, 1786; the *CC* 5 assumes that this version was the original one.

13 Froidcourt, p. 144; Grétry refers to *basse-taille* and *taille*, not *baryton*. See discussion of this in chapter 1.

31 *Le Comte d'Albert*

1 Mme Vigée-Lebrun (1755–1842), 'Peintre du Roi'; she had painted a portrait of Grétry in 1785 (now in the Musée de Versailles) and hosted many musical evenings in Paris. Grétry's dedication is in the form of an eight-line poem.

2 The score specifies the window; the libretto (Paris, Brunet, 1787) omits the window.

3 Incipits: (1) 'Sans doute' (2) 'Ah, ma bonne' (3) 'Quand j'entends un homme sensé' (4) 'Arrêtez! Ciel!' (5) 'Qu'opposez-vous?' (6) 'Quelle fatale journée (7) 'Assuré de ton innocence' (8) 'Quoi, mon papa' (9) 'Non, mon devoir' (10) 'Ah, mon Dieu' (11) 'Coquin, si tu fais des cris' (12) 'Sentirsi dire' (13) 'Non, laissez-moi' (14) 'De mes tendres vœux' (15) 'Où courez-vous donc?' (16) 'Chantons Monseigneur' (17) 'Je suis heureux' (18) 'Ah! mon ami' (20) 'Non, non' (21) 'Laissez les bergères' (22) 'Tous nos cœurs'.

4 Brunet's libretto has 'Chambre de Prison royale'; the score omits 'royale'. Grimm (xiv:488) simply calls it 'the Bastille', claiming Sedaine indicated its identity merely by 'referring to the name of the quarter of Paris in which it is situated'. In act 2 sc. 9 Antoine (making himself known) says, 'C'est vous, Monsieur, que j'ai vu dans le Faubourg St. Germain.'

5 CC, p. xxvii, identifies the words as from Metastasio's Semiramide; the Mémoires omit mention of it.

6 Score says 'Septuor', i.e. septet.

7 Louis-Sébastien Mercier, Tableau de Paris, extracts ed. Jeffry Kaplow (Paris, 1979), pp. 137–42.

8 George Rudé, The Crowd in the French Revolution (Oxford, 1959), p. 21.

9 Grimm:xv:9; Mémoires secrets, xxxiv, pp. 141–2 (13 February 1787).

10 Louis-Sébastien Mercier, Tableau de Paris (12 vols., Amsterdam, 1782–8), viii, p. 214.

11 Letter of 4 February 1793 to the Comédie-Française requesting restoration of speeches earlier censored. See Margaret Ann Rayner, 'The Social and Literary Aspects of Sedaine's Dramatic Work', unpublished dissertation, University of London, 1960, pp. 122–3. A duel also forms the mainspring of Sedaine's comedy Le mort marié (1777, rev. 1782).

12 Jean de La Fontaine, Fable xi. The Avertissement in Brunet's libretto of the opéra-comique gives Sedaine's intention: 'I am persuaded that few fables of La Fontaine might not be the germ of a dramatic production; but instead of the Fable indicating its moral point overtly, it suits the theatre to force the hearer to draw those conclusions himself which the poet has desired to impart.' (Cf. the Jupiter and Semele myth in relation to Wagner's Lohengrin.)

13 An anonymous translation of Goldoni as Les femmes curieuses: F:Po, Registre de l'Opéra-Comique vol. 118, 24 September 1785.

14 'In Le Comte d'Albert as in many other pieces, to attempt to write in praise of madame Dugazon is to wish to explain nature' (i:415); see also Sedaine's Avertissement.

15 That is, Grétry points to these words and others, but stops short of drawing the connection with Christ.

16 Rayner, 'Sedaine's Dramatic Work', p. 194.

17 John Lough, Paris Theatre Audiences in the Seventeenth and Eighteenth Centuries (London, 1957), p. 268.

18 Raymond Williams, Culture and Society 1780–1950 (Harmondsworth, 1963), p. 59. An indication of the change in France emerges when comparing the 1787 work with Sedaine's Le déserteur (1769), an earlier working of related ideas. The heroine Louise cuts a more instinctual, sentimental figure than the Countess.

19 Ruth Graham, 'Rousseau's Sexism Revolutionised', in Paul Fritz and Richard Morton (eds.), Women in the Eighteenth Century and Other Essays (Toronto and Sarasota, 1976), pp. 134–7.

20 Le mariage de Figaro, act 3 sc. 16.

21 Mémoires secrets, xxxiv, p. 57 (20 January 1787). Paisiello's opera, translated from Il re Teodoro in Venezia, was seen at Fontainebleau on 20 October 1786 and at Versailles the following 18 November.

22 Journal de Paris, 27 December 1787; 3 February 1788; 25 March 1793. CC 48–9 is only partly based on the autograph score in the Musée Grétry, Liège. The source used for the partially-edited score available to Ernest Closson when he took over the editorship of Le prisonnier anglais for CC proved impossible to find. Closson therefore produced an attempt at a conflated edition. Both the lost and the Liège sources appear to incorporate extensive

clarinet and trumpet parts; these instruments were not permanent until 1790 and special hirings were not made for *Le prisonnier anglais* in 1788. Until a critical edition of the music is made, all conclusions must be provisional. A further part-autograph score has recently been acquired by the Bibliothèque Royale Albert 1er, Brussels.

23 *Journal des théâtres*, 2ᵉ trimestre no. 16 (23 nivôse an III), pp. 241–3.

32 Confident rivals

1 Letter to L. P. de Croix in Lille: Froidcourt, p. 144.
2 Incipits: (1) 'Ici, lorsqu'on est heureux' (2) 'Je crains un tel homme' (3) 'Loin de mon fils' (4) 'Qui peut déplaire à Rosalie' (5) 'Non, je dois résister' (6) 'Lubin ne vient pas' (7) 'Quelqu'un est là-haut' (8) 'Quand on est sans reproche' (9) 'Pour faire l'homme d'importance' (10) 'Oui, Monsieur l'homme de justice'.
3 Daniel Heartz, 'The Beginnings of the Operatic Romance: Rousseau, Sedaine, and Monsigny', *Eighteenth-Century Studies*, xv (1981–2), pp. 149–78.
4 Grétry writes 'plus pleines d'harmonie' but this cannot mean 'richer in harmony' since this reasoning goes against his fundamental tenets of style.
5 The story, based on a factual report, is simply the decision of three tenant farmers to lend their *seigneur* enough money not to have to sell his land to a new owner. It is an act celebrating continuity of tradition and also friendship.
6 Antoine D'Origny, *Annales du Théâtre Italien depuis son origine jusqu'à ce jour* (3 vols., Paris, 1788, reprinted Geneva, 1970), iii, pp. 92–3.
7 An epitome of this sophistication would be the central section of Babet's act 3 'Ah, si parfois', which is in B flat minor.
8 F:Po, Registre de l'Opéra-Comique vol. 115.
9 F:Po, Registre de l'Opéra-Comique vol. 118. Dalayrac does not seem to have set it.
10 Earlier version in 3 acts as *Mathieu ou les deux soupers* (libretto, Paris, 1783).
11 It was Philip Augustus who defeated Richard the Lionheart in 1199. The librettist, Monvel, had already produced *Les amours de Bayard* at the Comédie-Française, complete with staged contest in act 2. Actually the chronicle of Brito says that Philip Augustus, having been unhorsed in battle, was defended in this way by one Peter Tristan. See Alexander Cartellieri, *Philipp II August, König von Frankreich* (4 vols., Leipzig and Paris, 1899–1922), iv, p. 467.
12 Alfred Cobban, *A History of Modern France* (3 vols., Harmondsworth, 1963), i, pp. 130–1.
13 George Rudé, *The Crowd in the French Revolution* (Oxford, 1959), p. 30.
14 Letter to L. P. de Croix in Lille, 4 April 1789; Froidcourt, p. 148.
15 F:Po, Registre de l'Opéra-Comique vol. 122. Incidentally, some opéras-comiques may have utilised timpani without that part appearing in the printed score, e.g. Dezède's *Alexis et Justine*, of which Grimm wrote (xiv:90–1): 'We found that the ceaseless employment that he made in his accompaniments of the noisiest instruments of the orchestra, above all the timpani, almost always went contrary to the expression of the words and even the emotion that the situation ought to have had command over.' That was in 1785.
16 Jean Mongrédien, *Jean-François Le Sueur* (2 vols., Berne, 1980), i, pp. 207–15; Louis Péricaud, *Théâtre de 'Monsieur'* (Paris, 1908). During 1789 performances were in the Salle des Machines in the Tuileries, but after the royal family's return from Versailles (see chapter 34) the company was obliged to move for its 1790 performances to the theatre of the Variétés-Amusantes, at the Foire St-Germain.
17 Remo Giazotto, *Giovan Battista Viotti* (Milan, 1956), p. 238.

33 Raoul Barbe-bleue

1 A close friend of Grétry (i:315) who had accompanied the composer to Liège in 1776: Froidcourt, p. 151. The main title-page of the score reads only BARBE BLEUE but after the overture (p. 11) RAOUL BARBE BLEUE.

2 Incipits: (1) 'Il m'enlevait' (2) 'Vergy, Vergy' (3) 'Moi, je serais infidèle' (4) 'Non, le serment fait'; 'Est-il beauté' (5) 'Ah! je vous rends' (6) 'Vivent, vivent' (8) 'Je te trouve bien pitoyable' (9) 'Jurez-moi' (10) 'Vergy, ton souvenir' (12) 'Il n'est plus' (16) 'Cher Vergy, sauvez vos jours' (17) 'Perfide, tu l'as ouverte!' (18) 'Vergy . . . ma sœur, ne vois-tu rien venir?'

3 *Mercure de France*, 14 March 1789, pp. 93–9. As late as 1811 the opera was described as 'the monstrous source of the bad taste which has corrupted the stage with disgusting butcher-shop melodramas': *Les tablettes de Polymnie*, ii (5 January 1811), pp. 225–7.

4 Charles Perrault, *Histoires ou contes du temps passé. Avec des moralitez* (Paris, 1698).

5 *Bibliothèque universelle des romans*, October 1775, ii, pp. 190–3 with biographical notes on Perrault p. 204ff.

6 Two versions are in the Bibliothèque Nationale: Ms.fr.9248 'La Barbe-bleu, tragédie' in verse, and Ms.fr.9318 'La Barbe-bleue', pantomime, 1746.

7 J. C. Le Vacher de Charnois (ed.), *Costumes et annales des grands théâtres de Paris*, iv, Issue ix [1789], pp. 75–7. Nevertheless, 'When this piece was first performed in Paris, the public applauded Chenard's costume loudly. We are not surprised by that; his costume is fine, rich, and the colours of its material have some analogy with that hardness of character that Raoul's personage contains. But aside from the fact that the costume is not true, it is, further, composed of parts absolutely estranged from one another' etc.

8 'Regardez cette femme changée en statue; celle-ci au désespoir d'avoir indiscrètement ouvert la botte qui lui a été confiée . . .'

9 Grétry's friendship with the very musical artist is described in *Mémoires*:ii:62.

10 *Carl Maria von Weber: Writings on Music*, ed. John Warrack (Cambridge, 1981), pp. 222–5. Weber reported that *Raoul*, *Richard Cœur-de-lion* and *Zémire et Azor* were Grétry's most popular works in Germany, 'endlessly in demand'.

11 There is an offstage trumpet-call, on the dominant note B, that brings with it the final short Allegro of the duet. Raoul's approach is close. This is possibly the earliest example in France of a musical *coup* used or adapted later by Dalayrac (*Léhéman*), Méhul (*Héléna*), and Beethoven (*Fidelio*); but a similar effect is found in *Clarice et Belton* (1793), undated manuscript in *CC* 48–9, possibly deriving from an inspiration in *Le prisonnier anglais* (1787).

12 This public letter forms evidence for dating the score in 1790: *The New Grove* suggests 1791. See *Journal de Paris*, 2 January 1791, supplement.

13 *La quotidienne*, no. 35, 26 October 'An Premier de la République', p. 4.

14 Margaret Ann Rayner, 'The Social and Literary Aspects of Sedaine's Dramatic Work', unpublished dissertation, University of London, 1960, p. 220. Printed libretto with manuscript corrections 'd'après le nouveau manuscrit de l'auteur et telle qu'elle se donne l'an 3ème de la république', Bibliothèque de l'Arsenal, Rf.13.770. Undated manuscript prompt copy (stamped on cover *Théâtre de l'Opéra Comique*) crediting the part of Vergy to Cretu, not Michu, Archives Nationales A.J.XIII, 1101.

15 Cf. *Journal de Paris*, 3 March 1789, p. 285: 'les frères arrivent, délivrent leur sœur, et immolent le sanguinaire *Raoul*'; in any case (19) had contained a quartet section for the brothers, Isaure and Vergy.

34 *Pierre le Grand*

1 Peter I the Great (1672–1725), tsar 1682 and emperor 1721. Grew up outside the court in a progressive atmosphere; built Russian fleet 1695 then a large navy; defeated the Turks and captured Azov, 1696. Went abroad in 1697 with the 'Grand Embassy' to gather information about European economies and culture. Worked incognito in Dutch shipyard of East India Company at Saardam, then in the Royal Navy's dockyard at Deptford.

2 François Lefort (1656–99), Genevan officer; became Peter's teacher and friend after he ascended the throne, led the 'Grand Embassy' to Europe and created the Russian fleet, becoming its first admiral, 1694. Defeated Turks at sea, 1696.

3 Catherine I (1684–1727), daughter of a Lithuanian peasant, originally Marta Skowronska.

Married a Swedish dragoon but was imprisoned 1702 during the Swedish evacuation of Marienburg. Sold to Prince Menshikov, in whose house Peter became her lover. Publicly married Peter 1712; crowned empress 1724. She was not related to Catherine II 'the Great'.

4 The part is in the tenor clef. However the rôle was created by Mlle Renaud *la jeune*.

5 Incipits: (1) 'Travaillons et chantons' (2) 'Oui, tes services' (3) 'Oui, mes amis' (4) 'J'étais au bord de la fontaine' (6) 'Morgué! sans m'vanter' (7b) 'Célébrons cette journée' (8) 'Célébrons cette journée' (10) 'Je vais m'unir' (11) 'Que je bénis ma destinée' (12) 'Jadis un célèbre empereur' (13) 'O ciel! que viens-je entendre?' (14) 'Qu'entends-je!' (16) 'Qu'entends-je!' (17) 'Oui, Pierre est not' prince' (18) 'Ah! soyez notre souveraine' (19) 'Pour nous instruire'.

6 For a recent survey see David Galliver, 'Jean-Nicolas Bouilly (1763–1842), Successor of Sedaine', *Studies in Music*, xiii (1979), pp. 16–33. The basic biographical source is Bouilly's *Mes récapitulations* (3 vols., Paris, [1836–7]).

7 F:Po, Registre de l'Opéra-Comique vol. 119, 7 June 1789. 'Le Comité a trouvé dans cet ouvrage un Stile pur et soigné de l'intérêt des choses agréables une marche chaude et l'a admis à la lecture de l'assemblée.' Bouilly says the reading in assembly was held around 12 July (*Mes récapitulations*, i, p. 133).

8 Louis Moland (ed.), *Œuvres complètes de Voltaire* (52 vols., Paris, 1877–85, reprinted Nendeln, 1967), xvi, pp. 276–7, 519.

9 There is a seeming connection with the *Marseillaise* in the unusual temporary recourse to the tonic minor just before the refrain. Rouget de Lisle had in fact met Grétry in February 1790 and became his firm friend, not to say future collaborator in *Cécile et Ermancé*, 1792. See Georges de Froidcourt, *Grétry, Rouget de Lisle et la Marseillaise* (Liège, Paris, 1945), p. 10. Froidcourt reports that both Grétry's *Les mariages samnites* (9) and Dalayrac's *Sargines*, as well as Mozart's piano concerto no. 25, have variously been seen as contributing to the *Marseillaise*.

10 *Mercure de France*, 23 January 1790, pp. 188–92.

11 *Charmante Gabrielle* here taken from Henri Davenson, *Le livre des chansons* (Neuchâtel, 1946), pp. 213–14. Davenson points out that the refrain's words date from *c*1602 while the melody in question appeared only in 1706.

12 [N. E. Framery,] *De l'organisation des spectacles de Paris ou essai sur leur forme actuelle* (Paris, 1790), p. 122.

13 The key, B flat, and even the main orchestral theme evoke the trust and friendship that was heard in (2) between Pierre and Le Fort.

14 *L'esprit des journaux*, cited in *CC*, p. iv. Research has yet to identify the dance.

15 F:Po, Registre de l'Opéra-Comique vol. 119.

16 Alfred Cobban, *A History of Modern France* (3 vols. Harmondsworth, 1963), i, p. 136.

17 Avant-Propos to *Pierre Le Grand, Comédie en Quatre Actes* (Paris, Tours, 1790), pp. 1–2.

18 *A Diary of the French Revolution by Gouverneur Morris 1752–1816*, ed. B. C. Davenport (2 vols., London, 1939), i, p. 592.

19 *Moniteur universel*, 17 January 1790, cited in *CC*, p. iv.

20 *Mercure de France*, 23 January 1790, pp. 189, 192. 'Quelques personnes auroient désiré plus d'analogie entre Pierre le Grand et ce Couplet sur notre Monarque.'

21 Froidcourt, p. 150. Bouilly suppressed mention of the four-act version in *Mes récapitulations*, i, pp. 29ff.

22 Incipits: Le Fort, 'Ah! livrez-vous'; duet, 'On dit qu'lorsqu'on s'marie'; Catherine, 'O toi que j'adorais'.

23 F:Po, Registre de l'Opéra-Comique vol. 122, 11 August 1790.

35 The entr'acte (II) and overture (III)

1 'Avec deux morceaux de drap liés aux baguettes'. See p. 244.

2 Information on the overture in France in theory and practice is in Basil Deane, 'The French Operatic Overture from Grétry to Berlioz', *Proceedings of the Royal Musical Association*, xcix

(1972–3), 67–80, and David Charlton, *The Overture in France, 1790–1810* in Barry S. Brook (ed.), *The Symphony 1720–1840*, series D, vol. vii (New York, London, 1983).

3 [anon.], 'Ranz des vaches', *The New Grove*. Grétry's use of it prefigures also works by Berlioz, Schumann and Liszt.

4 There is no mention of it in the Registres de l'Opéra-Comique in F:Po, although these do mention other purchases of instruments at this time, such as a harp and a 'grande trombone' in 1798. One would like to know whether any musical or other connection linked Grétry's 'corne' with the simple brass instruments used fifteen months later for the first time as neo-classical accessories in the Voltaire funeral cortège in Paris. See *The New Grove*, 'Buccin', 'Tuba corva'.

5 When the libretto was published he thought the music 'not pronounced enough to indicate what I desired people should feel, that at the raising of the curtain one was in a Swiss valley'.

6 J. N. Bouilly, *Mes récapitulations* (3 vols., Paris, [1836–7]), i, p. 431.

36 *Guillaume Tell;* conclusions

1 Incipits: (1) 'Ah! nous serons bien heureux' (2) 'On ne peut de trop bonne heure' (3) 'Bonjour, ma voisine' (4) 'Noisette, noisette' (5) 'Puisses-tu, ma fille' (6) 'Le mariage est un bonheur' (7) 'Grands dieux' (9) 'O ciel! Quoi!' (10) 'Non, jamais' (11) 'Seigneur, seigneur' (12) 'Nous vivons . . . et nous souffrons' (14) 'O ciel! où sont ces scélérats?' (15) 'Je suis altéré de vengeance' (16) 'A Roncevaux' (18) 'Servons aux siècles à venir'.

2 The detailed footnote found in the libretto (Paris, Maradan, An 2) has been translated in chapter 35.

3 Sedaine proposed a supplementary patriotic ending in which, to the *Marseillaise*, French *sans-culottes* arrive and show solidarity with the Swiss.

4 'Mais ton art plus fatal au pouvoir despotique / Fit mieux, en nous offrant la grandeur helvétique. / Dans un tableau frappant, dans ton Poème altier / Tu fis voir à la France un Peuple tout entier, / Qui se lève, aux accens de la Liberté fière.'

5 See chapter 1, above, and John Lough, *Paris Theatre Audiences in the Seventeenth and Eighteenth Centuries* (London, 1957), p. 239ff.

6 However, proof of its popularity with the reading public is shown in the play's repeated printings. The preface to the Neuchâtel edition of 1783 points out that Lemierre's numerous changes had been enshrined in the Paris edition of 1776, but that pirated editions at Avignon and The Hague had reproduced the old 1767 text. The mimed inclusion is not in the printed text but is generally accepted.

7 Margaret Ann Rayner, 'The Social and Literary Aspects of Sedaine's Dramatic Work', unpublished dissertation, University of London, 1960, pp. 27, 222.

8 Cited in *CC* 24, p. iii.

9 Robert L. Herbert, *David, Voltaire, 'Brutus' and the French Revolution: an Essay in Art and Politics*, Art in Context, ed. John Fleming and Hugh Honour (London, 1972).

10 Michel Brenet, *Grétry, sa vie et ses œuvres* (Paris, 1884), p. 215.

11 J. N. Bouilly, *Mes récapitulations* (3 vols., Paris, [1836–7]), i, p. 348.

12 Bouilly, *ibid.*, claims that Grétry went to Geneva and the mountains to absorb the necessary local colour.

13 A lengthier extract from this is in Martin Cooper, 'Opera in France', in *The Age of Enlightenment 1745–1790, New Oxford History of Music*, vii, ed. Egon Wellesz and Frederick Sternfeld (London, 1973), pp. 219–20. It is followed by an extract from the combat music (17), closely resembling Beethoven's music for Goethe's *Egmont*, composed 1809–10.

14 J. B. Weckerlin, *Chansons populaires du pays de France* (2 vols., Paris, 1903), i, pp. 85–8. Méhul was to write a Roland song for Duval's play *Guillaume le Conquérant* (1803).

15 Arthur Pougin, *L'Opéra-Comique pendant la Révolution de 1788 à 1801* (Paris, 1891), p. 43.

16 F:Po, Registre de l'Opéra-Comique vol. 122, 29 October 1790. The assembly of the Comédie-Italienne actually declined to mount *Tell* before *Grisélide* (8 January 1791).

17 Froidcourt, pp. 160, 169-70.
18 *Le barbier de village, ou le revenant* (Paris, Huet, An V), Avertissement.
19 Musical details discussed in Albert Vander Linden, 'La première version d'*Elisca* de Grétry', *Académie Royale de Belgique, Bulletin de la classe des Beaux-Arts*, xxxv (1953), p. 135.
20 A. J. Grétry, *Grétry en famille* (1814); Joachim Le Breton, *Notice historique sur la vie et les ouvrages de A. E. M. Grétry*; L. V. Flamand-Grétry, *L'Ermitage de J. J. Rousseau et de Grétry* (1820), etc.
21 Julian Rushton, 'An early essay in "Leitmotiv": J. B. Lemoyne's *Electre*', *Music & Letters*, lii (1971), pp. 387-401.
22 E. de Jouy, 'Les obsèques de Grétry' in *L'Hermite de la chaussée-d'Antin*, iv (7th edn, Paris, 1818), p. 239.

Select bibliography

Pre-1800 sources

Bibliographical particulars of librettos are given in the notes.

Bibliothèque universelle des romans.

Burney, Charles, *The Present State of Music in France and Italy* (London, 1773, reprinted New York, 1976).

The Present State of Music in Germany, The Netherlands, and United Provinces (2 vols., London, 1775, reprinted New York, 1969).

Desboulmiers, [Jean Auguste Jullien], *Histoire anecdotique et raisonnée du Théâtre Italien* (7 vols., Paris, 1770).

D'Origny, Antoine, *Annales du Théâtre Italien depuis son origine jusqu'à ce jour* (3 vols., Paris, 1788, reprinted Geneva, 1970).

Etat actuel de la Musique du Roi et des trois spectacles de Paris (Paris, 1771).

[Framery, N. E.], *De l'organisation des spectacles de Paris ou essai sur leur forme actuelle* (Paris, 1790).

Grétry, André-Ernest-Modeste, *Mémoires, ou Essais sur la musique* (3 vols., Paris, An v, reprinted New York, 1971).

Réflexions d'un solitaire, ed. Lucien Solvay and Ernest Closson (4 vols., Brussels, Paris, 1919–24).

Grimm, Friedrich Melchior, *et al.*, *Correspondance littéraire, philosophique et critique par Grimm, Diderot, Raynal, Meister, etc.*, ed. Maurice Tourneux (16 vols., Paris, 1877–82).

Journal de musique, par une société d'amateurs.

Journal de Paris.

La Borde, Jean Benjamin de, *Essai sur la musique ancienne et moderne* (4 vols., Paris, 1780).

La Harpe, Jean François de, *Correspondance littéraire* (6 vols., Paris, 1801–7).

Le Vacher de Charnois, J. C. (ed.), *Costumes et annales des grands théâtres de Paris* (Paris, 1786–9).

Marmontel, Jean-François, *Elemens de littérature*, in *Œuvres complettes [sic] de Marmontel* (10 vols., Paris, 1787).

Mémoires, ed. John Renwick (2 vols., Clermont-Ferrand, 1972).

Mercier, Louis Sébastien, *Tableau de Paris* (12 vols., Amsterdam, 1782–8).

Mercure de France.

Momigny, Jérôme Joseph de, 'Opéra' in *Encyclopédie methodique. Musique, publiée par MM. [N. E.] Framery, [P. L.] Ginguené et [J. J.] de Momigny* (2 vols., Paris, Liège, 1791, 1818).

[Nougaret, P. J. B.], *De l'art du théâtre, où il est parlé des différens genres de spectacles, et de la musique adaptée au théâtre* (2 vols., Paris, 1769).

[Petit de Bachaumont, Louis, *et al.*], *Mémoires secrets pour servir à l'histoire de la république des lettres en France, depuis 1762 jusqu'à nos jours* (36 vols. London, 1777–89).

Recueil des fêtes et spectacles donnés devant Sa Majesté, à Versailles, à Choisy & à Fontainebleau, pendant l'année 1771 ([Paris,] 1771).

Rosoi, Barnabé Farmian de, *Dissertation sur le drame lyrique* (The Hague, Paris, 1775 [1776]).

Sedaine, Michel-Jean, 'Quelques réflexions inédites de Sedaine sur l'opéra comique', in *Théâtre choisi de G. de Pixérécourt* (4 vols., Paris, Nancy, 1841–3).

Post-1800 sources

Bouilly, Jean-Nicolas, *Mes récapitulations* (3 vols., Paris, n.d. [1836–7]).

Breitholtz, Lennart, 'Le théâtre historique en France jusqu'à la Révolution', *Uppsala Universitets Årsskrift*, xii (1952).

Select bibliography

Brenet, Michel, *Grétry, sa vie et ses œuvres* (Paris, 1884).

Brenner, Clarence D., 'Dramatizations of French Short Stories in the Eighteenth Century with Special Reference to the "Contes" of La Fontaine, Marmontel and Voltaire', University of California Publications in Modern Philology, xxxiii (1947), pp. 1–34.

The Théâtre Italien, its Repertory 1716–1793, University of California Publications in Modern Philology, lxiii (1961).

Brookner, Anita, *Greuze, the Rise and Fall of an Eighteenth-Century Phenomenon* (London, 1972).

Campardon, Emile, *Les comédiens de la troupe italienne pendant les deux derniers siècles* (2 vols., Paris, 1880).

Charlton, David, 'Orchestra and Chorus at the Comédie-Italienne (Opéra-Comique), 1755–1799' in Malcolm H. Brown and Roland John Wiley (eds.), *Slavonic and Western Music: Essays for Gerald Abraham* (Ann Arbor, Oxford, 1985), pp. 87–108.

Closson, Ernest, 'Les notes marginales de Grétry dans l' "Essay sur la Musique" de Laborde', *Revue Belge de Musicologie*, ii (1948), pp. 106–24.

Cobban, Alfred, *A History of Modern France* (3 vols., Harmondsworth, 1963).

Cucuel, Georges, 'Le Moyen Age dans les opéras-comiques du XVIIIᵉ siècle', *Revue du Dix-Huitième Siècle*, ii (1914), pp. 56–71.

'Notes sur la Comédie Italienne de 1717 à 1789', *Quarterly Magazine of the International Musical Society (Internationale Musikgesellschaft)*, xv, part 1 (1913), pp. 154–66.

'Sources et documents pour servir à l'histoire de l'opéra-comique en France', *L'année musicale*, iii (1913), pp. 247–82.

Culot, Paul, *Le jugement de Midas, opéra-comique d'André-Ernest-Modeste Grétry* (Brussels, 1978).

Fiske, Roger, *English Theatre Music in the Eighteenth Century* (London, 1973).

Froidcourt, Georges de, *La correspondance générale de Grétry* (Brussels, 1962).

Kelly, Michael, *Reminiscences*, ed. Roger Fiske (London, 1975).

Lepeintre Desroches, Pierre Marie Michel, *Suite du répertoire du théâtre français* (81 vols., Paris, 1822–3, reprinted Geneva, 1970).

Long Des Clavières, Pauline, *La jeunesse de Grétry et ses débuts à Paris* (Besançon, 1920).

Lough, John, *Paris Theatre Audiences in the Seventeenth and Eighteenth Centuries* (London, 1957).

Martine, [J. D.], *De la musique dramatique en France* (Paris, 1813).

Nagler, Alois Maria (ed.), *A Source Book in Theatrical History* (New York, 1959).

Pougin, Arthur, *Un directeur d'opéra au dix-huitième siècle* (Paris, 1914).

Quitin, José, *Les maîtres de chant et la maîtrise de la collégiale Saint-Denis à Liège, au temps de Grétry: esquisse socio-musicologique*, Académie royale de Belgique, Classe des beaux-arts: Mémoires, 2nd series, xiii, fasc. 3 (Brussels, 1964).

Rayner, Margaret Ann, 'The Social and Literary Aspects of Sedaine's Dramatic Work', unpublished dissertation, University of London, 1960.

Renwick, John, *Marmontel, Voltaire and the 'Bélisaire' affair*, Studies on Voltaire and the Eighteenth Century, cxxi (Banbury, 1974).

Rudé, George, *The Crowd in the French Revolution* (Oxford, 1959).

Smith, Kent M., 'Egidio Duni and the Development of the *Opéra-Comique* from 1753 to 1770', unpublished dissertation, Cornell University, 1980.

Soubies, Albert, *Soixante-neuf ans à l'Opéra-Comique en deux pages* (Paris, 1894).

Voltaire's Correspondence, ed. Theodore Besterman (107 vols., Geneva, 1953–65).

Wichmann, Heinz, *Grétry und das musikalische Theater in Frankreich* (Halle, 1929).

Index

Index

Index

Index

Index

Index